Lifespan Issues

One of the major questions facing special educators is what happens to their students in secondary school and beyond. To what extent do they find jobs? To what extent are they personally independent?

TRANSITION FROM SCHOOL TO WORK

Several studies have been conducted that look at the transition experiences from school to work of youth with disabilities. One study in the state of Washington tracked more than 4,000 students who graduated between 1978 and 1986 (Neel, Meadows, Levine, & Edgar, 1988). One hundred sixty of these students had behavior disorders, and the researchers compared them with more than 500 nonhandicapped students of the same ages and from the same schools. Only 60 percent of the students with disabilities were currently working, compared with 70 percent of the nondisabled group. Moreover, those who were working had found their jobs themselves or with the help of family. No social or rehabilitation agency was actively working on their problems.

The authors concluded that school programs are not teaching children with behavior disorders the skills they need to find jobs. And a large number of parents agreed. One-third were dissatisfied with the programs their children had in school or with the jobs their children found. One of the most important responsibilities special educators have is helping students cope with the transition between school and the workplace. The main function of school is to prepare youngsters to live as independent adults. Mithaug, Martin, and Agran (1987) identified four skills that should be part of the secondary curriculum for exceptional children:

1. Choosing among available job options
2. Performing independently (a learning to learn strategy that allows students to

TRANSITION TO ADULTHOOD

What happens to emotionally or behaviorally disturbed individuals when they reach adulthood? Figure 7.4 compares the employment rates of emotionally disturbed youth with the rates of youth in eleven categories of disability (Wagner et al., 1991). The figure presents some modest good news and motivation for the establishment of effective and intense programs for such students with emotional disturbance.

Figure 7.4 shows that about 72 percent of youth with emotional disturbance "had a paid job last year"; the corresponding percentage among youths in the "all conditions" group was slightly lower—70 percent. This is a positive and somewhat unexpected finding. About 45 percent in each group are "currently competitively employed." Half or more of the emotionally disturbed youth are employed in some fashion, and there is little doubt that more effective and more efficient training programs and support features could improve those figures.

Something about the school environment appears to be particularly unsuitable for these students. Research with smaller samples seems to yield consistent findings. Feldman, Denhoff, and Denhoff (1984) carried out a ten- to twelve-year follow-up study on forty-eight adults who had been diagnosed as hyperactive children. The researchers found that by age twenty-one 91 percent were in some form of school or special training or working and seemed to be performing in a reasonably effective

Excerpts from Chapter 7.

are examples of the Lifespan and Family coverage found in the categorical chapters.

Educating Exceptional Children

EIGHTH EDITION

Samuel A. Kirk
Late of University of Arizona

James J. Gallagher
University of North Carolina at Chapel Hill

Nicholas J. Anastasiow
Emeritus, Hunter College, City University of New York

HOUGHTON MIFFLIN COMPANY   BOSTON   NEW YORK

Senior Sponsoring Editor: Loretta Wolozin
Assistant Editor: Lisa Mafrici
Project Editor: Nicole Ng
Design/Production Coordinator: Jennifer Waddell
Senior Manufacturing Coordinator: Priscilla Bailey
Marketing Manager: Dave Lenehan
Cover design by Darci Mehall. Cover photo: "Images © 1996 PhotoDisc, Inc."

Chapter opening photo credits: Chapter 1, Hugh Rogers / Monkmeyer Press Photo
Service; Chapters 2, 11, 12, Lydia Gans; Chapter 3, Jean-Claude Lejeune; Chapter 4, Joel
Gordon; Chapter 5, Paul S. Conklin; Chapter 6, James Carroll; Chapter 7, Mimi Forsyth /
Monkmeyer Press Photo Service; Chapter 8, Irene Bayer / Monkmeyer Press Photo Service;
Chapter 9, George Bellerose / Stock Boston; Chapter 10, Larry Kolvoord / Texas Stock.

Excerpt on pp. 34–35 from F. Warren (1985) in H. Turnbull and A. Turnbull (eds.),
Parents Speak Out: Then and Now, p. 227 (Columbus, OH: Merrill). Reprinted by
permission of Prentice-Hall, Inc., Upper Saddle River, NJ.

Excerpt on pp. 141–142 from J. Gallagher and S. Gallagher, *Teaching the Gifted Child*,
pp. 11–12. Copyright © 1994 by Allyn and Bacon. Reprinted by permission.

Excerpted dialogue on pp. 434–435 from M. Orlansky (1980), *Encouraging Successful
Mainstreaming of the Visually Impaired Child* (MAVIS Sourcebook No. 2). Boulder:
Social Science Education Consortium, pp. 9–10. Reprinted by permission.

Printed in the U.S.A.
Library of Congress Catalog Card Number: 96-76919
ISBN: 0-395-78051-9
123456789 -DH - 00 99 98 97 96

contents

Chapter 3   Early Intervention: Priorities and Programs   90

Chapter 4 Children Who Are Gifted and Talented 125

Chapter 6   Children with Learning Disabilities   231

Chapter 8 Children with Communication Disorders in Speech and Language 326

Chapter 10   Children with Visual Impairments   412

Special education is no longer the exclusive domain of special educators. At some time or other, practically all schoolteachers will have exceptional children in their classrooms. And with the emphasis on inclusion and the marked decrease in the institutionalization of persons with exceptionalities, as a society we are becoming increasingly aware that these individuals are important members of the human community.

Audience and Purpose

Meeting the special needs of children with exceptionalities is the shared responsibility of regular classroom teachers, special education teachers, therapists, psychologists, and other members of the education team, which also includes the parents and families of exceptional children. Our objective in writing this textbook is to assist in the preparation of those individuals for their roles in meeting the educational needs of people with exceptionalities.

Themes

In the eighth edition of our text we emphasize two themes: (1) an ecological approach to special education and (2) promotion of critical thinking by students using this textbook. Central among the emphases in the field is increasing awareness of the exceptional child first and foremost as a human individual who is influenced by and must cope with the broad contexts or environments of family, school, and society. *Educating Exceptional Children* perceives the family's role as central to the education of the child and shows why resolving family needs is critical to successfully educating children with exceptionalities.

We address the ecological theme in several ways. Chapter 3, on early childhood intervention, illustrates the importance of environment early in life. We provide an extensive discussion of risk factors, risk prevention, and the personnel involved in early intervention, as well as detailed examples of model programs. The chapter is oriented to the needs of both teachers and parents.

The ecological theme is reinforced by "The Child in Context" article in each chapter. It allows us to highlight an exceptional individual's interactions with his or her family, school, or society and address issues that go beyond the classroom. The commentary that accompanies each article invites discussion in the classroom.

The skill of critical thinking is vital for people who will be making decisions about students' special needs. In this book we strongly encourage readers to think critically about the field of special education and to explore what it means to teach and learn with exceptional children. To achieve this goal, we discuss extensively the debate over inclusion, the development of collaborative teaching methods, and the possibilities offered by new technologies. In the "Unresolved Issues" section in each chapter we identify additional topics for discussion, and the new "Questions for Thought" in each chapter ask students to think analytically, creatively, and practically about the issues raised in the chapter.

In this new edition of our book we continue our mission of presenting research and information on the best practices from multiple theoretical orientations, to encourage readers to do likewise as a method for formulating their own substantiated views. Acknowledging that education is part of change at large in society, we invite readers to embark on critical thinking and decision making, using as a springboard the text's new afterword, "Perspectives on Educating Exceptional Children in the Future."

Organization of the Text

Chapter 1, "Educating the Exceptional Child," focuses on the nature of exceptional children and their relationships with their families. We offer an overview of perspectives on exceptionality, including a general discussion of the characteristics or groupings of exceptional children, and we emphasize the significance of individual differences in exceptional children. The chapter addresses how the changes in prevalence of certain exceptionalities reflect changing attitudes of society toward exceptional children. In addition, the chapter discusses the impact of an exceptional child on his or her family, examining the ways in which stress affects the child's parent and siblings and the critical role parents play in the nurturing and education of their child.

Chapter 2, "Exceptional Children and Their Environment," discusses how society and school influence the lives of exceptional individuals, offering historical background on the field of special education and an overview of issues and trends that have affected the development of programs for exceptional individuals throughout their lifespan. State and federal legislation mandating services for exceptional individuals and the role of the courts in implementing these laws are covered in depth. The chapter also offers coverage of the various steps in the process of assessing and identifying the exceptional learner and in the planning of an individualized education program (IEP). We consider the effect of cultural diversity on special education practices and its significance as an inter-individual difference among children that teachers must address in each child's education program.

Chapter 3, "Early Intervention: Priorities and Programs," addresses the impact of recent legislation on services for exceptional children from birth through age 5. The concepts of risk, early identification, and the range of programs and personnel involved in early childhood special education are discussed.

The eighth edition of *Educating Exceptional Children* continues to provide basic information about the characteristics and distinctive problems of learners with exceptionalities, using the appropriate categorical terminology. Chapters 4 through 12 focus on the various clusters of children with exceptionalities. For children in each cluster the chapters cover the topics of definition, prevalence, causes, characteristics, classification, intervention, identification and assessment, special educational adaptations, and lifespan and family issues.

Revisions in This Edition

We have thoroughly updated the coverage in each categorical chapter and reorganized chapters to present a more logical, consistent sequence within and among them. In particular, Chapter 4, "Children Who Are Gifted and Talented," addresses the expanding definition of giftedness, encompassing discussions of multiple intelligences, knowledge structures, and creativity, and emphasizing the skills of problem finding and problem solving. Chapter 5, "Children with Mental Retardation," redefines mental retardation by placing new emphasis on adaptive behavior and the concomitant roles of teaching techniques and inclusion in education for children with mental retardation.

Chapter 6, "Children with Learning Disabilities," discusses changes in diagnoses of learning disabilities and in the subtypes of learning disabilities, and it addresses the neuropsychological/developmental and the academic/achievement perspectives. Chapter 7, "Children with Behavior Problems," addresses ADHD, functional assessment, the necessary support personnel for the classroom teacher, and the postschool prognosis for children with emotional and behavioral disorders.

Chapter 8, "Children with Communication Disorders in Speech and Language," covers the more transactional approaches to language instruction and remediation, discusses techniques that classroom teachers can use to assist students with language disorders, and presents the new auditory integration training. Chapter 9, "Children Who Are Deaf or Hard of Hearing," contains a new discussion on the deaf community and the expanded role of the educational audiologist. Chapter 10, "Children with Visual Impairments," discusses the increasing number of children who have disabilities in addition to visual impairments and the special challenges this combination presents to educators. It also addresses the decision that parents must make about whether to encourage their children's social adaptation through inclusive classrooms or to seek special learning environments that focus on mastery of braille and orientation and mobility skills. Chapter 11, "Children with Multiple and Severe Disabilities," presents techniques and augmentative devices for educating children who have more than one disability and addresses whether the disabilities call for supportive human or technical assistance. Chapter 12, "Children with Physical Disabilities and Health Impairments," provides new information on epilepsy, Tourette syndrome, asthma, and the effect of maternal substance abuse on the child.

This edition of the text concludes with an afterword, which provides some essential criteria for consideration of systemic change now making an impact on current and future possibilities for educating children with exceptionalities.

Features in the Eighth Edition

- **Focusing Questions** for each chapter help readers set goals and establish purposes for their reading of each important topic.
- **Introductions** to each chapter offer an overview of the chapter's content and give students a framework into which they can fit new ideas.
- **Marginal notes** within the chapters call out important points being discussed.
- **Educational Adaptations** in every categorical chapter offer suggestions for teaching to the strengths of the exceptional child by varying the learning environment, content, or teaching approach. These sections are color-tabbed for easy reference.
- **A Lifespan or Family section** in every chapter allows students to view the individual throughout the lifespan and focus on issues such as the role of the family, work, and higher education opportunities, social adjustments in adulthood, and integration into the community.
- **Summaries of Major Ideas** conclude each chapter and highlight in a clear, point-by-point format the major concepts presented in the chapter.
- **Unresolved Issues** encourage students to discuss and propose solutions for problems that are still being debated in the field of special education.
- **Key Terms** listed at the end of each chapter are cross-referenced to the place in the text where the terms are boldfaced and discussed.
- **Questions for Thought** ask students to gather, analyze, and apply information about a range of issues in special education.
- **References of Special Interest** provide for each chapter an annotated list of resources that students can pursue.
- **A Glossary** at the end of the book offers definitions of all key terms.

Instructor's Resource Manual

New to the eighth edition, the Instructor's Resource Manual (IRM), prepared by Krista Swensson of Eastern Mennonite University, combines into a single tool the formerly separate Study Guide, Instructor's Manual, and Test Bank. The IRM complements the students' and instructors' use of the text and class experiences by emphasizing the skills of organizing, reinforcing, evaluating, and expanding knowledge. Contents include a transition and planning guide; model syllabi; extensive learning and teaching resources for each chapter, including study handouts for students and instructor's support; an assessment section containing for each chapter 50 multiple-choice items (at least 30 percent conceptual), divergent essay questions, and an answer key; and professional resources.

Acknowledgments

We are grateful to a large group of our colleagues and specialists in various exceptionalities for their criticisms and suggestions during the revision of the text. Their critical comments and ideas helped shape and improve our presentation.

Alfred A. Baumeister, Vanderbilt University

Libby G. Cohen, University of Southern Maine

Shirley Cohen, Hunter College

James R. Delisle, Kent State University

Kay Alicyn Ferrell, University of Northern Colorado

Sr. Rosemary Gaffney, Hunter College

Katherine Garnett, Hunter College

Carole R. Gothelf, Jewish Guild for the Blind, New York

Emma C. Guilarte, Positive Approach Consultants

Tim Lackaye, Hunter College

John T. Neisworth, Pennsylvania State University

Lillian C. Patterson, Community College of Rhode Island

James L. Paul, University of South Florida

Judith Smitheran, St. Vincent Hospital, Santa Fe

Janet W. Stack, University of South Florida

Sheri D. Trent, Middle Tennessee State University

Frank H. Wood, University of Minnesota

Naomi Zigmond, University of Pittsburgh

We also wish to acknowledge the help provided by Sarah Helyar Smith, developmental editor, Don Braswell, Roberta Parry, Pat McConnell, Kim Summerville, and the staff of Houghton Mifflin, including Loretta Wolozin, Lisa Mafrici, and Nicole Ng. Their assistance was instrumental in bringing this volume to its present condition.

Our families deserve thanks for their tolerance of the necessary time and energy that this text required.

Nick Anastasiow and I were saddened to hear of the death of the senior author of this volume, Sam Kirk, in July 1996. Sam was a true giant in the field of education—scholar, teacher, writer, mentor, policy maker, colleague, and friend. His passing is a loss to all of us who care for children.

James J. Gallagher
Nicholas J. Anastasiow

Educating the Exceptional Child

Who are the children with exceptionalities?

How have approaches to treating individuals with special needs changed over time?

How do siblings respond to the presence of a child with disabilities in the family?

Children with disabilities may come from many different cultural backgrounds. How do cultural differences affect the future of such children?

How do we define and measure inter-individual and intra-individual differences?

How do we help the families of exceptional children cope effectively with their exceptional child?

I t's not easy to be different. We've all felt the sting of not belonging, of not feeling a part of the group. We've all felt overwhelmed when asked to do things beyond our skills and capabilities, or bored when asked to do simple things that do not challenge us. Of course, being different is not always negative: It is what makes us interesting. But it also forces us to adapt to meet social expectations. And when being different means that a child is not able to receive information through the normal senses, is not able to express himself or herself, or processes information too slowly or too quickly, special adaptations in the education program are necessary.

Despite the philosophical commitment to individualization in our education system, classrooms all too often are filled with grade-level textbooks, grade-level lessons, and grade-level expectations that assume that students deviate very little from their age norm—that is, they are "normal." What happens when students are different, when they cannot adapt to the standard education program because of their exceptionalities? The consequences are serious and have lifelong implications.

Adapting to educational programs is precisely the problem that exceptional children face, and some form of special education is necessary for these children to reach their potential. In this book we focus on the specific educational needs resulting from exceptionalities among different groups of children and the range of educational programs developed especially for them.

The Exceptional Child as a Special Learner

Our focus is the individual exceptional child and his or her development—including how the forces around that child (family, school, peer culture, and society) adapt to meet his or her needs. We will discuss in some detail the family and its adaptations, the school and special education, and other external forces, always with the goal of understanding and helping the special child to cope effectively with the outside world.

WHO IS AN EXCEPTIONAL CHILD?

We consider a child to be exceptional when his or her differences or disabilities occur to such a degree that school practices must be modified to serve the child's needs.

Many have attempted to define the term *exceptional child.* Some use it when referring to the bright child or the child with unusual talent. Others use it when describing any atypical child. The term is generally accepted, however, to include both the child with developmental disabilities and the child who is exceptionally able. Here we define as *exceptional* a child who differs from the average or normal child in (1) mental characteristics, (2) sensory abilities, (3) communication abilities, (4) behavior and emotional development, or (5) physical characteristics. These differences must occur to such an extent that the child requires a modification of school practices, or special educational services, to develop his or her unique capabilities.

Of course, this definition is very general and raises several questions. What is *average* or *normal*? How extensive must the difference be for the child to require special education? What is special education? What role does the child's environment play in the definition? We ask these questions in different forms throughout this text as we discuss each group of exceptional children.

CHARACTERISTICS OF EXCEPTIONAL CHILDREN

If we define an exceptional child as one who differs in some way from a group norm, then many children are exceptional. A child with red hair is "exceptional" if all the other children in the class have brown or blond hair. But that difference, though interesting to a pediatrician or geneticist, is of little concern to the teacher. Educationally speaking, a child with red hair is not an exceptional child, because the educational program does not have to be modified to serve the child's needs. Children are considered educationally exceptional only when it is necessary to alter the educational program—for example, if their exceptionality leaves them unable to read or to master learning in the traditional way or places them so far ahead that they are bored by what is being taught.

The term *exceptional child* may mean very different things in education, in psychology, or in other disciplines. In education, we group children of like characteristics for instructional purposes. For example, we put 6-year-olds in the first grade. In the same way and for the same reasons, we create subgroups of exceptional children. The following groupings are typical:

1. Intellectual differences, including children who are intellectually superior and children who are slow to learn
2. Communication differences, including children with learning disabilities or speech and language disabilities
3. Sensory differences, including children with auditory or visual disabilities
4. Behavioral differences, including children who are emotionally disturbed or socially maladjusted
5. Multiple and severe handicapping conditions, including children with combinations of impairments (cerebral palsy and mental retardation; deafness and blindness)
6. Physical differences, including children with nonsensory disabilities that impede mobility and physical vitality

Figure 1.1 indicates two major trends in the prevalence of high-incidence disabilities: a decrease in services to students with mental retardation and a sharp increase in services to those with learning disabilities. The category of learning disabilities contains more children than the other three categories combined. The reasons for these trends (only mental retardation has gone down) will be discussed more extensively in the individual chapters. Figure 1.2 shows the trends in the numbers of students with low-incidence disabilities: a growth of the number of children with multiple disabilities and children with other health impairments. These trends appear to be the result of improvements in medical science which can now help children to survive serious health problems early in life. In the past many of these children would have perished. Now they survive, but often with serious developmental problems.

Figure 1.1
Prevalence of high incidence disabilities

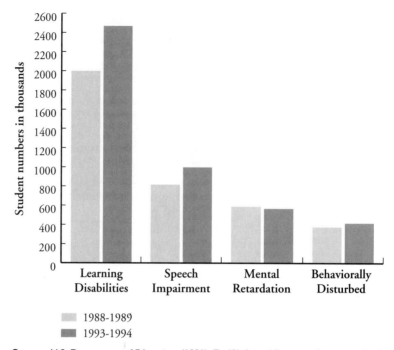

Source: U.S. Department of Education, (1991), *Twelfth Annual Report to Congress on Implementation of the Education of the Handicapped Act* (Washington, D.C.: U.S. Department of Education) (1995). *Seventeenth Annual Report to Congress on Implementation of the Individuals with Disabilities Education Act* (Washington, D.C.: U.S. Department of Education).

▮▮ *The Context of the Exceptional Child*

When discussing the child as learner, we believe that it's important to paint a complete portrait of the child, including the social and family context in which he or she lives. Even as the lead actor on the stage captures our attention, we are aware of the importance of the supporting players and of the sets to the play itself. Once we recognize the individuality of each child and the complex and unique forces and circumstances that act on and surround him or her, it is easier to choose or create the most appropriate instructional strategies and the most suitable learning environment. Figure 1.3 portrays the child at the center of successive layers of influence. The family is the first and often the most influential, but there are other influences: School, peer culture, and society also play a role, often interacting with the family. This is what we refer to as the *context* of the exceptional child. These life circles fold into one another and collectively comprise the child and the child's ecology, both of which we must understand if we are to make wise decisions about the child's education. Both the family and the society in which exceptional children live are essential to their growth and development. And it is in the public schools that we find the full expression of society's understanding and commitment: the knowledge, hopes, fears, and myths that are passed on to the next generation.

Figure 1.2
Prevalence of low incidence
disabilities

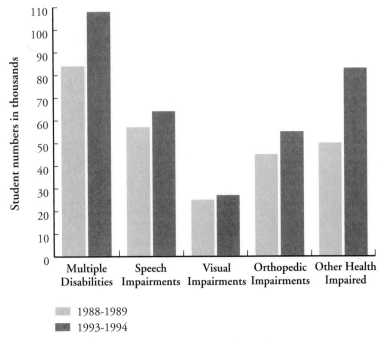

Source: U.S. Department of Education, (1991), *Twelfth Annual Report to Congress on Implementation of the Education of the Handicapped Act* (Washington, D.C.: U.S. Department of Education) (1995). *Seventeenth Annual Report to Congress on Implementation of the Individuals with Disabilities Education Act* (Washington, D.C.: U.S. Department of Education).

ECOLOGY AND THE EXCEPTIONAL CHILD

In the past few years a major shift has taken place in how educators perceive children with exceptionalities. For many years we have known that the environment surrounding an exceptional child can influence how well that child will adapt to his or her life situation (see Figure 1.3). We now realize that the environment, or ecology, can play a significant role in the initial development of an exceptionality.

In the 1950s, it was a well-accepted proposition that the exceptionality was embedded within the child. A child was deaf or blind because of injuries to his or her sensory systems. Cerebral palsy was caused by injury to the central nervous system. As educators expanded the concept of exceptionality to include mild manifestations of exceptionality, students who would have been referred to as having borderline mental retardation, mild behavior problems, or a less severe but still manifest learning disability were found where their "exceptionality" was partially created by their environment as well as their personal characteristics. It became clear that the ability of a child to adapt successfully depended on the nature of the child's environment, as well as on the child's own special characteristics. Increasingly, the approach that educators are taking to cope with the milder forms of

Figure I.3
The Context of the Exceptional Child

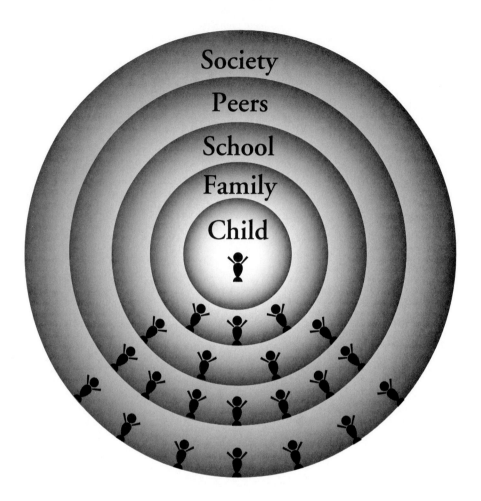

exceptionality is to try to aid the child's adjustment by modifying the life circles around the child, in addition to attempting to attack the child's developmental delay problem.

For example, George, age 7, was identified in kindergarten and first grade as being developmentally delayed and as not performing as well as his classmates. The school psychologist suggested that George might be mentally retarded. A more thorough evaluation of the life circles around George revealed a barren environment for learning. George's family had many adjustment problems of its own, including the drug problems of the parents. There was also a suggestion of child abuse. George had few friends or few opportunities to learn outside the school setting.

Instead of focusing entirely on the remediation of George's reading problems in school, George's individualized education program (IEP), a plan for the student's education devised by teachers and the parents, suggested that changes be made in George's environment. The school social worker arranged for George to be moved at least temporarily to the home of his uncle. The uncle and his wife were diligent providers, exposing George to a consistent and warm family life and accepting him as a member of their family. George's response to the change was a much improved attitude toward school and increased diligence to his lessons. The psychologist, observing these changes, modified his judgment that George was mentally retarded.

This is not to say that the exceptionality of every child can be removed through improvement of the environment. But in cases where ecology appears to play a significant part in the original identification of the exceptionality, making significant changes in the environment can improve the functioning of the child and may cause the exceptionality itself to disappear.

Perhaps the most dramatic change in educators' view of how to teach young children has resulted from the adoption of the ecological approach to child development (Bronfenbrenner, 1979). With this recognition of the role of the environment, the field moved from a **medical model**, which assumes that the physical condition or disease exists within the patient, to an **ecological model**, in which we see the exceptional child in complex interaction with many environmental forces.

The ecological approach seeks to modify the child's behavior directly by improving the context in which the child lives, learns, and plays.

The ecological approach tries not only to modify the exceptional child's learning and behavior through direct contact with the child, but also to improve the environment surrounding the child, including the family and the neighborhood—the entire context of the child. This ecological approach became the strategy of Head Start and other programs targeted at children from economically disadvantaged families. Head Start pays much attention to the family in addition to the child (Zigler, 1995). The ecological model also helps us understand what we can realistically expect to accomplish through intervention programs.

Most educational programs, by themselves, cannot change enough of the ecology or the larger environment to make a substantial difference in the lives of children. To be of greatest effect, the educator has to join hands with those who specialize in the family and the larger environment. As Zigler points out, "no amount of counseling, early childhood curricula, or home visits will take the place of jobs that provide decent incomes, affordable housing, health care, good schools, or safe neighborhoods where children encounter positive role models" (1995, p. 31). One can repeat such a sentence for exceptional children as well.

THE INFLUENCE OF FAMILY

One of the major forces that influence the exceptional child, or any child, is the family. If we expect to be effective in special education, we have to work with the family system in which the child lives, not just with the child. The trend toward early intervention (before the age of 5) increases the importance of the family. Much of the intervention with young children is directed toward changing the family environment and preparing the parent or parents to care for and teach their child. At the very least, intervention tries to generate more constructive parent-child interactions. Later in this chapter we present the role of family in caring for and supporting an exceptional child, and Chapter 3 focuses specifically on early childhood intervention from a variety of perspectives.

Families of exceptional children play an important role in early intervention. Parents can teach their children some of the skills and learning tools that will later be reinforced in a school setting. (© *Lora E. Askinazi/The Picture Cube*)

The increasing interest in the family can be attributed to a series of basic assumptions about the exceptional child and his or her family (Bailey, Buysee, Edmondson, & Smith, 1994):

1. Children and families are inextricably intertwined. Intentional or not, intervention with children almost invariably influences families; likewise, intervention and support with families almost invariably influence children.

2. Involving and supporting families is likely to be a more powerful intervention than one that focuses exclusively on the child.

3. Family members should be able to choose their level of involvement in program planning, decision making, and service delivery.

4. Professionals should attend to family priorities for goals and services, even when those priorities differ substantially from professional priorities.

The purpose of this **family-focused approach** is to help parents become more autonomous and less dependent on professionals, to be able to form their own support networks as appropriate instead of being told by "experts" how to raise their children (Zigler & Black, 1989).

Whenever the helping professions (such as medicine, education, and social work) make a major shift from an almost exclusive emphasis on the child to an emphasis on the family, a lot of professionals find themselves in unfamiliar territory. These are the teachers, psychologists, occupational therapists, and others who have been trained under the old "treat the child" model. They now have to shift their procedures and practices to take into account this family-focused approach. Many professionals do not feel adequately prepared for this shift (Bailey, Palsha, & Simeonsson, 1993).

THE SOCIAL CONTEXT: THE INFLUENCE OF THE ENVIRONMENT

The child's social context includes environmental forces beyond the family that interact with the child: the school, peers (neighborhood), and the larger society. Culture plays an important role as well, especially when the values of the home come into conflict with those of school and society. Children from diverse cultural backgrounds often encounter conflicting expectations and values in the home and in the school. Teachers can help these children by being acutely aware of the wide range of norms represented in their classrooms. When values honored by the school, such as competitiveness and willingness to work at a desk with a minimum of talking, conflict with a minority subculture's preference for cooperation and for lively discussion about problems, then tensions arise between families and school. Such tensions are often increased by the presence of an exceptional child.

The strength of environmental forces varies as the child grows: Initially the family is predominant in caring for the child and acts as a link between the child and the larger environment. Children from diverse cultural backgrounds may be confused by differences between family values and school or societal values, an issue that the child often confronts for the first time when entering school. The support of the family continues to be important but is joined by other factors as the child grows.

As the child grows older, the peer group becomes a major force. Adolescence, with its focus on social development and career orientation, is a special challenge for the exceptional child. Potential rejection by the peer group can have a powerful influence on the adaptation of the child with disabilities or the child with special talents, as it can on any vulnerable and self-conscious adolescent.

Finally, society, which includes the community and work environment, influences the adult who is trying to make the transition to a relatively independent lifestyle. Throughout their lives, many exceptional adults will be in contact with a support system that includes advocates, educators, friends, and service providers. In addition, representatives of the larger society (such as government leaders) often make rules that determine whether the exceptional child gets needed resources or is given an opportunity to succeed at some level of independence. (We discuss these environments further in Chapter 2.) All of these forces contribute to the full picture of the exceptional individual.

THE INFLUENCE OF CULTURE

Culture refers to the attitudes, values, customs, and language that family and friends transmit to children. These attitudes, values, customs, and language have been passed down from generations of ancestors and have formed an identifiable pattern or heritage. The child is embedded in the family, its habits and traditions, and this is as true for the child with special needs as for one who does not show

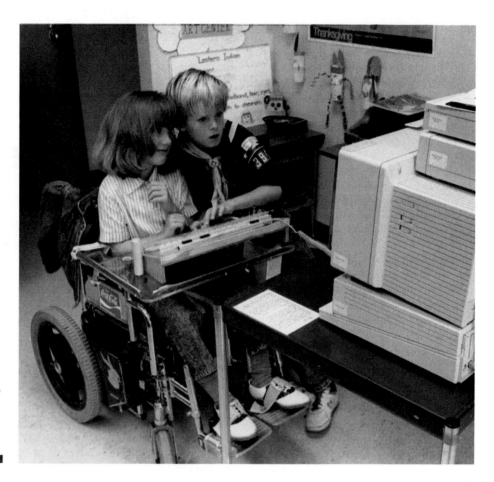

The support of the family in caring for the child continues to be important as the child grows, but it is joined by other factors, especially the school, peers, and the larger society. (© *Richard S. Orton/The Picture Cube*)

special needs. Although the child may be only dimly aware of these cultural influences, it makes a world of difference to the child's experiences if his or her family is fourth-generation American or first-generation Italian, Nigerian, or Taiwanese.

Respect for the breadwinner, attitudes toward religion, child-rearing practices, and even political choices or tendencies may reflect the attitudes of the cultural group to which the family belongs. So it is important to consider cultural factors as one more dimension needing study and understanding if we as teachers are to be effective in helping these children fulfill their capabilities.

Here are some examples of how cultural values impact on the child with special needs: If a family comes from a culture that emphasizes a dominant masculine role, how will the father of a child with disabilities respond to a female professional? Will he reject her advice and suggestions just to maintain his own masculine self-image? And what does he feel about his son who has disabilities that are so serious that the father despairs of the boy ever being able to play that masculine role? Such issues are not easily talked about but can rest at the heart of parental concerns for many years.

THE SIGNIFICANCE OF LANGUAGE AND TERMINOLOGY

Precise language is important when referring to exceptional children. The specific words used in legislation or educational standards define the ways in which needed resources are directed to the appropriate children and families. Legislative language also helps advocates, teachers, and parents be clear about what special education services the law provides.

Another important aspect of language is the role it plays in creating individuals' self-image and identity. For example, the term *handicapped children* was extensively used in legislation providing assistance for such children in the 1960s. That term was replaced with *children with handicapping conditions* in the 1970s to express our understanding that they are *children* first, that the handicapping condition is only *part* of their total being. We currently use the term *children with developmental disabilities* to indicate the potential, rather than the limitations, of the individual.

As our understanding of exceptionalities and educational techniques has increased, we have tried to find terms that express our respect for these children and families and our hopes for their successful adaptations in adulthood. With time, no doubt, the current terminology will change and will again reflect growing understanding and more effective educational programs. As an educator, you have the responsibility to consider your choices of terminology and the meanings you convey.

■ ■ *Individual Differences and Their Assessment*

Terminology is important because it is the means by which we acknowledge the exceptionality itself. But it is often only a springboard for learning about the individuality of the exceptional child. We are all aware of how children of the same age vary physically. Some are tall and thin, others are short and chubby, and there is much variation in between. We find this same variation in other areas: intelligence, educational attainment, emotional maturity, and social development. Individual differences are the rule rather than the exception. Regardless of the exceptionality, children with their exceptionality will show impressive differences from one another on these characteristics.

One dimension of individual differences important to our abilities and performance is our individual genetic makeup. The field of genetics has advanced remarkably since the 1960s, and we now know that more of our behaviors are influenced by our genes and chromosomes than we had previously realized. Some characteristics clearly linked to heredity are intelligence, temperament, mental illness, alcoholism, criminal behavior, and vocational interests (Plomin, 1989).

Genetic influence only increases or decreases the probability that a certain behavior or condition will occur.

Except in the case of rare single-gene dysfunctions or defects, genetic influence isn't felt directly. Instead, the influence of multiple gene interactions seems to nudge development in one direction or another, often in complex interrelationships with the environment and cumulative experience. Therefore, genetic influence is only one of a number of factors leading to particular behaviors. It does not guarantee a certain outcome (for example, alcoholism) but only increases or

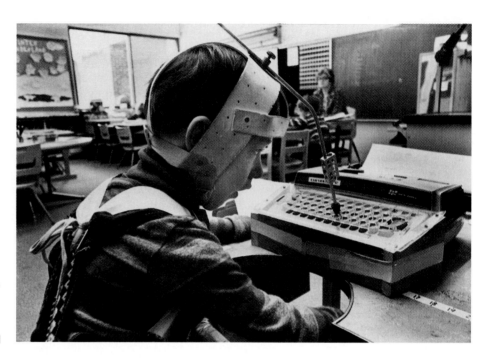

When students in the same classroom are markedly different from one another, teachers need assistance from a special education program in helping them reach their educational potential. (© *George Bellerose/Stock Boston*)

decreases the probability that it will occur. The role that genetic influence plays in each of the separate exceptionalities is discussed in subsequent chapters.

INDIVIDUAL DIFFERENCES AND THE CLASSROOM

Individual differences can create a serious problem for the classroom teacher. If a third-grade lesson is directed at average 8-year-olds, what happens to the child in the class whose intellectual development is at age 5? Or to the child with the social maturity and cognitive abilities of an 11-year-old? Or to the youngster with the emotional maturity of a 4-year-old? The teacher has a problem: The lesson is going to be too difficult for one child and too easy for the other, and the third child is creating a behavioral control problem.

When youngsters in the same classroom are markedly different from one another, it is difficult for the teachers to help them reach their academic potential without some kind of assistance. The differentiated program and services that the schools devise for children who differ significantly from the norm is called **special education**. The responsibility for providing an appropriate education to exceptional children, however, is shared by all educational staff of the school. Cooperation and joint planning between regular and special education personnel are important to reach the goal of appropriate educational strategies for all children.

THE ROLE OF ASSESSMENT

We examine the issue of comprehensive assessment in more depth throughout this book. But it is important to realize that a child is developing on many different physical and psychological dimensions at once. To understand a child's problems, we must keep track of individual differences in each of those dimensions.

The task of determining how an individual child is different, and along which dimensions, has become a major step in identifying and educating exceptional children. Such assessment serves two purposes. First, it identifies which children are eligible for special services. Second, it may provide information by which an individualized plan to meet the child's particular needs can be formulated.

Teachers can use five general approaches to provide an assessment of a child: norm-referenced tests, diagnostic achievement tests, interviews, observations, and informal assessments. Each approach has its advantages and shortcomings, which we summarize in Table 1.1. Generally, a combination of these tests and procedures is used to detect and thoroughly evaluate a child's inter-individual and intra-individual differences. These differences and their assessment are discussed in the following sections.

Inter-Individual Differences

Inter-individual differences are substantial differences among people along key dimensions of development. Special educators assess inter-individual differences along key dimensions such as academic aptitude, academic performance, language development, psychomotor skills, and psychosocial development.

Academic Aptitude. One area in which inter-individual differences show up is academic aptitude. The measure of children's aptitudes can tell teachers and schools a great deal about their student population and about how students are performing in relationship to their potential.

For decades the standard measure of academic aptitude has been the intelligence test. These tests measure the development of memory, association, reasoning, evaluation, and classification—the mental operations so important to school performance. In fact, these tests are accurate predictors of academic performance: Those who score high on intelligence tests generally do well in school; those who score low generally do poorly. You probably recognize these sample items from tests you've taken:

Mental Operations

Memory	Who was the first president of the United States?
Association	Glove is to hand as shoe is to _____.
Reasoning	If Paul is taller than Sam and Sam is taller than Tom, then Tom is _____ than Paul.
Classification	Which of the following does not belong? chair, sofa, table, red.
Evaluation	Why should we not tell lies?

Any serious problem with—or developmental delay in—the mental operations that these tests evaluate can create major difficulties in school. Intelligence tests

TABLE 1.1	Assessment strategies: Strengths and weaknesses	
Strategy	**Advantages**	**Disadvantages**
Norm-referenced test	It provides a comparison of a particular child's performance against the performance of a reference group of children, as in intelligence and achievement tests.	It does not provide reasons for the results; for culturally different children, the reference groups used for comparison may be inappropriate.
Diagnostic achievement test	It is designed to provide a profile of strengths and weaknesses, analyses of errors, etc., in arithmetic or reading to pinpoint specific academic problems of the student for remediation.	The scores generated by such instruments often have limited or suspect reliability; consequently, the profiles may not be very valuable.
Interview	Information from the child, parent, teacher, or others can provide perspective and insight into the reasons for the child's current performance.	All interviewees see the child through personal perspectives that may be limited by scope of experience or personal bias and, in particular, reference to themselves.
Observation	It can provide information based on the child's spontaneous behavior in natural settings and a basis for intervention planning.	The child may not reveal significant behaviors during the observation; the meaning of the child's behavior may be unclear.
Informal assessment	Information from teacher-made tests, particular language samples, portfolios, or descriptions of significant events in the life of the child may yield valuable insights leading to effective educational planning.	It is rarely possible to match a particular child's performance with the performance of others on these measures or observations. Such measures should be used with caution.

assume a common experience base for most children (and the desire of the child to do well). The results of such tests for youngsters for whom English is a second language or youngsters who have had atypical early childhood experiences need to be used with caution. An example of the areas measured by an intelligence test is seen in Table 1.2. The often-used test described in the table is the Wechsler Intelligence Scale for Children—Revised (WISC-R).

Intelligence tests have come under severe attack in recent years. One reason is that there is strong disagreement over the use and meaning of intelligence quotient (IQ) scores. In the past, those scores have been used (1) to indicate innate intellectual potential, (2) to predict future academic performance, and (3) to indicate a child's present rate of mental development compared with that of same-age children. The sharpest criticism has been raised over the use of IQ scores to indicate intellectual potential. Intelligence tests are not pure measures of intellectual potential and never should be used to try to demonstrate the innate superiority of one sex or ethnic or racial group over another. But they are valuable predictors of academic performance and indicators of current academic aptitude. They are useful when employed for these purposes.

One other criticism has been that standard IQ tests yield a single IQ score, when in fact many people believe that intelligence is multidimensional. Gardner's theory of multiple intelligences (1992) is the most well-known proposal of a multifaceted view of intelligence. Gardner has proposed seven major dimensions of intelligence: *linguistic, musical, logical-mathematical, spatial, bodily-kinesthetic, social awareness,* and *self-awareness.* These dimensions provide some basis for differentiating curriculum, but we have yet to see the full development of educational programming based on Gardner's model of intelligence.

Among the puzzles regarding intelligence are where it comes from and to what extent we can expect to change it with educational interventions. Perkins (1995) has presented a plausible answer to these questions in summarizing what is known about the construct. He proposes three separate aspects of intelligence:

- *Neural intelligence:* some kind of neural efficiency composed of the speed and precision of information processing in the neural system
- *Experiential intelligence:* the knowledge we gain through extended lived experience in academic areas like physics or nonacademic areas like raising a family
- *Reflective intelligence:* thinking strategies, positive attitudes toward investing oneself in good thinking, and metacognition-awareness and management of one's own mind

If Perkins's perception is close to the truth, we then have reason to believe that we can provide the stimulus for students to *improve* their intelligence by enlarging on the experiential domain and by helping students learn to be more reflective and to use more of their metacognitive capabilities than they have done previously.

Academic Performance. Two well-accepted approaches to describing inter-individual differences in academic performance are standard (norm-referenced) achievement tests and diagnostic achievement tests. **Standard (norm-referenced) achievement tests**

Intelligence tests are not pure measures of intellectual potential; rather, they are valuable predictors and indicators of academic ability and performance.

TABLE 1.2	Areas Measured by the Wechsler Intelligence Scale for Children–Revised

Verbal Section

Information (30 items). This subtest measures the student's knowledge of general information and facts. Examples include "What do we call a baby cow?" and "What are hieroglyphics?"

Similarities (17 items). This subtest measures a student's ability to perceive the common element of two terms. Examples include "In what way are an apple and a banana alike? anger and joy? mountain and lake?"

Arithmetic (18 items). This subtest measures the student's ability to solve problems requiring arithmetic computations and reasoning. This is primarily an oral subtest requiring concentration.

Vocabulary (32 items). In this subtest, the student is told a word and must orally define it. Items range in difficulty from *knife*, *umbrella*, and *clock* to *obliterate*, *imminent*, and *dilatory*.

Comprehension (17 items). This subtest measures the social, moral, and ethical judgment of the student, who must answer questions such as "What are you supposed to do if you find someone's wallet or pocketbook in a store?" and "Why are criminals locked up?"

Digit Span (14 items). This subtest includes two parts: Digits Forward and Digits Backward. The student is given a series of digits at a rate of one digit per second. Digits Forward requires the students to say them back exactly. Digits Backward requires the student to say the numbers in reverse order. There are seven progressively longer series of digits for both sections.

Performance Section

Picture Completion (26 items). In this subtest, the student is shown a picture in which an important element is missing. The student must either verbalize or point to the missing element.

Picture Arrangement (13 items). In this subtest, the student is given a series of pictures that represent a story but are in incorrect order. The task is to sequence the pictures in the correct order.

Block Design (11 items). In this subtest, the student must look at pictures of certain designs and reproduce these using red and white blocks. This subtest basically measures visual analysis and synthesis.

TABLE 1.2	Areas Measured by the Wechsler Intelligence Scale for Children–Revised (cont.)

Object Assembly (4 items). This subtest for visual organization and synthesis requires the student to put together four jigsaw puzzles.

Coding (45 items). This subtest requires the student to copy geometric symbols that are paired or coded with other symbols within a certain time limit. There are two parts, A for children under age 8, and B for individuals of age 8 and over.

Mazes (supplementary, 4 items). This subtest requires the child to use skills in visual planning to complete a number of progressively more difficult mazes.

Source: Ronald L. Taylor. *Assessment of Exceptional Students: Educational and Psychological Procedures.* Copyright © 1989 by Allyn and Bacon. Reprinted with permission.

measure the student's level of achievement compared with that of students of similar age or grade. These tests tell whether the student is achieving at expected levels of performance, but usually they do not tell *why* the student is not performing as well as he or she might. **Diagnostic achievement tests** help determine the process the student is using to solve a problem or decode a reading passage so that we can understand why this particular student is not mastering some aspect of the school curriculum—that is, why he or she is not performing at the level of other students. Figure 1.4 shows four diagnostic arithmetic items.

Language Development. Language, one of the most complex of human functions, is particularly vulnerable to problems affecting the development of children. Because using language effectively is one of the keys to academic success, it is one dimension to be carefully analyzed, particularly when a student is not performing well.

Both receptive language (listening) and expressive language (speaking) often need separate assessment. The Test of Adolescent Language—2 (Hammill, Brown, Larsen, & Weiderholt, 1987) is used to examine the dimensions of listening/vocabulary, listening/grammar, speaking/vocabulary, speaking/grammar, reading/vocabulary, reading/grammar, writing/vocabulary, and writing/grammar. This comprehensive measure allows the special educator to find areas of relative strength and weakness in the child's linguistic processes and to develop some specific plans for an individualized program of instruction.

Psychosocial Development. Another area of inter-individual difference is the individual child's ability to respond to the social environment, or how well the child is able to adapt. Does the child show aggressive tendencies when frustrated? Is he or she able to work cooperatively with others? How does the child react when things don't go right? How well the child is able to do these things when faced with increasingly complex social interactions (for example, with teachers or peers) strongly influences how well he or she will adapt as an adult.

Social adaptation also greatly influences how the exceptional child responds to remediation. Many children who fail to respond to special programs have behav-

Listening and speaking need to be addressed separately from one another.

Figure I.4
Diagnostic Arithmetic Items

143 − 28 125	The student subtracts the smaller digit in each column from the larger digit regardless of which is on top.
143 − 28 125	When the student needs to borrow, he adds 10 to the top digit of the current column without subtracting 1 from the next column to the left.
140 − 21 121	Whenever the top digit in a column is 0, the student writes the bottom digit in the answer; i.e., $0 - N = N$.
662 −357 205	Once the student needs to borrow from a column, s/he continues to borrow from every column whether s/he needs to or not.

Source: J. Brown and R. Burton (1978). Diagnostic models for procedural bugs in basic mathematic skills. *Cognitive Science, 2,* p. 182.

ioral and social problems, not academic ones. It is difficult to remediate a reading disability if a child has a severe attention problem or becomes aggressive when frustrated. For this reason, special educators often focus on behavioral and social problems at the same time as they tackle academic difficulties.

To assess psychosocial development, we often rely on the observations of others—parents, teachers, and caregivers—for information on how the child behaves in different settings. Rating scales can be used to bring some order to these judgments.

Another strategy is to systematically observe the child at home or school so that we can catalog the child's typical patterns of behavior. When children are able to articulate, we can ask them about their feelings or perceptions of themselves. These self-reports can be very revealing. They might show that a gifted child has a very low self-concept even though people around him say he is well adjusted. Or they might show that a child with retardation has a very unrealistic view of her own abilities.

Tests of adaptive behavior such as the AAMD Adaptive Behavior Scale, the Vineland Social Maturity Scale, and the System of Multicultural Pluralistic Assessment (SOMPA) are also available (Mercer & Lewis, 1977). Table 1.3 shows sample items from the Vineland Adaptive Behavior Scales that measure degree-of-coping ability and socialization. Such tests, together with interviews, can also explore histories of violent or antisocial behavior and of eccentric or unacceptable habits and measure both self-direction and responsibility. From the results of the tests and interviews, educators are able to tell how a child is adapting in terms of social and cooperative behaviors, which helps them create an individualized program to meet the child's needs. The accumulated information may sometimes be placed in a developmental profile such as shown in Figure 1.5 to provide a quick portrait of the child's development.

TABLE 1.3	Sample items from the Vineland Adaptive Behavior Scales
Domain	**Sample Items**
Communication	Turns eyes and head toward sound (ages <1 to 2 years) Uses sentences of four or more words (age 2 years)
Daily living skills	Uses sharp knife to cut food (ages 12 to 15 years) Washes own clothes (ages 16 to 18+ years)
Socialization	Makes own friends (ages 7 to 10 years) Has a hobby (ages 13 to 14 years)
Motor skills	Runs with some falling (age 2 years) Throws ball (ages 5+ years)
Maladaptive behavior	Has temper tantrums Displays behaviors that are self-injurious

Source: "Sample Items from the Vineland Adaptive Behavior Scales." J. Sattler (1988). *Assessment of Children* (3rd ed.) (San Diego, CA: Author). Copyright © 1988. Used by permission of the author.

Intra-Individual Differences

What sometimes goes unnoticed is that some students differ substantially from others not only along key dimensions of development (inter-individual differences), but also within their own abilities (intra-individual differences). A child may have the intelligence of an 11-year-old but the social behavior of a 6-year-old. Both inter-individual and intra-individual differences are the concern of special educators.

Understanding a child's **intra-individual differences**—the differences in abilities *within* the same child—can help us develop individualized programs of instruction. These programs are tailored to the strengths and weaknesses of the individual child. They do not necessarily consider how that child compares with other children.

Intra-individual differences can show up in any area: intellectual, psychological, physical, or social. A child may be very bright but unable to see or hear. Or a child may be developing normally physically but be unable to relate socially to his or her agemates. It is just as important for teachers to know the child's unique pattern of strengths and weaknesses as it is to know how the child compares with other children.

DEVELOPMENTAL PROFILES

How are inter-individual and intra-individual differences monitored and explored? Developmental profiles provide one way to track the range of an individual's differences. Figure 1.5 shows the developmental profiles of two children. Joan is

Figure 1.5

Profiles of a Child with Intellectual Gifts and a Child with Mental Retardation

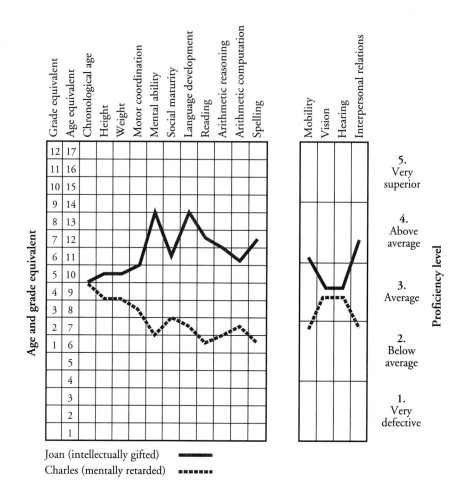

Joan (intellectually gifted) ▬▬▬▬
Charles (mentally retarded) ▪▪▪▪▪▪▪

an intellectually gifted 10-year-old. Her mental ability tests at age 14; her achievement in reading and arithmetic tests at from one to four grades beyond her fifth-grade classmates. These are the inter-individual differences between Joan and her classmates. But notice that Joan's performance shows many intra-individual differences. Although mentally she has the ability of a 14-year-old, her physical development is about average for a girl her age, and her social maturity is only slightly higher. If her parents or teachers expect her to behave like a 14-year-old in every dimension of development because her mental development is at that level, they are going to be disappointed.

The second profile in the figure is of Charles, a child with mental retardation. His profile shows him to be behind in development and performance in almost every dimension. Although he is 10 years old, his mental ability and academic performance are at first- and second-grade levels. These inter-individual differences distinguish Charles from his classmates. In addition, Charles shows substantial intra-individual differences, ranging from the 6- and 7-year-old level in academic achievement to the 9- and 10-year-old levels in physical development and life age.

Joan and Charles have very different exceptionalities. Yet both present similar problems for their teachers and schools: Their inter- and intra-individual differences set them apart from their classmates and require special educational attention.

CULTURE AND ASSESSMENT

When cultural values and attitudes differ substantially from the middle-class values that so strongly influence and direct the activities of the public schools, then predictable adaptation problems arise for children from culturally different circumstances and for their educators (Good, 1987). Consider Jorge, a 10-year-old Hispanic child with learning disabilities that prevent him from grasping the reading process. Jorge comes from a rich tradition of a close-knit family with common interests and loyalty. The family is also wary about the Anglo schools that Jorge is attending. When teachers and psychologists from a different culture tell the family that something is wrong with Jorge's approach to school, are they reflecting a prejudice against Jorge because of his Hispanic background and his bilingual family? Are they going to help Jorge, or is this a way to prevent Jorge from getting a proper education? Will Jorge's father, misunderstanding the school's message, put even *more* pressure on Jorge to do well in school, assuming that his son is not giving proper effort to his school lessons? The opportunities for misunderstanding from one culture to another are great and can substantially complicate the original learning problems faced by the exceptional child.

One of the observations that can be quickly made is that students in special education programs are often disproportionately of one gender or ethnic or racial background (or a combination). This observation applies whether we are viewing programs for children with mental retardation, with intellectual giftedness, or with emotional disturbance. Such a result has raised many questions in the minds of educators and the general public. Why should there be an excess of African-American students in programs for the mentally retarded (Heller, Holtzman, & Messick, 1982), an excess of Hispanic students in programs for learning disabilities (Cummings, 1986), and an excess of Asian students in programs for the intellectually gifted (Gallagher, 1991)? Some answers to these questions can be found in the nature of the assessment itself, the environmental conditions in which the child was raised, and differing family and school values.

Culture-Bound Assessment Measures

One possible explanation for these discrepancies has zeroed in on the assessment measures that help determine the eligibility of students for these special services. The standard intelligence test, for example, is based on assumptions of a common past experience base for the students. It is expected that the 9- or 10-year-old student has come into reasonably frequent contact with such words as *letter, diamond,* and *iron.* If personal experience has not brought the child into contact with such linguistic symbols, however, then the child's ability to learn, which is one of

Children vary greatly within their own abilities. For example, a child with a physical disability may have above-average intelligence. Such intraindividual differences are a prime concern of special educators. (© Alan Carey/The Image Works)

the key goals of intelligence tests, is possibly being underestimated, and the student may be inappropriately referred to special education.

An incorrect diagnosis can also be made if a teacher misinterprets a culturally different child's behavior as disturbing or resistant. Our expectations for students' behavior are shaped by the norms of the majority culture, and those expectations influence our evaluation of students' performance. Gage and Berliner (1988) used punctuality as an example:

> If we have grown up believing that punctuality demonstrates interest and concern, we are offended when someone is late. In cultures where time is a resource to be conserved, punctuality is important. In cultures where time is just a convenient reference for organizing activities, punctuality is far less important and being late is not a sign of disrespect. We may think that children who consistently arrive at school late are unmotivated or uninterested. But we should ask whether time simply has a different meaning for them. Although lateness may be disruptive in school and we may want to correct the problem, we have to be careful about our attributions. Our response to the children should vary according to the causes to which we attribute their behavior. (p. 196)

Environmental Conditions

A second explanation for the disproportionate representation of minority children in special education programs has to do with unfavorable environmental conditions. Many minority youngsters are born and raised in conditions such as poverty that predispose them to identification as children with mild mental retardation, emotional disturbance, or learning disabilities.

With poverty, for example, come malnutrition and inadequate health care, which can affect physical development. Family disorganization, stress, single-parent families, and mothers working outside the home are other byproducts of poverty. These factors may limit the verbal exchanges between parents and children and the opportunity for children to learn basic skills because their parents are not available to teach them or are under such pressure to survive economically that they have little time for them. Developmental problems caused by environmental deficits are believed to be progressive. Garber (1988) described them as *cumulative deficits,* or elements that gradually lower the functional intelligence of youngsters and increase their adaptive problems.

Conflicting Values

Another reason for the disproportionate number of minority children in special education programs is the general perception of "education" that the subculture that includes the particular child and the family may hold. For those who work in the field of education, it is often surprising that not all groups share our generally positive attitude toward education. Think of the child who is brought up in a culture that sees the educational system as a meaningless or obnoxious requirement that yields few benefits. Alternatively, think of the child who is brought up to view the educational system as a means by which the white cultural majority tries to subvert or suppress certain important cultural values of the subgroup. How different would that student's attitude be if he or she were raised in an environment in which education is seen as the major highway to the social improvement of self and family?

Clearly, a child's raw native ability needs substantial help from those persons important in his or her life to crystallize into the hard work, persistence, and anticipated rewards necessary for school success. Such cultural values as those just noted set the expectations of student performance and may well determine the amount of time and effort students are likely to put into schoolwork, before that time when they are driven by their own developing interests in a topic.

Child-Family Interaction

The various forms of assessment and developmental profiles are highly useful in understanding and charting specific characteristics of children. Recall, however, that we stress the importance of viewing the child in the *context* of family and societal forces. Although less easily measured than inter-individual and intra-individual characteristics, these forces nevertheless have a powerful impact on a child's development.

Let us think of two youngsters, Dan and Pablo, each of whom has been born with a moderate case of cerebral palsy, a disorder caused by damage to the parts of the central nervous system that control motor movements. This condition is certain to cause mobility and communications problems for both children. Each will surely find his way into some form of special services that exist in practically all school systems in the United States.

Dan's family viewed his arrival as a true disaster. Dan's mother sees his disability as a serious hindrance to her pursuing her own career goals. Despite her efforts to put such feelings aside, the resentment of what Dan's presence means to her and her interests is hard to submerge entirely. Similarly, Dan's father, struggling in his own career, sees Dan as a heavy and continuing burden of special expenses and needed therapies and, in the end, perhaps dependence on the family far into the future. These feelings, too, are hard to contain.

In Pablo's family, however, after the initial disappointment of the diagnosis of cerebral palsy, his arrival was accepted as a special challenge. His mother and father told Pablo's siblings that he will have some problems developing and that it is the responsibility of everyone in the family to help him develop as best he can. Both his mother and his father have felt the sting of social rejection in the past, and they are determined to do whatever they can to make sure that Pablo is accepted as a normal child.

Now think about Dan and Pablo at age 6: Which child do you think is more likely to be responsive to peers and teachers, and which child will become more quickly discouraged by failure and need more external support?

Differences in family attitudes, actions, and support result in variations in how children with special developmental problems such as cerebral palsy adjust to education or cope with their special condition. Thus, it is essential to consider familial and societal variables, in addition to assessing children's developmental profiles, to better understand what has happened to them in their family life before they entered school, or even what is happening in their life now beyond the school environment. Interviews can provide important information about the context of the child.

PARENTAL RESPONSE

As the example of Dan and Pablo shows, parents nearly always react strongly (whether positively or negatively) to the birth of an exceptional child. And it is important to consider these responses, because they happen to every parent, regardless of his or her educational background or socioeconomic level.

Most parents who must cope with a child with serious disabilities face two major crises. The first is the "symbolic death" of the child who was to be. When their child is first diagnosed as having a serious disability, most parents feel shock and then denial, guilt, anger, and sadness before they finally adjust (Peterson, 1987). Some parents react with severe depression (Bristol, Gallagher, & Schopler, 1988). Many move through a type of grieving process, as though their child had died (Farber, 1986), and they may wish to share their experience with others. This common sharing of problems is the basis for forming relationships with other parents experiencing similar situations. Members of groups composed of parents of children with similar disabilities are quite effective in helping new parents by sharing how they have coped with these problems.

Parents of a child with serious disabilities must face two crises: the symbolic death at birth of the child-who-could-have-been and the difficulty of providing daily care for the child-who-is.

The relationship between an exceptional child and his or her family is lifelong and complex. Basic family responsibilities include economics, domestic and health care, recreation, self-identity, affection, socialization, and educational and vocational choices. (© *Robert Crandall/Medical Images*)

The second, quite different, crisis that many parents of exceptional children face is the problem of providing daily care for the child. The child who has cerebral palsy or is emotionally disturbed is often difficult to feed, dress, and put to bed. It is the continual, day-by-day responsibilities for care that often weigh families down and require sympathetic professional attention. The realization that their child will not go through the normal developmental process or may never become an independent adult often weighs heavily on the parents.

FAMILY RESPONSIBILITIES

The relationship between an exceptional child and his or her family is lifelong and complex, beginning with the disclosure of the exceptionality. When a child with disabilities is added to the family, the daily responsibilities grow larger. There is the additional expense, the time, and the energy needed to care for the child; the extra concern for the child's safety; the difficulty of helping the child develop a good self-image and social skills; and the problems of seeing that the child receives an appropriate education. Many ordinary tasks become more difficult and more stressful. Consider Pablo's care:

The responsibilities of two-parent working families are awesome enough without adding the special condition of a child with disabilities. Pablo's father and mother are awakened at 6:30 in the morning by the cries of Pablo's sister. Pablo has to be washed and dressed, a task of considerable difficulty because of his cerebral palsy. Meanwhile Pablo's mother is setting out breakfast while beginning to think about her own workday as a teacher at a local school.

Pablo's father has gotten Pablo washed and dressed and down to the breakfast table and now begins to think about a shower and shave before going to the construction company where he works. Before work, he must deliver Pablo to the developmental day-care program, where he is in an integrated program with his age peers. The family is fortunate in that Pablo's sister goes to school where the mother teaches, so one transportation problem is solved.

Breakfast is a wild round robin with no one sitting down at the same time. Pablo needs extra help from one of the adults because of his inability to totally control the tools needed to bring cereal and milk to the proper resting place. Mother puts the breakfast dishes in the dishwasher, and father is off with Pablo while mother makes the beds before being off to school.

In the late afternoon and evening the same procedure is reversed. This time mother has to stop by and pick up Pablo because father is at a construction site on the other side of town. She is delayed further by the teacher describing an incident at the day-care center that involved Pablo's conflict with another child over possession of some toy. There is still dinner to prepare and baths to give and reading of stories before the children are tucked in. Is it any wonder that the parents are weary at the end of the day and are not looking forward to tomorrow when Pablo is to receive a medical checkup on top of the normal daily activities? Which parent is going to see to it that the medical visit gets done?

Imagine, first of all, this type of routine with only one parent present to do all of the tasks required. How much more harried and tired such a mother (most of the time the one parent) is at the end of the day. Imagine further what would happen if there was not some tacit agreement between the parents about who was supposed to do what, or if there were interpersonal tensions between mother and father because they cannot agree about the proper way to discipline Pablo or just because their own personal needs continually take second place to the requirements of the children. It is not hard to see that this family is a key to positive experiences for the exceptional child or why all of the family members need understanding and support from time to time.

When considering basic family responsibilities, it is important to realize the enormous diversity of families themselves. There has been a substantial increase in one-parent families, both through divorce and through lack of marriage. Because many single mothers live in poverty, their children are less likely to receive good prenatal and postnatal care, which increases their chances of having children with physical, academic, and emotional problems.

Even in two-parent families that have a child with disabilities, fathers generally do not come to the aid of mothers by increasing their presence, helping around the house, or taking care of the child (Gallagher & Bristol, 1986). The father may get a second job to help pay for the additional expenses and, as a consequence, not be in the home very much at all. A mother who thinks that this is an appropriate and loving thing to do accepts this behavior. A mother who sees such behavior by the

Anatomy Is Not Destiny

Today most nondisabled people assume that a baby with a permanent disability will lead a damaged life. They place the label "handicapped" on such a baby and think that the child's physical condition will in and of itself limit and define the person she will grow to be. If nondisabled men and women spent more time talking to disabled men and women, they would learn that anatomy is not destiny and never has been.

My own disability was not detected in infancy. It was only when I became a toddler who did not toddle, a wild grabber with no grip, that the unusual word *athetosis* was spoken. Perhaps now, with sophisticated reflex tests, athetosis, which is a form of cerebral palsy and which arises from a momentary lack of oxygen to an infant's brain during the birth process, can be detected almost immediately. I hope not. I am convinced that I benefited from those months of being treated as a normal baby. Moreover, since my parents had been successfully caring for me as well as my older brothers for a while before they heard the news, it was easier for them to realize that my problem, though unfortunate, was not a family disaster.

Although my disability affected my gait, coordination, and speech, few of my early memories concern disability. What I remember are trips to the beach and trips to the park, a new baby in the house, vying with my older brothers for the dog's attention, Halloween pumpkins, Christmas trees, and a baby sitter for New Year's Eve who came equipped with party hats and noisemakers. There were times when I was baffled at why people thought I called my best doll by the dumb name "Aya," when I had really named her Amelia. I wondered, too, at the proverbs that seemed to float my way. One was, "Slow and steady wins the race."

Another was, "If at first you don't succeed, try, try again." I repeated that one often because it always got applause. Yet it was beyond me why anyone would want to "suck a seed." My moments of puzzlement never lasted very long. . . . I was too busy being a kid.

Much of the credit for all this goes to my parents. They were devoted to me and untiring in their efforts to give me every advantage. I can say so much about them that it is probably best if I say very little. However, partial credit also goes to my orthopedist. He was extraordinary. Unlike many orthopedists of that time, he eschewed surgery and bracing. Unlike many doctors specializing in the physical effects of neurological injuries, he was connected with an outpatient rehabilitation center rather than a teaching hospital. He did only incidental research. He had no residents to keep occupied. His main professional goal was to help people with disabilities live up to their potential.

My orthopedist believed that athetosis could not be cured for the simple reason that it was not a disease but a functional impairment. However, just as a dancer through consistent exercise could surpass what would otherwise be her physical limits, so could a person with athetosis. He advised moderate amounts of physical therapy, occupational therapy, and speech therapy. More important, he emphasized that I would do all right as an adult, provided that as a child I was given the same opportunities I would have been given had I not had a disability.

The doctor felt it was crucial that physically disabled children attend regular school classes. Special education was inferior, segregated education that could handicap anyone for life. Thus, when I was 6, I started first grade at the public school down the block. →

27

Most of my teachers were open-minded and tolerant. The fact that I did well in my schoolwork may have earned me an acceptance that I might not have had if I'd been one of the poorer students in the class. Some of my teachers might not have been so gracious about giving me special help in getting my coat from the closet if I had also needed special help in reading. As for the other children, they could see that I used my body differently from the way they did, but once they got used to the unusualness of it, they accepted my disability just as we who lived in "regular" families accepted the fact that, for reasons we did not understand, little Dolores Hannings had a working mother and no father. I had friends. I was invited to birthday parties.

Later, in seventh and eighth grades, I did have some problems with other kids. We were all so terribly insecure. The fat girl who taunted me for not having a boyfriend and who sang "Miss Pop-U-larity" whenever she saw me coming did not have a boyfriend herself. I laughed at kids, too, usually the ones labeled stupid. "Mock and be mocked" seemed to be the slogan of those times. By high school, we all had grown up a bit, and things ebbed back to normal. . . . I became a senior [at Wellesley College] in heady 1974. It was the height of the women's movement, and the emphasis was on careers with a capital C. It seemed as if half the women I knew were applying to law school. . . . At Harvard [Law School] I was on my own more than ever before while still having the structure and security of an academic community. I did adequately, though not brilliantly, in my courses. I loved living in Cambridge. I had a social life involving men. I wanted law school to go on and on. Unfortunately—or so it seemed at the time—it ended after three years.

Since 1977 I have been employed in the law department of a major insurance company. I specialize in the state regulation of automobile and homeowners' insurance, contract drafting, and copyrights. Working for a corporation is better for me than working in a law firm because I work with the same people over and over again, and I do not have to worry about drumming up clients. My job is not especially thrilling, but it is a good job, and I don't take it for granted.

In the past few years I have become increasingly involved in disability rights. This is a movement composed of both disabled and nondisabled individuals who believe that the biggest problem disabled people face is prejudice. Our goals are equal rights and the full integration of people with disabilities in today's society. . . . My idea of physical well-being is simply living up to one's physical potential, and I hope to live up to mine. I have taken yoga, and I now have an exercise program supervised by a physical therapist whose approach is holistic. I walk like a drunken turtle, but I do walk, sometimes for substantial distances. My increase in physical self-esteem has had side effects: I used to buy clothes for work in discount stores. No polyester shift in size 10 was too cheap or too large. Now I buy many of my clothes in dress shops and only in my correct size, which is 6. . . . A few weeks ago, when I was having lunch at a coffee shop, I spilled some ketchup. The woman at the table next to mine shook her gray head sadly. I remained silent and just mopped up the ketchup. Yet I wanted to tell her that she shouldn't be so concerned. For who among us has not spilled ketchup?

father as a device for avoiding the problem and dodging responsibility may be quite unhappy in that situation.

The perception that each partner is taking responsibility for the family in an acceptable way determines **family harmony** (Bristol, Gallagher, & Schopler, 1988). The important factor for family harmony is whether the mother and father come to some form of understanding about the roles and responsibilities that each will hold in the family. The specific actions of one or the other parent are less important than the understanding that those behaviors have been agreed upon as appropriate at a particular stage in the family life cycle.

You should not imagine that, just because there are many stresses in the lives of families who have children with disabilities, such lives are joyless or without laughter and fun. These children can light up your heart with a smile just as any child can, and parents of children with disabilities have their own favorite stories of their young child's adventures in development as other parents do. The child is always a child first and a child with problems second. The task of the professional is to allow that child to bloom and grow to the limit of his or her capabilities.

Only when both parents understand and accept what each person's role and responsibilities will be in caring for a child with disabilities will there be family harmony.

CHANGING FAMILY ROLES

Recently, traditional family roles have undergone substantive changes. We now shift our focus to some of the causes of these changes—the external forces influencing the family of an exceptional child.

Working Mothers

Perhaps the greatest change in family roles has been in the movement of women into the work force. In 1948, less than 11 percent of mothers with children younger than age 6 worked. In the 1990 census, the median figure for the fifty states was 62 percent of mothers with children younger than 6 years of age (Zill & Nord, 1993).

When we spoke in the past of family-professional relationships, we were speaking mainly of *mother*-professional relationships. Traditionally, fathers have not played a large role in continuous relationships with professionals. Only recently have fathers become a source of study in the families of children with disabilities (Lamb, 1986). This development reflects the way in which families adapt to the necessity and reality of dual careers.

Parent Empowerment

Parent empowerment refers to the parents no longer passively and unthinkingly taking advice from a professional or team of professionals about the treatment of their child with special needs. Parents of exceptional children are now expected to play a major and determining role in their child's care, and the professionals are to provide needed counsel and specialized advice.

The expected change in the relationship between the professional (physician, social worker, psychologist, teacher, and so on) and the family of a child with disabilities is often subtle but meaningful. Table 1.4 provides the contrasting approaches of past and present. According to the traditional view, the professional plays the role of the kindly but firm holder of knowledge who tries to provide needed information and skills to the parents. Parents are expected to receive this advice and counsel and carry out that advice in the best interests of their child. This traditional doctor-patient relationship puts family members in a passive and expectant attitude, waiting for the wisdom of the professional to be delivered before they feel free to act.

The current approach has the family actively seeking and collecting information from many different sources, particularly other parents of children who have disabilities and have had experiences similar to their own. In this approach, the parents draw on the expertise of the professional community but make many of their own decisions about what is best for their child. These and other differences between the traditional and active approaches are described in Table 1.4.

Parents as Team Members

Many intervention programs for children with disabilities are developed and monitored by a multidisciplinary team. The team may include the child's teacher, special educators, doctors, therapists, and parents. Parents serve three primary functions as team members. First their observations of the child are a valuable source of information to the professional. This information becomes part of the basis for the child's educational program and the evaluation of that program. Second, parents—especially the parents of preschoolers—often take an active part in the teaching process. They may be trained by team members to teach specific skills (such as living skills, preacademic skills, mobility skills, and communication skills)

TABLE 1.4   Changing Views of Family Participation

Traditional Approach	Current Approach
1. Parents' greatest need is to accept the burden of raising their child and to become realistic about his or her limitations.	1. Families need to be encouraged to dream about what they want for themselves and their child with a disability, and they need assistance in making those dreams come true.
2. Parents' difficulties in coping with the child are largely psychological or psychiatric in nature, and the proper intervention is psychiatric or psychological counseling.	2. Families can benefit from each other. One benefit that almost all families need is the emotional resiliency and information that other families have acquired about life with disabilities.
3. Mothers need respite to alleviate the stress and burden of caring for their child.	3. Families need for the child with disabilities to have friends and integrated recreational options.
4. Mothers need the professional to provide clinical information about disability.	4. Families need information about and inspiration from people with a disability who are successfully integrated into community life.
5. Mothers need training related to skill development and behavior management so they can be follow-through teachers for their child.	5. Families need encouragement and ways to ensure that the child has a functional education taught in natural environments by natural helpers in those environments (e.g., family, friends, store clerks, bus drivers, scout leaders).
6. Many families are financially unable to meet their child's needs and should seek out-of-home placement.	6. Many families need new policies (e.g., direct subsidies and new tax credits) to help meet the financial demands associated with disability.

Source: From "Changing Views of Family Participation," in *Supporting Families with a Child with a Disability* by A. Gartner, D. K. Lipsky, and A. P. Turnbull. Baltimore: Paul H. Brookes, pp. 2–3. Used by permission.

to their child. Third, with training, parents are able to reinforce learning. They are able to see that the functional skills that the child learns in school are applied in the home. The shift over time has been to move the parent closer to the decision-

Parents are active members of the multidisciplinary intervention team for children with disabilities. They can make valuable observations of the child, teach specific skills, and reinforce learning. (© *Jerry Howard/Positive Images*)

maker role in each of these areas, at least to encourage the parents to share their child's interests and capabilities with other parents.

Parents as Advocates

The recognition that society and schools have a responsibility for exceptional children stemmed in large measure from the activities of some of those children's parents. Parents who were unable to get help for their children from local governments created their own programs in church basements, vacant stores, and any place that would house them. These informal groups, loosely formed around the common needs of the children, often provided important information to new parents struggling to find help for their children with disabilities. They were also a source of emotional support for parents, a means of sharing and solving the problems of accepting and living with exceptional children.

These groups quickly realized that fundamental changes were needed in the allocation of educational resources at local, state, and federal levels. A casual, haphazard approach was not going to provide the kind of help that parents or their exceptional children needed. Accordingly, in the 1940s and 1950s, large parents' groups, such as the National Association of Retarded Citizens, the United Cerebral Palsy Association, and, in the 1960s, the Association for Children with Learning Disabilities, began to form. Parents of children with Down syndrome, autism, and other specific conditions have also formed groups to ensure attention to their children's special needs. These parent organizations have successfully stimulated legislation at the state and federal levels providing for additional trained personnel, research, and other programs that have brought children with disabilities to the attention of the general public and have attracted more qualified people into the field.

Organized parents' groups for children who are gifted have only recently been formed and have not yet had the same political influence as the national organizations for children with disabilities. Still, these groups are helping the parents of children who are gifted cope with the problems of precocious development (Gallagher & Gallagher, 1994).

SIBLINGS

We now know enough about the family environment to dismiss the proposition that two children experienced the *same* environment when they were growing up merely because they lived in the same household. Obviously the home environment is not the same for a child with disabilities as it is for his or her normal sibling, or for an older daughter as it is for a younger daughter. We should study the home environment through the eyes of the particular child with whom we are concerned. It is less important to know how much income the family has or how many siblings than it is to know how each family member perceives other family members (McCall, 1987).

Assumptions often made about families with a child with disability are that the nondisabled sibling is inevitably neglected because the parents must pay so much attention to the child with disabilities, and that as a result the sibling becomes resentful of the child with disabilities. It is now clear that although this set of events may happen, it certainly doesn't have to happen, particularly when the parents are sensitive to sibling rivalry and the needs for attention for the siblings as well as for the child with disabilities (McHale & Gamble, 1989).

As McHale and Harris (1992) point out, siblings of the child with disability spend at least the same amount of time with their mothers and receive the same type of discipline as their brother or sister with disabilities receives, although they do perform a greater amount of household tasks. The sibling who appears most vulnerable for special adjustment problems seems to be the older sibling to whom the parents have given special child-care responsibilities. As in other family situations, it is not so much the actions of the parents that count, as how the sibling interprets those actions. If the sibling is sure of being loved and cared for by the parent, then being given additional responsibilities for the child with disabilities does not seem to matter (Powell & Gallagher, 1993).

Answering the siblings' questions is an important part of the parents' responsibilities. For example, consider the following questions, which are examples of what lies just below the surface in the concerns of siblings (Powell & Gallagher, 1993):

Why does he behave so strangely?

Can he grow out of this?

Will other brothers and sisters also have disabilities?

Will he ever be able to live on his own?

Will I be expected to take care of him as an adult?

Am I loved as much as my brother?

How can I tell my best friends about my brother?

What am I supposed to do when other children tease my brother?

Will my own children be more likely to have a disability?

Just because a sibling doesn't verbalize such questions doesn't mean that he or she is not thinking about them. It is the parents' responsibility to try and answer even unverbalized questions that the brother or sister may have about the child with disabilities and how that special child is affecting, and will affect, the family system.

Also, the number of questions that the sibling has does not diminish over time, and the content of, and the concerns evident in, the questions reflect developmental changes. For example, an illness or death of one of the parents may heighten the sibling's concern about his or her own responsibilities. If the parents are gone or no longer able to care for the special child, will the sibling be expected to share in the care of the child with disabilities throughout his or her lifetime? Each family has to answer these questions in its own way, but the answers must be clear and unambiguous for all family members. What kind of questions would you have if your brother or sister was a child with disabilities?

What happens when a younger sibling begins to surpass an older brother or sister with disabilities or begins to be ashamed of his or her deviant behavior? One sister described the guilt and love like this:

> I have a short story to tell. It is one of many stories of happiness and sorrow. It is a story of which I am not very proud, and one I have never told my parents. I will tell it now because it is time, and I have learned from my mistakes, as all people can.
>
> George is 21 years old today. He is a frequently happy, often troubled young man who has grown up in a society reluctant to accept and care for him even though he cannot fare for himself.
>
> I am very lucky. My crime was easily forgiven by someone who loved me very much, without reservation. George and I were very young. I was his frequent babysitter. As an older sister more interested in ponies and playing outdoors, I felt a great deal of resentment toward George and, of course, toward my persecutors, my mother and father. It was a day like any other day when I had been told to take care of George. They always seemed the same, those days, because I had no choice in the matter, and if I had one, I would have refused. It was that simple for me. I had better things to do.
>
> We were waiting in the car for our mother to come with the groceries. The recurring memory breaks my heart every time I think of it. He was antagonizing me again. Those unbearable, unreal sounds that haunted and humiliated me. They were the nonsense noises that made the neighborhood children speculate he was from Mars. I could hear their taunts, and rage welled up in me. How could I have a brother like this? He was not right at all. He was a curse. I screamed at him to "shut up." He kept on. He wouldn't stop. My suppressed anger exploded. I raised my hand and slapped him again and again across his soft, round baby face. George began to cry,

low, mournful whimpers. He never once raised a hand to protect himself. Shaking with fear and anger, [unable to think clearly,] I just looked at him. In that swift instance I felt more shame and revulsion for myself than I have ever felt toward anyone. The rude ugliness of it will never leave me. I hugged him to me, begging for forgiveness. And he gave it to me unconditionally. I shall never forget his sweet, sad face as he accepted my hugs.

In that instance I learned something of human nature and the nature of those who would reject people like George. I had been one of them: sullen, uncaring, unwilling to care for someone who came into the world with fewer advantages than I myself had. Today, I am a better person for having lived through both the good times and the bad times that our family experienced as a result of my brother's autism. I have a sense of understanding and compassion that I learned from growing up with George. Best of all, I have my brother, who loves me with all the goodness in his heart.

My message is simple. Look into your hearts and into the hearts of all people to see what is real, what makes them real people. For we are all the same. Accept people for what they are and work to make the world a receptive place—not just for those who are perceived as normal. (Warren, 1985, p. 227)

Identifying and Coping with Family Stress

How do families cope with the stress of providing for a child with disabilities? Research tells us that some families cope quite well but others do not: Divorce and suicide rates in families with exceptional children are higher than those rates in other families (Washington & Gallagher, 1986). Research, however, has also identified several forces that determine how well a family adapts to the presence of a child with disabilities or to other stressful situations (Hill, 1959; McCubbin & Patterson, 1983):

1. *The stressor event.* The stressor event is the condition that evokes stress. In this case, it is the presence of a child with disabilities. The degree of stress that the event generates is a function of the child's disability or need for care. The greater the disability or continued need for care and attention, the greater are the stress and the chance of a negative outcome.

2. *The family's resources.* The family may have economic resources and an extended family whose members are a source of comfort and support. The presence of professional support services can also be important. The more resources the family has, the greater is the probability of a positive outcome.

3. *The family's perception of the situation.* Families can feel many different ways about having a child with disabilities. Some see it as a disaster, and they retreat; others think of it as a challenge. The way people define a situation has a great deal to do with how well they cope with it and with the outcome.

The amount of distress that a family actually displays is a blend of these three major factors, so the mere presence of a child with disabilities (the stressor) does not automatically result in a predictable family response. Many families *are*

Because exceptional children often require extra attention, time, and special adaptations in the home, family members must draw on inner resources as well as external supports to ease the increased stress on the family. (© *Frank Siteman/Monkmeyer Press Studio*)

adapting well (Bristol, Gallagher, & Schopler, 1988), and in the following sections we discuss the resources that these parents call on for the strength to deal with the special needs of their children.

The family's internal resources (financial, social, and emotional) are one major factor in its reaction to stress. Since each family will perceive the situation differently, it is often necessary to have a considerable number of discussions with family members to determine how they are viewing the situation and to find out where possible strengths are (religious beliefs, a strong husband-wife bond, and so on).

Although the family's own resources are a critical factor in the way family members cope with stress, they are not the only factor. External support such as community agencies, service providers, and special educators can help them cope with the stress of having and caring for a child with disabilities.

One of the primary stresses of life with a child with severe disabilities is the day-to-day feeding, dressing, and toileting. A dependent child must have someone's help to survive. Often, the emotional and physical demands of that care leave the caregiver (usually the mother) with little strength for other relationships or activities. Community agencies now offer services such as *respite care* to families with children with disabilities. A trained individual comes into the home for a certain number of hours a week or for a week or a weekend a month to relieve the primary caregiver.

Special educators are an enormously important resource for families with children with disabilities. First, they function as facilitators, often introducing parents to a support network of professional service providers and coordinating their activities. Second, they can teach family members strategies that help the child learn and lessen the probability of behavioral problems.

Most important, the special educator needs to remember that each family has its own needs that extend beyond the exceptional child. As one parent was reported to have said when asked if her child with disabilities was causing problems in the family:

> Is this child causing me trouble? My mother is upstairs dying of cancer, my alcoholic uncle is coming to live with us, and my husband thinks he will be laid off from work in two weeks. And you want to know if this little child is causing trouble????

Each family reacts differently to the stressors. Some families need a great deal of support and information; others need very little. The task of teachers and other professionals is to listen to a family's perception of its needs and to individualize services to each family to optimize the fit between its needs and its unique characteristics (Bailey et al., 1986, p. 157).

Problems of Parents of Children with Special Gifts and Talents

Parents with children who are gifted (children who are developing intellectually far in advance of their agemates) have a set of concerns different from those of parents of children with disabilities. Although these concerns do not involve a child's survival or a child's ability to become an independent adult, they can cause worry and conflicts in family life.

Among the concerns common to parents of a child who is gifted and talented is whether they are doing enough to nurture and cultivate their child's talents. Are they, through inaction or the wrong actions, causing their child's obvious talents to wither and diffuse into mediocrity? Once parents realize that they have a child who is gifted, they often become extremely concerned about their parenting. Is their child's ability like a crystal vase that will shatter if they make a false move? These parents often seek counsel and advice to make sure they are doing the right thing. Parents in a cohesive family unit who emphasize optimum achievement for the child as well as high self-esteem do seem to produce more children who are high achievers (Olszewski, Kulieke, & Buescher, 1987). Parents are justified in believing that they are an important influence on their child's development and performance.

Parents who emphasize optimum achievement and high self-esteem seem to produce more children who are high achievers.

Many parents are aware of the importance of education in nurturing the talents of a child with special gifts. How can they be sure that their child is getting a "good education"? They are often concerned about whether the public schools can provide good educational experiences for a gifted child. Such concerns are reinforced when parents are informed that their child cannot enter elementary school until he or she reaches a certain age even though the child can perform at the second- or third-grade level in academic subjects, or that the local school has no special program for children who are gifted but are not yet 9 or 10 years old (Gallagher & Gallagher, 1995).

Another concern is whether their child's obvious differences will lead to rejection by the child's agemates. Many parents remember the fate of other gifted individuals at the hands of their peers (Socrates and Galileo, for example) and, as a consequence, do not want any special attention directed to their child. They may turn down special programs designed to enhance their child's education because such programs would cause the child's special talents to be revealed to the larger (and perhaps unfriendly) peer society.

Undoubtedly, many parents of children with disabilities would willingly exchange places with the parents of a child who is gifted, but we should not assume that the presence of such a child in the family is a source of uncomplicated joy and pleasure to conscientious parents.

In the next chapter, we explore institutional outside forces (such as school, legislation, and the courts) and their effects on the exceptional child.

Summary of Major Ideas

1. The exceptional child differs from the average child to the extent that he or she needs special educational services to reach full potential.

2. The major categories of exceptionality within the field of special education include children with intellectual differences (unusually fast or slow); communication differences; sensory differences including auditory and visual impairments; behavioral differences including problems with emotional and social adaptation; multiple and severe handicaps; and physical differences.

3. Special educators have moved from a medical model, which stresses that the physical condition exists within the patient, to an ecological model, which focuses on the individual's interaction with the environment.

4. The success of the family-focused approach depends on its acceptance by professionals.

5. We now know that heredity influences (but does not finally determine) intelligence, temperament, personality, and behavior.

6. The needs of the individual exceptional child can be assessed through norm-referenced tests, interviews, observations, and informal assessment.

7. Exceptional children show both inter-individual (among children) and intra-individual (within a child) differences. Both kinds of differences require special adaptation by the teacher and the school.

8. The adjustment of siblings of children with disabilities depends on parental sensitivities to their needs.

9. The families of children with disabilities face special stressors in meeting their responsibilities and in moving through family stages.

10. How the family of a child with disabilities copes with stress depends on three major factors: the nature of the stressor, the family's available resources, and the way the family interprets the situation.

11. The new movement toward parent empowerment gives parents more influence on the special or remedial programs established for their child. It also is causing a rethinking of the traditional roles played by professionals.

12. Parents of a child with intellectual gifts do not have the same problems as parents of a child with disabilities, but they do have concerns about how to maximize their child's potential, how to protect against social isolation, whether the school is providing appropriate services for their child, and so on.

Unresolved Issues

Every generation leaves, as its legacy to the next generation, certain problems for which solutions have not been found. There are many issues in the field of special education that today's professionals have been either unable or unwilling to resolve. The end-of-chapter sections entitled "Unresolved Issues" briefly describe widely debated topics as a beginning agenda for you, the current generation of students, who will face these problems in your professional or private lives.

1. *The search for exceptional children.* The boundary line separating exceptional children from nonexceptional children has become blurred where children with mild disabilities are concerned. Yet legislation and the courts call for eligibility standards to clearly separate those who should receive special help from those who should not. How do we distinguish, for example, between the child who is emotionally disturbed and the child who is suffering a temporary behavior problem?

2. *The family system.* For many years special educators have focused only on the exceptional child and excluded the child's environment. Increasingly we have become aware that the child is only one component in a complex family system and that many elements within that system can have a positive or negative impact on the child. Interacting constructively with the family system is a new objective of special education that has yet to be incorporated fully in our personnel preparation or educational programs.

3. *Lifespan development and transition.* Most special educators see exceptional children only for a limited period of time: the school years. They miss two significant stages of development: early childhood, in which important patterns of behavior are set, and adulthood, the period for which special programs supposedly prepare exceptional children. We are seeing a new awareness of the importance of transitions in the psychosocial life of the individual at whatever point in the developmental sequence it occurs.

4. *Measuring individual differences.* The term *individual differences* seems to refer almost exclusively to differences among children in intellectual and academic abilities. Although other areas of development (social, motivational, and self-concept) are clearly important for educational planning, the measurement of these factors is difficult and often ambiguous. We need an extensive, systematic effort to develop better instruments and procedures for cataloging all of the exceptional child's major developments, as well as efforts to assess the family's strengths and needs.

5. *Uncertain funding.* A chronic problem facing those who provide services for children with exceptionalities is obtaining the financial support necessary to conduct such programs. There is often disagreement about which level of government (federal, state, local) should pay for these special services. Taxpayers are often reluctant, and sometimes court action or legislative mandates are needed to provide necessary support. Uncertain funding makes it difficult to develop long-range, multiyear plans.

Key Terms

academic aptitude p. 13
culture p. 9
diagnostic achievement tests p. 17
ecological model of exceptionality p. 7
family-focused approach p. 8
family harmony p. 29
inter-individual differences p. 13

intra-individual differences p. 19
medical model of exceptionality p. 7
parent empowerment p. 30
special education p. 12
standard (norm-referenced) achievement
  tests p. 15

Questions for Thought

1. When is a child considered to be educationally exceptional?   p. 3

2. What caused the movement from a medical model of exceptionalities to an ecological model?   p. 5

3. Why is the trend toward early intervention increasing the importance of the family in intervention programs?   p. 7

4. Are inter-individual differences and intra-individual differences ever the same? Explain.   pp. 12–19

5. Why have intelligence tests come under attack in recent years, especially in connection with exceptional children and children who are culturally different?   p. 15

6. How are inter-individual differences in academic performance tracked?   p. 15

7. How can instructors obtain reliable information when measuring the psychosocial development of exceptional children?   p. 17

8. What are the special burdens of families with children who are disabled? p. 25

9. What role have parents played in the expansion of services for exceptional children?   pp. 32–35

10. What are three forces that determine how well a family adapts to the presence of a child with disabilities?   p. 35

11. What special role do educators play in supporting families with disabled children?   p. 35

12. What are the special concerns of children who are gifted?   p. 37

References of Special Interest

Dunst, C., Trivette, C., Starnes, A., Hamby, D., & Gordon, N. (1993). *Building and evaluating family support initiatives.* Baltimore: Paul H. Brookes Publishing Co.
> This book is a report on a nationwide study of the application and effectiveness of family support programs whose purpose is to enable and empower people by enhancing and promoting individual and family capabilities that support and strengthen family functioning. The authors point out many political, bureaucratic, and economic factors that impact on the family support initiative and argue that the belief systems of the families and of the service providers are also key to the implementation of family support policies.

Lesar, S., Trivette, C., & Dunst, C. (Eds). (1996). Families of Children and Adolescents with Special Needs. Special Issue, *Exceptional Children, 62*(3), 197–182.
> This special issue contains a series of articles that focuses upon the families of children and youth with disabilities. The emphasis of most of the articles is on the ecological role played by forces within and outside the family. Issues such as additional stress on the family unit, various strategies for helping families cope with the special needs of their children, and a desirable social policy for families are covered.

Odom, S., McConnell, S., & McEvoy, M. (1992). *Social competence of young children with disabilities.* Baltimore: Paul H. Brookes Publishing Co.
> This book is an excellent compilation of the latest information on the construct of social competence in preschool and young school-age children, and it provides a good history of the emergence and growing importance of this construct. It contains separate chapters on topics such as the development of social competence in children with developmental disabilities, visual impairment, hearing impairment, and specific learning impairments.

Powell, T., & Gallagher, P. (1993). *Brothers and sisters* (2nd ed.). Baltimore: Paul H. Brookes Publishing Co.
> This volume provides an excellent synthesis of what is known about an important but often neglected aspect of the families of children with disabilities: the siblings. The authors address the special problems of brothers and sisters adapting to the presence of a child with disabilities. Among their important conclusions is that the quality of family relationships depends more on how the parents treat the various members of the family than on the particular presence of an exceptional child.

Rutter, M., & Rutter, M. (1993). *Developing minds.* New York: Basic Books.
> This remarkably clear, readable, and concise portrait of what we know about the development of children and adults provides a fine basis for the consideration of what exceptionality, as a departure from normality, means.

Simeonsson, R. (1994). *Risk, resilience and prevention.* Baltimore: Paul H. Brookes Publishing Co.

Most efforts to improve the conditions of children focus on coping with crises that have become too serious to ignore. This book addresses the issue of preventing problems from occurring in the first place. Problems such as adolescent pregnancy, child abuse, drug use, dropping out of school, and behavior disorders are discussed by experts.

Exceptional Children and Their Environment

focusing questions

How has the educational reform movement affected exceptional children?

In what ways can cultural differences affect special education students and programs?

What are some of the different learning environments being used today for exceptional children?

How are special educators using technology to teach exceptional students?

How have the courts influenced the development of educational services for exceptional children?

What a society feels about its diverse membership, particularly about citizens who are different, is expressed through the institutions of that society. A close look at the major institutions of our society—the schools, the legislatures, and the courts—should tell us a lot about the place of exceptional children in our society.

■ The *schools* design programs to prepare these students for a productive and satisfying adult life.

■ The *legislatures* provide the money and authority for the special arrangements necessary to meet the special needs of these students.

■ The *courts* rule on what is fair and just and equitable with regard to these students.

Schools, legislatures, and courts are social institutions that have a major impact on the education of children with special needs.

Each of these social institutions has its own rules and traditions that influence how decisions are made and conclusions reached in its domain. This chapter touches briefly on how each of them impacts on the child who is exceptional in our society. Take, for example, Dan.

Dan is a 5-year-old with Down syndrome, a genetic condition that will affect his entire life. He has mental retardation and other problems caused by this genetic accident. Yet how Dan will fare in life will depend to a large degree on the environmental circumstances around him.

Will Dan do better in a loving, rather than a rejecting, family? Will he do better in a neighborhood with some comfort and resources than he would do in a slum or urban ghetto? Will Dan do better in a school program that recognizes his problems and adapts the program to his needs instead of unfairly expecting him to meet some kind of "normal" standard? Of course!

No matter what the degree of exceptionality, how the child will eventually adapt to life is determined in large measure by how the environmental forces outside the child facilitate or inhibit his or her development. That is why we spend so much time studying these outside forces, or the *context* of the child.

In Chapter 1, we stressed the importance of understanding the context of the exceptional child as well as his or her individual characteristics. The family ranks first among influences on the growing and developing child, and the subculture in which the family lives contributes much to his or her development as well. Many other external influences help shape the child's development, particularly later in life. Neither Dan nor his family, though, will likely know the degree to which the actions of legislatures and courts have played a role in his education.

How the exceptional child adjusts to adulthood is determined in large measure by his or her interactions with these forces and the way in which they are mediated by family and by the child's unique characteristics. It is difficult, if not impossible, to predict the outcome of special education services for a specific individual because of the range of each child's response and potential.

We begin with an overview of society's attitudes toward the education of exceptional individuals. By looking at how society has viewed exceptional students and directed its resources to them, we can better understand how schools treat these youngsters and what is expected from them.

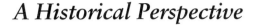

A Historical Perspective

During the last century, there have been enormous changes in the way society treats exceptional children, moving from rejection and the charitable isolation of children with disabilities to acceptance of them as contributing members of society. The current level of acceptance has few precedents, representing a much more enlightened view than was evident even in the immediate past.

As we look back in time, we find that the notion of educating *every* child to achieve his or her greatest potential is a relatively new idea. The current use of the term *exceptional* is itself a reflection of radical change in society's view of people who differ from the norm. The world has come a long way from the Spartans' practice of killing infants who didn't meet their standard of normalcy, but the journey has been slow, moving from neglect and mistreatment, to pity and over-protection, and finally to acceptance and integration into society to the fullest extent possible.

In the United States, attitudes toward individuals with disabilities have followed a similar pattern of development. Before 1850 there were few public provisions for children or adults with special needs. They were "stored away" in poorhouses and other charitable centers or left at home and given no educational opportunities. It was estimated that as late as 1850, 60 percent of the inmates of this country's poorhouses were people who were deaf, blind, "insane," or "idiots."

ESTABLISHING RESIDENTIAL SCHOOLS

Nineteenth-century reformers such as Horace Mann, Samuel Gridley Howe, and Dorothea Dix gave impetus to the establishment of residential schools. From 1817 to the beginning of the Civil War, a span of more than forty years, many states established residential schools for children who were deaf, blind, mentally retarded, or orphaned, patterning them after similar schools in Europe. In 1817, the American Asylum for the Education and Instruction of the Deaf, a residential institution, was opened in Hartford, Connecticut. Today it is called the American School for the Deaf. In 1829, the New England Asylum for the Blind—later renamed the Perkins School—was founded in Watertown, Massachusetts. Thirty years later, a residential school for the mentally retarded, the Massachusetts School for Idiotic and Feebleminded Youth, was established in South Boston. This school is now called the Fernald State School for the Mentally Retarded. These schools offered training, but equally important they provided an environment that often protected the individual throughout life.

ADAPTING PUBLIC SCHOOLS

The first special class for deaf children in a public school was held in Boston in 1869. Not until 1896 was the first special class for children who were mentally retarded organized, in Providence, Rhode Island. It was followed in 1899 by a class

The exceptional child's adjustment to adulthood is determined in large measure by his or her interactions with the school, culture, and society and the way in which these interactions are mediated by the family and the child's unique characteristics. (© Paul S. Conklin)

for children with physical impairments and, in 1900, by a class in Chicago for children who were blind. Since 1900, special programs and services for exceptional children have been organized in the majority of public schools throughout the nation.

The Exceptional Child and the School

Certainly one of the most significant of all the social institutions is the schools. Schools in large measure are a mirror of our society as a whole. Most of the values taught there reflect the values of the dominant sectors of society. Many of the problems encountered in the schools, such as lack of motivation, drug use, and violence, are part of the larger societal fabric.

INTEGRATION

Four processes (normalization, deinstitutionalization, mainstreaming, and inclusion) reflect our society's efforts to integrate exceptional persons into the community.

The thrust toward greater social and educational integration has brought many exceptional children and adults into the regular educational system and community from segregated settings and focused efforts on extending services to include early childhood and adulthood.

The changing social environment of exceptional children has spawned a new and different vocabulary. Four terms that are in common use today are *normalization,*

"One Child Is Included"

Within the process of systems change there are always individual children who are, by virtue of opportunity, catalysts for change. Our daughter Kate is a "pioneer" in New Jersey, as a second-grader fully participating in Mrs. Johnson's class at McKinley School in Westfield. Since she has been participating in regular classes, it is very difficult to capture the changes in Kate without a "before" and "after" video, but I will try to paint a picture of the differences.

Kate has been receiving intensive special education services since she was eight months old, when our family began participation in an early intervention program. Joining a program which had at its heart the belief that parents are the experts regarding their children was tremendously empowering and got us off to a good start. It was in this first three years that we created a vision for our family which included the determination that one day Kate would grow up in a world of close friends, that she would have meaningful employment, and that she would contribute to her community.

Even then, we adopted the philosophy of "integrate early and often," though at the time we were not aware of the concept of "inclusion." We just went ahead and enrolled Kate in Baby Dance (an exercise program) and in family day care with typical children two mornings a week. Saying "we just enrolled Kate" grossly minimizes the real level of concern we had about whether we and Kate would survive the experiences, but we made the decision anyway in spite of our fears that we would not find acceptance. In fact, people always reached out to Kate.

After graduating from early intervention, Kate entered a preschool which again focused on creating a "normalized" experience for her. Despite the objections of very caring professionals—"Two programs will be too much for her!"—we registered Kate in a dual program. In the morning she attended our neighborhood Montessori School, and in the afternoon she was bused across the city to a public school program for children with blindness and multiple disabilities. The need for the two programs occurred because it was not possible for her to receive the related services of speech, occupational, and physical therapies and orientation and mobility training within the private school.

ONE FLASH OF INSIGHT!

Family members have what I would call "lightning rod" experiences, when they are struck with insight in a flash. The dual program provided us with just this sort of experience. The Montessori school teachers were concerned with educating the "whole child," and sought to develop in children skills of communication, concern for others, and an eagerness to accept new experiences.

Geri Kennedy, Kate's Montessori teacher, wrote of her that "the emergence of spring and warm weather led to the blossoming of friendships between Kate and her classmates. During our daily trips to the playground, we discovered that although she did not yet walk independently, Kate loved to be physically active. The children naturally and enthusiastically included her in their turns on the swing, on the slide, and in the sandbox. Through this increased involvement with the other kids, Kate's language ability expanded much more quickly than it had through contact with her more doting teachers. The children expected Kate to let them know what she wanted, and Kate constantly surprised us with her improving ability to tell them." ➔

Andrea Lo, the newly appointed integration facilitator, realized very soon that we would need to meet regularly to fine-tune the program. She brought Kate's schedule to an early meeting and we problem solved—literally moment by moment—how Kate could be included and actively participate in all aspects of classroom life.

We tried to build in supports by the typical children whenever possible instead of always relying on adults to assist Kate. The integration strategies were prepared by Mrs. Lo and included in Kate's Individualized Education Program. It is important to stress that Kate is working on her own goals and objectives within the regular classroom.

FLEXIBLE, CAPABLE TEACHERS

Mrs. Johnson is Kate's regular teacher. She watched Kate grow from across the hall and "volunteered" to have Kate join her second-grade class. She is challenged by our daughter and has risen to the task. She attended computer classes and a program offered by the Commission for the Blind for teachers in the community. She is a seasoned teacher and approaches her work with a good sense of humor.

What makes Mrs. Johnson just right for Kate is that she "owns" Kate's education. She views herself as the person primarily responsible for our daughter's education and draws upon the consultants who visit her room to guide her. Administrative support from the school principal, Mr. Braynock, has enabled Mrs. Johnson to set aside time to learn new skills.

SPECIAL EDUCATION: A SERVICE, NOT A PLACE

Currently, Kate attends a regular second-grade class. She is greeted each morning by a friend who serves as a "sighted guide," helping Kate get from the playground to her class, acting as Kate's partner for the week, and sitting next to Kate. Because there was too much daily discussion among all the children about who would be chosen to be Kate's

guide, a schedule had to be devised to designate who could be her buddy.

The New Jersey Commission for the Blind provides a braille teacher and an orientation and mobility specialist who are consultants to the regular education teacher and work directly with Kate. Kate has been able to learn most of the alphabet. Now when we go shopping and find a can of peaches, Kate takes a braille stick-on label with the letter "p" and attaches it to the can. When we get home and she puts it away, she remembers that the can with the "p" is for "peaches." It is not necessary for Kate to learn to read "Plato" in school (though who knows what her interests will be!) but we want our daughter to have some functional reading skills.

Kate gave her class a braille lesson, completing a spelling assignment on her braille machine. The children were impressed because Kate knows this special code, and they wanted to learn how to write their names. Her braille teacher showed them how this was done. This past spring, Kate sent each child a valentine that she had signed herself.

The orientation and mobility specialist is very important to Kate. She is teaching Kate how to find her way around her school and the neighborhood by using her cane and good reasoning skills. It's not that easy to learn how to "map" a community in your mind and travel safely.

For forty minutes each day, Kate receives resource room services to work on "survival skills" (activities of daily living), as well as language and math instruction. Recently, after learning about coins during her math lesson, Kate accompanied her resource room teacher, Mrs. Mankowski, across the street to the little convenience store, where she bought her own oatmeal cookies. This "functional" instruction is very important because it helps Kate understand how what she is learning has direct and practical application in the real world.

Whenever possible, related services (those that help Kate benefit from her educational program) have been provided by including other typical kids within her class. For example, the occupational therapist visits Kate's classroom during recess just after lunch. She works with Kate on a game that involves other children. Kate is learning how to play and take turns, which is a very big challenge for children with blindness.

Kate's speech therapist spent a summer researching software for the classroom computer. She was responsible for the installation of an ECHO, which helps Kate recognize what appears on the computer screen. The ECHO is equipped with a voice output so that when Kate types an "a," for example, the machine says "a." The speech therapist has been teaching keyboard skills and invites another child to work with Kate. This has proved beneficial for everyone: The other children learn keyboarding and Kate has good language models around her.

The person with the most demanding job in support of Kate is the teaching assistant, Mrs. Vincenti. She has been Kate's aide over the past four years. Initially, her role was to remain with Kate and guide her throughout the day in the segregated program. Kate views Mrs. Vincenti as her "grandmother" and they have grown very close. At this point, however, we are asking Mrs. Vincenti to step back a bit so that the regular education classroom teacher is primarily responsible for interacting with Kate.

Because changing roles and expectations is very difficult, teaching assistants need support in learning about different ways to assist students. Now Mrs. Vincenti can be more available to help other children in the class while identifying situations where Kate might need a small modification in instruction—a science lesson, for example, during which Mrs. Vincenti hands Kate a live plant when talking about the parts of a plant.

SOCIAL GROWTH . . . FOR EVERYONE

In a planning session last week, Ted Kozlik, our director of special education, was reminiscing about a day four years ago when Kate was in a segregated class outside our district. He recalled Kate walking down the hall with her physical therapist, screaming at the top of her lungs. This was not an unusual sight in those days. He remarked that Kate has made tremendous progress in the way she manages her feelings.

"The children in turn had the too rare opportunity to ask questions openly about Kate's blindness and special needs. They began to understand when and where she would need help, and when she would not. They had a chance to explore and ask questions about adaptive aids, such as braille story books, and a 'beeper ball' that became a favorite toy for everyone." There was an overall sense of joy and great expectations.

Kate gradually learned all twenty of the children's names and could recognize many of them by voice cues alone. By contrast, in the afternoon she was treated as if she were severely disabled. She was in a classroom (which had previously served as a storage closet) that included four other children with total blindness and little verbal communication. A series of therapists would interact with Kate in order to provide services. While I know that her teacher loved her and did offer Kate some new experiences designed for a tactile learner, it was very difficult to find a sense of joy in the class.

It was that perception of the absence of joy that really disturbed me, combined with a very uneasy feeling that Kate was, in fact, "learning helplessness." In the morning Montessori program, Kate learned how to negotiate the complex environment of a large Victorian-era school building and became independent in the bathroom to such an extent that she learned where to put her paper towel after she washed her hands. In the afternoon program, she was always guided by an adult and "assisted with toileting." We heard little from Kate about her classmates in the afternoon.

The contrasts in the expectations of Kate were so profound that we were struck—literally clobbered—with the insight that maybe Kate belonged in the real world of regular education. However, it was not until three years later, when Kate taught us another lesson, that we fully acted on this insight.

OPENING THE DOORS

Hank and I wrote a letter to our director of special education and our superintendent of schools requesting an opportunity for Kate to be included in a regular grammar school in our town. We emphasized our wish to work collaboratively with the administration, child evaluation team and Kate's educators. We reviewed our reasons for wanting an integrated program for Kate. Our reasons then were the same as they are now:

First, we want Kate to have friends. Just being with others creates opportunities for friendship. Sometimes the process of building friendships needs a little support from helping adults and, even better, from peers. Think of the most important moments in your life. Your friends very likely were part of those moments.

Second, we want Kate to contribute to our community. People in our society have many misconceptions about persons with disabilities; being with typical kids gives people a chance to see the strengths in Kate and get beyond some of her challenges. Kate sings in church choir and takes regular swimming lessons at our YMCA. Last year she was invited to join the Brownie troop and learned and taught others about being a good citizen.

Third, we want Kate to learn more in general. Kate participates in an environment which stresses social and academic growth through a wide range of activities. She is exposed to the entire second-grade curriculum with modifications as needed. She is not stuck "getting ready" for the mainstream. She is getting ready for adult life by being included in ordinary places with ordinary people just like anyone else.

Source: Diana Cuthbertson, "One Child Is Included," *Children Today*, 20 (March–April 1991), p. 6. Reprinted by permission. Diana Cuthbertson is the director of the SPAN program in Westfield, New Jersey.

---

commentary

What Is the Context? School is a powerful link between the contexts of family and the community. In this article, the three contexts are interrelated: Kate's parents argued for her right to be included; her parents supported her by creating a "vision" of success for the family. The integrated school environment and caring teachers encouraged Kate to make friends and learn more. The social and academic preparation she has received may allow her to avoid a life of sheltered workshops and dependence and instead become a contributing member of the community.

Pivotal Issues. Discuss the roles of each teacher-specialist. What are some criteria for successful integration experiences that you can infer from this article?

deinstitutionalization, mainstreaming, and *inclusion.* All reflect the interest of society in trying to integrate exceptional children and adults more effectively into the community at large.

1. **Normalization** is the creation of a learning and social environment as normal as possible for the exceptional child and adult.

2. **Deinstitutionalization** is the process of releasing as many exceptional children and adults as possible from the confinement of residential institutions into their local community.

3. **Mainstreaming** is the process of bringing exceptional children into daily contact with nonexceptional children in an educational setting.

4. **Inclusion** is the process of bringing exceptional children of whatever condition into the general classroom for their education.

In recent years special educators have taken a lifespan perspective toward the provision of special education services. This involves the extension of special education services from the traditional school years back to early childhood and forward to adulthood.

LIFESPAN PERSPECTIVE

Early Childhood

At one time, most children with special needs did not receive special services before the third or fourth grade, after they had failed in the regular school program or had demonstrated that the regular school program was not appropriate for their level of development and learning. Fewer services were available in secondary school, and most ended in the eighth grade. Special educators found themselves looking through a narrow window (from ages 8 to 17) at the development of exceptional children, knowing little about their formative years or families and even less about what happened to them after high school. Today, our view has expanded. We have legislation that allows states to mandate that children with identifiable needs and their families receive special services from the child's birth or earliest time of identification (Odom & Karnes, 1988).

Transition Services

Another clear trend is the development of **transition services,** or programs that help exceptional students move from school to the world of work and the community. About 300,000 students who have received special education services leave the school system each year. Until recently, few attempts have been made to follow up on what has happened to these students and see whether the long-range goal of special education services—adjustment to the community—was met. With the new interest in the lifespan of exceptional individuals has come new interest in transition services.

Adjustment to the community seems to consist of three major components: the ability (1) to seek and hold gainful employment, (2) to live independently, and (3)

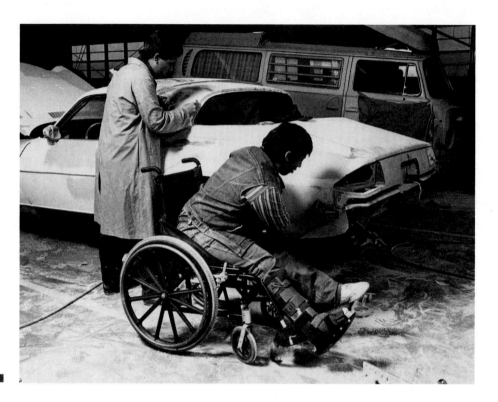

With the new interest in the lifespan of exceptional individuals has come new interest in transition services that help exceptional students move from school to the world of work and the community. (© Bob Daemmrich/Stock Boston)

to move around the community without help (Schill, 1988). Even those with severe disabilities can approach these goals. If they cannot work independently, they might find employment in a subsidized industry. If they cannot live independently, they might live in a group home under supervision.

Today there is widespread agreement that transition services are necessary, that many exceptional children cannot adapt to adult life without some help beyond the school years. The new emphasis on transition services is encouraging special educators to work with professionals in other fields such as vocational educators, members of the business community, psychologists, and counselors. In addition, cooperation between special educators in the secondary schools and those who provide adult services can improve the outcomes of special education programs (Edgar, 1987).

The school environment is where all of the many forces acting on exceptional children interact and influence each other. Laws regulate who receives services; courts interpret those laws and apply them to specific circumstances; and families support (or sometimes fail to support) the child's efforts and provide goals, values, and expectations that generally reflect the family's cultural background. The school is particularly important for exceptional children who may need very special kinds of help to become productive adults.

Here we provide an overview of how the schools have tried to organize themselves and their resources to meet the challenges of accepting and educating excep-

Instruction can be adapted to the differences found in exceptional children in several ways—by varying the learning environment, the content of lessons, and the skills being taught, and by introducing technology that can meet special needs. (© Meri Houtchens-Kitchens/The Picture Cube)

tional children. In Chapters 4 through 12 we describe specific adaptations for children with specific exceptionalities.

SPECIAL EDUCATION ADAPTATIONS

Special education provides to exceptional children necessary services that are not available in the regular school program.

The nature of special education is to provide exceptional children with services not available to them in the regular education program. Special education programs are different from regular programs because they try to take into account the child's inter-individual and intra-individual differences (see Chapter 1). It's important to realize that special education does *not* exist because regular education has failed. Classroom teachers and typical educational programs simply cannot respond fully to the special needs of exceptional children without a substantial change in the structure, program, and staffing of the typical classroom.

Instruction can be adapted to the inter-individual and intra-individual differences found in exceptional children in several ways: We can vary the learning environment to create an appropriate setting in which to learn. We can change the actual content of lessons or the specific knowledge being taught. We can modify the skills being taught. And we can introduce technology that meets the special needs of exceptional students.

Figure 2.1
Special Learning Environments for
Exceptional Children

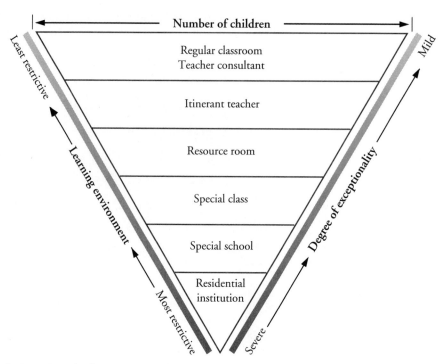

Source: "Special Education as Development Capital" by E. Deno, 1970. *Exceptional Children, 37,* pp. 229–237. Copyright 1970 by the Council for Exceptional Children. Reprinted with permission.

Note: Hospital and homebound services provided for children with disabilities who may be confined for long periods of time fall within the realm of the residential institution setting on the scale of special education learning environments.

Learning Environment

Often, a special learning environment is necessary to help exceptional children master particular content and skills. Making changes in the learning environment, however, has repercussions throughout the entire educational system. This may be one reason why environmental modifications are the subject of greater controversy than are changes in either content or skills.

When we decide to move youngsters from the regular classroom to a resource room for an hour a day, we generate a series of activities. First we have to allocate space in the school for the resource room. Then the classroom teacher must modify instruction to accommodate the students who are out of the class for part of the day. And, of course, a whole battery of special personnel must be brought into the system to identify eligible children and to deliver special services. Figure 2.1 shows some of the most common learning environment modifications for exceptional children, from limited interventions in the classroom to a total change of residence for the child.

The concept of **least restrictive environment** means that teachers attempt to educate a child in the environmental setting that maximizes the chances that the child with exceptionalities will respond well to the educational goals and objectives set for him or her—that is, as close to the top of Figure 2.1 as possible. Thus, the resource room is preferred to the part-time special class, and the teacher consultant is preferred to the resource room. This concept may mean that the program or setting in the regular classroom must be changed to lessen the likelihood of students being referred to special education in the first place (Chalfant, 1985; Will, 1986).

Recent legislation such as the Individuals with Disabilities Education Act (IDEA) requires that a continuum of placement options be available to meet the needs of students with disabilities. The law also requires that,

> To the maximum extent appropriate, children with disabilities . . . are educated with children who are not disabled, and that special classes, separate schooling, or other removal of children with disabilities from the regular environment occurs only when the nature of severity of the disability is such that education in regular classes with the use of supplementary aids and services cannot be attained satisfactorily. (IDEA Sec. 612[5][B])

The clear intent is to bring the exceptional child as close to the normal classroom setting as is feasible. But the educator must be aware that a special environment may be the most appropriate for a particular child at a particular point in his or her development.

The decision of where the child will receive the best education is aided immeasurably by the availability of these options. Sometimes a school system will have only one option (for example, a resource room); in such a case, special education means exercising that option or receiving no special services at all. The term *comprehensive services* usually refers to a variety of options (but rarely to the full range of possibilities) that can be applied to meet the individual needs of each child.

The recent emphasis on the *regular education initiative* and on *mainstreaming* often leaves the impression that practically all exceptional children are now back in the regular classroom. Such is far from the case. Figure 2.2 summarizes where students with disabilities are served. The most popular of the learning environment adaptations remains the resource room or pull-out program, followed by placement in a regular class. One of every four exceptional children is being educated in a totally separate class, 5 percent are being educated in a separate facility such as a separate school, and a very small number of exceptional children are placed in residential or hospital settings.

These data indicate that the schools are using a wide range of placements to try to find the proper setting for maximizing the education of exceptional students. The important question may well be not "Where are they?" but "What special services are being provided for them, wherever they are?"

A continuum of services has been designed to meet the needs of individual children with disabilities.

Content

Some exceptional children require modifications in the content of the curriculum. For children who are gifted, we can accelerate content or provide different kinds

Figure 2.2
Where Children with Disabilities
(Ages 3 to 21) Are Served

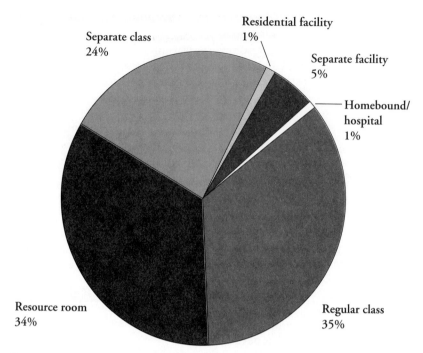

Source: U.S. Department of Education, Office of Special Education Programs (1994). *Sixteenth Annual Report to Congress: Implementing the Individuals with Disabilities Act (IDEA)*. Washington, DC: Author.

of learning experiences. We can adapt to the limited conceptual abilities of students with mental retardation by relating lessons through direct, concrete experiences to their homes, families, and neighborhoods. Instead of teaching about civilizations of the past or countries in Asia or South America, we can create lessons about their own towns and cities. We can make linguistic changes in the curriculum for children with hearing problems. We can minimize the presentation of visual-channel information for children with visual problems.

Skills

One educational objective is the mastery of reading, arithmetic, and writing skills. Most students spend their first three years in school mastering these basic skills, which are often taught in ways that encourage students to practice other skills like punctuality, attentiveness, and persistence that can lead to better social adaptation. Exceptional children often need to be taught the skills that average students master without special instruction. In addition, they sometimes must learn special skills to cope with their disability. A blind student may learn braille; a deaf student, finger spelling. These are critical communication skills. Even gifted children can learn additional techniques for finding and solving problems. All exceptional children require some kind of skill training appropriate to their special needs.

Computers and Technology

Special education has often led the way in the acceptance and use of technology in education. This achievement may well be due to the unique problems special educators face. Because they are educating children with special needs, they have been willing to try new devices that promise help: modified typewriters, hearing aids, print magnifiers, and machines that trace eye movements as the student reads. Perhaps the most important of these technological devices is the computer.

Technology for Children with Disabilities. There are two quite different uses of technology for children with disabilities: assistive and instructional uses. **Assistive technology** consists of tools that enhance the functioning of people with special disabilities. For the person who is blind, it provides braille readers and typewriters; for the person who is deaf, hearing aids; for the person who cannot speak, communication boards for pointing to and composing messages (see Table 2.1). Assistive technology can be as sophisticated as a Kurtzweil reading device that translates print into oral language or as simple as a headband and a pointer allowing students who have cerebral palsy to point to text or to their communication boards to extend their ability to communicate. Such devices have dramatically improved individual children's ability to receive and transmit information effectively and are most often used with children with moderate to severe disabilities that create major barriers to communication.

New technologies in the classroom can both assist and instruct the student who is disabled.

Instructional technology involves the computer and related tools that support and expand the computer's usefulness. Instructional technology is developed primarily as a means to deliver content and instruction in an appropriate manner to exceptional children.

Major attempts are being made to go beyond the traditional transmission of knowledge and to use technology as a means to aid thinking and problem solving by exceptional children. This is particularly important in view of the difficulty many such students have in transferring knowledge and information from one situation to another. Students both with and without disabilities have major problems with **inert knowledge** (Whitehead, 1928), which is knowledge stored in memory but not linked to other knowledge or applied to problems. Hasselbring (1994) points out that a student may understand how the special characteristics of a camel may help the animal survive desert sandstorms, yet fail to understand that this survival is one illustration of the phenomenon of *adaptation*. Thus, when this student is asked about the concept of adaptation, the individual may not realize that his or her knowledge of camels is relevant or is a good illustration of adaptation.

There is good reason to believe that problem-oriented instruction is much more likely than fact-oriented instruction to produce transferrable knowledge (Perkins & Salomon, 1989). That is why major efforts are being made to use technology not just to master specific information but as a tool to help in problem solving. It becomes especially important for teachers who work with children with exceptionalities to receive instruction in how to apply technology to their instruction. Currently, few expenditures of funds have been made to prepare teachers to fully utilize this equipment. For the most part, teachers have been left on their own to

Table 2.1	Uses of Technology
Assistive Technology	**Instructional Technology**
Tools for enhancing the routine functioning of people who have physical or sensory disabilities ■ Communication boards ■ Computer screen readers ■ Braille printers ■ Head pointers ■ Kurtzweil reading devices for the visually impaired	Use of computers or related technology for the delivery and support of instruction ■ Computers ■ Phone/fax ■ Internet ■ Data compression ■ Techniques ■ CD-Rom ■ Video discs

Source: Hasselbring, Ted (1994). *Florida's Future in Special Education: Applications of Technology.* Vision 2000 Conference. University of South Florida, Tampa. Reprinted by permission of the author.

learn as best they can, or they have been given short-term training introducing them to the technology but rarely allowing them sufficient time to explore the full potential of these new tools.

The Use of Computers.   The computer has the ability to create files for storing information; to organize and present text, video, and numerical data; and to provide access to data and programs. It allows children to learn at their own rate and provides immediate feedback and reinforcement. It makes the process of learning more active and self-directed. The computer has become particularly important in special education because it offers specific advantages to exceptional children:

1. Computer programs are available to teach basic reading and arithmetic skills, which are two important problem areas for many exceptional children.

2. Many computer activities use a gamelike format that special educators have found effective for teaching visual motor skills and specific academic skills.

3. Youngsters who learn to operate the equipment have the satisfaction of being independent and controlling their own environment, not an everyday experience for most exceptional children.

4. The computer can create conditionally branched or nonlinear interactions. The branching capability means that a slow-learning student can be given more items that provide additional practice on the concept to be mastered while the student who demonstrates understanding of the concept can be taken forward in the program without additional unnecessary examples (Barr, 1991).

The most important technological device used with children with special difficulties is the computer. It allows children to learn at their own rate and provides immediate feedback and reinforcement, making the process of learning active and self-directed. (© Paul S. Conklin/ Monkmeyer Press Photo Service)

5. The computer makes record keeping much easier. Its tracking system allows the school to keep updated records on tests that students have taken, their progress in individualized programs, and a host of evaluative reports.

The computer is a constantly evolving tool, and we are finding new uses for it on a regular basis.

REFERRAL AND ASSESSMENT

Before an effective instructional program can be developed, the child's needs, strengths, and weaknesses must be carefully assessed.

The traditional first step toward the development of an effective instructional program for each exceptional child has been to determine the child's individual needs, strengths, and weaknesses. This determination is made through the process of assessment. Test data, interviews, past records, and so on are assembled to draw a portrait of special children once they have been referred to special education services. In recent years an additional step has been taken—the prereferral system by which student problems are confronted *before* a formal referral is made. A child has often been referred to special education services because of his or her persistent inability to respond to the general education program. Sometimes the reason for this inability lies in the student's exceptionality (a serious behavior problem or developmental delay), but sometimes the reason is the limited and inflexible nature of the educational program itself.

Paul, age 8, has been referred to special education because his third-grade teacher, Mrs. Parker, claims that he is insolent, talks back to her, isn't mastering his reading and math skills, and is constantly disturbing the other children. Maybe Paul acts this way because he has a serious learning or behavioral disability, but maybe he and the teacher have gotten off on the wrong foot. He may be reacting in a predictable way to his inability to do the schoolwork (which seems pretty uninteresting to him anyway), and Mrs. Parker doesn't know how to cope with Paul's frustrations. How can a special education teacher sort out the correct answer? Can it even be done?

Chalfant and his colleagues (Chalfant & Pysh, 1989) have devised a prereferral system, called *teacher assistance teams,* designed to cope with situations like Paul's prior to a child's referral to special education. The team consists of the classroom teacher, the special education teacher, the school psychologist, the principal, and other school staff as appropriate. Team members thoroughly discuss the situation and suggest several alternative instructional strategies to the teacher (in our example, Mrs. Parker). A trial period is determined in which the teacher will apply these approaches in the classroom.

If the child continues to show no improvement, then a referral to special education may be made. Many times, however, the prereferral meeting and prescriptions seem to be all that is necessary to put the child and teacher on the right track (Chalfant, 1989). The team meeting prevents many unnecessary referrals to special education and strengthens the general program of education as well.

One strategy for reducing the number of referrals to special education is the teaming of teachers, a process called *peer collaboration.* Teachers in teams of two or three learn how to discuss a student's problem among themselves and seek an answer prior to referral for special help (Pugash & Johnson, 1995). The teachers learn how to present a problem and pose clarifying questions to explore the dimensions of a problem such as a student throwing tantrums or failing miserably on tests. On the basis of these problem explorations, they redefine the problem and design three or more possible interventions to address it. Finally, they establish an evaluation plan to determine if the intervention succeeded.

Pugash and Johnson (1995) compared 95 teachers who had received the special peer collaboration training with 96 teachers who had not and found the number of referrals for special help had been reduced by half in the group receiving the training while remaining the same for the teachers who did not receive such training. This outcome demonstrates again the untapped potential existing in the regular school staff, which can, with preparation, learn to cope with classroom problems without referring them to someone else.

Assessment

Through the assessment process, we get an educational portrait of the child that helps us create an individualized educational program. An ongoing assessment allows us to evaluate how well that program is working. In special education, then, **assessment** "is the systematic process of gathering educationally relevant information to make legal and instructional decisions about the provision of special services" (McLoughlin & Lewis, 1991, p. 3).

Assessment looks at whether a school performance problem exists; determines the child's strengths and weaknesses, the content areas affected, and the relationship of any academic problems to learning; and prescribes educational goals and objectives and strategies to help teachers and students meet them. (© *Jerry Howard/Positive Images*)

An assessment starts with the general issue of whether a school performance problem exists and then moves on to the child's strengths and weaknesses, the content areas affected, and the relationship of any academic problems to the child's learning environment. We finish with a prescription of educational goals and objectives and with strategies to help us meet them. Ongoing evaluation (for example, asking, How effective is the educational program?) gives us the necessary information to revise the educational program.

Assessment specialists use extensive tests, interviews, observations, and ratings to determine the child's inter-individual and intra-individual differences, (Some of these assessment tests are discussed in Chapter 1.) Their analysis of those differences allows them to make better educational decisions about the child. The assessment process involves five steps:

1. *Screening:* quickly and economically finding those children who need more thorough (and costly) examination

2. *Diagnosis, classification, and placement:* collecting additional information to determine which special program the child needs or for which the child is eligible

3. *Instructional planning:* using diagnostic information to design an individualized education program based on the child's needs

4. *Pupil evaluation:* administering tests to determine whether a particular student is indeed making expected progress and meeting the objectives that were originally established

5. *Program evaluation:* determining the effectiveness of a special program through tests and observation (Ysseldyke & Shinn, 1981)

A comprehensive assessment includes measurements or data collected across a number of developmental domains, including intelligence, academic achievement, social behavior, self-image, perceptual-motor abilities, vision, hearing, and other areas appropriate to the particular child. We can see how the process works in the case of Diane, a 7-year-old. Diane was a slim child, somewhat small for her age. She was promoted to second grade mainly because of the hopes of her first-grade teacher; her actual performance was not good. In the second grade, Diane was having trouble with basic reading and arithmetic skills. She was an unhappy child who did not talk a lot and who did not have many friends in the classroom.

In some school systems, screening before kindergarten or at the beginning or end of first grade might have picked up Diane's problems. In this kind of screening, every child is examined quickly for major problems in vision, hearing, and learning ability. If a difficulty shows up, the child is referred for an intensive evaluation. In Diane's school system, academic performance takes the place of the screening process. In fact, most students find their way into special education through academic failure or through the perceptive observation of school personnel. As Bailey and Harbin (1980) pointed out,

> Children are not usually referred for evaluation on a teacher's whim. A referral indicates a significant educational problem that is unlikely to be remedied without some form of additional intervention with the teacher or child. (p. 595)

Diane's second-grade teacher recognized a problem and referred the child for diagnostic evaluation. Diane was given a series of tests and interviews to determine whether she did have a problem and to identify that problem. In the process, the diagnostic team eliminated a number of factors that might have caused Diane difficulty. They looked for signs of physical disabilities, of serious emotional disturbance, of mental retardation, of environmental disadvantage. The goal of the assessment and referral is to identify the support Diane needs to maximize her potential. This is done through the individualized education program.

The Individualized Education Program

One of the many innovations brought forth by the Education for All Handicapped Children Act is the requirement that every handicapped child have an **individualized education program (IEP)**, a clearly documented and carefully monitored plan setting forth how to differentiate the curriculum and experiences of the exceptional child to meet the individual needs of that child. The instructional plan must include the following:

1. The nature of the child's problem
2. The program's long-term goals
3. The program's short-term objectives
4. The special education services the child will receive
5. The criteria for gauging the effectiveness of those services

The individualized education program describes the nature of the child's problem, the program's objectives and goals, the special education services the child will receive, and the criteria for gauging the effectiveness of those services. (*D and I MacDonald/ The Picture Cube*)

Despite the additional time and effort required of teachers, implementing IEPs has increased family involvement in students' instructional programs.

In Diane's case, after the initial diagnosis and classification, a more thorough analysis of specific learning problems or difficulties was carried out. Earlier examinations had defined Diane's abilities and disabilities; now the educational team analyzed those abilities and disabilities to design a specialized program and teaching strategies for the child. Once the program goals were set and the individual program was implemented, a plan was set up to measure Diane's progress at subsequent points to see if these objectives had been met.

A recent literature review (Gallagher & Desimone, 1995) shows evidence that the implementation of the IEP in school systems across the nation has had both positive and negative outcomes. On the positive side are evidence of better relations between teacher and family and improved understanding by the family of the special education program; there is also more information for parents about academic achievement and gains made by their child, as well as general agreement between school and family about the goals and program directions for the child.

On the negative side is much evidence that the implementation of this idea has not gone smoothly in many places. The IEP is often seen as paperwork with no substantive meaning or use in the classroom. It places great demands on teachers' time, may replace the regular curriculum, and, in short, is seen as one more meaningless requirement that must be fulfilled.

Although there are voices calling for the abandonment of the IEP, few wish to abandon the gains that it has brought. How can we get rid of the nonessentials of the process and keep the things that are good? A continual problem for educators!

Table 2.2 shows examples of goals and objectives written for two IEPs. The vocational and independent living goals for Karen, a child with moderate retardation, illustrate the types of goals and objectives written for the IEP of a teenage girl focusing on job-related activities. In contrast, the goals and objectives for Norman, a boy with mild retardation just beginning school, are linked to social behavior and to some reasonable academic standards. These examples represent only a small segment of the overall IEP process, which focuses much attention on the collection of information and diagnostic material on the child and also discusses the evaluation of the individualized program to see whether the goals and objectives have been carried out.

Educational Restructuring

The adaptations described earlier in this chapter are one aspect of school responses to the needs of exceptional children. Changes in societal structures, attitudes, and values in recent decades have led schools to accept their role more positively and often have resulted in new methods to carry out their responsibilities to exceptional children.

These changing attitudes come at a time when Americans increasingly believe that the public school system is not as effective as it should be and would benefit from new methods and approaches. Substantial efforts have been made to change or modify the overall system (Goodlad, 1985; Sizer, 1986). These reforms promise to change the educational landscape and create a very different educational environment for the exceptional child.

In many ways, special education has been defining its services to children with disabilities, and to children with special gifts and talents, on the basis of the established patterns of general education. Given the structure and programs of general education, special education has been defined by how it differs from the normal pattern of general education. Then major restructuring efforts in general education begun in the early 1990s made it necessary to redesign special educational services. This section briefly touches on some of the major elements of that restructuring effort.

THE REGULAR EDUCATION INITIATIVE

The regular education initiative (REI) seeks to integrate regular and special education.

One of the major recent movements to restructure the school environment has its origin in special education—the regular education initiative (REI). Ideally, a good education model has special educators joining with other educators to advance a broad program of adaptive education for all students (Reynolds, Wang, & Walberg, 1987). The ideal product is one unified system instead of two parallel systems (regular and special) existing side by side. This idea has attracted many special educators who question the efficacy of current programs and are concerned

TABLE 2.2 | IEP Goals and Objectives

Case Study: Karen (CA = 15-1, IQ = 47)

	Annual Goals	Sample Short-Term Objectives
Vocational	Karen will acquire skills appropriate for jobs in the food service industry.	When asked to fill the sink for dish washing, Karen will fill the sink to the halfway point with warm water without error on 9 out of 10 trials.
Independent living	1. Karen will place local telephone calls.	Given a written telephone number, Karen will push the correct buttons on the telephone without error on 4 out of 5 trials.
	2. Karen will safely cross a busy street at a traffic light.	Given a computer-simulation of a busy street corner with a traffic light, Karen will press the correct YES/NO response button on the computer on 10 out of 10 trials.
Leisure	Karen will buy movie tickets.	Upon arriving at the movie box office, Karen will successfully purchase a ticket for her preferred show without error on 5 out of 5 trials.

Case Study: Norman (CA = 5-5, IQ = 64)

	Annual Goals	Sample Short-Term Objectives
Social	Norman will demonstrate cooperative behavior with peers during group activities.	When asked to do so, Norman will pass food from the person seated on his right to the person seated on his left, for 10 consecutive snack breaks at school.
Self-help	Norman will independently eat with spoon and fork.	When handed a spoon, Norman will hold it between his thumb and index finger to scoop food for 10 consecutive lunches.
Academic	Norman will read, count, and name the values of numbers 1 through 10.	When presented with 5 cards, each containing a printed number between 1 and 5, Norman will achieve 100 percent accuracy per session for 5 consecutive sessions in naming the number.

Source: L. Hickson, J.A. Blackman, and E. Reis (1995). *Mental retardations: Foundations of educational programming,* pp. 159, 162. Copyright © by Allyn and Bacon. Reprinted by permission.

about the misclassification and overreferral of exceptional students (Biklin & Zollers, 1986; Gartner, 1986; Stainback & Stainback, 1988). The REI actually challenges some of the basic assumptions of special education, as summarized by Kaufman (1989) in Table 2.3.

The REI implies that there should be a broad support system for regular education—including reading specialists, psychologists, and speech-language pathologists—which would enable mildly handicapped children to be included within the regular education framework. It is an attempt to transform the concept of mainstreaming into operational terms.

The REI concept has been challenged on several fronts. First, although it is called a "regular education initiative," it was designed by special educators. General educators have contributed very little to the debate (McKinney & Hocutt, 1988). Also, the proposals do not spell out how they would work, what they would cost, and what administrative problems would have to be overcome. This lack of specifics has led to calls for caution before any major restructuring is done (see Hallahan, Kaufmann, Lloyd, & McKinney, 1988).

Reynolds, Wang, and Walberg (1987) have called for "experimental trials of integrated forms of education for students who are currently segregated for service in separate special, remedial, and compensatory education program" (p. 394), and many school systems are trying out the elements of REI, although not often in the systematic way that the REI advocates suggest. The immediate effect of the REI movement, however, has been to increase the alternatives to current practice and to introduce new service delivery models for exceptional children and general education students as well, as we try to balance the needs of students and professionals.

As you can see by the sharp differences noted in Table 2.3 for and against special education, a major challenge is being presented to special education programs and procedures as they now exist. The basic assumptions that exceptional children need additional services outside the regular classroom, and specially trained personnel to provide them, are being questioned for the first time. Proponents of the REI propose doing away with the special education establishment but stop short of doing away with special education services or personnel who they believe can be useful for children with disabilities within the regular classroom setting (Wang & Reynolds, 1989).

The strongest proponents of *inclusion* (the newest of the reform movements), however, would have the special education movement disappear as a wrongheaded approach to the learning problems of students, an approach that delays the proper attention to these children in the regular classroom.

THE INCLUSION MOVEMENT

Supporters of the inclusion movement believe that all children, regardless of ability, should be educated in general classrooms.

Proponents of inclusion believe that *all* children—regardless of disability or intensity of exceptionality—should be educated in general education environments. They assume that all students—including those with mild, moderate, or severe disabilities—should be educated with peers of the same age and in schools in their neighborhoods. The inclusion movement is a major departure from the REI, which

TABLE 2.3 REI Challenge to the Basic Assumptions of Special Education

Principles of Special Education	Counterarguments to Special Education
Some students are very different from most in ways that are specific regarding education, and special education is required to meet their needs.	Students are more alike than they are different. The same basic principles apply to the learning of all students. Consequently, no truly special instruction is needed by any student.
Special expertise is required by teachers of exceptional students, because such students present particularly difficult instructional problems.	Good teachers can teach all students; all good teachers use the same basic techniques and strategies.
Students who need special education must be clearly identified to ensure that they [such children] receive appropriate services.	All children can be provided a high-quality education without identifying some students as different or special and without maintaining separate budgets, training programs, teachers, or classes.
Education outside the regular classroom is sometimes required for some part of the school day to meet some students' needs.	Education outside the regular classroom is not required for anyone. All students can be instructed and managed effectively in regular classrooms.
The options of special education outside the regular classroom are required to ensure equal educational opportunity for exceptional students.	If handicapped students are educated alongside their nonhandicapped peers, then and only then can they be receiving an equal education opportunity.

Source: From "The Regular Education Initiative as Reagan–Bush Education Policy: A Trickle-Down Theory of Education of the Hard-to-Teach" by J. Kaufman, 1989, *Journal of Special Education, 23*, pp. 256–278. Copyright © 1989 by PRO-ED, Inc. Reprinted by permission.

supports some differential placement for exceptional students based on their individual needs.

If we defined *disability* so that it no longer exists, and if we decoupled schools from the old thinking, we might be able to develop a new system that would accept all individuals and find ways to teach them. That, at any rate, is the basic philosophy and goal of many of those who wish to abandon the special education model in favor of a more inclusive educational model (Edgar, 1995).

To some advocates of inclusion (Stainback & Stainback, 1992) any placement other than in the regular classroom poses a serious threat of putting a child at risk for an inferior education and deprives the child of the social relationships that can be nurtured in the general education setting. The overarching concern for those supporting the inclusion movement seems to be the social relationships of the child with disabilities, rather than mastery of certain academic and technical skills. This is the position of the Association for Persons with Severe Handicaps. The policy of full inclusion follows this path of reasoning: If we are to have, as a major goal, the *social integration* of persons with disabilities into the adult society, then the school environment should foster the development of such skills, personal friendships, and relationships with children with disabilities. These skills are available to nondisabled persons in the natural course of their educational experiences (Snell, 1988).

The attitude of the Learning Disabilities Association of America (LDA) toward inclusion is quite different. LDA believes that the regular education classroom is *not* the appropriate place for many students with learning disabilities—those who may need alternative instructional environments or teaching strategies that cannot or will not be provided within the context of the regular classroom. Neither group denies the legitimacy of the other's priorities. The issue is which should have precedence.

Evans (1995) points out that the inclusion philosophy requires the application of a variety of other strategies that can maintain a diverse group of students in the general education environment. These strategies include consultant teacher models, collaborative consultation, collaborative teaching, cooperative professional development, and prereferral consultation. In other words, it is not enough merely to decree that all exceptional children will be placed in the general education environment. If inclusion is to work, there must be a wide variety of support personnel to help the general education teacher to provide a healthy educational environment for *all* students. Table 2.4 describes the differentiated program advocated by proponents of inclusion. A special education teacher, two paraprofessionals, and considerable planning to meet individual needs will be necessary to achieve the results expected in this inclusive classroom.

How much inclusion is "included"? There has been a great deal of confusion about just how much time the child with disabilities must spend in the regular classroom to be considered "included." Must it be 100 percent of school time to justify the term *inclusion*? One answer is that the child with disabilities should be based in the regular class. Another is that the child is recognized to be a member of the class where he or she starts the school day. The child with disabilities need not spend all of his or her time with that class, but that class is the child's group, and everyone knows it (Brown et al., 1991). As Brown and his colleagues (1991) say, "It is better to be an 'insider' who goes out for short periods of time, than it is to be an 'outsider' who comes in" (p. 40). Figure 2.3 shows the trends over a 5-year period for enrollments of students in various types of environmental settings.

Do friendships result from merely placing students in proximity to one another? Does the fact that some students are modeling appropriate behavior mean that the exceptional child will imitate such behavior? Probably not. Friendships generally grow between students who perceive similarities with one another. Students who are withdrawn gravitate toward others who are shy; an aggressive student often chooses another aggressive student to bond with (Dision, Andrews, & Cosby,

TABLE 2.4	Necessary Conditions for the Integration of Children with Disabilities in Regular Classrooms

All of the school personnel have attended inservice training designed to develop collaborative skills for teaming and problem-solving. Mrs. Smith and the two paraprofessionals who work in the classroom also received special training on disabilities and on how to create an inclusive classroom environment. The school principal, Ben Parks, had worked in special education many years ago and has received training on the impact of new special education developments and instructional arrangements on school administration. Each year, Mr. Parks works with the building staff to identify areas in which new training is needed. For specific questions that may arise, technical assistance is available through a regional special education cooperative.

Jane Smith teaches third grade at Lincoln Elementary School. Three days a week, she co-teaches the class with Lynn Vogel, a special education teacher. Their 25 students include 4 who have special needs due to disabilities and 2 others who currently need special help in specific curriculum areas. Each of the students with a disability has an IEP that was developed by a team that included both teachers. The teachers, paraprofessionals, and the school principal believe that these students have a great deal to contribute to the class and that they will achieve their best in the environment of a general education classroom.

Mrs. Smith and Miss Vogel share responsibility for teaching and for supervising their two paraprofessionals. In addition to the time they spend together in the classroom, they spend 1 to 4 hours per week planning instruction, plus additional planning time with other teachers and support personnel who work with their students.

The teachers use their joint planning time to problem-solve and discuss the use of special instructional techniques for all students who need special assistance. Monitoring and adapting instruction for individual students is an ongoing activity. The teachers use curriculum-based measurement to systematically assess their students' learning progress. They adapt curricula so that lessons begin at the edge of the student's knowledge, adding new material at the student's pace, and presenting it in a style consistent with the student's learning style. For some students, preorganizers or chapter previews are used to bring out the most important points of the material to be learned; for other students, new vocabulary words may need to be highlighted or reduced reading levels may be required. Some students may use special activity worksheets, while others may learn best by using media or computer-assisted instruction.

In the classroom the teachers group students differently for different activities. Sometimes, the teachers and paraprofessionals divide the class, each teaching a small group or tutoring individuals. They use cooperative learning projects to help the students learn to work together and develop social relationships. Peer tutors provide extra help to students who need it. Students without disabilities are more than willing to help their friends who have disabilities, and vice versa.

Source: ERIC Digest. "Including Students with Disabilities in General Education Classrooms." *Clearinghouse on Disabilities and Gifted Education.* Council for Exceptional Children, July 1993. Reprinted with permission.

FIGURE 2.3

Percentage of students age 6 through 21 with disabilities serviced in different educational environments: school years 1988–89 through 1992–93

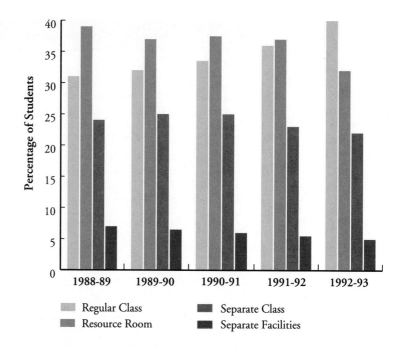

Source: U.S. Department of Education, (1995), *Seventeenth Annual Report to Congress*, (Washington, D.C.: U.S. Department of Education, Office of Special Education Programs, p. 15).

1995). Reflect on your own youth! Did you always form friendships with peers whom your parents wished you to be friends with in the hope that they would be good role models for you? Or were your parents occasionally horrified to see whom you brought home, which friends stirred in you some bond of interest or some common feeling about the school or world around you?

One device encouraging closer social contact is known as the **circle of friends,** in which nondisabled children under the leadership of a teacher or counselor or inclusion facilitator (Boathouse, 1993) take the responsibility for communicating with the children with disabilities on a social level and spend time finding out about their likes and dislikes. To their surprise they may find little difference between themselves and the child with disabilities, and this discovery is the beginning of wisdom and a degree of social acceptance.

Out of such experiences can come substantial benefits for the nondisabled child. Table 2.5 shows some ways in which students who help a child with disabilities gain something from the experience. The students' comments are clear indications that healthy interactions in school with children with disabilities can reduce the fear of differences and increase tolerance for differences, when the integration is done with clear purpose and sensitivity.

TABLE 2.5	**Growth in Nondisabled Students from Inclusion**
Self-concept	"I'm a lot more patient than I was before, and I understand a lot more things than I did. . . ."
Social cognitive growth	"Well, the nonhandicapped kids learned that (the kids with disabilities) are just like themselves, they're all alike, and they really are teenagers and they do a lot of the same things and like the same things you do. When you get to know them, you really understand that they really are the same people that you are."
Reduced fears of differences	"I had learned something different . . . to just know that you can talk to anyone if you really want to and you can be comfortable with anyone if you just take the step—not just your normal peer group."
Increased tolerance	"I think the 4 days that we spent (on a retreat with peers who had disabilities) were the most valuable teaching that I've ever had in my life because it not only opened up the doors for me to deal with people that have disabilities but everyone in general."
Development of principles	"(How has this affected your other attitudes?) Well, like a new person I meet, you know you don't like to go judging a book by its cover . . . you got to understand them and know them before you can really judge them . . . you got to know them personally."
Relaxed and accepting friendships	"She was nicer than most of the people I've met, you know. That's the funny thing about it. She seemed gentle and kind, never a harsh word, never a harsh word."

Adapted from C. Peck, J. Donaldson, and M. Pezzoli (1990). *Journal of the Association for Persons with Severe Handicaps,* 15(4), pp. 241–249.

RESTRUCTURING IN GENERAL EDUCATION: AMERICA 2000

The reform and restructuring movement of the 1990s has several elements that especially affect exceptional children (see Table 2.6). These include possible changes in the administration of special programs, the location of special education classes, and the training that special education teachers (and regular teachers) will receive. Reforms that impact special education are in middle schools, cooperative learning, site-based management, academic standards, effective assessment tools, accountability, and state and federal legislation.

Middle Schools

One result of the movement to restructure schools is a move away from the traditional junior high school program, with its imitation of the senior high school in establishing categorical content fields (such as chemistry and history), one-hour periods, and teachers prepared in those special fields but rarely schooled in educational strategies or developmental psychology. Advocates propose to replace the junior high school with the middle school, which would emphasize (1) the affective life of the student (recognizing the major physical changes the student is undergoing in this time period), (2) an interdisciplinary curriculum to indicate how bodies of knowledge interrelate, (3) team teaching to allow for the use of the special skills and knowledge of the teachers, (4) flexible scheduling, and (5) the organization of small to large student groups depending on the lesson and the time (George, 1988).

One current emphasis in middle schools is heterogeneous grouping, the deliberate mixing of all levels of students in the instructional program. This strategy raises serious concerns among special educators about whether the special needs of exceptional children will be adequately addressed (Oakes, 1985).

Restructuring regular education also requires major changes in special education.

Cooperative Learning

Although cooperative learning is a set of instructional strategies rather than a major administrative shift or structural change, it has come to symbolize a new emphasis in U.S. education toward cooperation, as opposed to competition or isolated learning. Cooperative learning organizes students into groups of three to six and gives them a task to solve cooperatively. The goal of such strategies is to help students learn problem-solving techniques and how to work with others in a constructive manner (Johnson, Johnson, & Holubec, 1990).

The child with exceptionalities can be expected to participate as a member of a cooperative learning team. In ideal circumstances, the task that is presented to the group has a meaningful role for the exceptional child. A problem such as "How did our community come to be?" might provide the child with mental retardation the task of searching newspaper files for information while the child with intellectual giftedness might go over courthouse records or conduct oral interviews of early residents. The use of cooperative learning has been reported to have increased the social acceptance of some exceptional children in regular classrooms

TABLE 2.6   Goals 2000: Educate America Act

Title I: National Education Goals

Codifies into law eight National Education Goals and their objectives. The goals state that, by the year 2000,

1. All children in America will start school ready to learn.

2. The high school graduation rate will increase to at least 90%.

3. American students will leave grades four, eight, and twelve having demonstrated competency over challenging subject matter, including English, mathematics, science, arts, foreign languages, history and geography, civics and government, and economics.

4. The Nation's teaching force will have access to programs for the continued improvement of their professional skills and the opportunity to acquire the knowledge and skills needed to instruct and prepare all American students for the next century.

5. U.S. students will be first in the world in math and science achievement.

6. Every American will be literate and will possess the knowledge and skills necessary to compete in a global economy.

7. Every school in America will be free of drugs, alcohol, and violence, and will offer a disciplined environment conducive to learning.

8. Every school will promote partnerships that will increase parental involvement and participation in promoting the social, emotional, and academic growth of children.

Source: U.S. Department of Education.

(Johnson, Johnson, & Holubec, 1990). An emphasis in some cooperative learning programs on organizing the groups by heterogeneous mixing (Slavin, 1991) has caused some educators of gifted students to question the level of challenge that their students would meet in such groups (Robinson, 1991).

Site-Based Management

Many people in the reform movement believe in shifting the power of educational decision making back to the teacher and the local school and away from distant administrators in the "central office" who may not be aware of local issues or problems. With site-based management, the state department of education, the local school administrators, or institutions of higher education exercise less power and decision making. Site-based management is one of a number of attempts to empower teachers, to recognize their expertise, and to support them in their own decisions about what is best for the students in their charge.

How such a move will affect children with special needs will probably depend in large measure on whether a specific site has people knowledgeable about the

Cooperative learning is a set of instructional strategies that helps students learn problem-solving techniques and how to work with others in a constructive manner. (© *David Pratt/Positive Images*)

special problems of such children and what educational strategies they can use to deal with these problems. If no one on the local site-based team knows about the special learning problems of children with learning disabilities, then there is concern that necessary services will not be delivered.

Academic Standards

One of the fundamental parts of the educational reform movement involves the development of academic standards (National Council on Educational Standards and Testing, 1992). Such standards, representing expectations of what students are expected to do at a certain level of schooling, are designed to counteract a supposed slippage of expectations in America's schools (Berliner, 1992). By establishing state or national standards for mastery of mathematics or history or science, we are able to assure ourselves that the schools in a community have been performing their educational job effectively.

Although the term *high academic standards* has an attractive ring to it, several questions should come to mind: How will we determine if students have met such standards? Are we calling for a major new testing program to determine if students meet minimal or challenging academic standards? Some people clearly hope that the establishment of standards and the tests to measure their attainment will be an effective motivator for upgrading school performance. (Simmons & Resnick, 1993). It has not escaped the notice of educators that teachers will teach whatever is on *high-stakes tests* (tests whose results are translated into meaningful action by the schools such as entrance to college or promotion to the next grade).

How these new standards impact on exceptional children is a key question that we need to concern ourselves with. Will a child with mental retardation be held back in the regular grades for a number of years until he or she masters basic material? Will a child with specific learning disabilities be allowed to take a modified version of a test—a version that takes into account the disability? How will this approach affect the movement to include children with disabilities in the regular classroom? We will revisit each of these issues as we consider each area of exceptionality.

The increasing concern about standards has raised an important point about what action should be taken with students who don't meet the standards. Suppose, in the interests of higher standards, the schools establish a minimum standard of performance to be achieved before a student moves on to the next grade. Many exceptional children will not be able to meet that standard. What happens then? All too often the answer is retention or holding the student back a grade in the hope that the student will, with the extra time, be able to master the basic skills or knowledge. Retention, however, has been long demonstrated to be one of the least useful of techniques. In general, students who are retained tend to drop out of school more and do not learn the necessary material that was the goal of the retention in the first place. Such results are also found in a research synthesis with children with learning disabilities (McLeskey, Lancaster, & Grizzle, 1995). There is little reason to believe that mere retention will do anything to help the student. The standards issue promises to be problematical for children with special needs.

Effective Assessment Tools

Also, there is the important question of whether we have the correct tools for the tasks of program assessment and evaluation. Elaborate goals such as improving productive thinking or increasing the scope of knowledge structure sound impressive, but do we have the means of demonstrating that such goals have been met?

Some new approaches have appeared to take the place of the standard achievement tests. They bear names like *performance assessment*, *authentic assessment*, and *real-life assessment*. Since performance is knowledge in use, **performance assessment** is a measure of the applications of knowledge. If a student is asked to write an essay on a particular topic, that essay could form the basis for a type of performance assessment. If a student is asked to conduct a research project or produce an oral presentation on a topic, this assignment could be a basis for performance assessment (Wiggins, 1992).

Authentic assessment, involves the regular classroom performance of the student, rather than a contrived task such as described above. Quite typically, it might be an examination of a student portfolio providing evidence of student performance over time. In this way, we have an assessment in real time, using classroom work and assignments as the basis for evaluation.

These forms of evaluation still leave the task of determining just what performance is acceptable or outstanding. Often such judgments are rather crude three-point or four-point scales ranging from *excellent* to *unacceptable*. Added to that would be a substantive critique of writing style or scientific procedures revealed through the authentic assessment. These approaches are good news for programs for gifted students because they give students considerably greater leeway to show what they know, and what applications they can make of what they know, than would be possible in a multiple-choice test. If these performance assessment or authentic assessments turn out to be high-stakes testing (an important decision regarding the student's life will be made as a result of their outcome), then considerable attention has to be paid to the scoring standards to ensure fairness and equity in the procedures from one place to another.

Accountability

The word accountability throws a mild chill into every educator. The general public tells us that we are to be held responsible for the products that we release from the educational system. No longer will the general public take the educator's word about what progress is being made in education; it wants to be shown. The public wants proof that education and special education produce good results, and it does not react well when told how hard it is to produce that proof, however valid the reasons.

In the field of exceptional children, the goals of the individualized education programs might be quite different from one child to another, and so aggregating results into a total report on the special education program may be hard. For example, if Mary is trying to achieve social acceptance goals and Sam is working on spelling, it would be hard to assess Sam's progress with a social acceptance scale or Mary's progress with a spelling test or to add up all the scores of the special students on these measures as a way of judging progress.

As currently constructed, the standard achievement test does not adequately measure the attainments of many exceptional children. The child with mental retardation may be learning many practical sets of skills and knowledge that are not covered by the standard curriculum and standard test, and the gifted child will surely have his or her abilities and attainments underestimated because of the lack of depth and conceptual complexity of most of these measures. Programs for exceptional children must be accountable—as must all education programs—but special efforts must be made to ensure that the measurements fit the exceptional student's program goals.

State and Federal Legislation

In many instances what is happening in the schools with children with special needs has legislative ancestors. Many of the resources and finances that schools need to conduct special services for such children have come from state or federal legislation. While providing these resources, the legislatures sometimes make certain requirements about where and how to educate such children. To access those funds, local schools modify their programs to meet the demands of the legislation. Thus, what you are observing in the schools may be designed not so much by educators as by legislators eager to have their say about the best way to modify the general education program for children with special needs.

An Overview. One of the ways we express society's needs and intentions in a democracy is through legislation. At the turn of the century, individual states became involved in a limited way in subsidizing programs in public schools for children with sensory disabilities (blindness, deafness) and physical impairments. Some states helped organize and support classes for children who were mentally retarded or who had behavioral problems. After World War II, many states expanded their involvement, providing financial support for special classes and services in local schools for children with all types of disability. This expansion caused two problems that many believed could be solved only by federal legislation.

First, these new and larger programs created a personnel scarcity in the late 1940s and early 1950s. Professional special educators were in short supply, and the field of special education was not firmly established. Second, because not all states expanded their involvement in special education, organized parents' groups began asking why children with disabilities and their parents should be penalized through the accident of birth in a particular state or a particular region of the state.

Were not U.S. citizens (in this case the parents of children with disabilities) entitled to equal treatment anywhere in the United States? Should parents, in addition to the burdens of having children with special needs, be forced to move their family to a community where special education resources were available, or to send their children to some institution far away from home and family because no local resources existed? The blatant unfairness of the situation called out for attention.

Legislation has provided resources for children with special needs.

Federal legislation clearly was needed, both to bring qualified people into special education and to equalize educational opportunities across the country. But that legislation was not easy to obtain. It violated the strong tradition in the United States that education is a state and local responsibility. Still, organized parents' groups with the support of other interested citizens convinced Congress that they needed help.

Public Law 88-164. After much debate, in the late 1950s Congress began to pass limited measures directed toward research and personnel training in the fields of mental retardation and deafness. In 1963, PL 88-164 authorized funds for training professionals and for research and demonstration. The law represented a strong initiative by President John Kennedy, whose interest was heightened by his sister's mental retardation. Those first efforts were followed by many others, and from that small beginning emerged thirty years of legislation to ensure that all children with disabilities have access to an appropriate education.

Public Law 94-142. That flood of legislation served notice that the federal government accepted responsibility for providing support and resources for children with disabilities and for encouraging the states to carry out their basic responsibilities. Still, programs and resources were not consistent from state to state. To deal with that inconsistency and to help the states handle the costs of court-mandated programs, Congress in 1975 passed PL 94-142, the Education for All Handicapped Children Act. The measure, which took effect in 1977, was designed

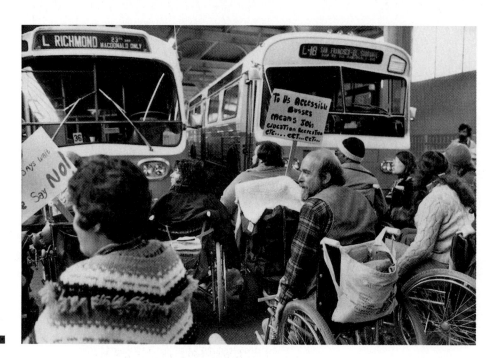

By pressuring their representatives and speaking out themselves, exceptional individuals have been instrumental in getting new laws passed and new programs established. (© Rose Skytta/ Jeroboam, Inc.)

to assure that all handicapped children have available to them . . . special education and related services designed to meet their unique needs . . . to assure that the rights of handicapped children, and their parents or guardians, are protected, to assist states and localities to provide for the education of all handicapped children, and to assess and assure the effectiveness of efforts to educate handicapped children. (House of Representatives, 1975, p. 35)

Six key principles at the heart of PL 94-142 have shaped special as well as general education during the last two decades:

1. *Zero reject.* All children with disabilities must be provided a free and appropriate public education. This means local school systems do not have the option to decide whether to provide needed services.

2. *Nondiscriminatory evaluation.* Each student must receive a full individual examination before being placed in a special education program, with tests appropriate to the child's cultural and linguistic background. A re-evaluation is required every three years.

3. *Individualized education program.* An individualized education program (IEP) must be written for every student with a handicap who is receiving special education. The IEP must describe the child's current performance and goals for the school year, the particular special education services to be delivered, and the procedures by which outcomes are evaluated.

4. *Least restrictive environment.* As much as possible, children who are handicapped must be educated with children who are not handicapped. The

philosophy is to move as close to the normal setting (regular classroom) as feasible for each child.

5. *Due process.* Due process is a set of legal procedures to ensure the fairness of educational decisions and the accountability of both professionals and parents in making those decisions. These procedures allow parents to call a hearing when they do not agree with the school's plans for their child, to obtain an individual evaluation from a qualified examiner outside the school system, or to take other actions to ensure that both family and child have channels through which to voice their interests and concerns.

6. *Parental participation.* Parents are to be included in the development of the IEP, and they have the right to access their child's educational records.

To carry out the provisions of the law, the federal government authorized the spending of up to $3 billion by 1982, promising much larger sums of money to aid the states than had previously been provided. By 1990, the government was still spending about $1 billion a year. In return for that aid, states are required to show evidence that they are doing their best to help children with disabilities receive needed services. Specific provisions in the law placed substantial pressure on public school systems, demanding more in the way of assessment, parent contact, and evaluation than most school systems had been accustomed to providing.

Not surprisingly, many educators have protested the burden that these requirements place on them. But the law has become part of the educational landscape. In less than three decades, the federal government moved from little involvement in special education to become a major partner in local and state programs for students who have disabilities. Federal education policy for children with disabilities is summarized in Table 2.7.

Public Law 99-457 and IDEA (Public Law 101-476). The Education for All Handicapped Children Act was, in fact, misnamed. It wasn't for all children at all ages. As it became increasingly evident that early intervention was important, both for the exceptional child and for his or her family, pressure grew for a downward extension of the law.

PL 99-457 (Education of the Handicapped Act Amendments), passed in 1986, provided that opportunity by allocating federal funds for the states to develop plans and programs for children and their families from birth on. PL 101-476, passed in 1990, changed the title of the Education of the Handicapped Act to the "Individuals with Disabilities Education Act" or IDEA. As was true of the earlier legislation, embedded in these laws were numerous attempts to reform or restructure the service system. For example, PL 99-457 included the following:

■ A requirement for an Individual Family Service Plan, which would provide a program of services to the child and family as appropriate and would recognize the rights of parents to influence their child's program.

■ A call for the integration of various services. Agencies were required to work together so that the resources of health, social, and family services and education blend their efforts to the common benefit of child and family.

TABLE 2.7	Highlights of Federal Education Policy for Children with Disabilities
Title	**Purpose**
PL 85-926 (1958)	Provided grants for teaching children with handicaps; related to the education of children who are mentally retarded
PL 88-164, Title III (1963)	Authorized funds for teacher training and for research and demonstration projects in the education of persons with handicaps
PL 89-10 (1965)	Elementary and Secondary Education Act; Title III authorized assistance to children with handicaps in state-operated and state-supported private day and residential schools
PL 89-313	Amendments to PL 89-10; provided grants to state educational agencies for the education of children with handicaps in state-supported institutions
PL 90-538 (1968)	Handicapped Children's Early Education Assistance Act; provided grants for the development and implementation of experimental programs in early education for children with handicaps, from birth to age 6
PL 91-230 (1969)	Amendments to PL 89-10; Title VI consolidated into one act—Education of the Handicapped—the previous enactments relating to children with handicaps
PL 92-424 (1972)	Economic Opportunity Amendments; required that not less than 10 percent of Head Start enrollment opportunities be available to children with handicaps
PL 94-142 (1975)	Education for All Handicapped Children Act; required states to provide by September 1, 1978, a free appropriate education for all children with handicaps between the ages of 3 and 18
PL 98-199 (1984)	Amended the Handicapped Children's Early Education Assistance Act (PL 90-538); provided funds for planning statewide comprehensive services for children with handicaps through age 5
PL 99-457, Part H (1986)	Amended the Education of the Handicapped Act; permitted comprehensive multidisciplinary services for

TABLE 2.7	Highlights of Federal Education Policy for Children with Disabilities (cont.)
Title	**Purpose**
	infants and toddlers (birth through age 2) and their families.
PL 101-476 (1990)	Individuals with Disabilities Education Act (IDEA); required schools to provide transition services to all students with disabilities
PL 101-336 (1991)	Americans with Disabilities Act; reaffirms the rights of disabled individuals to equal access to facilities and opportunities.

■ A call for personnel preparation standards and plans, so that capable and well-trained persons would be working with these families.

■ A requirement that states pool existing sources of funds to provide for these programs (the federal government no longer took responsibility for paying more than a small part of the services bill).

IDEA added a requirement for transition services, a coordinated set of activities to promote movement from school to post-school activities such as secondary education, vocational training, independent living, and community participation. Many other provisions of this law provided services for preschool children with disabilities and their families and made clear that the service system for young children would be redesigned in a more appropriate fashion—with comprehensive services, in a multidisciplinary pattern with interagency cooperation.

Federal Actions for Students Who Are Gifted. Except for a brief period in the 1970s, there had been little movement at the federal legislative level to provide resources to aid in the education of children who are gifted. The Javits Act (Public Law 100-297), named after New York Senator Jacob Javits, who showed early interest and support, provided a small sum of money to support research and demonstration programs that focused on the special needs of gifted students from economically disadvantaged circumstances, from different cultures, or with special physical disabilities. The new support of such programs seems linked to the general dismay of the American public at how far behind American students are in content fields such as mathematics and the sciences (see Chapter 4 for specific comparisons), when compared with students from other industrialized countries. This law also noted the limited number of gifted students being identified from cultural minorities and urged action on that issue.

THE ROLE OF THE COURTS

Another important player in the establishment and design of programs for children with special needs has been the courts. The basic issue here is that children with special needs deserve a free and appropriate education just as all children do in the United States. If that right is being abridged, or if other inequities are being created, citizens can appeal to the courts for justice and equity. During the 1970s and 1980s there were a series of legal cases that have solidified the position of exceptional children and their right to a free and appropriate education.

Courts have confirmed the right of children with special needs to a free, appropriate public education (FAPE).

The movement toward judicial action was, in part, a recognition of the success of minority groups in using the courts to establish their educational rights. In 1954 with the classic school desegregation case, *Brown* v. *Board of Education*, the courts began to reaffirm the rights of minority citizens in a wide variety of settings. If court decisions could protect the rights of one group of citizens, they should do the same for another group: those with disabilities. Soon, supporters of people with disabilities were working to translate abstract legal rights into tangible social action through the judicial system.

Class action suits have been influential in changing the status of children with disabilities in the United States. A *class action suit* provides that legal action taken as part of the suit applies not only to the individual who brings the particular case to court but to all members of the class to which that individual belongs. This means that the rights of all people with disabilities can be reaffirmed by a case involving just one child.

The rulings in several court cases have reaffirmed the rights of those who are handicapped and have defined the limits of those rights:

■ A child with disabilities cannot be excluded from school without careful due process, and it is the responsibility of the schools to provide appropriate programs for children who are different (*Pennsylvania Association for Retarded Children* v. *Commonwealth of Pennsylvania*, 1972; *Goso* v. *Lopez*, 1974; *Hairston* v. *Drosick*, 1974).

■ The presumed absence of funds is not an excuse for failing to provide educational services to exceptional children. If sufficient funds are not available, then all programs should be cut back *(Mills* v. *Board of Education*, 1972).

■ Children with disabilities who are committed to state institutions must be provided a meaningful education in that setting or their incarceration is considered unlawful detention (*Wyatt* v. *Stickney*, 1972).

■ Children should not be labeled "handicapped" or placed into special education without adequate diagnosis that takes into account different cultural and linguistic backgrounds (*Larry P.* v. *Riles*, 1979).

■ Bilingual exceptional children need identification, evaluation, and educational procedures that reflect and respect their dual-language background (*Jos P.* v. *Ambach*, 1979).

■ An individual with learning disabilities has a right to services whatever his or her age (*Frederick L. v. Thomas*, 1980).

■ A child with disabilities is entitled to an appropriate, not an optimum, education (*Board of Education v. Rowley*, 1982). The *Rowley* decision was the first court decision that suggested there was a limit to the resources that exceptional children could expect.

Recently, the attention of the courts has turned to the issue of *inclusion* and the *least restrictive environment* and what an appropriate program for exceptional children should be. The results are a mixture of rulings, some supporting a strong version of inclusion and some supporting a continuum of services (McCarthy, 1994):

■ A child with a hearing disability was allowed to attend a school several miles from home instead of a neighborhood school because the centralized program at the special school better met the child's needs (*Barnett v. Fairfax County Board of Education*, 1991).

■ A child with a serious attention deficit and acting-out behavior should be placed in a special school rather than in the general education classroom (*Clyde & Shela K v. Puyallup School District*, 1994).

■ A child with Down syndrome was placed in a general education program rather than in a special education class because of the presumed priority of mainstreaming in IDEA (*Greer v. Rome City School District*, 1991).

■ A court ruled that it is the responsibility of the school district to demonstrate that the child's disabilities are so severe that he or she will receive little benefit from inclusion or will be so disruptive as to keep other classmates from learning (*Oberti v. Board of Education of the Borough of Clementon School District*, 1993).

Clearly, these rulings reflect the specifics of each individual case and the interpretation of local or district courts. It may take a Supreme Court decision to provide more general guidance on the issue. Nevertheless, when the courts speak, people listen because court decisions represent the law as we currently know it and must be obeyed.

Numerous attempts have been made through court cases to determine just what the phrase *least restrictive environment* really means. Yell (1995) reviewed the many case decisions on least restrictive environment and concluded

> For a school to survive a legal challenge to the placement of a student in a segregated setting, it must show that the student would not benefit academically or socially from an integrated placement, or that the student would disrupt classroom learning. (p. 402)

Just as laws have to be enforced and money has to be appropriated, so court decisions have to be executed. These court decisions therefore created the expectation that something would be done, but they did not guarantee it. Closing down state institutions, reorganizing public schools, and providing special services to all children with disabilities were substantial and costly changes. They raised a serious problem for program administrators: From where would the money come for implementation? Ultimately, school and local leaders turned to Washington, pressuring Congress to appropriate funds to help pay for the changes that the courts were demanding. Even with federal assistance, implementation has come slowly.

Much of the change that has been formalized in legislation and court decisions protects the rights of youngsters with disabilities. But laws and court rulings are subject to interpretation. Special educators have a unique responsibility to see that these laws and rulings are implemented as they were intended: to guarantee that all children receive an appropriate education.

THE ROLE OF ORGANIZED RELIGION

In the nineteenth and early-twentieth-centuries, organized religion played a significant role in the education of children with disabilities. Thomas Gallaudet, famous for his innovative work in educating children with hearing impairments, was a graduate of a theological institute, and many of the early schools and leaders in the effort to provide education for children with mental retardation and with sensory impairments were linked to religious institutions and backgrounds (Moores, 1987). Organized religion and religious institutions considered it their duty to educate children with disabilities in their particular traditions, despite the children's various impairments, which ordinarily would have denied them the opportunity for formal education.

Many of the major religions continue their interest and commitment to children with special needs, but the concept of separation of church and state has severely limited the presence of church-related activities in the public schools, which began to take on the responsibility for special education in the middle third of the twentieth century. Also, the additional cost of educating children with disabilities became a heavy burden on the limited financial resources of church-related education, so the public schools gradually took the lead in special education.

■■ ■ *Conclusion*

We discuss the education reform movement throughout this text. Because these reforms were not specifically designed for exceptional children, however, their impact on such students was rarely considered in the initial stages of the intended reform.

As we said, the exceptional child must be viewed in a context that includes family, neighborhood, school, and society. All of these forces impinge on the child and on his or her family, and they either enhance or inhibit the efforts of special educators to provide an appropriate education. The goal of special education teachers is to create the most favorable environment possible so that the child's capabilities are maximized.

In the next chapter we focus on the early years of exceptional children. How these children and families develop during the period from birth to age 5 has a great deal to do with how the children react to later schooling.

Summary of Major Ideas

1. Changes in society's attitudes toward exceptional children are reflected in the processes of normalization, deinstitutionalization, mainstreaming, and inclusion.

2. Instruction can be adapted to the individual needs of exceptional students in several ways: We can vary the learning environment, change the lesson content, and modify the skills taught.

3. Many exceptional children come from different cultural backgrounds and have distinctive values, attitudes, and languages. It is the responsibility of special educators to take these differences into account in their special educational plans.

4. We can make innovative use of technology to meet the needs of exceptional students. Children with disabilities may face special challenges in living up to the adult role expected in their culture.

5. Teacher assistance teams can sometimes help the regular class teacher deal with difficult students prior to their referral to special education and, perhaps, can eliminate the need for such referrals.

6. Technology can serve two separate purposes for children with disabilities. Assistive technology enhances routine functioning. Instructional technology aids in the delivery and support of instruction.

7. The assessment of exceptional children involves screening, diagnosis, classification, and placement; instructional planning; and pupil and program evaluations.

8. An individualized education program (IEP) defines the nature of a child's problem, the program's long-term goals and short-term objectives, needed services, and criteria for evaluation. The IEP has received positive comments (it improves relations between teacher and parent) and negative comments (it places time demands on the teacher without helping the child).

many do not know about services that are available to them—services that did not exist even a few years ago. In the next sections, we discuss the origins and significance of early diagnosis and intervention, why early intervention is important, who are the children at risk, how some disabilities can be prevented and detected, and the major programs and services that are available.

Overview and Origins of Early Intervention

DEFINITIONS AND GOALS

Early intervention is designed to prevent deficits or to improve an existing disability.

Early childhood intervention consists of "sustained and systematic efforts to assist young, disabled, developmentally vulnerable children from birth to age five and their families" (Meisels, 1990, p. 151). Early intervention is designed to prevent deficits or to improve an existing disability by providing therapies (such as speech-language) or devices to help the child move (such as wheelchairs or braces for damaged limbs), and, most important in the new view of children with disabilities, building strength through teaching and learning experiences.

According to the current literature, the time for early childhood intervention ranges from birth to 8. However, many programs distinguish between *infancy* (age 0–2), *early intervention* (EI; 3–5), and *early childhood* (EC; also 3–5). Thus, although "early" intervention occurs as soon as the disability is suspected or identified, the field prefers to use *EI* to refer to children from birth to age 3 and *EC* to refer to children from 3 to 5 years of age.

ORIGINS OF EARLY INTERVENTION

Early intervention programs are a logical extension of early childhood programs, which have a long history in the United States, beginning in the late 1930s (Safford, Sargent, & Cook, 1994). Early childhood programs, known as nursery schools or preschools, were an outgrowth of psychologists' concerns for children's mental health (Cairns, 1983), which psychologists believed was fostered by positive child-rearing practices in the early years of life (Anastasiow & Nucci, 1994). Children with disabilities, however, were excluded from most of these programs. Many children with severe disabilities or mental retardation were sent to live in large state-run, hospital-like settings. These institutions provided custodial care and little training. Parents who could afford the alternative of a private residential school sent their children with disabilities there.

The prevailing opinion was that little could be done for a child with disabilities because intelligence and skills potential were fixed at birth. However, programs were developed for children who were deaf, hard of hearing, blind, or experiencing some loss of vision. Before 1900, children usually entered such programs at age 10; thereafter, they started as young as age 5. Not until the 1930s and 1940s

Early intervention programs are a logical extension of early childhood programs, which provide a sound base for the development of a secure and competent child who is ready for a successful regular school experience. (© *Jerry Howard/Positive Images*)

were programs initiated for children with physical disabilities and cerebral palsy (Safford, Sargent, & Cook, 1994). But these programs were not widely dispersed throughout the United States.

The belief that nothing could be done for children with disabilities was challenged by the children's parents, special educators, and members of allied therapeutic professions. This belief changed markedly as a result of Skeels and Skodak's work with orphanage children in the 1930s. These researchers found that children who were placed in foster homes or were adopted fared much better than a comparable group who remained in the orphanage (Skeels, 1966). The adopted group achieved normal intelligence while many of the orphanage children were classified as mentally retarded. In addition, Kirk (1950, 1977) demonstrated that preschool experience could increase the rate of mental development and the social skills of children who were classified as mentally retarded (see also Bricker, 1993, for a more detailed history).

Hunt's book *Intelligence and Experience* (1961) was extremely influential by summarizing research studies. It led directly to the development of **Head Start**, an educational program for children living in poverty. One of the assumptions was that children from families with higher economic status had higher intelligence quotient (IQ) scores because of their more privileged environments. Once Head Start was established, families of children with disabilities pressed schools, communities, and Congress to establish programs for their children as well. They cited the principle that had led to the creation of Head Start: If children with disabilities were taught early in their lives, then their lives could be improved. As a result of pressure exerted by the families of children with disabilities, early intervention was born.

LEGISLATIVE SUPPORT FOR EARLY INTERVENTION

Early intervention led to the development of early childhood special education.

Early intervention led to the development of early childhood special education, or the special training of teachers to work with infants and toddlers (from birth to age 2) and children from 3 to 5 years of age. Before 1968, few training programs prepared special educators or other specialists such as psychologists to work with infants and young children. In addition, few training programs prepared educators to work with speech-language therapists, physical therapists, physicians, and the host of other specialists who could intervene to improve the life outcomes of a child with disabilities.

Congress established the Bureau for the Education of the Handicapped in 1967 and in 1968 passed the Early Childhood Special Education Assistance Act. Early intervention programs were first started by a separate act or law, but they soon became one of the bureau's ongoing responsibilities and became known as HCEEP (Handicapped Children Early Education Program), later referred to as the First Chance Network (De Weerd, 1974). This act set up programs in every state of the United States to serve as models of how to work with children with disabilities and improve their lives. The programs usually were categorically oriented: There would be one program for children with visual losses, one for children with hearing losses, one for those with cerebral palsy, and so on. The intent was to demonstrate to others in the state how to work with children with disabilities early in their lives to make them to the greatest extent possible like children of the same age who do not have disabilities. HCEEP later became a regular program in the bureau, and by 1980 a budget of more than $20 million had been allocated to support early intervention programs throughout the United States. The bureau's name was changed to the Office of Special Education and Rehabilitation Services in the 1980s.

In more recent years, as we saw in Chapter 2, Congress passed Public Law (PL) 94–142, which provides services to all handicapped children between ages 6 and 21 in regular or special schools. PL 99-457 expanded the mandate to include children younger than 5 years of age (including newborns). Both of these laws were extended to provide service to all persons with disabilities through the Individuals with Disabilities Education Act (IDEA) of 1990. PL 99-457 (Part H), enacted in 1986, was a major national step to ensure that infants and toddlers who were at risk for disabilities, were developmentally delayed, or possessed an identifiable disability received the total range of services that they and their families required (Gallagher, Harbin, & Clifford, 1994).

The Ad Hoc 619 Workgroup (1995) perceives that Part H of PL 99-457 has been effective in:

1. Creating and maintaining effective family-provider partnerships
2. Ensuring quality of services
3. Providing services in community-based inclusive settings
4. Promoting seamless transitions for infants and toddlers to preschool
   (pp. 8–10)

Early intervention markedly improves the functioning of children with disabilities.

The fourth point is especially crucial because at the state level different agencies often handle the funding and administration of the 0–3 program and the preschool program. However, amendments to IDEA in 1991 (PL 102–119) were designed to provide effective transitions between the Part H and the preschool grant program. More than half of the states have passed special legislation to provide collaborative transitions between programs. Still unresolved is the setting in which the children should be served: an inclusive setting with children without disabilities or a school designed for children with specific disabilities.

In summary, the Ad Hoc 619 Group (1995) reports

The impact of guaranteeing every child ages 0–5 with a disability the right to special education has been dramatic and stands as the greatest success of preschool grant programs. In fiscal year 1994, 528,000 preschool-age children with disabilities were receiving special education and related services, more than double the 261,000 children who had been served in 1986. (p. 7)

Why Early Intervention?

Because children are born able to learn and to respond positively to the effects of a supportive, stimulating environment, in this section, we go into more detail about why early intervention is important: to help children who are developmentally delayed achieve higher levels of intellectual and social function and to prevent secondary deficits in children with disabilities or sensory deficits. Then we look at some of the research that supports the effectiveness of early intervention.

AVOIDING DEVELOPMENTAL DELAYS

Infants develop at varying rates. Some sit at 6 months of age, others at 4 months, and still others at 8 months. Some walk early, and some walk late. These variations are the major reason for being cautious when deciding whether an infant is developmentally delayed. Delays must exist in more than one area to be considered a problem.

Delays in development are spotted by comparing an infant's development of physical, emotional, and intellectual skills to the development of other children of the same age.

Delays in development are identified by comparing an infant's development of physical, emotional, and intellectual skills to the development of other same-age children. The average ages of a task's accomplishment are put together in a developmental scale. If, for example, a child does not sit, stand, walk, or speak at the age when most children in his or her culture have acquired these skills, a disability or developmental delay is suspected.

It is well known that children with sensory deficits such as vision or hearing impairments, damaged limbs, or genetic disorders linked to mental retardation do not achieve all of their developmental skills as quickly as nondisabled children. In fact, without extra help in the form of therapies or educational stimulation, the child with disabilities may develop very slowly and, as an adult, reach a much lower level of functioning than the child with disabilities who has had the benefit of early childhood special education. Because some deficits are irreversible, not all children with disabilities can achieve what the average child achieves easily (Guralnick, 1996).

PREVENTING ADDITIONAL DEFICITS

Another major reason for early intervention is to avoid the development of secondary problems that can result from the lack of stimulation to the child because of a disability or sensory deficit. These secondary problems, which are usually called *self-stimulation* or *challenging behaviors* (such as hitting and biting), are discussed fully in Chapter 11.

Murphy (1983) warns that once these aversive secondary problems are established, it is almost impossible to eliminate them. Murphy suggests that self-stimulation behaviors begin because of a lack of environmental input (for example, children with visual impairments cannot receive light; those with hearing impairments cannot receive sound) and serve to stimulate the parts of the brain near the pleasure areas. Thus, Murphy feels that self-stimulation is a self-induced pleasure for the child, and others in the environment must interact with the child early to enable him or her to find pleasure in the dual interaction of infant and basic caregiver. Touching the child and providing a great deal of physical contact will prevent the appearance of these behaviors in most children with visual impairments.

What seems most important in the long run is the quality of physical and emotional care provided by the family in early childhood.

Effective child-rearing practices can sometimes greatly improve a child's development and help overcome at-risk conditions present at birth. One of the best sources of knowledge is the Kauai Longitudinal Study, conducted from 1952 to 1992 (Werner & Smith, 1992). In this study, the developmental courses of individuals were followed from the time their expectant mothers made their pregnancies known (usually at 2 to 3 months) to when they were 30 years of age (Werner & Smith, 1992). The Kauai study demonstrated that many children who are at risk for developmental delays from conditions such as lack of sufficient oxygen during birth (*anoxia*, usually occurring when the cord is around the baby's neck) or being born feet first (*breech birth*, highly associated with cerebral palsy) can achieve what the average child achieves, given a home that provides psychological warmth, low physical punishment, responsiveness, verbalness, and encouragement to develop. The phrase "encouragement to develop" can be defined as the knowledge the parent possesses about normal development and the parent's (or caregiver's) assistance to the child in achieving normal developmental milestones. These childrearing practices tend to help heal the negative effects of abnormal birthing processes (Kolvin, Miller, Scott, Gazonts, & Fleeting, 1990).

Child-rearing practices can help offset the effects of disabilities.

Other researchers have also noted the importance of a supportive environment. For example, Parmelee and Sigman (1984) have shown that children born with irregular brain-wave patterns can obtain normal IQ scores when they are raised in home environments that are psychologically supportive and responsive to their needs. Infants with similar birth irregularities raised in nonresponsive and nonsupportive homes tend to have school achievement and adjustment problems (Werner & Smith, 1982).

ARE EARLY CHILDHOOD INTERVENTION PROGRAMS EFFECTIVE?

Many authors have reviewed the effectiveness of early childhood intervention projects. We suggest that the *Handbook of Early Intervention* (Meisels & Shonkoff, 1990) and the *Handbook of Infant Mental Health* (Zeanah, 1993) are the best current sources of statistics and research results on early intervention. In general, mild retardation can be improved through early intervention programs so that these children can enter regular education classrooms (McNulty, Soper, & Smith, 1984); speech and communication problems can be remediated or markedly improved (Shonkoff & Hauser-Cram, 1989); social and behavioral problems can be controlled (Upsur, 1990); and motor problems can be improved (Shonkoff & Hauser-Cram, 1987).

Early intervention is important because it provides quality physical and emotional care that promotes self-esteem and self-efficacy.

Many studies support early intervention's effectiveness. Guralnick and Bricker (1987) reviewed studies of children with Down syndrome and concluded that these children made more significant gains in intervention programs than they would have made had they not experienced early intervention. In a large study (McNulty, Soper, & Smith, 1984) in which 3- to 5-year-olds identified as children with special needs did not receive early intervention, all children were placed in special education classes in first grade. In contrast, in a follow-up study in which children identified as disabled received early intervention services, 31 percent of the children were able to enter regular educational classes in first grade, and an additional 38 percent entered regular classes with special services such as speech or physical therapy.

The importance of early intervention (besides lifesaving techniques) is to provide those protective factors of quality physical and emotional care that promote self-esteem and self-efficacy. These factors are the keys to a positive outcome for children in any intervention program, whether it be for the disabled or nondisabled (Rutter, 1989; Kolvin, Miller, Scott, Gazonts, & Fleeting, 1990). Once these elements are in place, they appear to provide individuals with the lifelong skills they need to face and deal with various kinds of adversity (Vaillant & Milofsky, 1980; Werner & Smith, 1992).

The Infant Health and Development Program is an example of an attempt to prevent developmental problems usually associated with low-birth-weight, premature infants. In this program, 985 low-birth-weight children were followed from birth to age 3. The children were widely dispersed throughout the United States at eight sites representing every geographical region except Alaska and Hawaii. The program also included a comparison group that received all medical treatments but no preschool intervention. Infants were assigned to groups randomly and by birth weight. The heavier ones weighed from 2,001 to 2,500 grams (4–5.5 lb); the smaller ones weighed 2,000 grams (4 lb) and less. Services provided to as many as 135 children at each site included the following: all medical care necessary for individual infants; home visits in which the family was provided with developmental information and cognitive, linguistic, and social curriculum; and parent curriculum to help parents manage self-acknowledged problems. At 12 months (adjusted for gestational age, or time at which the infant should have been born), the children began early intervention programs, which they attended five days a week until they were 3 years old. All the programs had the same basic curriculum plus additional training and instruction to meet individual needs.

These children received pediatric follow-up examinations (as did the controls) and were referred for special services when needs were detected. In addition, parents of these children were enrolled in a group in which they were provided with information on child rearing, health, and safety, as well as some degree of social support. A control group received the pediatric care but not the home visits, parent group, or early childhood program.

The results indicate that the children in the intervention program, including the smallest babies, had higher IQ scores, fewer behavior problems, and fewer infant illnesses and deaths. In most cases, the average IQ score in the intervention group was from low-normal to normal (81.0 to 102.5, with a group average across the eight sites of 93.5). The heavier babies did better than the lighter ones on all measures. For example, the heavier babies gained a mean of 13 IQ points, and the lighter babies gained a mean of 6.6 IQ points.

The superior IQ scores of the intervention group were maintained to 3 years of age (Blair, Ramey, & Hardin, 1995). At 5 years of age, however, the original effects for the lighter group (less than 2,000 gm) were washed out, and the difference between the program's heavier infants and the control group was only 3 IQ points. All other differences were not statistically significant (Baumeister, in press). Further insight into the elements that positively contribute to low-birth-weight children achieving normal IQs appears to point to the caregiver's involvement and interest in the intervention tasks (Fung-ruey Liaw, Meisels, & Brooks-Gunn, in press).

In looking at the results across the eight sites, one notices the effects of the respective communities and the overall impact of their socioeconomic status on the findings. For example, although the intervention groups made significant progress in both Harlem and New Haven, the New Haven infants (Yale Hospital) did better than those in Harlem (Infant Health and Development Program, 1991). A likely reason is that more of the Harlem infants lived in adverse socioeconomic conditions than did the New Haven infants.

What Puts Children at Risk?

An at-risk infant is one who, because of low birth weight, prematurity, or the presence of serious medical complications, has a heightened chance of displaying developmental delays or cognitive or motor deficits (Rossetti, 1986, p. 2). Researchers have identified three general categories of conditions that put children at risk: genetic disorders, events occurring during pregnancy and birth, and environmental conditions (Garwood & Sheehan, 1989).

GENETIC DISORDERS

More than one hundred genetic disorders are associated with lower developmental functioning and mental retardation (Kopp, 1983). They include mental retardation, Tay-Sachs (an incurable disease leading to early death), and Turner syndrome (a condition that occurs only in women—a missing x-sex chromosome leads to short height and either normal intelligence or retardation). Although children with these disorders require immediate attention, they account for less than 1 percent of the school-age population with disabilities. Of sixteen infants born, in only one can the disability be traced to genetic causes (Batshaw & Perret, 1992). One reason why few children are born with genetic defects is that fetuses with genetic defects usually result in miscarriages or spontaneous abortions (Batshaw & Perret, 1992). Most disabilities are caused by events that occur during pregnancy and after birth.

EVENTS DURING PREGNANCY AND BIRTH

The second broad category of conditions that put infants at risk is events that occur in the womb during pregnancy or during the birth process. A mother who contracts German measles during the first trimester of pregnancy is likely to have an infant with visual or hearing impairments, mental retardation, or a combination of two or three of these disabilities (Appell, 1977). Mothers older than 35 also have an increased risk of having a child with disabilities (Rossetti, 1986).

ENVIRONMENTAL RISKS

The third category is environmental risks—factors in the life of the infant or child that interfere with development. They are the major cause of disabilities of children by age 6. Some well-known environmental factors that interfere with development are child abuse, poverty, and parental substance abuse. Parents who are unaware of the child-rearing strategies that facilitate development are particularly at risk in rearing low-birth-weight or premature babies, conditions that are known to be associated with disabilities. Other risks are when family resources that are too limited to provide adequate nutrition, medical care, and housing. These are briefly discussed in the following sections.

Child Abuse

Many of us may find it hard to understand the fact of child abuse, whether the child is with or without disabilities. How can an adult physically harm a baby or a young child, particularly one with disabilities? Yet most of us cannot imagine the stress that parents of children with disabilities endure. Imagine a child who screams constantly. For hours during the night, the parents try everything they can think of to calm him. They walk him, feed him, and bounce him, but nothing works. Throw into the equation a shaky marriage, pressures at work, and no prospect that tomorrow will be any better than today. If the child is perceived as the cause of all this, the formula for child abuse is in place.

Nothing justifies child abuse, of course, but by understanding what causes it, perhaps we can prevent it, which is far better than just condemning the adult who has lost control. Certainly if individuals or organizations are available to ease the daily pressure by counseling the parents or helping with the child, then the likelihood of child abuse can be reduced. Zirpoli (1990) states that many studies have found relationships between specific disability groups and disproportionate incidences of abuse (p. 9). Money (1984) has shown that some severely physically abused children will stop growing physically, intellectually, and emotionally, not because of any genetic predisposition but because of the extreme cruelty. When these children are rescued from the destructive environments, they begin to make rapid developmental gains.

Lower Socioeconomic Conditions (Poverty)

Prenatal care allows a physician to detect and treat potential disorders.

Women who live in poverty are likely to have insufficient medical care (including prenatal care), poor housing, and inadequate nutrition. A pregnant woman's poor nutrition rarely affects her fetus; a fetus acts like a parasite, drawing on the mother for what it needs (Batshaw & Perret, 1992). However, the poorly nourished mother may have an infant that is very small at birth.

In the absence of prenatal care, potential disorders that a physician could detect and treat are missed. For example, vitamin B_{12} or B (biotin) can cure one inborn defect in fetuses. If untreated, the child may be born with mental retardation and experience repeated episodes of vomiting (Batshaw & Perret, 1992, p. 165).

If the expectant mother is a teenager living in poverty, she is at great risk of having a premature or low-birth-weight infant, who itself is at great risk for a variety of disabilities. Teenage mothers who live in economically advantaged homes, have good prenatal care, and receive emotional support from their spouse or family are more likely to give birth to normal infants (Anastasiow, 1982).

Substance Abuse

Substance abuse by the mother or father can be linked to behavior problems and disabilities in children. A woman's heavy use of alcohol during pregnancy may result in her infant's having **fetal alcohol syndrome.** Such children have facial abnormalities, droopy eyelids, heart defects, small size, and usually some degree of mental retardation (Batshaw & Perret, 1992). Physical anomalies and growth deficiencies such as these persist in later childhood and adulthood.

Expectant mothers who use heroin may give birth to premature or low-birth-weight infants. The infant may go through severe withdrawal symptoms and will be at risk for disabilities. Heroin and cocaine appear not to cause disabilities in utero but may cause premature births. The problems associated with the conditions at birth of low birth weight and prematurity may lead to physical or behavioral irregularities as the child matures (Hansen & Ulrey, 1992). In their study of forty-nine children who were exposed to drugs prenatally, Cohen and Erwin (1994) found that half did not display any of the negative behaviors that one-quarter of the group did: anger, aggressiveness, and unoccupied behavior. It appears that there is wide behavioral variability among children prenatally exposed to drugs.

If the expectant mother smokes at least two packs of cigarettes a day, she risks giving birth to a premature or low-birth-weight infant. Major national campaigns have been mounted to discourage pregnant women from smoking and using substances that may harm their fetuses. Physicians and other health-care workers caution expectant mothers to avoid the use of drugs.

Caution, however, should be exercised in talking about any risk condition. A single risk factor may not be predictive of developmental delay. For example, a physically disabled child may make normal cognitive and emotional progress. In the Kauai Longitudinal Study, Werner and Smith (1982) found that some children with as many as four environmental or genetic risk factors managed to develop without debilitating disabilities. The concept of *invulnerability* has been constructed to describe those individuals who are at risk but do not acquire disabilities. For example, Werner and Smith (1982) found that the loss of a basic caregiver, usually the mother or father, was a high risk factor for young children. Some at-risk children, however, were able to overcome the loss and develop in a healthy manner. In examining the data, Werner (1988) found that in some cases a relative, teacher, neighbor, or friend could help the child adjust to the loss of the mother or other family member.

Primary Prevention

Primary prevention involves genetic counseling and prenatal care.

The aim of primary prevention is to have a child without disabilities. Primary prevention involves two major activities: (1) genetic counseling, which includes an interview with the prospective parents to determine if the family has a history of disorder and, if so, what is the risk of their child having disabilities, and (2) prenatal care, which involves carefully monitoring the mother's health and fetal development to ensure that the infant is born healthy.

GENETIC COUNSELING

The first opportunity to detect potential disorders is **genetic counseling**. A counselor interviews the prospective parents about their families' histories of disabilities and analyzes samples of the clients' blood to determine if their gene pool contains defective genes that might be passed on to their children. Parents may choose to receive this counseling before the child is conceived. Some genetic disorders are most prevalent among certain racial groups, such as Tay-Sachs disease among Eastern (Ashkenazic) Jews, Couley's anemia among Mediterranean Greeks and Italians, and sickle cell anemia among African Americans (Anastasiow, 1984). Individuals from populations at particular risk for these and other disorders may seek genetic counseling to determine the likelihood of their having a child with disabilities.

A genetic counselor can calculate the probability or odds of a couple's having a child with a disabling condition or genetic disorder (March of Dimes, 1990), but the counselor cannot confirm whether the child will be born with or without disabilities. If, however, the parents have a high probability of having a child with disabilities, the expectant mother may choose to have a test that may detect if the child she is carrying is disabled.

PRENATAL CARE

In providing **prenatal care,** the physician checks the mother's health, monitors the progress of her pregnancy, and warns her about dangerous practices such as the use of alcohol, tobacco, or other drugs that can harm the fetus. Prenatal care can significantly reduce the number of premature or low-birth-weight babies. Even benign neglect—if, for example, the mother does not take iron or vitamin supplements or have other medical assistance during pregnancy—can have an adverse effect on the health of an infant. The physician can detect some deficiencies in the expectant mother's diet and prescribe the vitamins and minerals she and her baby need.

Teaching prospective parents good child-rearing practices can prevent disabilities from developing, even when the infant is at risk. For example, parents can learn that paint that contains lead should not be used where a young child can get at it because ingesting chips of this paint can cause lead poisoning and mental retardation.

In the United States Armed Services, prenatal care is provided uniformly to all pregnant women in the service and to wives of servicemen. It has been found that these women have the lowest instances of prematurity, low-birth-weight infants, and infant mortality in the United States. Interestingly, there are no racial differences in the infant death rates in this population. This finding is atypical of all other populations in the United States, where large racial differences exist (Pear, 1992).

An integral part of prenatal care is the tests that are available to screen the fetus for various disabilities. Some of the major prenatal tests are discussed below.

Alpha-fetoprotein Test

The **alpha-fetoprotein** test is a blood test that is offered to all pregnant women. Fetuses pass substances into the mother's blood, which can be examined to detect some disabilities. The blood sample is taken at sixteen weeks' gestation and can identify women who are at risk of having a fetus with a neural tube defect (a defect involving the spinal column or brain), Down syndrome, or some other birth defect (Batshaw & Perret, 1992; Blackman, 1983).

Because all women have some risk, however small, of having a child with a disability, some states require the alpha-fetoprotein test to alert the parents about the condition of their child before birth. If Ann and Bryan had taken the test, they

Figure 3.1

Sonogram of a Fetus at 20 Weeks
(*Courtesy of Kara Reardon-Navan*)

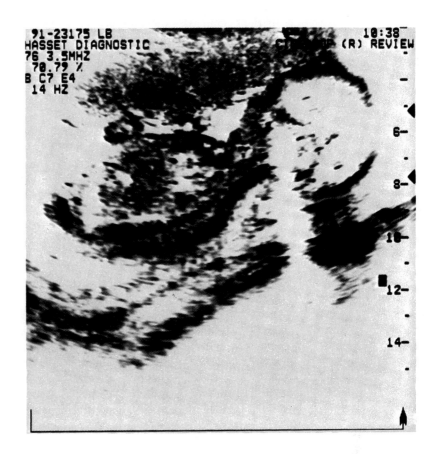

would have known that their infant would be born with Down syndrome. They would have had time to decide how to deal with the situation. If the results of the alpha-fetoprotein test indicate the possibility of a disorder, two other steps—sonography and amniocentesis—are taken to determine whether the disorder actually exists.

Sonography

Sonography, or ultrasound, is the use of sound waves to take a picture (like an x-ray) of the fetus (see Figure 3.1). This picture allows specialists to determine the position of the fetus and possibly detect defects such as microcephaly (small head). It also detects the sex of the child and indicates whether there is more than one fetus.

If a neural tube defect is suspected, it is important to rule out twins, for twins cause higher levels of spinal fluid than does a single fetus. Therefore, extra fluid in the mother's bloodstream does not necessarily indicate a neural tube defect. Pediatricians often ask expectant mothers to have an ultrasound test in the third month of pregnancy to determine the position of the fetus, and another one at five months to monitor the progress of fetal development. If a disorder is suspected, it is usually confirmed by amniocentesis.

Amniocentesis

Amniocentesis is a relatively safe test in which a needle is inserted into the placenta (with the help of ultrasound to ensure that the needle does not damage the fetus) at 4 to 17 weeks' gestation (Batshaw & Perret, 1992). The fluid can be analyzed to determine a number of (but not all) disabilities, such as Tay Sachs, Down syndrome, and spina bifida. If an incurable disability is detected, the prospective parents must choose between having the child and having an abortion, which is a personal family decision.

Chorionic Villus Biopsy

A test usually not available or not recommended by many physicians is **chorionic villus biopsy**. In this procedure, some tissue is removed from the uterus of the pregnant woman during the first trimester. When this tissue is examined under a microscope, some disabilities, such as Down syndrome, can be detected. The major drawback of this procedure is that it increases the risk of miscarriage, and it can also lead to internal bleeding and infection in the expectant mother (Batshaw & Perret, 1992). Batshaw and Perret (1992), however, suggest that if these risks can be reduced, chorionic villus biopsy would be very useful. It can be performed early in pregnancy, it is less expensive than amniocentesis, and it is less emotionally traumatic for the expectant mother, who may be afraid of having a needle inserted into the placenta.

■ ■　*Detecting Disabilities After Birth*

If the infant is born with a defect that can be cured, treatment must begin early in life. For example, phenylketonuria (PKU) causes toxic accumulations of phenylalanine in the brain that, if untreated, will lead to multiple disabilities and mental retardation. Although infants have no obvious symptoms, PKU can be detected by a simple blood test, preferably when the infant is a week old. The treatment is to restrict the infant's diet to reduce the intake of phenylalanine (Batshaw & Perret, 1992).

SCREENING AT BIRTH

When a child is born, the physician administers the Apgar test to determine if the infant has any identifiable problems or abnormalities.

How can a physician or other professional tell whether an infant is disabled or at risk for a disabling condition within the first few minutes of the child's birth? When a child is born, the physician administers the first screening test to determine whether the infant has any identifiable problems or abnormalities (Meisels, 1987). Screening tests are simple tests that are easy to administer and that separate

TABLE 3.1	Apgar Score Criteria		
Sign	**0**	**1**	**2**
Heart rate	Absent	Slow—less than 100	100 or more
Respiratory effort	Absent	Irregular, slow irregular	Normal respiratory, crying
Muscle tone	Limp	Some flexion	Active motion
Gag reflex	No response	Grimace	Sneeze, cough
Color	Blue, pale	Blue extremities	Pink all over

Source: M. L. Batshaw and Y. M. Perret, *Children with Handicaps: A Medical Primer* (2nd ed.). Baltimore: Paul H. Brookes, 1988, table 6.1, p. 70.

infants without serious developmental problems from those who have a disability or are suspected of being at risk for a disabling condition (Anastasiow, Frankenburg, & Fandall, 1982). The first infant screening is done in the hospital at one and five minutes after birth. It is known as the **Apgar test**, after Virginia Apgar, who developed it in 1952 (see Table 3.1).

In administering the Apgar test, the physician examines the infant's heart rate, respiratory effort, muscle tone, and general physical state, including skin color. A blue caste to the skin, for example, may indicate breathing or heart problems. Jaundice at birth is indicated by a yellow caste to the skin and eyes. A serious disorder, jaundice reflects the failure of the liver to process adequately because of its immaturity; as a result, bilirubin can accumulate. Many infants with jaundice recover in about a week. In more serious cases, the infant is placed under fluorescent lights for a day or two. This light treatment helps the infant process the bilirubin until the liver can function normally (Batshaw & Perret, 1992).

An infant with a below-average Apgar score at one minute or five minutes after birth is monitored by the physician to determine if a disability or medical problem exists and if medical intervention is needed. Lower-than-average Apgar scores are not necessarily predictive of disabilities, but they do serve to alert the physician that the infant may have special needs.

MEDICAL INTERVENTION

Additional medical screening includes blood and urine tests to determine if the infant has known curable disorders that should be treated immediately to prevent the occurrence of a disability. Hypothyroidism, or the failure of the thyroid gland to function, can lead to *cretinism*, an irreversible condition of severe mental retardation. If thyroid supplement is given at birth and continued throughout life, however, the condition can be prevented and the child will develop regularly. The

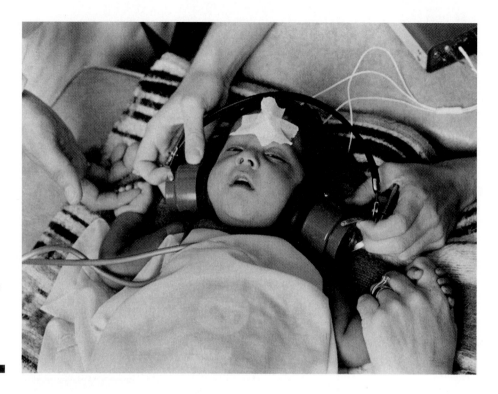

Early screening tests can determine whether an infant has any identifiable problems. If the infant is born with a defect that can be cured, treatment must begin early in life. (© *David E. Kennedy/Texas Stock*)

success in preventing mental retardation associated with a thyroid gland deficiency has done much to encourage research in the prevention of occurrences of developmental conditions identifiable at birth.

DEVELOPMENTAL SCREENING

After the first screening tests, which are usually medical in orientation, other tests assess a broad range of infant capacities, including development in cognitive, social, emotional, physical, communicative, language, and self-help skills. Usually the tests are administered only if a problem is suspected.

Developmental screening is a brief assessment of a sampling of a child's developmental progress to determine whether the child is at risk for a delay, possesses an identifiable disability, is delayed in development, or is proceeding at the expected pace for his or her age (Meisels & Provence, 1989). The critical dimension of any screening test is its accuracy in not identifying children as being at risk who are normal (false positives) or labeling children as normal who are at risk (false negatives).

There has been a proliferation of infant screening devices in recent years, but many of them fail to achieve acceptable levels of confidence. Many practitioners rely on the Bayley Scales (1993) or on the Connecticut Infant and Toddler Assessment procedure (IDA), which provide more complete diagnostic assessments. Others administer some form of family assessment and gain critical information from the caregiver (Henderson & Meisels, 1994). There are a number of screening instruments for children from 3 to 5 years of age. The Early Screening Inventory (Meisels, Wiske, Henderson, Marsden, & Browning, 1992) is among the most accurate.

Intervention Programs

The goal of intervention programs is to help the child with disabilities develop to his or her maximum potential. An outstanding example of intervention is recent research with Down syndrome, a disorder associated with mental retardation (Guralnick & Bricker, 1987). Untreated children with this disorder who were placed in institutions rarely learned more than fifteen or twenty words, whereas those who were reared in supportive homes and received early childhood special education developed language to the level of persons without disabilities and a high degree of competence in all other developmental areas (Hayden & Haring, 1977). Although this genetic condition does not go away, the child with Down syndrome who is reared in an enriched environment in the home or center will have an IQ score as many as 30 points higher than the score of a child who is untreated or raised in an institution (Guralnick & Bricker, 1987).

In this section we look at some intervention programs: where they take place and their strategies, how curriculum is developed, and model programs. Some conditions can be prevented and others remediated, but many can be neither prevented nor remediated entirely. With most disabilities, however, improved conditions can be achieved through carefully planned and implemented intervention programs. The basis for planning intervention is the individualized family services plan.

THE INDIVIDUALIZED FAMILY SERVICES PLAN

Part H of PL 99-457 and IDEA require that an **individualized family services plan** **(IFSP)** be developed for each child from 0 to 3 years of age who is diagnosed as disabled, developmentally delayed, or at risk for delay. McGonigel, Kaufman, and Johnson (1991) note that

> Section 677 of the regulations describes the IFSP as a written plan developed by a multidisciplinary team, including the parent(s) or guardian(s), that contains the following:
>
> ■ A statement of the child's present levels of physical development (including vision, hearing, and health status), cognitive development, language and speech development, psychosocial development, and self-help skills, based on acceptable objective criteria
>
> ■ A statement of the family's strengths and needs relating to enhancing the development of the family's handicapped infant

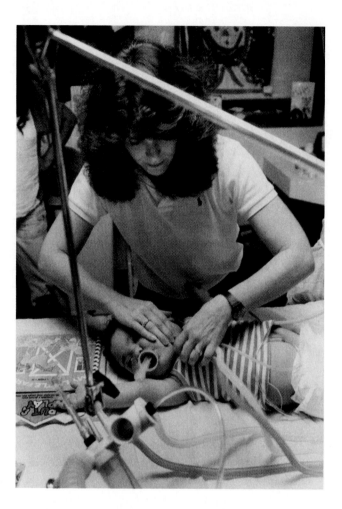

The individual family service plan acknowledges that a child with disabilities is a child in a family and that family members may need educational, financial, or emotional support to help the child achieve his or her potential. (© *Michael Weisbrot*)

◼ A statement of the major outcomes expected to be achieved for the child and family; the criteria, procedures, and timelines used to determine the degree to which progress toward achieving the outcomes is being made, and whether or not revisions of the outcomes or services are necessary

◼ A statement of specific early intervention services necessary to meet the unique needs of the child and family, including the frequency, intensity, and method of delivering services

◼ The projected dates for initiation of services and the anticipated duration of the services

◼ The name of the service coordinator (from the profession most immediately relevant to the child's or family's needs) who will be responsible for implementing the plan and coordinating with other agencies and persons

◼ The steps to be taken supporting the child's transition to Part B preschool services, if appropriate. (p. 47)

The focus on the *family* is an important outgrowth of the findings of early childhood intervention programs: A child with disabilities is a child in a family, and family members may need educational, financial, or emotional support to be able to provide the best setting, support, security, and stimulation to help the child with disabilities or developmental delays achieve his or her potential (Turnbull & Turnbull, 1986).

The law also recognizes that families need more than friendly neighbors or relatives to help them. They may need a variety of services from specialists as well as a service coordinator to help them locate, obtain, and implement the services specified in the IFSP. Children who qualify for services under IDEA must have been identified, screened, and diagnosed by a multidisciplinary team as having a disability known to be associated with developmental delays or be at risk for the occurrence of developmental delays. The term *multidisciplinary* means that more than one professional needs to work with the child. The child may need physical therapy for damaged limbs, speech-language therapy for poor control of the muscles involved in speech, and an educational program. Thus, a **multidisciplinary team** working in an early intervention program might include a member of each of these professions. Disciplines that are designated by law to be able to work with infants and children with disabilities are listed in Table 3.2.

An ideal team includes a physician or health-care worker who examines the child and reviews his or her medical record for any signs of disorder. A special educator or developmental psychologist assesses the child's physical, emotional, cognitive, language, and social development. A special educator, social worker, or psychologist interviews the family members to determine their health history, child-rearing practices, and concerns for the child. The ideal team also includes specialists as necessary. For example, a physical therapist assesses muscle tone and development, a language pathologist determines whether speech patterns are abnormal or delayed, an audiologist evaluates the hearing function, and in some cases a geneticist determines if the child has a genetic abnormality not detected previously.

The assessment may also include a visit to the home to view the child's living space. Bradley and Caldwell (1984) have developed the Home Observation Measure of the Environment (HOME) scale, which examines the quality of the home-care environment and its potential for assisting or arresting development. The HOME scale assesses the basic caregiver's emotional and verbal responsiveness to the child, the amount of physical punishment administered to the child, the organization of the home, and the amount of play and stimulation that caregivers provide to the child. These factors are predictors of a child's developmental progress. If negative factors exist, social workers or home visitors help the family develop facilitating strategies so that the child can make the best possible developmental progress (Gottfried, 1984).

When all the information on the child and the child's family has been gathered, the multidisciplinary team, including family members, discusses the case. The specialists might prescribe therapy or recommend an early intervention program. Their conclusion might be that the child should be re-evaluated at a later age; or, if no disabilities or risk factors have been identified, perhaps the child should be

TABLE 3.2	Multidisciplinary Team Members
Specialist	**Function**
Audiologist	Determines if hearing losses are present
Ophthalmologist	Determines if vision losses are present
Early childhood special educator	Plans and administers program for remediation of deficits and coordinates special therapies
Physician	Determines if a biological or health deficit exists and plans treatment
Nurse	Provides a plan for adequate health care
Occupational therapist	Promotes individual development of self, self-help skills, play, and autonomy
Physical therapist	Enhances motor development and suggests prostheses and positioning strategies; provides needed therapies
Psychologist	Provides a comprehensive document of the child's strengths and weaknesses and helps the family deal with the stress of having a child with disabilities
Social worker	Assists the family in implementing appropriate child-rearing strategies and helps families locate services as needed
Speech and language pathologist	Provides necessary assessment plan for needed therapies and delivers services in appropriate cases

discharged or monitored periodically. In cases in which the environment is the at-risk factor, the team may recommend parental counseling or identify sources of income assistance for the family.

The Connecticut Infant and Toddler Assessment procedure (IDA) (Erikson, 1989; Hutchinson, 1995), which uses a multidisciplinary team to assess the child's health, development, and family situation, meets the requirements of PL 99-457, Part H. A typical case might be handled as follows.

A pediatrician, a relative, or parents may raise concern about a child's development. The family calls the state department of health, the state department of special education, or some other agency for help. The family is referred to a center where screening (a quick assessment of the child's current developmental status to determine whether the child needs further tests) is performed. (The child should not be labeled at any time, particularly after the screening.) Because the results suggest a potential problem, the IDA is administered by at least two persons from different professions. They conduct an interview with the family to collect a health history and a history of disabilities within the family. They request permission to examine the child's health records. They assess the child's motor, social, speech and language, and cognitive (intelligence) skills to determine whether the child can perform age-appropriate developmental tasks (such as stacking small colored blocks).

After collecting all the information from the family interview, the health history, and the developmental assessment, the team meets with the family to develop an IFSP and decide which of the following best describes the situation: The child is all right and needs no special assistance; the child appears to be somewhat delayed but not to such a degree that assistance is needed now, but he or she should be brought back for another evaluation in three to six months; the child has a particular problem and should be in an intervention program; or the family needs economic assistance, job training, or training in how to deal with this child and his or her disabilities.

The family may agree or disagree with the decision. If agreement is reached, a service coordinator is assigned to assist the family in finding the services they and their child need, such as an early intervention program for speech delays. This is the ideal situation and fulfillment of the hopes embodied in PL 99-457, Part H, and in IDEA. If the family disagrees, they may remove their child from services. Most states do not have mandatory education for children from birth to age 3, whether they are with or without disabilities. So the parents can decide not to place their infant or preschooler in early intervention.

SETTINGS AND STRATEGIES

An early intervention program can take place in a hospital, at home, or in an early childhood intervention center. The intervention strategies in each of these settings vary. A measure for assessing the characteristics of room environment, available curriculum, staff training, and so forth is available from Harms and Clifford (1989). Early intervention programs can be operated privately, by national organizations such as United Cerebral Palsy, by churches, by means of government grants or state funds. Not all locations will have a program for a specific disability, and parents may have to search for an appropriate place for their child.

In a Hospital

Assistance for a child with disabilities may begin in a hospital on the first day of his or her life. Assistance may also begin in the early weeks through medical intervention such as surgery (for example, to close the open spine in cases of spina bifida), the administration of drugs, or the use of diagnostic tests to determine if a disability exists.

Hospitals provide medical intervention to premature and low-birth-weight, medically fragile, and sick infants until they can be sent home. The treatment in

Assistance for a child with disabilities may begin in a hospital on the first day of his or her life or may begin in the early weeks through medical intervention such as surgery, administration of drugs, or the use of diagnostic tests. (© *Jerry Speier/Design Conceptions*)

the hospital is usually lifesaving in that the child was born before he or she was biologically ready to be in an environment other than the womb. Most babies at the time of discharge should be able to survive without continuous medical treatment in a hospital, although sometimes it is necessary to prepare the home in some way, such as for an oxygen-dependent child (one who needs a tube to obtain extra oxygen from a tank).

Many hospitals have tried a variety of techniques to help premature infants, including providing an environment that simulates the womb by means of water beds, darkened rooms, and low stimulation. Most neonatal intensive-care units where at-risk infants are housed, however, are noisy; contain many adult contacts for health, feeding, and hygiene services; and are generally overstimulating and aversive to the newborn (Field, 1984).

A major movement is under way to establish intervention programs to follow the infant from the neonatal intensive-care nursery to the home. These programs aim to provide education to the parents, give them support, and help them find the services that their infant requires (Affleck, Tennen, & Rowe, 1991; Beckwith,1988; Infant Health and Development Program, 1991).

At times, hospitals continue to provide services to infants who are abandoned and become boarder babies. Babies are abandoned for a variety of reasons, not the least of which is the high cost of keeping a very-low-birth-weight baby alive. Parents can become responsible for thousands of dollars of hospital bills before their baby is ready for discharge. Current costs exceed $2,000 per day and can amount to \$54,000 before the child is discharged (Gustaitis & Emle, 1986; Rosenthal, 1991). Unable to face these debilitating costs, some parents abandon their babies. Some babies born to drug-addicted parents need to remain in the hospital, but when the infant is ready for discharge, the parents cannot be located. In this situation, the child must remain in the hospital. Many hospitals have set up early childhood programs for these children and make serious efforts to find foster parents for them. Finding foster homes is extremely difficult; thus, some children remain in the newly created "orphanage"—the hospital.

Home

Therapists, teachers, and other interventionists often provide services in the home for a number of reasons. A common belief among many educators is that education should take place in the setting in which the skills will be used; hence the home is the functional setting for very young children. Infants spend most of their time sleeping, and it is not practical to take them to an early intervention program that offers educational and therapeutic practice. In addition, mothers who are going through the process of accepting their child's disability may not be ready to take the child into public places. In some rural areas, early childhood special education centers are a long way from the home, and mothers would spend much valuable time traveling instead of interacting with and caring for the child. Furthermore, the mother's or caregiver's primary responsibility is to establish in the home routines that will facilitate the child's development. Attachments grow out of joint interactions with the child and are of fundamental importance to the infant's well-being.

Home programs emphasize helping the caregiver learn how to deal with the child in the child's setting.

Home programs tend to offer comprehensive services (therapies and education) and are very effective in assisting families with children at risk, the developmentally delayed, and those with disabilities (Shonkoff & Hauser-Cram, 1987). The data from research on home programs indicate positive gains for children as well as their parents. These strategies emphasize helping the caregiver learn how to deal with the child in the child's setting, thereby establishing a daily routine that is therapeutic.

The first person to visit the home may be a social worker who works with the caregivers in the home and helps them locate services to facilitate the child's development. Home visitors provide caregivers with information about the child's disability, child development in general, parenting practices, therapies, and a curriculum for the child (Affleck, Tennen, & Rowe, 1991; Beckwith, 1988). In the process, the home visitor provides emotional support and contact with the family. The home visitor can also act as a service coordinator and help the parents apply for additional services for the child or the family. An example of additional services is an occupational or physical therapist who visits the home once or twice a week to teach the caregivers to position, carry, sit, bathe, feed, and generally care for the child.

Rarely, if ever, does the home visitor act as a therapist. If the need for therapy is indicated, the home visitor will help the family locate the necessary personnel. Home programs tend to teach the mother to be the teacher or therapist for her child. Many home programs have declined as a consequence of the increased employment out of the house by women with young children (Moores, 1996).

In an Early Childhood Intervention Center

When the child is 3 to 6 months old, a popular solution is to combine parent and child home education with education at an early childhood intervention center. The best early childhood intervention centers have a well-trained staff sensitive to the needs of the children they serve and the needs of their parents, a well-developed curriculum, and appropriate multidisciplinary team therapies for the children. A center should be light and pleasant and not overcrowded with adults and children.

Early childhood centers provide families with a variety of personnel to assist them and their child. The infant program has the necessary therapists to work with the infant from 30 to 45 minutes a day. A physical therapist works with children who have motor disabilities, and an occupational therapist might teach a child how to eat with a spoon or drink from a cup.

As infants move into the toddler stage, they usually need additional services. For example, it is expected that the children will begin to speak. Speech and language therapists are usually available to work with the child who has any identified problem. As more infants and toddlers whose conditions require the use of technological equipment (oxygen tanks, respirators, and gastrostomy tubes) are entering public schools (this development is discussed more fully in Chapter 12), specialists who know how to regulate the equipment are needed, as are personnel trained to catheterize the child who is paralyzed from the waist down.

Centers offer supplies and resources to the family, providing ample toys for the child to manipulate and explore. The natural (genetic) manner in which all human beings learn is through play (Lerner, 1986). It is particularly crucial for young children, who are innately curious, to look at objects, manipulate (for example, shake or rattle) them to see what they will do, and then play with them. Play is used in most early childhood programs (Fewell & Rich, 1983; Linder, 1994).

Concern over the education of young children led the National Association for the Education of Young Children (NAEYC) and the National Education Association (NEA) to publish guidelines called Developmentally Appropriate Practice (DAP) (Bredekamp, 1984). These guidelines encourage early childhood teachers to do the following:

1. Match early childhood practices to the ways children learn.

2. View the time of early childhood not as discrete age/grade levels.

3. Create classrooms that encourage exploration and facilitate learning and development.

4. Consider parent involvement as a critical and essential element in the curriculum.

5. Use ongoing evaluation for decision making and curriculum development. (Gullo, 1992, p. 11)

Although special educators tend to agree with the goals of DAP, their list of suggested practices tends to include more teacher-directed suggestions. For example, the *Activity Based Intervention Program* (Bricker & Cripes, 1992), though consistent with the goals of DAP, looks for opportunities for the teaching of specific skills that the child has not mastered (Novick, 1993). The major difference between the programs resides in how one engages the child. Child engagement is defined as the amount of time the child spends in developmentally and contextual appropriate behavior (Fox, Hanline, Vail, & Galant, 1994). Special educators recognize that children with disabilities do not always readily engage and have to be taught to do so.

Children with disabilities tend to be less active (passive) and less curious about the world around them (Field, 1989). They have fewer coping skills with which to respond to environmental demands (Zeitlin & Williamson, 1994). Thus, an interventionist may have to teach a child with disabilities how to play so that the child can use play to learn (Anastasiow, 1995).

In some programs, psychologists are available to hold group meetings for parents to work through their grief and the personal problems resulting from having a child with disabilities. These groups also provide a forum for sharing information, providing emotional support, and learning about children's disabilities. In rare instances, Saturday classes are held so that fathers can attend group sessions with a psychologist. There are many half-day programs and some full-day ones.

The child's preparation for early intervention usually begins at home and in the center. The preparation should begin as soon as the child is diagnosed as having a disability and, in some cases, should continue throughout the lifespan. Some professionals in the field of special education advocate functionally training children with multiple or severe and profound disabilities in a community setting, where the child learns skills such as toileting, hygiene, social interactions, buying things at fast-food restaurants, leisure-time activities, and independent living (Meyer, Peck, & Brown, 1991). Model early intervention programs for 3- to 5-year-olds are beginning to do more in the community and are focusing on functional skills rather than on so-called enrichment skills such as visiting a museum, which may mean little or nothing to a 3-year-old.

EVALUATION AND CURRICULUM

In school, teachers and therapists evaluate a child's progress in gross and fine motor development, speech and language, cognitive, social and emotional development, and self-help skills.

Most children go through comprehensive assessments before they are assigned by a committee on special education. These assessments are conducted with a variety of instruments and personnel such as those we described earlier in the chapter. Once a child is in school, the term *evaluation* is more appropriate than *assessment*. Teachers and therapists evaluate a child's progress in motor development, fine motor development, speech and language, social and emotional development, and self-help skills. The special education teacher's role is to coordinate therapies, provide age-appropriate in-class experiences, and assist the student to capitalize on his or her abilities to attain, insofar as possible, the skills of a child of the same age without disabilities.

The first curriculum issue is that most infants and toddlers with disabilities are subject to increased risks of health problems. Thus, they may need special equipment (such as wheelchairs, hearing aids, braces) and an individualized treatment program. In Chapters 5 through 12 we describe modifications for specific disabilities. What we want to stress here is that an effective curriculum that takes these needs into account must be designed and begun early in the child's life, as soon as the disability is diagnosed. The following plans are frequently used as a basis for designing an individual child's curriculum.

The Hawaiian Early Learning Profile (HELP) (Furuno et al., 1989) is a popular and well-designed developmental scale used by special educators. The HELP contains nine scales and describes discrete tasks (such as drinking from a cup) and the average age at which most children accomplish the skill. By comparing an infant's or toddler's general profile across the nine areas, the teacher can pinpoint areas of delay and identify the areas that will constitute the curriculum. A version of the HELP is available for 3- to 5-year-olds.

The Carolina Curriculum (Johnson-Martin, Jens, Attermeier, & Hacker, 1991; Johnson-Martin, Attermeier, & Hacker, 1990) is similar to the HELP in that it provides an assessment as well as a curriculum to assist the child in accomplishing skill development. It is now available in two volumes. The first is designed for children from birth to age 3, the second for children from ages 3 to 5.

Both of these curriculums are in essence large developmental scales, breaking down each area of development into small, discrete steps. The teacher presents each task and determines whether the child is able to accomplish it, such as identifying a cup and spoon and, later, naming objects presented in a series of pictures or actual toys. If the child is able to accomplish a task, the teacher moves on to the next task, until reaching a task that the child is unable to accomplish. This process provides the teacher with information on where to begin instruction. Both the Carolina Curriculum and the HELP have suggestions for instruction at each skill level. Thus, these curriculums both evaluate the child's level of performance and provide the teacher with guidance on where to begin. After instruction has been provided and the child has mastered the skill, the teacher moves on to the next step.

The HELP and the Carolina Curriculum are two of many curriculums (see the catalogs of PRO-ED, 8700 Shoal Creek Road, Austin, TX 78758-6897, and other educational publishers for suggestions). They are valuable because they were developed by multidisciplinary teams and established a sequence for skills reflecting the order in which a child who is not disabled would acquire those skills. For each curriculum, there are recording forms on which the teacher can enter and share with family members, and with the next teacher, the child's progress. The major principle underlying both of these curriculums is that the child moves from being a very globally oriented infant to a youngster whose skills become more and more differentiated and complex. For example, an infant is expected to shake a rattle and, later, hold a cup and drink from it, and a 3- to 5-year-old is expected to be able to pretend to give a doll a drink from a cup.

Play is another major mode of gaining access to the child's strengths and needs (Linder, 1994). Linder's two books provide guidance on assessment and suggestions for intervention.

MODEL PROGRAMS

There are many model intervention programs; at least one can be found in every state and territory. Most states have or are in the process of compiling a resource directory of available services. (To locate model programs in a particular area, call the local or state department of health, education, or human services.) Stayton and

The Making of a Miracle

My 3-year-old son started preschool this fall. Soon after, he started riding the bus. Significant but routine events in the life of an American child—unless the child has, as my son does, cerebral palsy.

For parents of disabled children, every "routine" milestone reached is a miracle, bringing with it excitement, joy and, at least in this case, a small degree of trepidation. And this particular miracle will seem unusual to many readers because of its source. It was planted by the social activism of special-needs parents in the 1960s and 1970s. Its roots grew from special-education legislation. And its cultivation can be attributed in large part to the hard work and dedication of publicly funded educators, as well as parents and others who care. It is an example of the good that can and does spring from legislative policymaking and government spending.

Ben is a smiling, energetic, funny little boy (also quite handsome according to this unbiased source) who cannot walk, cannot sit up by himself, cannot reach his arms very far, cannot feed himself and can speak only in difficult-to-understand single words. His disability was caused by a congenital defect; a small "drain" in his brain is too narrow, resulting in a condition commonly called hydrocephalus or "water on the brain." Doctors gave him an auxiliary drain (a "shunt") when he was 6 days old, correcting the underlying problem but leaving Ben with brain damage that occurred during pregnancy.

Trying to be a good parent—a challenge with any child—to a son who cannot communicate or learn the way typical children do can be a very frustrating and isolating experience. Not only do my husband and I have to attend to and contain our own feelings of guilt and grief; we also need to find ways to teach Ben things that typical children learn through their own physical independence. We are enormously proud of our Ben, but his birth drove home the reality that no matter how emotionally or financially independent you are, there are some challenges you cannot face alone.

Enter the special-education system, mandated by state and federal law. Upon diagnosing Ben, doctors referred us to an early-intervention center (serving children from birth to 3 years) in our home state of Massachusetts. We were referred to another one when we moved to New Hampshire several months later in order for my husband to take a new job. These centers are staffed by some of the most creative, bright, warm, and supportive people, I have ever met. They helped us learn how best to teach Ben, how to motivate him and how to help him explore the world around him. Just before he began school, Ben's case manager, an occupational therapist, found a piece of equipment that helps him "crawl"—supporting his upper body on a sling so that his stronger legs can push the wheels attached to the sling's frame. Ben has begun to have the independent mobility that we had only dreamed of.

PREREQUISITES TO SUCCESS

Ben's preschool, run by our town's school system, is building on Ben's experience with early intervention. Although it has been some time since the school has had a child with Ben's level of physical disability, the teachers and students have truly welcomed him to the school, a welcome that does not come cheap. Like all children, Ben needs a happy family life, a roof over his head, clean and appropriate clothes, good nutrition and caring teachers as prerequisites to success in school. But Ben's special needs don't stop there. He requires a full-time classroom aide to help him move, play and eat with the other children. He and some of his classmates receive physical occupation and speech therapy so that they can reach their maximum development. The school will need to purchase special equipment. In a time of dwindling resources, educators, politicians, and parents of typical children may well ask whether the expense is worth it.

I can answer with an unqualified yes. Obviously, it's worth it to my family—especially to Ben. No child deserves a disability and Ben should be able to dream of being anything he wants to be, just as we encourage other children to do. But it is also worth it to Ben's community and especially to his peers. Ben has the potential to be a citizen in the true meaning of the word, very possibly a self-sufficient one who will not, as an adult, need to rely on the government for all or most of his financial support. But more important, Ben will provide his peers with a window to a world few of them would otherwise see, teaching them acceptance, tolerance, perspective and creativity. He may also turn out (and I hope this for him more than anything else) to be a best friend to someone who really needs his friendship.

The early reports from preschool are amazing, especially when compared with what Ben was able to do just a year ago. Ben is happy, watching his classmates closely, and in his fashion, participating in games, singing and story time. The other kids are curious about him, but once told that his muscles just don't work like everyone else's, they accept the information and figure out how they can play with him. They are happy that he likes to share his special equipment. The teachers and aides are warm, supportive, and, most important, very enthusiastic about Ben.

This small miracle of a routine beginning is not the stuff of made-for-TV movies, where the child walks despite the dire predictions of all the doctors. It is a miracle created by activists through government. And it is a miracle that requires money; without the dollars, the network of professionals who create and develop the information and experience that will cultivate a little boy like Ben into an integrated member of our society simply wouldn't exist. And it is a miracle that few parents could afford to create on their own, no matter how willing they might be.

Sometimes government spending does make a difference. Sometimes it can create miracles.

Source: Maggie Wood Hassan, "My Turn: The Making of a Miracle," *Newsweek*, January 6, 1992, p. 7. Hassan, a lawyer, lives in Exeter, New Hampshire. Reprinted by permission of the author.

---

commentary

What Is the Context? This article discusses the importance of a supportive societal context, which has been developed through the efforts of many parents and activists. In the author's view, the family cannot provide a self-sufficient environment; ideally, the family is a link to other support systems or contexts in the school or community. The author emphasizes to parents and families that "there are some challenges you cannot face alone." A major responsibility for families is understanding that they need support and finding out how to get it.

Pivotal Issues. How does the family's experience with early intervention show the benefits to "regular" kids as well as to kids with disabilities? How does one become empathic and sensitized to the value of services for children with disabilities? How do the services described in this article demonstrate early childhood legislation in action?

With toddlers and children 3 to 5 years old, toys and play are the primary mode of teaching the names of objects and colors and the concepts of gravity, volume, and space, and of overcoming weaknesses in motor skills and physical ability. (© *Lydia Gans*)

Karnes (1994) define a model program as one "in which content and operational strategies are clearly conceptualized and defined [to ensure] internal consistency and coherence" (p. 33). Model programs should have the following characteristics:

1. Clearly stated philosophy and theoretical orientation
2. Identified population and their families
3. Well-qualified personnel for multidisciplinary team functioning and staff development
4. Specific service delivery options
5. Established intervention procedures
6. A model for family involvement and family-centered activities
7. Rigorous program evaluation

Obviously these are extensive programs.

Families

A major movement in the United States is under way to give parents more authority in decisions related to their child with disabilities. Called *parent empowerment*, this movement aims to increase parents' control over decisions relevant to their child. For example, the UCLA Family Development Service Intervention Roles Profile for parents attempts to do the following:

1. Consolidate a helping working relationship between the interventionist and the caregiver

2. Enhance communication of the caregiver and enhance the caregiver's personal adaptation

3. Enhance alternative approaches to caregiver-child interactions (if needed)

4. Provide direct affirmation and support (Heinicke, 1992)

All parents suffer from stress (Gallagher, Beckman, & Cross, 1983). Dryson (1991) found that parents of children with disabilities are under greater stress than are parents of children without disabilities. For the caregivers of children with disabilities, the key challenge is to develop the hope and conviction that they will need to cope with their stress as well as find the benefits they will need (therapeutic and educational services for the child, financial and emotional support for the caregiver) throughout the child's life.

Several writers have suggested that there are developmental stages in grieving (see Anasastiow, 1984); however, these stages have not been borne out by further research (Affleck, Tennen, & Rowe, 1991). Persons under stress may be at any stage and may resolve their problems without experiencing all the stages that have been proposed. There are, however, several national programs designed to teach parents how to cope cognitively—that is, to learn how to think positively about a problem and to enhance self-esteem (Turnbull, Paterson, Behr, Murphy, Marquis, & Blue-Banning, 1993).

Recall Colin's mother, whom we introduced at the beginning of this chapter. After eight days in the hospital, Ann accepted that her child was disabled. However, she was not ready to realize that her life would have to change completely to accommodate Colin's needs. During the next two years, she actively sought services for her child with disabilities. Not only did she seek and find the services he needed, she also attended to the needs of her nondisabled 3-year-old. Knowing that other families tend to avoid a family with a disabled child, Ann and Bryan planned backyard barbecues, birthday parties, mothers' get-together, and dinner parties without children present to maintain the social network they had enjoyed before Colin was born. Ann was even able to laugh when a friend said that Colin, who had facial abnormalities, looked just like his father.

It was not an easy process, for she had to give up her career aspirations to provide the attention that Colin needed. Her husband was very supportive and involved in Colin's development. The outcomes for Colin at 10 years of age were an inspiring example of what devoted parents and early childhood special education can accomplish. Colin speaks in clear, comprehensible sentences, skis and participates in other sports, and attends school with resource room help. The long-term prediction is that Colin will be able to work in supportive employment (see Chapter 11) and perhaps in independent competitive employment.

Affleck, Tennen, and Rowe (1991) suggest that the key to a mother's successful management of her disabled child appears to be the extent to which she perceives that she has control of the child's development, the degree of positive outcomes that she perceives, the finding of emotional support and needed services, and her acceptance of the child's disability without seeking to blame anyone for it. Mothers who cannot accept their child's disability are likely to seek a cause for it, and in most cases they attribute it to their own behavior (pp. 130–132).

Remember that the human body is genetically programmed to remain healthy and to ward off or overcome illness. Thus, children who are at risk have their body's systems helping them overcome their risk state. In addition, persons in the environment can greatly assist the child's biological system by providing support in the form of positive child-rearing practices (Werner & Smith, 1992). As Sandra Scarr (1982) writes,

> In this view, humans are made of the newer plastics—they bend with environmental pressure, resume their shapes when the pressures are relieved, and are unlikely to be misshapened by transient experiences. When bad environments are improved, people's adaptations improve. Humans are resilient and responsive to the advantages the environment provides. (pp. 852–853)

Similarly, Affleck and associates (1991) quote Taylor (1988) as follows:

> Despite serious setbacks . . . the majority of people facing such blows (e.g., personal tragedies) achieve a happy quality of life or level of happiness equivalent to or even exceeding their prior level of satisfaction. Not everyone readjusts, of course, but most do. (p. 142)

In addition, care for at-risk, developmentally delayed, or disabled children does not end in infancy. Many of these children require continual monitoring and support. For example, as children with disabilities grow, bigger wheelchairs or braces may be required. Although many children experience a diminishment or outgrow of their earlier at-risk states—particularly children with mild retardation who have the benefit of an early intervention program—most children with sensory disabilities will need long-term assistance. The employment rate of adults with disabilities is very low—less than 30 percent.

Another stress-inducing issue is that a child with disabilities is likely to outlive his or her parents, and this poses the real problem of who will care for the child later in life. Fortunately, many national associations have been established to serve as guardians for children with disabilities when the need arises. Parents bequeath their estates to these associations to cover the cost of caring for their child, and the associations assume the responsibility for placing the individual in a foster home, group home, or independent living situation, and they monitor his or her needs as necessary.

Summary of Major Ideas

1. Early intervention programs can be very effective in facilitating the development of children who are at risk, developmentally delayed, or disabled.

2. Early intervention should begin as soon as the child has been diagnosed as having a disability or being at risk for a disability.

3. It is assumed that early intervention is effective because of the ability of the central nervous system to adapt early in life and its openness to environmental input in the early years. (The ability of the brain to adapt early in life is called *plasticity*.)

4. Some disabling conditions cannot be cured, but they can be improved to the point that the child can function in many environments and learn how to learn.

5. Early intervention is multidisciplinary in orientation at every step of the process: screening, diagnosis, therapies, and teaching.

6. Families of children with disabilities undergo stress as a result of not having the ideal child they expected. Some overcome this condition readily, but others need a great deal of help in accepting that their child is disabled. Family support groups are recommended as part of any early childhood special education service.

7. Low-birth-weight and premature infants are at high risk for disabling conditions. The increase in lifesaving techniques for very small babies is increasing the number of infants who are disabled.

8. Parenting strategies can be very healing and do much to cure or improve the conditions of a child with disabilities.

Unresolved Issues

1. *New lifesaving techniques.* New lifesaving techniques are keeping very-low-birth-weight (under 1,500 to 2,000 g), low-birth-weight (under 2,000 to 2,500 g), and premature infants from dying. However, large numbers of these children acquire disabilities as a result of being born too soon and too small. This will mean an increase in the number of infants to be served by early intervention.

2. *Prenatal care.* Primary prevention through prenatal care is not available to all expectant mothers, particularly those who live in poverty. Even when it is available, some individuals—adolescents, for example—do not take advantage of it. If prenatal care were provided universally, as it is in the United States Armed Services, it would markedly reduce the number of premature and low-birth-weight children, who are at risk for disabilities, thereby saving millions of dollars despite the costs of prenatal care.

3. *Inclusion.* Inclusion of children with disabilities in Head Start, day care, or private preschools for the nondisabled has been a very slow process, and to meet the requirements of federal law, massive training of Head Start staff must be undertaken.

4. *Difficulty of finding day care for children with disabilities.* Many women work outside the home because of preference or economic necessity. Among mothers of infants, 49 percent are employed outside the home. Among mothers of 3- to 4-year-olds, 55 percent are employed outside the home. Among mothers of 6- to 14-year-olds, 75 percent are employed outside the home. The primary caregiver of a child with disabilities, however, may not have the choice to continue working because of the difficulty of finding appropriate child care. Personnel of day-care centers are usually not trained to care for children with disabilities, and extended day care is not widely available.

5. *High turnover.* Consistency is an important feature of successful intervention programs. Yet the yearly turnover of some staff is 100 percent in Head Start, 81 percent in licensed day care, 75 percent in private early childhood programs, and 63 percent in public schools. The high turnover is usually attributed to low pay. High turnover in early childhood special education is usually attributed to the stress and strain of working with children with disabilities, particularly among those working with persons who have severe and profound disabilities.

6. *Teenage pregnancy.* Unmonitored teenage pregnancy (without prenatal care) continues at a very high rate, and these young mothers bear a great number of children who are disabled or at risk for developmental delays.

7. *Drug abuse.* The continued use of toxic substances (heroin, crack, alcohol, tobacco) by many pregnant women places infants at risk for disabilities or developmental delays. Educational, drug treatment, and other programs are important to combat this problem.

Key Terms

alpha-fetoprotein test p. 102
amniocentesis p. 104
Apgar test p. 105
at-risk infant p. 98
chorionic villus biopsy p. 104
developmental scale p. 95
developmental screening p. 106
early childhood intervention p. 92

fetal alcohol syndrome p. 100
genetic counseling p. 101
Head Start p. 93
individualized family services plan (IFSP) p. 107
multidisciplinary team p. 109
prenatal care p. 102
sonography p. 103

Questions for Thought

1. How has the history of early childhood programs influenced current ideas about early childhood special education? pp. 92–94

2. How effective are early intervention programs? pp. 97–98

3. What three conditions put children at risk? What are examples of each condition? pp. 98–99

4. Why is prenatal care important, and what does it involve? p. 102

5. What tests are currently available to screen the fetus? What disabilities can they detect? pp. 102–104

6. What does the Apgar test measure? When is it applied? p. 105

7. What does the IFSP contain? pp. 107–108

8. Who should be on a multidisciplinary team, and why? pp. 109–112

9. What characteristics must early childhood intervention centers have, and what do they offer to families? pp. 114–115

References of Special Interest

First start for caregivers of infants and children with special needs. Learning Managed Designs, P.O. Box 3067, Lawrence, KS 66043.

These materials cover a wide range of disabilities, providing information about conditions as well as techniques (such as positioning) for treating them. They were prepared under the leadership of Marilyn Krajicet, Ed.D., R.N., at the University of Colorado School of Nursing.

Furuno S., O'Reilly, K. S., Hosaka, C. M., Inatsuka, T. T., Allman, T. & Zeisloft, B. (1989). *Hawaiian early learning profile (HELP).* Vort Publishers, P.O. Box 60132, Palo Alto, CA 94306.

A multidisciplinary team working in a model program in Hawaii constructed this comprehensive curriculum. The curriculum is divided into areas of development (self-help, cognition, communications, and so on). A teaching manual provides suggestions on how to work with a child who has been determined to be at a given level through the use of HELP. Also available from the same publisher is *Understanding My Signals: Help for Parents of Premature Infants.* This guide has many pictures to help parents note and reinforce the basic nonverbal communication system that leads to speech.

Johnson-Martin, N., Jens, K. G., & Attermeier, S. (1991). *The Carolina curriculum for handicapped infants and infants at risk.* (2nd ed.). Baltimore: Paul H. Brookes. Johnson-Martin, N. Attermeier, S., & Hacker, B. (1990). *The Carolina curriculum for preschool children with special needs.* Baltimore: Paul H. Brookes.

These are two comprehensive curriculums prepared so that each item is clearly stated, in small steps for children with disabilities to master, and each section is based on sound development of nondisabled children. The books are oriented not toward therapies but toward education in the domains of cognition, communication, self-help, motor development, and independence. They can be purchased separately from Paul H. Brookes, P.O. Box 10624, Baltimore, MD 21285-0624. Booklets to record progress are available with the curriculums and can be purchased separately for each child.

chapter 4

Children Who Are Gifted and Talented

focusing question

How do public schools define children who are gifted and talented?

What have studies shown to be some of the characteristics of children who are gifted and talented?

How can we modify curriculum content to accommodate a student's special gifts and talents?

What are some special problems of girls who are gifted?

How has the educational reform movement affected programs for students who are gifted?

Ever since a senior member of the tribe brought a few children into the cave to teach them about survival in prehistoric times, it has been evident that some youngsters learn faster than others, remember more easily than others, and are able to solve problems more efficiently and creatively than others. It has also been obvious that these youngsters are often bored with the pace of instruction, a pace geared to "average" children, and that they pose a challenge to their teachers, occasionally an embarrassing one. Picture a bright child in the prehistoric cave innocently asking, "What happens if the spear misses the saber-toothed tiger?"

Society has a special interest in children who are gifted, both as individuals and as potential contributors to society's well-being. As individuals, they have the same right to full development as do all children. In addition, many of the leaders, scientists, and poets of the next generation will come from the current group of children who are gifted and talented. Few societies can afford to ignore that potential.

In this chapter, we discuss the special characteristics that set these students apart from average students. We explore how the schools attempt to adapt programs to meet the special needs of students who are gifted, in what ways educational reform movements have been affecting their education, and what is currently being done to find "hidden giftedness" in our schools to help those students reach a higher level of proficiency.

One of the strong motivating forces supporting special educational opportunities for students who are gifted has been the flood of negative reports about how U.S. students perform in comparison with students of other countries. One can add to these findings a devastating comparison of U.S. students with Chinese and Japanese students in mathematics in 120 classrooms in Taiwan, Japan, and Minneapolis. Among the top 100 first graders in mathematics, there were only 15 American children. And only 1 American child appeared in the top 100 fifth graders (Stevenson, Chen, & Lee, 1994). Many observers are calling for more emphasis and excellence in the mathematics instruction for all students, especially for those with exceptional talents.

Of special interest to us is that when the performance of the top 1 percent of students from each group is compared, we see the same discouraging findings: Our best students, in an academic sense, do not compare favorably with the best students from other countries. We have come to assume that Americans are in first place in everything. However, a series of international comparisons indicates that that assumption is far from accurate. Ross (1993) reports in a study on national excellence the following:

> Americans assume that our best students can compete with the best students anywhere. This is not true. International assessments focused attention on the relatively poor standing of all students. These tests also show that our top-performing are undistinguished at best and poor at worst when compared with top students in other countries. (p. 8)

Also of particular educational relevance is that when the task demands higher-level thinking processes, a domain in which students who are gifted supposedly have the greatest advantage over average students, additional poor results are reported by the National Assessment of Educational Progress. One natural question about these results is, "Do these other countries have programs for students who are gifted?" Although the answer varies from country to country, all countries funnel students into separate educational channels at or around early adolescence, creating in effect ability- and performance-grouping for their higher-ability students. The total portrait is one of students in the United States, both those who are gifted and those who are not, not being well prepared for our complex, information-based world.

■■■ *Definitions*

The term *gifted* has been traditionally used to refer to people with intellectual gifts, and we use it here in the same way. Each culture defines *giftedness* in its own image, in terms of the abilities that culture values. Ancient Greeks honored the philosopher and the orator, and Romans valued the engineer and the soldier. From a society's definition of giftedness, we learn something about the values and lifestyles of the culture. We also learn that the exceptional person often is defined by individual ability and societal needs.

In the United States, early definitions of giftedness were tied to performance on the Stanford-Binet Intelligence Test, which Lewis Terman developed during World War I. Children who scored above an agreed-upon point—such as 130 or 140—were called gifted. They represented from 1 to 3 percent of their age-group population.

Essentially, a high score on the Stanford-Binet or on other intelligence tests meant that children were intellectually developing more rapidly than their age-mates. What was unique was not so much *what* they were doing as *when*, developmentally, they were doing it. A child playing chess is not a phenomenon, but a child playing chess seriously at age 5 is. Many children write poetry, but not at age 6, when most are just learning to read. Early rapid development is one of the clear indicators of high intellectual ability, and that is what intelligence tests measure.

Over the past few decades, periodic efforts have been made to broaden the definition of giftedness to include more than abilities directly related to schoolwork. Table 4.1 presents two definitions, separated by twenty-one years, of children who are gifted. There are many similarities in the definitions. Both maintain that students can be of high potential without revealing that potential in actual performance, and both stress characteristics beyond the standard intellectual aptitude, such as creativity and achievement in the visual and performing arts. Yet the 1993 Ross definition talks about needed *services* rather than about a single *program*, as in the 1972 Marland definition, and stresses that individuals in all cultural groups and economic strata possess outstanding talents. These differences represent the shift in emphasis to a broad strategy of talent development and the seriousness of the search for hidden talent in neighborhoods and families not ordinarily associated with students who are gifted.

Children from all cultural groups, economic levels, and areas of human endeavor show outstanding talents.

TABLE 4.1	Contrasting Definitions of Students Who Are Gifted
Marland (1972)	**Ross (1993)**
Gifted and talented children are those identified by professionally qualified persons who by virtue of outstanding abilities are capable of high performance. These are children who require differentiated programs and services beyond those normally provided by the regular school program in order to realize their contributions to self and society. Children capable of high performance include those with demonstrated achievement and/or potential ability in any of the following areas: 1. General intellectual aptitude 2. Specific academic aptitude 3. Creative or productive thinking 4. Leadership ability 5. Visual and performing arts	Children and youth with outstanding talent perform, or show the potential for performing, at remarkably high levels of accomplishment when compared with others of their age, experience, or environment. These children and youth exhibit high performance capability in intellectual, creative, and/or artistic areas, possess an unusual leadership capacity, or excel in specific academic fields. They require services or activities not ordinarily provided by the schools. Outstanding talents are present in children and youth from all cultural groups, across all economic strata, and in all areas of human endeavor.

Other definitions of giftedness try to include the way an individual defines and then tackles a problem—the ability to *problem-find* and *problem-solve* (Gardner, 1985; Getzels, 1978; Siegler, 1985; Sternberg, 1986). In the real world, problems do not come in neat packages ready for solving. Usually, they are hard to define and organize—they are what Simon (1978) called *ill structured*. The ability to take an ill-structured problem and organize it so that the issue is clear is one indicator of giftedness.

Despite the addition of creativity, problem-finding and problem-solving skills, and different types of intelligence to our definition of giftedness, emphasis is still placed on intelligence tests as one means of identifying children who are gifted. Why? Because these tests have been effective in predicting performance in school-related activities. Since school lessons often rely on memory, association, and reasoning, they do not often demand creativity or the ability to identify and solve problems in novel ways. Also, all of these mental processes—such as memory, reasoning, association—are developmentally related: A measure of any one of them is likely to be a reasonably good predictor of the others.

The term *giftedness* refers to exceptional ability in academic areas and to exceptional creativity, artistic talent, leadership capacity, and problem-solving abilities. (© Nita Winter/The Image Works)

Components of Intellectual Competence

What are the components of intellectual competence? What does a student who is gifted need to be productive, and what must the schools offer to such a student? As noted in Chapter 1, Perkins (1995) believes that competence reflects three major factors:

1. The power of a person's neurological computer
2. The tactical repertoire or cognitive strategies that a person can bring to bear
3. Context-specific content and know-how

Students who are gifted appear to have advantages across the full range of information processing. They grasp new ideas faster, they see more associations between ideas, and they have a rich storehouse of concepts and systems of ideas to apply to individual problems. They also have a superior ability to use cognitive strategies, which increases their ability to cope with difficult assignments. In most instances, their ability to reason—that is, to use existing information to generate new information—is at a level from two to three years or more beyond that of their agemates.

In short, this cluster of abilities allows students who are gifted to be likely winners in academic competition, and, like most winners, they like to pursue the activities at which they are successful. Their eager pursuit of academic knowledge allows them to hone their already-superior skills. This phenomenon has been called the "Matthew Principle," referring to the Biblical proposition that the rich get richer. Under ordinary circumstances, clearly the intellectually rich ought to be able to get richer. That is the good news for these students. The bad news is that their potential will not be realized without a favorable context that provides support and encouragement from family, school, and society.

It is the responsibility of the schools to help students develop a tactical repertoire and content mastery. The notion that the student who is gifted will automatically learn these strategies or knowledge, however, is an idea that dies hard. The tactics or strategies that these students employ as they try to cope with difficult problems must be explicitly taught because they will not be spontaneously discovered. These strategies are often referred to as the *executive function*.

The student will not naturally stumble on the process of multiplication (which, after all, is a strategy for processing information), principles of logical analysis (synectics), and a number of other devices that are useful tools to the serious thinker. All these strategies must be taught. Occasionally, a student who is gifted will intuitively solve a problem in an innovative fashion, but unless the student explicitly recognizes the method, he or she will not likely have full use of the strategy (Glaser & Rabinowitz, 1986). Schools should deliberately attempt to teach the use of thinking strategies in many different content areas and tasks, because the conceptual transfer of a thinking strategy from one task to another is not as easy as many persons think.

One Gift or Many?

Should giftedness be regarded as one overriding mental ability or as a series of special abilities? Howard Gardner is one of the latest of a group of psychologists to view giftedness as a series of special abilities (1985). He has proposed a list of seven distinct and separate abilities that need specific educational attention (see Table 4.2).

Everyone knows persons who are particularly good at one or two of the abilities listed in Table 4.2 but who are not superior in them all. Think of a fellow student who is a math wiz but is not expert in linguistic or interpersonal intelligence. Some students seem to be particularly gifted in spatial intelligence but have only above-average ability in other areas. Whereas all of these abilities seem to be positively correlated with one another, and students who have outstanding talents in one area are usually good in the other areas as well, we can find concrete examples of specialists in outstanding performance. Consequently, the educational issue becomes not only how to plan one *overall* program for students who have talents in many of these areas, but also what should be done with students who have

TABLE 4.2	**Gardner's Multiple Intelligences**
Linguistic intelligence	The ability to use language in written and oral expression to aid in remembering, solving problems, and seeking new answers to old problems (novelist, lecturer, lawyer, lyricist)
Logical-mathematical intelligence	The ability to use notation and calculation to aid with deductive and inductive reasoning (mathematician, physicist)
Spatial intelligence	The ability to use notation, spatial configurations; important in pattern recognition (architect, navigator, sculptor, mechanic)
Bodily-kinesthetic intelligence	The ability to use all or part of one's body to perform a task or fashion a product (dancer, athlete, surgeon)
Musical intelligence	The ability to discriminate pitch; sensitivity to rhythm, texture, and timbre; the ability to hear themes; production of music through performance or composition (musician)
Interpersonal intelligence	The ability to understand other individuals—their actions and motivations—and to act productively on that knowledge (teacher, therapist, politician, salesperson)
Intrapersonal intelligence	The ability to understand one's own feelings and motivations, cognitive strengths, and styles (just about anything)

Source: From H. Ramos-Ford and H. Gardner (1991). "Giftedness from a Multiple Intelligences Perspective." In N. Colangelo and Gary Davis (eds.), *Handbook of Gifted Education*. Copyright © 1991 by Allyn and Bacon. Adapted with permission.

There seem to be several types of intelligence.

specialized talents in a single area such as mathematics, visual perception, or interpersonal perception.

Students who are gifted provide a fine example of the need to view exceptional children *in context*. Although abundant evidence suggests that we are born with differing neurological systems that are differentially responsive to outside experience (Plomin & McClearn, 1993), factors within the family and the society also help determine the full extent of the development of the child who is gifted (Bloom, 1986).

Students with high native ability still need support and help from the family, schools, and society to make the most of their outstanding abilities. The failure of these outside forces to provide this support may result in such a reduction of usable talent that the student may no longer be referred to as "gifted" (Frasier, 1987).

All other exceptional children have deficits in one or more areas of development. Children who are gifted are the only group of exceptional youngsters with a surplus of ability or talent in certain areas of development. That very surplus can create unique educational challenges for these children, their families, and their school systems.

Factors That Contribute to Giftedness and Talent

Are children born gifted and talented? Do outstanding abilities emerge no matter what opportunities or education a person has? What role does heredity play in giftedness? How important is the context of the child who is gifted?

HEREDITY

More than one hundred years ago, Francis Galton, in a study of outstanding Englishmen, concluded that extraordinary ability ran in families and was genetic in origin. (Galton overlooked the environmental advantage of being born into an upper-class family.) Ever since, there has been a strong belief in the powerful role that heredity plays in producing mental ability. Certainly, studies of twins and the close relationship of the abilities of adoptive children to the abilities of their natural parents demand that we recognize a hereditary element (Plomin & McClearn, 1993).

Krutetskii (1976), a distinguished mathematician in the former Soviet Union, suggested that mathematically gifted individuals have a unique neurological organization—a hereditary condition that he called a "mathematical cast of mind." He claimed that this "cast of mind" appears by age 7 or 8 and later acquires broad transfer effects: "It is expressed in a striving to make the phenomenon of the environment mathematical . . . to see the world 'through mathematical eyes'" (p. 302).

ENVIRONMENT

Students who are gifted appear to have both favorable hereditary and favorable environmental factors in their early development.

Although researchers make a strong case for the importance of heredity in giftedness; environment, or the context of the child, is important as well. Extraordinary talent may be shaped by heredity, but it is nurtured and developed by the environment. We've discussed the role that society plays in defining gifts and talents and rewarding them. A more powerful influence, because it is closer, is the family.

Extraordinary talent may be shaped by heredity, but it is nurtured and developed by the environment — by how society and the family defines and rewards gifts and talents. (© *Elizabeth Crews*)

Benjamin Bloom and his colleagues (1985) attempted to uncover the factors that are linked to extraordinary ability. Bloom conducted a retrospective study of the early life of world-class swimmers, pianists, mathematicians, and other persons who are gifted. He identified the participants through consultations with authorities in the fields and evidence of success (awards in national and international competitions, special prizes, fellowship awards). In interviews with the subjects, their parents, and their former teachers, he found that several general characteristics seem important whatever the talent area:

1. Willingness to do great amounts of work (practice, time, effort) to achieve a high level or standard

2. Competitiveness with peers in the area of talent and determination to do the best at all costs

3. Ability to rapidly learn new techniques, ideas, or processes in their area of talent

Bloom suggested that the group's high motivation was stimulated in a powerful way by the early recognition of talent by parents and friends, who went out of their way to obtain special instruction and to encourage and nurture the talent. The enthusiasm and support of the family seemed to be a critical element in the emergence of these gifted persons into world-class performers.

More information on the family's role in producing gifted children comes from a survey of MacArthur Fellows (Cox, Daniel, & Boston, 1985). These distinguished adults were singled out at an early age for their accomplishments in the arts and sciences. When asked about the major influences on their lives, they paid tribute to their parents. Virtually all the parents had let their children know the value of learning through personal example:

> The parents supported without pushing. Their homes had books, journals, newspapers. They took the children to the library. The parents themselves read, and they read to their children. Most important, they respected their children's ideas. (p. 23)

Another strong influence on these students was their teachers. If children do not receive the support of their families, the school and individual teachers have a responsibility to recognize and help them develop their special abilities. Obviously, a complex blend of heredity *and* environment produces students such as Cranshaw and Zelda, who are profiled later in this chapter.

■■ ■ *Studies of Students Who Are Gifted*

What sets students who are gifted apart from their nongifted agemates? How do those characteristics affect the way teachers plan their education? To answer these questions, we look for general patterns among youngsters who are gifted and for deviations from those patterns (the variance of characteristics within the group). Our objective, then, is to identify and study over time groups of students who are gifted to see what form their development takes.

After his revision and the publication of the Binet-Simon Tests of Intelligence in 1916, Lewis Terman, a professor of psychology at Stanford University, turned his attention to children who are gifted. In 1920 he began a study of 1,528 of such children, which was to continue for more than sixty years as he and his colleagues followed them into maturity and old age.

Terman conducted his search for children who are gifted in California's public schools. He used teacher nominations and group intelligence tests to screen subjects. (Those procedures are now thought to limit the findings because they tended to eliminate children whose behavior irritated teachers, children who underachieved, and children who showed gifts in realms other than academic work.) Terman based the final selection of children on their performance on the Stanford-Binet Intelligence Scale. Most had IQ scores of 140 or higher; the average IQ score for the group was 151. Table 4.3 summarizes Terman's findings. The results, on average, were favorable in practically every dimension. The group did well not only in school and career but also in areas such as mental health, marriage, and character.

TABLE 4.3	Characteristics of Students Who Are Intellectually Gifted: The Terman Longitudinal Study

Characteristics	Findings
Physical	Above-average physique and health; mortality rate 80 percent that of average
Interests	Broad range of interests in abstract subjects (literature, history, mathematics)
Education	Rates of college attendance 8 times that of general population; achieved several grades beyond age level throughout school career
Mental health	Slightly lower rates for maladjustment and delinquency; prevalence of suicide somewhat lower
Marriage and family	Marriage rate average; divorce rate lower than average; group's children obtained an average IQ score of 133
Vocational choice	Men chose professions (medicine, law) 8 times more frequently than did the general population
Character	Less prone to overstatement or cheating; appeared superior on tests of emotional stability

Source: Adapted from *Genetic Studies of Genius* (Vols. 1, 4, 5) by L. Terman (ed.), 1925, 1947, 1959, Stanford, CA: Stanford University Press. Used by permission.

Until recently, the follow-up on the Terman sample gave us the only systematic data available on what happens to gifted children when they grow up. Now the findings of two other longitudinal studies are helping us determine whether gifted children fulfill their early promise.

The Speyer School, a special elementary school in New York, was established through the work of Leta Hollingworth (1942), a pioneer in the education of gifted children. White and Renzulli (1987) recently conducted a forty-year follow-up of graduates of the school. Twenty-eight students were found; twenty of them returned questionnaires, and eight were interviewed in depth.

Like the subjects in the Terman study, the majority of the men had entered professions, and the women tended to combine career and family. Their memories of the school were vivid. And "they all believed that their experience at Speyer School was instrumental in providing them with peer interaction for the first time, exposing them to competition, causing them to learn and like school for the first time, giving them a strong desire to excel" (White & Renzulli, 1987, p. 90).

Kaufmann (1981) conducted a follow-up study of Presidential Scholars—a select group of students (two per state) chosen on the basis of the National Merit Scholarship Qualifying Test. She found that in the ten to fifteen years after their selection, the students continued to do well academically (89 percent received honors in college, and 61 percent went on for graduate degrees) and that most were professionals (doctors, lawyers, professors). Although no one in the group had made an earth-shaking discovery or contribution (the same was true of Terman's group and the Speyer School group), most seemed to be contributing substantially to the quality of society in what they were doing. (Remember that individuals can be extraordinarily successful in their own field such as business, science, the arts, or religion and still be virtually unknown to the general public. Can you name three of the country's outstanding biochemists? Can you name one?)

One of the recurring questions regarding longitudinal studies such as the one that Terman and his associates did is "Are the results due to the students or to the culture and times (the context) in which the study took place?" A more recent study provides some information on this issue (Subotnik, Kassan, Summers, & Wasser, 1993). In the 1940s a special elementary school was established at Hunter College in New York City. The school was highly selective of the students that it enrolled. Each year fifty students with IQ scores ranging from 122 to 196 were enrolled (their average IQ score was 157). A survey closely following the Terman questionnaires was taken of the six hundred students who attended the school from 1948 to 1960. Researchers found 210 persons who had attended and who completed the questionnaire. They interviewed 74 members of this group.

In educational attainment the results were similar to those reported by the Terman group. Over 80 percent held a master's degree, and 68 percent of the men and 40 percent of the women held a doctorate in medicine, law, or some other area. They were in good health, mentally and physically, and were earning an income as impressive as their educational attainments would suggest. Over half of the sample mentioned receiving one or more awards for professional work or community service.

One major difference in the Terman and Hunter Elementary samples was in the activities of the women. The vast majority of the women in the Hunter Elementary sample were employed and were satisfied with their careers. Less than 10 percent were homemakers exclusively. The interviews made it clear that the women's movement (context again!) had had a decided effect on their becoming more oriented to work outside the home.

Subotnik and the other authors of this study were somewhat disappointed by the lack of drive for success or for extraordinary achievement that they found in the Hunter College group. Most members of the group seemed perfectly content to do their professional job and enjoy their social life and the opportunities that their vocational success provided for them. The well-rounded students had become well-rounded, complacent adults. One of them remarked,

On average, children who are gifted grow up to become well-adjusted adults, successful in their chosen careers.

This is a terrible thing to say, but I think I'm where I want to be—terrible because I've always thought that there should have been more challenges. I'm very admired and respected where I work. . . . I don't want to be a senior vice president. . . . I want to have time to spend with my family, to garden, to play tennis, and see my friends. I'm very happy with my life. (p. 78)

The authors raise the interesting point that perhaps some degree of unhappiness or dissatisfaction may be necessary to create the obsessive concern with a particular goal and the single-minded drive and motivation to achieve that goal that lead to great attainments. On the other hand, the vast majority of these students became productive and useful citizens, and we might well ask if we should expect more of them than that.

The Burden of Giftedness

Despite their demonstrated ability to make friends and generally to adapt well, people who are gifted shoulder some difficult burdens that stem from their exceptionality.

Increased attention has been paid to the personality of gifted students. One popular theory about self-development comes from a Polish psychologist, Dabrowski (see Silverman, 1993). Dabrowski maintains that some persons have what he calls "overexcitabilities," by which he means a heightened capacity to respond to stimuli of various types. He identifies five major areas—*psychomotor, sensual, imagination, intellectual,* and *emotional*—that can be stimulated. These super-stimulations carry positive connotations such as an unusual capacity to care for others, an insatiable love of learning, vivid imagination, and so on. Therefore, overexcitability means an abundance of energies in these five areas. Many students who are intellectually gifted also reveal emotional overexcitability and are referred to as "sensitive." Two examples from Silverman's files at the Gifted Child Center illustrate these feelings:

■ R had early awareness and empathy with others' feelings. . . . She has amazing tolerance and was emotionally beyond her age. She wears her heart on her sleeve and is honest with her feelings with adults as well as with other children (age 4).

■ M is a very loving and compassionate child, cannot stand to hear a baby crying, puts his hands over his ears if he hears anything too loud or too violent, his feelings are hurt in an instant. Concerned about the welfare of others (age 3¾). (Silverman, p. 16)

One common adjustment problem of students who are gifted is dealing with the boredom that comes from sitting through classes in which something that they already know is being taught. Imagine yourself faced with learning the multiplication tables over and over, and you might begin to understand their dislike of a nondifferentiated educational program. A 9-year-old girl expressed her frustration with boredom in this poem:

Oh what a bore to sit and listen,
To stuff we already know.
Do everything we've done and done again,
But we still must sit and listen.

Over and over read one more page.
Oh bore,
Oh bore,
Oh bore.
Sometimes I feel if we do one more page
My head will explode with boreness rage
I wish I could get up right there
and march right out the door.[1]

A less recognized issue facing many students who are gifted is selecting from among their many talents. Table 4.4 presents a passage from a Thinking Log entry by a girl who recognizes the problem with a sense of humor.

Some additional difficulties that gifted students often have are unrealistic expectations placed on them by people who believe that everything comes easily to them and finding people who share their interests.

Developmental Profiles

We would like you to meet two children, Cranshaw and Zelda. Both are 10 years old and in the fifth grade. Cranshaw probably meets the criteria for intellectual,

TABLE 4.4 Excerpt from the Thinking Log of a Gifted Girl

I wish I could still draw. When I was in grammar school (junior high school included), I used to draw pretty decently. I still have some stuff I drew then. I love to draw—in pencil and in chalk. Art of all kinds intrigues me. I love music, paintings, carpentry and metal working, dancing, sewing, embroidery, cooking. I miss this stuff at school. I would love to take art classes again. I want to *so* badly. But I have my college-bound electives (I like these, too, they just don't leave time for anything else!), foreign language (German), and Band. Sometimes I want to draw so badly, or play with clay, or work in metal shop or wood shop, that it almost hurts I can feel it so much. But it's really hard to make myself sit down and draw. I'm so out of practice and I don't like to mess up! It's really scary to draw after a few months of not drawing at all. I'm so jealous of people like Todd, who bring their sketch pads everywhere with them; they take lots of art classes like I wish I could.

   I want to dance in my old ballet class, play my clarinet, draw thousands of pictures (*good* ones), create beautiful pieces of woodwork, cook and sew for my children, decorate my home, be an astrophysicist, go to Mars, and understand all of my questions about life. That's not so much to ask, is it?

Source: Stephanie Morris, *Thinking Log.* Copyright © 1991. Reprinted by permission of Illinois Mathematics and Science Academy.

[1]From *Gifted Kids Speak Out* (p. 55) by J. DeLisle, 1987, Minneapolis: Free Spirit. Reprinted by permission.

THE CHILD IN CONTEXT

On Going to College Early

Two years ago, I had the great fortune to interview the poet and author Dr. Maya Angelou. Something she said to me has come back to me over and over since we first met: "Everybody born is born with talent. They may not know it, they may not show it, but they are born with it. It's the rare person, however, who has the intelligence, the discipline, the forthrightness, and the perseverance to architect a dream."

What I think I got out of going to college early and, in particular, attending Simon's Rock College, is not so much any single intellectual achievement. What I believe I gained was a positive focus for my considerable energies; through the professors, mentors, and friends I met here I was given the tools with which to architect my dreams.

It is imperative that, as educators and concerned citizens, we not forget the needs of black and Latino students who are gifted and talented. On a recent show about black men Oprah Winfrey poses the question, "Why is it easier for black men to get into San Quentin that it is for them to get into Stanford?" So I pose the question to you—why is it easier for 15- or 16-year-old black youths to get into the criminal justice system than it is for them to get into Simon's Rock, Johns Hopkins, or the University of Chicago?

Some of the typical questions posed about early college entrance are: Do you miss not attending the prom? Does going to college early make you grow up too fast? Let me say this: When there are guns in your school and metal detectors at the front door, then I would suggest that, no, missing the prom is not a big deal. As to the question of growing up too fast, I believe that the elements of racism, poverty, the hustle of the inner city—one or some combination of all three—rob far too many kids of their childhood. I know because I was one of them. And for me, going to college early was a chance to do what I couldn't do at home—focus on my school work and socialize like the teenager I was.

Expectation plays a large part in all of our development. Too often, the expectation of young black people is criminality and stupidity. I grew up in the New York City public school system. One thing I remember very clearly is that the gifted and talented classes were always the ones with the most white kids. My friend Retha, who grew up in Queens, remembers exactly the same thing. More was expected of the white students. Period.

We moved often. Every time we did, I was put into the C or average class despite the fact that I'd always been in the gifted and talented classes before we began moving so much. After a couple of weeks, I would go up to my teacher and ask if there was a "harder class," and I would be moved. I was only 9 and 10 years old, but would have, somehow, to find a humble way to point out to a teacher that I wanted to be challenged more. No teacher ever asked why I, sitting in the C class, completed the math test in 10 minutes and sped through my reading assignments. "Did you do this yourself?" was a frequent and upsetting question. The expectations for me were low, and as long as I didn't cause trouble my overworked teachers ignored me. I had to challenge myself. And for that desire to learn I don't credit any sort of super-intelligence, but instead a high self-esteem that I was able to nurture and protect despite my circumstances. But think of how many young black students sit in C classes, needing more work but not receiving it! After all, they are just kids. Maybe some of them say, "Cool.

This is gonna be a breeze." And it is. Maybe some of them don't want to be seen as a smarty pants, so they play it low-key. Maybe some of them play dumb to fit in with their friends. Regardless, if you're poorly tracked by the fourth grade, you stop trying so hard. You don't go to college early. Perhaps, you don't go to college at all.

Like many black parents, like many immigrant parents, my mother and father trusted the school system to do right by their kids. All of us here know that lack of involvement can be a trust misplaced. Standing at the elevator bank at the *New York Times*, where I work, the other day I overheard two women, both white, both upper class, discussing their children's education. "We're trying to get our son into a lab school," said one woman, "but there's also a gifted and talented class we could get him into. And if worse comes to worse, thank God we've got the money for private school." Think about it. Then ask yourself why it is easier for young black persons to get into jail than it is for them to get into Simon's Rock. The answer shouldn't be because jail is free.

I urge you to do better by students of color. And I do not ask of you what I don't demand of myself. If there is something I can do on behalf of your students or your institution, call me. Our African-American neighborhoods are always more full of basketball recruiters than college recruiters. These days, record producers are also a known force—searching the streets for the next great gangsta rapper, the next platinum-selling Snoop Doggy Dogg. A message is being sent to our young black people that there are only three trades open to them—the dope trade, the basketball trade, and the rap trade. College recruiters need to make their voices heard and let these kids know that their gifts and talents are not limited to the streets, the basketball courts, and the rap studios.

I know there are many, many students like me— poor and black—who are biding their time for college while struggling with difficult situations. The ability to go to college early is the ability to keep your dreams alive before they are snuffed out by any number of traps that await children in urban areas—teenage pregnancy, drug dealing, under-education, and under-employment. For students like me, going to college early was not about missing the prom but about saving our own lives.

I come from a race of people that has given this country some of its best and brightest leaders: Children's Defense Fund head Marian Wright Edelman, attorney and White House insider Vernon Jordan, writers James Baldwin, Rita Dove, and Toni Morrison, astronaut Mae C. Jemison. When you are in your classrooms and universities, ask yourself: Where are the black faces, the Latino faces, the poor and the disadvantaged of all races? Then ask yourself what you can do to get these students what they need. We know where talent can go when it is nurtured, and we know what happens when the gift sits idle.

Source: Veronica Chambers, "On Going to College Early," speech presented at the Conference on Adolescence, Acceleration, and National Excellence at Simon's Rock College of Bard, Great Barrington, MA, June 19, 1994. Reprinted by kind permission of the author. Veronica Chambers is story editor at the *New York Times Magazine*.

commentary

What Is the Context? In this speech, a young woman who is gifted addresses the many challenges she has faced in the neighborhood, in school, and in college. The constant tumult of the inner city and exposure to racism, drugs, and poverty force children to grow up very fast. College became the sanctuary where she could concentrate on studying and have the opportunities to socialize. Negative expectations by society for inner-city youths become self-fulfilling prophecies. Veronica Chambers came to understand that it was vital to protect and nurture her self-esteem and to assert herself whenever teachers assumed that she belonged in unchallenging classes. Faced at times with conflicting pressures from violent neighborhoods and schools, she has come to understand herself as a talented, focused, whole person and to take responsibility for improving the opportunities of poor, inner-city children.

Pivotal Issues. What are some of the pressures that black and Latino students who are gifted face when placed in low-level classes? What other pressures, difficulties, and needs do black and Latino students who are gifted and talented face? Why are they more highly regarded for their athletic and musical ability than for their academic ability? How did the accelerated academic program help Veronica Chambers?

creative, and leadership giftedness; Zelda, the intellectual criteria. Their developmental profiles are shown in Figure 4.1.

Cranshaw is a big, athletic, happy-go-lucky youngster who impresses the casual observer as the "all-American boy." He seems to be a natural leader and to be enthusiastic over a wide range of interests. These interests have not yet solidified. One week he can be fascinated with astronomy, the next week with football formations, and the following week with the study of Africa.

His past history in school has suggested that teachers have two very distinct reactions to Cranshaw. One is that he is a joy to have in the classroom. He is a cooperative and responsible boy who can not only perform his own tasks well, but be a good influence in helping the other youngsters to perform effectively. On the other hand, Cranshaw's mere presence in the class also stimulates in teachers some hints of personal inferiority and frustration, since he always seems to be exceeding the bounds of the teachers' knowledge and abilities. The teachers secretly wonder how much they are really teaching Cranshaw and how much he is learning on his own.

Cranshaw's family is a well-knit, reasonably happy one. His father is a businessman, his mother has had some college education, and the family is moderately active in the community. Their attitude toward Cranshaw is that he is a fine boy, and they hope that he does well. They anticipate his going on to higher education but, in effect, say that it is pretty much up to him what he is going to do when the time comes. They do not seem to be future-oriented and are perfectly happy to have him as the enthusiastic and well-adjusted youngster that he appears to be today.

Zelda shares similar high scores on intelligence tests to those manifested by Cranshaw. Zelda is a chubby girl who wears rather thick glasses that give her a "bookish" appearance. Her clothes, while reasonably neat and clean, are not stylish and give the impression that neither her parents nor Zelda have given a great deal of thought to how they look on this particular child. Socially, she has one or two reasonably close

Figure 4.1

Profiles of Two Gifted Students

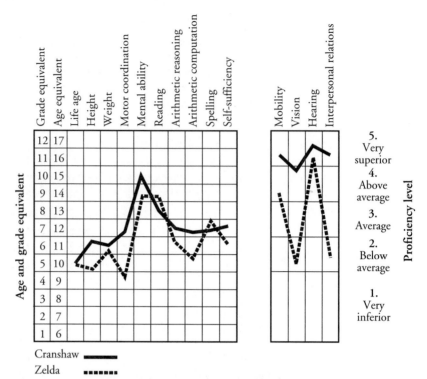

Cranshaw ▬▬▬
Zelda ▪▪▪▪▪

Source: From J. Gallagher and S. Gallagher, *Teaching the Gifted Child*, 4th ed., p.12. Copyright © 1994 by Allyn and Bacon. Reprinted by permission.

girl friends, but she is not a member of the wider social circle of girls in her classroom and, indeed, seems to reject it.

Teachers respond to Zelda with two generally different feelings. They are pleased with the enthusiasm with which Zelda attacks her schoolwork and the good grades that she gets. At the same time, they are vaguely annoyed or irritated with Zelda's undisguised feeling of superiority toward youngsters who are not as bright as she is; they tend to repel Zelda when she tries to act like an assistant teacher, or to gain favors that are more reserved for the teachers.

Zelda and her family seem to get along very well with each other. The main source of conflict is that the family has values which Zelda has accepted wholeheartedly but that are getting her into difficulty with her classmates. Her father is a college professor and her mother has an advanced degree in English literature. They seem to value achievement and intellectual performance almost to the exclusion of all other things.

Their social evenings are made up of intellectual discussions of politics, religion, or the current burning issue on the campus. These discussions are definitely adult-oriented, and Zelda is intelligent enough to be able to enter occasionally into such conversations. This type of behavior is rewarded much more by the parents than is the behavior that would seem more appropriate to her age level. (From J. Gallagher and S. Gallagher, *Teaching the Gifted Child*, pp. 11–12. Copyright © 1994 by Allyn and Bacon. Reprinted by permission.)

Any program for identifying children who are gifted in a school system should include both subjective and objective methods of evaluation. Classroom behavior, for example, can point up children's ability to organize and use materials and can reveal their potential for processing information. (© *Thomas Cheek/Stock Boston*)

Cranshaw's adjustment is as good as his academic achievement; Zelda has social difficulties. She is not accepted by her agemates and doesn't understand why.

The teachers of gifted students face several basic challenges: holding the interest of youngsters whose abilities are several years beyond their grade level, encouraging them to work in areas that may not interest them, and helping them deal with the social problems of being gifted.

Identification

Before we can provide children who are gifted with special services to match their special needs, we have to find them. Identification is not an easy task! In every generation, many such children pass through school unidentified, their talents uncultivated. Who are they? Many come from low socioeconomic backgrounds or from subcultures with values and emphases that differ from those of the mainstream of U.S. society. Others may have emotional problems that disguise their intellectual abilities (Baldwin, 1987).

We generally expect that teachers can spot these children and do something for them. But studies have shown that teachers do not always recognize children who are gifted, even those with academic talent (Parke, 1991). The identification of these students requires an understanding of the requirements of the program for which they are chosen. If we want to choose a group of students for an advanced mathematics class, our approach would be different than if we are looking for students with high aptitude for a creative-writing program. Specific program needs and requirements shape the identification process.

Any program for identifying children who are gifted in a school system should include both subjective and objective methods of evaluation. Classroom behavior, for example, can point up children's ability to organize and use materials and reveal their potential for processing information, sometimes better than can a test. Products, such as superior essays, term projects, etc. that can be kept in a student portfolio, can serve as identification of special gifts.

The products of creative performance are a good guide for finding talented students. But what about those with unfulfilled potential? Potential has largely been measured by extracting originality or other important elements from the creative process and using them to create a test or rating scale that focuses on several abilities:

1. *Fluency:* the ability to give many answers to a given question
2. *Flexibility:* the ability to give many different types of responses or to shift from one type of response to another
3. *Originality:* the ability to provide unique yet appropriate responses

Suppose a question asks, "How many different ways can you use a brick?" A long list of answers focusing on the types of buildings in which bricks are used would receive credit for *fluency.* Answers that point out that bricks can be used as decorations, weapons, or weights would receive credit for *flexibility.* And an answer that a brick can be crumbled up and used as a coloring agent would get credit for *originality.*

In the visual and performing arts, talent usually is determined by the consensus of expert judges, often in an audition setting. Experts in the arts are not enthusiastic about tests of artistic ability or musical aptitude. They trust their own judgment more, although their judgment is susceptible to bias. Sometimes, it is possible to judge the quality of a series of products or a portfolio of drawings or compositions that students produce over a period of time (Clark & Zimmerman, 1989).

Most schools have test scores available from group intelligence tests or group achievement tests. Such data can serve as a starting point for selecting candidates for a special program, but they have limitations:

1. Group intelligence tests are not as reliable as individual tests.
2. Group tests seldom differentiate abilities at the upper limits because they have been designed largely for the average student.
3. Group tests rarely measure creative thinking or cognitive areas beyond academic aptitude.
4. Some children do not function well in a timed testing situation.

Despite those limitations, group intelligence tests are a practical means of screening large numbers of students, unless the students come from culturally diverse

The visual and performing arts use expert judgment to identify talented students.

settings. If they do, their scores are likely to be underestimated. It is financially prohibitive, however, to give all children individual examinations.

Achievement tests are even less discriminating. They detect only the children who are achieving well academically. Emotional disturbance, family problems, peer-group values, poor study habits, a foreign-language background, and many other factors can affect a child's ability to perform academically. And because of family pressures, good study habits, or intense motivation, some children will achieve at a higher educational level than is consistent with their other abilities or their apparent mental level.

Another approach used to identify students who are gifted is to start with a particular program and find youngsters with the special abilities that meet program requirements. Stanley (1989) used this method to initiate a talent search for mathematically and verbally precocious youngsters—the Study of Mathematically Precocious Youth, now referred to as the Center for Talented Youth at Johns Hopkins University.

The Scholastic Aptitude Test and other aptitude tests are used to screen students who are extraordinarily capable in mathematics. Other characteristics—motivation and academic efficiency—determine the type of special attention suitable for those who score at the highest level on these tests. Most special education programs for students who are gifted now use a combination of aptitude tests, teacher ratings, nominations, portfolios, and scholastic records to help identify eligible students. A committee of teachers and other specialists often will try to match the child's talents with the special services that are available.

The reasons for identifying children who are gifted are complex. Identification should be the first step to a differentiated program. It can also be used to determine eligibility for state financial aid that may provide a subsidy for local programs or to satisfy state or federal guidelines.

Special Groups of Children Who Are Gifted

The category of children who are gifted and talented contains many subgroups. How well individuals in these groups are adapting depends to a major degree on how their families raise them, how their schools utilize their special gifts, and how society sees them.

GIRLS WHO ARE GIFTED

It seems strange in one respect to identify girls who are gifted as a special group, for girls make up more than 50 percent of the student population. But sufficient evidence shows that members of this group differ meaningfully on a number of indices from their male counterparts. The differences appear to rest in their perceptions of the world around them, often formed by the attitudes of those close to them. If trusted Aunt Millie tells her niece that girls are not supposed to be good in mathematics, and if other family members or other persons whom the child trusts

The belief is growing that girls who are gifted represent one of the largest groups of untapped intellectual potential in this country. (© Jerry Howard/Positive Images)

The limited number of girls being identified as gifted seems to be the result of societal preconceptions that girls do not have special abilities.

share that viewpoint, then what is the girl likely to believe—particularly if such a stereotype is repeated in the popular media and in the girl's peer group?

Gender differences in self-perception appear to limit girls' intellectual performance, so it is extremely important for teachers to be aware of such differences and try to do something about them. These differences appear to be related to societal expectations. Although there is reason to believe (Hollinger, 1995) that attitudes toward girls and women are changing, the forces at work to limit achievement of girls appear still powerful. The National Assessment of Educational Progress (Gallagher, 1993) reported relatively equal math achievement by boys and girls in the early elementary school years, but by the time these groups reach age 17 there is an enormous difference in favor of the boys. What has happened?

One study (Cramer & Oshima, 1992) places the key at about sixth through ninth grade, finding that girls who are gifted began, at that level but not before, to attribute math success to greater ability on the part of males and less to effort than males did. Such a belief can have a smothering effect on girls' efforts to achieve in mathematics. Another study showed a relationship between the mathematics self-concept of high-ability girls and their parents' belief in the ability of their daughters (Dickens & Cornell, 1993). Girls with a high mathematics self-concept had parents who had a similarly high perception of their daughters' ability and high expectations for their performance. This finding seems to indicate the importance of high parental expectations in dampening the societal bias against girls doing well in mathematics.

The fact that society still has a long way to go is made clear by Reis and Callahan (1989). They point out the relative absence of women in positions of power and prestige in our society—in business, the media, the Supreme Court, Congress, corporations, universities, symphony orchestras, and so on. The relative scarcity of female role models is another stumbling block, although that problem is easing now as more women become visible in desirable occupations.

Several experimental programs have been designed to overcome this societal bias. Some have grouped girls who are gifted for special instruction in mathematics (Rand & Gibb, 1989). By using female role models and keeping the intimidating element of male students out of the classroom, these programs hope to build students' confidence in their own abilities. It is too early to judge the impact of gender-linked segregation on this kind of instruction. The goal is to ensure that girls who are gifted receive the education that will allow them to choose what they want to do, not what others believe they should do. Table 4.5 reveals a set of rules proposed to aid girls in their science interests. These suggestions are designed to aid the girls' self-concepts and mastery of necessary skills.

CHILDREN OF EXTRAORDINARY ABILITY

It is generally accepted today that superior intellectual ability predicts high academic performance and personal adjustment. But doubts linger about the youngster of extraordinary ability—the 1 in 100,000 at the level of an Einstein. What happens to the student who is seven or eight years ahead of his or her age group in development?

Is there a relationship between extraordinary intelligence and later development? As IQ scores increase, do we see an increase in later accomplishments? Feldman (1984) compared two groups of adults among Terman's subjects. As children, one group obtained IQ scores of more than 180; the other, randomly selected from the average range of scores, had IQ scores in the area of 150. There was some evidence that men in the "very high IQ" group had accomplished more than men in the "high IQ" group. For example, one was an internationally known psychologist, another a highly honored landscape architect. Still, many of the men in the lower group were successful, if not eminent. Feldman also found a difference between the women in the two groups. Those with IQ scores around 180 tended to have full-time careers; those in the lower group tended to be homemakers. Despite the difference he found between the groups, Feldman concluded that *genius* is not solely a function of intelligence, but rather reflects a combination of intelligence, personality, motivation, and environmental variables.

Certainly Feldman's conclusions seem accurate when we look at the stories of two American prodigies, William Sidis and Charles Fefferman. Sidis was a mathematical prodigy who knew algebra, trigonometry, geometry, and calculus by age 10. He was admitted to Harvard University at age 11 and graduated cum laude at age 16. Despite his scholastic success, Sidis's emotional adjustment was always a problem. He retreated into social isolation, strenuously avoiding all academic life and publicity. He died in his middle forties, penniless and alone (Montour, 1977).

TABLE 4.5	Strengthening the Science Interest of Girls Who Are Gifted

1. *Remember: Do not overhelp young girls.* Let them gain valuable experience by thinking through a problem and trying various solutions. Encourage self-reliance or independence.

2. *Encourage girls to trust their own judgment.* Discourage girls from seeking constant approval or verification from others before making decisions or moving to the next step. They need to develop confidence in their own abilities.

3. *Insist that girls use tools and equipment.* They should feel confident in their ability to identify and use equipment from basic hand tools to sophisticated computers and microscopes.

4. *Introduce female role models whenever possible.* This includes historical as well as women currently in science fields. Remember also that women such as mothers and teachers exert a strong influence on a young girl's life; examine your own approaches to the areas listed above.

Source: D. Rand and L. Gibb (1989). A model program for gifted girls in science. *Journal for the Education of the Gifted, 12*(2), p. 153. Chapel Hill: The University of North Carolina Press.

Many believe that that is what happens to prodigies: "The faster the rocket goes up, the faster it comes down" and "Early ripe, early rot." Much more typical, however, is the story of Charles Fefferman, the youngest person in recent history to be appointed to a full professorship at a major university. He received that appointment at the University of Chicago at age 22. Encouraged by his father, a Ph.D. in economics, he was taking courses in mathematics at the University of Maryland by the age of 12 and entered college as a full-time student at age 14. He combined his studies with a normal social life; his friends were in junior high at the time. He won a number of prizes for his work in mathematics and at age 27 was the first recipient of the $150,000 Allan Waterman Award of the National Science Foundation (Montour, 1978).

It is unrealistic to think that any educational system is going to reorganize its program to fit children like these, who may appear once in a lifetime. Still, the potential impact of these children on society is so great that some degree of attention such as individualized tutoring and apprenticeship to other talented individuals is called for.

Extraordinarily precocious students represent one of our greatest and rarest natural resources. We must learn more about them to understand the origin of their giftedness and ways to help them adapt to an often difficult social environment.

UNDERACHIEVERS WHO ARE GIFTED

One of the many myths surrounding children who are gifted is the cannonball theory. The idea, simply put, is that such children can no more be stopped from achieving their potential than a cannonball once fired can be diverted from its path. Like most simplistic ideas about human beings, this one, too, is wrong.

A substantial proportion of children never achieve the level of performance that their scores on intelligence and aptitude tests predict for them. In the Terman longitudinal study, the researchers identified a group of 150 men who had not achieved to the level of their apparent ability and compared them with 150 men who had done well (Terman & Oden, 1947). In their self-ratings and in ratings by their wives and parents, four major characteristics separated the underachieving men from the achieving men:

1. Greater feelings of inferiority
2. Less self-confidence
3. Less perseverance
4. Less of a sense of life goals

More striking was an examination of teacher ratings made on the men twenty years earlier, while they were in school. Even at that time, their teachers believed that the underachievers lacked self-confidence, foresight, and the desire to excel.

Whitmore (1980) summed up the literature on the distinctive personality and behavioral traits that describe many underachievers:

> A negative self-concept, low self-esteem, expectations of academic and social failure, a sense of inability to control or determine outcomes of his efforts, and behaviors that serve as mechanisms for coping with the tension produced by conflict for the child in school. (p. 189)

Most teachers are able to describe at length the characteristics of underachievers. But what they really want to know is what to do about them. Whitmore (1980) reported on a special program at the primary-grade level. A group of twenty-seven underachievers who were gifted was placed in a special class, where the children were encouraged to express their feelings and concerns. The teacher met monthly with child and parents. After a year, twelve of the students had gained from 1½ to 3 years in reading scores; only three failed to reach grade level in reading or arithmetic. Social behavior and work habits also improved. Whitmore pointed out that many of the children had shown signs of emotional disturbance, but the creation of a warm, accepting environment had apparently overcome the outward symptoms of those problems.

In a carefully designed experiment with elementary school students, Butler-Por (1987) placed thirty-six underachievers in a program that stressed three elements:

A warm, accepting, supportive environment can significantly improve the academic and social performance of underachievers.

1. Acceptance of the individual child
2. Recognition by the child and the parents that a change in the school situation was necessary
3. Willingness of the child to take responsibility for change

Each of the twelve teachers in the study used diagnostic profiles to help the students recognize the need for change. At weekly meetings, teacher and student agreed to a written *contract* that spelled out goals for the coming week and

Students can be challenged by participating in Outward Bound activities, such as these high-schoolers sailing in Boston harbor. (© *Walter S. Silver/The Picture Cube*)

rewards for achieving them. Goals included preparing homework, organizing a social event, and reducing classroom disruptions. At the end of the program, teacher and student evaluated the success of their joint efforts and agreed that progress would continue without structured meetings. In comparing the students in the experimental group with a similar group of youngsters who received no special attention, Butler-Por found that the experimental group showed improvement in grades, in positive social experiences, in attitudes, and in school attendance.

Both Whitmore and Butler-Por have shown that carefully designed programs, over an extended period of time, can make a positive difference in the academic and social performance of underachievers. Yet very few school systems offer these programs. Why? Because underachievers who are gifted do not often come to the attention of special educators. They don't fail in school, yet they can't perform at the level that would place them in programs for students who are gifted (see also Supple, 1990).

CULTURALLY DIFFERENT CHILDREN WHO ARE GIFTED

Each of the subcultures in this country has contributed children and adults of high intellectual and artistic ability to the benefit of the larger society. Because these subcultures have their own values and reward different kinds of behaviors, the children often show their gifts in ways not typical of the mainstream society. One of the tasks of the school is to discover and nurture their talents (Frasier, 1987).

One way to expand the number of culturally different children who are gifted is to adopt alternative policies for state and local schools. Coleman and Gallagher (1992) analyzed the special changes that the fifty states made in their standard identification procedures to try to discover in nontraditional families and cultural groups children who are gifted. These strategies included

- Developing student profiles and case study examples of nontraditional gifted students
- Using multiple identification criteria with the clause "no single criterion should prevent identification"
- Using portfolios of student work samples to document giftedness

Such measures seemed necessary because cultural differences often mask outstanding talent. All too often, the student will not reveal talent to a peer group that might be unsympathetic to talent (Ogbu, 1992).

Wolf (1981) used a unique approach to qualify urban minority students for advanced work in the visual and performing arts. The identification process was in two stages. First, the top 15 or 20 percent of the student body was identified by performance on standard tests. That group was enrolled in a theater techniques program that emphasized expressive and communication skills. At the end of the program, the staff rated the students along a number of dimensions. Those who rated high graduated to an independent study and seminar program at the Educational Center for the Arts, which provides training in music, dance, theater arts, and graphic arts.

Once culturally different students who are gifted are found, by whatever method, we must develop an educational plan for their special needs and circumstances. One objective for minority group youngsters is to encourage their understanding of and respect for their own cultural background. Biographies and the works of noted writers or leaders from the particular cultural group are often the basis of special programs. Because there are so many groups with such diverse backgrounds, these programs are usually unique (Baldwin, 1987; Bernal, 1979).

The families of successful (in academic performance) minority group students also play a major role. Shade (1978), in a study of the families of African-American children who are gifted, found that the parents demanded better-than-average school performance while providing a warm, supportive home environment. Close family ties, a structured home life, moderate amounts of discipline, and help when needed all marked the families of high-achieving African-American children.

As minority groups gradually assimilate into the larger community, educational programs carry the difficult task of encouraging youngsters to respect their cultural heritage and, at the same time, to take on those characteristics of the larger society that can help them succeed within that society. The balance is a delicate one (see Figure 4.2).

One of the most difficult issues for minority students to cope with is their own self-identity, particularly if there appears to be a gap between the majority white

Figure 4.2
Sadness in My Heart
by Vena Romero, 13 years old

My thoughts flow vigorously
through my mind
as I see the tears fall endlessly
because we, the younger generation, are
blind.
Blinded by the white world
and what it brings,
we forget about our world
and all our sacred native things.
We have held our tradition
for so very long.
The elders are praying, wishing,
that it will live on.
We're forgetting about them
and our future.
Slowly we're losing them
and our culture.
We can't see how we're hurting ourselves
by losing our identity,
our culture, tradition, heritage, and ourselves.
We are not Native Americans
without our world.
We are just dark-skinned Americans
in a white world.

Source: Romero, Vena, (1994) in C. Callahan and J. McIntire, *Identifying Outstanding Talent in American Indian and Alaska Native Students*. Washington, DC: U.S. Department of Education, p. i.

culture and the culture of the family from which the student comes. Black students who are gifted and who are perceived as acting white because they accept the Protestant work ethic are likely to have a difficult time achieving good peer adjustment (Ford, Harris, & Schuerger, 1993) or finding a way to feel good about themselves.

Some special counseling has been suggested as a means of helping individual students come to terms with the differing values, attitudes, and norms of the dominant culture and the parent culture. Special multicultural counseling strategies are needed, together with use of mentor and role models. The ordinary school counseling program by itself does not seem adequate for this special task, and in any case, black students currently underutilize such standard counseling services.

One of the major controversies in the early 1990s pit the *assimilation approach* against the *pluralistic approach*. Proponents of the assimilation approach believed that students who are gifted and from minority backgrounds should learn about the majority culture and what behaviors and knowledge are necessary to make an academic and economic success within the rules of the majority culture (Frasier, 1992). Proponents of the pluralistic approach focused on how to modify the majority culture to better take into account the needs of the various subcultures

(Kitano, 1992). It is likely that elements of both positions will find a way into the school curriculum and into programs for nontraditional students who are gifted.

Maker (1989, p. 301) summarized the program suggestions from a wide variety of specialists concerned with children from different racial and ethnic backgrounds:

1. Identify students' strengths and plan a curriculum to develop these abilities.
2. Provide for the development of basic skills and other abilities students may lack.
3. Regard differences as positive, rather than negative, attributes.
4. Provide for involvement of parents, the community, and mentors or role models.
5. Create and maintain classrooms with a multicultural emphasis.

CHILDREN WITH DISABILITIES WHO ARE GIFTED

Through the remainder of this book, we discuss children who have various disabilities. They may not be able to see or hear or walk, but this limitation does not mean that they are not intellectually gifted. It only means that they stand a good chance of having their special talents overlooked. Whitmore (1981) described a child who not only went unrecognized as gifted but was actually considered mentally retarded:

> Kim. At seven years of age, this child with cerebral palsy had no speech and extremely limited motor control. In a public school for severely handicapped students, she was taught only self-help skills. Her parents, who were teachers, observed her use of her eyes to communicate and believed there was unstimulated intellect trapped in her severely handicapped body. Upon parent request, she was mainstreamed in her wheelchair into an open-space elementary school. After two months of stimulation and the provision of a mechanical communicator, Kim began to develop rapidly. She learned the Morse code in less than two days and began communicating continuously to the teacher and peers through her communicator. Within four months, she was reading on grade level (second), and subsequent testing indicated she possessed superior mental abilities—an exceptional capacity to learn. (p. 109)

It is not hard to imagine what Kim's world would have been like if she had not been given the opportunity to learn and communicate.

One of the areas of disabilities to which researchers have given particular attention is the child who is both gifted and learning disabled. Some students can be gifted and also have neurologically based attention problems or visual perceptual problems that can cause reading or spelling errors.

Coleman (1992) studied the coping strategies used by students with learning disabilities who were gifted, as opposed to average students with learning disabilities. She found that the students who were gifted, had many more constructive coping strategies—that they developed problem-solving plans—whereas the average student with learning disabilities often displayed *learned helplessness* ("there's nothing I can do"), *escape/avoidance* ("go out and play instead of do homework"), or *distancing* ("just shrug it off"). Coleman recommended that all students with learning disabilities be directly instructed in coping strategies as a way of helping them survive the educational environment. Whitmore (1981, p. 112) presented three conditions she believes are necessary for better service for these students who have disabilities and are also gifted:

1. The reintegration of special regular and gifted education with a significant amount of cooperation and collaboration
2. More regular and effective use by educators of the expertise of professionals in community agencies, especially those in the medical and psychological professions
3. Early identification and intervention, preferably at the preschool age

Education Reform and Its Effects

Many changes are taking place in the schools today. Even though most are not initiated for students who are gifted, they are having a profound effect on them. Education for these students is a relatively small part of the huge U.S. educational establishment. Whenever major change takes place in the overall educational establishment, it reverberates through the system and affects all of the smaller parts. This is true of the educational reform efforts of the early 1990s (see Chapter 2 for a discussion of them).

Table 4.6 summarizes some of the major movements in that reform effort and their apparent effects on education for students who are gifted. The *excellence movement* to combat international economic competition stirred interest and influenced a key national goal: taking steps to ensure that the United States is first in the world in mathematics and science by the year 2000. This goal, plus the realization that American students were substantially behind students from other countries in science and mathematics, energized a variety of special programs for talented students, from the establishment of state residential schools (like the Illinois Mathematics and Science Academy) to summer enrichment programs. Various curriculum reform movements also began.

Ironically, two of the other reform elements, *cooperative learning* (Slavin, 1989) and the *middle schools movement* (George, 1988), stress the importance of heterogeneous grouping as part of the most desirable and equitable practice to provide students who are gifted with the opportunity to experience and understand students at all levels of ability and cultural backgrounds. As a result, many schools have reduced the number of advanced classes or honors classes, which previously had served and stimulated children who are gifted.

Site-based management—making many educational decisions at the school level, where students are best known and planned for—is a reform that can work

TABLE 4.6	Educational Reform and Students Who Are Gifted	
Reform	**How Reform Is Revealed**	**Implications for Education of Students Who Are Gifted**
The excellence movement	Concern that U.S. has lost competitiveness and we, as a nation, need to encourage our best and brightest students	Emphasis on strengthening curriculum in math and science; raising standards
Cooperative learning	Techniques for group or team learning often stressing diversity of ability or cultural background in group formation	Gifted students often placed in tutorial roles in small group work, may not be challenged by tasks
Middle schools movement	Focus on affective learning, interdisciplinary content, thinking processes, team teaching, and flexible scheduling; features heterogeneous grouping in many schools	Potential loss of advanced classes, honors programs; academic challenge may be lessened
Site-based management	More key educational decisions are made at school level; teachers are empowered	Will children with special needs be recognized? Will district-wide programs (e.g., magnet schools) be discontinued?
Accountability	Schools are expected to demonstrate or display the results of their work	Usual measures grossly underestimate gifted students' performance; too low a ceiling

Source: Adapted from J. Gallagher (1991). Educational reform, values, and gifted students. *Gifted Child Quarterly, 35*(1), pp. 12–19.

well if educators at the site understand the special needs of exceptional children. In a backhanded way, *accountability* (the last reform listed in Table 4.6) may increase attention to students who are gifted. The results of an evaluation can reveal the poor results on achievement tests for all students and put pressure on the schools to raise standards and challenge the best of the students. As is the case with many complex movements to change the schools, the overall impact of accountability on the education of students who are gifted remains uncertain.

Educational Adaptations

A school program for students who are gifted involves modifications to the learning environment, to content, and to cognitive strategies.

No one special program can meet the individual needs of all the children we've described. The diversity we find among youngsters who are gifted is reflected in the number and type of adaptations the schools are making to meet their special needs. Educators, however, agree on three general educational objectives for special programs or services for students who are gifted and talented:

1. These children should master important conceptual systems that are at the level of their abilities in various content fields.

2. These children should develop skills and strategies that enable them to become more independent and creative.

3. These children should develop pleasure in, and excitement about, learning that will carry them through the drudgery and routine that are inevitable parts of the learning process.

Although regular classroom teachers, in collaboration with other teachers and specialists, can help children who are gifted meet some of these goals, special programs are deemed essential to consistently achieve in all three of them. We can modify the school program for any group of exceptional children in three areas: learning environment, content, and cognitive strategies. A special type of change in learning environment involves moving the student more rapidly through school—educational acceleration. In this section, we explore these topics, focusing on children who are intellectually gifted.

MODIFICATIONS TO THE LEARNING ENVIRONMENT

Teachers can change the learning environment in many ways, but most are designed to bring children who are gifted together for instruction for a period of time. Our aim is threefold:

1. To provide students who are gifted with an opportunity to interact with one another and to learn and be stimulated by their intellectual peers

2. To reduce the spread of abilities and performance within the group on instructionally relevant dimensions (past achievement, for example) to make it easier for the teacher to provide instructionally relevant materials

3. To place students who are gifted with an instructor who has expertise in working with such students or in a relevant content field

Because changes in the learning environment affect the entire school system, they have received more attention at the school district level than have changes in skills and content, which remain primarily classroom issues. Still, the three elements are closely related: Changes in the learning environment for students who are gifted are often necessary to meet the instructional goals of special skills and differential content development.

Table 4.7 summarizes some of the adaptations that educators can make for students with special gifts and talents: flexible pacing, grouping and organization of

Changes in the learning environment for gifted students are necessary to meet the instructional goals of special skills and differential content development.
(© Michael Zide)

special courses. The choice of which if any of these options to implement depends on the characteristics of the student and the context in which he or she is placed.

Flexible pacing allows students to move through material at their own pace. Such a strategy sometimes accelerates the student to a level in the school program that is higher than the level of his or her agemates. If Cranshaw is in a school where few of the other students have aptitudes similar to his, then some form of course or grade acceleration might be considered, especially in view of Cranshaw's good social and personal adjustment.

Grouping by performance or aptitude is usually done to reduce the range of ability that the teacher must face in teaching subject matter. Having all students with high performance ability in one group allows the teacher to proceed much more swiftly and in greater depth than otherwise might be possible. There is a continuing debate in American education about the advantages and disadvantages of grouping. But it seems clear that students with high ability profit from such arrangements even though other students might not—an outcome that creates a considerable dilemma for the school administrator.

The magnet school, which draws students who excel in a given subject, is a recent addition to the options available to bright students and is a type of performance grouping. These schools often specialize in subject matter such as mathematics or

TABLE 4.7   Placement Options for Educating Students Who Are Gifted

Flexible Pacing	Flexible pacing is any provision that places students at an appropriate instructional level and allows them to move forward in the curriculum as they achieve mastery of content and skills.
Early entrance	Students enter elementary, middle, high school, or college earlier than their agemates.
Continuous progress	Continuous progress allows students to progress at their own rate. It requires a high level of individualization.
Course acceleration (subject skipping)	Students are allowed to "test out" and bypass specific subjects or skill levels. They might receive some instruction at a higher level with another group of students yet remain with their peer group for most of their instruction.
Grade acceleration	Students move ahead one or more years, skipping levels in the normal sequence of promotion. This has traditionally been used successfully with students who are highly gifted.
Concurrent (dual) enrollment	Students can be enrolled in two levels of schooling at the same time. This option is appropriate for secondary students who might be enrolled in courses at postsecondary institutions.
Credit by examination	Students are allowed to "test out" of a course and receive credit on satisfactory completion of an examination or certification of mastery.
Compacted courses	Course content is covered in a shortened period of time, leaving students to pursue projects of special interest.
Grouping	Grouping by performance of aptitude has been used to meet individual instructional needs since the late 1800s. There continues to be a need for some grouping in order to meet the diverse needs of students who are gifted.
Cross-age grouping (Multiage)	Multiage students are grouped within a school by interests or skills—no more than a two-year age span.
In-class flexible grouping	Students in each class are assigned to a small group for instruction. These groups may be homogeneously grouped according to skill level.
Cluster grouping within a regular class	A cluster group (4 to 10) of students who are gifted is assigned to a regular heterogeneous class. The cluster teacher receives extensive training in gifted education and works closely with a specialist in giftedness.
Subject grouping	Students are grouped for specific subjects based on their aptitude or performance. Grouping may not be limited to identified gifted students but may include other high achievers.

TABLE 4.7	Placement Options for Educating Students Who Are Gifted (cont.)
Part-time special class with integration	Students who are gifted attend classes for enriched or accelerated work part-time, and they attend regular classes the rest of the day. This allows them to receive differentiated instruction in the appropriate academic area.
Full-time special class	Students who are gifted are assigned to a special class for all of their instruction. It is important that the curriculum in such classes be truly differentiated.
Magnet program	Special programs may be designed to have a special focus or be of particular interest to students. Students may be bused into a school from other schools.
Special Courses	
Honors courses	Honors courses are advanced courses that cover traditional content but also focus on issues, problems, and themes related to topics. They are designed to help students to apply knowledge at an advanced level.
Advanced Placement courses	The Advanced Placement program consists of college-level courses and examinations for high school students. AP courses are usually taught by teachers who have received special training.
International baccalaureate courses	International baccalaureate programs provide an excellent opportunity for acceleration. They are usually designed as two-year high school programs that emphasize international concerns and foreign language.
Special school	Selected students attend a special school all day. Eligibility requirements may be based on aptitude and performance or on interest, depending on the nature of the program.
Residential high school	Such schools offer advanced courses or specialized curriculum not available in most high schools. Such schools are committed to having a culturally diversified student body and consider geographic representation.

in an activity such as art, and they encourage interested and qualified students to attend. Students who are gifted are interested in magnet schools that allow them to study at advanced levels and with other highly motivated students.

At the secondary school level various **special courses** often address the increasing diversity of achievement and aptitude found in that student body. Honors courses or Advanced Placement courses for which students may earn college credit are very common and popular. Over ten states have advanced residential schools for high-performing students. The North Carolina School of Science and Mathematics, the Illinois Math and Science Academy, and other schools focus on math and science.

Regardless of the attractiveness of the context of learning, however, unless there are clear modifications in content and process (for example, in thinking strategies), not much is likely to be accomplished by merely grouping youngsters of high ability together (Kulik & Kulik, 1991).

The great current interest in the strategy of *inclusion* for children with disabilities has also influenced the education for the students who are gifted. Educators have renewed efforts to find strategies for effectively teaching students who are gifted within the framework of the general classroom (Maker, 1993; Parke, 1991). Devices such as *cluster grouping* and the use of a *teacher-consultant* have been revisited in an effort to avoid the physical separation of students who are gifted from their peers, particularly at the elementary level. Despite efforts at inclusion, many school systems rely on pull-out programs and resource rooms conducted by specially qualified teachers to modify the regular program in important ways to meet the educational needs of students with special gifts and talents.

We want to stress that all of these strategies can be useful in the right circumstances. If a school system is near a major computer company, the availability of knowledgeable mentors could lead local schools in that direction. If experienced master teachers are available, the teacher-consultant approach could work well. A middle school program using teams of teachers with differing skills can be helpful (George, 1988). No one model is best, although certain methods clearly are more popular than others.

MODIFICATIONS TO CONTENT

Educators can use content acceleration, enrichment, sophistication, and novelty to individualize a student's curriculum.

Suppose you were told again and again how to write simple noun-verb combinations or you had to practice simple spelling lists after you have mastered all of the words. You'd be bored. Boredom is a real problem for children like Cranshaw and Zelda, who are often forced to "learn" material they already know.

Renzulli, Smith, and Reis (1982) describe a process called **curriculum compacting**, which allows gifted youngsters to move ahead. The process has three steps:

1. Find out what the students know before instruction.
2. Arrange to teach, in a brief fashion, the remaining concepts or skills.
3. Provide a different set of experiences to enrich or advance the students.

Renzulli and his colleagues used Bill, a sixth-grade student with a straight-A average in math, as a case in point:

> After two days in math class Bill explains to the teacher that he knows how to do the math. He describes his interest in working on logic problems and shows his teacher the beginning of a logic book that he is putting together for other students.
>
> Bill's teacher administers the chapter tests for units 1–3 . . . [and] Bill scores 100 per unit. (p. 190)

The teacher responds to Bill's needs by arranging time for him to work on his logic book and to meet with people from a nearby computer center to develop his logic capabilities further. What Bill's teacher was doing was creating a differentiated curriculum for him. Gallagher and Gallagher (1994) described how teachers can use *acceleration, enrichment, sophistication,* and *novelty* (see Table 4.8) to individualize the curriculum of the student who is gifted.

The purpose of **content acceleration** is to move students through the traditional curriculum at a fast rate. The process allows students to master increasingly complex sets of ideas. For example, by learning calculus in ninth grade, students have the foundation to begin physics and chemistry, subjects that require the skills of calculus. Table 4.8 shows how content can be accelerated in mathematics and other subject areas.

Content enrichment gives students the opportunity for a greater appreciation of the topic under study by expanding the material for study (exploring additional examples, using specific illustrations). Having students read the diaries of Civil War soldiers on both sides, for example, enriches their perspective on the war. This form of differentiated content for students who are gifted is often used in the regular classroom because it requires no change in content, just additional assignments.

The failure to recognize *time* as the enemy of teachers and teaching is at the heart of many teachers' disputes. The question is often posed, "Cannot the average student learn what is being taught to students who are gifted?" The answer is 'Yes,' if you disregard the time factor. For example, middle school students who are gifted can be taught about the solar system and the various theories about its

Limited time often prevents teachers from presenting a sophisticated curriculum to students.

TABLE 4.8	Curriculum Modifications for Students Who Are Gifted			
	Math	**Science**	**Language Arts**	**Social Studies**
Acceleration	Algebra in fifth grade	Early chemistry and physics	Learning grammatical structure early	Early introduction to world history
Enrichment	Changing bases in number systems	Experimentation and data collecting	Short-story and poetry writing	Reading biographies of persons for historical insight
Sophistication	Mastering the laws of arithmetic	Learning the laws of physics	Mastering the structural properties of plays, sonnets, etc.	Learning and applying the principles of economics
Novelty	Probability and statistics	Science and its impact on society	Rewriting Shakespeare's plays to give them happy endings	Creating future societies and telling how they are governed

Source: From J. Gallagher and S. Gallagher, *Teaching the Gifted Child* (4th ed.). Copyright © 1994 by Allyn and Bacon. Adapted by permission.

origin in an enrichment lesson because they have already mastered the required curriculum in less than the time allotted. Could average students also master these theories? Of course, if they are given enough time. But they have not yet mastered the required lessons of the regular curriculum, and they also have greater difficulty with the concepts of distance, of orbits, and of centrifugal force—difficulty that will extend further the time they need to master the theories.

Time is a fixed constant. Between 180 and 200 days are available in a school year, so there is not an unlimited period in which students can master needed knowledge and skills. Youngsters who learn faster than others will be able to master more knowledge and practice more of the necessary skills than will other students in the same amount of time. Such differences are a fact of life that we, as educators, must adjust to, instead of pretending that they don't exist.

Content sophistication challenges students who are gifted to use higher levels of thinking to understand ideas that average students of the same age would find difficult or impossible to comprehend. The objective is to encourage children who are gifted to understand important abstractions, scientific laws, or general principles that can be applied in many circumstances. One example is *values,* an area rarely explored in regular educational programs. The diversity in our society often causes us to overlook important common principles that we share with one another. This oversight can lead idealistic youngsters to believe that they live in a valueless society, a society dominated by selfish people acting against the public interest.

How would you go about teaching values? You could assign students to look for those ethical standards held in common by classmates or neighbors and then discuss how these common values bind the nation together. For example, Gardner (1978) identified several fundamental values held in common in our society:

1. *Justice and the rule of law.* The attempt to provide justice for all, though often falling short in practice, represents one of the most common themes of U.S. society.

2. *Freedom of expression.* The right to speak one's mind, regardless of who is offended, is another proud tradition. Without it, many of our other freedoms would likely vanish.

3. *The dignity and worth of each person.* Equality of opportunity—giving all a chance to reach their potential—is a consistent theme. The insistence on special education for all children with disabilities is a clear reflection of this value.

4. *Individual moral responsibility.* Each of us is responsible for the consequences of our actions. Even making allowances for differences in background and opportunities, in the end we are assumed to be the captains of our fate and are judged as such by our friends, neighbors, and communities.

5. *Distaste for corruption.* The larger purposes of society may be betrayed by hatred, fear, envy, the misuse of power, or personal gain. We agree that these things should not be, and we array our legal and social institutions to protect the larger society against personal frailty.

You can encourage vigorous discussions about clashes involving these accepted values in the "real world."

Content novelty is the introduction of material that normally would not appear in the general curriculum because of time constraints or the abstract nature of the content. Students who are gifted are often able to see relationships across content fields. Because of this ability a teacher could describe one or two examples and have the students think of others. Table 4.9, for example, explores the impact of technology (automobiles and television) on society. The teacher could encourage students to think about the consequences of other technological advances (air conditioning, computers) or to produce alternative sequences that yield more positive results (television gives us greater empathy for human suffering in faraway places). Because technology and science are central elements in modern society, it makes sense to teach their social impact to youngsters, many of whom will be in positions to implement new discoveries when they are adults.

Computers are another tool to use to introduce content novelty into the curriculum. As Papert (1981) pointed out, computers allow children to be active, not passive, learners. Computers demand the use of systematic procedures. In the process of learning how computers think, children explore the ways they themselves think.

TEACHING COGNITIVE STRATEGIES

One objective of all educators who work with children who are gifted and talented is to increase or enhance those students' capability in productive thinking. The ability to generate new information through the internal processing of available information is perhaps the most valuable skill that human beings have. Practically all students at the elementary school level can solve this simple puzzle:

Mary is taller than Ruth.
Ruth is taller than Sally.
Sally is _____ than Mary.

Given the first two pieces of information, the students generate the third piece by themselves. Students who are gifted can use the reasoning process much more effectively and in far greater complexity than can children of average ability, and they are also usually superior in the tasks of problem finding, problem solving, and creativity.

Children who come from very different family cultures and values face not only the limited opportunity to learn the knowledge that the school feels is important but also a psychological struggle over whether they want to become part of mainstream America and participate in the same fashion as middle-class white children. Recall Figure 4.2, the poem written by a Native American girl. It is an expression of this conflict and of the desire to hold onto the values of another culture. Such ambivalence is not favorable to achievement in the traditional school sense.

TABLE 4.9   Unintended Consequences of Technology

Automobile

First-order consequences: People have a means of traveling rapidly, easily, cheaply, privately door to door.

Second-order consequences: People patronize stores at greater distances from their homes. These are generally bigger stores with large clienteles.

Third-order consequences: Residents of a community do not meet one another as often and therefore do not get to know one another well.

Fourth-order consequences: Strangers to each other, community members find it difficult to unite to deal with common problems. Individuals find themselves increasingly isolated from their neighbors.

Fifth-order consequences: Isolated from their neighbors, members of a family depend more on one another for satisfaction of most of their psychological needs.

Sixth-order consequences: When spouses are unable to meet the heavy psychological demands that each makes on the other, frustration occurs. This can lead to divorce.

Television

First-order consequences: People have a new source of entertainment and enlightenment in their homes.

Second-order consequences: People stay home more, rather than going out to local clubs and bars where they would meet other people in their community.

Third-order consequences: Because they are home more, people do not get to know one another well. They are also less dependent on one another for entertainment.

Fourth-order consequences: Strangers to each other, community members find it difficult to unite to deal with common problems. Individuals find themselves increasingly isolated from their neighbors.

Fifth-order consequences: Isolated from their neighbors, members of a family depend more on one another for satisfaction of most of their psychological needs.

Sixth-order consequences: When spouses are unable to meet the heavy psychological demands that each makes on the other, frustration occurs. This can lead to divorce.

Source: Adapted from *The Study of the Future* (1977) by E. Cornish. Washington, DC: World Future Society. Used by permission.

One of educators' favorite adjustments to both content and process is Renzulli's *enrichment triad* (Renzulli, 1992). It consists of three steps that the teacher can take a class through (see Table 4.10). Step 1 is the introduction of the topic to be studied—in this case, "How did our city or town begin?" In Step 1 the teacher lists exploratory activities such as field trips and interviews with citizens with special knowledge to intrigue and pique students' interest with stories about the beginnings of the city. In Step 2 students learn methods by which they can find answers to questions that they themselves have posed as a result of Step 1. They might learn how to search for the early records of the town or for early newspapers that may have ceased publication and how to handle historical information and check the validity of information. In Step 3 students choose a real problem using the skills they learned in Step 2. The teacher can accommodate individual differences by encouraging Cranshaw and Zelda to tackle problems that are more difficult than the problems that many of the others in the class work on. Such *enrichment triad experiences* can be very exciting to students, encouraging active rather than passive learning. They also place a considerable burden on the classroom teacher to monitor and supervise the students' various projects.

The enrichment triad is a device for encouraging active learning.

Problem Finding and Problem Solving

Gallagher (1994) defined **problem finding** as "the ability to review an area of study and to perceive those elements worthy of further analysis and study." **Problem solving** is "the ability to reach a previously determined answer by organizing and processing the available information in a logical and systematic fashion."

We teach problem solving but rarely teach problem finding.

The approach to enhancing problem-finding and problem-solving skills—which can be taught in the regular classroom, resource room, or special class—is to provide students with a set of strategies by which a problem can be attacked more efficiently. For example, to help students increase their problem-finding skills, we can have them ask questions like these:

1. How many people will be helped by the solution to this problem?
2. What negative things will happen if the problem is not solved?
3. What are the benefits of solving this problem?

Parnes, Noller, and Biondi (1977) developed a model for creative problem solving that has been much used. The creative problem-solving steps are as follows:

1. *Fact finding:* collecting data about the problem
2. *Problem finding:* restating the problem in solvable form, using data from Step 1
3. *Idea finding:* generating many possible solutions
4. *Solution finding:* developing criteria for the evaluation of alternatives
5. *Acceptance finding:* convincing the audience who must accept the plan that it can work

TABLE 4.10	The Renzulli Enrichment Triad: How Did Our City or Town Begin?

Step	Teacher Activity	Student Activity
1	These are general exploratory activities that introduce students to a major topic. Field trips, special speakers, etc., help to stir students' interest.	Students are asked to consider why their town started and developed here. They may read old newspapers and documents to stir their curiosity.
2	Students are introduced to methods by which they can find answer to these questions.	Students learn how to find historical documents, how to use school and community libraries, how to deal with conflicting information.
3	Students take a real problem and conduct an independent investigation using some of the skills they learned in Step 2.	Cranshaw uses diaries and other reports to study the role played by the initial settlers in establishing the community. Zelda studies the role played by trade via the roads and rivers that shape and determine community growth.

The creative problem-solving model might be used to think about the need to conserve energy resources in this country, for example.

The Importance of Knowledge Structure.   Do certain personal characteristics help us find and solve problems? The ability to store and access complex networks of associations seems to be one important basis for productive thinking. A set of experiments comparing the memory of children who were skilled chess players with adults who had little or no experience with the game yielded important information (Chi, 1978).

In one experiment, chess pieces were placed on a chessboard in various combinations. Each person was allowed to look at the board for a short time and then was asked to remember which pieces were on the board and where they were placed. The chess-playing children outperformed the adults on this task. Did the children have a special ability in memory? Was this why they were so good at chess? To answer these questions, researchers tested the youngsters and adults on short-term memory ability. The purest test of short-term memory is the ability to reproduce a string of numbers—such as 4-7-2-8-3-9—given orally. When the participants were given this kind of test, the adults did better than the children. Clearly, simple memory alone was not at work. Did the children's familiarity with the chess pieces give them the advantage? In another experiment, the chess pieces were placed on the board randomly, not as they would be placed in a game (deGroot, 1965). Under these conditions, the adults outperformed children.

By eliminating alternative theories, we begin to see why the chess-playing children did better than the adults on the original task. They were not remembering just the individual chess pieces; they were remembering *patterns of pieces*, pieces in recognizable game positions. They had a **knowledge structure**, or a bank of interrelated information in long-term memory that helped them recognize and recall patterns to use in solving problems. In this case, the patterns consisted of patterns of chess pieces.

Studies comparing the problem-solving capabilities of experts and novice professionals in the fields of engineering, computer programming, physics, medical diagnosis, and mathematics all yield similar results. The experts relied on their past knowledge structure to solve problems, whereas the novices were limited to the specific elements of the problem presented. Effective problem solving depends strongly on the nature and organization of knowledge available to the problem solver (Bransford, Sherwood, Vye, & Rieser, 1986).

The way to develop problem-solving skills in individuals who are gifted and those who are not is *not* to drill them on unconnected facts but to help them build a knowledge structure of interrelated information. And the key to this is

> practice, thousands of hours of practice. . . . There may be some as yet undiscovered basic abilities that underlie the attainment of truly exceptional performance . . . but for the most part, practice is by far the best predictor of performance. (Chase & Chi, 1980, p. 12)

Building a usable knowledge structure that is more complex and sophisticated than the knowledge structure one's agemates is one of the marks of a student who is gifted. The investigations of the differences between experts and novices illustrate one type of difference between students who are gifted and students who are average. The experts may be persons experienced in medical diagnostics, persons knowledgeable about physics, or veteran chess players. Whatever their expertise, they have in common many characteristics that separate them from novices in their domain of expertise. According to these studies (see Gallagher, 1994), students who are gifted can see large, meaningful patterns in the information or problem available to them. These students have superior long-term and short-term memories and can draw on their knowledge to solve problems, whereas the students who are not gifted are limited to the information available in the presentation of the problem.

Suppose the teacher presents a problem related to the Battle of Saratoga in the Revolutionary War. The average student (likely unknowledgeable on the subject) is limited to the materials the teacher makes available. By contrast, Cranshaw has read much about the Revolutionary War and can draw on a number of sources to enrich his answers and products. The development of these knowledge structures, and linking them with one another, are a teacher's prime goals with all students.

The developed knowledge structures of students who are gifted, and the ease with which these students add to existing structures, make such tasks relatively easy and quick for them.

Enhancing Problem-Finding Skills. An alternative approach popular with teachers of students who are gifted is to engage the students in the search for a solution to a problem presented to the class or to a subgroup of the class. In effect, the teacher asks the students to learn a variety of search techniques so that they can function as autonomous learners who can operate without the continued assistance of an adult mentor or teacher (Betts, 1989).

This approach is know as *problem finding, anchored instruction, creative problem solving,* and/or *cooperative learning.* It begins with the presentation of a problem that students are expected to solve. The problem is presented in ill-structured form, as one would find it in the real world. It can range from how to transport a wounded bird for treatment (Bransford et al., 1992), to whether to drop the atomic bomb, to the steps leading to the discovery of a new disease (Stepien, Gallagher, & Wakefield, 1994). A variety of information and information sources are provided to the students, who are expected to organize an attack on the subject by considering various strategies, weighing their usefulness, and selecting one to be followed. Students are expected to defend their choice and to organize themselves for a group attack on the problem.

There are several manifest advantages to this problem-finding approach, beginning with heightened student interest. Students become intrigued with the question and spend a substantial amount of time working on the discovery of the real problem and the design of a solution. They also experience various types of incidental learning about how to organize an attack on a problem and how to shape a problem into manageable size.

The disadvantage is our old friend *time.* Students often need a great deal of time to organize themselves into a working group and to find relevant information. For students who are gifted, time constraints are less likely to be a serious matter because the students have probably completed the regular unit or have shown mastery through curriculum compacting. Time limitations are much more serious in a heterogeneous class, in which the teacher has to worry about whether the average students have mastered the basic learning expected of that grade level.

Creativity

Superior intellectual talent enables students to generate new and better solutions to problems.

Creativity is "a mental process by which an individual creates new ideas or products, or recombines existing ideas and products in a fashion that is novel to him or her" (Gallagher, 1985, pp. 268, 303). More attention has probably been paid to creativity than to any other single objective in the education of children who are gifted and talented. We expect that superior intellectual development or talent gives students the ability to generate novel and better solutions to problems.

Gallagher (1992) reported that the recipe for creative production in students depended on the presence of four main ingredients:

■ A strong knowledge base

■ High motivation for distinctive achievement

■ Willingness to be different, to oppose the status quo

■ Cognitive strategies for solving difficult tasks

Even the most facile mind cannot operate without a strong knowledge base. A student may be asked a classical divergent-thinking question such as "How many ways can we suggest to save the salmon in the Columbia River?" If the student has no knowledge of salmon or the Columbia River, no matter how intelligent or creative the student is, he or she will have a hard time generating many "creative" answers. Even if a lot of off-the-top-of-the-head answers are produced, they are unlikely to be of any serious use. One must begin creative thinking with a good knowledge base.

Although it has been traditional to picture a creative person working independently at his or her craft or special product, many researchers believe that it is impossible to consider most acts of individual creativity apart from the culture and environment in which the creator works (Csikszentmihalyi, 1990; Gardner, 1993; Starko, 1995). Csikszentmihalyi views creativity as an interaction among persons, products, and environment. This change from focusing intense attention on the creative individual to focusing on the interaction between individual and environment helps us focus more on how to create a more fruitful environment for the creative child. We realize that by teaching children how to behave independently, and how to search for new ideas, we can help *many* students to become more creative, not merely the few with the highest measured intelligence.

The stimulation of creativity in the classroom has to be arranged with the context in mind. A creative student is not necessarily a solitary student left alone in a corner with his or her creative muse. Creativity is a product that can be stimulated by appropriate small-group work and interaction with other people and by additional resources. For example, a student working on the "How Did Our City or Town Begin?" project could be encouraged to produce creative work on what the city might have been like if it did not have a major river flowing through it. Innovative ideas can be stimulated by the reports of other students and the research that the class has done.

Starko (1995) presents a series of topics devoted to the preparation of students to be more independent:

■ Uses of independent work time

■ What to do if you are stuck and don't understand a task

■ How to signal a teacher for assistance or for a conference

■ Choice of activities and what to do when tasks are completed

It is increasingly clear that many general education classrooms with their standard curriculum, worksheets, and restrictive management are destined to impede the development of independent thinking without meaning to do so. It is also clear that if one of your instructional goals is student independent thought, then you will need to plan carefully to bring about this desired result.

Another accepted practice for extending intellectual fluency is **brainstorming** (Osborn, 1957). A group of people or a whole class that is brainstorming discusses a particular problem (for example, how to improve local government) and suggests as many answers as possible. You can use this activity with students of a wide range of abilities because many answers are "right" or acceptable. Here are some ground rules for brainstorming:

1. *No criticism is allowed.* Nothing should stop the free flow of ideas. Neither teacher nor students should criticize or ridicule a suggestion. Let students know in advance that evaluation comes later.

2. *The more ideas the better.* When a lot of ideas are suggested, it is increasingly likely that a good one is among them. Place a premium on unusual or unique solutions.

3. *Integration and combinations of ideas are welcomed.* Be sure everyone understands that it's acceptable to combine with or add to previous ideas.

4. *Evaluation happens after all ideas have been presented.* Judge when the fluency or inventiveness of the class is lagging. At that point, encourage evaluative thinking by students.

Divergent thinking requires fluency, flexibility, and originality.

Notice that evaluation becomes an important part of the process after the **divergent thinking**—that is, producing many different answers to a question—takes place. Once the ideas are produced, the group can choose those that seem most likely to solve the problem. Brainstorming, then, requires divergent thinking; judgment is more evaluative.

Our exploration of how to allow the human spirit and imagination to soar in the classroom while achieving other educational objectives is only beginning. We know what *not* to do (lecture interminably, ridicule fresh ideas, discourage alternatives), but we still have much to learn about the most effective ways to stimulate productive thinking.

STUDENT ACCELERATION

We can also adapt the educational program by abandoning the traditional practice of going from grade to grade and varying the length of the educational program. As more and more knowledge and skills must be learned at the highest levels of the professions, students who are talented and gifted can find themselves still in school at age 30 and beyond. While skilled workers are earning a living and starting a family, students who are gifted are often dependent on others for a good part of their young adult life. The process of **student acceleration**—passing students through the educational system as quickly as possible—is a clear educational objective for some children. Stanley (1989) described six ways of accelerating students:

Brainstorming helps students extend their intellectual fluency by discussing a particular problem and suggesting as many answers as possible for the problem. During brainstorming, criticism and evaluation are delayed until all ideas have been presented. (© *Jerry Howard/Positive Images*)

1. *Early school admission.* The intellectually and socially mature child is allowed to enter kindergarten at a younger-than-normal age.

2. *Skipping grades.* The child can be accelerated by completely eliminating one semester or grade in school. The primary drawback here is the potential for temporary adjustment problems for the student.

3. *Telescoping grades.* The child covers the standard material but in less time. For example, a three-year middle school program is taught over two years to an advanced group.

4. *Advanced Placement.* The student takes courses for college credit while still in high school, shortening the college program.

5. *Dual enrollment in high school and college.* The student takes college courses while still in high school.

6. *Early college admission.* An extraordinarily advanced student may enter college at 13, 14, or 15 years of age.

Stanley (1989) found that acceleration, particularly through dual enrollment in high school and college and early admission to college, is most effective for many students who excel in mathematics. In a field like mathematics, in which the curriculum content can be organized in sequential fashion, it is possible for bright students to move quickly through the material. Stanley developed a program for accelerating students in mathematics courses and for awarding college credit to children from 12 to 14 years of age. He described one student:

> Sean, who is 12 1/2 years of age, completed four and one-half years of pre-calculus mathematics in six 2-hour Saturday mornings compared with the 810 forty-five or fifty-minute periods usually required for Algebra I through III, plane geometry, trigonometry, and analytic geometry. . . . [D]uring the second semester of the eighth grade he was given released time to take the introduction to computer science course at Johns Hopkins and made a final grade of A. . . . While still 13 years old, Sean skipped the ninth and tenth grades. He became an eleventh-grader at a large suburban public high school and took calculus with twelfth graders, won a letter on the wrestling team, was a science and math whiz on the school's television academic quiz team, tutored a brilliant seventh grader through two and one-half years of algebra and a year of plane geometry in eight months, played a good game of golf, and took some college courses on the side (set theory, economics, and political science).
> (p. 175)

All this work allowed Sean to enter Johns Hopkins University as a sophomore with 34 credits at the age of 14. And Sean was just one example. Stanley reported that a number of youngsters with extraordinary talent in mathematics had academic programs that were shortened by accelerating either the student or the content.

Many students who are gifted can be moved ahead a year or two without serious negative effects.

From early admission to school to early admission to college, research studies invariably report that children who have been accelerated, as a group, have adjusted as well as or better than children of similar ability who have not been accelerated. Despite these findings, some parents and teachers continue to have strong negative feelings about the practice, and some educational administrators do not want to deal with these special cases. The major objection to the strategy is the fear that acceleration can displace individual children who are gifted from their social and emotional peers, affecting their subsequent social adjustment (Southern, 1991). The result of these misgivings is that many students who are gifted spend the greater part of their first three decades of life in the educational system, often locked in a relatively unproductive role, to the detriment of themselves and society.

Lifespan Issues

The economic and vocational futures for most individuals with gifts and talents are bright. The vocational opportunities awaiting them are diverse, including the fields of medicine, law, business, politics, and science. Only in the arts, where a limited number of opportunities exist to earn a comfortable income, do people who are gifted encounter social and economic barriers to their ambitions.

It is virtually certain that when most students who are gifted finish secondary school, they will go on to more school. They often have from eight to ten *more* years of training before they can expect to begin earning a living. This is especially true if they choose careers in medicine, law, or the sciences. The delay in becoming an independent wage earner creates personal and social problems that researchers are just beginning to study. Prolonged schooling means that individuals who are gifted must receive continued financial support. The most common forms of financial support are assistance from family and subsidies from private or public sources. If financial aid takes the form of bank or government loans, then a man or woman who is gifted will begin his or her career with a substantial debt. This period of extended schooling also tends to postpone marriage and raising a family.

The psychological problems that result from remaining dependent on others for financial support for as much as thirty years remain unexplored. We need to consider these issues before we burden students who are gifted with more schooling requirements intended to meet the demands of this rapidly changing world.

Summary of Major Ideas

1. Children who are gifted may show outstanding abilities in a variety of areas, including intellect, academic aptitude, creative thinking, leadership, and the visual and performing arts. They also can show talent in superior self-knowledge and interpersonal relationships.

2. Heredity plays a major role in intellectual giftedness, but the full development of the student who is gifted depends on his or her environmental context, strong encouragement, and support from family and social groups.

3. Longitudinal studies indicate that most children who are gifted are healthy and well adjusted and achieve well into adulthood. There are some exceptions (called underachievers).

4. A series of international comparisons of U.S. students with students from other countries in mathematics and science revealed even top-level U.S. students lag behind top-level students of other countries.

5. The great differences in the motivation, experience, and family and cultural backgrounds of students who are gifted require flexibility in the schools in choosing the appropriate learning environment, content, and cognitive strategies to teach.

6. There are many ways to change the learning environment, all of which can be effective under certain circumstances. Most of the changes include grouping students who are gifted together for learning for part of the school experience.

7. Ability grouping, combined with a differentiated program, has been demonstrated to be an effective strategy that results in improved performance by students who are gifted.

8. Cognitive strategies—problem finding, problem solving, and creativity—are the focus of many special programs for students who are gifted. Effective problem-finding and problem-solving skills depend on the individual's flexible use of his or her knowledge structure.

9. Creativity depends on the individual's capacity for divergent thinking, a willingness to be different, strong motivation, and a favorable context.

10. Society's traditional expectations for girls have limited their willingness and opportunities to succeed and the areas in which they try to succeed.

11. The characteristics of underachievers who are gifted (feelings of inferiority, low self-confidence, expectations of failure) can be modified through carefully planned and intensive educational programs that focus on the child and allow the child to take control of his or her learning.

12. To uncover the abilities of children who are members of cultural subgroups, special identification methods and procedures that depend less on prior knowledge and experience and more on reasoning and creative thinking are necessary.

13. Children with physical and sensory handicaps can be intellectually gifted, but often their abilities are undiscovered because educators do not search for their special talents.

14. Prolonged schooling (perhaps as much as twenty-five years) can create personal and social problems for the individual who is gifted. It also denies society the contributions of that individual while he or she is in school.

Unresolved Issues

1. *Societal love-hate relationships with gifted students.* Many people who support special education for children with disabilities are reluctant to extend special programming to students who are gifted. These people define exceptionality in terms of deficits. They believe that because children who are gifted are not lacking in ability, they warrant no special attention. It is critical that we accept responsibility for these students, a potential source of so many of tomorrow's leaders.

2. *Special teachers and classroom teachers.* One problem facing special educators is the often difficult relationship between the classroom teacher and the special education teacher. Theoretically, they should work together as a team, but personal problems of professional status and authority often create a chasm

between them, ultimately hurting the child who is gifted. A greater effort at collaboration and teamwork is required.

3. *Undiscovered and underutilized talent.* For many reasons, including different cultural values, students who are gifted or potentially gifted are being overlooked in public schools. Standard tests for identification are not helping the situation to any significant degree. We need more and better approaches to discover this hidden talent and, just as important, special programs to enhance it.

4. *Young children who are gifted.* Very little is being done on a systematic basis to help young (preschool) children who are gifted, even though the parents of these children are aware of the need and are asking for help. Most of these children are not allowed to enter public schools before a certain age—whatever their intellectual maturity—and often are unable to go beyond their grade level despite manifest achievements.

Key Terms

brainstorming p. 170
content acceleration p. 161
content enrichment p. 161
content novelty p. 163
content sophistication p. 163
creativity p. 168
curriculum compacting p. 160
divergent thinking p. 170

flexible pacing p. 157
grouping p. 157
knowledge structure p. 167
problem finding p. 165
problem solving p. 165
special courses p. 159
student acceleration p. 170

Questions for Thought

1. How do heredity and environment interact in those with special talents? pp. 132–134

2. What is the significance of Terman's longitudinal study? p. 134

3. From the developmental profiles, list five characteristics each for Zelda and Cranshaw that are associated with giftedness. pp. 141–142

4. In what ways has social bias affected the achievement of girls who are gifted? pp. 145–147

5. According to the longitudinal study conducted by Terman and Oden (1947), four characteristics separate underachievers from achievers. How do these findings compare with the results of the Butler-Por study (1987)? p. 149

6. How might the definition of giftedness differ from culture to culture? How can students who are gifted be discovered in diverse cultural groups? p. 151

7. How does the assimilation approach differ from the pluralistic approach for culturally different students? p. 152

8. What three basic challenges do students who are gifted pose for teachers? p. 156

9. Describe four ways in which teachers can adjust curriculum content to meet the needs of students who are gifted and talented. pp. 160–163

10. What part does practice play in the development of problem-solving skills? p. 165

11. How can teachers use brainstorming to develop divergent thinking? p. 170

12. Briefly explain the six ways to accelerate students described by Stanley. p. 171

References of Special Interest

Bloom, B. (Ed.). (1985). *Developing talent in young people.* New York: Ballantine.
This book describes a major effort to identify factors that influence the development of notable talent in young people. The people studied were 120 world-class performers, including concert pianists, sculptors, research mathematicians, research neurologists, Olympic swimmers, and tennis champions. The book focuses on the long, intensive process of encouragement, nurturing, education, and training that these young people needed to achieve the highest levels of capability in their chosen fields.

Gardner, H. (1985). *Frames of mind: The theory of multiple intelligences.* New York: Basic Books.
This influential book argues that there are many different forms of intelligence: linguistic, musical, logical-mathematical, spatial, bodily-kinesthetic, sense of self, and sense of others. The author describes each form, the reasons he believes it is distinct, and the implications and applications of his theory.

Karnes, F., & Marquardt, R. (1991). *Gifted children and the law.* Dayton, OH: Ohio Psychology Press.
The authors synthesize an extensive array of legal cases filed to ensure the rights of children who are gifted to an appropriate education. Although most observers have long been aware of the use of the courts to obtain appropriate educational services for children with disabilities, a similar attempt with students who are gifted received little publicity until the publication of this volume. The authors cover topics such as mediation, due process, and educational opportunities.

Maker, C. (Ed.). (1993). *Critical issues in gifted education: Programs for the gifted in regular classrooms* (Vol. 3). Austin, TX: Pro-Ed.
A variety of experts explore how to modify a program within the regular classroom for students who are gifted. The emphasis is on school-wide management and programs, classroom management systems and techniques, curriculum differentiation, and so on. These writers follow the current trend to find ways to educate the child who is gifted without using pull-out programs or special classes.

Perkins, D. (1995). *Outsmarting IQ: The emerging science of learnable intelligence.* New York: Free Press.

> This very readable book brings the reader up-to-date on current thinking about the concept of intelligence. Though written for the general reader and containing many interesting examples, the text is well supported with scholarly research. The author views intelligence as composed of a complex combination of *neural intelligence*, inherited abilities; *experiential intelligence*, the range of experiences that a person has had; and *reflective intelligence*, the collection of strategies that a person uses to direct his or her own intellect. Because the last two types of intelligence can be modified, Perkins concludes that people can improve their intelligence, and he has some suggestions about how to achieve that goal.

Ross, p.(Ed.). (1993). *National excellence.* Washington, DC: U.S. Department of Education.

> This report on the current status of the education of students in the United States who are gifted and talented points out that studies have indicated American students fall behind students from other countries in areas such as mathematics and science and that the provisions for such students in the United States are fragmentary and not well supported. Recommendations for improving the situation are included.

Shore, B., Cornell, D., Robinson, A., & Ward, V. (1991). *Recommended practices in gifted education: A critical analysis.* New York: Teachers College Press.

> This volume reviews 101 common practices in use for educating students who are gifted, and it provides a review of the available research to support each practice. The authors also provide implications of the state of knowledge for the implementation of each practice and suggestions about what research is needed to improve the knowledge base for that particular practice. This is destined to be a much-read book because it provides guidance on where the supportable practices are.

Starko, A. (1995). *Creativity in the classroom.* White Plains, NY: Longman.

> This fine review of the theories of creativity contains many useful translations of those theories into practical classroom use. There is a particular attempt to blend changes in process and in instructional strategies with important content ideas. The author's belief that creativity is influenced by culture and surroundings, as well as by the characteristics of the creative person, is a relatively new idea.

Children with Mental Retardation

focusing questions

How do educators define mental retardation?

What are the two major groups of children with mental retardation?

What four areas of instruction generally comprise the special education programs for students with mild or moderate retardation?

How have the regular education initiative (REI) and the push for inclusion influenced the education of children with mental retardation?

How can teachers prepare students with mental retardation to function in the workplace?

Awareness of the existence of children with mental retardation—children who learn more slowly than their agemates and have difficulty adapting to social and educational demands—has been present for centuries, but the exact nature of the condition, its identification, and societal attitudes toward it have been constantly changing. Above all, we are trying to discover what can be done educationally for children and youth with the condition. Ideas about appropriate educational adjustments also have been changing as we add to our knowledge of the condition and what can be done to cure or ameliorate it.

Definition

Definitions of what constitutes learning disabilities or mental retardation are not cast in concrete. As we learn more about a condition and its treatment, we modify how we refer to it and to the individuals the condition affects. Table 5.1 highlights the current definition of mental retardation set forth by the American Association on Mental Retardation (AAMR). It refers to two separate domains where limitations must be found before we refer to a person as having mental retardation. The first is significantly subaverage intellectual functioning existing concurrently with related limitations in two or more of ten separate indicators of adaptive skills. The second domain reflects limitations in adaptive behavior.

Four key assumptions are essential to the definition. Any assessment of an individual needs to take into account

1. Cultural differences in individual circumstances
2. The influence of community environments on the development of adaptive skills
3. Individuals' relative strengths in various domains of development
4. The improvement in life functioning that can occur with appropriate supports.

In short, the context of the child can determine his or her eventual ability to adapt, positively or negatively. It is possible, therefore, for a youngster to be labeled mentally retarded in one city but not in another, if the urban environments are sufficiently different from one another.

INTELLECTUAL SUBNORMALITY

The definition of mental retardation must include retardation in intellectual development and in adaptive behavior.

No definition, no matter how comprehensive, is worth much unless we can translate its abstractions into concrete action. Intellectual subnormality has traditionally been determined by performance on intelligence tests. Children with mental retardation are markedly slower than their agemates in using memory effectively, in association and classifying information, in reasoning, and in making sound judgments—the types of performance measured on intelligence tests. One of the earliest of these tests was developed by Alfred Binet for the express purpose of finding children who were not capable of responding to the traditional education program in France at the turn of the twentieth century.

TABLE 5.1   Definition of Mental Retardation

Mental Retardation refers to substantial limitations in present functioning. It is characterized by significantly subaverage intellectual functioning existing concurrently with related limitations in two or more of the following applicable adaptive skills areas: communication, self-care, home living, social skills, community use, self-direction, health and safety, functional academics, leisure, and work. Mental retardation manifests before age 18.

Application of the Definition

The following four assumptions are essential to the application of the definition:

1. Valid assessment considers cultural and linguistic diversity as well as differences in communication and behavioral factors;
2. The existence of limitations in adaptive skills occurs within the context of community environments typical of the individual's age peers and is indexed to the person's individualized needs for supports;
3. Specific adaptive limitations often coexist with strengths in other adaptive skills or other personal capabilities; and
4. With appropriate supports over a sustained period, the life functioning of the person with mental retardation will generally improve.

Source: R. Luckassson, D. Coulder, E. Polloway, S. Russ, R. Schalock, M. Snell, D. Spitalnik, and I. Stark (1992). *Mental retardation: Definition, classification, and systems of support.* Washington, DC: American Association on Mental Retardation, p. 1.

Later on, individual tests of intelligence developed by David Wechsler (1974) became popular and widely used. Part of the popularity of the Wechsler scales is that they provided for ten subtests (for example, similarities, information, and block design) scale scores that allowed psychologists to develop a profile of the skills of the individual tested and allowed teachers to distinguish between verbal IQ and performance IQ (see chapter 1). Other group tests of intelligence were designed to test large numbers of students in a shorter period of time. Though considerably less expensive than the individual tests, they are also less reliable and less valid and should be used only for screening.

ADAPTIVE BEHAVIOR

The current emphasis on the environment and the context of the child has resulted in an extended attempt to distinguish among various categories of adaptive behavior. Table 5.2 indicates ten areas of adaptive skills that can be described and rated. To be considered to have mental retardation, a child or adult must be significantly

TABLE 5.2 Adaptive Skills and Mental Retardation

Category	Skills
Communication	Skills include the ability to comprehend and express information through symbolic behaviors (e.g., spoken word, written word/ sign language) or nonsymbolic behaviors (e.g., facial expression).
Self-care	Skills involved in toileting, eating, dressing, hygiene, and grooming.
Home-living	Skills related to functioning within a home, which include clothing care, housekeeping, food preparation, and home safety.
Social	Skills related to social exchanges with other individuals, including initiating interacting and terminating interaction with others; responding to pertinent situational cues; recognizing feelings.
Community use	Skills related to the appropriate use of community resources, including traveling in the community; shopping at stores and markets; purchasing or obtaining services (e.g., gas stations, doctor's and dentist's offices; using public transportation and public facilities.
Self-direction	Skills related to making choices; following a schedule; initiating activities appropriate to the setting; completing necessary or required tasks.
Health and safety	Skills related to maintenance of one's health in terms of eating; illness, treatment, and prevention; basic first aid; sexuality; basic safety considerations (e.g., following rules and laws).
Functional academics	Cognitive abilities and skills related to learning at school that also have direct application in one's life (e.g., writing, reading, using basic practical math concepts, awareness of the physical environment and one's health and sexuality).
Leisure	The development of a variety of leisure and recreational interests (i.e., self-entertainment and interactional) that reflect personal preferences and choices.
Work	Skills related to holding a part- or full-time job or jobs in the community in terms of specific job skills, appropriate social behavior, and related work skills (e.g., completion of tasks; awareness of schedules; ability to take criticism and improve skills.

Source: Adapted from R. Luckasson, (Chair) (1992). *Mental Retardation: Definition, Classification and Systems of Support.* Washington, DC: American Association on Mental Retardation, Ad Hoc Committee on Terminology and Classification, pp. 40–41.

deficient in at least two of these areas. This delineation of ten areas of adaptation is much more extensive than past efforts to define adaptive behavior and reflects the growing concern for adaptive skills as a key element in special education programs. Thus, it is possible to have a low IQ score and still possess usable adaptive skills, be self-sufficient in the community, be able to interact reasonably with other citizens, and maintain a part-time or full-time job. Under such circumstances, an individual would still be considered intellectually subnormal but would not be considered mentally retarded.

The identification of ten areas of ability in assessing mental retardation shows the emphasis now put on adaptability.

Whether deficits in adaptive behavior are seen as a key component in the definition of mental retardation or as merely one of the characteristics that many of these children possess, adaptive behavior is a critical element in their adjustment as adults. Bruininks, Thurlow, and Gilman (1987) summarized the available literature and estimated that "20–40 percent of mentally retarded people in various samples and service programs consistently exhibit behaviors that are perceived by others in their environment as serious problems" (p. 76). Further, they observed that "deficiencies in social skills are frequently primary factors in the failure of handicapped individuals to be successfully integrated into community and work settings" (p. 78). These factors of adaptability clearly call for a strong emphasis on the development of constructive social skills and the elimination of maladaptive behaviors as a key part of any educational or training program for these children.

Despite the problems that the AAMR definition poses, most educators and psychologists see the wisdom of using the dual criteria—*intellectual subnormality/developmental delay* and *deficits in adaptive behavior*—as important to identifying mild mental retardation.

LEVELS OF MENTAL RETARDATION

Historically, psychologists and educators have distinguished among levels of intensity of mental retardation by assigning students to various categories (first *idiot*, *imbecile*, and *moron*; later *educable*, *trainable*, and *dependent*; then *mild*, *moderate*, or *severe*). *Mild* indicated development at between one-half and three-fourths of the normal rate; *moderate*, development at about one-half of the normal rate; and *severe*, development at less than one-fourth of normal cognitive growth. Now, what psychologists and educators assess is how well these children are adapting to their environment in the ten categories of adaptability listed in Table 5.2, as well as their level of measurable intelligence.

In addition to degree of severity, mental retardation is defined by whether it has a biological cause.

Although there has been a movement away from the designation of a child by level of development (educable, trainable, and so on), there remains a division of children with mental retardation into one of two groups (Hodapp, Burack, & Zigler, 1990). The *organically injured group* consists of children whose retardation can be attributed to some specific organic damage. The *familial retarded group* consists of individuals whose retardation is not accompanied by any known organic insult. These individuals appear to come predominantly from families at the lower socioeconomic levels, and their problems seem to stem from lack of stimulation or opportunity to learn rather than from, or in addition to, a fundamental defect within the individuals themselves.

The child who is mildly retarded because of delayed mental development has the capacity to develop academically, socially, and vocationally. (© *Jerry Howard/ Positive Images*)

The reason for the division between the organically injured and the familial retarded groups is that evidence seems to indicate that developmental processes are somewhat different for the two groups, and different even in the various subgroups within the organically injured classification. It has been observed, for example, that Down syndrome children are more delayed in language development than in other areas of development, that children with fragile X syndrome seem to have a decline in IQ scores around puberty, and that autistic children have more severe delays in psychosocial development (Dykens & Leckman, 1990).

Although progress within a developmental area such as perceptual-motor skills seems to follow an invariant and orderly path like a regular stairway, the rate at which each child moves along that developmental stairway can vary according to the etiology. Teachers, in particular, need to be alert to the specific developmental patterns to be expected from the etiology of a child with mental retardation. Students in the familial retarded group have problems with understanding and interpreting their context—their surrounding environment. For mental structures to grow, there must be psychological and educational nourishment just as there must be nourishment for physical growth (Sameroff, 1990). Familial retardation, as it reveals itself in the schools, probably represents a combination of lack of experiences plus limited genetic potential (Plomin & McClearn, 1993). The lowest score on an IQ test that a child with an intact, undamaged nervous system (the familial group) would achieve is not zero but about 60 or 70. Any score lower than that is generally a sign of some type of organic pathology.

Biological Factors That Contribute to Mental Retardation

CHROMOSOMAL ABNORMALITIES

The question of how a tiny gene can influence the complex behavior of children and adults has puzzled scientists for many years. The breakthroughs of James Watson and Francis Crick help to explain the functions of DNA and RNA, and it is now possible to provide a general answer to that question. According to McClearn (1993), "Genes influence the proteins that are critical to the functioning of the organ systems that determine behavior" (p. 39). Thus, genes can influence anatomical systems and their functions—the nervous system, sensory systems, musculature, and so on.

Do certain patterns of genes predetermine certain types of behavior? Are we unwittingly automatons driven by mysterious bursts of chemicals? Not really. No particular gene or protein forces a person to drink a glass of whiskey, but some people have a genetic sensitivity to ethanol that may increase their tendency to become alcoholics if they drink a lot. The relationship between genes and behavior is complex, and environmental influences are almost always an important factor.

According to Plomin, DeFries, and McClearn (1980), human genetic abnormalities are common, involving as many as half of all human fertilizations. They don't show up in the general population because most genetic abnormalities result in early spontaneous abortion. About 1 in 200 fetuses with genetic abnormalities survives until birth, but many of these infants die soon after they are born. So although many deviations occur, most are never seen. More than 100 genetic disorders have been identified. Fortunately, most of them are relatively rare. Here we look at three of the most common ones: Down syndrome, phenylketonuria, and fragile X syndrome.

Down Syndrome

One of the most common and easily recognized genetic disorders is **Down syndrome.** This condition was one of the first to be linked to a genetic abnormality (Lejeune, Gautier, & Turpin, 1959). People with Down syndrome have forty-seven chromosomes instead of the normal forty-six (see Figure 5.1). The condition in most instances leads to mild or moderate mental retardation and a variety of hearing, skeletal, and heart problems. The presence of Down syndrome is related to maternal age; the incidence increases significantly in children born to mothers age 35 and older. According to current figures, more than 50 percent of children with Down syndrome are born to mothers older than 35. We do not know exactly why age is related to the condition. We do know, however, that the mother is not the exclusive source of the extra chromosome. The father contributes the extra chromosome in 20 to 25 percent of all cases (Abroms & Bennett, 1980). The age of the father does not seem as significant as the age of the mother.

Figure 5.1
Chromosomal
Pattern of a Girl
with Down
Syndrome,
with an Extra
Chromosome
in Pair 21

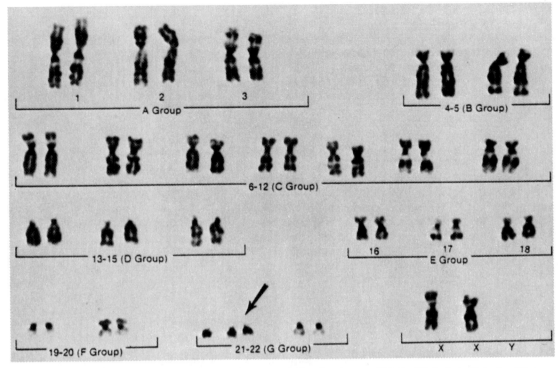

Source: From "The Child with Down Syndrome," by S. Pueschel (1983), in *Developmental-Behavioral Pediatrics* by M. Levine, W. Carey, A. Crocker, and R. Gross (Eds.). Philadelphia: Saunders. Copyright 1983 by W. B. Saunders & Co. Reprinted by permission.

Down syndrome can also be caused by a chromosomal abnormality called *translocation*. The child may have forty-six chromosomes, but one pair breaks, and the broken part fuses to another chromosome. The incidence of Down syndrome is from 1 to 2 of 1,000 births.

Before the 1970s, the diagnosis of Down syndrome and a number of other pathological conditions was not made until the child was born or even later. **Amniocentesis,** a procedure for drawing a sample of amniotic fluid (the fluid that surrounds the fetus in the uterus) from the pregnant woman, has made earlier diagnosis possible. Fetal cells in the fluid are analyzed for chromosomal abnormality by **karyotyping,** a process in which a picture of chromosomal patterns is prepared (see Figure 5.1). Tests of prenatal maternal alpha-fetoprotein and ultrasonography can also reveal the presence of a fetus with Down syndrome. Such early diagnosis has posed a major dilemma for families and physicians (Pueschal, 1991). It allows parents to decide whether the pregnancy should be terminated. The decision is not an easy one, generating questions about the right to life and genetic selection.

The effects of Down syndrome extend well beyond the child's early development. Research shows that persons with Down syndrome are at substantial risk in later years for Alzheimer's disease and dementia. Systematic efforts to prevent or control this later risk have yet to be made (Epstein, 1988).

Figure 5.2
Children with Down Syndrome
Before and After Plastic Surgery

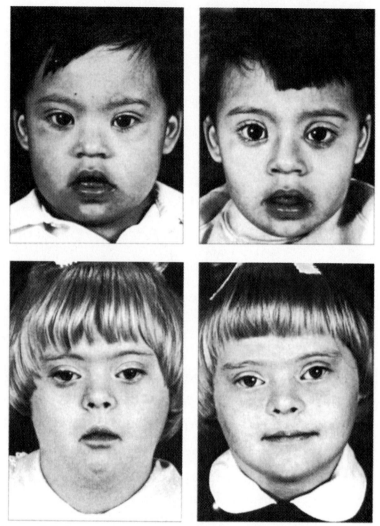

Source: C. Turkington, Special talents, *Psychology Today* (September 1987), pp. 42–46.

Part of the context of the child with Down syndrome is the distinctive physical appearance of the child, which may evoke negative responses from other children and adults. Recently, suggestions have been made for plastic surgery to remove some of the distinctive physical features (see Figure 5.2).

Phenylketonuria

Normal growth and development in the embryo and fetus depend on the production of enzymes at the right time and place. When enzymes are not produced or fail to perform their normal functions, a number of conditions can result.

These conditions are called *inborn errors of metabolism*. One of them is **phenylketonuria (PKU)**, a single-gene defect that can produce severe retardation. In PKU the absence of a specific enzyme in the liver leads to a buildup of the amino acid *phenylalanine*.

The effects of PKU and other metabolic disorders such as hyperthyroidism can be controlled by modifying the child's nutritional intake. But such modification must begin early in infancy. Fortunately, the conditions can be detected in the newborn's blood.

Fragile X Syndrome

Prenatal tests can now determine if a fetus has any genetic abnormalities.

Although basically undiscovered until 1969, **fragile X syndrome** (so named because of a constriction near the end of the X chromosome) is now recognized as one of the leading causes of mental retardation and developmental disabilities (Bailey & Nelson, in press). Its most serious influence is on males, although females can carry the genetic basis for the disorder. Girls seem not generally affected in general IQ scores, as are males, but girls may reveal specific learning disabilities in their school performance.

The major effect of fragile X syndrome is impaired intellectual performance. A study of 250 males with the syndrome found only 13 percent with IQ scores over 70, and there was a tendency for the IQ scores of males with this disorder to decline in measured ability over time (Hagerman et al., 1990). Some physical characteristics that appear with the syndrome include a slightly larger-than-normal head together with a long, narrow face, loose connective tissue, and a high, arched palate. Such physical anomalies do not show up until two years or more after birth.

There is considerable diversity in the behavior patterns of children with fragile X syndrome. But there are consistent problems with social relationships, delays in communication skills, and marked tendencies toward perseveration or repetition of words or phrases.

TOXIC AGENTS

The remarkable system whereby a pregnant mother transmits nutrients through the umbilical cord to her fetus is also the highway by which many damaging substances can pass to the developing child. Our increasing ability to monitor fetal development and the rapidly growing body of research from studies of animals have raised concerns about the effects on the unborn child of substances ingested by the mother. A **teratogen** (from the Greek, meaning "monster creating") is a substance that adversely affects fetal development. Drugs (including alcohol) and cigarette smoke are prime examples of teratogens. The heavy use of alcohol or other drugs creates a prenatal and postnatal environmental context that is unfavorable for the infant's and child's early development.

Fetal Alcohol Syndrome

For centuries we have been generally aware of the unfavorable effects that alcohol consumption by the mother has on her unborn child. But only in the past few decades have those general concerns been replaced by specific statistics and

According to the "least restrictive environment" principle, children should be moved from the mainstream of education only as far as necessary to meet their special needs. (© *Lydia Gans*)

FAS is a leading cause of organic mental retardation.

detailed descriptions of the consequences of what is now referred to as **fetal alcohol syndrome (FAS)**. Most of these findings have stirred even more alarm and concern.

Obviously, not every fetus is affected by maternal drinking; otherwise we would be awash with children with fetal alcohol syndrome (FAS), however, it is sufficiently prevalent to be a major cause of concern. Also, milder effects of alcohol consumption during pregnancy, known as *fetal alcohol effects (FAE)*, include distractibility and hyperactivity, which may go unnoticed because they do not have FAS's catastrophic impact on the child.

One of the distressing aspects of FAS is that it directly affects the development of the brain, and its results last long into adulthood. FAS is currently considered one of the leading causes of moderate or severe organic mental retardation (Menke, McClead, & Hansen, 1991).

Heavy Metals

Ingesting heavy metals such as lead, cadmium, and mercury can result in severe consequences including mental retardation. Most attention is currently focused on lead, and much of the lead that enters the brain comes from the atmosphere. One of the most effective steps that has been taken, on a societal level, was the reduction of lead amounts permitted in gasoline. This reduction resulted in a lowering by one-third of the average lead levels in the blood of U.S. men, women, and children. This reduction in lead levels paralleled the declining use of leaded gasoline (Mahafey, Roberts, & Murphy, 1982).

Also, legislation has restricted the use of lead in paint and mandated that lead paint be removed from the walls and ceilings of older homes—a common source of lead poisoning in youngsters. Some children are born with high levels of lead in their blood (prenatal exposure to lead can be determined by examining the umbilical cord). On tests of intelligence, these children scored 8 percent below children who had lower levels of lead in their blood (Bellinger, Levitan, Waternaux, Needleman, & Rabinowitz, 1987). Children, who will place anything in their mouths, are known to ingest peeling paint chips with some regularity. Davis (1988) pointed out that good nutrition can prevent lead-related damage by reducing lead absorption in the body. The susceptibility of many children from low economic backgrounds to lead poisoning may, in part, reflect a combination of poor nutrition and the greater availability of lead in their environment, another contextual feature. Also, medications can be prescribed which can have the effect of flushing the system of lead, once it has been discovered (Pueschel, Scola, Weidenman, & Bemeer, 1995).

INFECTIONS

The brain begins to develop about three weeks after fertilization. Over the next several weeks, the central nervous system is highly susceptible to disease. If the mother contracts **rubella** (German measles) during this time, her child will likely be born with mental retardation and other serious birth defects. Children and adults are at risk of brain damage from viruses that produce high fevers, which, in turn, destroy brain cells. Encephalitis is one virus of this type. Fortunately it is rare, as are other viruses like it.

One of the viruses that is having an enormous effect on the entire world in the last decades of the twentieth century is acquired immune deficiency syndrome (AIDS). As the name implies, this virus interferes with the body's immune system, allowing it to become vulnerable to a host of fatal infections that the body is normally able to ward off (Scola, 1991). The AIDS virus is spread through sexual contact with an infected person, through exposure to infected blood or blood products, and from an infected mother to her child before and during birth. At this writing, there is no known cure.

Although the presence of HIV, the virus that causes AIDS, is often a death sentence to adults, it is not certain whether the same discouraging statement can be said about children with HIV. Many individual cases, however, demonstrate that children with the virus can become mentally retarded, although the extent to which this occurs is not yet known. What is known is that children with AIDS and their families need massive help from the health and educational communities.

The Family and Other Environmental Factors That Affect Mental Retardation

There has long been an enormous gap between what we know about the brain and its function and the set of behavioral symptoms by which we define mental retardation. With current advances in our understanding of the central nervous system, however, we are able to make some reasonable assumptions about the links between that system and behavior. Huttenlocher (1988) suggested that experience influences the development and maintenance of certain structures in the brain. The implications here are exciting. If the development of the nervous system is not preset at fertilization by genetic factors, the nervous system can grow and change as the individual experiences new things. This means that environment and human interactions can play a role in neurological and hence intellectual development.

Sameroff (1990) raised the issue of possible biosocial influences on the child, or the effect of the interaction of the environment with the biological state of the child. He pointed out that many children with birth complications actually grow up to show no evidence of their unhappy start, and he concluded that "social conditions were much better predictors of outcome for those children than either their early biological status, as measured by birth and pregnancy complications, or their psychological status, as measured by developmental scales" (p. 95).

When children who tested in the "low" or "mentally retarded" range as preschoolers are retested at ages 10 to 12, the correlation between the two measurements tends to be very high. Researchers have often interpreted this high correlation as an indication of the consistency with which the slow developmental rate of intellectual growth is maintained. When Sameroff tested the influences of external environment over time, he found similarly high or higher correlations between the preschool child's unfavorable environmental conditions and the preadolescent's environmental conditions. So the environmental conditions that the child experienced were as consistent as the measurements taken of the child's intellectual performance. Sameroff observed (1990):

> When predictions on how children will turn out are based on their early behavior, the predictions are generally wrong. When such predictions are based on their life circumstances, the predictions are generally right. In this domain, an understanding of the context may have greater developmental importance than an understanding of the child. (p. 97)

Sameroff (1990) identified a set of ten environmental risk factors (such as breadwinner employed in unskilled work, poor maternal health). Only in families with *multiple risk factors* did the child's competence seem to be in jeopardy. The multiple pressures of (1) the amount of stress from the environment, (2) the family's resources for coping with that stress, (3) the number of children who must share those resources, and (4) the parents' flexibility in understanding and dealing with their children play a role in fostering or hindering the child's intellectual and social competencies.

The family's role in creating the context or environment in which the child with mental retardation grows up depends on whether the child is in the organically injured or the familial retarded group. When the child is at the low end of the intellectual distribution but is without observable pathology, the family often creates a context in which poor education, poverty, and a barren neighborhood create additional problems for the child, who in turn creates problems for the teachers trying to educate him or her.

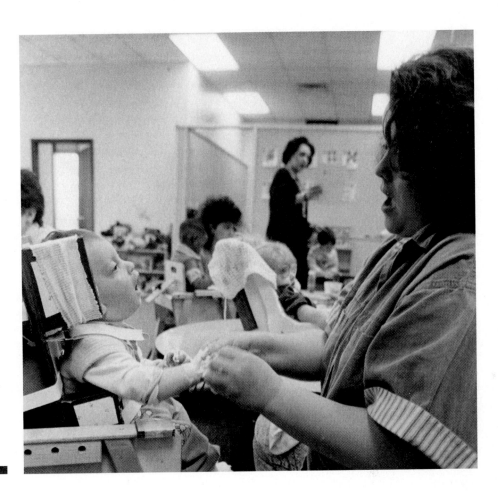

Researchers have shown that early childhood intervention can lead to modest but meaningful changes in children's development. (© Patrick Watson/The Image Works)

Respite care is one of the simplest and most effective aids to families.

The impact on the family of having a child with mental retardation can be great. Some families seem to mourn the death of the child-that-was-to-be and go through a period of grief (Farber, 1986). The stress that families experience is evident in an increased rate of divorce in families with a child with retardation or other handicaps (Bristol, 1987). There are numerous accounts of the problems that families suffer from (Turnbull & Turnbull, 1994), but not all families collapse. The majority of families seem to be able to cope well if they receive reasonable professional support services and support from extended families and friends (Bristol, Gallagher, & Schopler, 1988).

One of the strategies that professionals use to help families cope with the extra stress that often accompanies living with children with disabilities is respite care. **Respite care** is the provision of child-care services so that the parents are freed, for a few days, of their constant care responsibilities. Parents who may not have had a "day off" from child-care responsibilities for years greatly appreciate such assistance. Respite care is an effective way of reducing parental depression and stress and enabling parents to be more effective in their role (Botuck & Winsberg, 1991).

With organized training programs and support services, many young people with retardation can adjust well in employment and community settings. (© *Frank Siteman/The Picture Cube*)

Characteristics of Children with Retardation

Special programming for children with mild and moderate retardation is shaped in part by the characteristics that distinguish these children from their agemates. There are marked differences in factors linked to level of intellectual development, such as the ability to process information, the ability to acquire and use language, and emotional development.

ABILITY TO PROCESS INFORMATION

To help children learn, we must know how they process information.

The most obvious characteristic of children who are mildly or moderately retarded is their limited cognitive ability—a limitation that inevitably shows up in their academic work. These children may lag by two to five grades, particularly in language-related subjects (reading, language arts). To help children who are not learning effectively, we must understand what is preventing them from learning. To do this, we must understand how they think—how they process information.

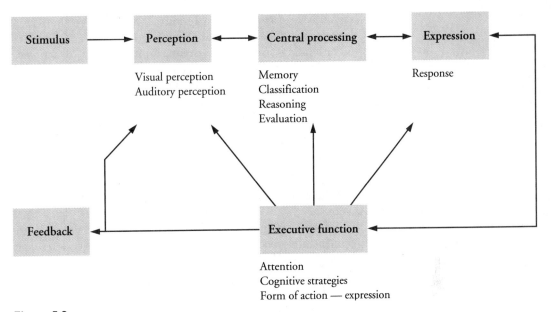

Figure 5.3
The Components of Information Processing

We look at how children with retardation process information to identify the areas that are most affected. Does the child's inability to learn stem from an inability to perceive stimuli effectively? Does the difficulty lie with the child's problem-solving abilities? Does the child lack expressive skills? Is the child's executive function operating? Or does the child have problems in all of these dimensions? The components of information processing are shown in Figure 5.3.

Many children who are retarded have problems in **central processing**, or the classification of a stimulus through the use of memory, reasoning, and evaluation. *Classification*— the organization of information—seems to be a special problem for children who are mentally retarded. School-age children quickly learn to cluster (or group) events or things into useful classes: A chair, a table, and a sofa become "furniture"; an apple, a peach, and a pear become "fruit." Children who are retarded are less able to group things. They have difficulty telling how a train and an automobile are alike.

Memory, another central-processing function noted in Figure 5.3, is also difficult for children who are retarded. Memory problems can stem from poor initial perception or poor judgment about applying what has been stored to a given situation. Most children use "rehearsal" as a memory aid, saying a string of words or a poem to themselves until they remember it. Children with retardation are less likely to rehearse information because their ability to use short-term memory appears limited.

Executive function—the decision-making element that controls reception, central processing, and expression—is one key factor in the poor performance of children who are mentally retarded (Baumeister & Brooks, 1981; Sternberg, 1982; Borkowski & Day, 1987). It is not so much that these children cannot perceive a stimulus as it is that they cannot pay attention to the relevant aspects of a problem. It is not so much that they cannot reason as it is that they do not have the metathinking strategies to organize information to a point where reasoning can take place. And it is not so much that they do not have a repertoire of responses as it is that they too often choose an inappropriate response. Their teachers often say that they lack good judgment.

For these children, learning problems are not limited to a specific cognitive function; instead, the whole information-processing system substantially breaks down. Most children whose IQ score is 50 or lower suffer from neurological damage that can make information processing very difficult.

ABILITY TO ACQUIRE AND USE LANGUAGE

Children with mental retardation seem to have a general deficit in language development and specific problems using interpretative language. Researchers do not know how much of language delay is due to impaired cognitive abilities. Does the development of language in mentally retarded children follow the same sequence of development as it does in other children but at a slower rate? Or are there qualitative differences in the development of language in those who are mentally retarded? Evidence appears to support both positions.

The language of children who are mildly retarded is sparse in structure and content. The problems in language development for children with moderate retardation tend to be much more severe. In addition to slow development, problems stem from the neurological or physiological cause of the retardation. Damage to the brain, for example, can have a devastating effect on a child's language development.

EMOTIONAL PROBLEMS AND SOCIAL ACCEPTANCE

For many years there has been a modest understanding of the link between emotional and social problems and the condition of mental retardation. But what that link signifies and what should be done about it remain issues of some dispute (Korinek & Polloway, 1993). We know that emotional and social difficulties can undermine vocational and community adjustment. We are also aware that emotional and behavioral problems probably lower the level of social acceptance experienced by children with mental retardation in comparison with their peers in the classroom. It is entirely possible that this low level of social acceptance is related to the behavioral and social problems rather than to the condition of mental retardation itself.

Certain skills appear to be important for social acceptance. They include sharing, turn-taking, smiling, attending, and following directions. A person with social competence uses such skills appropriately in social situations. Despite the widespread acknowledgment of the problems of social adaptation and social skills development that confront young mentally retarded students, however, individualized education programs often do not address those problems. McBride and Forgnone (1985) found that less than 5 percent of the IEP objectives written for middle school students with mild retardation reflected either a career vocational or a social behavioral emphasis. This situation seems particularly serious in light of research indicating that a minority of the graduates of programs for students with mild mental retardation are employed (Edgar, 1988; Wagner et al., 1991). We may be missing a real opportunity to help others make good adjustments to adulthood.

Korinek and Polloway (1993) have called for a major emphasis in the curriculum on the development of social skills and social competencies. This means a goal not only to improve social adaptability in order to increase academic efficiency, but also to develop social skills for their own sake and because of their importance in adult adjustment. Indeed, students who do not have social skills are ill prepared to adapt to the inclusive classroom or school. One serious remaining problem involves the specific curriculum for teaching social skills. How can such a program fit into the regular classroom activities and objectives? If most of the general students have already learned these skills without specific instruction, then how can the teacher take the time to engage in this training with just a handful of students with mental retardation?

Developmental Profiles

Figure 5.4 shows the developmental profiles of Bob, a child with mild familial retardation, and Carol, a child with moderate organic retardation. Both children are 10 years old. The patterns revealed in the figure are not unusual for children of their intellectual development, although individual differences from one child to another within each of these groups may be great.

Bob's physical profile (height, weight, motor coordination) does not differ markedly from the profiles of others in his age group. But in academic areas such as reading, arithmetic, and spelling, Bob is performing three and four grades below his age group. Depending on his classmates and the levels at which they are performing, Bob would fall at the bottom of the regular class group or be placed in a special program in a resource room or special class. Bob's mobility, vision, and hearing are average, but he is having problems with interpersonal relationships. Although he is a likable boy under nonthreatening conditions, he is quick to take offense and fight on the playground. In the classroom he has a tendency to interrupt other children at their work and to wander aimlessly around the room when given an individual assignment. All of these characteristics add up to a situation in which Bob has only a few friends, although he is tolerated by his classmates. With special help, he is able to maintain a marginal performance within the regular class.

Carol is moderately retarded and has a much more serious adaptive problem. Her development is at the level of a 4-year-old (her IQ score is in the 40s). Like many other children with Down syndrome, she shows poor motor coordination and some minor vision and hearing problems that complicate her educational adaptation.

Carol's developmental profile shows that her academic performance is well below first-grade level; indeed, at maturity, Carol's reading and arithmetic skills

Figure 5.4

Profiles of Two Children with Mental Retardation

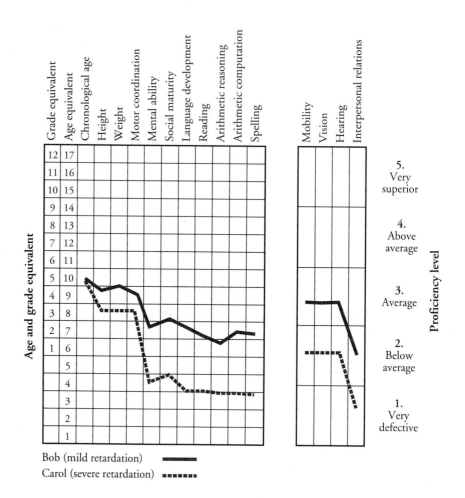

Bob (mild retardation) ▬▬▬▬
Carol (severe retardation) ▪▪▪▪▪▪▪

may not exceed a first- or second-grade level. She can learn important skills or concepts in an educational setting, but the standard academic program is clearly inappropriate for her. To develop her capabilities to their maximum potential, Carol will need some special experiences with specially trained personnel.

Prevention of Mental Retardation

As we learn more about the causes of mental retardation, we are in a better position to prevent it. Scott and Carran (1987) described three levels of prevention: *primary*, *secondary*, and *tertiary*. Table 5.3 lists objectives for each level and strategies for achieving them.

Primary prevention focuses on the developing fetus. The objective is to reduce the number of children born mentally retarded or with conditions that could lead to mental retardation. Good prenatal care—teaching pregnant women about the dangers of drugs, alcohol, and smoking, for example—is one important strategy.

Jon Will's Aptitudes

Jon Will, the oldest of my four children, turns 21 this week and on this birthday, as on every other workday, he will commute by subway to his job delivering mail and being useful in other ways at the National Institutes of Health. Jon is a taxpayer, which serves him right: he voted for Bill Clinton (although he was partial to Pat Buchanan in the primaries).

The fact that Jon is striding into a productive adulthood with a spring in his step and Baltimore's Orioles on his mind is a consummation that could not have been confidently predicted when he was born. Then a doctor told his parents that their first decision must be whether or not to take Jon home. Surely 21 years later fewer doctors suggest to parents of handicapped newborns that the parental instinct of instant love should be tentative or attenuated, or that their commitment to nurturing is merely a matter of choice, even a question of convenience.

Jon has Down syndrome, a chromosomal defect involving varying degrees of mental retardation and physical abnormalities. Jon lost, at the instant he was conceived, one of life's lotteries, but he also was lucky: his physical abnormalities do not impede his vitality and his retardation is not so severe that it interferes with life's essential joys—receiving love, returning it, and reading baseball box scores.

One must mind one's language when speaking of people like Jon. He does not "suffer from" Down syndrome. It is an affliction, but he is happy—as happy as the Orioles' stumbling start this season will permit. You may well say that being happy is easy now that ESPN exists. Jon would agree. But happiness is a species of talent, for which some people have superior aptitudes.

Jon's many aptitudes far exceed those few that were dogmatically ascribed to people like him not long ago. He was born when scientific and social understanding relevant to him was expanding dramatically. We know much more about genetically based problems than we did when, in the early 1950s, James Watson and Francis Crick published their discoveries concerning the structure of DNA, the hereditary molecule, thereby beginning the cracking of the genetic code. Jon was born the year before *Roe* v. *Wade* and just as prenatal genetic tests were becoming routine. Because of advancing science and declining morals, there are fewer people like Jon than there should be. And just in Jon's generation much has been learned about unlocking the hitherto unimagined potential of the retarded. This begins with early intervention in the form of infant stimulation. Jon began going off to school when he was three months old.

Because Down syndrome is determined at conception and leaves its imprint in every cell of the person's body, it raises what philosophers call ontological questions. It seems mistaken to say that Jon is less than he would be without Down syndrome. When a child suffers a mentally limiting injury after birth we wonder sadly about what might have been. But a Down person's life never had any other trajectory. Jon was Jon from conception on. He has seen a brother two years younger surpass him in size, get a driver's license and leave for college, and although Jon would be forgiven for shaking his fist at the universe, he has been equable. I believe his serenity is grounded in his sense that he is a complete Jon and that is that.

SHADOW OF LONELINESS

Some of life's pleasures, such as the delights of literature, are not accessible to Jon, but his most poignant problem is that he is just like everyone else, only a bit more so. A shadow of loneliness, an irreducible apartness from others, is inseparable from the fact of individual existence. This entails a sense of incompleteness—we *are* social creatures—that can be assuaged by marriage and other friendships, in the intimacy of which people speak their hearts and minds. Listen to the wisdom whispered by common locutions: We speak of "unburdening ourselves" when we talk with those to whom we talk most freely.

Now, try to imagine being prevented, by mental retardation and by physical impediments to clear articulation, from putting down, through conversation, many burdens attendant on personhood. The shadow of loneliness must often be somewhat darker, the sense of apartness more acute, the sense of incompleteness more aching for people like Jon. Their ability to articulate is, even more than for everyone else, often not commensurate with their abilities to think and feel, to be curious and amused, and to yearn.

Because of Jon's problems of articulation, I marvel at his casual everyday courage in coping with a world that often is uncomprehending. He is intensely interested in major league baseball umpires, and is a friend of a few of them. I think he is fascinated by their ability to make themselves understood, by vigorous gestures, all the way to the back row of the bleachers. From his season-ticket seat behind the Orioles dugout, Jon relishes rhubarbs, but I have never seen him really angry. The closest he comes is exasperation leavened by resignation. It is an interesting commentary on the human condition that one aspect of Jon's abnormality—a facet of his disability—is the fact that he is gentleness straight through. But must we ascribe a sweet soul to a defective chromosome? Let us just say that Jon is an adornment to a world increasingly stained by anger acted out.

Like many handicapped people, Jon frequently depends on the kindness of strangers. He almost invariably received it, partly because Americans are, by and large, nice, and because Jon is, too. He was born on his father's birthday, a gift that keeps on giving.

Source: George F. Will, "Jon Will's Aptitudes," *Newsweek,* May 3, 1993, p. 70.

---

commentary

What Is the Context? This article discusses Jon Will's capabilities, wants, and joys as he progresses from the inner circle of family to the outer circle of society. His father describes Jon's abilities and inabilities, joys, and frustrations but above all shows how Jon's life is simple but whole. Jon copes with a difficulty to articulate his thoughts by showing resolve and gentleness in adversity.

Pivotal Issues. What does the author value about Jon and his abilities? How is Jon's personality affected by Down syndrome? How has the way Jon's family raised him affected Jon's current abilities and attitudes? How does Jon's love of baseball give a sense of wholeness to his life? Now that Jon has reached adulthood, what does he contribute to society, and in what other ways might he contribute?

Genetic counseling for couples whose children are at risk is another. Research is essential to finding causes of, and possible treatments for, conditions that can lead to retardation. The effects of rubella, for example, have been largely eliminated through antibody screening and immunization programs (Crocker & Nelson, 1983).

The objective of *secondary prevention* is to identify and change environmental conditions that could lead to retardation. By screening newborns for PKU, we can

TABLE 5.3	Preventing Mental Retardation

Prevention Level	Objective	Strategy
Primary	Fewer children born with mental retardation	Prenatal care Genetic counseling Scientific research Improved family planning
Secondary	Early identification and effective treatment	Intensive neonatal care Parental education Long-term social services Screening Diet management
Tertiary	Adaptations to achieve maximum potential and highest quality of life	Increased educational and social services over lifespan

Source: Adapted from K. Scott and D. Carran (1987), The epidemiology and prevention of mental retardation, *American Psychologist* 42(8), pp. 801–804. Used by permission.

begin treatment and prevent retardation. By eliminating sources of lead, we can reduce brain damage from lead poisoning. By providing youngsters from disadvantaged homes with strong preschool programs, we can begin to counteract the elements that can cause environmental retardation.

Tertiary prevention focuses on arranging the educational and social environment so that people who are born with or who develop mental retardation can achieve their maximum potential and highest quality of life.

While biomedical scientists have been looking for genetic and metabolic causes of moderate and severe retardation, social and behavioral scientists have been concentrating on mild mental retardation. They reason that if environmental context, family context, and social factors can have an unfavorable impact on the child's early development and lead to retardation, then reversing or preventing harmful conditions could reduce the intellectual subnormality and poor adaptive behavior that led to a classification of mild mental retardation. (Recall our discussion of early intervention in Chapter 3.)

Early intervention projects approach the problem in the same way. They start with youngsters who seem to be at risk for retardation at an early age and try to sharpen their perceptual abilities, encourage the use of expressive language, and give practice in classification and reasoning. Some urge parents to continue and extend these activities at home. All attempt to strengthen the thinking processes of young children who are delayed in development, and all succeed to a degree. Preschool programs with strong staff and valid objectives can make a modest positive difference in intellectual and social growth, but they are not a cure-all in the face of continuing poverty, hunger, and social disorganization in the home.

Primary prevention of mental retardation occurs before birth, secondary prevention occurs in early childhood, and tertiary prevention occurs throughout the lifespan.

Educational Adaptations

Organized attempts to help children who learn slowly began less than two hundred years ago, when Jean Itard, a French physician, tried to educate a young boy who had lived by himself in the woods—the so-called Wild Boy of Aveyron. Although Itard failed to achieve all of his objectives, one of his students, Edward Seguin, later developed Itard's approaches and became an acknowledged leader of the movement to help mentally retarded children and adults.

Political turmoil in Europe brought Seguin to the United States in 1848. His work had a marked effect on this country's efforts to provide education for mentally retarded children. Over the years, the care and education of children who have mental retardation has moved gradually from large state institutions to the public schools and within the schools to the least restrictive environment.

One other person worth noting is Maria Montessori (1912), who worked with retarded children in the physiological tradition, using what is now called *sense training*. Her work was so successful that her teachings were applied to the teaching of young normal children. Today she is best known for her educational play materials and methods, even though her original work was with children who were retarded.

Since the 1970s, thanks to major investments in research by the federal government, there have been significant advances in discoveries and attempts to find ways to aid in the development of the children with disabilities and in the support available to their families (see Chapter 2). The context in which children with mental retardation have been growing up has also changed. The context of modern life, with its increasing emphasis on advanced education and complex understandings, has not always been kind or favorable to children and adults with mental retardation. Opportunities for employment seem to be shrinking at the same time that acceptance of such individuals as a part of our society appears to be growing.

Probably no exceptional children have been more affected by the various educational reform movements than have children with mental retardation, and it is in this rapidly changing context that we discuss the educational needs of these youngsters and strategies to meet those needs.

IDENTIFICATION

The IEP has brought both positive and negative effects to the education of children with mental retardation.

The first step in adapting the standard educational program to meet the needs of children with mental retardation is to identify those children who need special help. How does a child find special education services? Although referrals can come from many different sources, most students with mental retardation come to the attention of special education services because they fail in school. The inability of the child to adapt academically or socially to the expected standards of his or her age group sets off alarm bells in the teacher and calls for action.

Until recently, the response to such alarm bells was a diagnostic examination by the school psychologist to determine if the child was eligible for some form of special education. Now, many school systems use a *prereferral team*, which includes the classroom teacher, the principal, someone from special education, and relevant other special personnel. The team tries to see if it can help the classroom teacher devise some adaptation of the regular classroom program to cope with the student's problems without more intensive (and more expensive) intervention (Chalfant, 1989). If the student makes no apparent gain as a result of the recommendations of the prereferral team, the child may be referred for more detailed diagnostic examination by the psychologist and, if found eligible, placed in more intensive special education services with an individualized education program decided by the IEP team working with the child's parents.

The diagnostic examination assesses the child's intellectual development and adaptive behavior, the two key elements in the AAMR definition of mental retardation (see Table 5.1 on p. 180). The individual intelligence test remains the most common instrument used to determine intellectual subnormality. A student whose scores fall below those of 98 percent of his or her agemates is considered intellectually subnormal, unless cultural differences call these results into question.

Adaptive behavior is more difficult to assess because behavior can differ depending on the environment. Adaptive rating scales may indicate that a child is adapting well to the larger environment, but the child is acting out in the classroom. The Adaptive Behavior Scales of the American Association on Mental Deficiency (AAMD) and the Adaptive Behavior Inventory for Children (ABIC) measure adaptation to the community (Leland, 1991). Most children do well on these and similar scales because they are not asked to perform academically and constraints on their behavior are minimal. But a total measure of adaptation should measure how well students respond in the school environment, where they spend five or six hours a day, five days a week. The school edition of the AAMR scale does focus on behavior in the school setting (Lambert & Windmiller, 1981; Salvia & Ysseldyke, 1988) and therefore may be the more appropriate measure to use.

An addition to the measures of adaptive behavior has been the Vineland Adaptive Behavior Scales (Sparrow, Balla, & Cicchetti, 1984). The scale covers four domains and appears to have good reliability and validity:

Despite the availability of formal tools to assess adaptive behavior, assessment may still depend on the judgment of teacher and counselor.

1. *Communication:* What the individual understands (receptive), says (expressive), and reads and writes (written)

2. *Daily living skills:* How the individual eats, dresses, and practices personal hygiene; performs household tasks (domestic); and uses his or her time, money, telephone, and job skills (community)

3. *Socialization:* How the individual interacts with others, plays, uses leisure time, and demonstrates sensitivity and responsibility to others

4. *Motor:* How the individual uses arms and legs for movement and coordination and uses hands and fingers to manipulate objects (Leland, 1991)

Despite the availability of such formal tools for assessing adaptive behavior, the school assessment may still depend on the judgment of teachers and other educators who have had direct experience with the child.

Many of the current methods of identifying children with retardation are based on medical procedures for diagnosis, which include identification, diagnosis, and treatment. Today, many educators want to bypass most of the diagnostic and classification procedures and get right to work educating the child.

As Forness and Kavale (1984) pointed out: "The essential diagnosis of a child's needs usually takes place only *after* the special education teacher or resource specialist has worked with the child in the special or regular classroom over a period of weeks" (p. 243).

Fuchs and Deno (1992) introduced an interesting alternative to the use of intelligence or aptitude tests to determine the student's performance level. Their curriculum-based measurement uses readings from various textbooks and asks students to read aloud from a hundred-word passage from the text. The number of words said correctly in one minute is the index of performance of the student. A variety of texts of differing levels of difficulty can fix the approximate reading level of the child. Such a simple method seems to correlate highly with standard measures of reading skills. It also provides the teacher with a clear sense of the student's developmental level of reading. If the teacher uses material of several grade levels to determine the proper reading level for the student, then the teacher should be able to adjust the difficulty level of the lessons that he or she provides to the student.

DIFFERENTIAL PROGRAMMING

How should the educational program be adapted to meet the needs of children with mental retardation? One intriguing aspect of the reform movement for inclusion is that it highlights principles of interpersonal interaction that are designed for life in the larger society. Proponents of inclusion wish the child with disabilities to be welcomed into a community of equals in the classroom, no one to speak disparagingly about others, everyone to be helpful to one another, and no one to be put down by others because of an inability to do certain things. But can such a philosophy of fairness and love be implemented in the school as we know it, particularly when the school has a number of competing academic goals that may make achieving such interpersonal goals difficult? Implementation would be particularly difficult in the absence of support personnel to assist the classroom teacher, who otherwise would have to bear sole responsibility for inculcating such values.

Stainback, Stainback, and Johnson (1992, p. 13) describe the way inclusion should be. Teachers in inclusive classrooms should be able to call on reading specialists, compensatory education personnel, students in the classroom, school counselors, physical and speech therapists, other classroom teachers, math and science teachers, and a variety of other people to provide suggestions or participate in the classroom to make classes more flexible and relevant to the needs of all students.

Those who worry about a terrible traffic jam as these counselors, special teachers, and psychologists bump into one another trying to get to the classroom teacher need not be concerned just yet. The availability of these personnel is uncertain, to say the least. It is not the ideals of inclusion that are being argued, but the ability to achieve or implement them. All three of the major areas of change—learning environments, curriculum content, and skills mastery—seem to require attention for students with mental retardations.

INDIVIDUALIZED EDUCATION PROGRAMS

One of the first efforts to develop long-range plans for child and family came forth from the Individualized Education Program (IEP), mandated in 1975 by the Education for All Handicapped Children Act (PL 94-142) to increase the collaboration between professionals and parents and to ensure some thoughtful consideration about how children would be served within the special education program (Gallagher, 1972). Although that program was an attempt to marshal educational resources to meet the needs of special children, many potential community and agency resources were not drawn into the process. Consider, for example, the transition from school to community and the supports that are needed to help students reach a healthy adaptation to work and life.

A new concept in use for children with mental retardation is the development of social supports that are necessary to help the individual move toward independence and interdependence in the community. They may include everything from financial planning, to technology assistance, to carpooling, to mobility training.

LEARNING ENVIRONMENTS

Regular Classroom

In special education, it often appears necessary to change the learning environment to provide the special curriculum or skills required to meet students' special needs. According to the "least restrictive environment" principle, the child should be moved from the mainstream of education only as far as necessary to meet those needs. Nevertheless, many students continue to be removed from the regular program for part or all of the school day, and that practice has generated major controversy within and outside special education.

Teacher Consultants or Facilitators

Just about everybody agrees that simply placing a child with special needs into a regular classroom, without making additional and necessary resources available to the classroom teacher, is a recipe for failure. A *support facilitator* may be used to encourage and organize support networks for the child with special needs, to serve as a resource locator for the regular classroom teacher, or to play the role of *team teacher*. A support facilitator can help broaden regular education curriculum:

> The curriculum in mainstream education requires expansion to meet the needs of all students. Curriculum areas, such as daily life and community living skills, competitive and supportive employment, sign language, braille, speech reading, and other similar areas, need to become an inherent part of regular education. (Stainback & Stainback, 1988, p. 76)

TABLE 5.4   Arguments For and Against Integrating Regular and Special Education

In Favor of Integration	Against Integration
Special students are not clearly defined: Trying to distinguish students eligible for special education from those who are not eligible can be extremely problematic.	Students with special needs require a differentiated program and different lessons to fit their level and style of learning—which they will not get from integration.
When students are categorized by the term *mentally retarded* or other labels, the label gains attention; we tend to forget that the child is a human being, with many desirable qualities, and instead focus on the label.	Integration has not demonstrated effective results; its arguments are persuasive but not yet backed by evidence.
The presence of a dual system fosters inappropriate attitudes among both groups of students; these students can be viewed as special charity cases because of their special condition.	Integration is strictly a special education invention; few regular education personnel support this effort.

Statements like that, as well as the following, may be making regular educators somewhat nervous about the implications of the regular education initiative (see Table 5.4) or inclusion, given the diverse responsibilities that they have already:

> Because a student cannot read, multiply, or write does not necessarily preclude the functionality of, and importance of, him or her taking core regular education high school courses such as science, history, and literature. (Stainback & Stainback, 1988, p. 81)

Few high school teachers would willingly take into their science or history classes students who could not read or write, even if doing so were socially beneficial for these students.

The acceptance of any new child into a classroom group is rarely an easy process. When various characteristics make a child discernibly different from the other children, as a child's special needs would, then the task requires special attention. Therefore, the mainstream placement of Bob or Carol needs careful planning.

A device that seems to encourage children to develop an accepting attitude toward a child with special needs is the use of Circles. Figure 5.5 shows a sample dialogue that might take place as a facilitator tries to prepare the way for May, the new child. Read the dialogue carefully. You will see that the facilitator (1) acknowledges May's differences; (2) accepts the child; and (3) allows the students time to express their own ideas of how to facilitate the acceptance.

Nor is the task done when the initial acceptance has been completed. May is not an easy person to get along with, and the children in the classroom may react negatively to her; these negative feelings must then be counteracted. The use of team learning strategies such as cooperative learning can foster feelings of acceptance and belonging (Johnson & Johnson, 1986).

Figure 5.5

Circles of Friends: A Support Network

Consultant (C): Hi. I've come to talk to you about May, who is coming to your class next week. You met her last week when she visited with her mother. For years, May has gone to a segregated school or been in a self-contained life skills class. What does that mean?

Students (S): Places for retarded people.

Schools for kids who are really bad.

Like the one near my house where all the wheelchairs go.

C: Well, May is coming here and I'll tell you a secret. Everyone is really scared. Her mother and father are scared, Mr. Gorman [teacher] is scared. Mr. Cullen [principal] is scared. I'm scared. Why do you think all of us are so scared?

S: You all think we'll be mean to her.

You think we'll tease her and be mean to her.

You think she'll be left out.

C: There are some things we don't want you to do when she arrives. What do you think these are?

S: Don't treat her like a baby.

Don't pity her.

Don't ignore her.

Don't feel sorry for her.

C: Why are we doing this? Why is May coming to this class?

S: Why not? She's our age, she should be here.

How would you feel if you were 12 and never were with kids your own age?

It's dumb for her not to be here.

She needs friends.

She needs a boy friend.

C: What do you think we want you to do?

S: Treat her like one of us.

Make her feel welcome.

Help her make friends.

Help her with her work.

Call her and invite her to our parties.

C: I want to switch gears for a few minutes and ask you to all do an exercise with me called "circle of friends." I do this very same thing with teachers and parents and I think you are all grown up enough to handle it.

(The consultant handed out a sheet with four concentric circles on it. After the first circle, each circle was a little larger and farther away from the center of the page, where a stick person was drawn.)

There are four circles. On each circle, you are to list people you know. I want you to think about whom you would put in your first circle. These are the people closest to you, the people you really love. You can do this privately or in pairs, and you can tell us or keep it private.

Source: M. Forest and E. Lusthaus (1989). From "Promoting Educational Equality for All Students," *Educating All Students in the Mainstream of Regular Education,* edited by S. Stainback, W. Stainback and M. Forest. Reprinted by permission of Paul H. Brookes Publishing Co.

There is also the task of helping May adopt more constructive coping skills. It is the rare classroom teacher who has the training or the time to devote to such objectives. This calls for a team of professionals working together.

Resource Room

A resource room provides children with mild or moderate retardation an opportunity to work with special education teachers and focus on particular learning problems that are interfering with their performance in the regular classroom. These children leave the classroom for about an hour a day to take part in special lessons. The number of children in the resource room at any one time is usually much less than the number in the regular classroom, giving the resource room teacher an opportunity to work individually or in small groups with children who are retarded. In some schools, resource room programs combine other children with mild handicaps who are at a comparable developmental level with the children with mild retardation, allowing the teacher to plan for them in small groups. Although the resource room has come under increasing criticism, it still is a highly popular model for delivering special educational services (16th Annual Report to Congress, 1994).

Special Classes

The greater the degree of disability, the more likely is a child to need a special learning environment to learn distinctively different material. In the special class, a trained teacher provides a distinctive curriculum for a small group of children, typically no more than fifteen. The curriculum may include exercises in personal grooming, safety, preprimary reading skills, or any subject not appropriate for the normally developing child in the regular classroom but highly appropriate for a child like Carol, whose cognitive development is half or less of what is normal for her age. The argument against the special class is that such a setting does not allow for social interaction with general education students.

Middle School

The middle school offers students with mental retardation the opportunity to participate in the regular activities of the school and classroom.

One of the rapidly moving educational reforms in U.S. education is the *middle school movement* (George, 1988). The middle school is replacing the junior high school in many school systems. The middle school philosophy places a strong emphasis on counseling and affective education, team teaching with typically a team of four or five teachers for a group of one hundred students, an interdisciplinary curriculum, and often a commitment to mainstreaming children with limited achievement or aptitude into these teams. In many ways, the middle school represents an upward extension of the elementary school even as the junior high school represents a downward extension of the high school.

All of the consequences of this movement for children with mental retardation are not clear, but the middle school does offer the opportunity for such students to participate in the broader school program and to be drawn into the regular program with instructional strategies such as *cooperative learning* (Slavin, 1988;

Kagan, 1988; Johnson & Johnson, 1987), which stress team or group performance and are inclusive of low-ability and low-performing children.

At the secondary school level, special remedial classes or basic skills classes may enroll some mildly retarded children. Both mainstreaming and the resource room strategy appear better suited to the elementary school or the middle school than they do to the secondary school, where the day is divided into separate classes by content field (English, history, math).

CURRICULUM CONTENT

There has been much discussion about the most desirable curriculum for children with mental retardation. Should the content be different from that given to the average child? If so, where in the educational sequence should the branching take place? In secondary school? In middle school? Or should the curriculum be different right from the beginning? The important questions to be answered in the development of curricula for students with mental retardation are, "What are our goals? What are our immediate objectives to reach that goal?"

For students who have moderate or severe retardation, reasonable goals are to learn to read at least to the "survival words" level (*stop, poison, restroom,* and so on); to do basic arithmetic, to understand the various denominations of money; to learn social skills, such as the ability to work cooperatively with others; to have some leisure-time skills; to be able to communicate with persons such as storekeepers and community helpers; and to be able to learn some work skills to be partially or fully self-supporting in adulthood, if possible.

The more difficult curriculum decision involves children with mild mental retardation, who can be expected to reach a medium-to-high elementary school level of skills and knowledge. This decision is particularly difficult if the child is mainstreamed. The curriculum will be the mainstream curriculum—which may or may not meet the needs of the child, except for the social contacts the student will be having in the regular program. Patton (1986) suggested that it is possible to infuse relevant career education topics into regularly assigned lessons. Though possible, such a process would require more knowledge and teamwork between special education and regular education than are often present.

At what point does the student with mild mental retardation branch off into a separate secondary school program that is designed to provide work skills rather than help the student reach the next level of education? Even advocates of the REI do not expect students with mild or moderate retardation to take advanced high school physics or calculus. It is in the secondary program where attention is traditionally paid to community adjustment and work skills.

Oddly, the recent national emphasis on educational excellence may be a special problem for marginal students such as Bob. They may face academic difficulties when confronted with policies that do not tolerate academic mediocrity and insist on a minimal competence level in order to continue in middle school or secondary school programs.

Arithmetic concepts taught to individuals with mental retardation should be related to daily living, such as telling time and using money. (© Paul S. Conklin/ Monkmeyer Press Photo Services, Inc.)

In most programs for children with mild and moderate retardation—particularly for those who are grouped with other students of limited abilities or performance—differential instruction takes place in four major areas:

1. *Readiness and academic skills.* With preschoolers and elementary school children, basic reading and arithmetic skills are stressed. Later these skills are applied to practical work and community settings.

2. *Communication and language development.* The student gets practice in using language to communicate needs and ideas. Specific efforts are directed toward improving memory skills and problem-solving skills at the level of the student's ability.

3. *Socialization.* Specific instruction is provided in self-care and family living skills, beginning at the preschool level with sharing and manners, then gradually developing in secondary school into subjects like grooming, dancing, sex education, and avoiding drug abuse.

4. *Prevocational and vocational skills.* The basis for vocational adjustment through good work habits (promptness, following through on instruction, working cooperatively on group projects) is established. At the secondary level, this curriculum can focus on career education and include part-time job placement and field trips to possible job sites.

We will examine each area separately. Because of current awareness of the value of early intervention, many of these skills are being included in the school curriculum at various levels.

Basic Academic Skills

To develop a curriculum for primary-grade children with mental retardation, we use **task analysis**—breaking down a complex task into simple subtasks that are within the child's abilities. Reading, for example, combines auditory perception (auditory discrimination and sound blending) and visual perception (matching letters and letter-word recognition) (Wolery & Brookfield-Norman, 1988). By helping the child master these basic skills, we are preparing the child to read.

In much the same way, we prepare the child to think about numbers in sets and to match numbers and objects by first teaching the child how to count. And we prepare the child to write by focusing on simple visual-motor activities (imitating a specific stroke, then tracing letters). The process offers dual benefits. First, the subtasks are the source from which academic skills will develop. Second, mastery of the subtasks gives the child with retardation an opportunity to succeed and gain self-confidence.

When we teach reading to Carol and other children with moderate retardation, we focus on functional reading (Snell, 1987). Although these individuals are unlikely to ever read for comprehension or recreation, they need to be able to identify key words in simple recipes, to develop a protective vocabulary (*walk*, *don't walk*, *stop*, *men*, *women*, *in*, *out*), and to recognize the skull and crossbones that denotes poisonous substances (see Table 5.5 for a list of essential words). Traditionally, we use the whole-word method to teach moderately retarded students. It helps them recognize words in context. Students may be asked to "read" television schedules or directions on food boxes or to travel around their community looking for key words.

Children such as Carol, with moderate retardation, are not often taught the formal arithmetic usually presented in the primary grades. They can learn quantitative concepts (*more* and *less*, *big* and *little*) and the elementary vocabulary of quantitative thinking. They can be taught to count to 10 and to identify quantities in small groupings. As they grow older, these children can learn to write numbers from 1 to 10 and understand time concepts, especially the sequence of activities during the day, telling time, and an elemental understanding of the calendar. They often show surprising mastery of television schedules. Some can recognize and remember telephone numbers, their own ages, and simple money concepts. In general, the arithmetic they are taught, like the reading, is related to everyday living.

Language and Communication

There is a substantial effort in elementary schools to help children with moderate retardation use language as a tool for communication. Students may be asked to describe a simple object such as a table (it is round; it is hard; you put things on it;

TABLE 5.5	Survival Words and Phrases		
50 Most Essential Survival Words		**50 Most Essential Survival Phrases**	
1. Poison	26. Ambulance	1. Don't walk	26. Wrong way
2. Danger	27. Girls	2. Fire escape	27. No fires
3. Police	28. Open	3. Fire extinguisher	28. No swimming
4. Emergency	29. Out	4. Do not enter	29. Watch your step
5. Stop	30. Combustible	5. First aid	30. Watch for children
6. Hot	31. Closed	6. Deep water	31. No diving
7. Walk	32. Condemned	7. External use only	32. Stop for pedestrians
8. Caution	33. Up	8. High voltage	33. Post office
9. Exit	34. Blasting	9. No trespassing	34. Slippery when wet
10. Men	35. Gentlemen	10. Railroad crossing	35. Help wanted
11. Women	36. Pull	11. Rest rooms	36. Slow down
12. Warning	37. Down	12. Do not touch	37. Smoking prohibited
13. Entrance	38. Detour	13. Do not use near open flame	38. No admittance
14. Help	39. Gasoline	14. Do not inhale fumes	39. Proceed at your own risk
15. Off	40. Inflammable	15. One way	40. Step down
16. On	41. In	16. Do not cross	41. No parking
17. Explosives	42. Push	17. Do not use near heat	42. Keep closed
18. Flammable	43. Nurse	18. Keep off	43. No turns
19. Doctor	44. Information	19. Keep out	44. Beware of dog
20. Go	45. Lifeguard	20. Exit only	45. School zone
21. Telephone	46. Listen	21. No right turn	46. Dangerous curve
22. Boys	47. Private	22. Keep away	47. Hospital zone
23. Contaminated	48. Quiet	23. Thin ice	48. Out of order
24. Ladies	49. Look	24. Bus stop	49. No smoking
25. Dynamite	50. Wanted	25. No passing	50. Go slow

Source: From "Survival Words for Disabled Readers" by E. A. Polloway and C. H. Polloway (1981). *Academic Therapy, 16*, pp. 446–447. Copyright 1981 by PRO-ED. Reprinted by permission.

it is brown). And they may learn to communicate feelings of happiness, anger, and sadness by using language.

An Israeli educator, Reuven Feuerstein, developed a training program called Instrumental Enrichment (Feuerstein, Rand, Hoffman, & Miller, 1980), which is designed to improve the problem-solving skills of children who are developmentally delayed. The program includes a series of exercises to help children identify the nature of the problem, draw conclusions, and understand relationships. For example,

Draw a square next to the rectangle. ▭

Be sure that the square is not above the triangle. △

This kind of exercise requires students to pay careful attention to directions and relationships.

Feuerstein's program was able to improve the cognitive processes of adolescents, even though most training of this type had focused primarily on preschool and primary-grade children. The assumption was that this kind of training would have little effect on teenagers. Other educators have applied Feuerstein's program in the United States with some encouraging results (Arbitman-Smith, Haywood, & Bransford, 1984).

The functional use of language is a critical goal for children with mental retardation.

Language exercises for children with moderate retardation aim to foster the development of speech and the understanding and use of verbal concepts. Communication skills such as the ability to listen to stories, discuss pictures, and tell about recent experiences are stressed. Two important areas of study are the home and the community. Children learn about holidays, transportation, the months of the year and days of the week, and contributions to home life. Classes make use of dramatization, acting out a story or a song, playing make-believe, engaging in shadow play, and using gestures with songs, stories, and rhymes.

Socialization

Social skills are a critical component of the primary school curriculum for children who are mentally retarded. But instruction at this level should be informal. Children can learn to take turns, share, and work cooperatively as part of their daily activities. The lunch table is an excellent location for teaching social skills. Here, youngsters learn table manners as well as how to pass and share food, help others (pouring juice, for example), and wait their turn. The lunch table is also a good place to review the morning's activities and talk about what is planned for the afternoon or the next day. Although the teaching is informal, it is both effective and important to the child's social development.

Children with retardation have difficulty transferring or applying ideas from one setting to another. Thus, we teach needed social skills directly. We do not expect the children to automatically understand these skills and apply them from experience.

Part of the process of growing up in our society is gradually mastering social skills to establish effective communication and relationships with others. We rarely think about these skills because they emerge through adult and peer modeling without our being conscious of them. If we are asked how we meet strangers, break unpleasant news, communicate with someone we haven't seen for a long time, or tell someone that he is intruding on our space and time, it is likely that we will have to think for a while before we can recall the coping strategies that we use without conscious effort. These skills, however, are the lubrication that allows each of us to move smoothly through our daily contacts and tasks. Someone who is markedly deficient or awkward in such skills stands out in a crowd. Many children with mental retardation lack these social skills and need direct instruction in them if they are to establish a useful personal and community adjustment.

Bob, for example, usually got too close to the person he was speaking to. He made the other person uncomfortable but was not aware of this reaction. Through role-playing a number of social situations with Bob and others, the teacher was able to establish that each person has a personal space that is not to be invaded without permission (for example, to kiss an aunt good-bye). Such social rules may seem trivial, but their importance is magnified substantially when they are violated.

It is important that the sense of privacy is established and understood when the child begins to cope with sexual relationships. Parents and other adults worry about the susceptibility of young people with mental retardation to sexual abuse or unwanted sexual contact merely because they lack the skills to fend off others in sexual encounters. The closer the student is brought to the mainstream, the more likely is he or she to have a variety of contacts with members of the opposite sex. Therefore, some type of counseling and role-playing of relationships or situations with the opposite sex are often part of the curriculum for students with mild or moderate retardation.

The **social learning approach** (Bandura, 1989) aims to foster critical thinking and independent action by those with mild retardation. Lesson experiences focus on psychological needs (for self-respect, mastery), physical needs (for sensory stimulation), and physical maintenance and social aspects (dependence, mobility). For example, in the middle school, lesson experiences teaching the importance of economic security could include the following objectives: (1) choosing a job commensurate with skills and interests, (2) locating and acquiring a satisfactory job, (3) maintaining a job, and (4) effectively managing the financial resources earned from a job.

An important issue related to full-inclusion schools is the social status of children with disabilities. In a research project conducted in a large western community, when researchers asked students whom they liked best and whom they liked least in the class, children with disabilities received significantly more negative choices and significantly fewer "liked" choices than children without disabilities in the comparison group (Sale & Carey, 1995). When interpreting these results, we should take care, for they are from a single school system; but they are consistent with previous findings of a relative lack of acceptance of exceptional children. These results remind us that the task of gaining social acceptance for children with disabilities in the inclusive class is not easy and requires special planning.

Prevocational and Work-Study Skills

When students with mental retardation reach middle school, their special education programs often begin to emphasize work skills.

As the child with mild retardation reaches middle school or junior high school, many special education programs focus on the development of work skills. The skills may be related to a specific occupation (assembling transistor radios) or to general work skills (cooperation, punctuality, persistence).

For the preadolescent child, lessons often take the form of prevocational experience, focusing on the knowledge and skills that are the basis for vocational competence. For example,

1. Given a road map, the student can demonstrate the route from one point to another.

2. Given an assigned work task involving two or more students, the participants work together until the task is completed.

3. Given a newspaper, the student demonstrates the ability to find specific information when requested to do so (Kolstoe, 1976).

Such specific, observable behaviors often are the crux of the individualized education programs that must be completed for all children with mental retardation.

Table 5.6 presents important knowledge and skills to be mastered in five areas—consumer economics, occupational knowledge, health, community resources, and government and law. Listed in the table are examples of the concrete and practical knowledge that persons with mental retardation need, such as how to fill out forms, read a city or town map, and get a driver's license. This approach is preferable to teaching generalizations or abstract principles that the child then has to apply to specific situations—a skill in which children with retardation are not proficient. The problem for the teacher comes when other students in the classroom are learning different materials more appropriate for their age level. It takes a good deal of joint planning with the classroom teacher or the middle school teaching team to integrate functional competencies with the standard educational program.

Vocational training focuses on dimensions beyond the job itself: banking and using money, grooming, caring for a car and obtaining insurance, interviewing for jobs, and using leisure time. Adjustment to the work world involves adapting to the demands of life as well as to a specific job.

Some programs try to build a set of vocational skills progressively over time, involving a variety of social agencies in the educational activities. Fundamental activities and skills are taught in a special class setting. Then specific areas of prevocational and vocational training, including on-the-job training, are covered in the adolescent years. Finally, with the help of vocational rehabilitation, attempts are made to provide a useful work experience in either a sheltered workshop facility or a competitive employment setting. This plan has the merit of establishing developmental tasks and long-range goals that those who are moderately retarded can approach step by step.

The recent movement toward the inclusion in regular classes of children who are mildly retarded has created a difficult conflict. As long as children with retardation are in regular classrooms, they are receiving the regular curriculum or some variation of it. But the secondary school curriculum of content subjects (English, history, science) may not be the most appropriate for them. These students could profit more from a program that emphasizes the practical and vocational skills needed for independent living.

USES OF TECHNOLOGY

Instructional technology in the classroom has many possible applications for students with mental retardation, as well as for other students. Table 5.7 lists some instructional uses of computers. Serna and Patton (1989) indicated that the computer can be used for *drill and practice*—in reading and arithmetic particularly—*tutorials, simulations,* and *problem solving.* A disadvantage of using computers is

TABLE 5.6	Model of Junior High School Functional Competency: Examples of Tasks

	Consumer Economics	Occupational Knowledge	Health	Community Resources	Government and Law
Reading	Read an ad for a sale locating name, location, and phone number of store, and price of item	Read a job description	Locate poison control numbers in telephone book	Use telephone book to locate recreational program in community	Locate and read lists of members of state and U.S. Congress
Writing	Fill out a magazine order form completely	Practice writing abbreviations for words	Write a menu for a balanced diet	Write a letter to television station about a program they just canceled	Fill out voter registration card
Speaking, writing, viewing	Discuss saving versus spending money	Discuss reasons why we work	Listen to positive and negative feedback on personal appearance	Call library to find out if it has a certain book	Discuss why we need to vote
Problem-solving	Given $10 for the evening, which activity would you choose: movies, bowling, or pizza	Decide on job environment: inside, outside, desk, travel, etc.	Role-play appropriate behavior for various places (movies, church, restaurant)	Locate the skating rink on a city map and decide the best way to get there	Decide what items have state or local tax
Interpersonal relations	Ask a salesperson for help in purchasing jeans	List questions to ask in job interview	Discuss honesty, trust, and promise; define each	Call skating rink to inquire about hours	Call to find out what precinct you live in
Computation	Compute the sales tax on a pair of jeans	Compute net income	Calculate and compare the prices of hair grooming products	Calculate bus fare to and from the teen center	Calculate the cost of getting a driver's license (fee, gas)

Source: G. Robinson, J. Patton, E. Polloway, and L. Sargent (1989). *Best Practices in Mild Mental Disabilities*. Reston, VA: Council for Exceptional Children. Used by permission.

TABLE 5.7   Computer Applications for Students with Mental Retardation

Type of Use	Description	Features	Cautions
Drill and practice	Reinforces previously learned information and provides student with practice	Many students need extra practice Best used as adjunct to ongoing instruction	Does not teach new concepts Best to have students work independently
Tutorial	Presents new or previously presented material, and then assesses the student's understanding of the information	Additional instruction for those who need more time to grasp concepts	Not the most effective way of presenting new information to special learners
Simulation	Allows students to experience vicariously real-life events that are not easily shown in a traditional setting	Powerful Can provide more concrete examples of abstract concepts	Problems can arise if students do not possess prerequisite knowledge, skills, or both Students may need help in generalizing computer-displayed events to real world
Problem solving	Use of the computer to solve real-life problems; can include programming	Helps students understand problems and the processes needed to solve them	May be too difficult Often requires teacher assistance and monitoring

Source: Adapted from L. Sernal and J. Patton (1989). *Science*. In G. Robinson, J. Patton, E. Polloway, and L. Sargent (Eds.), *Best Practices in Mild Mental Retardation* (Vol. 5). Reston, VA: Council for Exceptional Children, pp. 197–199. Used by permission.

that the teacher cannot merely point to the computer and say, "Bob, go and do your exercises." Students who are retarded need consistent monitoring, and some need considerable instruction in the use of the computer and in the use of some of the simulation and problem-solving programs.

Parette (1991) pointed out that some state-of-the-art *hypermedia*—an information storage and usage design that enables text, graphics, animation, and sound to be combined to suit individual needs—can be adapted for use with children with mental retardation. Such approaches may help students who otherwise would have problems linking ideas and thoughts.

This increasingly available technology can be a valuable adjunct to the well-prepared teacher, particularly when the student becomes stuck in the mastery of a particular skill or set of information. It has the additional social value to students with retardation of signaling their ability to use sophisticated equipment, just as the other students do (Gardner & Bates, 1991).

SKILLS MASTERY

One of the most important questions facing the teachers of children with mental retardation is how to motivate them to learn. There are a lot of reasons for them not to be motivated in school. Bob, for example, comes from a home in which there is little interest in school learning. He is 10 years old and has had a few years' experience in school. But those years have not been full of positive experiences. Bob has known a lot of failure, and failure is a distinct turnoff for most children and adults.

People who believe they are likely to fail can develop a condition known as *learned helplessness*. They think, "I can't do anything about my situation, and I know things are going to turn out badly" (Dweck & Leggett, 1988). Students who experience this feeling tend to avoid situations in which they think they probably will fail. They avoid the very learning situations that they need to experience if they are going to improve their situation. Such individuals need a strong dose of *self-efficacy* (Bandura, 1989)—the belief that they are competent at some tasks. But if failure is their constant diet, then how can they develop feelings of competence? Finding an answer to that question is the basic challenge facing the educator who will work with Bob.

Carol will face a somewhat different situation. Her local school practices inclusion. For nearly all of the students in the school, the fundamental educational goals are learning important information and mastering relevant skills that will enable them to interpret and move about in the world. In order to maximize this goal, students also must learn some proactive social skills and be motivated to learn their lessons, for doing so will improve the likelihood of success in achieving the fundamental goals.

Carol, however, faces a different situation. Many special educators believe that their students' fundamental goal is not the mastery of knowledge or skills but the mastery of adaptive behaviors such as social skills, communication skills, and work skills. After all, they ask, who cares very much if Carol reaches third-grade or fourth-grade mastery of academic skills? What is important is that Carol develop adaptive skills that will serve her well in adulthood and in the world of work. Thus, it is important for Carol to participate in cooperative learning exercises, not necessarily to learn what the other students learn, but to experience positive social interaction and learn how to work constructively with others. Many special educators are less interested in the middle school academic curriculum and more interested in how they can help students like Carol become effective workers.

A large part of the positive experience of school stems from success in learning how to learn and learning how to work constructively with others. Such skills, if they become habits, serve the individual well beyond the school years. So the mastery of social skills becomes a major objective of programs for exceptional children. It is unwise to assume that students with mental retardation absorb these skills any more readily than they do the academic skills that we mentioned earlier.

It is much more likely that teachers need to design activities to help students achieve social-skill goals and replace disruptive behavior such as aggression, excessive talking, and out-of-seat behavior with prosocial skills.

McGinnis and Goldstein (1984) identified a series of prosocial skill areas that teachers need to plan for. We list a few of them here as examples:

Classroom survival skills

- Asking for help
- Following instructions
- Deciding on something to do

Friendship-making skills

- Beginning a conversation
- Offering help to a classmate
- Sharing
- Apologizing

Skills for dealing with feelings

- Knowing your feelings
- Recognizing another's feelings
- Expressing concern for another

Skill alternatives to aggression

- Using self-control
- Problem solving
- Negotiating

Skills for dealing with stress

- Making a complaint
- Dealing with losing
- Reacting to failure
- Dealing with group pressure

One goal of teachers is to help students develop a sense of competence. Self-confidence comes in part from being able to do well the work that is expected of you. The teacher can build students' self-confidence by presenting lessons that are challenging but within the range of their ability to perform.

The teacher also needs a variety of skills that will help her or him to nurture positive, prosocial skills and diminish negative patterns of behavior that a student may be showing. In the next section we describe teaching strategies designed to build these important nonacademic skills.

TEACHING STRATEGIES

Special education draws heavily on learning theory to help children achieve a level of constructive behavior. Many of the learning principles that we use to help children with retardation associate ideas or remember events have been used intuitively in classrooms and families for years. One popular approach, Premack's principle (Premack, 1959) is to attach a wanted but low-probability behavior to a high-probability behavior, which then becomes a positive reinforcer. Practically, the teacher says, "If you clean up your workplace on time, you can do a puzzle or listen to records." (Premack's principle has been called "Grandma's law": "First you eat your vegetables, and then you get dessert.")

The special learning problems that children with mental retardation have require special teaching strategies. Two of these strategies are scaffolding and reciprocal teaching. In **scaffolding** the teacher models the expected behavior and then guides the student through the early stages of understanding. As the student's understanding increases, the teacher gradually withdraws aid (hence the name "scaffolding"). The goal is to have the student internalize the knowledge and operate independently. The goal is unlikely to be reached, however, without the teacher's help and assistance, which is gradually withdrawn (Brown & Palinscar, 1989). For example, in teaching division, the teacher does some problems and talks about the steps she or he is taking. When the student first attempts the problem, the teacher is at hand to prompt but then gradually moves away to allow the student to do the problems on his or her own.

In **reciprocal teaching** small groups of students and teachers take turns leading a discussion on a particular topic. This exercise features four activities: questioning, clarifying, summarizing, and predicting. In this strategy (as in scaffolding) the teacher models how to carry out the activities successfully. The students then imitate the teaching style while the teacher plays the role of the student. In this way students become active players in a role they find enjoyable.

Behavior Modification

Behavior modification is a term describing techniques designed to reduce or eliminate obnoxious or nonadaptive behaviors and to increase the use of socially constructive behaviors. It is based on principles developed by B. F. Skinner (1953), who found that the systematic application of **positive reinforcement** after a behavior tends to increase the likelihood of that behavior occurring in the next similar situation. **Negative reinforcement** (the application of a negative stimulus immediately after a response) causes unwanted behaviors to decrease. The absence of reinforcement, either positive or negative, causes a behavior to disappear or be extinguished. The quickest way to eliminate an unwanted behavior, then, is to ignore it while responding positively to a more acceptable behavior.

The educational strategy here is to arrange the environment so that the particular behavior the teacher wants the child to repeat will occur. When the behavior does occur, it receives a positive reward (food, praise, a token, or some other symbol of recognition). If possible, the teacher does not respond to the unwanted behavior. Gresham (1981) noted a variety of techniques that use these principles:

1. *Differential reinforcement.* **Differential reinforcement** follows the basic behavior modification procedures by rewarding behaviors that are appropriate and ignoring the target behavior (for example, aggressive behavior). In a variation of this approach, the teacher provides rewards if the student can increase the time between displays of unacceptable behavior. If the child is acting out a great deal, the teacher rewards a ten-minute period of acceptable behavior if it reflects an increase in the elapsed time between periods of unacceptable behavior.

2. *Time-out.* **Time-out** is the physical removal of a child from a situation for a period of time, usually immediately after an unwanted response. A child who has shown unacceptable aggressive behavior in the classroom may be asked to leave the classroom or may be moved to a section of the classroom in which he or she is left alone with some reading or work materials, essentially isolated from the group for a period of time. The child is asked to return when he or she feels in control of the unacceptable behavior. This procedure has proved effective in decreasing disruptive, aggressive, and inappropriate social behaviors.

3. *Contingent social reinforcement.* Some teachers who work with young handicapped children use **contingent social reinforcement,** or a token system, to teach appropriate social behavior. Tokens are handed out in response to the appropriate use of certain social skills (greeting another child, borrowing a toy in an acceptable manner). If a child displays unacceptable behavior, tokens may be taken away. Children save tokens and cash them in for toys or time to do a puzzle or play a game. This kind of extrinsic reward program appears to be effective in controlling social behavior within special groups of children and, to some extent, within the context of a mainstreamed class.

The use of behavior modification techniques with exceptional children has helped increase academic response rates and attendance, achievement, and grades and has encouraged verbal interchange and the following of instructions (Sabatino, Miller, & Schmidt, 1981). Despite these positive results, however, the procedures are controversial because they accomplish the goal without the cooperation of the child and thus strike some observers as being overly manipulative.

Intrinsic Motivation

There is general acceptance of the finding that children with mental retardation seem to be motivated more by **extrinsic motivation** (If you are good, I will buy you an ice cream cone) than by **intrinsic motivation** (If you do your homework, you will feel much better about yourself). This finding is translated into educational strategies through the use of various extrinsic rewards—such as positive social reinforcement by means of praise, gold stars, or tokens to be cashed in for toys—

to motivate the student to greater effort. Some, however, maintain that an intrinsic motivational approach is helpful to children with special needs (Switzky & Schultz, 1988). They maintain that children with intrinsic motivation work harder and longer on tasks than do those with extrinsic motivation and that therefore it is important to help instill an attitude of intrinsic motivation in youngsters. The problem with extrinsic motivation, they point out, is that someone will not always be present and ready to give immediate and tangible rewards for proper behavior, and then what will extrinsically motivated youngsters do?

Students who are intrinsically motivated work harder and longer on tasks than do students who are extrinsically motivated.

A number of educators have devised approaches to stimulate intrinsic learning (Feuerstein, Rand, & Hoffman, 1986; Haywood, Brooks, & Burns, 1986). These approaches require extensive modeling of task-intrinsic behavior by the teacher and positive motivation. They attempt to foster in students an active learning style and to correct problem-solving deficits by having the teacher use a mediational teaching style and teach cognitive processes and strategies even if they are not among the students' strong points at the outset.

Counseling

Classroom teachers cannot do everything. They often need the help of support personnel, special educators, counselors, and school psychologists. There are a number of indications that adolescence, for example, is a particularly difficult time for students with retardation. Zetlin and Turner (1985) conducted an eighteen-month study of twenty-five adults with mental retardation and their parents. The subjects, in their twenties and thirties at the time of the study, were asked to reflect on their feelings, attitudes, and problems during their adolescent years. They identified two major concerns—parent-child relationships and identity issues—identified by many adolescents but sharpened and intensified by retardation.

Those adults with mental retardation resented parental protectiveness and reluctance to allow them to venture into new activities, and they became aware of their "differentness" and its effect on their social life. They reported that schoolmates and neighborhood children teased them. At least 84 percent of them had some type of emotional or behavioral reaction in secondary school—drug or alcohol abuse, temper tantrums, destructive behavior, or withdrawal. Zetlin and Turner concluded: "A limited or unclear set of normative expectations by parents as well as the absence of a peer support network available to most non-retarded adolescents seems to have exacerbated adjustment disturbances" (p. 578).

Most schools now recognize that special programs for children with retardation are the responsibility of a team that includes classroom teachers, special education teachers, and other professional personnel working together to help these children learn and adapt.

Cooperative Learning

Interestingly, emphasis has switched from a focus on a one-on-one type of instruction for the individual student with special needs, as represented in the policies for an individualized education program, to the importance of student participation in *cooperative learning* or *team-assisted individualization*. With the inclusion of many children with special needs in regular classrooms has come the need to develop strategies that will help the teacher integrate students with disabilities with the other students. Cooperative learning is one of these strategies. There are many versions of it (Kagan, 1994; Slavin, 1993; Johnson & Johnson, 1992), but all have some characteristics in common.

In **cooperative learning**, the teacher gives a task to a small group of students (typically from four to six), who are expected to complete the task by working cooperatively with one another. The teacher may assign different responsibilities to different members of the group or ask each child to play a specific role (such as recorder, reporter, searcher, or praiser). Although group members are expected to work cooperatively, most advocates of cooperative learning insist that the students be evaluated individually. The child with disabilities may have the same overall objective as other students but be operating with a lower level of task expectations, a reduced workload, or partial participation. As long as the child feels a part of the enterprise, some good social interactions can occur.

Group instruction may actually be more advantageous than one-on-one instruction because of the economy of teacher effort, students learning how to interact with peers, and students learning from peers. Small-group instruction is the mode for the regular classroom if the students are to be mainstreamed (Collins, Gast, Ault, & Wolery, 1991).

Special Olympics

Important additions to overall programs for children with mental retardation have occurred outside the school program. An outstanding example is Special Olympics, begun by Eunice Kennedy Shriver, the sister of former president John F. Kennedy. This program, which conducts competitions in many cities across the United States and holds national and international meets, allows children with disabilities to participate in a type of miniature Olympics with races, field events, and games. This experience allows the children to gain a sense of participation and achievement that they rarely attain elsewhere, particularly in school. Special Olympics receives broad community support and approval and is a bridge between such children and the mainstream society.

Can Special Education Make a Difference?

Researchers have made numerous efforts to assess in students with mental retardation the nature and level of change that accompanies changes in their learning environment, curriculum, or skills mastery. Does the type of learning environment make a difference in the academic achievement, adaptive behavior, or cognitive development of children with mild and moderate retardation? Research findings suggest that changes in the learning environment alone do not make a striking difference. A large number of studies have tested the effectiveness of mainstreaming children with

One outstanding bridge between children with disabilities and mainstream society is the Special Olympics Program. Its national and international meets encourage children with disabling conditions to compete in races, field events, and games. (© *Jonathan A. Meyers*)

mental retardation (Gottleib, Alter, & Gottleib, 1991), but the information derived from such studies is not often educationally significant. The reason is that few of the studies discuss the nature of the program that the students received—and that, surely, is just as important as, if not more important than "where" the student has been placed.

The diversity of programs included under the "mainstreaming" umbrella is probably another reason for the disparity of results obtained. Studies rarely found major differences in academic achievement between students in mainstreamed versus those in special education programs. In addition, there was often poor social acceptance of special education students in the mainstream. We do not know, however, whether there was careful preparation for the entry of children with mental retardation into the classrooms, or whether they were assigned to the classes without the preparation that advocates of mainstreaming insist on.

Intervention programs result in moderate improvement in the development of adaptive behaviors.

Although most of the intervention programs that have been assessed have focused on children with mild mental retardation, some assessments have attempted to test the impact of programs for children with moderate mental retardation as well. In one such program, eleven centers were devoted to the education of children with Down syndrome and other developmental delays in Washington state (Delwein, Fewell, & Pruess, 1985). The eleven centers emphasized enhancing five skill areas: gross motor, fine motor, cognitive, communicative, and social/self-help. The Developmental Sequence Performance Inventory (DSPI), a developmental checklist for children from birth to age 8, was used to test the effectiveness of the program. The children with Down syndrome exceeded developmental expectations in cognitive and communication areas and showed modest progress in the gross and fine motor areas. Only in the social/self-help areas were no substantive developmental gains noted.

It seems that teachers can accelerate developmental trends by giving specific instruction to children with moderate handicaps. This point is echoed by Casto (1987), who reviewed seventy-four intervention studies for all levels of disabling conditions and found evidence supporting the usefulness of special intervention programs for a wide variety of students.

Lifespan Issues

What happens to children with mental retardation when they finish their schooling? Do they find work? At what kinds of jobs? Where do they live? What kinds of support do they need to adapt to society?

TRANSITION FROM SCHOOL TO WORK

In the not-too-distant past, after students with mental retardation left school, little or no information about their progress was available. Today, a growing number of studies indicate how these students are doing in adult life. The news is mixed.

Edgar (1987) found that just five of thirty-nine graduates of programs for mildly retarded students in Washington were working. Sixteen of the graduates were involved in some form of vocational training; twenty-three were doing little or nothing. Another study indicated that fully one-third of mildly retarded teenagers in five major urban areas had no vocational activity at all (Kerachsky & Thornton, 1987). Moreover, lack of coordination among community agencies made it very difficult to see what, if anything, was being done to help these people (Stodden & Boone, 1987).

A major study looking at 8,000 youths with disabilities was begun in 1987—the National Longitudinal Transitional Study of Special Education Students (Wagner et al., 1991). Researchers used a careful sampling design to ensure that their sample was nationally representative and generalizable to the population as a whole as well as to students in eleven disabilities categories. Large samples of youngsters with disabilities from 300 public school districts and from 25 state-operated schools for children who are deaf or blind were surveyed and interviewed. In addition, a subsample of more than 800 parents of youth who had been out of secondary school between two and four years was interviewed.

What happened to youths identified as mentally retarded? Let's look first at performance in secondary school and then at performance in the working world and postsecondary schools.

One indicator of student problems in secondary school is absenteeism. When researchers combined all eleven categories of students with disabilities, they found that 48 percent of the students had been absent *eleven days or more* during a school year. The rate among students with mental retardation was 47 percent. More than 1 out of every 10 students with mental retardation had been retained in grade during the last school year. Sixteen percent of the students with emotional disturbances had been retained in grade during the last school year. Half of the mentally retarded students graduated from high school; the rest either dropped out or aged out of school. The reasons for dropping out of school appeared to be related to behavior rather than to academic performance. Twenty-eight percent of the students with disabilities who dropped out were identified as individuals having serious discipline problems.

What about social relationships? About 1 out of every 4 individuals with mental retardation was identified as a social isolate in school. But the percentage of students with mental retardation who regularly saw friends was no lower than the percentage among those who were visually impaired, speech impaired, or learning disabled. Children with mental retardation were less likely than other students with disabilities to be members of organized groups such as the Boy Scouts or church youth groups or sports teams. Only about 1 out of every 3 of the students with mental retardation was identified as belonging to, or having some regular membership in, a group.

What about the arrest rate of youth with disabilities? Children with mental retardation ranked fourth in the eleven categories of youth with disabilities who were arrested while they were in secondary school, and they ranked fifth in the "out of school" arrest category. Roughly 1 out of every 10 of the school youth with mental retardation had an arrest record. A factor significant to the arrest record was gender: Males were arrested four times more often than females.

What about responsibilities at home? Youth out of school with mental retardation had roughly the same amount of household responsibilities as youth in other disability categories. Although the number of students with mental retardation who were performing in an unsatisfactory fashion was not encouraging, their adaptation seemed to be similar to that of students with disabilities.

What about living independently? In the first or second year after secondary school, fewer students with mental retardation were living independently than were students with other disabilities. For example, 9 percent of the mentally retarded students, 22 percent of the students with learning disabilities, and 26 percent of the visually impaired students were living independently.

Figure 5.6

Employment Rates of Youth with Disabilities and with Mental Retardation

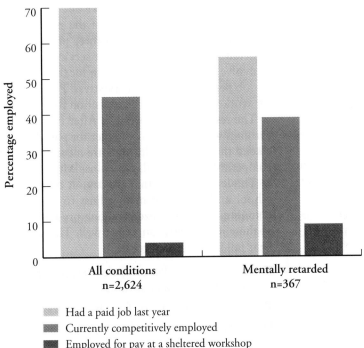

Had a paid job last year
Currently competitively employed
Employed for pay at a sheltered workshop

Source: M. Wagner, L. Newman, R. D'Amico, E. Jay, P. Butler-Nalu, C. Marder, and R. Cox (1991). *Youth with Disabilities: How Are They Doing?* Washington, DC: U. S. Department of Education, Office of Special Education Programs.

TRANSITION TO ADULTHOOD

Figure 5.6 compares the employment rates of people in all eleven categories of disabilities with the rates of people in the specific category of mental retardation. The figure shows that 56 percent of the adults with mental retardation and 70 percent of those in all eleven categories "had a paid job last year." So the mentally retarded are somewhat less likely than others to secure a paid job. But, on the positive side, more than half of these former students did secure a paid job and thus demonstrated their capability to have a productive vocational adaptation.

Figure 5.6 also shows 46 percent of those in the "all conditions" and 28 percent of those in the "mentally retarded" category to be "currently competitively employed." Nevertheless, on the plus side, 1 out of 4 individuals with mental retardation is "currently employed" and another 9 percent are "employed for pay at a sheltered workshop." Such figures highlight the importance of special educational programs in both the vocational/academic and the social domains.

We know that adults with mental retardation want to work and to participate in society. The problem is helping them to do so. Kerachsky and Thornton (1987)

12. By reducing failure, increasing success, and modeling appropriate behaviors, teachers can improve the attitudes and behaviors of children with mild and moderate retardation.

13. Behavior modification and social learning theory are generating teaching strategies to help youngsters with retardation to learn.

14. A strong effort is being made to build intrinsic motivation for students with mental retardation as a way of improving their learning skills when no adults are present.

15. Planning and vocational training are needed to ease the transition from school to work of those with mental retardation.

Unresolved Issues

1. *The culture of poverty.* We still are not sure what factors within the culture of poverty are responsible for the slow development of children with mild retardation. Until we can determine the nature of the problem (lack of motivation, poor language, inattention and hyperactivity, lack of effective adult models), it is difficult to design effective methods for preventing it.

2. *The changing job market.* The future of students with mental retardation depends as much on the environment or context in which they live as on their education and training. The increasing complexity of modern society casts a shadow over the goal of independence for these youngsters, although they may be able to get jobs in the service sector. Do individuals with mild or moderate retardation have a place in a shrinking job market, or will they be part of a "surplus" population?

3. *The resilient family.* Some families are able to adjust to the problem of having a child who is moderately or severely retarded; others are shattered by it. Why? What gives some families the strength to adapt to the stress? There are two quite different approaches to the families of the handicapped: One wants them to be teachers of their children with disabilities; the second stresses professional help and respite care to allow periodic relief from the daily burden of care. Which approach is more appropriate for which families?

4. *Secondary education.* By mainstreaming mildly retarded youngsters at the secondary level, we limit them to a standard curriculum. Yet these students need special instruction in prevocational and survival skills. How do we balance the benefits of mainstreaming against these special vocational needs?

Key Terms

amniocentesis p. 185
behavior modification p. 218
central processing p. 193
contingent social reinforcement p. 219
cooperative learning p. 221

differential reinforcement p. 219
Down syndrome p. 184
executive function p. 193
extrinsic motivation p. 219
fetal alcohol syndrome (FAS) p. 188

fragile X syndrome p. 187
intrinsic motivation p. 219
karyotyping p. 185
mental retardation p. 180
negative reinforcement p. 218
phenylketonuria (PKU) p. 187
positive reinforcement p. 218
reciprocal teaching p. 218

respite care p. 191
rubella p. 189
scaffoldling p. 218
social learning approach p. 212
task analysis p. 209
teratogen p. 187
time-out p. 219

Questions for Thought

1. Why is the concept of adaptive behavior important to identifying mild mental retardation? pp. 180–182

2. Compare the development of children who are mildly retarded with the development of those who are moderately retarded. pp. 182–183

3. How do toxic agents influence the development of mental retardation? p. 187

4. How does the language acquisition of children who are mildly retarded differ from that of children who are not retarded? p. 194

5. What is being done to prevent mental retardation at the primary, secondary, and tertiary levels? pp. 188–189

6. Explain the role of central processing and executive function in information processing. p. 193–194

7. Why is adaptive behavior difficult to assess? p. 199

8. What roles do the prereferral team and the diagnostic examination play in identifying children who need special help? pp. 200–201

9. Describe the usefulness of each of the following environments for students who are mentally retarded: regular classroom, resource room, special class. pp. 203–207

10. What advantage does a middle school approach offer to the student with mild mental retardation? pp. 206–207

11. Describe three methods of behavior modification. p. 219

12. Why is intrinsic motivation important for persons who are mentally retarded? p. 219–220

13. How do intervention programs for mentally retarded children make a long-term difference? pp. 221–223

References of Special Interest

Borkowski, J., & Day, J. (1987). *Cognition in special children: Comparative approaches to retardation, learning disabilities and giftedness.* Norwood, NJ: Ablex.
   This is a synthesis of findings on the cognitive processes of children who are retarded, learning disabled, or gifted. The authors give special attention to how these three

groups differ in processing speed, memory, knowledge structure, problem solving, and metacognition. This work has many implications for educators and for the design of differentiated curricula for these groups.

Bradley, V., Ashbaugh, J., & Blaney, B. (Eds.). (1994). *Creating individual supports for people with developmental disabilities.* Baltimore: Paul H. Brookes Publishing Co.
This work is an attempt to present a new approach to developing individual supports for exceptional children. A push is made for an expanded partnership between many disciplines, for parents to design an individualized program, and for detailing the individualized planning process. The book has chapters written by professionals from different fields to illustrate a fundamental change in service delivery.

Matson, J., & Mulick, J. (1991). *Handbook of mental retardation* (2nd ed.). New York: Pergamon Press.
This is a major volume updating what we know about mental retardation. Forty chapters cover topics under major headings of philosophy of care, social developments, classification, assessment, prevention, treatment, basic cognitive processes, and methodology.

R. Simeonsson (Ed.). (1994). *Risk, resilience and prevention.* Baltimore: Paul H. Brookes Publishing Co.
This is a detailed description of the concept of prevention. Several professionals define what primary prevention is and discuss how to modify service delivery in ways that can enhance primary and secondary prevention. The text covers topics ranging from physical injury and child abuse to internalizing affective disorders and preventing school failures and dropouts.

Stainback, S., & Stainback, W. (1992). *Curriculum considerations in inclusive classrooms.* Baltimore: Paul H. Brookes Publishing Co.
The authors defend the inclusive school movement by presenting suggestions about how the school curriculum should be modified to take into account the presence of children with special needs. They attempt to answer the questions of critics of the inclusive classroom approach by presenting practical suggestions for curriculum adaptations in the classroom for exceptional children.

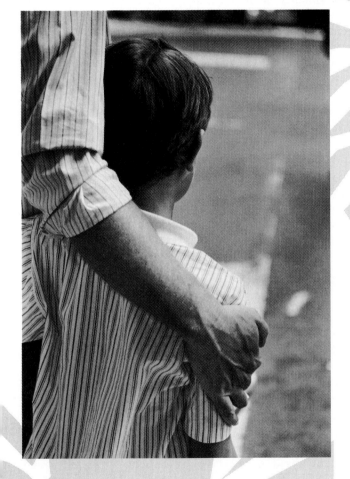

Children with Learning Disabilities

Not all learning problems are learning disabilities.

Perhaps no area of special education is generating so much multidisciplinary research and stimulating so much debate as learning disabilities. Researchers are intrigued by learning disabilities because children who possess them have average or higher intelligence quotient (IQ) scores but do not succeed in areas that the IQ scores predict, particularly in learning how to read and write. Essentially, persons with learning disabilities belie one fundamental assumption about human beings: If you do not experience mental retardation, mental disturbances, visual or hearing impairments, or environmental deprivations, you should be able to do well in school. Why children with learning disabilities do not do well has fascinated and baffled researchers in the fields of reading, cognition, speech and hearing, neurology, learning, vision, audition, and special education in general. Although not all evidence is in, some appealing hypotheses are being discarded for lack of research support, and others are gaining stronger support. What is clear is that there is no one cause of the difficulties experienced by all persons who are said to have learning disabilities. There appear to be multiple causes, and not all children with learning disabilities have the same set of deficits. Most have trouble learning to read and write. Others have trouble with math. Some have trouble with all three.

A Historical Overview

Children who have normal intelligence and no classifiable disability yet do not succeed in school have been a concern to teachers, parents, and researchers, and to the children themselves. Researchers began investigating the causes of the conditions now known as learning disabilities in the 1800s, and research continues today. Poor teaching and lack of effort by the student have been ruled out as causative factors, but many questions remain.

A number of intriguing hypotheses have been proposed to account for the disorder. Orton (1936) believed that the difficulty resides in the failure of the left hemisphere of the brain to take on the role of language as it typically does in human beings. He called students who had difficulty learning "minimally brain damaged." Kirk and Kirk (1971) and Myklebust (1954) perceived the problems as a specific language disorder and followed that line of reasoning in their research. Frostig (1964), Getman (1962), and others investigated perceptual and motor processes as possible factors. Fernald (1943) and Gillingham and Stillman (1960) believed that the disorder is primarily in the area of written language. These differences in opinion produced a fragmented body of research and no consensus among researchers as to the causes of the disorder or what to call it. At a meeting of concerned parents, Samuel Kirk (1966) proposed the term *learning disabilities* to describe the condition, and that term was widely adopted and is still used.

Today most of the older hypotheses about learning disabilities involving brain damage have been abandoned or revised, but the causes of the disorder are still largely unknown (Lyon, 1994; Stanovich, 1986; Torgesen & Wong, 1986). Many researchers are working to devise tests to determine the source of the disorder and curricula to remediate academic problems.

Researchers and parents are supported by organizations such as the Council for Exceptional Children (whose learning disabilities division was founded in 1972), the Orton Society, and the Learning Disabilities Association of America (LDA). These organizations provide a forum for research presentations and debate. They also serve as advocacy groups encouraging legislation such as the Specific Learning Disability Act of 1969 (PL 91-230) and the Individuals with Disabilities Education Act (IDEA) of 1990 (PL 101-476).

■■■ *Definitions*

The label *learning disability* refers to a syndrome and does not describe the specific deficit or dysfunction of the child or the specific academic/achievement problem of the child (National Information Center for Children and Youth with Disabilities [NICHCY], 1994). The label assists persons in identifying and classifying children who need special help.

Children with learning disabilities are children with unusual ways of perceiving the world. Their neurological patterns seem somewhat different from those of children of the same age without disabilities. Persons with learning disabilities have in common some type of failure in school or in the community. They are not able to do what others with the same level of intelligence are able to accomplish.

The *Federal Register* (1977) includes the regulations for identifying and defining students with learning disabilities under the Education for All Handicapped Children Act of 1975 (PL 94-142):

> "Specific learning disability" means a disorder in one or more of basic psychological processes involved in using language, spoken or written, which may manifest itself in an imperfect ability to listen, think, speak, read, write, spell, or to do mathematical calculations. The term includes such conditions as perceptual handicaps, brain injury, minimal brain dysfunction, dyslexia, and developmental aphasia. The term does not include children who have learning problems which are primarily the result of visual, hearing, or motor handicaps, of mental retardation, of emotional disturbance, or of environmental, cultural, or economic disadvantage. (USOE, 1977, p.650)

The *Federal Register* definition has four criteria that teachers must consider when identifying students with learning disabilities:

Learning disabilities are indicated by a great discrepancy between intellectual ability and actual school achievement.

1. *Academic difficulties.* The child with learning disabilities has difficulty learning how to read or do mathematical calculations, compared with other children of the same age.

2. *Discrepancy between potential and achievement.* The child with learning disabilities experiences a serious discrepancy between intellectual ability and achievement in school; this is known as an **aptitude-achievement discrepancy.**

3. *Exclusion of other factors.* A person may not be classified as having learning disabilities if the learning problem is caused by visual or hearing impairments, mental retardation, motor disabilities, emotional disturbance, or environmental factors.

"Learning disabilities" refers to a heterogeneous group of disorders manifested by significant difficulties in acquiring and using listening, speaking, reading, writing, reasoning, or mathematical abilities. (© *Gale Zucker*)

4. *Neuropsychological disorder.* Basic learning disabilities are the result of some type of neuropsychological disorder.

The revised regulations of the Individuals with Disabilities Education Act (IDEA) define "a learning disability in one of more basic psychological processes involved or in using spoken or written language, which may manifest itself in an imperfect ability to listen, think, speak, read, write, spell, or to do mathematical calculations" (NICHCY, 1994).

Summarizing the criteria in PL 94-142 and PL 101-476, one can say that the field can be divided into two distinct areas of activity. Researchers in one seek the source of the difficulty. Researchers in the other try to design curricula and teaching strategies to enable persons with learning disabilities to learn academic subjects in spite of the source of their difficulties.

The National Joint Committee for Learning Disabilities (1991) proposed the following definition:

Learning disabilities is a generic term that refers to a heterogeneous group of disorders that are manifested by significant difficulties in the acquisition and use of listening, speaking, reading, writing, reasoning, or mathematical abilities. These disorders are intrinsic to the individual and are presumed to be due to central nervous system dysfunction. Even though a learning disability may occur concomitantly with other handicapping conditions (e.g., sensory impairment, mental retardation, social and emotional disturbances, insufficient/inappropriate instruction, psychogenic factors), it is not the real result of those conditions or influences. (p.16)

"Central nervous system dysfunction" is currently more commonly called *neuropsychological dysfunctioning* or *differences*. These terms mean that the definition assumes that the brain or perceptional systems or both are not damaged but work in a way that is different from the way they function in children without learning problems. Learning disabilities are suspected to arise out of differences in brain and perceptual functioning rather than from specific damage to these systems.

Both definitions point to the need to present an alternative set of lessons to match the unusual neurological patterns of these children. Much of the special education designed for these children focuses on strategies to help them master lessons they cannot learn from the traditional curriculum.

It is important to bear in mind the following:

■ All children with learning disabilities have learning problems.

■ Not all children with academic problems have learning disabilities.

One should not say, for example, that children with Down syndrome have learning disabilities, although they may need special help because of their lower cognitive abilities caused by the disorder. And children who have trouble learning in academic settings because of the disorganized environment in which they live, or the emotional trauma they have experienced, are not considered by definition to have learning disabilities.

At this time, we can make the following general statements about learning disabilities:

1. *Learning disabilities* is a general term referring to a heterogeneous group of disorders that includes different subgroups.

2. Learning disabilities must be viewed as a problem not only of the school years but also of early childhood and adult life.

3. A learning disability is intrinsic to the individual; the basis of the disorder is presumed to be a central nervous system dysfunction.

4. Learning disabilities may occur with other handicapping conditions as well as within different cultural and linguistic groups (Kavale, Forness, & Bender, 1987, Vol. 1, p. 6).

Prevalence

The U.S. Department of Education reported in 1994 that more than 4 percent of all school-age children received special education for learning disabilities (NICHCY, 1994). Of these children, 54.2 percent were in special education programs; the rest, in regular education classrooms. The distribution in the United

Because reading and arithmetic are similar in many ways (e.g., numbers and words stand for concepts), a child with language difficulty is likely to have difficulty in learning to calculate. (© Alan Carey/ The Image Works)

States is not geographic and varies from state to state. For example, Rhode Island reported that 63 percent of the special education population in the state had learning disabilities; Alabama reported that 26 percent of its special education population had learning disabilities.

The problem with prevalence figures lies in the lack of a uniform definition of learning disabilities across the states and a failure to administer a complex multidisciplinary assessment that encompasses social, genetic, cultural, and educational factors. Because there is no single cause of school failure, some factors have to be ruled out (such as severe hearing impairments or cultural deprivation) before a child is considered as having learning disabilities (Interagency Committee, 1990, p. 140). Currently, the category of learning disabilities contains the largest number of students in special education (Kavale, Forness, & Bender, Vol. 1, 1987). Some schools tend to identify all students in academic trouble as having learning disabilities.

Keep in mind the concept of individual and intra-individual differences when thinking about children with learning disabilities. These children have some disabilities in common, but they may have other disabilities that are idiosyncratic characteristics of only a small subgroup of the population with learning disabilities. Although children in a subgroup may have characteristics in common, they will differ from one another on some dimension, some having several problems and some having only one. For example, Snowling and Perrin (1988) found that some children with learning disabilities had problems in reading, spelling, and writing, whereas others were excellent readers but poor spellers. Learning disabilities may be of a verbal or a nonverbal nature (Rourke, 1995).

Is There a Single Cause?

No one has discovered a single cause of learning disabilities. Rather, studies that focus on subgroups within the larger population of children with learning disabilities have identified some deficits associated with their learning problems (Rourke, 1994; Yule & Rutter, 1979). For example, although visual-perceptual-motor deficits do not appear to be a single cause of learning disabilities when researchers look at a large group overall, they do appear to be a factor for a small sample within the group. Satz, Morrison, and Fletcher (1985) wrote that "virtually all subgroup studies have revealed a subgroup of children with learning disabilities who have relatively intact language processing abilities but impaired performance on visual-perceptual-motor tasks" (p. 34).

Learning disabilities result from a variety of causes.

Research now clearly supports the rejection of a single cause or single deficit. The field recognizes multiple problems and teaches each child, keeping his or her particular deficit clearly in mind. Instruction varies from child to child, depending on the underlying subtype of problems he or she faces.

The search for the cause of a learning disability in one child or in many children is similar to a detective story in which many suspects must be eliminated one after another until the real perpetrator is found. This detective story has multiple solutions, however, as the true cause of learning disabilities for one child can be quite different from that of another child so labeled.

It is one thing to say that something is wrong with the way a child processes information and another thing entirely to expect that the same defect will appear in every child categorized as having a learning disability. Perhaps for one child the problem lies in how visual information available to that child is processed. Perhaps it may lie in auditory perception. Perhaps it is in how the information is stored and how the child organizes stored information. One must assume that every student with learning disabilities must be approached as if his or her problems are unique, idiosyncratic, and personal.

This major detective story is complicated because the child with learning disabilities is likely to have failed frequently in schoolwork in the past, and some of the presenting problems relate to that history of failure and the child's reaction to it as well as to the original condition.

Characteristics of Children with Learning Disabilities

Children with learning disabilities usually do not have difficulty in dressing themselves; they are toilet trained; and, until they begin to fail in school, they apparently are happy. In school they have difficulty making friends (Vaugh, McIntosh,

& Spencer-Rowe, 1991), and they do not seem to hear all that is said or respond quickly to questions (Curtis & Tallal, 1991). They have trouble learning the rules of games, but once they learn them, they insist on strict adherence to them (Valletutti, 1987).

In the literature on learning disabilities, authors have used many negative terms to describe children with learning *disabilities*. These terms, however, are equally descriptive of children with learning *problems*. The main point to keep in mind is that children with learning disabilities have normal intelligence and have difficulty in one or more school subjects—difficulty that is *not* associated with a known disability such as cerebral palsy or mental retardation. It is hoped that the earlier we identify a child with learning disabilities and institute a successful educational program, the less likely are boredom, lack of motivation, and lack of interest to set in. But if a child continues to fail in elementary school, problem behaviors may be established by adolescence.

Classification of Learning Disabilities

Researchers generally take one of two perspectives on learning disabilities: developmental or academic achievement. Those who take a neuropsychological/ developmental perspective seek an underlying cause for students' difficulties in academic subjects. The top part of Figure 6.1 contains the hypothesized neuropsychological/developmental disorders: biological/genetic, perceptual-motor, visual, auditory, memory, and attentional disorders. A large number of researchers are pursuing the source or causes of these disorders (Kavale, Forness, & Bender, Vols. 1–3, 1987, 1988).

Researchers who take the academic perspective investigate the specific problems that students have with the content and processes (executive functions) they need to learn to master academic subjects. The middle part of Figure 6.1 lists the academic areas that teachers are most concerned with: language and reading, writing, spelling, mathematics, and executive functions. A large group of researchers are focusing on how to solve these difficulties by developing teaching strategies and curriculum (see Adelman & Taylor, 1993; Kavale, Forness, & Bender, Vol. 3, 1988).

The developmental-academic model implies that the child with learning disabilities comes to school with a set of developmental problems in processing information. **Developmental learning disabilities** (also called **neuropsychological learning disabilities**) include attention problems, memory problems, and disorders in thinking and using language. These problems are rarely detected before the child enters school because no serious demands are made of the preschool child in these areas. The downward extension of schooling to ages 3 and 4 may result in more systematic observation and earlier identification of such children (see Wolery, 1992).

These developmental learning disabilities lead to **academic/achievement learning disabilities** in reading, spelling, writing, or arithmetic. Again, not everyone who has these academic problems has a learning disability, but a thorough examination can determine the presence of developmental learning disabilities (Lyon, 1994).

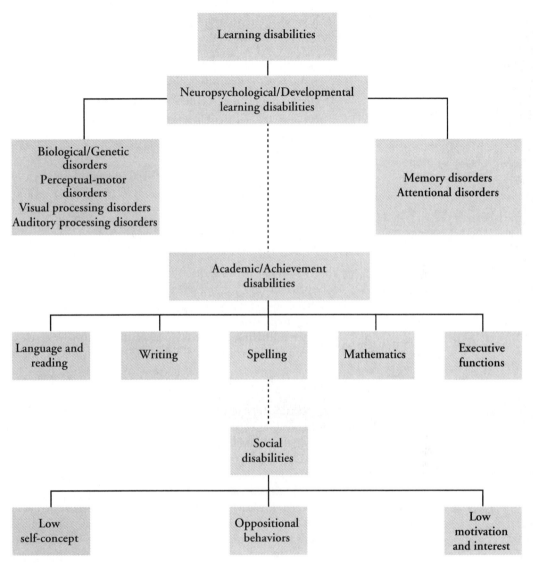

Figure 6.1
Types of Learning Disabilities

NEUROPSYCHOLOGICAL/DEVELOPMENTAL LEARNING DISABILITIES

Inherent in the term *learning disabilities* is the understanding that the disorder or disorders exist in the person, not in the environment. Hence, the first hypotheses proposed that these individuals suffered from brain damage, brain dysfunction, or brain differences resulting in disordered thinking skills, poor memory, poor attentive skills, and challenging behaviors (for example, lack of motivation, passive aggression). The neuropsychological/developmental model assumes that learning disabilities are due to the following:

1. Something wrong with or different in the child's brain or perceptual systems
2. Some type of neurological dysfunction
3. Disturbances in perceptual-motor functioning
4. An imbalance of intelligence abilities and academic achievement from some type of damage to the brain (Kavale, Forness & Bender, Vol. 1, 1987; Rourke, 1994)

Learning disabilities occur within the child, not within the environment.

We have already mentioned that most children with learning disabilities have trouble learning to read. Herein may be the source of many of the disputes about learning disabilities. Learning to read depends on several perceptional systems: vision, hearing (matching one's auditory system to print), attention, previous experience, and so on. Thus, a researcher who pursues one of these topics, may come to assume that one particular disability is the major source of learning disabilities. What is being discovered is that a researcher who makes this assumption is both right and wrong, overgeneralizing that all children with learning disabilities have vision problems, for example, and accurately perceiving that some of them actually do.

In the following sections, we look at attempts by researchers to discover a cause (or causes) of learning disabilities.

Biological and Genetic Explanations

Researchers have reported biological, hereditary, and genetic explanations for some subtypes of learning disabilities. Pennington (1994) demonstrated that some learning disabilities have a genetic base and are inherited. Greschwind (1985) proposed elevated hormone imbalances as a source of learning disabilities. Several researchers have demonstrated relationships between brain damage and some types of learning disabilities (Rourke, 1994).

Note that although it has long been known that persons with damage to the frontal lobe of the brain have problems in planning and using appropriate strategies in solving problems, it is not correct to assume that persons who display these problems have frontal lobe damage. By analogy, if a baseball player who is nearsighted misses a ball hit to him, this does not mean that everyone who fails to catch a fly ball is nearsighted. A player may or may not be nearsighted, just as students with learning disabilities may or may not have brain damage. The student's disability may be a brain dysfunction or a way of operating different from most other children.

Perceptual-Motor Problems

Recall that early researchers perceived perceptual-motor disorders as a major cause of learning disabilities. The hypotheses were that learning disabilities were due to disordered motor skills, perception, perceptional integration, balance, and tactile and kinesthetic disorders (Cruickshank, 1961; Frostig, 1964; Getman, 1964; Gillingham & Stillman, 1960; Kephart, 1964). Many remedial activities were suggested to increase perceptual-motor integration. Modern concern, however, tends to focus on techniques for remediating specific deficits—such as reading, spelling, or mathematical disorders—rather than on activities to increase proposed lacks in body integration. It is "unexpected underachievement" that is at the core of today's thinking about learning disabilities (Lyons, 1994, p. xv).

Visual Processing Deficits

Because reading depends partially on vision, many people assumed that visual deficits are the cause of learning disabilities. Children with visual deficits were observed to have difficulty moving their eyes from left to right to follow printed text, and they moved their eyes frequently back and forth across a line. These visual processing deficits were perceived to signal not a problem in seeing but instead a problem in how visual information was processed in the brain and how the children used their eyes to gain information. Visual processing deficits should not be ignored. Testing for them should be part of the diagnostic process so that children with these deficits can be identified and receive appropriate remediation (Atkinson, 1994; Satz, Morris, & Fletcher, 1987; Swanson, 1987).

Auditory Processing Deficits

Curtis and Tallal (1991), Tallal (1990), and Tallal, Miller, and Fitch (1993) suggested that auditory processing is slower in children with language delays. Language delays are common in children with learning disabilities. These children take longer to process auditory as well as visual information (Blakeslee, 1991). If the information takes longer to get into the short-term memory, it may not get into long-term memory. In addition, these children take longer to respond to questions or to solve problems. They differ from their peers in the rate at which they process sensory information (Tallal & Curtis, 1991). The impairments are perceived to be in the rate of processing (Torgesen, 1988) as well as slower access to long-term memory for response. These deficits have strong educational relevance, as we shall explain later in the chapter.

Memory Disorders

A deficit in auditory processing affects storage in short-term memory (Curtis & Tallal, 1991; Tallal, 1990). The slower auditory processing doesn't allow enough time for information to be entered into short-term memory. Hence much of what is presented to the learner is lost, not entering short-term memory and therefore not transferred to long-term memory (Tallal, Miller, & Fitch, 1993; Vellutino, 1970). The deficit related to learning disabilities appears to occur in semantic memory and affects encoding, cataloging, and recalling information that one has been taught (Mann & Liberman, 1984; Interagency Committee, 1990).

Attentional Deficits and Hyperactivity

It has long been thought that children with learning disabilities have attentional deficits and are easily distracted, impulsive, hyperactive, or poor listeners (Berger, 1978; Krupski, 1986; Torgesen & Licht, 1983). Some of the professionals who

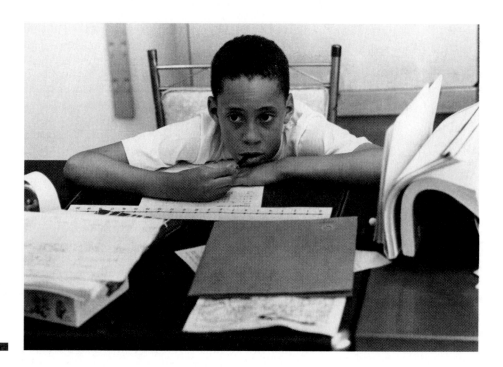

Children with learning disabilities are thought to have attentional deficits and to be easily distracted, impulsive, hyperactive, or poor listeners. (© *Alan Carey/The Image Works*)

Not all persons with learning disabilities have behavioral problems.

identify children as having learning disabilities prefer to regard the condition as an **attention-deficit hyperactivity disorder** (**ADHD**). The *Diagnostic Statistical Manual of Mental Disorders (DSM)* used the term *attention-deficit disorder (ADD)*, but added *ADHD* in the 1980 edition (American Psychiatric Association, 1980). The basic assumption was that attention deficits and **hyperactivity** (impulsivity, acting before thinking, excessive moving about) were the source of the academic problems. Silver (1990) suggested that *learning disability* should be used to describe persons whose brains interfere with their learning, not persons unavailable for learning because of their increased activity and inattention. There is no conclusive evidence that children with learning disorders are fated to develop antisocial behavior. Rourke suggests most students with learning disorders appear to achieve adequate behavioral control (Rourke, 1994).

Those who believe that ADHD causes learning disabilities might agree to use stimulant drugs to calm the individual. The most commonly used stimulants are Ritalin and Dexidrene (Gadov, 1985; Mercer, 1992). Although many professionals in the field of learning disabilities object to the use of these drugs, Forness and Kavale (1988) reported positive results in improving academic learning, and Hallahan, Kauffman, and Lloyd (1985) found that the effect of these drugs in improving learning is conclusively documented. Some believe, however, that the student's failure to learn at the same rate as his or her peers is the source of the behavioral problems.

ACADEMIC/ACHIEVEMENT LEARNING DISABILITIES

Lerner (1993) defined academic/achievement learning disabilities to include deficits in school subjects such as reading, writing, spelling, and mathematics. How to teach these subjects to students with learning disabilities has been the subject of a long debate; there is no general consensus about which model is best.

Language and Reading Disorders

Language disorders is a general term referring to difficulties in listening, speaking, phonological mastery, word recognition, reading, spelling, and writing (see Lyon, 1994, for a discussion of each area and its measurement). The most common difficulty identified for children with learning disabilities is mastery of phonological systems, which leads to deficits in reading, spelling, and writing (Liberman & Shankweller, 1985; Tallal, Miller, & Fitch, 1993).

About 80 percent of children with learning disabilities have difficulty in word and letter recognition or reading comprehension (Lerner, 1993). Becoming a skilled reader is so important in our culture that an unskilled reader is at a great disadvantage in school and the workplace. The following problems may prevent a child with learning disabilities from learning to read:

1. Faulty auditory perception without hearing impairment

2. Slow auditory and visual processing

3. Inability to perceive words (dyslexia)

4. Lack of knowledge of the purpose of reading

5. Failure to attend to critical aspects of the word, sentence, or paragraph

6. Failure to understand that letters represent units of speech (Clark, 1988; Perfetti, 1984; Liberman & Liberman, 1990; Curtis & Tallal, 1991; Goodman, 1976)

Dyslexia

Currently, dyslexia is accepted as a subgroup disorder within the learning disability population, and it has been widely studied (Liberman & Shankweiler, 1977; Deshler, Rudel, & Chapman, 1985; Clark 1988; Gray and Kavenaugh, 1977). The major conclusion is that children with **dyslexia** have a variety of deficits resulting from brain dysfunction (that is, the brain is not damaged, but it operates differently from the brain of a child without dyslexia) (Rourke, 1991).

Children who have been identified and classified as **dyslexic** have a combination of problems learning the relationships between sounds and letters (the abstract code representing sounds). Thus, they have difficulties recognizing letters, learning the names of letters, and breaking words down into the sounds of letters and letter combinations (phonemes); they also have difficulties with spelling and writing (Clark, 1988). In fact, they appear to have problems in all processing information, and the result is serious learning problems across all academic areas. Persons with dyslexia are not mentally retarded (Gray & Kavenaugh, 1985).

In the opinion of many professionals, dyslexia is simply a severe reading disability (Mercer, 1992). The term is still used, however, particularly among those who are medically oriented, and the condition does appear to have a genetic base (Rourke, 1991).

Despite the enormous problems children with dyslexia face, the general consensus among researchers and teachers is that they can learn (Denckla, Rudel, & Chapman, 1985; Clark, 1988). When the diagnosis of *dyslexia* is made in the first two grades, more than 80 percent of the children are brought up to grade level. However, if it is not made until fifth grade, only 10 to 15 percent are helped (Fletcher & Forman, 1994, p. 187).

It is important to remember that not all children with learning disabilities have dyslexia. Dyslexia is an extreme form of learning disability. The term *dyslexia* is overused in the popular press, which gives the inaccurate impression that everyone with reading or literacy problems is dyslexic.

A child with learning disabilities may have one or more academic disorders.

Writing Disorders

A disorder affecting written language is technically termed *agraphia*. The neurological basis is unknown; however, the disorder is known *not* to be associated with *aphasia*, the loss of speech. It is best described as a failure to produce visible, understandable, and legible language reflecting knowledge of the topic being written about (Montgomery et al; 1994, p. 377). It seems that good writers get better with experience and poor writers get worse. Researchers are far from establishing exact criteria defining disorders of written expression (p. 380).

Spelling Disorders

Many children with language and reading problems are poor spellers. However, that is not always the case; some excellent readers are poor spellers (Fisher, Shankweiler, & Liberman, 1985). This finding suggests that the skills involved in spelling and reading may not be entirely connected (Moats, 1994). Moats suggests that prior research has shown spelling to be a complex process that is not simply mechanical. A sign that a child may be learning disabled and not have a learning problem is the ability to read well coupled with poor spelling ability.

Mathematics Disorders

Mathematical learning disabilities have been studied far less than reading difficulties. The technical term *dyscalcula* refers to selective impairment in mathematical thinking or in calculation skills (Fleischner, 1994). Often mathematical learning disability occurs without deficits in reading or in other verbal skills. However, mathematics can be thought of as a language system with numeric symbols instead of words or letters. The brain's mathematic-arithmetic system is located in the same hemisphere as spoken, gestural, and other language systems (Bellugi, 1988). Reading and arithmetic are similar in many ways: Numbers and words stand for concepts; rule systems govern the correct use of the numbers and words, and so on. Thus, a child with a language difficulty may also have difficulty in learning to calculate.

A Student Helps Other Dyslexics

Writer's block was more than a passing problem for Joan Corsiglia. The only way she could write a paper was to cut out each sentence of the laborious first draft, put the sentences on a table like pieces of a jigsaw puzzle and sort them under topics to form coherent paragraphs.

Only when she was a junior at Harvard did she learn why it took her ten times as long as other students to do reading and writing assignments. She had assumed that she was not trying hard enough.

She was diagnosed by tests at the Harvard health office as a dyslexic, one of average or better intelligence who has difficulty learning to read, write and organize language because of abnormal interactions in the brain. But her problems did not stop there. She found that there was no policy of remedial counseling or help, such as untimed exams, for dyslexic students.

"The deans and the tutors congratulated me on my strategies of coping, and the Bureau of Study Skills people told me that my skills were as good as any, but I was concerned that there was no help for students who had the same problems. Two percent of each entering class at Harvard have dyslexia."

The determined student organized a group of students with the same disorder to talk with faculty on what to expect from them and how to accommodate their needs. She turned to the Orton Dyslexia Society for speakers and films about the disorder, which affects some 15 percent of the nation's schoolchildren.

Then, during her senior year at Harvard and while she was preparing for medical school, Corsiglia was tutored by Jean Chall, professor of education at the Harvard Graduate School of Education, and one of her students, Martha Freeman.

Now a third-year medical student at Dartmouth, Corsiglia has helped to develop support policies there for dyslexics. More than 150 educators from 20 colleges met at Dartmouth in mid-April for a symposium that she organized on dyslexia and learning disabilities, and many more were turned away for lack of space.

Corsiglia's success at Harvard and Dartmouth in establishing support policies for dyslexics earned her an award from the New England Branch of the Orton Society at a dinner April 25 to raise $200,000 for dyslexia research. Dr. Drake D. Duane of the Mayo Clinic in Minnesota told her that any medical residency program will be lucky to have such a highly motivated person.

She calls herself lucky to have had so much help from her parents, Joseph and Sharon Corsiglia of Darien, Conn., and teachers who gave her confidence to overcome her learning handicaps.

"My father owns his own business, so his hours were flexible," says Corsiglia. "He and my mother took us to historic sites all over New England on three-day weekends so that we could learn history that way, as well as by reading. He had a horrible time in school, and so did my brothers, but they weren't diagnosed as dyslexic until after I was.

"My biggest thing was how do things work and why things are the way they are. I asked a lot of questions in school." Corsiglia says teachers told her that she was careless with her spelling, although she spent hours memorizing words, but they praised her for good ideas and extensive reports that gave her a chance to build models and do creative artwork to supplement her essays. Her mother checked her homework and sent her to the dictionary. "But my biggest problem was getting as far as the first draft of a paper," she says.

In the ninth grade, teacher Joan Burchenal sparked Corsiglia's interest in biology. She and her husband, Dr. Joseph Burchenal, an oncologist, helped Corsiglia build an incubator in her basement for experiments on the effects of chemotherapeutic drugs for leukemia on chick embryos.

Determination and fascination with learning won high marks for Corsiglia and helped get her into Harvard, but, by her junior year, her coping strategies began to break down. There wasn't enough time to do every assignment over and over again.

Carroll Williams, her biology adviser, was helpful in getting a diagnosis because he has a son with the same disorder. He had recognized the discrepancy between her laboratory work and written work, and encouraged her. She worked in his laboratory on her honors thesis on "Hormonal Control of Molting in the Tobacco Hornworm." "He helped me to get back my confidence," she says.

Another mentor was Martha Freeman, a graduate student of Jeanne Chall's at the Harvard School of Education.

Corsiglia talks of the tutoring given by Martha Freeman. "She set me to reading editorials in the *Boston Globe* and the *New York Times* and writing summaries." Corsiglia says, "Then I had to turn my summaries into paraphrases without going back to the originals." Medical papers and literate essays such as those of Dr. Lewis Thomas' "Lives of a Cell" captured her attention during long hours of tutoring.

Sports are an important outlet for Corsiglia. She runs from 3 to 5 miles a day and makes time for varsity cross-country track as well as skiing, basketball, soccer, tennis and golf.

With her record of advocacy for and interest in dyslexia, Corsiglia has been doing research on the anatomical differences between dyslexic and nondyslexic brains. She has been working with Albert Galaburda, associate professor of neurology at the Harvard Medical School and director of the Orton Society's Dyslexia Neuroanatomical Laboratory at the Beth Israel Hospital. She plans to specialize in neurology and direct her efforts toward research and clinical practice.

"I want to work with patients as well as in the laboratory," she says. "I feel it is terribly important for young people with dyslexia to get help early so that they won't be discouraged from fulfilling their potential."

Source: Phyllis Coons, "A Student Helps Other Dyslexics," *Boston Globe*, June 14, 1987. Reprinted courtesy of The Boston Globe.

commentary

What Is the Context? Joan Corsiglia's support system at Harvard included organized advocacy groups like the Orton Society as well as her family and professors. The supportive context promoted the development of alternative methods of learning and evaluation to accommodate her dyslexia. Joan's experience demonstrates the importance of finding an approach to education that is tailored to the particular needs of students with learning disabilities, that focuses on their strengths rather than their weaknesses.

Pivotal Issues. Discuss the various methods of learning and evaluation that Joan and her teachers used. Why were they effective for Joan? How can teachers learn to adapt their teaching to the needs of individual students with learning disabilities?

Deficits in Executive Function or Cognitive Strategies

To be able to solve the problems that schools present as learning, children must master a set of skills known as **executive function, metacognition,** or **cognitive strategies;** these are the internal processes that children use to select, control, and monitor the strategies they use to solve problems or to learn (Torgesen, 1994). They include monitoring one's behavior, planning how to learn, and self-regulation (keeping oneself on task and not becoming distracted). These strategies are gained from experience, teaching, or learning and are stored in long-term memory. For most adults, they seem automatic. They are the way a person thinks about how to learn. Previous knowledge is essential for appropriate problem solving; for example, one must know the times tables to be able to multiply (Flavall, 1993). Some children with learning disabilities do not possess or do not use these strategies to solve problems and must be taught them (Stone & Conca, 1993; Denckla, 1994).

SOCIAL DISABILITIES

Children with learning disabilities are, by definition, intelligent but have difficulties in learning what the school expects them to learn. This failure, when often repeated, leads to depression, lack of motivation, oppositional behaviors, and a poor self-concept. These side effects are often interpreted to be part of the syndrome of learning disabilities, but evidence suggests that they are not (Rourke, 1994). Children with learning disabilities are likely to attribute their failure to their lack of ability and to lower their feelings of self-esteem (Stone & Conca, 1993).

Some children with learning disabilities may have mild-to-severe disturbances in socioemotional development. Most children with learning disabilities appear to achieve adequate psychosocial adaptation. There is no uniform pattern of personality characteristics, psychological adaptation, social competence, self-concept, or other indicators of socioemotional functioning (Rourke, 1994). Thus, social disorders of children with learning disabilities are *related* to learning disabilities and are not included in the syndrome of learning disabilities (Voeller, 1994).

Teachers can do much to help children with learning disabilities recognize that their academic problems are not due to a lack of effort or intelligence. Early intervention and identification of learning disabilities can do much to decrease social deficits.

■ *Developmental Profiles*

Distinguishing students who are learning disabled from those who have learning problems is not always easy. Individuals in both groups often present similar academic problems.

Learning problems are often confused with learning disabilities.

Ron, a fifth grader, was becoming the classroom clown. His wit and antics were clever and kept the class amused. His achievement was at grade level but with a major dip in spelling (see Figure 6.2). The psychologist's report revealed an IQ score of 179 and equal strengths in verbal and nonverbal scores. The teacher met

Figure 6.2
Developmental Profiles of Two Children

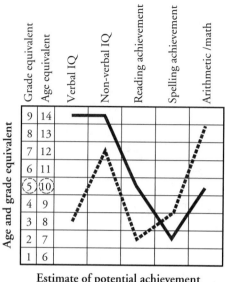

Estimate of potential achievement

Ron (learning problem) ▬▬▬
Yuet (learning disabled) ■■■■■■

with Ron's parents to explore these discrepancies. The meeting revealed intense parental academic pressure at home, strong dissatisfaction with Ron's academic achievement, and a suspicion that Ron might be cognitively delayed. The parents found the intelligence test scores difficult to accept. Each morning the father spent an hour with Ron before school, drilling him on spelling. The parents refused to seek counseling with Ron.

The teacher's greater acceptance of Ron, following the psychologist's report, was reflected in Ron's diminished attention-getting antics and some slight improvement in his reading scores. However, Ron's overall achievement remained well below what his IQ scores seemed to predict. His spelling achievement remained well below grade level. He had a learning problem, not a learning disability.

Yuet, a fifth-grade student, could read only extremely frequently appearing words such as her name, street signs, and the names of comic strip characters. Yet she was a talented artist and an excellent oral problem solver, and she possessed excellent fine motor skills. Her nonverbal IQ score was well above average, whereas her verbal IQ score was near the retarded range (see Figure 6.2).

Yuet was completely unmotivated to do most classroom work and, if allowed, spent her time drawing masterful three-dimensional pictures to accompany the current social studies lessons. A meeting with her parents revealed that they were as puzzled about Yuet as the teacher was.

The psychologist's report noted superior fine motor skills and suggested that Yuet be taught reading with a nonaural method that took advantage of her visual capacity, using pictures, stories, and a whole-word approach. This nonaural approach was effective with Yuet, and after two years of specialized help in the resource room her reading greatly improved as did her self-esteem and motivation.

Yuet is learning disabled. The wide difference between her nonverbal IQ and verbal IQ scores is often a sign of the disability. Her superior art work along with her poor reading is another signal of her disability. Yuet probably falls into the subgroup of children with learning disabilities who have damage to their left hemisphere.

Identification and Assessment

Identifying children with learning disabilities is not easy. First, learning disabilities must be distinguished from other conditions, and then the difference between potential and achievement must be evaluated. How large a discrepancy is acceptable? Must a child have an identifiable developmental learning disability that has contributed to educational underachievement? Who makes the decision?

School systems, according to the provisions of PL 94-142 and PL 101-476, are required to assemble a multidisciplinary team of professionals to examine the child psychologically, mentally, socially, and educationally and, with the parents, come to a decision about whether the child is eligible for special education. The identification process that most school systems follow includes these steps:

1. Someone such as a teacher or parent refers the child for evaluation.
2. A committee of teachers, including the special education teacher, evaluates the referral to determine whether a multidisciplinary team should assess the child.
3. Once an assessment is approved, parental permission for the assessment is obtained.
4. A multidisciplinary team including psychologists, social workers, the classroom teacher, and the special education teacher conducts the evaluation.
5. Team members hold a conference and decide whether the child is eligible for special education.
6. If the child is eligible, an individualized education program (IEP) is formulated, and the child is placed in the appropriate service.

To adequately assess the child with learning disabilities, specific deficits, dysfunctions, or difficulties, skilled personnel are needed to select the appropriate measure, whether it be in the neuropsychological domain or the academic/achievement domain. Lyon's book (1994) is a valuable tool for selecting specific measures in all of the subtypes of learning disabilities currently identified. Great care must be taken, for all too frequently the test does not measure what the title of the test suggests.

DIAGNOSIS

A **differential diagnosis** is used to pinpoint an atypical behavior, explain it, and differentiate it from similar problems of other children with disabilities. It allows teachers to determine the remedial program best suited to correcting or improving

A differential diagnosis pinpoints an atypical behavior, explains it, and differentiates it from similar problems of other children with disabilities. (© *Jerry Howard/Positive Images*)

the disability. Methods of identification and diagnosis are somewhat different for preschool children and school-age children. Preschoolers are identified through developmental discrepancies, or measured strengths and weaknesses in their developmental abilities. Schoolchildren are identified through discrepancies between aptitude and school achievement.

Educational diagnosis is different from identification of the type of a disability. As a teacher you will need to know what the academic deficit is and then plan a strategy to remediate it. Achievement tests based on national norms are the most commonly used and readily available in most school districts. A Curriculum-Based Measurement (Deno, 1985) is a technique in which the assessment is based on what has been taught specifically in the classroom (L. Fuchs, Fuchs, Hamlett, Phillips, & Bentz, 1994). A newer, comprehensive approach is the Work Sampling System (Meisels, Jablon, Marsden, Dichelmiller, & Dorfman, 1994). This approach offers guidelines about what to sample of children's classroom work and compares the sample to developmental age norms. These methods avoid the pitfalls of achievement tests that contain items and content that may not have been taught.

EARLY INTERVENTION

Obviously, the earlier we identify children with learning disabilities, the sooner we can begin intervention programs to help them. More important, if we can identify youngsters who are at risk for learning disabilities, we may be able to prevent those disabilities (Fletcher & Forman, 1994; Wolery, 1992).

Badian (1982, 1988) found that two tests—the information and sentences subtests of the Wechsler Preschool and Primary Scale of Intelligence—predict with a fairly high degree of accuracy the long-term performance of students in reading. (The information subtest assesses factual knowledge; the sentences subtest assesses the ability to repeat increasingly complex sentences.) Moreover, certain characteristics—troubled birth history, family history of learning disabilities, late order of birth among siblings, delayed speech development, and lower socioeconomic status—differentiate poor readers from good readers (Badian, 1982, 1988).

The identification of learning disabilities in preschool children depends on our being able to observe behavior on age-appropriate tasks. These tasks often involve preacademic readiness skills (cutting with scissors, holding a crayon, sharing an experience with a classmate). Some children have trouble with fine and gross motor development. Others are slow to develop oral language and reasoning abilities. These delays in information processing can affect the child's learning, ability to communicate, and social and emotional adjustment. The most common disorders among preschoolers are delayed language development, poor perceptual-motor skills, and lack of attention.

In diagnosing preschool children, examiners rely on the observations of parents and teachers, rating scales, informal clinical diagnoses, and norm-referenced and criterion-referenced tests. They function much like detectives, gathering clues and formulating and discarding hypotheses until they arrive at the solution that best fits the available evidence.

Language Disabilities

Language disabilities are the most common learning disabilities among preschoolers.

The most common learning disabilities noted at the preschool level are language disabilities. To diagnose a language disability, psychoeducational examiners follow a series of steps:

1. Obtain a description of the language behavior as observed by the parent, the preschool teacher, or both.

2. Review the medical record to see whether the disability can be explained medically.

3. Study the family situation to determine whether factors in the home contribute to the disability.

4. Using formal and informal tests, examine the child's abilities and disabilities in understanding language, relating things heard to past experiences, and talking.

5. Determine what the child can and cannot do in a specific area. For example, if the child functions well in most areas but does not talk, the next step is to find out if he or she understands language. If the child does not understand oral

language, the next step is to find out if he or she can discriminate among words, among phonemes, or among common sounds in the environment.

6. Organize a remedial program that moves the child step by step into areas in which the child could not initially perform.

To identify potential language difficulties early, an assessment of the infant's or young child's *prelinguistic* behaviors must be made. These behaviors before words are spoken include eye contact, mutual gaze, prespeech vocalization, and gesture (Dromi, 1993).

Perceptual-Motor Disabilities

Youngsters with **perceptual-motor disabilities** have difficulty understanding and responding to the meaning of pictures or numbers. In diagnosing perceptual-motor disabilities in a preschooler, psychoeducational examiners ask the usual questions about medical and home background, and through ratings, interviews, and formal tests they try to discover the contributing factors and areas in which the child experiences major difficulties. In the process, examiners try to answer several questions:

1. Can the child interpret the environment and the significance of what he or she sees?
2. Can the child match shapes and colors?
3. Can the child recognize visual objects and pictures rapidly?
4. Can the child assemble puzzles?
5. Can the child express ideas in motor (nonverbal) terms through gestures and drawings?

Attentional and Other Disabilities

Examiners use observation and formal and informal tests to diagnose attentional and other disorders. They are trying to answer these kinds of questions:

1. Can the child sustain attention to auditory or visual stimuli?
2. Is the child easily distracted?
3. Does the child persevere in the face of difficulty or initial failure?
4. Can the child discriminate between two pictures or objects (visual discrimination), between two words or sounds (auditory discrimination), or between two objects felt or touched (haptic discrimination)?
5. Is the child oriented in space? Does he or she have right-left discrimination?
6. Can the child remember immediately what was heard, seen, or felt?
7. Can the child imitate the examiner orally or with gestures? Can the child mimic?
8. Does the child have adequate visual-motor coordination? Is the child clumsy?

An individualized family service plan (IFSP) is especially important for families of children with learning disabilities because information from the family about how the child is functioning at home is critical in ruling out causes. (© *Michael Zide*)

THE INDIVIDUALIZED FAMILY SERVICE PLAN

An individualized family service plan (IFSP) can be particularly useful with children with learning disabilities. The service plan must be developed with the family and the evaluators of the child. An IEP or an IFSP is especially important for families of children with learning disabilities because information from the family about how the child is functioning at home is critical in ruling out causes. For example, if the family reports that the child has never had any difficulty at home but has difficulty in learning to read in the first grade, the evaluator learns when and where the problem occurred. Taking a family medical and social history can help determine whether other family members have experienced this problem or whether the child being evaluated is the first in the family to experience school failure. Observing the child and interviewing the parents about the child's strengths and weaknesses are among the most valuable tools that the evaluator possesses in determining what the developmental problem may be. As we saw with Ron and Yuet, the parent interview can be very helpful.

After the developmental assessment, an educational assessment must be conducted to determine the most appropriate way to teach this student. The field has no easy solution for the problems of all children with learning disabilities. Each individual must be evaluated by a multidisciplinary team and then by an educational team to determine the appropriate methods and place of instruction.

SCHOOLCHILDREN

To be able to work effectively with children with learning disabilities, two kinds of evaluations are necessary: one to identify (if possible), the source of the disorder and one to identify the kinds of academic or social difficulties the student is having. Appropriate multidisciplinary teams must conduct both evaluations. The law mandates such evaluations, and they are critical if a teacher is to devise or select the appropriate curriculum for the disorder and academic problem the student possesses.

In diagnosing children with learning disabilities, the examiner must take great care to rule out children who are low achievers because of factors excluded from the previously stated definition or because of cultural reasons related to ethnicity or bilingualism. Thus, identification consists of assessing school or social failures that are related to some unknown neurological cause. Researchers such as Shinn and Ysseldyke (1983) recommended directly measuring academic performance in reading, spelling, and writing. Others suggested that the ability to relate to peers, usually judged observationally, be assessed (Pearl, Donahue, & Bray, 1981).

Students classified as having learning disabilities should have had a multidisciplinary assessment to rule out problems other than the IQ score achievement discrepancy. School psychologists spend 70 percent of their testing time on these problems (Tindal & Marston, 1986). Once the child is assessed, the issue becomes one of how to teach the child, particularly how to teach reading, for three-fourths of these children have reading problems (Kirk & Elkins, 1975).

Educational Adaptations

Children with learning disabilities require an individualized teaching plan.

A large group of researchers in the field of learning disabilities have been focusing on the academic problems of children with learning disabilities. Their focus has been to analyze what the children must learn and to identify the problems they have in mastering the material. Although this trend has many proponents, there are still major differences in recommendations about how to adapt the educational process to help each child.

Historically, approaches to remediation of learning disabilities were based on multiple sensory techniques such as teaching children how to read, spell, write, and compute by using pictures, tracing letters in sand, and drill and practice. Many teachers in remedial instruction still use these techniques for children with learning disabilities and children who are developmentally delayed or mentally retarded. As Clark (1988) writes: "Despite the widespread inclusion of multisensory techniques in remedial programs for dyslexic students and the almost unanimous conviction among practitioners using these techniques is that they work, we have little empirical data to validate their effectiveness" (p. 49). From an educational point of view, the best help for teachers working with children with learning disabilities is to provide teachers with tools for identifying the academic and social problems that children with learning disabilities possess and a curriculum with strategies and materials that will help these children use their strengths to overcome their weaknesses (Adelman & Taylor, 1993; Lerner, 1993; Yule, Rutter, Berger, & Thompson, 1974).

MAJOR APPROACHES FOR TEACHING STUDENTS WITH LEARNING DISABILITIES

In this section we present an overview of procedures to use with children with all types of learning disabilities. It is beyond the scope of this chapter to discuss all the available instructional techniques; however, the approaches presented here can be adapted to subject matter, including mathematics, writing and spelling, and reading or dealing with dyslexia. These techniques can be used in the regular classroom, resource room, or special class.

Applied Behavioral Analysis

Applied behavioral analysis (ABA) is frequently called *behaviorism* because it grew out of earlier work on the modification of challenging behaviors and emotional disturbances. Behaviorism is based on the work of Skinner (1953) and has been used widely to control or modify unacceptable behavior in school. The same techniques are used for teaching academic skills and subjects (Trieber & Lahey, 1983). In theory, ABA is concerned with the causes of disorder only insofar as they help teachers to formulate a treatment plan (Tindal & Marston, 1988). The learning programs are based on individual analyses of the child's functioning rather than on the child's assumed biological problems. Before the steps of ABA can be implemented, the task to be learned must be thoroughly analyzed (*task analysis*), and the child's skill and academic strengths and weaknesses must be thoroughly assessed (Neeper & Lahey, 1983).

Koorland (1986) suggested the following steps in ABA:

1. Pinpoint the child's behavior to be targeted for change.
2. Measure the behavior directly and repeatedly.
3. Institute a change in events antecedent and consequent to the behavior (what happens in the environment immediately before and after instruction).
4. Evaluate and record results.
5. Try again if goals are not attained. (Koorland, 1986, p. 299)

To these, we add four steps:

6. If the child is successful, reward or reinforce the success.
7. If the child is successful, increase the demand with additional or more complex tasks.
8. Chart the results of the child's work.
9. Involve the child in identifying target behaviors.

Applied behavioral analysis uses demonstration, modeling, and feedback to teach and reinforce desired behavior.

Researchers recently have focused on analyzing what children must learn and identifying the problems children with learning disabilities have in mastering the material. (© *Paul S. Conklin*)

Demonstrating, modeling, and feedback are recommended antecedent and consequent strategies in ABA. The instruction is always direct and focused on the specific fact or skill to be learned. At times, prompting or cueing is used to help the student focus on the task (Koorland, 1986). Direct instruction can be used with individual children or with small groups of children who have similar problems.

Evaluation and recording of results are conducted for individual children, however, and are not combined for group results.

The following is an example of how to apply this approach to teach arithmetic:

1. Teach the concept of five.
2. Identify for yourself what are the smallest units of five. $1 + 4$; $4 + 1$; $3 + 2$; $2 + 3$; if zero is known, $5 + 0$ and $0 + 5$.
3. Present the concepts directly to the child, step by step (one at a time).
4. If necessary, use aids such as sticks or objects that can be placed in groups of five and counted.
5. Record results and reward or reinforce success.
6. Review and reteach any concept that is not mastered, such as $0 + 5$ or $5 + 0$.
7. If the child is successful, move on to the concept of six.
8. Follow the steps used in teaching the concept of five.

Figure 6.3 provides an example of how a child's success is charted on the basis of changing criteria—for example, completing more problems in each successful session.

Lerner (1993) found that direct instruction is effective with students who have learning disabilities and described how it can be combined with other teaching approaches. A child who lacks phonological awareness, for example, may have difficulty in learning phonics during direct instruction. This child may need more time to experience phonemes and syllables and to practice word segmentation.

Diagnostic Prescriptive Model

Teaching strategies are often modified for children with learning disabilities.

The diagnostic prescriptive model (Pressley et al., 1990) is designed to remediate what we have termed *executive functions, metacognitions,* or *organizational strategies.* The model, which focuses on the teacher's behavior as well as the student's, can be applied to all academic areas and to children with and without

Figure 6.3
Changing Criteria for Problems

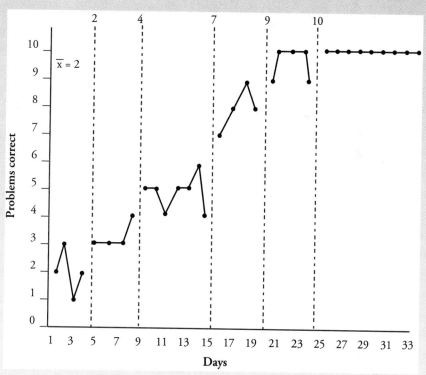

Source: P. Schloss, R. Sedlack, C. Elliott, and M. Smothers (1982). Application of the changing criterion design in special education, *Journal of Special Education,* 16, pp. 359–367. Copyright © 1982 by PRO-ED, Inc. Reprinted by permission.

learning disabilities. The approach uses many behavioral principles and includes teaching children strategies for approaching learning problems. Psychologists refer to these strategies as **metacognition,** or the ability to think about one's own thinking and monitor its effectiveness. The overall plan is presented in Table 6.1.

If the child is not successful in the task (such as learning how to answer questions), the strategy learning may have to be repeated. It may also be advisable to reconsider and perhaps modify the behaviors of the teacher, change the setting of the learning, or change the nature of the reinforcement (to ensure that it is rewarding).

The diagnostic prescriptive model approach can be applied to all subject areas from elementary to high school. It emphasizes self-monitoring by the teacher and the student. Facts, skills, and strategies may be taught in tutoring sessions, through peer teaching, or in small groups (Clark, 1988). The teacher may use prompts such as pictures of a word or of the idea of a story, object aids for counting or understanding fractions, or the actual object when introducing a word such as *ball*.

Mnemonic Devices

A **mnemonic** is a device or rhyme that helps people to remember words or concepts. The use of mnemonics is a popular way to help children with learning disabilities (Snowman, 1991). One simple example is this mnemonic sentence that helps us remember the planets in order of distance from the sun: Mary's (Mercury) violet (Venus) eyes (Earth) make (Mars) John (Jupiter) sit (Saturn) up (Uranus) nights (Neptune) period (Pluto). More sophisticated examples can be found in Snowman (1991).

Cooperative Learning

In cooperative learning, students of all levels of ability work together to solve a problem.

Cooperative learning is a teaching strategy involving students of varying ability levels working together to solve a problem. The students may ask the teacher for help if necessary, but for the most part the group works on the problem without the teacher. When used appropriately, cooperative learning has positive results. Students with difficulties are assisted by others who have mastered the skills needed to solve the problem; those students in turn have their understanding of the problem reinforced by helping others in the group.

Another form of cooperative learning is **peer tutoring,** in which a capable student works with a student who needs help on a specific topic. The success of peer tutoring depends on balanced interaction between the tutor and student, with the tutor teaching, rather than telling, the student what to do.

Cognitive Instruction

Other approaches for teaching students with learning disabilities are based on cognitive (information-processing strategies) and cognitive-learning theory (a combination of ABA and cognitive principles). The distinction between ABA and cognitive approaches is becoming blurred, for they use similar techniques. The

TABLE 6.1   General Model of How-to-Teach Strategies

■ Teach a few strategies at a time, intensively and extensively, as part of the ongoing curriculum.

■ Model and explain new strategies.

■ Model again and re-explain strategies in ways that are sensitive to aspects of strategy use that are not well understood.

■ Explain to student where and when to use strategies.

■ Provide plenty of practice, using strategies for as many appropriate tasks as possible.

■ Encourage students to monitor how they are doing when they are using strategies.

■ Encourage continued use of and generalization of strategies.

■ Increase students' motivation to use strategies by heightening students' awareness that they are acquiring valuable skills that are at the heart of competent functioning.

■ Emphasize reflective processing rather than speedy processing; do all possible to eliminate high anxiety in students; encourage students to shield themselves from distraction so they can attend to academic tasks.

Source: From M. Pressley and Associates (1990). *Cognitive Strategy Instruction.* Cambridge, MA: Brookline Books, p. 18.

major difference is that cognitive approaches rely more on theories of how children process information, along with direct and indirect teaching.

Wong (1986) emphasized that all cognitive approaches attempt to have the child with learning disabilities become aware of his or her own learning processes. Thus, in learning how to read, the child first focuses on the knowledge that words have meaning, that they are made of letters that stand for sounds, and that the sounds are part of the child's auditory system. Cognitive approaches combine knowledge of letter recognition, phonemes, syntax, word knowledge, and strategies for abstracting meaning from the printed page (metacognition) (Short & Ryan, 1984; Baker & Brown, 1984). Wong (1986) suggested that basic knowledge of four cognitive strategies aids reading:

1. Awareness of the purpose of reading

2. Knowledge of reading strategies

3. Self-monitoring comprehension

4. Spontaneous looking-back while reading (p. 21)

Teaching cognitive strategies has been popular with both cognitive and behaviorally oriented curriculum planners. One major project (Kline, Deshler, & Schumaker, 1991) teaches educators how to teach the strategies and also presents a curriculum for teaching students with learning disabilities.

Gagne (1985) approaches learning as a task of the person in an environment. He suggests nine instructional steps:

1. Gaining the student's attention
2. Informing the learner about what is to be learned
3. Reminding learners what they have already learned and its relationship to the current topic
4. Prescribing the lesson
5. Providing guidance—hints about how to approach the problem
6. Asking the learner to perform
7. Providing feedback on accuracy—giving information, reinforcement, correction
8. Evaluating performance—providing guidance about what corrections are needed, rewarding good performance
9. Suggesting how what was learned relates to other learning (transfer)

Some Approaches to Instruction

Preschool curriculum for those at risk for learning disabilities is not too different from the regular preschool curriculum. The major difference is the mode of presentation, which should focus directly, in a supportive manner, on the child's strengths as well as on deficits, allowing the child ample time to engage in the tasks. The tasks may need frequent repetition and review for the child with potential learning disabilities. Tasks include the following (see Lerner, 1988 & 1993, for other ideas):

1. *Gross motor:* walking forward, backward, and sideways; line walks
2. *Fine motor:* cutting, pasting, buttoning, tracing, and throwing; and assembling puzzles
3. *Communication:* listening, talking, explaining, rhyming, and engaging others
4. *Visual:* recognizing similarities and differences in pictures, objects, shapes, and letters
5. *Auditory:* phonological awareness, word games, rhyming games
6. *Cognitive:* learning relationships and differences, classifying objects by use, color, and shape
7. *Social:* communication with peers and adults, sharing, turn-taking, cooperative play

Reading. A child first learning to read matches his or her own auditory sound system to an abstract system of print. In English, the twenty-six letters of the alphabet are abstract symbols of a sound system consisting of consonants and vowels. The vowels (*a,e,i,o,u,* and sometimes *y*) combine with the consonants to make up forty-eight *phonemes,* the smallest units of sound meaning. Thus, "bat" has three phonemes (*b a t*), which are blended together. "Boat" also has three phonemes, for the *a* is silent and serves only to make the *o* long or sound its name. ("When two vowels go walking, the first one does the talking.")

To read, a child must have a rich store of auditorially perceived words that have meaning, such as knowing that a bat can be a flying rodent or a stick used in baseball. The child must next break the abstract code. Although words contain letters, it is not knowing the alphabet in sequence that helps in reading but understanding the relationship of the letters as phonemes and being able to decode (figure out the sound the letter stands for) and blend the letters into words (Mann & Liberman, 1984; Liberman & Shankweiler, 1977).

Approaches to teaching reading to students with learning disabilities are based on one of three philosophies of how children learn to read: bottom-up, top-down, and interactive. The *bottom-up approach* attempts to teach children phonics, letter-sounds combinations, and isolated words, and then how to use those skills to decode text. The *top-down approach* uses the child's prior knowledge and experience to construct meaning from a text. Programs that use whole-language or literature-based methods are examples of the top-down philosophy, which emphasizes that meaning and understanding can be generated only from within the reader in the context of working with real literature. The *interactive approach* combines the top-down and bottom-up philosophies. The student might be encouraged to use top-down strategies when the text is familiar, bottom-up strategies when the text is unfamiliar (Mercer, 1992, p. 501).

Many schools use basal readers in reading instruction. Basal readers are prepared by grade level and provide material for the development and practice of reading skills and reading comprehension. They try to select stories that will appeal to the age of the child and try to introduce skills in a sequential fashion. They usually have a teacher's manual for each grade that contains suggestions on how to present the story. Basal readers generally take an interactive approach; however, some series introduce bottom-up activities earlier than others.

Most basal readers suggest a *directed teaching approach;* the teacher introduces new words contained in the story, motivates children to read by telling them what kind of story it is (fairy tale, mystery, and so on), and lets them know in advance what to look for in the story. Students read silently, sometimes reading the story aloud after reading it silently. The teacher questions them about the content of the story and plans follow-up activities.

In the *language experience approach,* students dictate stories based on their experiences. The stories are usually written on a large chart, and students then copy from the chart into their own story books. The approach can be used with small groups, the members of which dictate a story. The goal is to have students read the words dictated from their own vocabulary and use them to make connections with the rules of phonics. Teachers can build more complicated stories by providing in-school experiences or field trips that can become the subject for students' stories. Later, as writing and reading skills improve, students may write their own stories and read them to the class or teacher. Burns, Roe, and Ross (1992) suggested that the language experience approach can be used effectively with bilingual students who are able to understand the stories they dictate and whose oral skills are reinforced by the use of written language.

For students with learning disabilities, any of these approaches may need to be used with one-to-one instruction so that the teacher can identify a student's learning style and the particular difficulties the student is experiencing.

Dyslexia is a severe form of language and reading disorder.

Many techniques have been used to teach children with dyslexia to read: tracing over letters, using the sense of touch, showing pictures along with the word, using toys along with the word, and using a general language enrichment program. Persons with dyslexia usually also have deficits in both vision and hearing as well as in the ability to process information into language or cognitive systems. Some teachers rely on tape recordings of books. After the tape has been played, the teacher asks the child a series of oral questions about its content. If the child has major problems with audition as well as dyslexia, however, this method may not work. Teachers need to try different approaches to determine which works best with the individual student.

Spelling and Writing.   Spelling is a more difficult skill to master than reading, for there are no clues, such as context, to help students spell (Lerner, 1993). In addition, the English language contains many exceptions (for example, *tough, through, thorough*) to orderly phonetic rules, and each exception must be taught separately. The rules listed in Table 6.2 will be helpful to many students who have difficulty with spelling. Word processors with spelling checks are invaluable for students with spelling difficulties. Remember that the resource the child uses to achieve the correct spelling is not as important as the fact that the child was able to select an appropriate source and solve the problem (this is equally true in mathematics and other subjects).

If a motor writing problem is also present, the teacher may ask an occupational therapist for techniques to help the child hold and control the pencil as well as techniques to make writing legible.

Mathematics.   Most children with math learning disabilities will profit from working with basic counting, matching, and measuring activities with real objects. Tongue depressors, small discs, and water pitchers are useful objects. Repeated counting to obtain the correct numerical sequence is basic. Recognizing how many objects are present without having to count them is a good exercise. Most arithmetic manipulatives help students gain a firm foundation for later arithmetic operations. Table 6.3 presents an overview of the four basic arithmetic operations and the sequential steps in teaching them. Once children have learned the basic signs of

TABLE 6.2   Spelling Rules

1. Rules governing the addition of suffixes and inflected endings:
   a. When a word ends in "e," the "e" is usually dropped when a syllable beginning with a vowel is added.

bake	baking
make	making

   b. When a word ends in "e," the "e" is usually kept when a syllable beginning with a consonant is added.

bake	baker
make	maker

   c. When a root word ends in "y" and is preceded by a consonant, the "y" is changed to "i" when suffixes and endings are added unless they begin with an "i."

fly	flies	fly	flying
study	studies	study	studying

   d. When a noun ends in "y" and is preceded by a consonant, the plural is formed by changing the "y" to "i" and adding "es."

baby	babies
puppy	puppies

   e. When a root word ends in "y" and is preceded by a vowel, the root word is not changed when a suffix or ending is added.

play	playful
monkey	monkeys

   f. Words that end in a consonant and are preceded by a single vowel usually require that the consonant be doubled before adding an ending.

run	running
sit	sitting

2. Capital letters are used in the following situations:
   a. The first word of a sentence (He went home)
   b. The letter "I" when used as a word (Jimmy and I went fishing)
   c. Proper names (Tommy, Jane, Canada)
   d. Words derived from proper names (Canadian, French)
   e. Titles before proper names (Sir Winston Churchill)
   f. The first and all important words of a book title, story, etc. (*The Return of the Native*)

3. Apostrophes are used in the following situations:
   a. An apostrophe and "s" to show possession after a single noun (the boy's coat)
   b. An apostrophe alone to show possession after a plural noun ending in "s" (the girls' coats)
   c. An apostrophe and "s" to show possession after a plural noun not ending in "s" (the children's coats)
   d. An apostrophe to show the omission of a letter or letters in a contraction (isn't, I'll)

TABLE 6.2   Spelling Rules (cont.)

4. Rules about the letter "s" and plurals:
   a. When adding "s" to words to form plurals or to change the tense of verbs: "es" must be added to words ending with hissing sounds ("x," "s," "sh," "ch").

   | glass | glasses |
   | watch | watches |

   b. When "s" is added to words ending in a single "f" to form plurals, the "f" is changed to "v" and "es" is added.

   | wolf | wolves |
   | half | halves |

5. Most abbreviations end with a period.

   | Ont. | Nov. |

6. The letter "q" is always followed by "u" in common English words.

   | queen | quiet |

7. No English words end in "v."

   | glove | move |

8. The letter "i" usually comes before "e" except after "c."

   | receive | receipt |

Source: M. Pressley and Associates (1990). *Cognitive Strategy Instruction.* Cambridge, MA: Brookline Books, p. 89.

the four operations, a simple calculator can be useful to assist them in accomplishing the calculations needed to solve mathematical concepts (Lerner, 1993).

Children with reading problems may need to have word problems read to them. This can be easily accomplished by a peer or in a cooperative learning group.

LEARNING ENVIRONMENT

The expression *learning styles* refers to the student's sound preference (noisy or quiet atmosphere), light preference (bright or dull), and preference for working alone or in a cooperative group or with a peer, for short bursts or long periods of work, and for moving around or staying quiet. Children achieve best when the learning environment matches their learning style (Schrag, 1994).

Where is the student with learning disabilities taught? Strong proponents of **inclusion** would have all students with learning disabilities spend all their time in regular classrooms. Today, students with mild disabilities may be in a regular classroom with special materials and equipment, tutoring, and access to a resource room staffed by a special education teacher and a diagnostic-prescriptive teaching center. A comparative study demonstrated that students with learning disabilities in regular classrooms achieved as much as students with learning disabilities in

Depending on the teacher's ability, students with learning disabilities can learn as much in a regular class as they can in a special class.

TABLE 6.3	Strategy Instruction for Four Mathematical Operations

Operation	Strategy Steps
Addition	1. Add down 2. Carry if needed 3. Repeat next column

Subtraction	1. Start with ones column
	2. Look at top number
	    Top number larger or same?
	    Subtract?
	    Top number smaller?
	    Borrow and rename
	3. Repeat next column

Multiplication: one-digit multiplier	1. Multiply bottom number and ones digit 2. Carry, if needed 3. Multiply bottom number and tens digit and add carried number 4. Repeat
Multiplication: two-digit multiplier	1. Multiply bottom ones digit and top number 2. Write zero as place holder 3. Multiply bottom tens digit and top number 4. Add
Division: one-digit divisor	1. Divide 2. Multiply 3. Subtract and compare 4. Bring down one digit 5. Repeat
Division: two-digit divisor	1. Estimate 2. Divide 3. Multiply 4. Subtract and compare 5. Bring down one digit 6. Repeat

Source: M. Pressley and Associates (1990). *Cognitive Strategy Instruction.* Cambridge, MA: Brookline Books, p. 155. Adapted from *A Learning Strategies Approach to Functional Mathematics for Students with Special Needs: A Special Education Instructional Guide.* Bel Air, MD: Hartford County Public Schools, pp. 52, 59, 66, 81. Adapted by permission.

special classrooms (Affleck, Madge, Adams, & Lowenbrau, 1988). The important factor appeared to be the teacher and his or her competence in dealing with these special students.

Whether children with learning disabilities are educated in the regular classroom, resource room, or special class depends on what state they live in. The 16th Annual Report to Congress (1994) reported that 94 percent of the children with learning disabilities in Vermont, 86 percent of those in New Mexico, and 68 percent of those in Idaho are educated in the regular class. However, 84 percent of the students with learning disabilities in Minnesota, 72 percent of those in Kentucky, and 78 percent of those in Colorado are educated in resource rooms. In thirty-nine states more than 40 percent of students with learning disabilities are educated in resource rooms.

Kauffman and Pullen (1989) and others objected to single-class placement because they believed that the students need a continuum of special education services that are more than the regular classroom teacher can provide. Schumaker and Deshler (1988) stated that high school students with learning disabilities need specialized instruction, not regular lecture-style high school lessons. Zigmond and Baker (1990) reported that students with major learning disabilities in their study did not make progress in the academic subjects in regular classrooms. Thus, the debate continues, with data and arguments supporting both sides.

Schuman and his colleagues (1995) indicated that elementary school teachers are more successful than high school teachers in providing for the individualized needs of the learning disabled student, because the high school teacher is under greater pressure to cover the course content. In addition, the Division of Learning Disabilities of the Council for Exceptional Children (1995) recommends that students with learning disabilities continue to have access to the full continuum of placements and the use of specialized instructional arrangements. A list of classroom adaptations to aid inclusion is given in Table 6.4. Garnett and Lackaye (1993) have prepared a manual to help teachers adapt materials by academic subject area to aid inclusion of the student who is learning disabled. These suggestions complement and repeat many of the suggestions made in the text. They highlight the need for careful diagnoses of the learning needs of the student and the selection of appropriate teaching strategy to remediate academic and social deficiencies. There are no conclusive answers. The student with learning disabilities has the right to be in the regular classroom, but the following question should be answered unequivocally: Is this the most appropriate place for the student to acquire the skills and knowledge he or she needs to lead an independent life?

Techniques such as peer tutoring can be used with some students, but the tutor must be prepared to work effectively with the student with learning disabilities. Cooperative learning (a mix of ability levels) is often successful, but it requires the full cooperation of the student without disabilities. Recall that the student with learning disabilities is frequently rejected socially, so cooperative learning techniques must overcome peer rejection if the student with learning disabilities is to derive the full benefit of the procedure.

TABLE 6.4   Adaptations for Mainstreamed Students

General Adaptations

Respect mainstreamed students as individuals with differences.

Establish routines appropriate for mainstreamed students.

Adapt classroom management strategies that are effective with mainstreamed students.

Provide reinforcement and encouragement.

Establish personal relationships with mainstreamed students.

Help mainstreamed students find appropriate ways to deal with feelings.

Communicate with mainstreamed students.

Communicate with the special education teacher.

Communicate with parents of mainstreamed students.

Establish expectations for mainstreamed students.

Make adaptations for mainstreamed students when developing long-range plans.

Make adaptations for mainstreamed students when developing daily plans.

Plan assignments and activities that allow mainstreamed students to be successful.

Allot time for teaching learning strategies as well as content.

Adjust physical arrangement of room for mainstreamed students.

Adapt general classroom materials for mainstreamed students.

Use alternative materials for mainstreamed students.

Use computers to enhance learning with mainstreamed students as a tool for practicing skills.

Monitor the mainstreamed students' understanding of directions and assigned tasks.

Monitor the mainstreamed students' understanding of concepts presented in class.

Provide individual instruction for mainstreamed students.

Pair the mainstreamed students with a classmate.

Involve mainstreamed students in small-group activities.

Involve mainstreamed students in whole-class activities.

Textbook Adaptations

Teach study strategies to improve retention of text material.

Work with students individually or in small groups to master textbook material.

Provide assistance for answering text-based questions.

Structure postreading activities to increase retention of content.

Summarize and reduce textbook information to guide classroom discussions and independent reading.

Read textbook aloud to students.

Demonstrate and model effective reading strategies and comprehension techniques.

Determine level of difficulty of textbooks.

Use film, video tapes, and recordings to supplement or substitute textbook reading.

Use computer programs to supplement or substitute textbook reading.

Use different colors to mark key words, definitions, and important facts throughout textbook.

Create interest in reading assignments to motivate students.

Explain textbook information thoroughly in classroom lectures and presentations.

Teach reading strategies to improve comprehension of text.

Pair students to master textbook content.

Teach students to use graphic aids.

Construct abridged versions of textbook content or use publisher's abridged versions.

Provide students with questions to guide their reading.

Determine students reading levels to identify students with potential problems with textbooks.

Avoid use of textbooks.

Develop a study guide or study outline to direct learning from text.

Preview reading assignments with students to orient them to a topic and budget reading and study time.

Substitute or supplement textbook reading assignments with direct experiences.

TABLE 6.4 **Adaptations for Mainstreamed Students (cont.)**

General Adaptations	Textbook Adaptations
Provide extra time for mainstreamed students.	Audiotape textbook content.
Adapt pacing of instruction.	Preview textbook with students to orient them to textbook organization and learning tools.
Keep records to monitor students' progress.	Provide students with purposes for reading.
Provide students with ongoing feedback about performance.	Place students in cooperative learning groups to master textbook content.
Adapt evaluations for mainstreamed students.	Use multilevel, multimaterial approach.
Adapt scoring/grading criteria for mainstreamed students.	Teach comprehension-monitoring techniques to improve ongoing understanding of text.
	Reduce length of assignments.
	Introduce key vocabulary before a reading assignment.

Source: J. S. Schumm, and S. Vaughn (1995). Getting ready for inclusion: Is the stage set? *Learning Disabilities Research and Practice 10* (3), 169–179 (pp. 178, 179). Reprinted by permission of Lawrence Erlbaum Associates, Inc.

For some students, one-on-one tutoring is the most appropriate instructional strategy, designed after the evaluation is complete and the IEP is written. For others, the resource room can provide a person specially prepared to work with students with learning disabilities. In the resource room or regular education classroom, augmented communication devices and computers can be useful, but most of them require the student to be able to read and follow direction. Thus, strategy learning (see Pressley, 1990) may be required before instructional technology is introduced.

SECONDARY SCHOOL PROGRAMS

In junior and senior high schools, we find students who have not yet mastered the basic skills sufficiently to cope with content subjects. English, mathematics, science, social science, and history require reading, and most of that reading is beyond the ability of youngsters with learning disabilities. These students also continue to have difficulty with tasks that require specific types of information processing. Many of them need the developmental programs that are appropriate for their age. Most schools offer these programs in resource rooms and self-contained classrooms.

TRANSITION PROGRAMS

Individuals with learning disabilities have their disabilities all of their lives. They may graduate from high school with a special diploma that indicates that they attended but did not meet all requirements, and they have very low employment

Teaching techniques use multisensory strategies to assist learning. (© *Paul S. Conklin*)

rates (Kavali, Forness, & Bender, 1988, Vol. 3). The U.S. Vocational and Rehabilitation Department has developed programs on the national and local levels to assist them in making a successful transition from school to work.

One effort to assist persons with severe and profound disabilities is *supportive employment* (see Chapter 11). Supportive employment places the individual in an actual work setting and provides a supervisor to assist in mastery of the required tasks. As the person masters the tasks, coaching is diminished, and the supervisor gradually is removed but may remain available for counseling and emotional support. Supportive employment grants pay for this on-the-job preparation and for the supervisor's time. Although strategies vary, most of these programs have a common goal: to enable the person with learning disabilities to be independent and self-supporting. Bear in mind that persons with learning disabilities vary greatly in skill performance. Some function quite adequately; others need a great deal of help.

A model program prepared by the National Center for Disability Services is shown in Figure 6.4. The plan provides for evaluation, job skills development, and individual counseling for personal and social skills, as well as on-site skills development with job-coach support. With students whose learning disabilities are severe, a variety of strategies are used: peer tutoring, functional skills development

Figure 6.4
Learn and Earn Program: Participant
Flow Chart

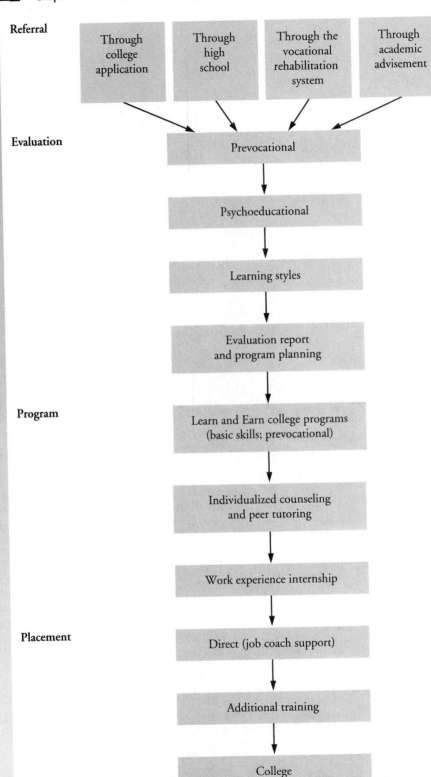

Source: C. A. Michaels (1990). *Learn and Earn Program.* Albertson, NY: National Center for Disability Services. U.S. Department of Education grant proposal 84.078C. Reprinted by permission of the author.

Referral

Through college application

Through high school

Through the vocational rehabilitation system

Through academic advisement

Evaluation

Prevocational

Psychoeducational

Learning styles

Evaluation report and program planning

Program

Learn and Earn college programs (basic skills; prevocational)

Individualized counseling and peer tutoring

Work experience internship

Placement

Direct (job coach support)

Additional training

College

(at the work site), counseling about social skills (how to dress, how to talk to coworkers and supervisors), and counseling about good work habits (low absenteeism, punctuality).

Some students with learning disabilities may enter community colleges or four-year colleges. Persons with learning disabilities who have mastered the acquisition of strategy skills and academic subjects are able to pursue higher education. Some may need extra support to complete academic tasks. Professors may allow those who have difficulty writing to dictate their responses to examinations. Garnett (1989) prepared a handbook of suggestions for college students with learning disabilities.

The person with moderate-to-severe learning disabilities presents a lifetime challenge to his or her family. We consider this issue next.

■ Families

The parents of persons with severe learning disabilities are constantly challenged to make adjustments. They must consider their own needs as well as the special needs of their children, which change as the children move into adolescence and adulthood.

Parents play an integral part in any plan to assist their child with learning disabilities. At times, parents and other family members need help to become fully empowered to make decisions for themselves. O'Hara and Levy (1987) suggested the questions listed in Table 6.5 to help practitioners determine who can best assist parents to function independently.

Families must be intimately involved in every aspect of the life of the child with disability, from diagnosis and intervention programs to transitional services, not only because of the law's requirements but because the family is key to the child's success. This is particularly true of families with children with learning disabilities. These children do not function as other children do, and they confuse the family. Too often the child is seen as lazy, not working hard enough, or resistant to instruction. From the earliest days of the child's life, children with learning disabilities tend to be less consistent, less flexible, unpredictable, and prone to temper outbursts (Breske, 1994).

The quality of the child-parent transactions, the extent to which the family provides diverse activities, influences the child's progress. Families of children with learning disabilities are at risk themselves if they lack social support and are undergoing stress due to having a child with disabilities. They may fall into the trap of teaching by being more "demanding" than "interacting" and using meaningless drills rather than *transacting* (taking turns in conversation, for example).

Harbin (1993) pointed out that families with children with disabilities have an ever-changing source of stress that affects the entire family. For children with learning disabilities, the struggle can be, and usually is, lifelong. Parents may feel guilt that they have genetically passed on the disability. However, families are

TABLE 6.5	Questions to Help Practitioners Determine How Best to Assist Parents of Children with Learning Disabilities

- How do parents describe their child? Do they use primarily positive or negative terms?
- What is their statement of the problem?
- What do parents expect from professionals? Remediation or cure?
- What do parents understand about the cause of the problem? Is it their fault that the child is learning disabled? Is it the fault of one parent? Is it genetically linked? Are parents blaming each other? Are they blaming professionals?
- What do parents understand about the child's ability to influence the problem?
- What diagnostic information have they heard previously?
- What is their understanding of their information on learning disabilities?
- What is their perception of their own relationship to the ongoing nature of the problem? To what extent do they believe that they can influence the course of the disability? How have they tried in the past to influence the situation?
- What has their experience been with other persons presenting problems similar to those of their child?
- What is the parents' assessment of how this problem affects their lives?
- How do they regard previous experiences associated with this problem? What was it like for them to take this child for diagnostic testing? Was their pediatrician supportive? What was diagnostic counseling like for them? How was the information presented? Were both parents present for the informing session? Were they able to support one another? What have their experiences been like with the school system thus far?
- What are their expectations for their own performances as it relates to the problem?
- How do parents feel about this situation? Are they angry or sad? Are they able to express any feelings at all?

Sources: D. O'Hara and J. Levy (1987) Family Intervention. In K. Kavale, S. Forness, and M. Bender (Eds.) *Handbook of Learning Disabilities.* Boston, MA: College-Hill, p. 215.

unique, and may display amazing strengths as well as needs. Many recognize that their children with learning disabilities need to be taught strategies (executive functions) for learning as well as information and facts. Families are key to convincing their children with learning disabilities that they are not "stupid" or "lazy," and families need to find ways to motivate their children to persist in the face of academic failure.

Teachers working closely with families can develop an individualized learning program appropriate for the child. Teachers can do much to help families use the appropriate teaching strategy for the particular child. At times this may require a revision of the family's child-rearing techniques; at other times it may require a reinforcement of the effective techniques the family has been using. Regardless, transaction occurs in four areas: (1) teacher-family, (2) teacher-child, (3) family-child, and (4) parent-teacher. Each influences the other as progress is made. The task, as Heinicke (1993) suggested, is to consolidate a helping working relationship in three areas: (1) encouraging communication, (2) providing mutual support, and (3) revising and evaluating child instruction and progress.

There is a particular distinction between families of children with learning disabilities and families of children with other disabilities. Learning disabilities are diagnosed later in life, and the child may exhibit emotional problems that grow out of difficulties in learning that occur before his or her condition is known (O'Hara & Levy, 1987). The family's way of life may therefore have to be altered once the diagnosis is made, and the change can disrupt the functioning of the family and its flow of development. Whereas the family of a child with other kinds of disabilities has to make changes early in the child's life, the family of a child with learning disabilities has to make changes much later.

Summary of Major Ideas

1. Although the cause or causes of learning disabilities are largely unknown, the most commonly accepted cause is a dysfunction in processing information at the neurological level (not damage to the system).

2. Many researchers are attempting to investigate subgroups of children with learning disabilities and to design teaching strategies that match specific deficits.

3. There is major movement in the field toward acceptance of the IQ-achievement deficit and designing instructional strategies that capitalize on the individual's strengths.

4. Accurate diagnosis of a student with a learning disability who has academic deficiency is key to planning appropriate instructional remediation.

5. In most cases, a student with a learning disability will need, regardless of instructional setting, individual, tutorial, peer, or cooperative instruction to become academically successful.

6. A student with a learning disability can profit most in regular class settings in areas of his or her competence.

7. All students with learning disabilities require a full range of support for their disability as well as instruction designed to utilize their strengths to resolve their academic deficits.

8. Most major approaches for teaching students with learning disabilities include teaching strategy as well as specific subject matter.

9. Transitional programs are needed for persons with moderate-to-severe learning disabilities.

10. Persons with learning disabilities face a lifelong problem, for the deficits are at the neurological processing level, and dysfunction will continue throughout the lifespan.

Unresolved Issues

1. *Learning disabilities defined.* The definition of *learning disabilities* is not uniform across the country. Some states may include the mildly retarded in this group, thereby inflating the prevalence figure.

2. *Cause of learning disabilities.* There is no consensus about the cause or causes of learning disabilities.

3. *Early intervention.* Techniques have not been fully developed for the early identification of individuals with learning disabilities. At present, we do not know if the development of deficits associated with learning disabilities can be prevented early in life. For effective intervention, attention must be given to indications of potential problems during the earliest stages of the brain's plasticity.

4. *Transitional programs.* There is a need for more programs throughout the United States to help individuals with learning disabilities make the transition from high school to work or college.

5. *Appropriate placements.* There is strong debate as to the appropriate instructional setting for students with learning disabilities. Some argue for full inclusion in the regular classroom. Others suggest partial inclusion with remedial instruction in the resource room. For some, individualized tutoring is deemed advisable. For others, the special class is still maintained in some settings. There is no consensus on where to most effectively educate students with learning disabilities.

6. *Full range of services.* Students with learning disabilities are a very heterogenous group with a wide range of individual needs. How schools can provide the multiple range of services for individual students strains financial resources. In addition, there are shortages in available trained personnel.

Key Terms

academic/achievement learning
   disabilities p. 238
applied behavioral analysis (ABA) p. 255
aptitude-achievement discrepancy p. 233
attention-deficit hyperactivity disorder
   (ADHD) p. 242
cognitive strategies p. 247

cooperative learning p. 257
developmental learning disabilities p. 238
differential diagnosis p. 249
dyslexia p. 243
dyslexic p. 243
executive function p. 247
hyperactivity p. 242

Questions for Thought

1. How does the *Federal Register* define *specific learning disability?*   p. 233
2. What four criteria must teachers consider when identifying students with learning disabilities?   pp. 233–234
3. Briefly compare the characteristics of a child who is mildly retarded (see Chapter 5) with the characteristics of a child who is learning disabled. pp. 233–235
4. Describe the differences between neuropsychological/developmental and academic/achievement perspectives on learning disabilities.   p. 238
5. According to the neuropsychological/developmental model, what are the causes of learning disabilities?   p. 240
6. Briefly describe how each of the following contributes to learning disabilities: biological and genetic factors, perceptual-motor problems, visual processing deficits, auditory processing deficits, memory disorders, attentional deficits, and hyperactivity.   pp. 240–242
7. Define *dyslexia*, and describe some of the techniques used to teach dyslexic children.   pp. 243, 261–262
8. In preschool children, the identification of learning disabilities is directly related to behavior on age-approximate tasks. What are these tasks, and how does the examiner get the information necessary for identification?   p. 251
9. What are the most common learning disorders among preschoolers? How are they diagnosed?   p. 251
10. What steps are involved in applied behavioral analysis?   p. 253
11. Describe three approaches to reading instruction for students with learning disabilities.   p. 261–262

References of Special Interest

Adelman, H., & Taylor, L. (1993). *Learning problems and learning disabilities*. Pacific Grove, CA: Brooks/Cole.

 The authors distinguish between students with learning problems and those with learning disabilities. This comprehensive text is a rich source of instructional techniques and intervention strategies.

Rourke, B. P. (Ed.). (1995). *Syndrome of non-verbal learning disabilities*. New York: Guilford Press.

The writings in this collection constitute a comprehensive overview of subtypes of learning disabilities whose assets and deficits have predictable academic outcomes.

Clark, D. B. (1993). *Dyslexia: Theory and practice of remedial instruction.* Parkton, MD: York Press.

The author presents a comprehensive view of dyslexia and the designing of educational strategies to assist dyslexic individuals.

Garnett, K., & Lackaye, T. (1993). *Modifying and adopting methods and materials for students with disabilities in mainstreamed classrooms.* New York: Hunter College.

In this valuable resource of techniques organized by academic subjects, specific suggestions are presented for teachers to use in a regular classroom with a child with learning disabilities.

Kavale, K. A., Forness, S. R., & Bender, M. (Eds.). (1988). *Handbook of learning disabilities: Vol. 1. Dimensions and diagnoses. Vol. 2. Methods and interventions. Vol. 3. Programs and practices.* Boston: College-Hill/Little, Brown.

The articles in these volumes cover all areas of the various theories and practices in the field of learning disabilities.

Lerner, J. L. (1997). *Learning disabilities: theories, diagnosis and teaching strategies, sixth edition.* Boston: Houghton Mifflin Company.

This text is a comprehensive introduction in the teaching of students with learning disabilities. Its balanced coverage of theory and practice has made it a standard in its field.

Lyon, G. R. (Ed.). (1993). *Understanding learning disabilities.* Baltimore: Paul H. Brookes Publishing Co.

This is an exploration of the theories and implications of practice for persons with learning disabilities.

Pressley, M., & Associates. (1990). *Cognitive strategy instruction.* Cambridge, MA: Brookline Books.

This is an excellent source of strategies for teachers and students and an excellent source of ways to design and conduct instruction for all children.

Torgesen, J. K., & Wong, B. Y. L. (1986). *Psychological and educational perspectives on learning disabilities.* San Diego: Academic Press.

This is a readable compendium of various theories and approaches for working with people with learning disabilities.

chapter 7

Children with Behavior Problems

What are several potential causes of behavior problems?

What can we do to deter an attitude of learned helplessness?

What techniques do we use to teach children to manage and control their own behavior?

How does functional assessment differ from other treatment programs?

How successful are special education programs in helping youngsters with behavior disorders make the transition from school to workplace?

F ew experiences are as disturbing to teachers as trying to teach children who are chronically unhappy or driven to aggressive, antisocial behavior. The teachers feel distressed, knowing there's a problem but feeling unable to do anything about it.

Children with behavior problems carry a burden that youngsters with other disabilities do not. We don't blame children who are mentally retarded or who have cerebral palsy for their deviant behavior. But many people assume that children with behavior disorders can control their actions and could stop their disturbing behavior if they wanted to. The sense that they are somehow responsible for their disability colors these children's interactions with those around them: their families, their agemates, their teachers.

Definition

It is not easy to define behavior and emotional problems in children. Most definitions assume that a child with a **behavior disorder,** or serious emotional disturbance, reveals consistent "age-inappropriate behavior" leading to social conflict, personal unhappiness, and school failure.

A behavior disorder implies that the child is causing trouble for someone else. Serious emotional disturbance can be merely manifest personal unhappiness. But almost all children reveal age-inappropriate behavior at one time or another. Moreover, a child's behavior is not the only variable that determines classification in this category. The person who perceives the child's behavior as "inappropriate" plays a key role in the decision. Clearly, some kinds of behavior such as physical attacks, constant weeping or unhappiness, and extreme hyperactivity are unacceptable in any setting. But the acceptability of a wide range of other behaviors depends on the attitude of the perceiver.

In our pluralistic society, behavior that is acceptable in some groups or subcultures is unacceptable in others. Our definition, therefore, must allow for cultural differences. Can we say that a child's behavior is deviant if the behavior is the norm in the child's cultural group, even though we may find the particular behavior socially unacceptable?

Wood (1982) suggested that a definition of *problem behavior*, or a set of actions that follows from the definition, should include four elements:

1. *The disturber element.* What or who is perceived to be the focus of the problem?
2. *The problem behavior element.* How is the problem behavior described?
3. *The setting element.* In what setting does the problem behavior occur?
4. *The disturbed element.* Who regards the behavior as a problem? (pp. 7–8)

These elements clearly suggest an environmental basis for the definition. The term *problem behavior* refers not just to the behavior itself but to the context in which the behavior is observed or judged. Debate continues among the various professionals who encounter children with behavior problems about how much

Because practically all children exhibit inappropriate behavior from time to time, criteria for identifying problem behavior depend largely on the frequency and intensity of specific behaviors. (© Lilyan Aloma/ Monkmeyer Press Photo Service)

Context often plays a role in defining problem behavior.

environment and how much personal characteristics influence the classroom and interpersonal problems.

This disagreement extends to the definition of *seriously emotionally disturbed (SED) persons* that is stated in federal law (PL 94-142), a definition that pleases few professionals but does help to determine who is eligible for special services. Forness (1992) summarized the key elements in that definition:

1. An inability to learn that cannot be explained by intellectual, sensory, or health factors

2. An inability to build or maintain satisfactory relationships with peers and teachers

3. Inappropriate types of behaviors or feelings under normal circumstances

4. A general pervasive mood of unhappiness or depression

5. A tendency to develop physical symptoms or fears associated with personal or school problems (p. 55)

In addition to those five individual characteristics, the definition of SED also includes three criteria: (1) *extensive duration* of the problem, (2) *severity* of the problem, and (3) *demonstrated adverse effect on school performance*. Excluded from the group (and therefore from special education services) are youths who are *socially maladjusted but not emotionally disturbed*.

The history of that exclusion suggests strongly that the lawmakers' intent was to prevent adjudicated delinquents from receiving special education services—on the grounds that they were being cared for under the provisions of other laws (Maag & Howell, 1992). Nevertheless, this exclusion causes much confusion within the school community. As an example, consider Pete, a 12-year-old doing quite poorly in school (third- or fourth-grade-level proficiency).

Pete is a constant trial to his teachers in middle school. He physically attacks other students when frustrated (which seems to be quite often), he is suspected of being part of a group of older boys stealing from local stores, and he is openly defiant to the teacher in the classroom. The teachers don't have any trouble reaching the conclusion that Pete needs some special attention—social skills training perhaps leads the list. But the school psychologist has trouble fitting him under the general category of seriously emotionally disturbed as just defined because Pete doesn't reveal a pervasive mood of unhappiness or depression. His role in life appears to be to upset other people. He can, without a doubt, be called socially maladjusted. But is he socially maladjusted *without emotional disturbance* and, hence, excluded from special education services?

This type of bureaucratic dancing around the problem infuriates teachers, who know Pete needs help. But the definition of SED has another problem that seems to be even more serious. A number of observers have pointed out that the federal definition places *all* responsibility for the problem on the child and none on the environment in which the child exists, thus making it the responsibility of the special education program to change the *child* but not the *learning environment*—which can be considerably flawed (Maag & Howell, 1992; Leone, 1989; Nelson & Rutherford, 1990).

The learning environment may be exactly what is at issue for youngsters who come to school from very different cultures with different lifestyles and values (Rueda, 1989). Juan, a newly arrived Hispanic child, has trouble with the different ways he is supposed to react to authority. He is expected to look teachers in the eye when they are talking to him ("Look at me when I am speaking to you!"). But if he did that at home, he would be severely reprimanded because such eye contact would be considered defiance of parental authority. Juan's reaction to this very different environment may cause him to exhibit behavior within the range of the current definition of behavior disorder. This behavior would be due not to some underlying pathology, however, but to the clash of cultural values of the school and home (Webber, 1992; Cline & Rock, 1992).

What treatment is prescribed for such a child? Should Juan be made to change his behavior patterns to fit the new environment or try and reach an accommodation between the two? The issue of an individual child with maladaptive behavior may turn out to be an issue of clashing societies with a very different prescription for social remediation that extends far beyond the reach of special education.

Even the student caught between two cultures, however, can still manifest behaviors that are certain to cause him trouble now and in the future in the school environment and in the community. In short, the problem may start out as a cultural clash, but it is transformed into a personal adjustment problem. Should the child receive some type of intervention to help in that situation? In this situation it is appropriate to think of the entire family as the focus of attention. Increasingly, the family unit is involved in the attempts at behavior change in the child.

There is a disturbing gap between the numbers of children who have both serious emotional disturbance and behavior disorders, variously estimated between 5 and 15 percent (Knitzer, Steinberg, & Fleisch, 1990) and the number being served. Less than 1 percent of children who fit this description are receiving special services (Sixteenth Annual Report to Congress, Office of Special Education Programs, U.S. Department of Education, 1994).

This category lacks the quantitative character of an index like the intelligence test (intelligence quotient [IQ] scores), and much of the judgments are subjective and left to local personnel. This is not to say, however, that there is not a core of youngsters who can readily be identified as having an emotional or behavior disturbance. A child who attacks another child with a weapon such as scissors, a knife, or a hammer leaves little doubt, and neither does a child who weeps five or six times a day without apparent cause. As always, confusion about whether a child is eligible for special services exists at the margin of the category.

Does it make any difference whether children with emotional or behavior disorders are identified? Could we be dealing with a temporary developmental immaturity that will go away with time? The clear answer is, unfortunately, no. The presence of emotional or behavior disorders in school strongly predicts future school failure, school dropout, delinquency, and adult psychiatric problems (Robins, 1966; Walker, Shinn, O'Neill, & Ramsey, 1987). Although not every child who is aggressive and violent in school will show such behavior in adulthood, it is hard to find an aggressive and violent adult who did not show that behavior in his or her youth (Simpson, Miles, Walker, Ormsbee, & Daining, 1991). It is in everyone's best interests that such youngsters are screened and identified early in their school career and positive steps are taken to modify these maladaptive behavioral patterns.

A child's emotional or behavior disturbances in school are strong indications of future difficulties in school and society.

Factors Related to Behavior Problems

Parents and professionals looking for the reasons why some children show disturbed behaviors must examine an array of potential influences, including the individual's biological makeup and cognitive ability and the family and its relationship to the larger society. More than adequate evidence has been collected about factors that predict whether a child is at risk for emotional disturbance. Figure 7.1 shows some of the factors that affect the lives of more than 30 percent of the children identified as emotionally disturbed (Nelson & Pearson, 1991).

Strong family-related factors put children at risk for behavior disturbance.

BIOLOGICAL RISK FACTORS

For a quarter-century, sociologists and psychologists pointed to the environment as the key factor in behavior disturbance. But today, a growing body of knowledge suggests that much abnormal behavior has a genetic base. Studies comparing the behavior of monozygotic (identical) and dizygotic (fraternal) twins clearly indicate

Figure 7.1
Factors That Put Children at Risk
for Social and Emotional Disorders

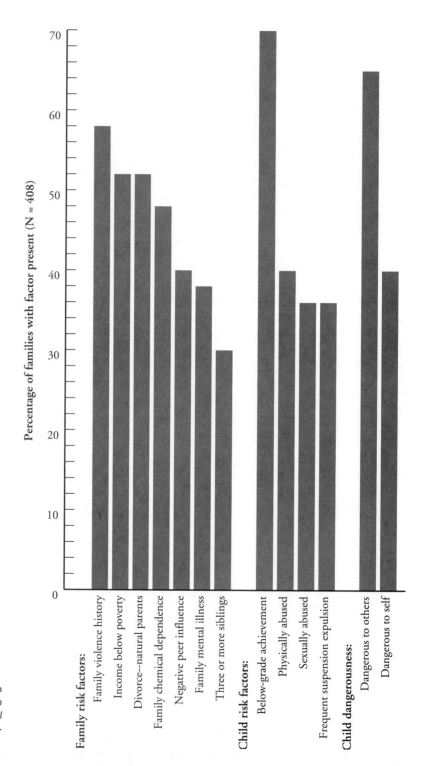

Source: C. Nelson and C. Pearson
(1991). *Integrating Services for Children
and Youth with Emotional and Behavioral
Disorders.* Reston, VA: Council for Exceptional Children.

Many behavioral disturbances have a biological cause.

that children who share an identical genetic background (the monozygotic twins) are more alike in terms of aggressive behavior—even when reared apart—than are the dizygotic twins (even when reared in the same environment) (Cantwell, 1982; Gershon, Hamovit, & Guroff, 1983).

The Influence of Genes

McClearn (1993) also found credible evidence of the important role that heredity plays in shaping behavior and personality, specifically the sex-linked differences in many behavioral conditions. Infantile autism, hyperactivity, and conduct disorders (alcoholism, antisocial behavior) occur in males four to eight times more often than they do in females. Depression and social phobias appear in postpubescent females two to three times more than they do in males. Of course, we can tie these differences—at least in part—to the very different ways in which society treats males and females. But they also suggest that a sex-linked genetic factor may be at work.

To what extent are deviant behaviors hereditary? To what extent are they environmental? We can probably say that all behaviors reflect some combination of heredity and environment. The task of behavioral geneticists is to sort out the contribution of these forces in specific behavioral areas.

The evidence of the genetic influence on behavior has been traced through the study of identical twins (identical heredity), adoptive children (Is the child more like the biological parents or the adoptive parents?), and statistical analyses of the prevalence of conditions in certain families or populations over generations (Plomin & McClearn, 1993).

Interaction Between Genes and Environment

Behavior is both genetically and environmentally controlled. According to Kagan, Arcus, and Snidman (1993),

> No human quality, psychological or physiological, is free of the contributions of events both within and outside the organism. No behavior is a first-order, direct product of genes. . . . Every psychological quality is like a pale gray fabric woven from thin black threads, biology; and thin white ones, experience. But it is not possible to detect any quite black or white threads in the gray cloth. (p. 209)

It is one thing to identify genetic characteristics in various areas of exceptionality and another to conclude that they are final determinants of behavior. Although there is clearly some genetic influence in conduct disorders, particularly those associated with hyperactivity, inattention, and poor peer relationships (Rutter, Silberg, & Simonoff, 1993), there is no reason to believe that environmental experiences cannot counteract those influences. After all, if you can get a lion to sit on a chair and a bear to ride a bicycle (hardly gene-driven behavior), as happens in many circuses, you can control the behavior of a child with tendencies to hyperactivity.

Perhaps the only condition in the field of behavior disturbance in which genetics plays an overwhelming role is autism (see Chapter 11). Strong evidence from family and twin studies indicates that genetics plays a significant role in the unusual behavior shown by children with autism. Even so, intensive treatment programs have been successful in ameliorating many of the symptoms of that condition (Rutter, Bailey, Bolton, & Le Couteur, 1993).

The Influence of Drugs

Another issue in the last two decades has been the increasing availability and use of illicit drugs. Does the presence of behavior or emotional problems predispose an individual to use drugs? If you are anxious, depressed, or angry, are you more likely to take drugs? Common sense would answer 'Yes,' but research is not clear.

Substance abuse is a growing problem in U.S. schools (Hawley, 1987). The prevalence of alcohol abuse and drug use is substantial, and Johnson (1988) theorized that exceptional children may be overrepresented among those who use drugs and alcohol. Think about the characteristics of drug users: low self-esteem, depression, inability to handle social experiences, and stress. These are the same characteristics that mark children with behavioral disorders. Johnson suggested a dual diagnosis: The primary handicap is a behavioral disturbance; the secondary handicap is a chemical dependency. Special educators, then, must know the signs of chemical dependency, what to do when they suspect drug abuse in their students, and how to work with drug treatment programs.

Children who are victims of abuse and violence often learn to inflict those behaviors on others.

FAMILY RISK FACTORS

The family risk factors shown in Figure 7.1 clearly indicate that problems within the family may help produce a child who is disturbed. One interesting indicator is family violence, which includes child abuse. Violence against children is a behavior that the children themselves are likely to display when they are old enough to inflict violence on those weaker than they.

The intergenerational aspect of this disorder is most distressing. A child with serious emotional disturbance rarely comes from a stable home with warm and loving parents. And the child who is abused is likely to be an abusive parent and to reproduce the entire negative pattern—unless the school or community intervenes.

Ramsey and Walker (1988) compared two groups of boys drawn, as pairs, from the same fourth-grade classrooms. The thirty-nine boys in one group exhibited antisocial behaviors; the forty-one boys in the other group did not. Data that came from structured family interviews confirmed that the antisocial children lived in an unstructured, negative environment where discipline was harsh and inconsistent. Although these factors may not have "caused" the antisocial behavior, they certainly did not contribute in a positive way to the child's social development. These factors, once again, indicate the importance of involving the entire family when possible.

A generation ago, feelings were strong that parents were in large part responsible for their child's behavior problems. Today, many believe that the child's atypical behavior may cause parents to react in ways that are inappropriate and make the condition worse in a downward spiral of unfortunate sequential events.

SCHOOL RISK FACTORS

As Figure 7.1 indicates, the child risk factor most frequently associated with social and emotional disturbance is below-grade achievement in school. Do these children act out *because* they are academically slow and not able to keep up with their classmates? Is their acting out a reaction to their failure in school? The idea is an interesting one, but the evidence does not seem to support it. For one thing, studies that measure the abilities of children with conduct disorders consistently find that, as a group, they score in the below-average range of intelligence (Kauffman, 1981). For another, the aggressive behavior that gets these youngsters into trouble in school is clearly observable *before* they enter school (Thomas & Chess, 1984).

Jim, for example, was in trouble in school right from kindergarten. His school records are peppered with teachers' statements: "He seems bright but doesn't want to apply himself." "He's unmotivated, and an angry little boy." "This boy will not take the time necessary to learn the basics."

In the general education literature, "time on task" is a well-established predictor of school success (Berliner, 1990). In other words, the common-sense conclusion that the more time you spend on learning a topic the more likely you will be to master it turns out to have solid research backing. This principle is relevant to the school performance of children who are seriously emotionally disturbed because they spend less time engaged in academic activities in the classroom—and probably outside the classroom as well (Walker, Stieber, & O'Neill, 1990).

SOCIAL RISK FACTORS

Bronfenbrenner (1979) focused on the family as a child-rearing system, on society's support or lack of support for that system, and on the effects of that support or lack of support on children. He maintained that the alienation of children reflects a breakdown in the interconnected segments of a child's life—family, peer group, school, neighborhood, and work world. The question is not, "What is wrong with children with emotional or behavior disorders?" The question is, "What is wrong with the child's social system?"

Although many of these children do not have feelings of anxiety or guilt about their behavior (especially children with socialized aggression or aggression stimulated by peer group actions or neighborhood values), the conflict between the values of those in authority in society (and in the school) and the values of their subculture can create tension. For example, what does a child who sees a friend cheating do? Honesty—a valued societal ethic—demands that the child report the incident. But loyalty—a valued subcultural ethic—demands silence. Even more serious in its impact is the situation in which the subgroup devalues education or pressures the individual to use drugs or violence.

Are criminals bred by family and social conditions? Are bad neighborhoods the source of delinquency? The easy answer is, Yes, but we should be careful about oversimplifying. We know that many youngsters emerge from what seem to be the most destructive social settings as effective adults. Individual patterns of development can overcome ecological forces, creating children who are invulnerable to their bad surroundings (Werner, 1979).

Viewing the ecological evidence linked to this condition should not cause us to leap to the conclusion that individual characteristics have nothing to do with the condition itself and that *only* environment is important.

▓▓▓▓▓▓▓   *Classifications and Characteristics*

Within the broad category of children with behavior disorders, many subgroups are educationally relevant. The purpose of classifying is to produce subgroups that either (1) improve our understanding of the origin or causes of a condition or (2) provide the basis for differential education and treatment. For example, Jim and Molly, an anxious and withdrawn child, can be classified as "children with behavior disorders," but they belong in different subcategories and would probably receive very different educational programming.

In the past, classification systems for children and adults with behavior problems emerged from psychiatry in response to the diagnostic patterns described by professionals in fields like clinical psychology and psychiatric social work. Two major classification systems were developed from that clinical perspective: the *Diagnostic and Statistical Manual of Mental Disorders*, fourth edition (*DSM* IV, 1994), and the classification system of Psychopathological Disorders in Children from the Group for the Advancement of Psychiatry (GAP). These systems also contain subgroups—for example, personality and developmental disorders, motor coordination disorders, and psychoneurotic disorders. But as useful as these designations may be from a psychiatric standpoint, they hold little value for educators.

A somewhat different approach involves the use of statistical techniques that isolate patterns of interrelated behaviors. By using checklists, rating scales, and other measuring devices to evaluate large numbers of children, it is possible to sort out clusters of responses that separate one group of characteristics or symptoms from another. This approach has yielded patterns of deviant behavior in children such as conduct disorders (including attention-deficit hyperactivity disorder), and anxiety-withdrawal (Quay & Werry, 1986).

CONDUCT DISORDERS

We find a common pattern in the families of children with conduct disorders. Often the father is aggressive and hostile and uses physical force for discipline. Jim's father treated what he thought was Jim's misbehavior with spankings that verged on beatings. Apparently hostility breeds hostility, and Jim became even more of a problem when his father walked out on the family, leaving Jim's mother to cope with Jim. Also, the mothers of these families tend to be inconsistent with discipline and preoccupied with financial survival (Wood, Combs, Gunn, & Weller, 1986). Obviously, the entire family can benefit from treatment, and attempts are made to involve key family members in treatment where possible.

Children with conduct disorders learn that aggressive behavior is a way of getting what they want, particularly when parental punishment is sporadic and ineffective and provides another model of aggressiveness. (© *Michael Weisbrot*)

There are many different opinions about the causes of the aggressive behavior that is typical of conduct disorders. One opinion based on social learning theory has gained wide acceptance. Patterson (1980) argued that, over time, children with conduct disorders (usually boys) learn that aggressive behavior is a way of getting what they want. They see it first at home, when parents give in to the aggressive youth. They use the response again and again in other situations, usually getting their way there, too. Parental punishment here is sporadic and ineffective and simply provides another model of aggressiveness. In short, these children are rewarded for aggressive behavior and thus continue to act out.

Children with conduct disorders are a serious problem in a school setting. They are easily distracted, unable to persist at tasks, and often disrupt class. Their inability to follow directions and maintain attention on a specific task is a source of constant irritation to teachers. As education has become more directly involved with these children, increasing concern has been expressed about their academic status. The problems of asocial and antisocial behavior, unless dealt with vigorously in childhood, can lead to antisocial behavior in adulthood, which in turn can create a new generation of antisocial children. And so the cycle continues.

Attention-Deficit Hyperactivity Disorder

As we learn more about behavioral disturbance and other conditions that we wish to study, we establish different descriptions of these conditions. We tend to separate out conditions such as infantile autism for the purpose of understanding their specific causes and identifying the most effective treatment. For **attention-deficit hyperactivity disorder (ADHD)**, the intent of establishing a new condition is to distinguish ADHD from other conditions that belong to the general category of developmental disorders or delay.

An ADHD child such as Dave, who is a compact and energetic 6-year-old, displays significant signs of inattention, distractibility, and disorganization but does not show the typical signs (such as delayed cognition) of a child with mental retardation. Such patterns of behavior show up typically in the preschool age. Dave's parents describe Dave like this: "He hits the floor running every day and has us all worn to a frazzle by midmorning." "He seems driven by some unseen force to be always on the go." "I never seem to be able to catch his attention to read him a story or get him to slow down to pay attention to what I want to tell him." It is not clear what the cause of such a condition is, but whether the cause is nutritional or neurological or an imbalance of neurotransmitter chemicals, the impact on the family and the teacher is predictable. Dave is hard to teach because he won't stand in one place long enough for a person to communicate meaningfully with him.

One standard possible treatment for ADHD is medication, primarily to slow the child down so that someone can catch his or her attention long enough to teach needed information. Drugs such as Ritalin, Dexedrine, or recently added Cylert have been prescribed, often with the desired result of increasing the child's control of his or her own behavior (Pueschel, Scala, Weidenman, & Bernier, 1995). Dave's parents are reluctant to give such powerful medicine to a 6-year-old, but his uncontrollable behavior may cause them to eventually give in.

Whether or not Dave responds positively to such medical intervention, he needs special educational programming, for he will miss many important educational experiences while he engages in this whirl of physical activity that can be so wearing to his parents and teachers.

Children with ADHD find it difficult to settle down to a particular task, particularly deskwork. Such students have been called learning disabled or even emotionally or behaviorally disturbed. Sometimes there is a case for classifying them under "other health-impaired." But whatever the classification, some standard intervention techniques can help teachers respond to such students:

- Providing a structured learning environment
- Repeating and simplifying instructions about in-class and homework assignments
- Supplementing verbal instructions with visual instructions
- Using behavioral management techniques
- Using tape recorders

Children who are anxious or withdrawn are more likely a danger to themselves than they are to others.

ANXIETY-WITHDRAWAL

Children who are anxious or withdrawn are likely to be a bigger threat to themselves than to others around them. Because they usually are not disruptive, they generally do not cause classroom management problems. But they are a source of worry for teachers.

In contrast to children with conduct disorders, who show too much behavior, children who are anxious and withdrawn show too little (Quay, 1979). Their problems are with excessive internal control; in all settings they maintain firm control over their impulses, wishes, and desires. Children who are anxious and withdrawn are rigid and unable to be spontaneous.

We find in children who are withdrawn and depressed, a **learned helplessness,** or the belief that nothing they do can stop bad things from happening. Learned helplessness results in severe deterioration in performance after failure, as though the children have said to themselves, "It's all happening again." These children often have such low self-concepts that failure in a school task or a social setting only confirms for them their worthlessness and helplessness in the face of an unfriendly environment (see Seligman & Peterson, 1986). These children's poor performance in the classroom may be much worse than they are capable of doing, simply because they are so pessimistic about themselves and their abilities. Low self-esteem seems to be at the heart of much of the underachievement of children who are anxious and withdrawn.

Where do fearful children come from? We know that many of them have parents with similar problems. In addition, most professionals agree that chronic anxiety in children comes from being in a stressful situation, not being able to get out of the situation, and not being able to do anything to improve it. This inability to change the situation adds to feelings of helplessness and reinforces low self-image.

Children develop chronic anxiety when they are frequently exposed to, and unable to control or remove themselves from, stressful situations.

For college students, a crucial examination looming on the horizon can create chronic anxiety. For younger children, anxiety can stem from homes where they feel unwanted or are abused. Children are often too young to understand that their parents may be working out their own problems or that their parents' actions have little to do with them. All they understand is that no matter what they do they are not getting praise or love from their parents.

One serious outcome of a prolonged intense period of anxiety or depression is suicide (suicide is also a problem among youngsters with other disabilities). Concern is growing about the prevalence of suicide in schoolchildren. It is the third leading cause of death in the 15-to-24 age group and the sixth leading cause for ages 5 to 14 (Guetzloe, 1991). Even these figures may be low because many suicides are listed as accidental deaths. If a teenager drives into a tree or off a bridge, it is difficult to know whether the crash was accidental or deliberate. Even accidents that are alcohol related may be a form of suicide if the use of alcohol was stimulated by depression.

Guetzloe (1991) reported a series of risk factors identified by many psychologists and psychiatrists to alert the observer to the possibility of suicide. One list points out that it is not just the *presence* of the characteristics but they should be in evidence nearly every day for a two-week period. At least five of these factors should be present:

1. Depressed or irritable mood
2. Loss of enjoyment or interest in normally pleasurable activities

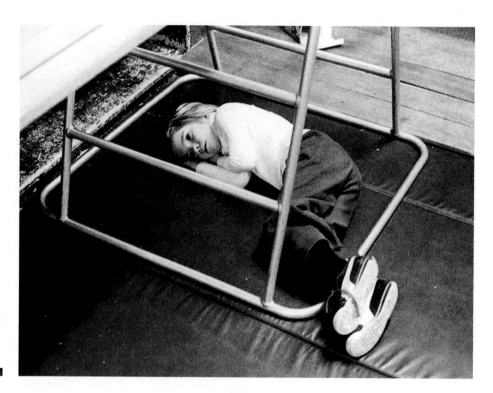

Children who are anxious and withdrawn have problems with excessive internal control and often feel helpless and unable to be spontaneous. (© *Michael Weisbrot*)

3. Change in weight, appetite, or eating habits

4. Problems with sleeping (insomnia or hypersomnia)

5. Psychomotor agitation or retardation (hyperactivity in children)

6. Loss of energy or feelings of fatigue

7. Feelings of worthlessness or excessive or inappropriate guilt

8. Diminished ability to attend, think, or concentrate (indecisiveness)

9. Recurrent thoughts of death or suicide

Although that list gives a strong impression that the problem rests within the individual, context factors can play a part. For example, there can be a significant increase in youth suicide following a front-page story on suicide or fictional accounts of suicide (Phillips & Carstensen, 1986). It is clear that some individuals are on a roof edge and can be pitched off by events in the community that cause them to lose control.

One effort to thwart suicide attempts has been the formation of crisis teams at both the school and the district level. Team members learn procedures to cope with suicidal individuals, and the team has access to resources that it can bring to bear quickly (Guetzloe, 1989).

A teacher who sees the danger signs has the immediate task of providing relief from the feelings of helplessness or hopelessness that the student may be expressing and instilling in the student some feeling of being in control (Guetzloe, 1988).

Some positive change, no matter how small, must be made to prove to the student that the situation is not hopeless. Shneidman (1985) called this change a "just noticeable difference."

Long-range treatment may demand services from community and mental health agencies, and teachers should be aware of good referral sources. For schools, the best method of prevention is an educational program that enhances feelings of self-worth and self-control. Explicit instruction in positive coping skills can be one way of providing feelings of self-control.

All of us have felt depressed at one time or another. Why do these feelings persist in some individuals and not in others? Schloss (1983) had three separate theories: learned helplessness, social skills deficiency, or coercive consequences. For each of these theories there is a predictable intervention technique. In the case of *learned helplessness*, we must convince children that they are capable of influencing their own environment. In the case of *social skills deficiency*, we can teach and reinforce effective interpersonal skills. In the case of *coercive consequences*, we can avoid reinforcing children's dependency and helplessness, focusing instead on positive aspects of their personality and performance.

Learned helplessness comes from low self-esteem and depression.

Developmental Profiles

Figure 7.2 shows the profiles of two youngsters. Both have behavior problems, and both are experiencing academic difficulties. The two children, however, manifest these problems in different ways.

Jim is an 11-year-old who seems sullen and angry most of the time. He rarely smiles and has a history of terrifying temper outbursts. When he is frustrated, he sometimes blows up and attacks the nearest person with such frenzy that other children give him a wide berth and hesitate to interact with him.

Stories in the neighborhood recount Jim's cruelty to animals, how he has tortured and killed cats and dogs. His language borders on profanity, and he has been known to challenge his teachers by asking, "What are you going to do about it?" Jim is a threat not only to his peers but also to his teachers' sense of their own competence. His physical skills are advanced, even though his interpersonal skills are not, and this tends to complicate the situation. As he grows older, he will become less manageable physically. Although we can tolerate the temper tantrums of a 5-year-old, the same outbursts from a 15-year-old are frightening.

School personnel are actively seeking alternative placement for Jim on the grounds that they are not capable, either physically or psychologically, of coping with his problems. Jim comes from a father-absent home; his mother is somewhat disorganized and seems to have given up trying to control her son. Attempts have been made to coordinate the program for Jim with mental health services for his mother in hopes of strengthening the family as a viable social unit. Although some progress has been made, the situation remains difficult. His social contacts are limited to a few other youngsters who have similar propensities for acting out when they become angry. Those who are close to Jim are worried about his future. Jim's

Figure 7.2

Profiles of Two Children with Behavior Disorders

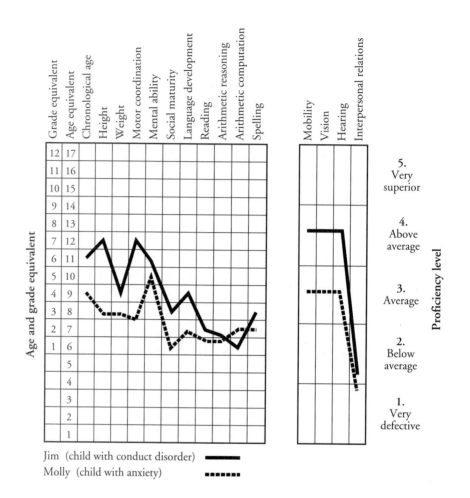

Jim (child with conduct disorder) ▬▬▬

Molly (child with anxiety) ▪▪▪▪▪▪▪

performance in school, as shown in the profile, is from two to five grades below his grade level, and his hostility and unwillingness to accept correction or help have caused his teachers much anxiety.

The second profile in Figure 7.2 is of Molly, a 9-year-old girl in the fourth grade who is having a difficult time at school. In contrast to Jim, who tends to externalize his problems, Molly seems to internalize hers. She is in tears and depressed much of the time. She is not able to make friends with the girls who have formed the major social group in the classroom, and she seems lonely and alone. Molly is so quiet that if it were not for the manifest unhappiness that shows in her face and physical demeanor, she would likely go completely unnoticed in school. She, like Jim, is seriously behind in her academic work. Jim is clearly externalizing his problems and, in the process, is causing problems for others. Molly is internalizing her problems and making herself miserable but is not directly confronting others.

Molly's middle-class parents are concerned about her and have taken many different steps to help her, including therapy, but so far their efforts have met with little success. She is a source of great frustration to her parents, who cannot understand why she is not like her older sister, who seems to succeed effortlessly in both academic and social spheres. Molly is not the personal threat to teachers that Jim is because she does not challenge their ability to control the classroom. But she does challenge those teachers who want the children in their classes to be happy in school and who are upset by their inability to modify her sadness and low self-concept.

Identification and Placement

The decision to refer a child for special education services is an important one; it must be made carefully. It is often difficult to distinguish between children with behavior disorders and those who just have a series of transient adaptation problems: Each child shows unacceptable behavior, but one shows it longer and more intensely than the other.

The placement of a disproportionate number of minority students in special education programs has raised questions about the process that many school systems use to identify students with behavior problems. Are these systems mistaking cultural differences for aberrant behavior? Are the personal biases of some decision makers playing a role in decision making? Or are some subgroups especially likely to show the symptoms of behavior problems?

Whatever the answer may be in individual circumstances, it is clear that some testing and an interview with the school psychologist are not enough to support a placement decision. Wood and Smith (1985) developed a five-step response and assessment process:

1. *Classroom or home adjustments.* The first level of response to a child's problems is the home or the classroom teacher. Usually a parent or teacher deprives a child of privileges or reprimands the child following asocial or antisocial behavior. If the problem is transitory, this action may be as far as the issue needs to be taken.

2. *Prereferral activities.* If a problem persists in the classroom, some school systems use a *prereferral team*—a group of specialists (psychologists, principals, speech-language therapists)—to work out a plan that the teacher can implement in the regular classroom with the help of the team. If the plan fails after a reasonable time, additional steps are necessary.

3. *Referral for special education services—collecting information.* With the parents' consent, information is gathered about the child. In addition to the standard intelligence achievement data and health information, direct observational data about the child in the classroom should be collected so that the problem is seen in the environment in which the solution must be implemented. Data are assembled through interviews, teacher rating scales, tests, and observations and usually are synthesized in a case study team approach.

It often is difficult to distinguish between children with behavior disorders and those who just have a series of transient adaptation problems. (© *Jean-Claude Lejeune/ Stock Boston*)

4. *Referral for special education services—placement.* At this stage the assessment team determines that the child is not profiting from the current placement and makes new recommendations. These can include a change in physical environment, different treatment schedules, or the employment of supportive services. The individualized education program (IEP) is developed at this stage.

5. *Implementing the IEP.* The plan developed during the earlier steps of the assessment is put into operation. Evaluative data on the child's progress continue to be collected.

The IEP, when used properly, is an effective guide for teachers who are trying to cope with children who show emotional or behavior problems. The IEP is shaped not only by the student's specific problem but also by available resources. The presence of professional consultants in the mental health area or an active remedial program in the school gives both the assessment team and the parents more options to consider.

Despite a liberal definition of children with behavior problems that includes the perceiver as well as the child, most diagnostic instruments now in use focus exclusively on the characteristics of the child and do not take into consideration the nature of the environment. Judgment about the role of the environment is still left to the discretion of the individual observer, clinician, or special educator.

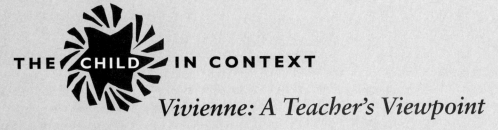

THE CHILD IN CONTEXT

Vivienne: A Teacher's Viewpoint

In my teaching career, I have taught all ages, I have known children far more apparently injured than Vivienne, even abused. I have known adolescents with fewer successes and, to an observer, deeper feelings of worthlessness who nevertheless survived. Even Vivienne's preoccupation with death, had I known of it, would not have shocked me. The idea of personal death has impact at any age, but for adolescents it has particular force. Many young people struggle to incorporate their new awareness and even toy with death as a possible means of controlling their own destinies. . . .

Vivienne did not send signals to any Cambridge School adult and her pain was not visible. Her deepest injuries had occurred before we knew her and she had become clever about concealing them. But suppose we had seen some of her most dramatic writing? It takes an experienced eye to detect the difference between fatal despair and sensitive introspection. Adolescents are often dramatic in their writing. To an adult, young people sometimes seem to lack an emotional thermostat, so heated and volatile are their responses. They can be anguished at one moment, restored and vivacious the next. One must know a great deal about them to judge how serious their struggles are. . . .

All of this certainly crosses a teacher's mind when a student shares tragic thoughts. Empathetic teachers are aware of the pride and dignity, the sense of privacy young people feel so keenly. Here, indeed, is that puzzling line that teachers sometimes face between themselves and other professionals. When should a teacher report troubling news? When would it drive a wedge between him and the adolescent who trusts no one else? Can any sympathetic adult handle the situation?

Knowing what we know now, the answer seems simple. Vivienne tried to strangle herself. . . . The family should have been alerted. A therapist should have been called in.

But, in my experience, these are not easy decisions. We hesitate to cut lines of communication that may, in the end, help to heal. The strangulation description in Vivienne's letter is followed by "I have decided to stick this life of mine out," and she went on to report that she was writing poetry again.

These are reassuring communications and seem to put the suicidal impulse in the past. . . .

The issues are difficult ones. Adolescents don't seem to be the best candidates for therapy. They tend to see adult counselors as official parental representatives and consequently as a threat to their unsteady independence. They often lack, too, the deep and continuing discontent that informs the motivation of older people. It is hard for them to commit themselves seriously to regular appointments. They are inclined to flee when sessions come closest to the heart of their suffering. They would rather turn to trusted teachers or other adults when they need a listener. They prefer to remain in control of the time and the extent of their own confidences.

But this poses another problem. Teachers have their limitations. They may be frightened of emotional crises. They may mistake what they are hearing. They may lack the personal insight and training that illuminate for psychologists, not only the meaning of confidences young people offer, but, perhaps even more important, their own blind spots and denials. Teachers are not professional psychologists. They need to know when to turn to the experts. There is a distinct line between what the counseling profession offers and what educators can do to prevent suicide.

The distinction between the two is entirely proper. In some ways, teachers represent reality and daily partnership. A teacher may see as "lazy" what a psychiatrist would label "paralyzed." A teacher could respond to "hostility" where a psychologist would see "depression." Young people need to know both aspects of themselves: the effect of their behavior and, when it is troubling, the emotional logic that causes it. Perhaps these two functions cannot be blended in one person, but it is safe to say that the two viewpoints ought to come closer together and that teachers should make new relationships with counselors.

In our school we have a training group for teachers, now in its fourth year. We meet once a week for two hours under the supervision of an experienced psychologist. There we talk about ourselves, our students, relationships and events that puzzle us. The group serves to enlighten and inform us, deepen our personal insight and enrich our understanding of young people. We can better recognize and handle normal adolescent turmoil. It does not, however, make us psychologists, and we learn to be very respectful of that line between us. . . .

Vivienne died at fourteen. No one close to her was able to keep her from suicide. As Marianne Moore wrote, "What is our innocence,/what is our guilt? All are/naked, none is safe." Shaken and changed, we review Vivienne's suffering and reconsider the plight of adolescents everywhere. Her death reminds us again: all children are under our care.

Source: *Vivienne: The Life and Suicide of an Adolescent Girl* by John E. Mack and Holly Hickler (1981). Boston, MA: Little, Brown and Company, Inc.

---

commentary

What Is the Context? Within the school context, teachers and psychologists see children from different perspectives but sometimes do not share these perspectives with one another. As a result, children with behavior disturbances may be in unrecognized danger. To best help students with disabilities, teachers need to create a shared context with psychologists and parents.

Pivotal Issues. Who is responsible for responding to a child with severe emotional disturbance? How can families, psychologists, and teachers work together to reach these children? When should a teacher intervene? What are teachers' limitations? How do special educators provide support for a teacher who observes such behavior?

Intervention Strategies

In earlier chapters, we discussed the various ways that educators can modify the standard educational program to meet the special needs of exceptional children. They can change the *learning environment* in which the child is currently placed, they can change the *content* of the lessons that are provided to the child, and they can teach the child *skills* to process information and to work effectively with peers and adults. In addition, teaching personnel must be given intervention strategies as well as training to accomplish these differential tasks. It is important to think of modifications in all of these areas for children with behavioral disorders.

Educators are using a wide variety of approaches to try to change behavior. Their objectives are to change behavior patterns, encourage constructive behaviors, and help children develop effective strategies for coping with their disorder.

Major strategies in this area have a base in what we have learned about operant conditioning and ecological strategies. Drug therapy may also be an option. Although we discuss each intervention strategy separately here, many are used in combination with one another. Table 7.1 summarizes some behavior reduction

TABLE 7.1   Behavior Reduction Strategies for Use with Children with Behavior Disorders

Type	Procedure	Example	Results
Environmental modification	Change environmental cues that trigger unacceptable behavior	Reducing student stress by giving tasks with shorter steps	Works well for mild problems but may not be sufficient for serious problems
Differential reinforcement	Reinforce appropriate behavior and ignore unacceptable behavior	Praise aggressive student for sharing with other students; don't "hear" verbal aggressive comments	Seems to reduce hyperactivity, aggressiveness, and self-injury; does not result in quick change
Time-out	Suspend child for a time period from sources of possible reinforcement	Child with temper tantrum is asked to go to "quiet corner"—an enclosed cubicle, for example—until he or she regains control	Although not universally effective, the utility of time-out is well documented
Overcorrection	Ask child to correct the consequences of misbehavior	Child who deliberately soils self may be asked to wash, clean, and wax affected classroom areas	Overcorrection appears to be an effective option
Aversive conditioning	The use of painful, distasteful, or undesirable stimuli to reduce inappropriate behavior	Giving student mild electric shocks when aggressing against peers	Seems to work when combined with other methods; use of this method is controversial
Corporal punishment	Any procedure for inflicting pain on body of offending child	Spanking child for manifest unacceptable behavior	Not generally considered as effective as other techniques

Source: Council for Children with Behavior Disorders (1990). Position paper on use of behavior reduction strategies with children with behavior disorders. *Behavioral Disorders*, 15(4), pp. 243–260.

strategies for use with children with behavior disorders. A number of these rely on operant conditioning.

OPERANT CONDITIONING

With **operant conditioning,** we control the stimulus that produces a response. For example, suppose a little boy sucks his thumb when he watches television. If his parent turns the television off when his thumb is in his mouth and on when it is not, the child will soon learn that if he wants to keep the television on, he must not suck his thumb. In this situation, the response (thumb sucking) is controlled by the stimulus (television off).

Operant conditioning is based on the principle that behavior is a function of its consequence. The application of a positive stimulus (television on) immediately following a response is called *positive reinforcement.* Now suppose instead that the parents turn on a loud alarm clock when the child sucks his thumb. When the boy takes his thumb out of his mouth, the clock is turned off. This is an example of *negative reinforcement.* The withdrawal of a negative stimulus (the clock) leads to the desired behavior. A common procedure is to establish a base line of behavior (observations prior to treatment) so that gains or improvement can be measured against the base line.

The most controversial operant conditioning methods are those that rely on aversive conditioning or corporal punishment. They are reserved for serious conditions that have been resistant to other approaches.

One byproduct of the increasing use of operant conditioning is a more precise description of target behaviors, the characteristics we want to change or enhance. Kerr and Nelson (1989) described several of those behaviors:

A wide range of behavior reduction strategies exists for use with children who have behavior disorders.

1. Kim does not comply with teacher requests.

   When asked by the teacher to do something, Kim will respond appropriately within 10 seconds without being asked again.

2. Andy is hyperactive.

   Andy will remain at his desk, without moving and with all four chair legs on the floor, for 20 consecutive minutes.

3. Fred can't ride the school bus appropriately.

   Fred will get on the bus without pushing, hitting, or shoving; walk to his assigned seat; remain there throughout the ride without disturbing others; and exit from bus without pushing, hitting, or shoving.

4. Betsy is aggressive.

   Betsy will play with other children during the entire recess period without hitting, kicking, pushing, or calling them names.

5. Billy is withdrawn.   Billy will initiate at least two peer
                                           interactions during any given 15-minute
                                           recess period (p. 25).

Notice that the clear description of a positive target behavior allows us to measure its occurrence with greater precision.

One of the key elements of a positive conditioning system is providing some type of external reward (extra time at recess, free time, a field trip) when the child exhibits the target behavior (Paul & Epanchin, 1986). Once the student starts behaving appropriately, the teacher can begin to use positive reinforcement. But a teacher can't reinforce behavior that isn't there! As one teacher commented, "I am more than ready to give positive reinforcement. When is *he* (the student) going to show some positive behavior that I can reinforce?"

One program designed to elicit positive behavior is called a *levels program* because it features identifiable levels of rewards and privileges that are available for students who behave appropriately. Mastropieri, Jenne, and Scruggs (1988) reported an example of the approach used in a secondary education resource program. Fifteen high school students identified as behaviorally disturbed were placed in an English program. The teacher identified four different behavioral levels, and colored nametags identified the level at which each student was performing. As the students' behavior improved—as judged by their peers—their privileges increased, and their colored nametags were changed.

At the lowest level, students with a blue nametag were expected to be prepared for their lessons, to raise their hands before speaking, and to be in their seats at all times. Students who showed appropriate behavior moved up to the next level. At the highest level (a red nametag), students were allowed to move around the room, study in a special room, and monitor their own behavior.

Did the program work? The students' academic and social behavior improved substantially during the four-week program, and a follow-up two weeks after the program was discontinued showed the same improvement.

Some object to the use of behavior modification techniques because they treat the child like a slot machine (insert a quarter, get good behavior) and have little impact on the child's basic personality. This criticism is not fair. The educational objective is to create in the child a positive response that can be expanded and used for better overall social adjustment.

The usual procedure for shaping behavior in the classroom is to establish goals and organize tasks in small steps so that the child can experience ongoing success. This procedure is referred to as *task analysis*. The child receives positive reinforcement for each step or part of the total task as he or she completes it (arithmetic, reading, or spelling, for example). Assignments are programmed in easy steps. After the child completes a task in a specified period of time, the teacher checks the work, praises the child (social reinforcement), and rewards the child with a mark, a grade, a token, or some other tangible reinforcement. In this way the child is able to work at assignments for longer and longer periods and to accept increasingly more difficult tasks.

FUNCTIONAL ASSESSMENT

Functional assessment is another intervention strategy to use with children with behavioral disorders. A functional assessment is a multistep procedure carried out for the purpose of understanding the intended objective or intent of the student's behavior as well as describing that behavior (Gibney & Wood, 1994). It is different from operant conditioning, which deals directly with the behavior itself regardless of what the behavior might signify to the individual.

Starting from the premise that even puzzling and self-destructive behavior has a rational purpose, functional assessment aims to shed light on that purpose. Much aberrant behavior is a reaction to fear or anger, but if we don't know precisely what the fear or anger refers to, we have difficulty knowing how to respond to the sometimes provocative behavior.

Table 7.2 presents a conversation in which a teacher uses some functional assessment methods to determine what might be behind a shoplifting incident that Melissa became involved in. It soon becomes clear that the incident involves not merely the theft of a jacket but a complex relationship between Melissa and her boyfriend and between Melissa and her mother. The teacher attempts to see the world through the eyes of the child in order to understand what this otherwise puzzling behavior means to the child. After all, we all react to the world as we see it, not as others see it.

TABLE 7.2   Functional Assessment About Shoplifting

I: Hello, Melissa. Would you tell me what happened yesterday at the store.

M: (*Looks surprised.*) Oh, you heard.

I: Yes. I'd like to hear more about it.

M: Well, I was walking through the store with my friend, Tim. He dared me to steal a leather jacket. That's all.

I: Shoplifting is no big deal?

M: You sound like my mom. Shoplifting isn't like regular stealing. You aren't hurting a person, and the store won't miss one stupid jacket.

I: So, it's O.K. to take something if you aren't hurting someone?

M: Yeah, I guess so.

I: But you got caught.

M: Yeah, so what? I know my mom told you to talk to me about this. What does it matter to you if I got caught?

I: Well, you know your mom is going to ask me about our talk. I think stealing is serious stuff, and I'm going to have to tell her about this.

M: I know, but she won't care. Ever since the divorce she hasn't been the same. She doesn't care what I do.

Source: C. Gibney and F. Wood (1994). *Why Would Anyone Do Something Like That?* Minneapolis: University of Minnesota, p. 23. Reprinted by permission of the author.

ECOLOGICAL STRATEGIES

The first behavior disturbance reduction strategy described in Table 7.1 is **environmental modification,** or deliberately creating a more responsive environment in which the children work. Ecological strategy assumes that the child is an inseparable part of a small social system, of an ecological unit made up of the child, family, school, neighborhood, and community. Supporters of this model maintain that behavior problems are a result of destructive interactions between the child and this social system, or the environment (family, agemates, teachers, cultural subgroups). Treatment consists of modifying elements in the ecology, including the child (through counseling), to foster more constructive interactions between the child and the environment.

Project Re-Ed

Hobbs (1996, 1970, 1979, 1982) and his colleagues implemented the ecological strategy with programs for emotionally disturbed children. They called their program Project Re-Ed (re-education). Two residential schools in the Re-Ed program were organized to house approximately forty children each, ages 6 to 12. The plan was to re-educate these children for a short period of time (from four to six months) and at the same time, through a liaison teacher, to modify the attitudes of the home, school, and community. The program was oriented toward re-establishing the children as quickly as possible in their own homes, schools, and communities.

In general, a program of re-education follows a number of principles:

1. *Life is to be lived now.* Every hour of the day children engage in purposeful activities and in activities in which they can succeed.

2. *Time is an ally.* Some children improve with time. But children should not remain in a residential setting for long periods. Doing so could estrange them from their families. Six months in the residential center is the stated goal of Project Re-Ed.

3. *Trust is essential.* How to inspire trust, according to Hobbs, is not something that can be learned in college courses. It is something that those working with emotionally disturbed children "know, without knowing they know."

4. *Competence makes a difference.* The arrangement of the environment and learning tasks must be structured so that children are able to gain confidence and self-respect from their successes.

5. *Symptoms can and should be controlled.* The treatment of symptoms, not causes, is emphasized.

The teacher-counselor is the key staff person in re-education programs and is qualified not only in special education but also in counseling methods designed for children who are disturbed. A liaison teacher-counselor works in the program to form effective alliances among home, school, and child. When a child is removed from a regular school and placed in a Re-Ed school, the liaison teacher-counselor keeps the school aware of the child's progress in the program and prepares the child and the school for his or her re-entry when the time approaches.

Time-Out

The time-out is frequently used to control the misbehavior of children.

One of the techniques used most frequently to control the behavior of children with behavior disorders is **time-out**—sending students who have violated classroom rules to a secluded place in the room or in a space nearby with instructions to come back when they feel that they have regained control of themselves. Time-out takes the student away from possibly negative interactions with other students and gives him or her a chance to cool off.

Most teachers consider time-out to be a neutral tactic, not expressing negative feelings to the student in question. Few people, however, have asked students how they feel about the procedure. When Wrobel and Wood (1992) did ask some students, they got some surprising responses:

Ed: It's a waste of time to go in there. They want you to write stuff down but you probably already knew what you did so it's just a waste of time, basically.

Fred: Just gets you _____ mad.

George: To me it's like a prison. It's like when you do somethin' it's always time-out this, time-out that, and it's just like to me . . . just a _____ prison.

It is clear that those students felt that time-out was an assertion of power by the school rather than an intervention that helped them deal with their problems. According to Wrobel and Wood, "Teachers can frequently discuss the general reasons for the use of time-out, recognizing and accepting the students' view that it is more often punishing than therapeutic in its immediate effects" (1992, p. 96).

THE CHALLENGE OF SUBSTANCE ABUSE

One of the serious side problems of many children with behavior disorders is substance abuse. The public's attention is often directed to the use of exotic drugs, but the use and abuse of alcohol and tobacco are much more common. There is evidence (Leone, Greenberg, Tricket, & Spero, 1989; Elmquist, Morgan, & Bolds, 1992) that children with behavior problems have rates of substance abuse much higher than the rates of their peers in special education or students in general education. Despite this information, there appears to be little systematic effort to include prevention programs in the school curriculum for these students.

A number of forces are inhibiting a direct educational attack on substance abuse for such students (Genaux, Morgan, & Friedman, 1995). Among these factors are limited interest shown by parents, lack of curriculum materials, and lack of time and funding. There appears to be a need to focus general education and special education teachers on the whys and hows of drug abuse and what they can do about it.

DRUG TREATMENT

One of the supplementary strategies for coping with children with ADHD has been the administration of drugs in order to dampen the hyperactivity or inattention so that the student is in a better personal context for learning. Forness (1992) studied seventy-one boys with ADHD and the effect of methylphenidate (Ritalin) over a five-week period on their reading comprehension. The effects on measured ability and achievement were quite modest. The only group that responded consisted of boys who had "ADHD with conduct disorders," and their reading comprehension improved. It does not seem that a magic pill will solve the academic problems of such students, although medication may be helpful in individual cases.

It was once thought that drug treatment was going to be an important answer. It is still clear that the right dosage of the right drug can result in marked improvement of hyperactive student behavior (Kauffman, 1989, p. 239). The problem is that the effects of medication are highly idiosyncratic and cannot be predicted in advance of trial. Also, enough negative side effects such as adverse effects on learning, growth, and health, and even a reducing of the students' sense of self-control ("It is the drug that is improving behavior, not me"), have been reported that caution and careful clinical monitoring are needed. Kauffman concluded (1989, p. 239):

> Responsible clinicians use drugs carefully as one approach to treatment when other solutions to the problem of hyperactivity are not feasible or when there is reason to suspect that drugs, in addition to other interventions, will produce a better result.

It seems to be increasingly clear that under the right circumstances and with certain individuals, drug therapy can be an important part of a total program of help. But it rarely if ever can be the sole method of treatment.

TREATMENT COMBINATIONS

To be effective, teachers must tailor treatments to the individual child's characteristics.

Each skills mastery technique or intervention strategy brings some benefits to children with behavior disorders and their families. Hinshaw, Henker, and Whalen (1984) studied the effects of combining several treatments into one multidisciplinary approach. Twenty-four hyperactive boys were taught how to work by themselves on academic tasks, how to control their anger, and how to evaluate themselves. In addition, they were given medication to control their hyperactivity. The results suggested that the educational program in combination with medication worked best.

There are few easy answers in the search for good educational programs for exceptional children. But we do know that we have to match the characteristics of the child with the characteristics of his or her environment, and we need to look for a variety of treatment options that will match the characteristics of individual students.

Educational Adaptations

THE ROLE OF THE CASE MANAGER (SERVICE COORDINATOR)

Prior to 1975, children with behavior disorders were seen as the clients of the mental health community. Then the schools took over the major responsibility through vehicles like the Education for All Handicapped Children Act (PL 94-142). Recognition is now growing that these multifaceted problems need multifaceted solutions and the professional services of many different fields.

One realization that has emerged from experiences with children with behavior disorders or emotional disturbance (or both) is that various professional skills are required to make a difference in the life situation for such students. Multidisciplinary teams that may include educators, counselors, social service personnel, mental health personnel, paraprofessionals, and parents are increasingly popular (Simpson, Miles, Walker, Ormsbee, & Downing, 1991).

The multidisciplinary team is coordinated by a *case manager* (also known as a *service coordinator*). This person may come from any of these professions and is directly responsible for seeing that the treatment program is carried out. Among the case manager's functions are coordinating the various services going to child and family, providing follow-up to ensure that goals are being met, and guiding the work of paraprofessionals and volunteers who work with the child. It is a substantial advantage to have one person who knows all aspects of the treatment program and who has responsibility to see that forward progress is being made (Johnson, 1989).

This may seem to be an enormous expenditure of staff for one student, but it has become increasingly clear that this type of approach is necessary to obtain positive results. Minor tinkering with one or another part of a student's environment is not likely to effect major changes in students prone to aggressiveness and violence.

One thing is certain. Failing to act can be very expensive in human lives and in scarce resources. Although the cost of treatment is substantial, it is nowhere near the cost of not treating the child and family. As of 1990, the state of Kentucky estimated that institutionalization in a psychiatric hospital cost taxpayers $72,000 per child per year. Similarly, the cost of incarcerating a juvenile is estimated at $30,000 per year (Allen-Hagen, 1992). Society is faced with a serious set of choices of the "pay me a little now, or pay me a lot later" variety.

LEARNING ENVIRONMENT

The learning environment for children with behavior disorders who have passed through the prereferral stage and have been determined eligible can include inclusion in the regular classroom, a resource room, a special class, and special residential schools where a total therapeutic environment is provided for children who do

TABLE 7.3 Comparison of Available and Proposed Services

Services	Current System	Proposed System
Hospitalization	•	•
Residential treatment		
Large setting	•	•
Group home	•	•
Professional parenting, specialized foster care		•
Supervised independent living		•
Day treatment		
High management—full day		•
Moderate management—full day		•
Moderate management with public school—half day		•
Therapeutic vocational placement		•
Therapeutic preschool (ages 0–6)		•
Evening treatment		
After school or work—half-day equivalent		•
Therapeutic camping		
Weekend, summer, or year round		•
Outpatient		
Individual treatment (office or home)	•	•
Family treatment (office or home)	•	•
In-school support services	•	•
Emergency services (available 24 hr./day)	•	•
Family preservation		
In-home crisis stabilization	•	•

Source: L. Behar (1990). Financing mental health services for children and adolescents (p. 129). *Bulletin of the Menninger Clinic, 54,* pp. 127–139. Copyright 1990, The Menninger Foundation, Topeka, KS. Reprinted by permission.

not seem able to cope with the regular school program, or vice versa. Table 7.3 gives a mental health viewpoint on the range of service settings that should be available. The range and intensity of problems presented by the child with serious emotional disturbance require a range of intensity of treatment. Unfortunately, as Behar (1990) pointed out, and as Table 7.3 shows, substantial gaps in the system of care and treatment still exist as we traverse the 1990s. In particular, there is a major gap between the school and what it can do and the residential treatment center or institutionalization.

This gap was most evident when the movement to deinstitutionalize youths and adults became most vigorous in the 1970s. Many individuals were released from large institutions into the community. Instead of being re-enrolled in a more moderate treatment program—through group homes or supervised independent living settings, which many professionals recommended—they were left on their own. A sudden move from total care to no care is not a reasonable strategy. Establishing new community treatment facilities is expensive, however, and budgets and the public may not be willing to bear these costs.

Inclusion

The goal of special education has been to place children with behavior disorders in the least restrictive environment, which is the regular education program, whenever possible. The reasons are to give these students a chance (1) to interact with children who do not have disabilities, (2) to have constructive models of behavior, and (3) to keep in step academically. Although teachers may desperately wish to remove some of these disruptive children from their classrooms, educators who stress inclusion as a strategy wish to keep them in.

One of the most serious barriers to the proper educational and mental health programming for students with behavior problems is that the intensity of the treatment does not match the intensity of the problem. These students did not acquire their dysfunctional patterns of behavior overnight. The dysfunctional patterns have been years in the making, and it is not realistic to believe that they can be eliminated and positive responses substituted for them as a result of an hour of remedial education two times a week or a stern lecture. We often shortchange such children because of staff or financial limitations and then wonder why they don't show more immediate improvement.

On the basis of phone interviews with over 130 programs across the country and site visits to twenty-six programs, Knitzer, Steinberg, and Fleisch (1990) concluded that the resource room strategy has generally been nonproductive. They recommended that it be replaced with direct supportive services brought into the general classroom, together with substantial collaboration between mental health services and educators.

There has been an unfortunate tendency for general education teachers to refer children to special services or special education as a way of getting themselves out of an awkward situation. The prereferral strategies that we have mentioned in previous chapters (see Chalfant & Pysh, 1989) seem also to be a preferred strategy here, with a team of personnel in the school building meeting with the teacher to see what adjustments or adaptations might be made in the regular classroom before a referral is made to special education. Substantial questions have been raised about whether sufficient support services will be available to support the general educator. Kauffman, for example, worries about whether there are sufficient general classroom resources to cope with the most violent or disturbed children in an inclusive classroom:

> Special education is intellectually bankrupt and morally derelict to the extent that it embraces a philosophy that insists on the same placement decision for all students. A second topic for discussion is how does this philosophy of inclusion and the practices derived from it fit with the nature of schools as they exist now, their changing priorities, and the processes of reform? At the same time that teachers are faced with increasingly difficult tasks, they are being asked to do more and to do better with less.
>
> Many of the students now identified for special education because of their emotional or behavioral disorders are kids with very serious problems who require intensive sustained services from many well-trained people who are continuously available. (1994, p. 14)

That view is echoed by a position statement of the Council for Children with Behavior Disorders (1989):

> Academic accommodation in general education is important but insufficient to meet the needs of most behaviorally disordered students. Behaviors which interfere with educational performance are *infrequently* merely a matter of low academic ability or poor teaching. Typically, the academic problems of behaviorally disordered students reflect basic behavioral-emotional problems which must be addressed if the academic deficit is to be resolved.

The issue surrounding inclusion of children with behavioral disorders essentially boils down to whether one has confidence that the schools will be able to provide the support personnel necessary to allow a particular child, the teacher, and other students to have a positive and constructive experience. Clearly, the consensus that emerges from the current literature is that necessary social skills instruction and behavior management support are not in place in general education environments, and general educators are not prepared to accept and teach students with challenging behaviors at this time (Lewis, Chard, & Scott, 1994, p. 288).

One technique that emerged from the field of mental health and has been used successfully by teachers is the **life space interview,** originally designed by Redl (1959) and updated by Wood and Long (1991). A life space interview with the student occurs directly after a particular crisis situation or event so that the child faces the consequences of the behavior immediately instead of waiting a day or more for a regular counseling session or visit to the principal, by which time the child has forgotten or has built sufficient defenses around the event for self-protection.

Let's look at how it works. On the playground Jim has been unmercifully teasing another youngster, Paul, who did something to irritate Jim in the classroom. Finally, out of desperation, Paul strikes out at Jim, giving Jim an excuse to hit back. The teacher immediately sits down with Jim quietly in a private setting and

It is possible to create a positive social environment through instruction and prior preparation, so that children in regular classrooms can reach out to children with disabilities in an informed, empathic way.
(© Elizabeth Crews/Stock, Boston)

discusses the incident in detail. The teacher might ask Jim to describe what happened and his role in creating the event. Jim would have full opportunity to verbalize his own attitudes about the situation and to express his feelings about Paul.

Ideally, a life space interview ends with specific steps for resolving the problem or for preventing similar problems in the future. Some evidence supports life space interviews as a means of reducing maladaptive behavior, not only by inhibiting undesirable behavior but also by generating alternative solutions.

It is not always possible for the regular class teacher, or even a team of teachers untrained in the special instructional strategies, to cope with students with behavior disorders in the regular education setting. In such instances the student spends a part or all of the school day with a specially trained teacher so that both social and academic goals can be met.

CURRICULUM CONTENT

For children with behavior disturbances, the path toward academic success is likely to be difficult and uncertain. Not only do they often have poor relationships with many of their teachers, but their personal and social problems distract them from academic tasks. Consequently these children often find themselves far behind in their academic work and in need of remedial attention (Kerr & Nelson, 1989).

The content of their curriculum may not be different from that of other children, but because they may be at an earlier developmental level, the curriculum may be two or three grade levels earlier in difficulty. The special education teacher in a resource room where a child with behavior problems may come for an hour a day often spends much time in a combination of remedial reading and arithmetic combined with empathic counseling.

Mark is an 8-year-old boy who was referred to a special class for emotionally disturbed children because his mother was concerned about his immaturity and learning problems. After a thorough evaluation, the special services committee in his school agreed that Mark was excessively rigid, inhibited, and anxious. Even after the evaluation, however, it was not clear why he was having learning problems. Mark was placed in a special class for academic work. His teacher formulated an IEP that involved remedial work in reading and math. The teaching materials included stories about children and how they felt in various circumstances. In addition, the teacher tried, whenever possible, to give Mark psychological permission to express his feelings.

One day when the teacher was very late getting to him, she said, "I'm sorry I'm late. If I had to wait as long as you've had to wait, I'd be upset. Are you a little upset?" On another day, when a child ripped Mark's paper off the bulletin board, she said, "It's too bad about your paper. That upsets me!"

Gradually, Mark began to express his feelings, and as he did it became increasingly evident that once he had vented his frustrations, he was learning and producing more efficiently. With this realization, the teacher began to teach Mark about himself—about how he behaved and how he could monitor himself.

Though Mark's problems were emotional in nature, they led to serious academic problems that could not be ignored. Even if, through some combination of drug treatment and psychotherapy, those emotional problems could have been "solved," Mark still would have been left with serious academic deficiencies that needed remediation.

One way to adapt a program content for children with behavior problems is to design a self-awareness curriculum that provides students with an opportunity to learn more about their own feelings and those of other children. The teaching tools include carefully chosen literature, role-playing, and class discussions in which the teacher stresses feelings and attitudes.

COMPUTERS: AIDING CONTENT MASTERY AND AVOIDING NEGATIVE RESPONSE

A computer can be an especially useful learning tool for a student with behavior problems because it provides an objective, neutral response to the child's sometimes provocative or challenging behavior. Children with a long history of social interaction problems may respond poorly to teacher feedback, particularly when criticism or correction is involved. The child who is adept at manipulating others can quickly change the focus of a discussion from his or her inadequate academic performance to the teacher's behavior. "Why are you always picking on me?" is a common theme. With a computer, however, the student must find a different approach.

Obviously, a computer isn't able to interact emotionally with the child. If the student has difficulty solving a problem, he or she must find out why and determine the right answer to proceed with the computer program. The student cannot resort to emotional manipulation or accuse the machine of being unfair.

Children who are hyperactive or who have an attention-deficit hyperactive disorder often have difficulty concentrating and can be helped by a computer. When working with a computer, they must pay some degree of attention to get results. The orderliness and sequence of the software programs can provide a systematic structure for students who have very little cognitive structure or self-discipline. Given the extensive possibilities for the use of computers with students who have behavior problems, it is surprising that little research on their impact with such students has been published.

SKILLS MASTERY TECHNIQUES

Specialists who work with children who have behavior disorders have focused much of their attention on behavior change, which can occur with or without the child's participation. This means reducing some unacceptable behavior or encouraging proactive, socially desirable behavior. Behavior change that occurs without the child's participation results from operant conditioning (which we discussed in the section on intervention strategies). Specialists apparently can also help youngsters to actively change their behavior. They can help youngsters (1) to see the signals in their environment that trigger their unacceptable behavior, (2) to inhibit the impulse to respond immediately, and (3) to develop a plan of action to meet different situations. In many respects, the goal of learning those three skills is as important to the education of youngsters with behavior disorders as are the academic goals of reading and arithmetic. Until these children are able to exercise self-control and to develop other social skills, they are unlikely to learn traditional academic skills.

Teachers can use various strategies with students who have behavior disorders, but each strategy imposes costs or demands on the teachers themselves (see Table 7.4)—whether they are trying to communicate with students, support desirable behavior, or control problem behavior. The strategies in Table 7.4 that are preceded by an asterisk are unusually costly in time or additional effort. For example, reminding a student about the rules of the classroom costs the teacher less in energy or effort than does conducting a group meeting on a problem behavior. High-cost teacher behavior, however, may be needed to bring some benefits to the situation. Teachers often find themselves having to decide whether to use these high-cost strategies, and all sorts of factors—professional and personal—can affect the final

TABLE 7.4 Strategies for Managing the Behavior of Students with Emotional or Behavior Disorders

Communication Strategies

Structure schedules—communicating expectations about the use of time.

Structure expectations that link behavior and reward—"If you choose to do this . . . you will receive this reward."

Define the relationship between unacceptable behavior and sanctions—"If you choose to do this . . . you will be penalized in this way."

Establish classroom procedures and routines—"Rules of the road."

*Discuss with students the meaning/value of what is to be learned. Solicit and respect a student perspective.

*Communicate regularly with students—conversations, notes, journals. (At secondary level, each student should be assigned to at least one teacher.)

*Communicate regularly with parents—notes, phone conversations, conferences.

Supporting Desirable Behavior

Verbally praise a student who is behaving appropriately.

Verbally encourage appropriate behavior.

Give grades and other recognition for achievement.

*Accommodate individual instructional needs by grouping.

*Organize "buddy" or peer tutoring assistance.

*Reward using individualized token/points system (entire group).

Controlling Problem Behavior

Remind student of expectations and rules being violated.

Use gesture or signal alert.

Move closer to student (proximity control).

Use verbal humor.

*Reinforce another student who is behaving appropriately to remind of expectations (also a support strategy for the student whose behavior is appropriate).

*Promise reward for return to appropriate behavior.

*Conduct tension-release activities.

*Conduct group meeting focused on problem behavior that has just occurred.

*Supervise time-out at special place in classroom.

Source: F. Wood (1991). Cost/benefit considerations in managing the behavior of students with emotional/behavior disorders. *Preventing School Failure, 35*(2), pp. 17–23.

* Involves extra time or effort by the teacher.

decision. A variety of strategies have been developed to cope with children who manifest these disorders.

Cognitive Strategy Approaches

In contrast to the operant conditioning approach (which does not necessarily rely on the child's cooperation to modify undesirable behavior) is the family of strategies known as the *cognitive strategy approach*. Whether called *self-monitoring*, *self-instruction*, or *self-control*, these methods rely on the cooperation of the child and encourage the development of effective conscious coping skills. With the development of the child's skills comes more self-confidence and a more positive self-image as the child achieves greater control over his or her own impulses.

Self-management for behavior change has received much favorable comment. One attraction of self-management techniques is that students who successfully apply them assume greater responsibility for their behavior, instead of being externally controlled or "forced" to change by various kinds of conditioning.

Suppose Jim has been having trouble staying in his seat. The first step is to teach him to recognize the behavior and then to record its frequency. Next, Jim negotiates a reward that is satisfying to him (perhaps some time to work a puzzle) for staying in his seat for a specified period. Once he has shown the ability to control the behavior, he can be given the opportunity to control his own schedule and make decisions about the content or skills he would like to work on in the time slot.

There are several self-management techniques:

Students using self-management assume greater responsibility for changing undesired behaviors.

- *Self-monitoring* requires students to determine whether a target behavior has occurred and then record its occurrence. For example, if Jim feels an aggressive attack coming on, he can note this in a journal. This helps him become increasingly aware of the clues identifying a potential outburst.

- *Self-evaluation* asks the student to compare his or her behavior to some criteria and make a judgment about the quality of the behavior being exhibited—for example, "On a scale of 1 to 5, am I paying attention to the teacher?"

- *Self-reinforcement* means that the student rewards himself or herself with a token or a tally after meeting some performance standard such as avoiding aggressive outbursts for a set period of time. For example, a timer set for ten minutes that goes off without an aggressive outburst earns for the student a token that he or she can cash in later for game-playing time or a specially designed activity.

- *Self-instruction* is a method by which students can, in essence, talk to themselves, encouraging themselves with verbal prompts to persist in solving an academic or social problem.

Those techniques are designed to increase students' awareness, competence, and commitment to eliminating negative behaviors and to encourage the acquisition of constructive ones. For Jim, this means that the teacher works with him to improve self-awareness skills that will enable him to increase his own control over his hyper-activity or distractibility. One practical way of increasing the student's personal responsibility is to let the student participate in developing his or her own IEP.

A review of eleven studies regarding the effectiveness of self-management has determined that such techniques were universally successful in changing the behavior of students with behavior disorders (Hughes, Ruhl, & Misra, 1989). The majority of the behaviors that changed, however, involved fairly simple tasks such as increasing on-task performance. Whether these techniques work as well with changes in more complex behaviors, or last over an extended period of time, remains to be determined.

The greatest advantage of this approach is that the child gains self-confidence by exerting control of his or her previously out-of-control behavior. There is an important additional advantage. Many children with behavior disorders spend part of their time in the regular classroom as a result of the least restrictive environment and inclusive philosophies. Many regular classroom teachers do not wish to, or feel that they cannot, engage in the complex monitoring and recording of individual student behaviors that some of the other behavior-shaping techniques require. Therefore, because students who use self-management monitor themselves, once the students learn what they are to do in a self-management program, they can proceed with only modest teacher supervision.

Much of the work with fearful or withdrawn children is still done by mental health professionals outside the public school program. Limited budgets do not allow most school systems to employ a battery of psychiatrists, psychologists, and social workers. The release of pent-up feelings and unspoken fears in a protected environment is one of the major goals of most child therapists. Classroom teachers often notice positive changes in children who have someone to talk to and relax with outside the school environment.

Developing Social Skills

Many children with behavior disorders not only engage in nonadaptive behaviors that cause them trouble with their peers and teachers but also lack positive social skills. One specific goal of a special education program is therefore to enhance the use and practice of socially acceptable behaviors.

Molly's periodic weeping "turned off" her peers, and she had no positive skills to re-establish social contact with one or more of her classmates so that she could experience desirable social contact. One positive skill that can be introduced to Molly and that she can practice is how to approach another child with a request to play or talk.

Kerr and Nelson (1989) described a sequence of activities by which such skills might be developed:

1. *Modeling.* The skill can be introduced through live, audio, or video modeling. Peers can demonstrate such skills.

Social skills can be developed through modeling, role-playing, performance feedback, and generalization and maintenance. (© *Michael Weisbrot*)

2. *Role-playing.* The skill can be played out in a pretend real-life situation. The role-play can be highly structured so that the person has a good chance of performing acceptably.

3. *Performance feedback.* Just as drama students are critiqued for their performance of a scene, so the teacher can discuss with the student the pluses (always first) and the minuses of the performance. The student might be asked to do the scene again after the critique, and the performance is almost always improved.

4. *Generalization and maintenance.* The student must be able to use the skill in a variety of situations. Self-monitoring techniques can be helpful in keeping the skill foremost in the student's mind.

The supportive atmosphere that teachers and peers can establish in this process can be extraordinarily helpful in its own right. This means that the teacher takes pains to set the situation up as a helping situation with perhaps more than one student as the focus of the social skills practice. Such extensive efforts require much time and attention on the part of the teacher and are best done with a teacher consultant in the classroom or in a small-group setting such as a resource room or special classroom. The increased pressure to place students in the least restrictive environment means that many children with behavior disorders will be in the regular classroom and raises the question of how much the regular classroom teacher can or will do to aid in these situations unless provided with professional support.

Modeling Acceptable Behavior

One of the strongest issues related to inclusion and children with behavioral problems has been the modeling of acceptable behavior. How, ask those supporting the inclusion model, can a child learn acceptable behavior in a group that is displaying a large amount of unacceptable behavior, as might be true in a special class with behavior problems? Stainback and Stainback (1980) pointed out that the behavior of a person with normal behavior patterns can be made abnormal if the person spends all day with persons with abnormal behavior. The Stainbacks suggested that placing children with maladaptive behavior patterns in a regular class in which many students reveal acceptable behavior patterns will encourage the child with deviant behaviors to seek a more socially acceptable pattern. This would be done through **vicarious learning**—that is, learning from observing other children being positively reinforced even though they themselves are not part of the event.

Such conclusions, however, have been brought into question by Halenbeck and Kauffman (1995), who reviewed the literature on observational learning and its effect on student behavior. They point out, among other things, that the child with behavior disturbance probably came from a classroom of students performing in a socially acceptable manner. Why hadn't the student learned the proper behavior through observing his or her classmates there? These three questions need answering in such a situation:

■ Under what circumstances will students imitate the desirable behavior of typical peers?

■ What types of models are these students most likely to imitate?

■ Under what conditions will models have vicarious effects on such students?

The answers to these questions are complex but basically confirm the notion that merely placing a youngster in a classroom in which much desirable behavior is being presented does not guarantee that the child with deviant behavior will imitate it. Data from observation suggest that people most readily imitate those whom they perceive to be similar to themselves in significant ways (Bandura, 1986). Indeed, within the regular classroom such a preference can lead to the formation of a subgroup of antisocial boys who see the youngster who is misbehaving as being more closely aligned to themselves than to the more properly behaved students.

The issue in the regular classroom is complicated by some other observations. Once a student has received negative judgments from other students, it is very difficult for that student to rid himself or herself of an undesirable reputation even if his or her behavior changes. Also, teachers' attitudes toward disruptive students do not necessarily change even when the students decrease their disruptive behavior.

By being included in a regular classroom, children who have behavioral difficulties can learn the desired behaviors vicariously by observing those behaviors in their classmates.

Activities such as participating in a community project or helping a charity, give students an environment where they can observe and model positive behavior.

Halenbeck and Kauffman (1995) concluded that children with emotional or behavior disorders, particularly those displaying aggressive behavior, need specific interventions and reinforcement programs. If they are to benefit from observing peer models, they will need instruction on what to pay attention to, how to remember and rehearse model behavior, and how to judge whether to produce imitative responses. These require an intensity of treatment unlikely to be available in the regular classroom, in their opinion.

In other words, students do not imitate every behavior that they observe. The imitation is selective and related to their own identification of similarity to the model and also to their own predetermined view of themselves. Students who have been told that they are aggressive and disruptive seem especially likely to model themselves after other students with the same label. Halenbeck and Kauffman (1995) suggested that a student with behavior disorders is more likely to imitate other students with behavior disorders who are making an attempt to modify and improve their behavior than they are to imitate peers with whom they think they have little or nothing in common.

An example of how social skills can become a part of an IEP is shown in Figure 7.3. The plan devised for Robert is one about which the parents and school

Child's Name __Robert Rimcover__

School __Washington High School__

Date of Program Entry __9/14/95__

Prioritized Long-Term Goals:

1. __Control temper when corrected by adult__

2. __Eliminate drug intoxication at school__

3. __Increase writing skills__

Summary of
Present Levels of Performance
Achieving slightly above
grade level in math,
history, science & shop.
Approx. 2 yrs. below in written
composition. Refuses to engage in
writing tasks.

Short-Term Objectives	Specific Educational and/or Support Services	Person(s) Responsible	Percent of Time	Beginning and Ending Date	Review Date
1.1 Given a direction, Rob will complete the required behavior within 10 seconds without committing a verbally or physically aggressive act.	Contingency contracting time-out procedures Role Playing	Reg. class & resource teacher	100	9/14/95 —6/12/96	12/20/95 & 6/12/96
1.2 When asked to redo careless or inaccurate work, R will comply without committing a verbally or physically aggressive act.	Same as above plus immediate feedback on academic assignments	Same as above	100	Same as above	Same as above

Percent of Time in Regular Classroom

83% (5 of 6 periods)

Placement Recommendation

Regular 11th grade
(non-accelerated)

Committee Members Present

E. Dokes, Principal

C. Dorsett, Counselor

Marrel Perez, Resource Teacher

F & R Rimcover, Parents

Dates of Meeting __8/17/95__

Figure 7.3
Individualized Education Program

personnel agreed. The focus of the IEP is to improve Robert's ability to gain control over his temper, which has been resulting in numerous fights with peers and confrontations with the school administration. Unless Robert is successful in reducing his violent outbursts, it is not likely that anything else he is able to do will be much valued. The progress of the plan needs to be monitored. A student teacher or aide might chart the progress of the plan, since the subject-matter teachers will be otherwise engaged.

Another device to aid in developing social skills is a written contract between the student and the teacher. This contract is developed by both the teacher and student, who agree on a particular goal toward which a student is striving. For example, Robert might agree to try to go a week without a major temper outburst; the teacher might then agree to provide some free time for him to read any book that he likes if that happens. The advantage of a contract is that it is written down and can be referred to in the future to see if an agreement has been kept. If Robert succeeds at this level, then a new contract might be written focusing on his writing skills and mentioning other contingent rewards for successful performance.

The emphasis in programs that stress positive reinforcement is that "work comes before play." This means that highly preferred activities (play) are contingent on less preferred activities (work). When successful, an additional advantage is that a sense of pride emerges in the child for accomplishing valued tasks—if the teacher is skilled enough to present tasks that Hobbs (1974) referred to as Just Manageable Difficulties (JMD), or tasks of sufficient difficulty that the student has a true sense of accomplishment when they are completed.

THE HELPING TEACHER

The helping teacher concept fits well into the inclusive classroom.

One innovative suggestion for helping beleaguered classroom teachers is the **helping teacher,** a person who comes into the general classroom and provides the teacher with support for children with special needs. Obviously, a classroom teacher with twenty-five or thirty children cannot cope with all aspects of the classroom environment without help. Who can provide that help? Morse (1976), based on his work with disturbed or disturbing children, proposed the "helping teacher" strategy. The strategy rests on five assumptions and principles:

1. Even a child who is very disturbed is not "disturbed all the time." There are *only certain periods* when the disturbed pupil cannot function in the larger group setting. These periods may be at certain regular times or in the press of a crisis. But most of the time, the child who is disturbed can benefit from and fit into the regular class.

2. Teachers need direct assistance. Consultation is one thing, but real help is something else. Psychologists and similar professionals might offer advice, but they do not know what it is like to try to administer a classroom that includes children who have behavior disorders.

3. The direct-service helping teacher should work full-time in the school to which he or she is assigned, should not be itinerant, and should be trained as a special teacher. The helping teacher should be able to respond to the child who is disturbed in crisis but also be able to help all children with academic and emotional problems. Many of these youngsters need direct counseling help with issues such as self-concept, but just as many can achieve growth through therapeutic tutoring.

4. Sometimes the helping teacher can assist best by taking over the classroom while the regular teacher works through a phase of a problem with a youngster.

5. Help should be based on the reality of how the child is able to cope with the classroom and not on categories, labels, or diagnostic criteria. Morse pointed

out that many normal children need help during a crisis in the classroom or in their lives, just as the chronically and severely variant youngster does (pp. 1–2).

The helping teacher generally uses techniques that are an extension of regular education procedures, emphasizing support and encouragement. In addition, the helping teacher is able to provide important liaison services that are not within the capabilities of the heavily burdened classroom teacher. Children with behavior problems often need the help of pediatricians, psychologists, and paraprofessionals, and the helping teacher can coordinate these sources of assistance. Morse summed up the nature of the relationship as follows:

> The plan envisions co-team teaching of the special and regular teacher. There is no intent to replace, only to supplement. The best staff education will come as a result of offering direct help; through service comes change. The job is overwhelming, all agree, but the direction has stood the test of time. (p. 8)

The concept of the helping teacher gains particular relevance with the emergence of the inclusion philosophy. It offers an alternative to resource rooms and brings needed assistance to an already heavily burdened classroom teacher.

Lifespan Issues

One of the major questions facing special educators is what happens to their students in secondary school and beyond. To what extent do they find jobs? To what extent are they personally independent?

TRANSITION FROM SCHOOL TO WORK

Several studies have been conducted that look at the transition experiences from school to work of youth with disabilities. One study in the state of Washington tracked more than 4,000 students who graduated between 1978 and 1986 (Neel, Meadows, Levine, & Edgar, 1988). One hundred sixty of these students had behavior disorders, and the researchers compared them with more than 500 nonhandicapped students of the same ages and from the same schools. Only 60 percent of the students with disabilities were currently working, compared with 70 percent of the nondisabled group. Moreover, those who were working had found their jobs themselves or with the help of family. No social or rehabilitation agency was actively working on their problems.

The authors concluded that school programs are not teaching children with behavior disorders the skills they need to find jobs. And a large number of parents agreed. One-third were dissatisfied with the programs their children had in school or with the jobs their children found. One of the most important responsibilities special educators have is helping students cope with the transition between school and the workplace. The main function of school is to prepare youngsters to live as independent adults. Mithaug, Martin, and Agran (1987) identified four skills that should be part of the secondary curriculum for exceptional children:

1. Choosing among available job options
2. Performing independently (a learning-to-learn strategy that allows students to respond to a new task without relying on others to help)
3. Self-evaluation (so that students can measure their own performance)
4. Adjustment (deciding what to do the next time they work at a task)

None of those skills is easy to master. This means students need extensive practice with them if they are going to make an effective transition from school to work.

The National Longitudinal Transitions Study of Special Education Students included more than 8,000 youths from ages 13 to 21 and was a nationally representative sample (Wagner et al., 1991). Persons who were classified as emotionally disturbed had adjustments to school that were manifestly unsuccessful. They had lower grade-point averages than students in other disability categories and the highest dropout rate of all students with disabilities.

One in five secondary school students with the designation "seriously emotionally disturbed (SED)" had been arrested, and 35 percent of the persons older than school age had been arrested. This group was least likely to belong to social and community groups after high school. Outside school, however, their adaptation was another matter. Students with emotional disturbances had among the highest employment rates while in school and earned wages comparable to the wages of students with learning disabilities who were living independently.

TRANSITION TO ADULTHOOD

What happens to emotionally or behaviorally disturbed individuals when they reach adulthood? Figure 7.4 compares the employment rates of emotionally disturbed youth with the rates of youth in eleven categories of disability (Wagner et al., 1991). The figure presents some modest good news and motivation for the establishment of effective and intense programs for such students with emotional disturbance.

Figure 7.4 shows that about 72 percent of youth with emotional disturbance "had a paid job last year"; the corresponding percentage among youths in the "all conditions" group was slightly lower—70 percent. This is a positive and somewhat unexpected finding. About 45 percent in each group are "currently competitively employed." Half or more of the emotionally disturbed youth are employed in some fashion, and there is little doubt that more effective and more efficient training programs and support features could improve those figures.

Something about the school environment appears to be particularly unsuitable for these students. Research with smaller samples seems to yield consistent findings. Feldman, Denhoff, and Denhoff (1984) carried out a ten- to twelve-year follow-up study on forty-eight adults who had been diagnosed as hyperactive children. The researchers found that by age twenty-one 91 percent were in some form of school or special training or working and seemed to be performing in a reasonably effective

Figure 7.4

Employment Rates of Youth with Disabilities and Youth with Emotional Disturbances

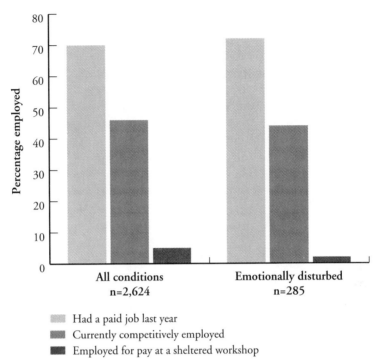

Had a paid job last year
Currently competitively employed
Employed for pay at a sheltered workshop

Source: M. Wagner, L. Newman, R. D'Amico, E. Jay, P. Butler-Nalu, C. Marder, and R. Cox (1991). *Youth with disabilities: How are they doing?* Washington, DC: U.S. Department of Education, Office of Special Education Programs.

manner, although they had lower self-esteem and less educational achievement than their nonhyperactive siblings who made up the control group.

Hechtman and Weiss (1985) studied seventy-six youngsters originally seen in a psychiatric department of Montreal Children's Hospital, where they were diagnosed as hyperactive at 6 to 12 years of age. These children were compared in young adulthood with forty-five control subjects, who were matched for gender, IQ score, and socioeconomic status with the hyperactive subjects. The control subjects had no observable behavior or academic problems. Hechtman and Weiss found that the hyperactive subjects in young adulthood attained lower academic grades, had more car accidents, and received somewhat more court referrals. On self-report scales they indicated higher levels of anxiety, grandiosity, and hostility. The researchers concluded that few hyperactive children become grossly disturbed or chronic offenders of the law when they become adults, but they do have adjustment problems related to their impulsiveness and inability to concentrate, two characteristics that created problems for them in school.

What seems to emerge from these studies is that early problems such as a difficult temperament or hyperactivity increase the risk of poor adult adjustment but do not, in any sense, guarantee it. Our treatments can be effective, and favorable environmental circumstances help a child cope more effectively with impulsiveness, lack of attentiveness, and feelings of hostility.

Summary of Major Ideas

1. Unlike children with other disabilities, youngsters with behavior disorders are often blamed for their condition. This affects their interactions with those around them.

2. The definition of *behavior disorder* takes into account the intensity and duration of age-inappropriate behavior, the situation in which the behavior is exhibited, and the individual who considers the behavior a problem.

3. Although less than 1 percent of schoolchildren are receiving special education services for behavior disorders, studies show that the number of children who actually need those services is at least 5 percent and may range as high as 15 percent.

4. Conduct disorders include aggressive behavior, hyperactivity, and attention deficits. They are far more common in boys than in girls. Often the punishments children receive for these kinds of behaviors actually serve to reinforce them.

5. Depression and learned helplessness are two characteristics of the child who is anxious and withdrawn. Intervention should have as its primary objective instilling a sense of self-worth and self-control. Positive experiences play an important role in preventing suicide—a serious problem among youngsters who are seriously depressed and withdrawn.

6. Both genetic and environmental factors interact in complex ways to produce problem behavior in children.

7. The decision to place a child in a special program should be considered only after adjustments have been made in the classroom and home, prereferral activities have been carried out, and information has been gathered.

8. We currently lack a graduated intensity of treatment programs and settings to cope with the various levels of behavior disorders.

9. Because computers do not react emotionally to children's behavior and force users to pay attention, they are an effective tool for students with behavior disorders.

10. Operant conditioning is an effective strategy that teachers can use to reinforce positive behaviors and reduce negative behaviors.

11. Inclusion appears to offer a viable setting for some students with behavior disorders, if the classroom teacher has received training in special instructional strategies, the other students have been alerted to the special needs of the student with behavior problems, and adequate support services are made available.

12. Ecological strategies focus on the interactions between children and their environment and attempt to design therapeutic settings for the children.

13. Drug therapy, in combination with educational intervention, is effective in the treatment of many hyperactive youngsters, although the reaction to drugs is a highly individual matter that needs careful monitoring.

14. The helping teacher adapts the learning environment to the needs of children with behavior disorders.

15. A key component of the special education program for students with behavior disorders is the development of skills to help these individuals make the transition from school to the workplace.

Unresolved Issues

1. *Increasing uses of paraprofessionals.* One serious condition limiting the delivery of quality educational services to children with behavior problems is the need for highly trained personnel. Unless a way can be found to use paraprofessional personnel, as has been done in behavior modification programs, it will not be possible to provide the help needed by the large number of youngsters identified as having behavior problems.

2. *Need for intervention.* Longitudinal studies of children who are socially maladjusted and act out their aggressive feelings suggest strongly that they do not outgrow these tendencies. Unless something significant is done with these children or with the environment surrounding them, we can predict that aggressive children who hurt people will become aggressive adults who hurt people. The need for large-scale intervention within the school, family, and neighborhood is clear.

3. *Understanding the causes of behavior problems.* Since World War II, the predominant thinking about causes of problem behavior has focused on psychological or sociological causes. Either the child was mentally ill because of unusual or bizarre psychic processes or was showing abnormal behavior as a result of some negative sociological or ecological condition. Now, with increasingly sophisticated analysis, the role of genetics in causing or influencing emotional behavior has been reintroduced. We need to sort out the roles that these various forces play in the creation of unproductive behavior.

4. *Placement of children with behavior disorders.* Within the field of special education, there is considerable disagreement about the feasibility of inclusion for children with behavior disorders. On the one hand, the classroom teacher without special education training is ill equipped to cope with such students. On the other hand, the clustering of students with behavior disorders often removes models of positive behavior from their view. Some careful descriptions of programs that have achieved success seem required.

Key Terms

attention-deficit hyperactivity disorder (ADHD) p. 288
behavior disorder p. 278

environmental modification p. 300
functional assessment p. 300
helping teacher p. 318

Questions for Thought

1. What five characteristics exhibited to a marked degree over a long period of time does PL 94-142 identify as behavior disabilities? p. 279

2. What family risk factors may contribute to producing a child with a behavior disorder? p. 284

3. What is the apparent relationship between substance abuse and behavior disorders? p. 284

4. What are the common patterns in families of children with *conduct* disorders? p. 286

5. What relationship, if any, do you see between anxiety and adolescent suicide? p. 288

6. Briefly describe the five-step assessment process that Wood and Smith developed for identifying and placing children who are behaviorally disturbed. p. 293

7. Briefly describe the assumptions behind operant conditioning. p. 298

8. Describe the use of drug therapy to treat academic problems. p. 303

9. Give two reasons why computers are an effective teaching tool for children with behavior problems. p. 309

10. Describe steps that students can take to monitor their own behavior. p. 312

11. List the sequence of activities by which socially acceptable behaviors might be developed, according to Kerr and Nelson. p. 313

12. Identify the four skills that can help exceptional children make the transition from school to the workplace. p. 320

References of Special Interest

Kauffman, J. (1993). *Characteristics of behavior disorders of children and youth* (5th ed.). Columbus, OH: Merrill.

> This popular basic text provides a comprehensive portrait of the history of, characteristics of, and treatment options for children with behavior disorders. The author provides a strong review of the literature and has some special suggestions for teachers.

Knitzer, J., Steinberg, Z., & Fleisch, B. (1990). *At the schoolhouse door.* New York: Bank Street College.

> This report details a major study on the effectiveness of various educational programs and practices designed to cope with children with behavior and emotional problems. The authors point out that many of the traditional methods of providing services for

such children have not demonstrated their effectiveness, and they describe programs that coordinate mental health and educational services to good effect. They also recommend ways to improve programs for such children.

Paul, J., & Epanchin, B. (1991). *Educating emotionally disturbed children and youth: Theories and practices for teachers*. Columbus, OH: Merrill.
This well-balanced textbook includes strong and impartial discussions of theories on emotional disturbance. In addition the authors make many helpful suggestions for teachers about how to deal with various problems. The text presents current trends very well.

Quay, H. (1994). *Disruptive behavior disorders in childhood*. New York: Plenum Press.
The author has written a solid review of the various issues relating to the special problems of students and children who violate societal norms and pose a special problem for teachers and parents. The book reviews past methods for coping with such children and provides suggestions about how teachers should attempt to deal with them. A strong scholarly and research base makes this book particularly authoritative.

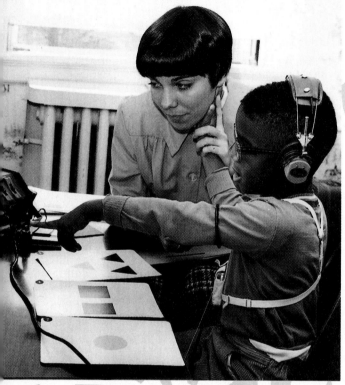

chapter 8

Children with Communication Disorders in Speech and Language

Nothing is more exciting to parents than their infant's amazing ability to begin to acquire speech and language in the first year of life. So it is not surprising that parents are often devastated if their infant fails to acquire the language of his or her home and to speak in a manner that is understandable.

Communication through speech and language is a complicated but natural human process that grows out of the child's prelinguistic communication through cries, grunts, smiles, and gestures (Dromi, 1992). It involves cognition (thinking) and audition (hearing). It means receiving information and sending information back. It means learning how to control air for sound production in words (speech) in a fashion that another person of the same culture can understand.

Speech and language development occurs in most individuals who are not disabled. Thus, failure to learn to produce sounds (words) that have meaning in a given culture (language) is indicative of almost all major communication disabilities. When such a disability is suspected, it must be identified and appropriate remediation initiated as early in the child's life as possible so that the child will be able to communicate with others and, at school age, learn to read and write.

Definitions

Communication is the exchange of thoughts, information, or ideas. Most commonly, we think of verbal communication occurring through speech or talking. Messages can be transmitted in other ways, however: through writing, reading, telegraphy, and the electrical impulses of the telephone (using a computer and a modem). Communication can be nonverbal, through gestures and facial expressions. Sign language uses an ordered form of gestures to convey meaning. Necessary for communication to take place are a sender, a message, and a receiver (see Figure 8.1).

Speech is the systematic oral production of the words of a given language. Sounds become speech only if they produce words that have meaning. Speech has a rhythmic flow with stress and intonation and words with stressed and unstressed syllables. Figure 8.2 presents a simplified overview of the production of speech. A

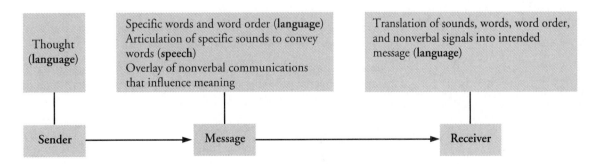

Figure 8.1
The Communication Process

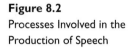

Figure 8.2
Processes Involved in the
Production of Speech

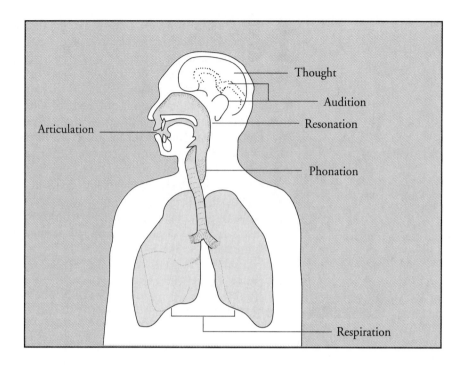

thought occurs in the brain; it is translated into symbols and sent to the breathing areas for resonation and phonation; then air is sent to be modified by movements of the tongue and passage over the teeth and lips, which combine to form the sounds, words, and sentences of a particular language (articulation). The thought transformed into words is received by a listener through hearing, in a process called **audition.**

The following four processes are involved in the production of speech:

■ **Respiration** (breathing) generates the energy that produces sound.

■ **Phonation** is the production of sound by the vibration of the vocal cords.

■ **Resonation** gives the voice a unique characteristic that identifies the speaker. It is the product of sound traveling through the speaker's head and neck.

■ **Articulation** is the movement of the mouth and tongue that shapes sound into phonemes (the smallest unit of sound) that make speech.

Damage to any of these processes can result in a speech disorder but does not necessarily interfere with language learning or reading and writing. Hearing losses can also cause speech disorders. A child will fail to produce speech if he or she cannot hear it spoken or hear his or her own sound production. Fortunately, most children with hearing losses have some audition, and they can learn to speak when provided with amplification through hearing aids (children who are deaf or hard of hearing are the subject of Chapter 9).

Language is an organized system of symbols that humans use to express and receive meaning. According to McNeill (1966) and Bates (1979), language systems

Speech therapists encourage production and understandable articulation. (© Joel Gordon)

evolved over time and largely replaced the innate communication system of emotions by means of gestures and facial expressions, which convey meaning, though the range of meaning they convey is limited. When a given community selects a series of sounds to convey meaning, it creates language. Language has many advantages over the expression of emotions, as it can convey meaning through speech and writing, and it can express the past and future as well as the present.

An infant is innately programmed to communicate through smiles, eye contact, sounds, and gestures (the prelinguistic system). The language system uses these talents, and parents teach the child that people and objects have names and particular sounds to identify them. Children learn that things have names early in life because they are rational beings (Bower, 1989) and are genetically prepared to learn a language. The language they learn is the one spoken in the home.

Differences Between Speech Disorders and Language Disorders

Communication may be oral (speech), gestural, or written.

A **communication disorder** is a disorder in both speech and language. It is important to distinguish between disorders in speech and disorders in language because they have different origins and require different interventions. A **speech disorder** is a disorder affecting articulation, voice, or fluency. A **language disorder** is the impairment or deviant development of comprehension or use (or both) of a spoken, written, or other verbal symbol system. Cromer's 1978 definition is still a standard. Cromer defined a language disorder as a disorder that exists without other disabilities, such as deafness, mental retardation, motor disabilities, or personality disorders. Language problems can coexist with all of these deficits, however, and need to be treated.

The professional organization of specialists in speech and hearing is the American Speech-Language-Hearing Association (ASHA). The ASHA definitions of communication disorders in speech and language are presented in Table 8.1.

The Elements of Verbal Language

Most verbal languages have elements in common.

Verbal language is language expressed in words—through speech and in writing. To be considered a verbal language, spoken or written words must have several elements in common so that members of the culture in which the words are used are able to understand what the speaker or writer wants to communicate.

There must be agreement about **semantics** (what the words mean) and **phonology** (how to pronounce the words). If the language is written, the words must be spelled in conformity with the alphabetic system and phonemes of the language.

There must also be agreement about morphology, syntax, and pragmatics. Rules about **morphology** determine the structure and formation of words, including the way affixes such as |s|, |ed|, and |pre| change a word's meaning (compare *cat* and *cats, want* and *wanted,* and *view* and *preview*). Rules about **syntax** specify word order in speech and writing. For example, an English-speaker says "white house" (putting the adjective before the noun), and a Spanish-speaker says "casa blanca" (putting the noun first). **Pragmatics,** the study of how language is used in different situations, yields rules that affect, for example, the words we use when greeting a friend or when greeting a stranger.

All human infants have language mechanisms that enable them to figure out the rules (syntax) and sounds (phonology) of their language (Pinker, 1991). The mechanisms that enable an infant to identify the sounds of his or her language begin to operate when the infant is about 6 months of age. The mechanisms that enable the infant to figure out the rules of the language (morphology, syntax, and pragmatics) begin to operate shortly before the child's second year of life (Bloom, 1991). These mechanisms may be similar to cognitive mechanisms, but they can exist when a child is mentally retarded and has faulty cognitive mechanisms but is linguistically sophisticated, as children with Wallace syndrome are (Bellugi, 1988; Pinker, 1991).

In summary, the production of meaningful spoken and written language depends on a multitude of working parts of the biological system. It also requires the child to learn rules of pronunciation, grammar, and usage. Children without disabilities generally master spoken language very quickly and display an amazing competence by the third year of life. Because our culture values proficiency in spoken language highly and expects everyone to master it, a great deal of research has been conducted to identify discrete disorders of speech, specialists are trained to remediate them, and curriculum is devised to improve them. Spoken language is

TABLE 8.1	**ASHA Definition of Communication Disorders in Speech and Language**

I. Communication Disorders: Speech and Language Disorders

A. *Speech disorder* is an impairment of voice, articulation of speech sounds, fluency, or a combination. These impairments are observed in the transmission and use of the oral symbol system.

1. A *voice disorder* is the absence or abnormal production of voice quality, pitch, loudness, resonance, duration, or a combination.
2. An *articulation disorder* is the abnormal production of speech sounds.
3. A *fluency disorder* is the abnormal flow of verbal expression, characterized by impaired rate and rhythm, which may be accompanied by struggle behavior.

B. A *language disorder* is the impairment or deviant development of comprehension or use (or both) of a spoken, written, or other symbol system. The disorder may involve (1) the form of language (phonologic, morphologic, and syntactic systems), (2) the content of language (semantic system), or (3) the function of language in communication (pragmatic system) in any combination.

1. Form of language
   a. *Phonology* is the sound system of a language and the linguistic rules that govern the sound combination.
   b. *Morphology* is the linguistic rule system that governs the structure of words and the construction of word forms from the basic elements of meaning.
   c. *Syntax* is the linguistic rules governing the order and combination of words to form sentences and the relationships among the elements within a sentence.
2. Content of language
   a. *Semantics* is the psycholinguistic system that patterns the content of an utterance, intent, and meanings of words and sentence.
3. Function of language
   a. *Pragmatics* is the sociolinguistic system that patterns the use of language in communication, which may be expressed motorically, vocally, or verbally.

II. Communication Variations

A. *Communication difference or dialect* is a variation of a symbol system used by a group of individuals that reflects and is determined by shared regional, social, or cultural and ethnic factors. Variations or alterations in the use of a symbol system may be indicative of primary language interferences. A regional, social, or cultural and ethnic variation of a symbol system should not be considered a disorder of speech or language.

B. *Augmented communication* is a system used to supplement the communication skills of individuals for whom speech is temporarily or permanently inadequate to meet communication needs. Both prosthetic devices and nonprosthetic techniques may be designed for individual use as an augmented communication system.

Source: American Speech-Language-Hearing Association (1982). Definitions: Communicative disorders and variations. *ASHA, 24,* pp. 949–950. Copyright © 1982. Reprinted with permission of the American Speech-Language-Hearing Association.

considered the hallmark of human functioning, and when it does not come naturally, a great deal of attention is paid to correcting it.

Prevalence of Communication Disorders

Because of the many systems and processes in which communication problems can originate, it is difficult to get an accurate picture of how many communication disorders are speech deficits and how many are language deficits. Language deficits are now considered to affect from 5 to 10 percent of schoolchildren in the United States (Rossetti, 1990). Not all children with language disorders are in special education classes. About one-fourth of all children in special education settings are there because of language and communication disorders (Leske, 1981).

Prevalence figures also tend to be distorted because mental retardation, cerebral palsy, and many other disabilities affect communication (Leske, 1981). Although a communication disorder may be secondary to another disability, it still requires treatment and therapy as part of a total special education program (see Table 8.2). Over 1 million children with speech-language problems were served in the 1992–1993 school year (U.S. Department of Education, 1994).

Some patterns in communication disorders have been found. Tallal, Curtis, and Kapland (1988) demonstrated that speech-language problems tend to run in families. They occur in about 33 percent of the children whose mothers have such problems and 18 percent of the children whose fathers have such problems. Knowing that a member of the family has a specific language problem alerts parents to the risk of their children having a similar problem.

Language Development: A Brief Overview

It is far beyond the scope of this chapter to list all aspects of language development. As you read this overview, keep in mind that a child is a hypothesis maker and an active creator of theories about his or her world and language (Bates, 1979). When children hear speech, they try to figure out the rules of speech. They do so without explicit instruction, for they are motivated to learn language on their own, and they monitor their own learning (Shatz & Ebeling, 1991; Pinker, 1991).

In this chapter, we discuss spoken language (speech). We discuss gestural languages more fully in Chapter 9.

CHARACTERISTICS OF LANGUAGE DEVELOPMENT

In most if not all societies, all children who are not disabled learn to speak the language of their culture very early in life. The sequence in mastering a language is similar across cultures. Language is social in origin, and it arises in the context of a close interaction with basic caregivers (usually the child's parents). Linguists generally agree that the infant learns language during interactions with his or her basic caregivers.

TABLE 8.2	Disabilities That Communication Disorders May Accompany
Disability	**Characteristic of Communication Disorder**
Mental retardation	Delayed language is a universal characteristic; disorders may be present in all aspects of language production and reception.
Cerebral palsy	Poor muscle control and impaired breathing of the child with cerebral palsy result in communication difficulties ranging from language delays and voice disorders to the inability to speak.
Learning disabilities	Major problems in learning to read, write, spell, and do arithmetic. The most likely hypothesis is that an unknown brain dysfunction interferes with auditory and visual perception and thus with all language reception and production.
Severe and profound multiple disabilities	Inability to speak; possibly able to learn a limited number of receptive words. Those without mental retardation may have no difficulties or may experience delays in language development; the child with severe physical disabilities may need a head pointer to type or some other form of augmented communication device to communicate by pointing to pictures, letters, or words.
Autism; childhood mental disturbance	Spoken language may not be present, but some can learn to communicate by using augmented and alternative communication devices. Autistic children with mental retardation and other severe mental disturbances may have disordered language in terms of syntax and semantics.

Most adults simplify their language (spoken or gestural) when communicating with a young child.

The caregiver's sensitive responsiveness to the child and to the child's requests greatly facilitates the child's acquisition of language. The interaction of caregiver and child in games such as "peek-a-boo" and "I'm going to get you" is enjoyable play for the child and encourages the child to fulfill his or her genetic push to learn language. Children learn language when interacting with caregivers in a setting (usually the home) in which they are provided with psychological warmth and encouragement. At first, the child's contribution may be smiles, gestures, and babbling, and the caregiver's role is to take turns and provide words.

Most parents in Western cultures use what psycholinguists call *motherese* to talk to their children. Motherese is a form of language in which the adult uses a high-pitched voice, which infants seem to respond to, speaks in simple sentences, repeats words and sentences, uses the present tense, and asks a lot of simple questions about what is going on in the context. Examples of these questions are "Where's Daddy?" "See the doggie?" "Where did the doggie go?" "More milk?" and "More cookies?" Motherese is spoken slowly and pronounced carefully (Baringa, 1992). The clear pronunciation may help babies learn sound categories, and the questions may help babies identify objects by name. The use of motherese seems to be widespread; it has been found in fourteen different languages (Bohannon, Warren, & Leubaker, 1985).

Thus, nature (genes) and parents combine to enable the child to master the language of his or her home.

Parents in many cultures use motherese to communicate with infants and toddlers.

THE SEQUENCE OF LANGUAGE DEVELOPMENT

By 2 to 3 months of age, infants begin to coo, make eye contact with their caregivers, and emit a socially communicative smile. By 2 months of age, they can detect the rhythm of the language of their home (Demany, McKenzie, & Vurpillot, 1977; Mencher & Gerber, 1983).

Around 5 to 6 months of age, infants babble and parents begin to match the sounds the infants produce to words in the home language. When the infant produces sounds such as "ba ba, da da, na na, ma ma," the mother will tend to select "ma ma" and reinforce it. Thus, the infant "learns" to say "ma ma." At 6 months of age, babies change from being "universal linguists" who can learn any language of the world into specialists in their own language (Baringa, 1992), and by 7 months, infants appear to recognize major features of their home language (phonology, syntax, and phrases) and lose the ability to distinguish sounds not found in their own language (Leonard, 1992).

Language development proceeds like this: Infants are programmed genetically to make sounds, and the caregivers give meaning to these sounds and repeat them. Consequently, the infant learns to repeat the sounds made by their caregivers in the way the caregivers say them. Caregivers tend to select sounds that occur in their home language. The most common babblings considered words by caregivers are the sounds the infant genetically produces at about 7 to 9 months of age. Most cultures have come to accept these sounds as terms for parents—*Mama, Dada, Gragra,* and so on.

At this point, the infant learns (cognitively) a major fact about the world: People and objects have names (Brown, 1988; Bower, 1989). The child appears to be able to abstract meaning from the environment and figure out the words associated with objects at home by looking where the caregiver is looking while saying a word—for example, the name of an object like *ball.* At this point in the infant's development, usually by the age of 9 months, the child's speech or oral sounds take on meaning, and they become language by the time the child is 12 months of age, when the first words appear.

The caregiver's sensitive responsiveness to the child and to his or her requests greatly facilitates the child's acquisition of language. (© *Jonathan A. Meyers*)

Learning language involves a combination of genetic and environmental inputs.

When the first word appears, the child may string together a series of nonsense syllables with the word. The child seems to understand that one word isn't enough, but combining words is beyond his or her ability at this age.

The child's first sentences are one-word sentences that convey the total meaning of what the child is trying to communicate. Thus, the word *ball* may mean "See the ball," "I want the ball," "Throw me the ball," or "Where is the ball?" For parents, deciphering meaning is a guessing game. They have to be in the same context as the child to determine what the child is communicating. All words have meaning only in a particular context.

Around 18 months, most children are speaking in two-word sentences, usually a verb and a noun, such as "See doggie," or "Daddy go." The verb in the two-word sentence conveys much of the meaning (Bloom, 1991). By 3 years of age, most children are speaking in multiple-word sentences and using generally correct syntax, although some common errors are present, such as overgeneralizations ("I runned" instead of "I ran") and errors in making plurals (*sheeps* for *sheep* and *deers* for *deer*). By 6 years of age, the child is a good communicator with a knowledge of several thousand words. He or she is using speech and language in various logical forms and has mastered most of the phonology of the community's language (see Table 8.3). Learning the rules of how to pronounce all the sounds of the home language extends through infancy and childhood into adulthood (Gleason,

TABLE 8.3   Development of Syntactic Skills

Age (Years)	MLU[a]	Syntactic Skills	Examples
1–2	1.5	One-word utterances called holophrases, and two-word utterances called duos. The child can express basic semantic relationships such as:	
		Recurrence	More ball.
		Nonexistence	All gone ball.
		Attribution	Big ball.
		Possession	My ball.
		Nomination	That ball.
		Agent-action	Adam hit.
		Agent-action-object	Adam hit ball.
2–3	2.25	Grammatical morphemes are added, such as:	
		Present progressive inflection	I walking.
		Locative prepositions	Kitty in basket.
		Plurals	Two balls.
		Possessive	Adam's ball.
		Past	It broke.
		Verb inflections	He walks.
3–4	2.75	Auxiliary verbs	I am walking.
			I do like you.
		Negative particles	I didn't do it.
			This isn't ice cream.
		Yes-no questions	Will it go?
			Do you want it?
		Wh questions	What do you have?
			Where is the doggie?
3–4	3.25	Sentence clauses	You think I can do it.
			I see what you made.
4–5	3.75	Conjunctions of two sentences	You think I can, but I can't.
			Mary and I are going.
Older than 5	More than 4	Reversible passives	The truck was chased by the car.
		Connectives	I am going although I don't want to.
		Indirect object–direct object	The man showed the boy the friend.
		Pronominalization	He knew that John was going to win the race.

Source: From Grover J. Whitehurst, Language development (1982). In B. B. Wolman (Ed.), *Handbook of developmental psychology.* Englewood Cliffs, NJ: Prentice-Hall, p. 371. Copyright © 1982. Adapted by permission of Prentice-Hall, Englewood Cliffs, NJ.

[a]MLU: average number of independent units of meaning (morphemes) in spontaneous utterances.

Articulation errors—misproductions of speech sounds associated with speech motor activity, including lisping—respond to therapy. This child and the clinician are using a mirror to practice sound articulation techniques. (© Alan Carey/The Image Works)

1993). Remember that children go through these language acquisition stages at roughly the same ages but with some degree of individual variation.

It is important to understand language development, for it is in the early stages of language development that disorders appear. Some elements of language, such as correct pronunciation and articulation, will improve with age. Problems with other elements indicate the need for early therapy if they are to be remediated.

■■ Classification of Communication Disorders

Communication disorders usually fall into four broad categories: disorders of (1) articulation-phonology, (2) disorders of fluency and speech timing, (3) disorders of voice, and (4) disorders of language. The first three classifications are traditionally considered speech disorders.

We want to emphasize that these classifications are not mutually exclusive. Individuals with one kind of disorder are by no means protected from having another. The relationship between articulation-phonology disorders and language disorders is well established, and researchers are exploring other connections among these areas.

DISORDERS OF ARTICULATION-PHONOLOGY

Articulation-phonology disorders are misproductions of speech sounds. They are the most common communication disorder among children in public schools. Although historically these disorders were considered speech disorders, they can be considered language disorders as well. We discuss them here as a distinct category of disorder and later as a subcategory of language disorders.

In recent years, the terminology used to describe articulation-phonology disorders has become more precise (Ingram, 1976). Today **articulation errors** indicates misproductions associated with speech motor activity, such as saying "ring" for "king." **Phonological errors** indicates misproductions of speech sounds associated with the dysfunctional use of the sound system of the language (Bernthal & Bankson, 1988; Newman, Creaghead, & Secord, 1985).

The number and kinds of misproductions and their effect on intelligibility are among the criteria for judging the disorder on a continuum ranging from mild to severe (McReynolds, 1986). Articulation-phonology disorders may range from a mild frontal lisp, a fleeting hesitation in words, to mispronunciations of speech sounds so severe that the speaker is unintelligible to listeners in his or her own community. Persons with severe and profound disabilities may never develop speech and must rely on learning how to use their prelinguistic system for communication (Holdgrafer & Dunst, 1986). Tallal, Galaburda, Llinas, and Von Enler (1993) propose that some children are unable to process auditorially the rapidity of speech. This failure to be able to process and integrate speech begins with phonological difficulties and eventually leads to defects in language development and difficulty in learning to read. This type of disability is usually labeled a learning disability rather than a speech or language disorder.

The Nature of Articulation-Phonology Disorders

According to a long-standing tradition, we describe imprecise phoneme production or articulation errors as substitutions, distortions, omissions, and, infrequently, the addition of extra sounds (McReynolds, 1986). When the intended phoneme is replaced by another phoneme, the error is one of *substitution*. Common examples are *w* for *r* (*wight* for *right*,) *t* for *k* (*toat* for *coat*,) and *w* for *l* (*wove* for *love*.) The influence of multiple substitutions on intelligibility becomes apparent when *like* becomes *wite*. In other instances, a misproduction makes a phoneme sound different, but the difference is not enough to change the production into a different phoneme. These productions are known as *distortions* (for example, *brlu* for *blue*.) When a disorder involves *omissions*, certain sounds are omitted entirely (*pay* for *play*, *ka* for *cat* or *cap*.)

Misarticulations are not always consistent. In some phoneme sequences, sounds are articulated correctly; in others, they are not. Often the position of a sound (at the beginning, middle, or end of a word) or the position of a word influences the production. Moreover, imitated productions and spontaneous productions can be different, and single-word productions may not reflect conversational productions (Creaghead & Newman, 1985).

Disabilities Associated with Articulation-Phonology Disorders

Obvious handicaps associated with disordered articulation are cleft palate, hearing loss, cerebral palsy, and other disorders of the central nervous system.

Cleft palate is a structural deficiency caused by the failure of the bone and soft tissue of the roof of the mouth to fuse during prenatal development. It is often associated with cleft lip. Historically, these clefts have been of special interest to speech-language pathologists. Hypernasality (excessively nasal-sounding speech) is the most familiar speech characteristic of children with clefts. Children with palatal clefts also make particular kinds of articulation errors related to impaired palatal function.

Sometimes an articulation-phonology disorder is associated with another speech disorder (for example, stuttering) or is part of a basic language disorder. Although researchers have examined many different causal factors, they have not reached a consensus.

DISORDERS OF FLUENCY AND SPEECH TIMING

Fluency is the flow of speech. The most common fluency disorder is **stuttering,** which is characterized by repetitions and prolongations of sound, syllables, or words; tension; and extraneous movement. In 1942, Wendell Johnson and his colleagues at the University of Iowa theorized that children become stutterers as a result of listeners' critical reactions to normal dysfluencies in their early speech. This view was widely accepted for years, but now most experts in stuttering do not accept it. Evidence indicates that "stuttering is not a neurotic disorder" (Andrews, Craig, Feyer, Hoddinott, Howie, & Nielson, 1983, p. 236) and that "psychoanalysis and traditional psychotherapy for the problem of stuttering, especially in adults, have not been effective on a large scale" (Shames & Rubin, 1986).

Today studies of stuttering are pursuing several productive paths. Evidence is accumulating that there is a genetic predisposition to stuttering and that a breakdown in speech-motor processes is involved (Cox, 1988; Smith & Weber, 1988; Wingate, 1986). Equally important, the influence of environment and the speaker's attitudes, which seem to affect stuttering, are being defined more clearly (Andrews, Craig, Feyer, Hoddinott, Howie, & Nielson, 1983; Daly, 1988; Gregory, 1986).

DISORDERS OF VOICE

Voice is the production of sound in the larynx and the selective transmission and modification of that sound through resonance and loudness. When we talk about voice, we usually think of three characteristics: quality, pitch, and loudness. We evaluate these characteristics in terms of the speaker's age, gender, and culture (Moore, 1986). A **voice disorder** is an inappropriate variation in voice quality, pitch, or loudness.

Disorders of voice quality, generally called **dysphonia**, can be related to phonation, resonation, or both. Breathiness, hoarseness, or harshness are disorders of phonation. Problems with resonation include hypernasality (excessively nasal-sounding speech) and hyponasality (speech that sounds as if the speaker has a bad cold). Often phonation and resonation disorders are present in the same person, but they can be separate disorders.

Pitch indicates whether the speaker is male or female, young or old. Pitch breaks, a common problem, occur in adolescents and affect boys particularly. High-pitched and variably pitched voices are common among children with severe hearing impairments or cerebral palsy (Boone & McFarlane, 1988).

DISORDERS OF LANGUAGE

As we explained earlier, culturally determined rules of correct usage govern the elements of language. Each element—phonology, morphology, syntax, pragmatics, and semantics—is a potential source of language disorder. For example, some children are able to express age-appropriate ideas in correct sentence structures but are not able to use accepted rules of morphology; they might have difficulty with pluralization (*foot-feet*), with verb tenses (*run-ran, walk-walked*), or with the use of prefixes (*pre-, anti-*).

Language involves both *reception* (taking in information) and *expression* (giving out verbal information), and in some manner it is processed internally during both reception and expression. Processing errors interfere with all types of learning, including language learning.

The stages and sequences of normal language acquisition (also discussed earlier in this chapter) give clues to language disorders. But it is often difficult to determine a specific cause for a specific language disorder in a specific child. Speech problems, developmental disorders, or other disabilities may all influence the child's ability to use language.

In summary, any deviation from linguistic competence involving the following is considered a disorder:

1. Producing understandable sounds (articulation and pronunciation)
2. Creating well-formed sentences and understanding grammatical structures (syntax and morphology)
3. Creating sentences with meaningful content (semantics)
4. Constructing logical sentences with appropriate knowledge (for example, saying "I see a bird," when the child actually sees a bird, not an airplane)
5. Speaking appropriately in context (pragmatics) (revised and adapted from Dore, 1986, p. 4)

■■■■ *Developmental Delay in Communication*

A major debate is now going on in the literature about a category of children who have been classified as language impaired. The major identifier of these children is that they talk later than their agemates in the same culture (Curtis & Tallal, 1990). Although these children have slower acquisition rates of learning language, they follow the same sequence of language development as their nondisordered

Figure 8.3
Profile of a Child with Mild Speech
and Language Disorder

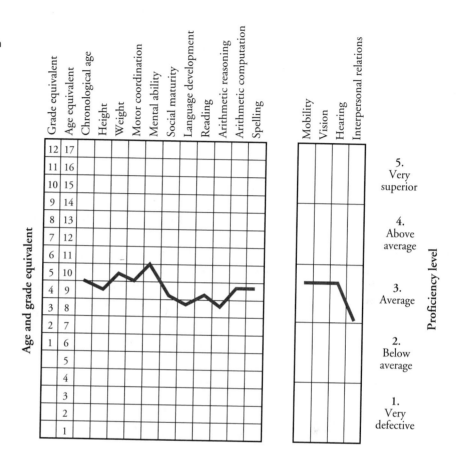

agemates. Thus, Curtis and Tallal raised the following question: If these children follow the same pattern of language development, are they deficient or merely delayed for some other reason? Curtis and Tallal found that these children have other problems in the timing of their learning. They believed that the deficiency is in short-term memory; these children need a longer time to take in information (reception), process it, and then return their part of the communication (expression). Curtis and Tallal found that these children have a normal language acquisition device (LAD) mechanism, but their impaired short-term memory interferes with it. Because the problem is not a language deficit but a delay from other causes, it is properly called a learning delay.

This work, as in the case of learning disabilities, may identify a subpopulation among children considered "specific language impaired."

■■ *Developmental Profile*

Figure 8.3 shows the developmental profile of Michele, a 10-year-old girl who has a moderate articulation-phonology disorder (she mispronounces specific sounds). Careful evaluation indicates that Michele has a language deficit as well. (Often a speech disorder signals an underlying language impairment.) Academically, she is performing below grade level on skills that require language mediation. Her sound substitutions and omissions are not so severe that she cannot be understood, but oral productions call attention to her speech and set her apart from her peers.

Michele's speech is characterized by consistent sound substitutions (*w/r* as *wabbit* for *rabbit*; *t/k* as in *tome* for *come*). She also sometimes omits sounds at the ends of words, including the sounds that represent verb tense and noun number (for example, the final /s/ in *looks* and *cats*.) Careful listening to her conversational language reveals that she omits articles and that her sentence structure is not as elaborate as that of most 10-year-olds.

Michele is in a regular classroom but seems reluctant to participate in class. It has not been determined whether this reluctance stems from her sensitivity to others' reactions, an inability to formulate speech and complex language to express her ideas, or both.

In contrast to Michele, many children with mild speech disorders seem to develop normally in other areas and do not differ markedly from other children in educational performance or social skills. Young children often make developmental articulation errors that continue into kindergarten or first grade then disappear as the child matures and acquires reading skills. Children whose misarticulations persist until about age 8 are less likely to correct inaccurate sound productions themselves. The teacher can do much to help Michele feel comfortable in spite of her disorder. The suggestions listed on page 351 would help Michele develop a more positive self-esteem.

■ *Identification and Assessment*

PRESCHOOL CHILDREN AND EARLY INTERVENTION

Although much of language development begins before a child says his or her first word, most tests for language delays or disorders are not administered until the child is 2 years of age (Leonard, 1992). Leonard stated that the criterion for administering diagnostic tests is the failure of the child to master fifty words by age 2. Mastery of fewer than fifty words may indicate that the child has a communication disorder or a hearing impairment.

Attention recently has been given to the nonverbal communication system (the prelinguistic system) that is a precursor to speech. Prior to the emergence of words, infants point to objects, respond to the caregiver's pointing, look at what the caregiver is looking at, and interact in basic play activities (Dromi, 1992). Infants also use gestures to make requests and to respond. If these prelinguistic competencies fail to develop at the expected time, a communication deficit may exist.

Irregularities in an infant's production of sound, sucking, swallowing, or breathing may portend a problem in the infant's development of spoken language.

Irregularities in the early nonverbal sound system (such as a strange infant cry) or in the sucking, swallowing, or breathing systems may predict a problem in spoken language development (Oller, 1985; Schiefelbusch, Sullivan, & Ganz, 1980). These difficulties will interfere with speech production. Deficient sucking or choking on fluids is an indicator of potential disorder, as is the child's swallowing excessive air or failing to chew by 18 months of age (Schiefelbusch, Sullivan, &

Ganz, 1980). A pediatric neurologist should be consulted to determine if a disorder exists. A physician or surgeon may need to determine if abnormalities are present in the mouth, throat, or breathing apparatus.

A multidisciplinary team composed of speech-language pathologists, physical therapists, physicians, audiologists, occupational therapists, special education teachers, parents, psychologists, and social workers may be formed to plan early intervention services. Because speech disorders so commonly accompany other disabilities, the speech-language pathologist has a role in many different therapies. That role may be major or minor in the delivery of service, but it is always major in assessment, diagnosis, and planning a program for the remediation or improvement of a communication disorder.

The speech-language pathologist should be primarily responsible for the identification, diagnosis (as part of a multidisciplinary team), and design of the treatment plan and curriculum for children with language and speech deficits. The speech-language pathologist sits down with the teacher and suggests or designs lessons to include in the individualized education program (IEP) or individualized family service plan (IFSP). The speech-language pathologist may formulate plans to encourage the spontaneous flow of language and assist non-English-speaking children in learning the English language. He or she may suggest activities to teach rhymes and jingles that contain words with consonant and vowel combinations that are troubling the student. For example, the jingle "Polly put the popcorn in a big iron pot until it went pop, pop, pop" introduces the child to the sounds of *p* with vowels in initial and end positions. The IFSP may include plans for the therapist or teacher to send home simple activities such as this for the parent to model for the child.

The teacher's primary role may be to encourage talk, expand talk, and model correct forms and usage. Rarely should children with speech and language disorders be placed in a special class. These children will be part of the regular preschool classes (inclusion) and perhaps have extra instruction outside class several times a week in a resource room.

The pace of human development is slower than that of other mammals, and the human infant's brain is relatively open to experience and change. Thus, it is easier to correct a problem early in life, and it is easier then to prevent an abnormal pattern from becoming fixed and unchangeable later in life.

SCHOOL-AGE CHILDREN

Many school systems use four procedures to identify children who have communication disorders (Neidecker, 1987):

1. Screening children who are suspected of having communication disorders and who may need additional testing or a full evaluation

2. Evaluating those identified during screening and from referrals with appropriate audiological, speech, and language assessment tools

3. Diagnosing the type and severity of communication disorder according to the criteria of the evaluation data

4. Making appropriate placement decisions for children who need speech or language intervention and developing an IEP or IFSP for them

Screening

Most school systems have formal screening programs for vision, hearing, and communication disorders. Often parents or teachers request that a child be screened. Speech-language pathologists may conduct screening in selected grades at the beginning of each year to identify children suspected of having disorders of articulation, fluency, voice, or language. Screening is sometimes a yes-no process: Yes, this child needs further evaluation; no, this child does not need further evalua-tion *at this time*. If there is any doubt, an assessment is conducted. The purpose of rapid screening is detection, not diagnosis; it must be well planned, fast, and accurate.

Federal regulations do not require a parent's permission before group screening; however, some school districts and some states require that parents be notified. Children who are identified through screening are then evaluated more thoroughly.

Evaluation and Diagnosis

Evaluating children who are suspected of having communication disorders and di-agnosing those disorders usually involve the following steps:

- ■ *Obtaining parental permission.* Federal law requires that parents or legally designated caregivers give permission before a child is formally tested for communication disorders.

- ■ *Taking a case history.* During the evaluation process, the speech-language pathologist often obtains information about other people's opinions of the child's communication abilities and disabilities. This history may include background information about the child's development, a health history, family information, a social history, school achievement records, and data from earlier evaluations.

- ■ *Assessing the disorder.* The clinician assesses the type and severity of the disorder with formal audiological, speech, and language tests and informal procedures (language sampling, analysis of conversation). The speech-language pathologist also evaluates the structure and function of the speech mechanism.

- ■ *Assessing other areas.* Assessing intellectual development may be particularly important for children with language deficits. Psychologists usually are responsible for intelligence testing. Often psychological tests are administered to evaluate cognitive skills and identify differences between verbal and nonverbal abilities. Educational assessment and its consistency with other assessment data are important. Physical therapists, occupational therapists, and other health professionals may also contribute important assessment information.

- ■ *Making a diagnosis.* Diagnosis has been called the art and science of distinguishing one disorder from another according to the signs and symptoms that characterize each disorder. The speech-language pathologist makes a written report about the kind of disorder(s) observed and describes the symptoms of the disorder(s) on which the diagnosis is based.

Developing the Individualized Education Program

The speech-language clinician may lead the school team in developing an IEP for the child with a communication disorder. Parental permission is required for the plan to be implemented. Intervention for the communication disorder outlined in the IEP is based on assessment data, the diagnosis, and other characteristics of the child (intellectual function, learning deficits).

LINGUISTIC DIVERSITY

As we have said, children learn to speak the language that is spoken in their homes and neighborhoods. They tend to use language to express their needs and thoughts as their parents or caregivers do. In some homes, parents use language in ways that are different from the language some teachers expect students to use. For example, teachers may demand explicitness in language (Anastasiow, Hanes, & Hanes, 1982). Whereas the two sentences "He took it" and "Arthur took my truck" convey the same meaning, the listener has to be in the immediate environment to understand the former, less explicit communication. Children who have not been exposed to explicit communication in the home may have difficulty when they encounter a teacher who does expect it.

Teachers must be aware that differences in language usage such as this are not treated as disorders. They can be addressed by teaching rather than by therapy. For example, Tough (1977) and Heath (1983) demonstrated that children can learn to use explicit language if they are taught to do so. Children will imitate their teacher if the teacher models the forms he or she expects them to use.

Assessment of Non-English-Speaking Children

Children from homes in which English is not the primary language are likely to encounter difficulty in using English in school. Language differences can and should be identified early, and language skills (how to relate to and speak to the teacher) should be taught to avoid failure by the child due to cultural differences in talking with adults. Children from communities that speak a language other than American English need assessments by speech-language pathologists who are skilled in the child's primary language. Services for these children are mandated in Parts B and H of Section 16 of the Individuals with Disabilities Education Act (IDEA) of 1990 (Anderson & Goldberg, 1991).

Children who are bilingual vary in their English competence. Any assessment of these children should involve a specialist who is bicultural and speaks the language of their home and who can answer three basic questions (Metz, 1991): Who speaks what language? When is that language spoken? For what purpose is that language spoken?

Great care must be taken that children from different cultures who speak a dif-

Saying "warsh" for "wash" is a sign not of a speech defect but of a regional dialect. If a child says "dog" for "cow," then a disorder may be suspected (though it may be that the child has not learned the new term).

Speech-language pathologists offer language, speech, and hearing services in hospitals and clinics, public and private schools, university speech clinics, and private offices. The treatment program must be an integral part of the formal school program so that students can generalize their newly learned communication behaviors to academic and social settings (Leonard, 1986). Professionals who help children with communication disorders often form a clinical team that provides many services to supplement the regular school program.

Inclusion is an important option for the child with communication disorders. Children with primary speech disorders typically respond to the regular education program if they receive additional help for their special communication needs.

INTERVENTION PRIORITIES

School systems must provide appropriate services to all students, but they can make decisions about types of services and where to offer them. A number of professionals have concerned themselves with the priorities in providing speech and language services within the educational program. Zemmol (1977) and Neidecker (1987) suggested the following continuum of services based on a model developed by ASHA:

■ *Communication disorders.* Children with moderate-to-severe articulation, fluency, voice, or language disorders require intensive intervention. These disorders often interfere with academic achievement and social adjustment, and a variety of professionals may be needed to plan a treatment program.

■ *Communication deviations.* Children with communication deviations have less severe handicapping disorders, but their communication can cause adaptation difficulties in school. Youngsters with developmental lags and mild mental retardation are often in this group.

■ *Communication development.* All children may need some effort by speech-language pathologists to prevent the progression of mild speech problems and to improve their primary linguistic skills and enrich their language.

INTERVENTION STRATEGIES

Therapy

The speech-language pathologist brings to each therapy session a considerable knowledge base and set of skills to recognize and remediate each child's specific problem (such as errors in articulation, syntax, and voice). The choice of therapy depends on the assessment of the child's need. The most common therapeutic procedure for most young children with deficits is play (sometimes called role-playing). Play, as we mentioned earlier, is the way children without disabilities learn speech and language. In the therapy sessions, therapists model the way children who are not disabled learn language. For example, the therapist introduces an age-appropriate toy, talks about it, and encourages the child to examine and manipulate the toy and discover its aspects and the word for it. The therapist asks questions about the toy ("What will it do?" "Can you push it?" "What color is it?" "Can you make it go?") and encourages the child to respond. If the child responds in one word, the therapist expands the child's response and models the correct pronunciation and language form (Fey, Catts, & Larrivee, 1995; Ogura, 1991; McCune-Nicolich, 1986).

Here is a sample dialogue between a therapist and a 3-year-old boy:

Therapist: Can you give the doll a drink?
Child: Dink (*while holding the cup to the doll's lips*).
Therapist: What a big boy. You gave the doll a drink. What does the doll say?
Child: Ank ou.
Therapist: The doll says thank you. The doll liked the drink. What kind was it?
Child: Juice.
Therapist: Oh, the doll likes juice. What kind of juice was it?
Child: Apple.
Therapist: Do you want some apple juice?
Child: Um (*holds the cup to his own lips*).

All of the child's language is not perfectly pronounced, but notice that the therapist models the correct form and expands the child's response. Rarely is it advisable to break a word into syllables or to stop the child's communication to correct the pronunciation. If the therapist can understand the meaning the child intends to convey, expansion and modeling are called for. If the therapist cannot understand the child, the adult may query the child about what he or she wished to communicate. If the word did not communicate (for example, if the child had said "cookie" instead of "juice"), the therapist would correct the response. Because a portion of the treatment and intervention program may be delivered by parents or the teacher, the speech-language therapist may be responsible for training the parent or teacher and modeling correct behavior for them. For example, if the child says "Wa doo," the parents may say, "I don't understand; tell me again." The child repeats "Wa doo," looking at the refrigerator. The parent then says, "Oh, you want some juice," and gives it to the child (Camarata, 1995, p. 70). Camarata also calls it *recasting* when the parent models correct pronunciation without correction. For example, a child says "a wion," and the parent says, "yes, a lion." At no time does the parent or teacher interrupt the child and tell him or her, "Say lion." These responses by the adult that build on what the child is communicating are also referred to as *following directives*. They have been shown to be positively associated with language development (McCathren, Yoder, & Warren, 1995).

Parents also need to be taught that their child with disabilities needs everything a child without disabilities needs, and perhaps something more in the form of aids or extra time.

Interactive Approaches

It was once quite popular to use operant conditioning to train a child to repeat words spoken to him or her. (*Operant conditioning* is a technique of behavior modification that works by controlling the stimulus that follows a response.) If the child repeated the word correctly, he or she was rewarded for doing so. Some interventionists achieved success in having the child master a list of words, but they were disappointed when the child did not use the words in his or her own free speech. The material learned in the training sessions did not transfer or generalize to other settings (Warren & Kaiser, 1988).

Bloom (1991) noted that these modeling procedures failed in part because children without disabilities imitate far less than was previously believed.

Most behavioristic approaches to teaching language have been replaced. Teachers and therapists now focus on the social use of language (pragmatics) and stress functional communication in natural language environments (Kaiser & Gray, 1993). Most interventions have changed from didactic, learning-principle orientations to ones based on natural language acquisition (Camarata, 1995).

A more popular form of treatment is the *interactive approach*. The interventionist—the parent, special education teacher, or speech-language pathologist—tries to capitalize on the natural inclination of the child to talk about what he or she is doing, plans to do, or wants to do. To encourage correct word use and language use, interventionists provide remediation sessions while the child is eating, playing, or visiting community settings such as a fast-food restaurant (Warren & Kaiser, 1989).

This natural approach is frequently referred to as *functionalism*, which means using speech and language in a functional way to acquire and satisfy one's needs. Other terms for this technique are *incidental teaching* and *social language learning*. The intent of these techniques is to increase the child's amount of talk (Bloom, 1991). The more the child talks, the more the child will gradually gain accuracy and increase his or her vocabulary.

Intervention for Fluency Disorders

Since the 1970s, intervention programs based on learning theory and principles of behavior have had a tremendous impact on all speech and language therapy, particularly for stuttering. Although parent counseling and training to change environmental stress continue to be important therapeutic tools for young children, direct speech intervention programs for children as young as age 2 have been developed and are working (Culp, 1985; Fey, Windsor, & Warren, 1995; Gregory, 1986). Whatever the therapeutic strategy, rarely are parents any longer told simply to ignore children's dysfluencies (Shine, 1985).

Peins (1985) and Shames (1986) provided detailed discussions of several therapies, including personalized fluency control and desensitization programs that use technology as a part of therapy. Many successful therapies recognize the importance of motivation, attitudes toward speech and self, and environmental interactions. In one successful approach, developed many years ago by pioneers in speech-language disorders at the University of Iowa, stutterers are taught to control stuttering, to reduce extraneous behaviors, and to stutter "normally." They are taught to face the problem rather than try to cover up their dysfluencies. The approach makes use of outside speaking activities (shopping, asking for directions, making telephone calls).

Classroom teachers can be particularly helpful to the child who stutters by working with the speech-language pathologist to plan opportunities for the child to participate in speaking activities that are appropriate for practicing newly acquired fluency skills at increasing levels of complexity. The classroom teacher can assist by

1. Reducing the rate of speech
2. Creating silence in interactions
3. Modeling sample vocabulary and grammatical forms
4. Modeling normal influences (Blance, Stedal, & Smith, 1994)

Furthermore, teachers can improve their students' self-esteem by

1. Disregarding moments of nonfluency
2. Showing acceptance of what the child has expressed rather than how it was said
3. Treating a child who stutters like any other member of the class
4. Acknowledging nonfluency without labeling the child
5. Helping the child feel in control of his or her speech
6. Accepting nonfluency (Blance, Stedal, & Smith, 1994)

Augmented and Alternative Communication

At times, children with severe motor problems cannot produce intelligible speech. A common instructional strategy is called *augmented and alternative communication* (see Table 8.4). **American Sign Language,** a system of gestures that contain meaning, is one example of this strategy. Another gesture system that is sometimes used is Signed English. Sign language is taught to some visually or motor-impaired children (Bower, 1989).

Other aids include communication boards of varying complexity, with letters or pictures to which the child can point to spell out a word or select a picture of the word (Beukelman & Miranda, 1992). The use of these aids has been shown to assist the child in acquiring language—many times without speech, but not always (Brady, 1984).

TABLE 8.4   Augmentative and Alternative Communication

Position Statement

It is the position of the American Speech-Language-Hearing Association that communication is the essence of human life and that all people have the right to communicate to the fullest extent possible. Furthermore, provision of augmentative and alternative communication (AAC) services is within the scope of practice of speech-language pathologists and audiologists (ASHA, 1990).

AAC refers to an area of clinical, research, and educational practice for speech-language pathologists and audiologists that attempts to compensate and facilitate, temporarily or permanently, for the impairment and disability patterns of individuals with severe expressive and/or language comprehension disorders. AAC may be required for individuals demonstrating impairments in gestural, spoken, and/or written modes of communication.

Source: American Speech-Language-Hearing Association (1982). Augmentative and alternative communication. *ASHA*, 33 (Suppl. 5), p. 8. Copyright © 1991. Reprinted with permission of American Speech-Language-Hearing Association.

Computers

Speech-language pathologists must be computer literate to be able to use some therapeutic tools.

Speech-language professionals are using computers as therapeutic tools. Today it is essential for speech-language pathologists to be computer literate. ASHA and a national group, Computer Users in Speech and Hearing (CUSH), both provide information about technological advances.

Computer programs are designed for a variety of specific purposes—for example, phonological evaluation and teaching children sentence structure. Another important use is word processing, which frees children from the burden of organizing bits and pieces of written language on the spatial confines of a page. Behrmann (1984, p. 96) pointed out the benefits of word-processing systems for children with disorders of written language (and for others as well):

1. There is no penalty for revising.
2. It is easy for students to experiment with writing.
3. Interest in writing is maintained.
4. Editing is simple: Spelling, punctuation, and grammar can be changed or checked.
5. Writing and editing are less time-consuming.
6. Frustration is minimized.
7. It is easy to produce perfect copy.

Computers provide highly structured, totally consistent stimulus materials and response acceptance. They give students independence in routine activities, and

For children with severe motor problems who cannot produce intelligible speech, a common instructional strategy is augmented and alternative communication by means of American Sign Language, Signed English, and communication boards. (© Alan Carey/The Image Works)

they help maintain interest in practice and drill, areas that traditionally have bored both students and clinicians. They are also designed to provide specific communication skill training (Schery & Connor, 1995).

In Chapter 11, on children with multiple and severe disabilities, we discuss Christy Brown, a severely spastic man with little muscle control who learned to type with his left foot and wrote several books. He had sufficient intellectual capacity to produce words and language but lacked the motor control necessary to produce speech. His story is beautifully told in his book *Down All My Days* (Brown, 1972) and in the motion picture *My Left Foot*.

Another youngster with severe motor impairments learned to type with a head pointer while his mother held his head to prevent spastic spasms. He won awards for his poetry and described his life in a fictionalized autobiography published under the pseudonym Christopher Nolan (Nolan, 1987).

Auditory Integration Training

A technique developed for treating hearing and communication disorders in France (Bernard, 1993) has been used in the United States with both success (Veale, 1994; Rimland & Edelson, 1994) and failure (Trace, 1994). The procedure involves playing ten hours of electronically modulated music over a period of ten to twenty days for children who are labeled as autistic, dyslexic, or having hypersensitive hearing. Usually, these sessions are held twice a day for a series of ten sessions. Frequencies in which the child is hypersensitive are identified and filtered out. Among the positive results for the child are increased attention to auditory stimuli, improved articulation, improved speech comprehension, increased mean length of utterances, reduced challenging behaviors, and decreased hypersensitivity to sound (Veale, 1994). The procedure works with some but not all children who are diagnosed as autistic (Trace, 1994).

Facilitative Communication

Created by Rosemary Crossley in Australia, facilitative communication was originally designed to assist children with cerebral palsy to communicate. Later, its use was expanded for teaching children with autism (Biklin, 1990, 1994). **Facilitative communication** requires the instructor (called the *facilitator*) to hold the arms and wrists of the individual to help him or her overcome tremors, apraxia (the inability to make voluntary motor movements in general), and other motor problems.

Many individuals with autism or cerebral palsy are able to perform these communicative tasks when aided by an instructor (facilitator) who supports their arms or hands and teaches them finger extensions (Biklin, 1990). It has been reported that some children have become independent of the facilitator and are able to type without assistance.

The success of facilitative communication challenges the view that all children with autism have mental retardation (Williams, 1994; Kaiser, 1994). However, not all research has demonstrated positive results (Green & Shore, 1994). Critics claim that the facilitator, not the student, controls the message (Wheeler, Jacobsen, Paglieri, & Schwartz, 1993).

Clearly, not all students with communication disorders can benefit from this technique, but some can. In many instances, it has changed parents' and teachers' perceptions of the child, giving them greater respect for the child's cognitive competence (Kaiser, 1994). (For extensive pros and cons, refer to *Journal of the Association for Persons with Severe Handicaps*, 19 (3), Fall 1994.)

IMPLICATIONS FOR TEACHERS

The speech-language pathologist and the teacher must work closely together to ensure that a child's disorder is treated appropriately.

Speech-language pathologists have specific terminology for some of the major disorders. These terms are listed in Tables 8.5 and 8.6. The terminology is necessary information for teachers. During the preparation of the IEP or the IFSP, speech-language pathologists use these terms to refer to common speech-language disorders, and teachers need to work closely with the speech-language pathologist to decide how to approach the child's disorder. Often the speech-language pathologist works individually with the child outside the classroom as well.

Speech-language pathologists use many techniques to promote the carryover of newly acquired communication skills into the classroom and everyday conversation.

TABLE 8.5	Terms That Speech-Language Pathologists Use to Describe Disorders
Term	**Disorder**
Apraxia	Inability to voluntarily perform coordinated movements
Aphasia	Impairment in the ability to communicate due to brain damage
Dysarthria	Articulation or voice disorder due to impaired motor control problems of throat, tongue, or lips
Anarthria	Loss of the ability to speak
Dysphonia	A disorder of voice quality
Stuttering	A disorder of fluency: repetitions, prolongations, and hesitations of sounds and syllables

These techniques include children's notebooks prepared by therapists that are kept in the classroom for the teacher's regular review, weekly conferences with teachers regarding specific objectives, the use of devices and props as reminders, and carefully planned in-class "talking" activities. A major task of the communication specialist is to help the classroom teacher use these tools effectively, because the teacher's help is vital to success.

Many children outgrow articulation problems when they are between 5 and 6 years of age. The teacher needs to be aware of what therapies the child has received in kindergarten and work with the speech-language pathologist to determine which therapies to continue. The multidisciplinary team should determine what therapies (if any) to include in the IEP or IFSP.

The success of intervention depends on the teacher's cooperation in scheduling time out of class for therapy and sending children to "speech lessons" regularly. Some speech and language changes (the production of particular sounds, language targets, fluency patterns) are best learned in individualized structured therapy sessions; however, the teachers' creativity in adapting classroom opportunities to foster ways of talking will help the student to generalize new skills. The classroom is often the most appropriate setting for incidental and interactive functional teaching (Fey, Windsor, & Warren, 1995).

TABLE 8.6	Terms That Speech-Language Pathologists Use to Describe General Disorders of Speech and Associated Behaviors
Disorder	**Behavior**
Voice disorder	A variation of speech from accepted norms in voice quality, pitch, and loudness (dysphonia)
Articulation-phonology	Mispronunciation, lisping, substitution (*toat* for *coat*)
Fluency	Stuttering (breaks in the flow of speech caused by repetitions and tensions in the speaking mechanisms)
Pitch	Voice too high or too low
Cerebral palsy and physical disabilities	Articulation deficits in as many as 80% of persons with these handicaps
Cleft palate	Nasal voice, articulation errors; multidisciplinary team needed to correct split lip, loss of teeth, or potential hearing loss; learns languages in normal fashion
Social disorders	Autism: fails to relate and develop speech and language

Teachers often participate in innovative alternatives to traditional speech-language lessons. It is common practice for the speech-language pathologist and classroom teacher to work side by side each day in a classroom, focusing on the language components of reading, language arts, and socialization (Cole, 1995).

Teachers recognize that there are differences between speech-language programs at the elementary and secondary levels. Often young children have therapy in their classroom, and older students have individual therapy. Because fewer standardized materials are available for students at the secondary level, the speech-language pathologist may have to design and develop or adapt materials for older students with speech and language disorders (Neal, 1976). However, computer programs are very useful in helping high school students master a wide variety of language skills (Schery & O'Connor, 1995).

Most children with communication disorders are in regular classrooms. Speech-language pathologists give direct service to these children individually, in resource rooms, and in regular and special classrooms. (© *Paul S. Conklin*)

SERVICE DELIVERY OPTIONS

The organization of programs for speech and language disorders in the schools varies with the size of the district and other local factors. Most children with communication disorders are in regular classrooms. Special language classes and other alternatives are available in some school systems, and school services may be offered in various combinations of delivery models.

Consultative Service

Consultative service provides a school system with a speech-language pathologist who serves as a consultant to regular classroom teachers, special class teachers, aides, curriculum specialists, administrators, and parents in organizing a speech and language development program. Specialized materials and procedures, inservice education, demonstrations, and other activities help educators, administrators, and parents improve the communication skills of children in natural settings—the classroom and the home. The educational audiologist is becoming more involved in assisting teachers in working with children with communication disorders (English, 1995). (See Chapter 9, on children who are deaf or hard of hearing.)

Itinerant Service

In the past, the most common delivery system was the itinerant service provider—that is, a therapist who went from room to room or took children out of the classroom. In some areas a speech-language pathologist still travels from school to school to give direct service to children in regular and special classrooms.

Intensive-Cycle Scheduling

Another method of service delivery is the *intensive cycle*, sometimes called the *block system,* in which children are scheduled for therapy four or five times a week for a concentrated period, usually from four to six weeks. This type of scheduling is sometimes used in combination with the itinerant service provider, particularly where more than one speech-language pathologist is on the staff (Neidecker, 1987).

Educational Setting

In the school year 1992–1993 more than 47 states predominantly used the regular classroom with resource room backup as the educational setting for children with speech and language disorders. Three states predominantly used the resource room as the place of service with the regular classroom as backup. Separate classes are infrequently used as the educational setting (16th Annual Report to Congress, 1994).

ADDITIONAL ROLES OF THE SPEECH-LANGUAGE PATHOLOGIST

A speech-language pathologist must be able to deal with a wide variety of disorders.

From the variety of settings and options for delivery of services to children with speech and language disorders, it's obvious that a speech-language pathologist must be able to serve in more than one capacity. An itinerant speech-language pathologist must be prepared to deal with a broad range of handicapping conditions—primary articulation, fluency, voice, and language disorders—as well as the problems found among children with cleft palate, mental retardation, cerebral palsy, learning disabilities, and emotional disturbance.

Speech-language therapists often work with parents of children with other disabilities. Researchers found that parents may not talk to a child with disabilities as much as they would talk to a child without disabilities, or they may overwhelm their child with talk. They appear to be more anxious about their child's progress, especially the progress of a low-birth-weight premature child who is less responsive to the parent and generally less fun to interact with than a child without disabilities (Field, 1983). Mothers of children with hearing-language impairments tend to be less flexible, permissive, and encouraging and more intrusive and didactic (Schlesing, 1983).

ASHA outlined the general responsibilities of speech-language pathologists in the schools (Project Upgrade, 1973):

- Supervise and administer programs for children with communication disorders.
- Identify and diagnose.
- Consult teachers and parents.
- Provide direct services.

Family Issues

What lies ahead for the child who has a communication disorder? The answer to this question depends on the nature and severity of the disorder. Children who have primary articulation disorders (that is, a speech or language disorder not associated with other disabilities) seem to have few special problems as adults. In contrast, follow-up studies of children with severe disorders show that those with language deficits, in spite of early intervention, continue to have problems in academics, interpersonal relationships, and work. Intelligence seems to be an important variable in determining the outcome among children who have language disorders from brain damage or mental retardation.

Families are concerned by any and all irregularities in their child's spoken language. They need information about their child's condition, and they need to be taught appropriate techniques to use at home. Teaching parents to recast the child's pronunciation, articulation, or incomplete sentences is critical. Parents will tend to correct communications that are understandable but not correct in form. The techniques for teachers that we suggested under fluency disorders need to be taught to parents. Language learning proceeds best in a setting in which language is used naturally (Fey, Windsor, & Warren, 1995).

Contemporary research is giving us evidence that speech and language intervention programs decrease the severity of communication disorders. In 1987, forty-three studies were analyzed with special techniques to assess the overall effectiveness of language intervention with individuals who have language-learning disabilities. The composite results indicated that the average language-disordered child moved from the 50th to the 85th percentile as a result of language intervention (Shriberg & Kwiatkowski, 1988).

The prospect for stutterers to learn good communication skills also seems to be brighter than it once was. For at least two professional generations very little direct therapy was provided for young children who stuttered. An important outcome of this practice was that most therapy was carried out with older, confirmed

Learning to Try

When the doctors and their staffs were evaluating my month-old son to recommend treatment programs for his cleft lip and palate, several of them remarked with surprise at the extent of my cleft palate surgery and therapy and complimented my near perfect speech. It was a timely morale booster to be reassured that the series of operations and the years of speech therapy I had undergone had been worth all the effort. Hearing this from the professionals in this field, which has grown so much in the last twenty-five years, not only reaffirmed my successful struggle to achieve normal speech, but also left me with greater hopes that my son's ordeal would be easier than my own.

It is not difficult to recall the days of frequently being misunderstood when I spoke. As a young child I think this self-consciousness developed earlier than the concern that my appearance was "different." I was not aware of the distinctions of tone and pitch, I just knew the words did not sound right. Sounds such as *s, z, l,* and *p* (and others) were distorted. I used to wish that my last name did not start with *s* (luckily it was a very common name) and that my birthday was not on the "sixth" of May, with its *s* and *x.* Naturally, time with family and friends was not threatening, but new people and school situations often were. Fortunately, I have mostly positive memories of teachers somehow conveying their understanding of my difficulties without singling me out as different.

Twenty-five years ago speech therapy was not available through the school system. My brother and I (my father and one brother also have cleft lip and palate) used to leave school early one day each week for speech therapy at a local rehabilitation center. We made a lot of progress in those early years with a wonderful speech therapist who filled our lessons with games, encouragement, and pa-

tience. The sessions ended when I achieved a level of passable communication skills and my motivation waned.

Adolescence brought all of the usual turmoil, including a renewed self-consciousness. Concern for my appearance was addressed through a series of cosmetic surgeries with results that did more for my self-confidence than I would admit at the time.

I also realized at this time that my speech was not good enough. When I was 15 a pharyngeal flap operation decreased the nasality of my voice, but I knew there was more work to be done on my part. There were probably many incidents that prompted me to reconsider speech therapy but one particular classroom scene highlights my predicament.

"Je m'appelle Lynn" was the way to begin any response in French class. "Je m'assie" was the closing before sitting down. I could only approximate this phrase because of the *s* sound in it. But the teacher kept having me repeat the phrase to correct my pronunciation. Didn't she know I could not pronounce it any more clearly? Finally, embarrassed, I said, "I can't say it." Then she let me sit down. Was she just insensitive to my difficulties, or was she pushing me not to accept such imperfect speech? Either way, it helped me find new motivation to resume speech therapy.

My parents and I were pleased to find my former speech therapist still in private practice in our area. He was able to tailor the sessions to my needs as an adolescent as skillfully as he had when I was a child. He explained to me how the various sounds are made and what the surgery had accomplished.

Most importantly, I learned that motivation and desire are the keys to success. My progress was swift during those sessions. Because I could recognize what I did not like in my speech, I was able to direct and concentrate my efforts. My goal was clear to me—to have as normal speech as possible. As long as I could see progress toward that end, I looked forward to the lessons and practiced on my own. Within a few months, I could hear the difference. It was a while before I could begin to take for granted the mechanics of proper speech and could think of what I wanted to say without having to worry about how to say it.

Today I am encouraged that my son will achieve this level of speech at a much younger age. Earlier surgeries and refined techniques will minimize his needs for speech therapy. For my part, I hope he learns to try, and to listen.

Source: "Learning to Try" was written expressly for this text by Lynn Smith Dennison, who lives in Brewster, New York, with her husband, Bob, and their son, Andrew.

commentary

What Is the Context? The school context described in this article is generally encouraging and supportive, but the author's clear memory of failure shows the fine line between motivation and humiliation. Teachers and staff need to encourage students with disabilities to learn to try, but they also must realize that the school is an inherently threatening environment in comparison to the home.

Pivotal Issues. What is the difference between a teacher who encourages students to exceed their own expectations and one who puts too much pressure on them, resulting in possible humiliation? How can a teacher effectively motivate students to speak more and use language more effectively? How might other factors in school (such as peer pressure and insecurity) affect the motivation of a child with a communication disorder?

stutterers, and success with permanent fluency carryover into social communication remained elusive. We know now that "the therapeutic success record is enviably better with children and best with preschoolers" (Shames & Rubin, 1986). Therapy with stutterers should begin by 3 years of age, at the first appearance of stuttering. Since the 1980s, serious research has focused on the problems of maintaining fluent speech and preventing relapse. Evaluation of these studies and others indicated that scientifically based therapy is clearly effective (Boberg, 1986). Rates of spontaneous recovery from stuttering are reported to vary from approximately 45 percent (Cooper, 1972) to 80 percent (Shames & Rubin, 1986). Information comparing the characteristics of those who recover spontaneously with the characteristics of those who do not will be useful in predicting the variables that increase children's risk for continuing problems with fluency (Lubker, 1986; Shames & Rubin, 1986).

Important changes have come about in helping students with language disorders make transitions from high school to college and the workplace. Many colleges and universities have support services and special programs for these students. Special clinics and help sessions are staffed by speech-language pathologists, learning disabilities specialists, and psychologists, and individualized techniques for note taking, class participation, and writing are available to help students who have written language deficits.

Summary of Major Ideas

1. Communication can be verbal or nonverbal or a combination of each. A sender, a message, and a receiver are necessary for communication to take place. Language is the system of symbols used to express and receive meaning. Speech is the systematic oral production of the words of a given language.

2. The processes needed to produce sound are respiration, phonation, resonation, articulation, audition, and symbolization/organization.

3. Communication disorders include speech disorders of articulation, fluency, and voice, and language disorders. Hearing loss can also cause speech disorders.

4. Impaired speech is conspicuous, unintelligible, and considered unpleasant. A child who is language impaired shows skills in the primary language that are markedly below the skills expected for the child's chronological age.

5. The prevalence of language disorders in the school-age population in the United States is between 5 and 10 percent. But data collection methods and classification procedures raise questions about the accuracy of this estimate.

6. Communication disorders can be secondary to other disabilities.

7. An understanding of normal patterns of language acquisition is an important part of identifying children with language disorders and developing remediation programs for them.

8. The process of identifying and assessing schoolchildren with communication disorders involves screening, evaluating, diagnosing, and making appropriate placement decisions.

9. Common models for the delivery of language and speech services are consultative services, itinerant services, intensive-cycle scheduling, and resource rooms—all of which fit well within the concept of mainstreaming as well as training parents and teachers to deliver services.

10. The role of the speech-language pathologist has expanded. In the schools, this professional is a member of the multidisciplinary team that develops and monitors the child's individualized education program or individualized family services program.

Unresolved Issues

1. *Individual versus group therapy.* Children with major speech disorders need one-on-one therapy. However, recent emphasis on inclusion raises questions on how individual therapy can take place in the classroom without disrupting the classroom program. The problem of incorporating full inclusion with individual therapy is still unresolved.

2. *Implementing early intervention.* Most speech disorders are not identifiable until a child reaches two years of age—the age when verbal language ability usually appears. Unfortunately, early signs of potential speech disorders in the prelinguistic stage are not frequently associated by parents as signs of a potential problem. How to make this information more available to both pediatricians and parents remains an issue.

3. *Multicultural language issues.* Large numbers of immigrants from many different non-English-speaking cultures have introduced major problems for U.S. schools. Because languages can vary up to eight different ones, some schools find it difficult to cope with the demands of this diversity. How schools can locate personnel who speak these languages and how the schools can afford to hire them are unresolved issues.

Key Terms

American Sign Language p. 351
articulation p. 327
articulation error p. 338
audition p. 328
cleft palate p. 339
communication p. 327
communication disorder p. 329
dysphonia p. 339
facilitative communication p. 354
fluency p. 339
language p. 328–329
language disorder p. 329
morphology p. 330

phonation p. 328
phonological error p. 338
phonology p. 330
pragmatics p. 330
resonation p. 328
respiration p. 328
semantics p. 330
speech p. 327
speech disorder p. 329
stuttering p. 339
syntax p. 331
verbal language p. 330
voice disorder p. 331

Questions for Thought

1. Explain the roles of speech and language in the communication process. p. 329

2. Between 5 and 10 percent of the school-age population is receiving services for speech or language problems. What two factors contribute to the uncertainty of that figure? What patterns of prevalence of speech-language problems have been documented?   p. 332

3. What is motherese, and how does it help children learn language?   p. 328
4. Briefly describe the four broad categories of communication disorders. p. 327
5. Briefly describe the causes of voice disorders.   p. 339
6. What prelinguistic irregularities may signal the existence of a communication disorder?   p. 342
7. What steps are involved in evaluating and diagnosing children who are suspected of having communication disorders?   p. 343
8. Briefly describe six intervention strategies.   p. 349
9. What can a classroom teacher do to help a student who stutters?   p. 351
10. Briefly describe seven general disorders of speech.   p. 356
11. What service options are available for dealing with communication disorders?   p. 357

References of Special Interest

Bloodstein, O. (1987). *A handbook of stuttering* (3rd ed.). Chicago: National Easter Seal Society.
   The text is a comprehensive easy-to-read overview written by an authority. The author summarizes history, theory, and treatment.

Fey, M., Windsor, J., & Warren, S. (Eds.). (1995). *Language intervention: Preschool through elementary years.* Baltimore: Paul H. Brookes Publishing Co.
   In this collection, authorities in the field offer teachers many practical suggestions based on sound research.

Kaiser, A., & Gray, D. (Eds.). (1993). *Enhancing children's communication.* Baltimore: Paul H. Brookes Publishing Co.
   The articles in this collection offer a rich array of intervention techniques, such as parent-implemented language intervention, for dealing with language disorders.

Lahey, M., & Bloom, L. (1988). *Language disorders and language development.* Columbus, OH: Merrill.
   The first edition was a classic in the field, and this edition with the title reversed is equally valuable. The authors provide a clear and succinct description of speech and language disorders and how to deal with them in the classroom or in special therapy situations. Highly recommended.

Neidecker, E. (1987). *School programs, in speech and language* (2nd ed.). Englewood Cliffs, N.J.: Prentice-Hall.
   A guide to designing and implementing speech and language services in the schools, this book contains information on caseload selection, programming and scheduling, team participation, and record keeping.

Newman, P., Creaghead, N., & Secord, W. (Eds.). (1985). *Assessment and remediation of articulatory and phonologic disorders.* Columbus, OH: Merrill.

An overview of contemporary practice with disorders of articulation-phonology, this book has specialized content, but the specialists who describe each of the major therapeutic procedures give information that is useful to educators and speech-language pathologists.

Watkins, R., & Rice, M. (Eds.). (1994). *Specific language impairments in children.* Baltimore: Paul H. Brookes Publishing Co.
This research-oriented collection sheds light on the genetic basis of language disorders and suggests intervention strategies.

chapter 9

Children Who Are Deaf or Hard of Hearing

focusing questions

What three factors are critical elements in the definition of hearing losses?

How do we identify children with hearing losses?

How do hearing losses affect a child's language development, and what can be done to maximize communication potential?

What are the trends in school placement for students who have hearing losses?

What is the deaf community, and how can it help a student who is deaf or hard of hearing?

Why is it critical to teach a gestural language to a person who is deaf and to his or her family?

Children who are deaf or hard of hearing have a much greater chance of achieving a communication system (gesture-manual, speech, or both) and academic success than at any time in the past. There is now much broader acceptance of persons who are deaf or hard of hearing in society. In the past decade, an actress who is deaf won a Tony award for her performance in a Broadway play, and another actress received an Oscar for her performance in the motion picture based on that play, as well as an Emmy for the leading role in a television series about a lawyer who is deaf. Miss America of 1995 is deaf. There is a player who is deaf on a major league baseball team, and one who plays professional football. Moreover, there are now doctors, lawyers, directors of government agencies, and other professionals who are deaf. There is a president of Gallaudet University who is deaf.

These advances have been greatly assisted by government mandates. Commissions established by Congress in 1986 and 1988 led to the establishment of the National Information Center on Deafness and the Helen Keller National Center for Technical Assistance, and to rules and regulations requiring statewide telephone relaying systems. In addition, all television sets sold in the United States now must be equipped to receive captioned broadcasts. The Individuals with Disabilities Education Act (IDEA; PL 101-476), the Americans with Disabilities Act (PL 101-336), the Rehabilitation Act (PL 102-569), and other laws and regulations have increased public awareness of the talents and educational needs of persons who are deaf and hard of hearing. Identification during infancy and early childhood has led to progress for parents and their children through early intervention and educational and communication training.

In spite of the gains, there is a lack of agreement in the field on several major issues, two of which are critical: what to teach and how to teach it. Our speech-language-oriented society has not readily accepted a gestural-language system. Thus, some educators of persons who are deaf and hard of hearing strongly advocate oral-speech language. Others advocate gestural language or some combination of both. In addition, professionals in the field differ about terminology. Some prefer the term *hearing impairment*, which has a mixed set of definitions and is sometimes seen as pejorative to persons who are deaf or hard of hearing (Moores, 1996). Throughout this chapter, we use a variety of terms, for there are strong feelings about these labels, and we wish to respect the opinions of all individuals.

While reading this chapter, keep in mind that the essential deficit is a partial or total lack of auditory reception and that language can be communicated orally (speech) or by means of gestures (manual-movement, visual).

■ *Definitions*

Hearing losses are defined in terms of the degree of loss, the age at which the loss occurs, and the type of loss.

DEGREE OF HEARING LOSS

The term *hearing impairment* has different meanings for different authors. For some, it describes a slight-to-moderate hearing loss (Moores, 1987, p. 1). For others, it describes any hearing loss, mild or severe (Paul & Quigley, 1990). We use the term **deaf** to refer to a profound or complete inability to hear and **hard of hearing** to refer to all other categories of loss.

The severity of hearing losses is determined by the individual's reception of sound as measured in **decibels (dB)**. A loss of 26 dB is within the normal range. A person with a loss of from 27 to 70 dB (slight to moderate) is considered hard of hearing. A loss of more than 71 dB is considered a severe and profound hearing impairment or, to use the more common term, *deaf* (Moores, 1987, pp. 40–41). Table 9.1 presents the range of classifications and levels of hearing impairment.

Individuals classified as hard of hearing may be able to hear and understand speech, or they can be assisted to do so with hearing aids. Persons who are severely hard of hearing may be able to hear speech with the assistance of some form of hearing aid. Only a small percentage (less than 1 percent) of persons who are deaf are unable to hear speech under any conditions.

To give you an idea of how to relate hearing losses to noises and sounds in the environment, Table 9.2 lists the levels of common environmental sounds. As the table indicates, a person with a hearing loss of 60 dB, and without amplification such as a hearing aid provides, has difficulty hearing conversational speech. An individual with a loss of 100 dB is not able to hear a power lawnmower without amplification.

AGE OF ONSET OF LOSS

Children experience hearing loss before they acquire speech and language when their hearing loss is genetic or is caused by an event during pregnancy; this

---

TABLE 9.1   Categories of Hearing Impairment

Degree of Impairment	Description	Label
Up to 26 dB	Normal	Normal hearing
27–40 dB	Slight	Hard of hearing
41–55 dB	Mild	Hard of hearing
56–70 dB	Moderate	Hard of hearing
71–90 dB	Severe	Hard of hearing, or deaf
91+ dB	Profound (extreme)	Deaf

Source: P. V. Paul & S. P. Quigley (1990). *Education and Deafness.* White Plains, NY: Longman, p. 41. Copyright © 1990 by Longman Publishing Group. Reprinted by permission of the authors.
Note: Decibel loss refers to results from the better, unaided ear averaged across the speech frequencies, according to the International Standards Organization (ISO).

TABLE 9.2	Hearing Threshold Levels and Some Common Environmental Sounds		
Hearing Threshold Levels		**Decibels**	**Environmental Sounds**
Pain		140	Shotgun blast
Discomfort		130	Jet takeoff
		120	Loud rock music
		110	Power lawnmower
		100	
		90	
		80	Party with 100 guests
		70	
Conversational speech		60	
		50	
		40	
		30	Inside a library
Whisper (5 feet)		20	
		10	
Threshold of hearing (1,000 Hertz)		0	

Source: P. V. Paul & S. P. Quigley (1990). *Education and Deafness.* White Plains, NY: Longman, p. 31. Based on Bess & McConnell (1981). Copyright © 1990 by Longman Publishing Group. Reprinted by permission of the authors.

phenomenon is called **prelinguistic deafness.** Loss after the child has acquired some speech and language is called **postlinguistic deafness.** Prelinguistic deafness is of great significance and often leads to serious educational problems (Boothroyd, 1988).

Chapter 8 (on communication) and Chapter 11 (on multiple and severe disabilities) note that children proceed through a prelinguistic (without speech) period of development that includes crying, comfort sounds (coos and pleasant noises), babbling, and then the first sounds that appear to be words (protowords such as *mama*, *dada*, *baba*, and *gaga*). The non–hearing impaired child typically speaks the first word around 12 months of age (Dromi, 1992). Infants with prelinguistic deafness also proceed through these same genetically determined stages and give the appearance of producing and acquiring normal sounds related to speech (Oller, 1984). After the last stage of producing sounds such as *mama* and *dada*, however, infants with prelinguistic deafness stop making speech-like sounds because they are unable to hear sounds, and they fail to speak their first word. It is quite common for parents to note the hearing loss at this time. But for some parents, it is not until their child is 2 years of age that they note and have assessed their child's prelinguistic deafness (Leonard, 1991).

Not until their child is age 2 do many parents notice that the child may have a hearing loss.

The identification of children who are deaf or hard of hearing during infancy and in early childhood special education programs helps children with hearing impairments increase their communication development and academic success (© *Bob Daemmrich/Stock Boston*)

THE STRUCTURE OF THE EAR AND TYPES OF HEARING LOSS

The ear is a complicated structure (see Figure 9.1), and it functions in a complex way. The middle ear is composed of the tympanic membrane, or eardrum, and the three ear bones: the malleus, the incus, and the stapes. The stapes lies next to the oval window, the gateway to the inner ear. The inner ear contains the cochlea and the vestibular apparatus, collectively called the labyrinth (Batshaw & Perret, 1992).

Although defects are possible in structure and function, they can be classified into four categories: conductive losses, sensorineural losses, mixed losses, and central losses.

A **conductive hearing loss** reduces the intensity of sound reaching the inner ear, where the auditory nerve begins. Sound waves must pass through the ear canal to the tympanic membrane (eardrum), where vibrations are picked up by the three bones of the middle ear (the malleus, the incus, and the stapes) and are then passed on to the inner ear. Any condition that impedes the sequence of vibrations or prevents them from reaching the auditory nerve causes a loss in conduction. The sequence of vibrations can be held up anywhere from the external to the inner ear. Wax or a malformation can block the external canal, the eardrum can be broken or punctured, or the movement of the bones in the middle ear can be obstructed. Conductive defects seldom cause losses of more than 60 to 70 dB. These losses can be effectively reduced through amplification, medical treatment, or surgery (National Information Center of Deafness [NICD], 1989).

Sensorineural hearing losses are caused by defects in the inner ear (cochlea) or the auditory nerve—particularly in the delicate sensory hairs of the inner ear or in the nerves that supply them. Those nerves transmit impulses to the brain.

Figure 9.1
Structure of the Ear

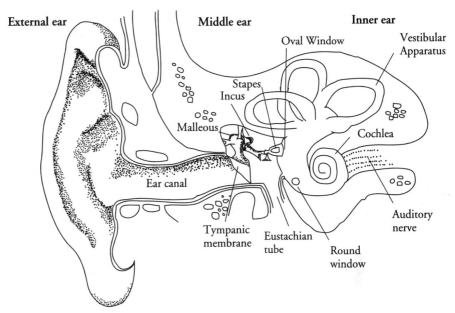

External ear   Middle ear   Inner ear

Oval Window   Vestibular
                     Apparatus

Stapes
Incus

Malleous   Cochlea

Ear canal

                  Auditory
                  nerve

Tympanic   Eustachian
membrane   tube   Round
                       window

Source: M. L. Batshaw (1992). *Children with Disabilities* (3rd ed.). Baltimore: Paul H. Brookes Publishing Co., p. 323. Used by permission of the author.

Tests with an audiometer can determine whether a hearing loss is conductive or sensorineural. Figure 9.2 shows the audiogram of a child with a conductive hearing loss. On the audiometer, the child heard airborne sounds at the 40-dB level at all frequencies; using a bone-conduction receiver, the child responded in the normal range. Notice that the hearing loss is fairly even at all frequencies.

We see a very different pattern in Figure 9.3. The audiogram in this figure is of a child with a sensorineural hearing loss. The youngster shows a profound loss of high frequencies (about 1,000 cycles) and a severe loss of low frequencies. In this case, the bone-conduction receiver gave no better reception because the defect is in the auditory nerve, not in the middle ear structure that carries the sound vibrations to the nerve. Even with amplification to increase the sound level, persons with this pattern may perceive speech sounds as distorted (NICD, 1989).

Mixed hearing losses result from problems in the outer ear as well as in the middle or inner ear (NICD, 1989). Persons with this type of loss may hear distorted sounds as well as have difficulty with sound level. **Central hearing losses** result from changes in the reception of hearing areas in the brain or damage to the pathways of the brain (NICD, 1989). Central hearing losses are not frequently encountered.

Prevalence of Hearing Loss

About 21 million persons in the United States, or 8 percent of the general population, have some degree of hearing loss. Of these, about 1 percent are deaf (Paul &

Figure 9.2
Audiogram of a Child with a
Conductive Hearing Loss

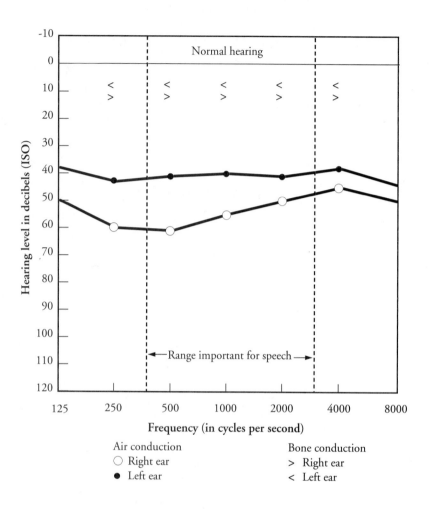

Air conduction
○ Right ear
● Left ear

Bone conduction
> Right ear
< Left ear

More students who are deaf are now being educated in local schools.

Quigley, 1990; NICD, 1989). Because of the impact of the Education for All Handicapped Children Act (PL 94-142) and IDEA, the education of children who are hard of hearing or deaf has moved from residential and day schools to local schools (see Table 9.3).

Causes of Hearing Loss

The causes of deafness or being hard of hearing are equally divided between genetics and the environment. Each accounts for about 50 percent of the causes (NICD, 1989). Table 9.4 lists some common causes of hearing losses. Note the number of illnesses, infections, or accidents that can lead to hearing losses after birth.

Figure 9.3
Audiogram of a Child with a
Sensorineural Hearing Loss

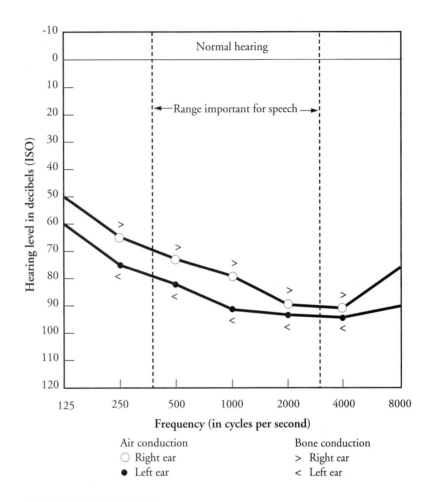

GENETIC CAUSES

The genetic causes are disorders inherited from one or both of the parents. More than two hundred different types of genetic deafness have been identified and can be inherited from either a hearing parent or a nonhearing parent (NICD, 1989).

Children with other genetic defects may have associated hearing disorders. For example, children with Down syndrome (a genetic disorder associated with mental retardation) have narrow ear canals and are prone to middle ear infections, which may cause hearing losses. Individuals with cleft palates (an opening in the lips and aboral ridge) may have repeated middle ear infections, which can result in conductive hearing losses (Batshaw & Perret, 1992).

Rh (hyperbilirubinemia) can develop incompatibility when a mother who is Rh-negative carries a fetus that is Rh-positive. The mother's immune system begins to destroy the fetus's red blood cells when they enter the mother's circulatory system. As a result, the fetus may become anemic and die in utero. If the child survives, he or she is likely to have a high-frequency hearing loss. The drug RhoGAM is

| TABLE 9.3 | Comparison of Enrollments in Schools and Classes for the Deaf in the United States, 1974–1994 | | | | | |

Schools and Classes	1974		1994		Enrollment Change 1974–1994
	Student Enrollment	Percentage of Total Enrollment	Student Enrollment	Percentage of Total Enrollment	
Residential schools	20,564	40.4%	9,772	22.3%	–10,792
Day schools	8,075	15.9%	3,704	8.5%	–4,371
Local schools	22,256	43.7%	30,347	69.1%	+8,091
	50,895		40,823		–7,077

Source: From D. Moores (1996), *Educating the Deaf,* 4/e. Boston: Houghton Mifflin, p. 37. Used with permission.

available to block the formation of antibodies in the mother's system. Usually, the first pregnancy is not affected, but all subsequent ones are if the condition is not identified and treated.

Boothroyd (1988) reminds us that not all hearing losses due to genetic defects appear at birth. Babies born with perfectly normal hearing may lose it in months or years as a result of heredity (p. 50). Teachers who suspect that a child may be exhibiting signs of a loss should be that loss can occur in a child who previously exhibited a normal range of hearing.

Some genetically based hearing losses occur during childhood and adolescence.

ENVIRONMENTAL CAUSES

The environmental effects that begin before birth are associated with illness or infections the mother may have had during pregnancy. For example, uncontrolled diabetes in the mother may cause a hearing loss in her child. More specifically, a group of infections that affect the mother but cause severe hearing losses in the fetus have been labeled *TORCHS*. The *TO* stands for toxoplasmosis, a parasitic disease common in Europe that may be contracted by handling contaminated cat feces or eating infected lamb that has not been cooked sufficiently (Gordon, Appell, & Cooper, 1982). The *R* stands for rubella (German measles), which, if contracted by the mother, can cause not only serious hearing losses in the child, but also blindness and retardation as well. With the advent of the rubella vaccine, very few cases are occurring (Batshaw & Perret, 1992). This vaccination must be renewed periodically. The *C* stands for cytomegalovirus (CMV), an infection in the mother's uterus, which is a major environmental cause of deafness in the United States (Hanshaw, 1982). CMV can go undiagnosed, or it can be misdiagnosed

Some infections that the mother has during pregnancy can cause deafness in her child.

TABLE 9.4	Some Causes and Conditions Associated with Hearing Loss in School-Age Children

Conductive Hearing Impairment

Otitis media (including middle ear fluid)	Perforation of the tympanic membrane
Otitis externa	Impacted cerumen (wax)
Discontinuity of the ossicles	Blockage of the external auditory meatus by foreign object
Congenital malformation of the outer ear	Cholesteatoma
Congenital malformation of the middle ear	Cleft palate
Genetic syndromes (e.g., Down syndrome, Hunter's syndrome)	Traumatic head injury
	Eustachian tube dysfunction

Sensorineural Hearing Impairment

Congenital viral infections	Meningitis
Maternal rubella	Encephalitis
Cytomegalovirus	Scarlet fever
Prematurity and low birth weight	Measles
Perinatal anoxia or hypoxia	Mumps
Hyperbilirubinemia	Influenza
Rh-factor incompatibility	Other viral infections
Maldevelopment of inner ear	Cerebrovascular disorders
Hereditary familial hearing impairment (congenital or acquired)	Drug ototoxicity
Noise-induced hearing loss	Congenital syphilis
Genetic syndromes (e.g., Waardenburg's syndrome, Hunter's syndrome)	Unexplained high fever
	Auditory nerve tumors (e.g., neurofibromatosis)

Source: B. Friedrith (1987). Auditory dysfunction. In K. Kavale, J. Forness, & M. Bender (Eds.), *Handbook on Learning Disabilities, Vol. 1*. Copyright © 1987. Used by permission of the publisher, PRO-ED, Inc.

(sometimes as the flu). A particularly harmful virus, it can pass through the placenta and affect the fetus. Specialists believe that some children with hearing losses caused by rubella may actually have been exposed to CMV (Gothelf, 1991). CMV is so strongly associated with low-birth-weight and premature infants that it has been considered as a possible cause of prematurity as well as of the resulting hearing loss (Stewart, 1986; NICD, 1989). The *HS* stands for herpes simplex virus, which, if untreated, can lead to the death of 60 percent of infected infants. Those who survive may have serious neurological problems and potential hearing loss. Some believe that CMV is a form of herpes virus (Pappas, 1985).

Noise pollution, particularly loud and persistent noises, can cause hearing loss. It is suspected that the noise produced by isolettes for premature babies is related to hearing loss, but this has not been proven (Batshaw & Perret, 1986).

Children who are born with hearing losses need assistive technology and instruction as early as possible. (© *Elizabeth Crews*)

Infections after birth, such as *meningitis* (an inflammation of the membranes covering the brain and spinal cord), can damage the auditory nerve. Because the antibiotics given to treat the infection may also cause damage to the auditory nerve, the dosage for the infant must be measured carefully (Batshaw & Perret, 1992). All infants should be inoculated against meningitis.

Otitis media, a common infection of the middle ear, may cause a hearing loss if it is persistent or recurrent and untreated. It is generally associated with mild-to-moderate hearing losses.

Asphyxia (lack of oxygen) during the birth process may bring about a hearing loss.

Premature and low-birth-weight infants weighing less than 4 pounds are at greater risk of hearing loss, and because of increasingly successful life-saving techniques now being used in neonate nurseries, we are seeing an increase in the number of infants with hearing losses (Robertson & Whyte, 1983).

When reading is taught visually or by a gestural method, deaf children are better able to learn how to read, write, and use language logic forms and to succeed in school. (© Betty Medsger)

Characteristics of Children with Hearing Loss

COGNITIVE DEVELOPMENT

Most children who are deaf or hard of hearing possess normal intelligence.

The most important thing to remember about children who are deaf or hard of hearing is that most of them possess normal intelligence (Schlesinger, 1983). They are not deficient or deviant in their cognitive abilities; they are simply children who cannot hear as well as children with normal hearing. They follow the same sequence of cognitive development as children without losses, but sometimes at a slower rate.

One of the major problems in the past in determining the intellectual level of children with hearing losses was that the intelligence tests used to measure their abilities were not appropriate for children with hearing losses. Orally (speech) administered intelligence tests greatly underestimate the abilities of a child whose primary language is gestural (Paul & Quigley, 1990). In addition, few psychologists have been trained to administer tests to children who are deaf (Vernon & Andrew, 1990). When nonverbal tests are used with a sign system familiar to the child, these children perform well within the normal range (Bellugi & Studdert-Kennedy, 1984).

A child who has not heard the sounds of the language will not be able to decode print if taught in the usual method of matching sounds to print. If reading is taught visually (Moore, 1971) or by a gestural method (such as American Sign Language or finger spelling, which are discussed later in the chapter), however, children who are deaf or hard of hearing are able to learn how to read, write, and use language logic forms (for example, past tense, questions, logical propositions such as if-then or either-or) and will be successful in school. Depending on the degree of hearing present, the child may learn how to use both the gestural system and the oral system of language.

In a series of studies, Iran-Nejad, Ortony, and Rittenhouse (1981) found that adolescents with hearing losses could be taught to understand figurative language, which is related to solving cognitive problems. Thus, cognitive ability is present in persons with hearing losses, but if they do not do as well as expected in acquiring reading, writing, and literacy skills, it is probably because the manner in which they are being taught is inappropriate for students with hearing losses.

Why most children with hearing losses do not develop literacy skills commensurate with their intelligence is still a matter of debate. The evidence strongly suggests that most should be able to do so. There are strong camps in the field of hearing loss with different opinions about how to teach children to enable them to succeed academically and vocationally. Although the various theoretical positions are closely aligned, major differences persist. There is also a genetic role in language development that has not been fully integrated into the field. In the future, this information should have a major impact on instructional strategies and the timing of intervention for children who are deaf or hard of hearing. What is clear is that children who are deaf or hard of hearing, who have parents who are deaf or hard of hearing, and who are taught a sign language (usually ASL) early usually do far better in school than other such children who have first been taught an oral system. Before discussing other controversies in the field of teaching children who are deaf or hard of hearing, let us look at some information from linguistics about how all children acquire language.

LANGUAGE DEVELOPMENT

Casper and Fifer (1984) presented evidence showing that fetuses begin to hear sounds in utero around the age of 7 natal months. After birth, they can distinguish their mother's voice from the voices of other women. Condon and Sander (1974) found that infants thrash (move their arms and legs) in time with the rhythm of the speech spoken around them. They appear to be learning the rhythm of the language of their home by moving their bodies in time with it.

Children with prelinguistic deafness do not move their arms and legs in this way, because at birth and in early infancy they do not receive the sounds that help them acquire the language of their homes. However, Petito and Marentette (1991) found that children with severe hearing losses gesture at about the same developmental age as non–hearing impaired children babble. They concluded that infants are innately predisposed to learn language and do so by stimulating the environment by babbling; if they cannot hear, they use babbling-like hand gestures that are sign equivalents of speech sounds.

Thus, for all children, language begins before birth and proceeds during the first year of life well in advance of the production of the first word at around 12 months of age. The gestures of infants with hearing losses are precursors to learning language in the form of manual signs, and parents must recognize and reinforce these gestures in much the same way that they would reinforce oral sounds.

These babbling-like gestures are seen in children of parents with severe hearing losses, who tend to reinforce them. Thus, the presence of both babbling and gestures tends to support the position of those who believe there is a strong, innate push to learn how to communicate in one's home, using the same mode of communication as the adults in the home (Goldwin-Meadow, 1985). Goldwin-Meadow and Feldman (1975) found that children who are deaf and who have parents who are deaf do better in learning language and later in academic tasks than do children with hearing losses who have hearing parents. We suspect that this is because the parent who has hearing losses recognizes the child's gestures as an initial form of nonverbal communication, reinforces them, and begins teaching the child sign language early in life.

Deafness may seriously hamper verbal language development.

As we said earlier in this chapter, the language learning patterns of children who are deaf or hard of hearing and of children who can hear are the same. Most children produce their first word by 12 months of age. By 18 to 22 months of age, they master the logic forms of the language used in their home (Bloom, 1991), and they begin on their own to figure out the rules of language from the spoken examples provided by their environment (Pinker, 1991; Shantz & Eberling, 1991). This ability to independently generate the rules of grammar (syntax or word order) tends to disappear after 6 years of age. If the child masters these rules of grammar by the age of 6, he or she can build on them through instruction. If the child has not acquired them by then, it is extremely difficult or almost impossible to teach them to the child.

Children with severe prelinguistic hearing losses who are not provided with amplification and early childhood special education are seriously deprived of the experience they need to use their innate mechanisms to figure out the grammar (syntax) and use (pragmatics) of their language. Not surprisingly, grammar and syntax are two aspects of language that children with prelinguistic hearing losses have difficulty mastering (Paul & Quigley, 1990).

For those who can hear no sounds, the introduction of sign language during the first year of life does much to encourage normal gestural language, which has most of the features of American English.

Our basic argument is that all children have a genetic push to acquire language (Chomsky, 1965). They can do so in rich language environments and in poor ones. If they cannot hear, they can develop an equally adequate system of gestural language (Goldwin-Meadow, 1985). If a speech or gestural system is not provided for children to master, however, each child develops a system that is unique, which is not considered normal (Paul & Quigley, 1991).

The National Information Center on Deafness (1989) stated the following:

> Deaf children have unique communication needs; unable to hear the continuous repeated flow of language interchange around them, children with severe hearing impairments are not exposed to the enormous amounts of language stimulation experienced by hearing children during the early years. For children with severe hearing losses, early, consistent, and conscious use of visible communication modes (such

All children have a genetic push to acquire language. For those with severe and profound hearing losses, the introduction of sign language during the first year of life does much to encourage normal gestural language, which has most of the features of American English. (© *Steven Stone/The Picture Cube*)

as sign language, finger spelling, and cued speech) and/or amplification and aural/oral training can help reduce this language delay. Without such assistance *from infancy*, problems in the use of English typically persist throughout the child's school years. With such assistance, the language learning task is easier but by no means easy. (p. 21; emphasis added)

These results point to the importance of *every* parent or teacher of a student who is deaf learning a signed system, particularly in infancy and the preschool years when the child's central nervous system is ready to learn language. The language of the child's culture, whether it be expressed in gestural or oral form, must be provided with strong parental involvement if the child is to learn to communicate (Solnit, Taylor, & Bednarczyk, 1992). The teacher's and parents' abilities to sign not only will aid the child in developing a communication system but also will enhance the child's social skills, peer interaction, and play (Luetke-Stahlman, 1994).

SOCIAL AND PERSONAL ADJUSTMENT

A hearing loss often brings with it communication problems, and communication problems can contribute to social and behavioral difficulties:

Personality inventories have consistently shown that deaf children have more adjustment problems than hearing children. When deaf children without overt or serious problems have been studied, they have been found to exhibit characteristics of rigidity, egocentricity, absence of inner controls, impulsivity, and suggestibility. (Meadow, 1980, p. 97)

People with serious hearing losses develop a sense of community and an awareness of their needs as a group that has been translated into political and social action to protect their individual and group rights. (© Bob Rashid/Monkmeyer Press Photo Service)

Lack of verbal language makes it difficult for children who are deaf to make friends with children who speak and do not sign.

Consider the boy with prelinguistic hearing loss who wants a turn on the playground swings. He cannot simply say, "I want my turn" or "It's my turn now." What does he do? He may push another youngster out of the way. Obviously this kind of behavior is going to cause the child difficulties with interpersonal relationships. And when it is repeated many times, it can create serious social adaptation problems.

These problems intensify in adolescence. Davis et al. (1981) reported the loneliness and rejection of children with hearing losses who were mainstreamed in a local school program. Most of these youngsters had just one or two close friends. Of course, adolescence is a difficult time for most young people, but for youngsters who have severe hearing losses, it can be especially hard:

> Hearing impairment, in rare cases, affects the ease with which communication occurs, and communication forms the basis for social interaction. The hearing impaired person's self-concept and confidence influence how rejection by others is perceived and handled. It is a rare hearing impaired child who does not perceive his social relations as inadequate and does not long for full acceptance by his peers. If being different is the worst thing that can happen, then the next worst thing is associating with someone who is different. One cannot always control the former, but one can control the latter. It is from this fact that social problems encountered by hearing impaired adolescents often stem. (Davis et al., 1981, p. 73)

It is not surprising that many children with severe hearing losses prefer to be with children like themselves, with whom they can feel socially accepted and comfortable (Anita, 1982).

The desire to cluster extends into adulthood, and in many large cities there is a culture of people with severe hearing losses, a group of individuals who socialize with one another and intermarry—the deaf community. This tendency to band together is not unusual. Most adults and children feel most comfortable with people like themselves. This does not mean that people who are deaf do not want to be or cannot be integrated into society. Nor does it mean that all people who are deaf are alike.

The Deaf Community

The cohesive deaf community helps its members overcome a sense of isolation from the mainstream society.

The deaf community exists as a separate cultural group within our society and has exhibited considerable cohesiveness for more than a century (Moores, 1996). Its members share similar values and traditions, and they have a common language—American Sign Language (ASL). As we have noted, parents who are deaf teach ASL to their children who are deaf. Many adults who are deaf learned ASL from their peers in residential schools.

The deaf community has state and local networks, holds world games for the deaf (Envo, 1995) and a Deaf Miss America Pageant (Moores, 1995), and publishes a newspaper as well as other material. The community is strongly bonded, and most deaf adults in the United States move toward membership and involvement in it. The deaf community has the status of a minority group within the mainstream culture. Its members are bilingual, using ASL for communication with others and American English for reading and writing. They provide one another with a sense of belonging and pride, and they help each other overcome their isolation from mainstream society.

Developmental Profiles

Figure 9.4 shows the developmental profiles of three children: Kiesha, Juan, and Raymon. All three children are 10 years old. Their profiles are similar in shape, but their intra-individual differences increase with the severity of hearing loss and age at the onset of deafness. Kiesha is hard of hearing, Juan has a postlingual hearing loss, and Raymon has a prelingual hearing loss.

The upper profile in the figure is Kiesha's. She has a moderate hearing loss of 45 dB. Like Juan and Raymon, Kiesha is of average height, weight, and motor coordination. She also shows average mental ability and social maturity for her age. Her speech development is slightly delayed. She has some difficulty in articulation and needs speech remediation. This speech problem has affected Kiesha's reading skills, but her achievement in arithmetic and spelling is at grade level.

When Kiesha was first fitted with a hearing aid, her special education program included instruction in its use. Now an itinerant speech-language pathologist gives her speech remediation, auditory training, and speech-reading lessons once a week.

Figure 9.4
Profiles of Three Children with
Different Degrees of Hearing Loss

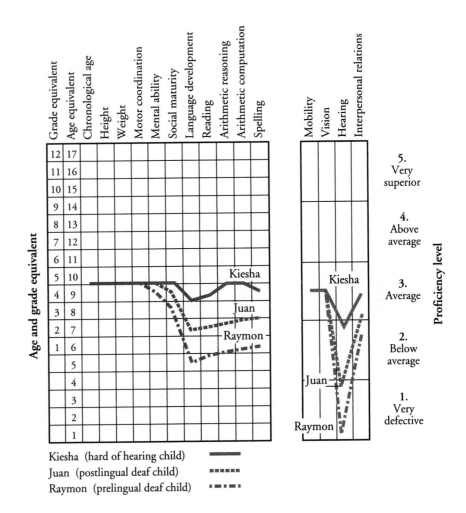

Kiesha (hard of hearing child) ————
Juan (postlingual deaf child) ▪▪▪▪▪▪
Raymon (prelingual deaf child) ▪—▪—▪

Even though Kiesha's development and educational achievement are close to that of her peers, she does need some special attention from the classroom teacher. Her hearing aid makes her feel different from her friends, which could become more of a problem when she is an adolescent. Kiesha's hearing fluctuates somewhat when the weather changes or when she has a cold. Teachers who are not aware of this fluctuation may think that she is deliberately ignoring them when in fact she simply cannot hear them.

The middle profile in Figure 9.4 shows the developmental pattern of Juan, who has a severe hearing loss. He was born with normal hearing but suffered a severe hearing loss in both ears at age 4. He is classified as having postlingual severe hearing loss. Although Juan is approximately normal in physical ability, intelligence, and social maturity, his speech and language have not developed normally. On an audiometer test, he showed a hearing loss of 75 dB even after he was fitted with hearing aids. Fortunately, Juan learned to talk normally before his loss of hearing and developed considerable language ability. This means that he can learn through the auditory channel with the help of hearing aids. Still, his reading and other academic achievement scores are at a second-grade level. His hearing loss has interfered considerably with his educational progress, but, with hearing aids, speech habilitation, and other special education services, he is moving ahead.

Juan relies a good deal on his speech-reading skills. For this reason, and to use his hearing aids to best advantage, he sits at the front of the classroom, facing the teacher. He needs extra help in developing social skills and making friends.

The bottom profile in Figure 9.4 is of a child with a profound hearing loss. Raymon was born with a severe hearing impairment. He has never heard a spoken word. Hearing aids might make him aware of environmental sounds but cannot help him develop speech and English. Because of the severity of Raymon's hearing loss—it tested at more than 90 dB—he is in a self-contained special class. He would need intensive tutorial services if he were integrated into the regular classroom.

Raymon's speech is difficult to understand. His English language development has not followed the pattern of hearing children. In reading and other academic subjects, he is about four grades behind his agemates.

Raymon's communication with his family and peers is limited; so are his sources of information and his social experiences. He often reacts to social situations in ways that are characteristic of a much younger child. If he were placed in the regular classroom, he would need help in making friends.

The School's Role in Identification

Children with severe hearing losses are usually identified through public health screenings or pediatric examinations before they enter school. Children with mild or moderate hearing losses often go undiagnosed until academic performance indicates a problem. Even then, an accurate diagnosis is not automatic. Many of the symptoms of a hearing loss are also indicative of other disorders. A child who stares blankly at the teacher may not be able to hear or may not understand what is being said. Alternatively, the child may be so emotionally disturbed that he or she blocks out communication.

THE CLASSROOM TEACHER

How does the classroom teacher identify a child with a possible hearing loss so that the child can be referred for comprehensive examination? Stephens, Blackhurst, and Magliocca (1982) suggested that teachers watch for several things:

A classroom teacher can help identify a child with a possible hearing loss by observing his or her articulation, need for a higher volume of sounds, requests that information be repeated, and inattentiveness or unresponsiveness.

▪ *Does the child appear to have a physical problem associated with the ears?*
   The student may complain of earaches, discomfort in the ear, or strange ringing or buzzing noises. Teachers should note these complaints and also be alert for signs of discharge from the ears or excessively heavy waxy buildup in the ear canal. Frequent colds and sore throats are occasional indicators of infections that could impair hearing.

■ *Does the child articulate sounds poorly and particularly omit consonant sounds?* Students who articulate poorly may have a hearing problem that is preventing them from getting feedback about their vocal productions. Omission of consonant sounds from speech is often indicative of a high-frequency hearing loss.

■ *When listening to radio, television, or records, does the student turn the volume up so high that others complain?* Because it is much in vogue among young people today to turn up the amplification of rock music almost "to the threshold of pain," this determination will sometimes be difficult to make. Teachers can often get clues, however, by observing students listening to audio media that are not producing music, such as instructional records and sound-filmstrips.

■ *Does the student cock the head or turn toward the speaker in an apparent effort to hear better?* Sometimes such movements are quite obvious and may even be accompanied by the "cupping" of the ear with the hand in an effort to direct the sound into the ear. In other cases, actions are much more subtle. Teachers often overlook such signs, interpreting them as symbols of increased inquisitiveness and interest.

■ *Does the student frequently request that what has just been said be repeated?* Although some students pick up the habit of saying "Huh?" as a form of defense mechanism when they are unable to produce what they perceive as an acceptable response, such verbalizations may also indicate a hearing loss. When a particular student frequently requests repeated instructions, teachers should further investigate the possibility of hearing loss.

■ *Is the student unresponsive or inattentive when spoken to in a normal voice?* Some students who do not follow directions or do not pay attention in class are frequently labeled as "troublemakers," which results in negative or punitive treatment. Often, however, these inappropriate school behaviors are actually caused by the student's inability to hear. They can also be caused if the sounds that are heard appear to be "garbled."

■ *Is the student reluctant to participate in oral activities?* Although reluctance to participate orally may be symptomatic of problems such as shyness, insecurity with respect to knowledge of subject matter, or fear of failure, it may also be due to hearing loss. The child might not be able to hear the verbal interactions that occur in such activities (pp. 43–44).

THE AUDIOLOGIST

With the passage of the Education for All Handicapped Children Act, the presence of the audiologist on the multidisciplinary team had an impact on the services that audiologists provide in the school setting (English, 1995). Audiologists continue to provide traditional clinical services—evaluating hearing level, recommending and fitting devices, and offering counsel on hearing conservation and room acoustics. In addition, they are involved in instruction in speech and in reading (listening skills as well as checking and monitoring all types of amplification devices), and they assist teachers in recognizing and resolving psychological issues of the child who is hard of hearing or deaf (English, 1995). In essence, audiology has developed a subspecialty—educational audiology.

■■ ■ *Means of Testing Hearing Loss*

PURE-TONE AUDIOMETRY

An audiologist is critical in assessing the degree, type, and extent of hearing loss.

Pure-tone audiometry, which is the most common means of determining hearing loss, can be used in children about 3 years of age and older. The **audiometer**—an instrument for testing hearing acuity—presents pure tones (not speech) to the individual, who receives the tones in a headset. The audiometer presents a range of sounds and measures the frequency (vibrations) and intensity (pitch) that the individual is able to hear through the earphones. The individual being tested responds to the sounds by raising his or her hand (or speaking into a microphone) if he or she can hear the tone. These responses are recorded on a graph called an **audiogram**. From an examination of the results, an audiologist can determine the degree and range of hearing loss. More elaborate audiometers can present and measure speech reception and discrimination (Paul & Quigley, 1990).

BONE-CONDUCTOR TEST

With infants and preschool children younger than 3 years of age, it is common to use both a **pure-tone test** and a **bone-conductor test**, which measure the movement of sound through the hearing system to the brain. The reception of sound in the brain (auditory brainstem recognition) is recorded on a graph that charts the brain's response in vibrations (Linden, Kankkunen, & Tjellstrom, 1985). The vibrations are received by electrodes placed on the child's ear. By comparing the test taker's responses to the responses of a population of hearing persons, the audiologist can ascertain hearing abilities or losses (Kankkunnen & Tjellstrom, 1985).

BEHAVIORAL OBSERVATION AUDIOMETRY

Audiologists use behavioral observation audiometry to test hearing in children younger than 3 years of age. The child is placed in an environment with attractive toys, and an outside observer notes the child's reactions as sounds are introduced into the room. Head turning, eye blinking, smiles, movements toward the sound source, and lack of response to presented sounds are recorded.

PLAY AUDIOMETRY

Play audiometry tests are conducted in a pleasant environment with toys that move and make sounds. The toys are used to elicit responses, such as eye blinks and changes in respiration or heartbeat (slower heartbeats indicate attention).

The child is brought into a room with his or her caregiver. An examiner distracts the child with an attractive toy. Sounds are piped into the room. A change in sound indicates that a curtain will be raised to reveal a more attractive toy. The child is not told that this will happen. Children without hearing losses hear the change of sound and turn to look at the hidden toy before the curtain is lifted to reveal it. If the child does not turn when the sound is changed, hearing losses are suspected.

Other play behavioral assessments are based on principles of conditioning children to respond to sound by rewarding them when they indicate that they hear it. The reward is usually allowing them to play with the toy. Paul and Quigley (1990) reported that play-conditioning audiometry is both reliable and an acceptable technique for assessing hearing in young children (p. 37). However, it is not suitable for infants (ASHA, 1991).

Technologies and Programs

HEARING AIDS

One of the most important developments in this century for those with hearing loss is the electronic hearing aid. Paul & Quigley (1990) explained how a hearing aid works:

> Three basic units are common to all amplification systems—the microphone, the amplifier, and the receiver. The microphone converts acoustic sound waves into a weaker but similar electrical energy. The amplifier driven by a power supply (usually a battery) increases the amplitude of the electrical signal. (pp. 45–47)

Thus the receiver in the ear receives an electrical signal which is transformed into speech.

The development of the transistor transformed hearing aids from heavy, cumbersome units to easily portable devices. And directional microphones have cut down on background noise, amplifying only the sounds coming from directly in front of the listener (Northern & Downs, 1978).

The following are additional devices to facilitate hearing:

1. Bone-anchored hearing aids.
2. Implantation techniques similar to hearing aids (Linden, Kankkunnen, & Tjellstrom, 1983).
3. Augmentative communication devices (symbolic black-and-white outline drawings, pictorial symbols, pointers) (MacDonald & Gillette, 1986).
4. Assistive listening devices (ALDs): These devices increase the volume of the voice received and reduce other sounds in the environment. They are wired or wireless and are small enough to be portable for use in vocational or recreational settings (Armstrong, Carr, Houghton, Belanich, & Mascia, 1995).

5. FM wireless systems: These systems send voices through a transmitter to a receiver worn by the listener. They can be used in a variety of noisy settings, indoors or outdoors (Armstrong et al., 1995).

6. Infrared and induction loop wireless and wired systems: Use of these devices is determined by degree of loss and individual needs (Armstrong et al., 1995).

COMPUTERS

The computer is a common sight in classrooms for students with hearing losses. The usefulness of computers for children with hearing losses is comparable to their usefulness for those who have learning disabilities (see Chapter 6). Applied computer technology has advanced to such an extent that special word-processing systems can be used to translate written English into graphic finger spelling signed on the computer screen. The computer enables the student with severe hearing losses to practice both signed and written English.

OTHER TECHNOLOGICAL ADVANCES

A major advance in technology for children and adults with serious hearing losses is the teletypewriter and printer (TTY), a device developed in 1964 by an orthodontist with a hearing loss. This machine enables persons with severe hearing losses to communicate by using a typewriter that transforms typed messages into electrical signals, then retranslates them into print at the other end of a telephone connector. To make a TTY call, the individual places an ordinary telephone receiver on a coupler modem or interface between the typewriter and the telephone. The acoustic coupler transforms the electrical signals into two sounds at different frequencies that are then transmitted over the telephone and converted back into printed letters on the receiving end (Flippo, Inge, & Baruis, 1995; Levitt, Pickett, & Houde, 1980). More sophisticated units that can work with a computer are available, and research is under way to determine how the TTY can be used to improve social language skills (Rittenhouse, 1985).

A series of similar systems, known as telecommunication devices for the deaf (TDD), have been generated over the past two decades. Currently, more than fifty thousand stations send, receive, and print messages on TDD systems. Although costs for the machines and the messages are high, the systems provide a very effective way for people with severe hearing losses to communicate across long distances (Rothstein & Everson, 1995; Schein & Hamilton, 1980).

We are also seeing major technological advances in medicine. One exciting breakthrough is the cochlear implant. The implant is an electronic device that simulates those nerves in the cochlea that are not impaired. The implant system—a microphone, sound processor, transmitter, receiver, and one or more electrodes—converts sound into electrical signals. Although the cochlear implant has helped some children and adults with serious hearing losses hear sounds, it has by no means made those sounds intelligible. According to Dr. William House (the physician who pioneered the cochlear implant), it "sounds like a radio that isn't quite tuned in." Users can make gross discriminations between sounds—distinguishing

Modern technology greatly facilitates communication for the deaf and hard of hearing.

Rachel Remembers

A Santa Fe, N.M., teacher received a small book in the mail one day. Its cover was made of blue construction paper. Inside, on pages cut from a loose-leaf notebook, were short poems written and neatly illustrated by one of the teacher's former pupils, a little girl I'll call Rachel.

> School means work
> and friends,
> quiet hours
> sitting at your desk
> listening to the rustle
> of papers.
>   That's school.

When Rachel had entered the teacher's fourth-grade class three years earlier, school had meant none of those things. Partly deaf since early childhood, Rachel wore two strong hearing aids. And the time she had spent in her hushed world when she was younger had left her reclusive and withdrawn. She also stood out because she was tall and thin with red hair, and couldn't catch a ball.

Rachel was bright, however, and early in her life had found refuge in books. In books she had friends. In books she had no handicaps. In books she could do anything.

> What if you had your own way
> every day?
> What would you say?
> I'd sail
> on a whale
> and go to a garage sale.
> Listen to an owl
> imitate a wolf's howl.
> And chase a goon
>   up to the moon!

During her earlier years in school, Rachel had developed the custom of turning off her hearing aids and sitting quietly in the back of the room reading. When a teacher tried to pull her back into the class-room, she would fly into such a rage that the other kids would stop whatever they were doing and gape at her. And so, more and more, her teachers gave up and left her alone to read.

Rachel's reputation preceded her into the fourth grade at a new school. Both her new teacher and the principal were worried about her effect on the class, and talked of placing her in a class for disruptive children. But Rachel's parents begged the teacher not to give up on their daughter.

So the teacher decided to do her best with Rachel. Whenever the teacher saw her slipping away into books, she made her come back into the lesson at hand. Three or four times a week, flying out of control, Rachel would shout "I won't do this!" and hurl her books off her desk. But no matter how many times Rachel exploded, the teacher would explain that she was not going to get away with it.

After two months, the outbursts became less frequent, and Rachel slowly began to take part in the class. She started acting like an ordinary student. More than ordinary, for she had read so much that there was hardly a subject to which she could not contribute.

> A tree is wisdom.
> They stand for centuries.
> They know everything.
> They quietly watch
> and learn and learn.
> They will never tell what they know;
>   which is lots.

The other children were still frightened of Rachel. They kept their distance. She had no friends.

So the teacher arranged for a demonstration of how a hearing aid works. The kids were fascinated. The teacher asked two little girls who seemed especially understanding to make friends with Rachel. And they did. ➜

Little fish, little fish,
come out of the reeds
on the stream's side,
and play with me.

The rest of Rachel's fourth-grade year got better. The two girls who made friends with her found her to be fun. Soon other children did too. Her enthusiasm for school grew, and when the year drew to a close, the teacher decided to teach fifth grade the next year. She made sure Rachel would be in her class.

That second year Rachel excelled. She had friends. She went on class field trips. Her work in class had few mistakes. But her most wonderful works were her stories.

The unicorn,
so graceful,
leaping across meadows,
playing by starlite,
stopping only
to touch noses
with a woodland creature;
Dawn pierces the sky,
the unicorn goes to
rest upon soft clouds.

Rachel was no longer in the teacher's class in the sixth grade. They would meet on the playground during recess, and it was clear that they both still cared about each other. But Rachel had many other things on her mind: new classes, new friends, perhaps even a boy or two. The teacher understood that Rachel was looking ahead.

In seventh grade, Rachel went off to junior high school. From time to time the teacher called Rachel's parents to ask about her. Cheered by good news, she promised to stay in touch. But her life and work kept her very busy. There were new children whose needs she had to meet.

Then one day, the little book of poems arrived.

A teacher is a friend
who helps you learn math,
English, social studies, science,
reading and fun things.
A teacher is like
another parent,
so caring,
and makes sure
you do your
homework,
and get it right
so you'll have
no trouble as you
grow up,
to maybe
be a teacher
also.

Source: Richard McCord, Rachel Remembers, originally published in *Santa Fe Reporter* (December 10, 1986). Condensation from *Reader's Digest*, 135: (812): pp. 170–172. Copyright © 1986 by Richard McCord. Reprinted by permission of the author.

commentary

What Is the Context? The determination and persistence of a classroom teacher to engage Rachel and encourage her to participate in classroom activities pulled Rachel out of her isolation. Three years later Rachel warmly showed continuing gratitude to her teacher by giving her a special volume of poems that she had composed.

Pivotal Issues. How did Rachel's early behavior affect her classmates? How did the teacher draw Rachel out of her solitary world? Why did Rachel resist the teacher's efforts to engage her in the class activity? What did the teacher do to encourage the other children to approach and befriend Rachel? What do Rachel's poems say about her?

LEARNING ENVIRONMENTS

In the not-too-distant past, most children with severe and profound hearing losses were educated in state residential schools. During the past two decades we have seen a movement away from residential education (see Table 9.3). Although approximately 22 percent of children with severe hearing losses are still being educated in residential settings, most are in public or private day schools or classes (segregated classes held in regular public or private schools). Of the children who are in residential settings, many are day students. A large majority of students with severe hearing losses in the United States are enrolled in programs that allow them to live at home. Some states—Texas, for example—have regional day schools for children with severe hearing losses.

Early Intervention

Teachers of students with severe hearing losses all agree on the importance of early intervention. Infants learn about communication from the facial expressions, lip and head movements, gestures, touch, and vocal vibrations of those around them. This is why it is so important for the parents of children who are deaf or hard of hearing to establish effective communication as early as possible.

Many of the early education programs for preschoolers with severe hearing losses focus on the parents. Some provide counseling to help family members accept and adjust to the diagnosis of the severe hearing losses and to understand the condition. Others train parents to take an active role in teaching their children, carrying out in the home developmental tasks that are part of the overall program. The extent of the parents' involvement is a function of their readiness to participate and the willingness of educators to include them.

Parent training and programs for very young children with severe hearing losses are often provided in the home by appropriate therapists and special education teachers. These programs are also available in nursery schools, day-care centers, and some public schools. Their primary objectives are

■ To train parents

■ To develop communication skills

■ To give children with severe hearing losses opportunities to share, play, and take turns with other children

■ To help children with hearing losses use their residual hearing (through auditory training or with hearing aids)

■ To develop readiness in Basic English, reading, and arithmetic

Intensive preschool training is a fundamental step in preparing children with severe hearing losses for school. One important part of that preparation for children and their parents is learning to use sign language.

Educational Adaptations

Involving parents in early intervention programs for the deaf or hard of hearing assists both child and parent.

Good emotional and behavioral adjustment is one of the greatest challenges for deaf children, who may experience social difficulties (© Freda Leinwand/Monkmeyer Press Photo Service)

Elementary School

The increasing popularity of inclusion, or integrating children with disabilities into the regular classroom, has triggered controversy among teachers of children with severe hearing loss. Obviously, any academic program that attempts to mainstream children with severe hearing losses must provide trained supplementary personnel who are accessible to parents as well as to children. The teacher must be skilled at some form of gestural communication (Solnit et al., 1992). The child's major responsibilities during the elementary years are to develop reading, writing, arithmetic, science, and social studies skills. Quigley and King (1981–1984) developed a reading series called *Reading Milestones* for children with severe hearing losses. They controlled the difficulty level of the language of the readers by applying the results of research with children with severe hearing losses (Quigley & Thomare, 1968). There are eight levels of reading difficulty arranged in sequence. A child who has mastered them all should be able to begin reading traditional basal texts at a fourth-grade level. *Reading Milestones* is the most widely used reading series for children with severe hearing losses (LaSasso, 1986). Decisions about the type of school placement and curriculum should be based on the needs of the individual child at his or her particular stage of development.

In addition, there is a movement to teach reading by the whole word method. First the student learns to read words that stand for persons or things that he or she is familiar with—for example, *ball*. Then, after the student has acquired a basic reading vocabulary, the teacher introduces phonics as a part of a continuing emphasis on teaching whole words (Abrams, 1991).

Secondary School

It is difficult to mainstream high school students with serious hearing losses because they are often several grade levels behind their agemates in achievement. When they are mainstreamed, these students need sign language interpreters in the classroom as well as supplementary resource assistance. Moores, Kluwin, and Mertens (1985) reported a tendency to mainstream children with severe hearing losses more in mathematics than in English, history, or science. Interviews with teachers and administrators revealed a consensus that there are fewer problems in mathematics achievement than in other academic areas.

Today, a number of large metropolitan and suburban school districts are also able to offer a wide range of special services by centralizing programs (Moores, Kluwin, & Mertens, 1985). Schools within a district or several districts working together can combine their resources to provide special services to accommodate students with severe hearing losses within a large comprehensive high school. This setting allows a range of environmental options, from self-contained classes for youngsters with severe hearing losses to mainstreaming in all academic courses.

Postsecondary Programs

In the mid-1960s, surveys of the vocational status of adults with severe hearing losses revealed some disturbing facts. The unemployment rate among the population was four times greater than that of hearing adults, and the level of employment was primarily fixed at unskilled or semiskilled positions (for example, see Moores, 1989). At about the same time, an effort to locate all persons with hearing losses who had enrolled in or graduated from regular colleges and universities was under way. It yielded just 653 persons, only 133 of them graduates, who had prelinguistic hearing losses (Quigley, Jenne, & Phillips, 1968). Clearly, one factor affecting the kinds of jobs that adults with severe hearing losses were finding was their limited educational opportunities.

Since the 1970s, the situation has changed. In that time, we have developed an increasing number of vocational programs for young adults with severe hearing losses. One major development was the establishment in 1967 of the National Technical Institute for the Deaf in Rochester, New York. The institute, which is supported by the federal government, was founded to provide technical and vocational training for adolescents and adults with severe hearing losses.

In 1990, the federal government funded postsecondary vocational programs in three community colleges in New Orleans, Seattle, and St. Paul. The schools offered training to a small group (65 to 100) of young adults with severe hearing losses in the graphic arts, metalworking, welding, automobile repair, food services, machine tool processing, and electronics (Craig, Newman, & Barrows, 1972). In an evaluation of programs, Moores, Fisher, and Harlow (1974) found positive results. For example, three-fourths of the graduates were able to find positions in technical, trade, and commercial industries. But the study did not reveal any major breakthroughs into new job areas. Instead, students tended to cluster in certain occupations: general office work for female students, printing for male students.

Persons who are deaf or hard of hearing are seriously underemployed.

New job opportunities would come with educational opportunities. One academic alternative for students with severe hearing losses is Gallaudet University in Washington, D.C., the only college in the world devoted to the liberal arts education of students with severe hearing losses. The school was established by Congress in 1864 and is still supported by the federal government. It is an accredited four-year liberal arts college and now includes a graduate school for students who are both hearing and deaf or hard of hearing. Gallaudet also operates the Kendall Demonstration Elementary School and the Model Secondary School for the Deaf.

Many state universities now have students with moderate-to-severe hearing losses on their campuses. They provide interpreting and note-taking services for these students. The impact of new educational opportunities is yet to be determined, but much depends on the quality of early education:

> It is doubtful that any postsecondary program, no matter how exemplary, can overcome the inadequate education most deaf individuals receive in the early intervention, elementary, and secondary years, despite improvements. Until education of the deaf, in general, begins to provide students with basic skills and helps them to develop to the limits of their potential, the economic position of deaf adults will continue to be below that which they are capable of obtaining. (Moores, 1987, p. 315)

COMMUNICATION SKILLS

The dispute over how to teach language to a child with hearing losses began in Europe, with Samuel Heinicke in Germany stressing oralism (speech) and Abbé de l'Eprée in France stressing manualism (gestures). A conference held in Milan in 1880 stressed oralism and claimed that gestural language impeded language development (Paul & Quigley, 1990).

In the United States, the gestural approach was taken up by Thomas Hopkins Gallaudet, who founded the first school for the hearing impaired in Hartford, Connecticut, in 1817. The school was moved to Washington, D.C., in 1884. The oral approach was advocated by Alexander Graham Bell, inventor of the telephone and the audiometer. Interestingly, both men had mothers with severe hearing losses, and each was firmly convinced of the correctness of his position.

Not until the 1970s did Bob Holcomb (Gannum, 1981), a college graduate with a severe hearing loss, advocate the use of both systems, oral and gestural, and coin the term *total communication method* to describe this dual approach. In total communication, some type of sign system is used simultaneously with speech.

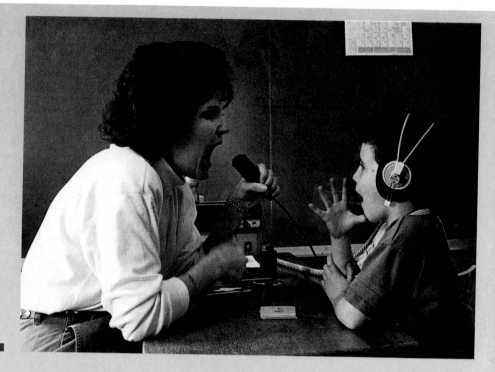

The combination of gestural and oral systems in a total communication approach is now being widely recommended for those with hearing losses, regardless of whether the impairment is moderate or severe. (© Grant LeDuc/Monkmeyer Press Photo Service)

However, according to Paul and Quigley (1990), most educators of persons who are deaf or hard of hearing do not use a sign system as an instructional technique. The simple fact is that our culture prefers that people learn to speak with correct pronunciation, correct word order, and interpretable meaning appropriate to the setting in which speech is spoken. Given this strong societal bias, educators of students who have hearing losses stress oral language, although the children do not succeed as well as expected. Many specialists in educating persons with hearing losses argue that it is more important to teach a communication system that the child can master whether it is gestural or oral. The combination of gestural and oral systems in a total communication approach is now being more widely recommended for those with hearing losses, regardless of whether the loss is moderate or severe (Moores, 1989).

In this section we first discuss oral and manual methods of communication, and then we look at two approaches to teaching communication that combine oral and manual methods.

Communication Methods

Oral methods of communication for persons who are deaf or hard of hearing use whatever hearing and speech abilities the person has. Oral methods include the oral-aural method and the auditory method. **Manual methods** include the various signing systems (American Sign Language, for example) and finger spelling. The effectiveness of all of these methods depends on the severity of the hearing loss and the availability of early intervention.

Oral-Aural Method. The **oral-aural method** uses residual hearing through amplified sound, speech reading, and speech to develop communication skills. Oral-aural programs do not use or encourage the use of sign languages or finger spelling, believing that manual communication impedes the child's adjustment to the hearing world.

One important skill in the oral-aural method is **speech reading,** the visual interpretation of spoken communication (also known as *lip reading*). It is one means by which people with severe hearing losses receive communication from those who can hear. Because few hearing people go to the trouble to learn a complex system of manual communication, individuals with severe hearing losses who want to keep in meaningful contact with the hearing world must learn to speech-read.

Speech reading is possible because many sounds in the English language bring a particular expression to the speaker's face. For example, the *n* sound looks very different from the *k* sound. A major problem, however, is sounds that are homophones—they are articulated in similar ways and look the same on the speaker's lips and face (for example, cite, height, night). The fact that half of the words in the English language have homophones is one reason why speech reading is so difficult.

The approach that is used to teach youngsters speech reading depends on the child's age. When the child is young, the teacher or parent talks in whole sentences. At first the child may not pick up any clues, but as the teacher or parent repeats the same expression over and over in the same relationship to something that the child is experiencing—an object, an action, a feeling—the child begins to get an idea of what is being said. At a later stage, these vague whole impressions are converted into lessons that emphasize details and into exercises that help the child discriminate among different words and sounds. Eventually, the special education teacher uses speech reading to present lessons in school.

Auditory Method. The **auditory method** (or **aural method**) makes extensive use of sound amplification to develop listening and speech skills. It involves auditory training—teaching the child to listen to sounds and to discriminate among different sounds. Although the method is used widely with school-age youngsters who have mild or moderate hearing losses, it has been most effective with preschoolers, particularly children with a severe loss. Parents play an important part in the early training process, and one of the goals of hearing specialists is to instruct them and include them in the training.

The auditory method is also called the **acoustic method,** the **acoupedic method,** and the **unisensory method.** Calvert and Silverman (1975) called it the **auditory global method** and claimed that the approach makes maximum use of residual hearing. They also recommended that it be used with amplification as early as possible.

Signing Systems. There are several signing systems of communication: **American Sign Language (ASL),** Pidgin Sign English (PSE), Seeing Essential English (SEE I),

The effectiveness of any communication method depends on the severity of a person's hearing loss and how early the loss is diagnosed and intervention is begun.

There are several sign systems to aid the child who is deaf in learning a language.

American Sign Language is the only signing system of communication that is a distinct language, with its own grammar and syntax that are both very different from English grammar and syntax. (© *Arlene Collins/Monkmeyer Press Photo Service*)

and Signing Exact English (SEE II). Of these, American Sign Language is the only distinct language (Bellugi & Studdert-Kennedy, 1984). The others are manual codes based on English.

Like all languages, ASL has its own grammar and syntax. It is a distinct language and is very different from the "home" language, be it American English, an Asian language, or Spanish as it is spoken in different parts of North and South America. The language of the deaf community, ASL is not easily learned by adults who learned another language first.

Because of the absence of teachers who are deaf from intervention, school, and college programs, teachers who can hear face the challenge of teaching ASL to students who are deaf.

Each sign has three elements: the position of the hands, the configuration of the hands, and the movement of the hands to different positions (Moores, 1996, p. 12). Moores (1996) reports that Gallaudet University requires faculty members to attain proficiency in ASL within six years. He feels it may be unreasonable to expect parents who hear to learn ASL in such a short period of time.

Differences in grammar and syntax between ASL and English have created a controversy over the use of ASL with students with severe hearing losses. Many educators believe that ASL inhibits the acquisition of English. Others, principally researchers, believe that ASL is (or should be) the native language of children with severe hearing losses and they should learn it *before* they learn English.

PSE, SEE I, and SEE II are manually coded systems that preserve the syntactic patterns of English. Of the three, PSE comes closes to ASL. It uses the same signs and occasionally omits English function words and inflections. SEE I and SEE II are similar. Both systems maintain strict English structural patterns. In both, one morpheme equals one sign. (For example, the word *cats* would be signed with two morphemes: *cat* plus *s*.) The major difference between SEE I and SEE II is the way each treats compound words (such as babysit, cowboy). SEE I borrows signs from ASL; SEE II treats each part of the word (*baby, sit*) separately.

Finger Spelling.   **Finger spelling** is writing in the air. The signs are presented in Figure 9.5. Instead of writing with a pencil, the child writes with his or her finger, spelling out each letter of the word. The practice was very common in the USSR in the 1970s and 1980s among preschool children who were hearing impaired; finger spelling was used in conjunction with speech (Gallagher et al., 1976; Moores, 1995). In the United States, finger spelling with speech is commonly known as the **Rochester method** (NICD, 1989). In Russia, finger spelling is a common way to begin teaching speech to preschoolers who are deaf or hard of hearing. In the United States, it is used to establish the letter-phoneme correspondence to reading.

Approaches to Teaching Communication

Total Communication Method.   The **total communication method**, also known as the **simultaneous method** or **combined method**, combines finger spelling, signs (one of the several signed English systems), speech reading, speech, and auditory amplification. The Conference of Executives of American Schools for the Deaf (1976) defined *total communication* as a "philosophy requiring the incorporation of appropriate aural, manual, and oral modes of communication in order to insure effective communication with and among hearing impaired persons" (p. 358).

Combining the oral and aural (auditory) methods, total communication is the most common method of classroom communication; the oral-aural method is the next most common. The two procedures together were used by more than 90 percent of the schools surveyed. Manual communication by itself was not reported as a major mode of instruction in any school (Paul & Quigley, 1990).

Bilingual Approach.   Some specialists in teaching people with hearing losses advocate postponing the introduction of speech. They believe that children should first be taught a gestural system and be introduced to oral language later, as if it were a second language (the first being the gestural one). Children with hearing losses who were taught in this manner would be considered bilingual.

This argument is much like any other that favors bilingual instruction—that is, it is best to begin by teaching the child to read and write in his or her native language, be it Spanish, Hebrew, French, or any other, and then introduce English after the basic literacy skills have been attained (around the third grade) (Anastasiow, Hanes,

Figure 9.5
The Alphabet of Finger Spelling

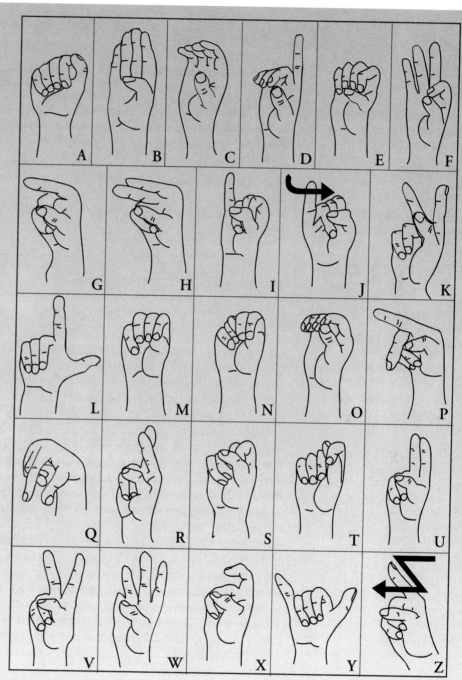

Source: T. Humphries, C. Padden, and T. J. O'Rourke (1980). *A Basic Course in American Sign Language.* Silver Springs, MD: T. J. Publishers. Reprinted by permission.

& Hanes, 1984). Advocates of the bilingual/native language approach argue for the following:

1. Provide instruction in the early grades in the first language only (gestural if the child is deaf or severely hard of hearing; oral if he or she is not).
2. Introduce reading and writing in the first language only.
3. During grade three, provide instruction in the first language and then in the second or target language.
4. Then introduce and develop reading and writing in the second language. (revised and adapted from Paul & Quigley, 1990, p. 14)

The principles apply to the instruction of any child whose native language is not American English.

Learning to read is critical and should lead to reading to learn.

ACADEMIC ACHIEVEMENT

Three factors are related to the academic achievement of children with hearing losses: the degree of hearing loss, the presence of language, and experiences in the environment with people and things. If amplification can provide a rich linguistic environment and the home a rich environment in terms of experiential language and activities, these children need not fail in school (Paul & Quigley, 1990).

National trends in the reading achievement of children with hearing losses are exciting. Moores (1987) reported on a study in which Allen (1986) found the reading comprehension of children with hearing losses to be higher in 1983 than it was in 1975 at every age from 8 to 18 (p. 274). Paul and Quigley (1990) reported that adolescents with severe and profound hearing losses read at about the average level of 9- and 10-year-olds without hearing losses (p. 180). New technology should help these students attain their age-appropriate academic levels.

Moores (1989) attributed some of these gains to the movement toward teaching reading and writing in a more functional (practical) and semantic (knowledge/meaning) manner. Many also affirmed that mainstreaming (placing children with hearing losses in regular classrooms) has increased their academic achievement. Table 9.5 indicates whether it is considered advantageous to mainstream children with various degrees of hearing loss.

About 65 percent of the graduates of Gallaudet College are going on to graduate school and doing as well as their classmates who do not have hearing impairments (Moores, 1996). However, this is not to say that the academic achievement problem has disappeared. Several factors should be mentioned for persons with hearing losses at all age levels:

1. Peer play and interaction are limited, for peers who can hear usually cannot communicate gesturally.

TABLE 9.5	Categories of Hearing Impairment and Educational Implications	
Degree of Impairment	**Label**	**Educational Implications**
Up to 26 dB	Normal	Regular education placement
27–40 dB	Slight	Regular education placement; favorable seating; may need training in speech and speech reading; may need other support services; academic progress should be monitored.
41–55 dB	Mild	Regular education placement; favorable seating; should use hearing aid; may need instruction in speech, speech reading, and auditory training; may need help in language and reading; may need other support services; academic progress should be monitored.
56–70 dB	Moderate	Regular education placement; favorable seating; training and use of hearing aid; instruction in speech and speech reading; special help in language and reading; use of other support services such as tutoring and note taking; progress should be monitored.
71–90 dB	Severe	Regular education placement if possible; favorable seating; full-time special education program may be necessary; part-time integration whenever possible; training in use of hearing aid; instruction in speech, speech reading, and auditory training; comprehensive support services must be available; academic progress should be monitored.
91+ dB	Profound	Special education program likely; training in both oral and signing communication skills; comprehensive support services must be available; part-time integration only for carefully selected children.

Source: P. V. Paul & S. P. Quigley (1990). *Education and Deafness.* White Plains, NY: Longman, p. 57. From Ross (1986a), Ross (1986b), Calvert (1978). Copyright © 1990 by Longman Publishing Group. Reprinted by permission of the authors.

2. Not all family members can use some form of gestural communication. Although 70 percent of students with hearing losses use some form of signing, only 35 percent of their families use it at home (Paul & Quigley, 1990, p. 163).

3. The experiences of young children with hearing losses are limited. They cannot go into the environment without supervision because they cannot hear approaching cars or other dangers and the general populace cannot communicate with them.

GENERAL TEACHING STRATEGIES

Research has supported several strategies to assist persons with hearing losses. Moores (1987, p. 297) described the following strategies.

Instructor Variables

Instructor variables are factors under the control of the teacher, such as knowledge of subject matter and skill in communicating with children with severe hearing losses. The following additional instructional variables also enhance the teaching and learning process:

1. *Reinforcement:* The teacher should provide appropriate reinforcement and positive feedback.
2. *Mastery learning:* The addition of teaching and feedback procedures to conventional instruction enhances learning.
3. *Graded homework:* Meaningful homework that is assigned, graded, and responded to will increase learning.
4. *Time on task:* There is a positive correlation between the time spent on a subject and the amount learned. This may seem a rather simplistic statement, but many teachers—particularly teachers of students with severe hearing losses in academic content areas—spend surprisingly little time on task.
5. *Class morale:* Teachers should strive to maintain cohesiveness, satisfaction, and goal direction in the classroom.
6. *Support:* Someone who can sign (the teacher or an interpreter) needs to be in the classroom.

Program Variables

Program variables are variables that are specific to a program rather than under the control of an individual teacher. In addition to fostering the teacher's individual efforts, programs should concentrate on the following components, found by research to be desirable:

1. *Reading training:* Over and above conventional reading instruction, a special program should train students with severe hearing losses in adjusting reading strategies for various purposes. After reading is mastered, emphasis should be placed on reading to learn (Moores, 1996; Kelly, 1995).

2. *Cognitive strategies:* The teaching of cognitive strategies should be an important part of the curriculum (Moores, 1996). Students use these strategies to select, control, and monitor how they learn and solve problems. According to Moores, they are frequently neglected in programs for students who are deaf or hard of hearing. (See Chapter 6 for specific techniques for teaching strategies.)

3. *Special programs:* Students with severe hearing losses who have high potential should be identified and should receive accelerated training.

4. *Tutoring:* Even if a one-to-one situation cannot be attained, with careful planning a low student-teacher ratio in programs for persons with severe hearing losses can lead to significant one-to-one and small-group instruction.

5. *Cooperative parent programs:* The alterable curriculum of the home can be manipulated to foster school achievement.

Home Variables

The idea behind the use of the alterable home curriculum is not to place the total responsibility for teaching on parents but to encourage academic achievement. The results have been excellent. Basic things that parents are asked to do include the following:

1. Keep television viewing to moderate levels—that is, twelve hours per week or less.

2. Monitor homework to see that it is completed.

3. Encourage leisure reading.

4. Discuss school with the child.

5. Express interest in the child's progress.

6. Learn a sign or gestural communication system if the child has a severe hearing loss.

Many programs at homes or with therapists, or early intervention programs, focus on teaching words and phonemes (the smallest units of sound with meaning) rather than on the broad set of literary skills. Children with hearing losses must be taught the following concepts:

◼ *Word meanings:* multiple meanings of the same word, such as *mole*, an animal, and *mole*, a spy whose task it is to collect classified information within an organization

◼ *Syntax:* variety of word order, such as in questions, declarative statements, and possessives

◼ *Figurative language:* similes ("he has a head like a rock"), metaphors ("she is a vixen"), and onomatopoeia ("the whir of the engine")

◼ *Idioms:* for example, "he pulled himself up by his bootstraps"

■ *Inferences:* for example, "the cold wind blew snow around the house," from which it can be inferred that it is winter. (after Paul & Quigley, 1990, pp. 181–186)

THE EDUCATIONAL TEAM

A child with a significant hearing loss faces problems that are so varied that no single professional can deal with them all. The child's needs demand a team of professionals to produce a comprehensive program of education and therapy. A clinical audiologist must carefully assess the hearing loss and its physical and functional dimensions. A speech therapist must help the child reach his or her potential in speech reading and production. A special education teacher trained to work with children with severe hearing losses must develop an individualized education program (IEP) and a sequence of lessons to help regular educators understand the special needs of the child.

That list is not exhaustive. The education of children with severe hearing losses is changing. Because of the recognition that instruction must adapt to the students' needs, and because their needs appear to include some form of manual interpretation, we find interpreters in the classroom and teachers trained not only in special education but in subject areas as well.

Parents are critical members of the educational team.

One critical segment of the educational team is not professional at all. More than 50 percent of the families of children who are deaf or severely hard of hearing use signs in the home (Trybus, 1985). In more than 80 percent of these families, parents and siblings do not have hearing losses (Rawlings & Jensema, 1977). In addition, family members are providing important reinforcement and even training throughout the critical preschool years.

between a strange voice and a familiar one, for example—but cannot understand what is being said. At present, the cochlear implant is still controversial.

SOME SPECIAL SERVICES

Numerous social service agencies extend their programs to clients with severe hearing losses. In addition, various agencies and organizations—related either to hearing losses or to disability in general—provide specific services to people with severe hearing losses. We discuss these special services in this section.

Captioned Films for the Deaf

Captioned Films for the Deaf lends theatrical and educational films captioned for viewers with severe hearing losses. It is funded by the Captioning and Adaptations Branch of the U.S. Department of Education. Its aim is to promote the education and welfare of people with severe hearing losses through the use of media. The

Captioning and Adaptations Branch also provides funds for closed-captioned television programs, including the live-captioned ABC television news (NICD, 1989).

Signaling Devices

Signaling devices that add a flashing or vibrating signal to the existing auditory signal are popular with hearing impaired users. Among devices using flashing lights are door "bells," telephone-ring signalers, baby-cry signals (which alert the parent that the baby is crying), and smoke alarms. Alarm clocks may feature either a flashing light or vibrating signal.

Registry of Interpreters for the Deaf, Inc.

A professional organization, The Registry of Interpreters for the Deaf (RID) maintains a national listing of persons skilled in the use of American Sign Language and other sign systems. The organization also provides information on interpreting and evaluation and certification of interpreters for people with severe hearing losses (NICD, 1989).

State Departments of Vocational Rehabilitation

Each state has specific provisions for the type and extent of vocational evaluation, financial assistance for education and training, and job placement help (NICD, 1989).

Telecommunications for the Deaf, Inc.

Telecommunications for the Deaf (TDI) publishes an international telephone directory of individuals and organizations that own and maintain TTDs for personal or business use (NICD, 1989).

Families

The most important inclusion required by law in educational programs for the deaf and hard of hearing is the family. Family-oriented approaches have resulted in children who are deaf or hard of hearing attaining better communication skills; moreover, when stress is reduced within a family, better interaction usually occurs among its members (Moores, 1996). IDEA stresses that the family is central to intervention programs.

Focusing on the family system requires recognition of its strengths and respect for its values, beliefs, choices, and aspirations. It helps the family to recognize the critical role that sign language plays in the development of children who are deaf or severely hard of hearing. The child's development is facilitated when family members adopt interactive strategies, encouraging the child to request, respond, or take the initiative. All these interactive patterns are important factors in effective learning (Jamieson, 1994). They also stimulate the child to use language rather than shifting to the visual mode.

The teacher is faced with a dual problem—how to recognize the strengths of the family and how to improve (when necessary) the transaction patterns if parents are not aware of how they should be used to maximize the development of a child who is deaf or hard of hearing.

When the parents of a child who is deaf are also deaf, they are likely to prefer having the child learn a sign-manual language, usually ASL, first. Children in this situation are fortunate because they learn a language early and probably develop more quickly than children who are deaf and born to hearing parents, who may not recognize their child's condition for some time.

Most parents who can hear have little or no experience with deafness and may not know how to proceed with a child who is deaf. Feelings of guilt and helplessness are common. In many instances, they initially misperceive the condition, believing it to be an inability to speak rather than an inability to hear. They tend to resort to spanking more often (the child cannot hear other commands) and exhibit a great deal of frustration. In turn, they also tend to be overprotective of the child, and the child tends to be more dependent.

Summary of Major Ideas

1. Children with hearing losses fall into several categories: those with mild hearing loss, some residual hearing (hard of hearing), and severe hearing losses, usually prelinguistically impaired (deaf). With sound amplification, the child who is hard of hearing can understand speech; the child with severe hearing losses (deaf) usually cannot and must depend on a sign system.

2. Prelinguistic deafness is the loss of hearing before speech and language develop; postlinguistic deafness is the loss of hearing after speech and language develop. The child who has prelinguistic severe hearing losses faces the most serious learning problems.

3. A conductive hearing loss reduces the intensity of sound reaching the inner ear. A sensorineural hearing loss is caused by a defect of the inner ear or auditory nerve. Conductive losses can be reduced through sound amplification; sensorineural losses cannot.

4. Severe and profound hearing losses are usually identified before the child enters school, but a mild loss may go unnoticed. Teachers should be aware of certain behaviors that could indicate that a child has a hearing loss.

5. The causes of hearing losses are equally divided between genetics and the environment. Environmental causes include complications during pregnancy and birth, childhood diseases, infections, and injuries.

6. Only one child in one thousand has a severe hearing loss (deafness), and only three or four in one thousand are hard of hearing.

7. Studies show that children with serious hearing losses are cognitively normal. Their poor reading performance stems from their difficulty in reading and writing the English language.

8. The difficulty children with severe hearing losses have in understanding the complex structure of the English language is a function of their limited opportunities to use that language on a daily basis.

9. The social adjustment of youngsters with severe hearing losses can be impeded by a lack of communication with those around them.

10. Most early intervention programs for youngsters with severe hearing losses make the parents a critical part of the process. Most elementary and secondary programs bring children who have severe hearing losses into the public schools, either in regular or in special classrooms. There are a limited number of postsecondary programs for young adults who have severe hearing losses. Most offer vocational training.

11. Methods of teaching communication skills to students with severe hearing losses include the oral-aural method, the auditory method, and manual methods. Approaches to teaching communication include the total communication method and the bilingual approach. The total communication method combines oral and manual communication and is currently the most popular approach.

12. The use of signs and auditory training during the child's early developmental years have a positive effect on academic performance and adjustment.

13. Technology is having an impact on children with mild-to-severe hearing loss. The electronic hearing aid is extensively used, and computers give students the individual attention they need. Advances in telecommunications are allowing people with severe hearing losses to communicate across long distances. Cochlear implants offer the promise of increased hearing in some individuals. And captioned films and television programs are making visual channels more accessible.

14. Many of the problems facing adults with severe hearing losses in our society are job related. Limited language skills, poor educational and vocational training, and employer prejudice make finding appropriate jobs difficult. The underemployment and low-level employment of adults with severe hearing losses gives them a financial handicap in addition to their physical disability.

Employment Issues

1. With respect to unemployment, occupational level, wage earnings, and opportunities for advancement, in all groups persons with severe hearing losses fare worse than the general U.S. population.

2. The favorable reports of most supervisors regarding the job performance of their employees who have severe hearing losses indicate that employed young adults who have severe hearing losses perform well in their jobs, as does the supervisors' willingness to have more subordinates who have severe hearing losses and to advance them if they receive further training.

3. The vocational preparation resources for persons who are deaf are limited.

4. The opportunities for young adults with severe hearing losses to advance are limited. In spite of their employers' ratings of "average" or "above average" in the performance of their jobs, only a few of the employed young adults with severe hearing losses can advance beyond their present occupational levels without retraining or relocation (or both).

5. An updating and upgrading of vocational training and ancillary services for young adults with severe hearing losses is long overdue.

6. A majority of current and former students who have severe hearing losses and their parents perceive a need for postsecondary training and indicate that they would support such programs if the opportunity were available. A majority of parents would prefer that postschool training for young adults who have severe hearing losses be provided in a facility for hearing students, with modifications including additional staff introduced to serve trainees who have severe hearing losses. Approximately 40 percent of the young adults with severe hearing losses have a preference for being educated with peers who have severe hearing losses (Moores, 1989).

Unresolved Issues

1. *Educating the multiply handicapped child with a hearing loss.* Approximately one of every four children with severe hearing losses has some other impairment. It is essential to design educational programs for these youngsters. At present, only a handful of pilot programs provide systemic education for children who are emotionally disturbed and have severe hearing losses or those with learning disabilities and severe hearing losses. If we want to see a change here, we must begin training teachers in the special needs of students who have multiple and profound disabilities as well as hearing losses.

2. *Stimulating language development.* The growing popularity of the total communication method reflects the importance of language to the academic performance of a child with a severe hearing loss. Our teaching of the structural and conceptual aspects of language must be organized in sequence so that the youngster can move from preschool to elementary to secondary programs that build on and reinforce earlier learning.

3. *Increasing occupational opportunities.* Although people with severe hearing losses are working, they are working at low-level, low-paying jobs. Even the availability of postsecondary vocational programs has not had a substantial impact on their employment. In a world where communication and language have become increasingly important, how do we broaden the opportunities of people with severe hearing losses so that they can communicate in the hearing world? Most people who have severe hearing losses still find that interaction with the hearing world is both painful and difficult. As a consequence, they segregate themselves as adolescents and adults. If we believe that integration is a valuable goal, then we must provide the means by which those with severe

hearing problems can be integrated successfully—both vocationally and socially.

4. *The factors that facilitate speech reading.* We must determine what factors are at work in the speech-reading process. "Speech reading, the hallmark of education for those with severe hearing losses, remains an enigma. Even those persons with severe hearing losses who are proficient lip readers are unable to explain how they acquired the ability or what factors enable them to use this method to understand speech" (Farwell, 1976, p. 27). Obviously, it is impossible to teach a skill efficiently if we do not understand the factors that operate in helping the individual master the skill.

5. *Improving teacher-training programs.* Most teacher-training programs reflect traditional philosophies and methodologies, not the innovative educational approaches suggested by research findings. All too often the preparation of teachers and the operation of research programs are mutually exclusive functions. Until teacher-training programs begin to integrate preparation and research through faculty appointments and university emphases, the students who graduate from traditional programs may continue to use methods that are not working.

6. *Teaching reading and English language to children with severe hearing losses.* Many adolescents who have severe hearing losses graduate from high school today with little control over the English language. Although the education of those with severe hearing losses has changed markedly over the course of this century, more improvements are needed. With new findings in language and cognitive research and new materials, we may see some changes in the achievement of youngsters with severe hearing losses. Of course this means that new findings and materials must be assimilated directly into teacher-training programs if we want them to be implemented as soon as possible.

Key Terms

acoupedic method p. 396
acoustic method p. 396
American Sign Language (ASL) p. 396
audiogram p. 325
audiometer p. 325
auditory method p. 396
auditory global method p. 396
aural method p. 396
bone-conductor test p. 325
central hearing loss p. 371
combined method p. 398
conductive hearing loss p. 370
deaf p. 368
decibels (dB) p. 368

finger spelling p. 398
hard of hearing p. 368
manual method p. 395
mixed hearing loss p. 371
oral-aural method p. 396
postlinguistic deafness p. 369
prelinguistic deafness p. 369
pure-tone test p. 386
Rochester method p. 398
sensorineural hearing loss p. 370
simultaneous method p. 398
speech reading p. 396
total communication method p. 398
unisensory method p. 396

Questions for Thought

1. Explain the difference between a conductive hearing loss and a sensorineural hearing loss. p. 370

2. What are three causes of conductive hearing loss and three causes of sensorineural hearing loss? p. 375

3. To be able to identify possible hearing problems, what should the classroom teacher watch for? p. 384

4. How have computers and other technological advances helped persons who are deaf or hard of hearing? p. 388

5. How are the teletypewriter and printer, telecommunication devices for the deaf (TDD), and captioned films used? p. 388

6. What are the primary objectives of early intervention programs? p. 391

7. Explain how speech reading is taught and why it is an important skill. p. 396

8. What is the bilingual approach to teaching persons who are deaf or hard of hearing, and how does it work? p. 398

9. What three factors still hinder the academic achievement of students who are deaf or hard of hearing? p. 400

10. What are several things that parents can do at home to help encourage the academic achievement of their child who is deaf or hearing impaired? p. 403

References of Special Interest

American Speech-Hearing-Language Association. (1991). **ASHA**, *Supplement H, 33(3)*.
This guide to position statements on children with hearing impairments or speech and language disorders is a must for all speech-language and hearing pathologists as a professional guide to practice.

Batshaw, M. L., & Perret, Y. M. (1992). *Children with handicaps: A medical primer*. Baltimore: Paul H. Brookes Publishing Co.
A comprehensive guide to all disabilities, with a focus on medical causes and treatments, this book includes both genetic and environmentally induced dysfunctions. It is amply illustrated with photographs and diagrams of aids for children with disabilities.

Dolnic, E. (1993). *Deafness as culture. The Atlantic Monthly, 272*, 37–53.
In an accessible article, the writer explains the meaning and importance of the deaf culture in American society.

English, K. (1995). *Educational audiology across the lifespan*. Baltimore: Paul H. Brookes Publishing Co.
The author describes the role of audiologists in the education of persons with hearing disabilities. The text includes suggestions for practice as well as ways in which an audiologist can contribute to collaborative teams.

Moores, D. (1996). *Educating the deaf: Psychology, principles, and practices* (4th ed.). Boston: Houghton Mifflin.

This comprehensive textbook on children with severe hearing losses provides a rich historical background and up-to-date reports on current research, educational trends, and preschool and postsecondary programs.

Moores, D., & Meadows-Orlan, K. P. (Eds.). (1990). *Educational and developmental aspects of deafness*. Washington, DC: Gallaudet University Press.

The articles in this collection cover a wide variety of topics on deafness.

Paul, P., & Quigley, S. (1990). *Education and deafness*. White Plains, NY: Longman.

This is a comprehensive, readable report on the various issues and controversies surrounding the education of children with mild-to-severe hearing losses. The authors offer an especially good review of essential research over the past decade and present the findings on the effectiveness of different communication systems in an evenhanded way.

Children with Visual Impairments

focusing questions

What effects do limited visual experiences have on the development of children with visual impairments?

Why is learned helplessness a problem for many children who are visually impaired?

How do we adapt the instructional program for youngsters with visual impairments?

What effects has technology had on the communication skills and mobility of children and youth with visual impairments?

How does the philosophy of inclusion affect the education of these special students?

About one child in ten enters school with some visual impairment. Fortunately, most of these problems can be fully corrected with glasses and have little or no effect on social or educational development. But for one child in a thousand, visual impairments are so severe they cannot be corrected. In this chapter, we discuss the special needs of children who are visually impaired and the educatonal adaptation that are, or should be, made for them.

Definitions

Visual impairments fall along a continuum ranging from normal vision to profound visual disability (blindness). The smallest number of children are found at the blindness end of the continuum. According to Barraga (1983), "a visually handicapped child is one whose visual impairment interferes with his optimal learning and achievement, unless adaptations are made in the methods of presenting learning experiences, the nature of the materials used, and/or in the learning environment" (p. 25).

Visual impairments can be classified in several ways. Legally, a definition distinguishes blind and partially sighted or low-vision children on the basis of tests of visual acuity. A child who is legally blind can see at only 20/200 or less, with correction. This means that the child can see only at 20 feet what someone with normal sight can see at 200 feet. Legal blindness does not necessarily mean that a child has no visual stimulation at all; the child may be able to sense light and darkness and may have some visual imagery. A child who scores between 20/70 and 20/200 on tests of visual acuity, with correction, is legally partially sighted. The term *low vision* refers to children and adults whose vision is 20/200 or less and who read print or braille when assisted by a variety of devices.

More and more, levels of visual impairment are being defined in educational terms, which are very different from legal terms that focus on distance of effective sight. Educational classifications are *moderate*, *severe*, and *profound* and are based not on tests of visual acuity but on the special educational adaptations that are necessary to help these children learn (Table 10.1).

A **moderate visual disability** can be almost entirely corrected with the help of visual aids, either in the regular classroom or in a resource room. A **severe visual disability** is helped only somewhat with visual aids; still, the child can use vision as a channel for learning. This classification is equivalent to the definition of a child with partial sight. A child with a **profound visual disability** cannot use vision as an educational tool. For this child, touch and hearing are the predominant learning channels.

Visual Interpretation and the Human Eye

Vision or visual interpretation is a function of the brain, experience, and the adequacy of the sense organ that receives stimuli from the outside world: the eye. Faulty visual interpretation can result from a defect in the brain, inadequate

TABLE 10.1 Educational Characteristics of Children with Visual Disabilities	
Level of Visual Disability	**Performance Capability**
Moderate	With use of special aids and lighting, can perform visual tasks almost like students with normal vision
Severe	In performance of visual tasks, may need more time and energy and be less accurate even with visual aids and modifications
Profound	Performance of even gross visual tasks may be very difficult, and detailed tasks cannot be handled visually at all

Source: Adapted from N. Barraga (1986). Sensory perceptual development. In G. Scholl (Ed.), *Foundations of Education for Blind and Visually Handicapped Children and Youth* (p. 86). New York: American Foundation for the Blind. Adapted from A. Colenbrander (1977). Dimensions of visual performance, *Transactions of the American Academy of Ophthalmology and Otolaryngology, 83*, pp. 332–335.

experience, or a defective eye. The process of visual interpretation is as follows: Light enters the eye, focuses on the retina, and is transmitted along the optic nerve to the brain, where visual information is interpreted. Two people with well-functioning sense organs can interpret a visual experience differently, depending on their training and experience.

Educators of children with visual impairments are concerned primarily with adapting instruction to the impairment. To accomplish this, they need to understand how healthy eyes operate and what some of the conditions are that can cause problems.

Vision is a function of the sensation and perception of light.

THE HUMAN EYE

The human eye is a complex system of interrelated parts (see Figure 10.1). Any part can be defective or become nonfunctional as a result of hereditary anomaly, disease, accident, or other causes.

The eye has been called a camera for the brain. Like a camera, the eye has a diaphragm, the **iris**. The iris is the colored muscular partition that expands and contracts to regulate the amount of light admitted through the central opening, or **pupil**. Behind the iris is the **lens**, an elastic biconvex body that focuses onto the retina the light reflected from objects in the line of vision. The **retina** is the light-sensitive innermost layer of tissue at the back of the eyeball. It contains neural receptors that translate the physical energy of light into the neural energy that results in the experience of seeing.

As Figure 10.1 shows, other protective and structural elements in the eye can affect vision. The **cornea** is the transparent anterior (front) portion of the tough

Figure 10.1
The Human Eye

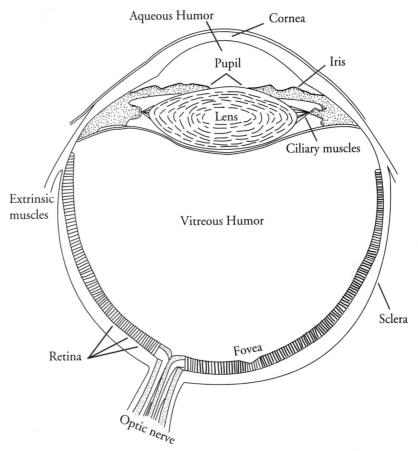

Aqueous Humor   Cornea

Pupil   Iris

Lens

Ciliary muscles

Extrinsic
muscles

Vitreous Humor

Sclera

Retina   Fovea

Optic nerve

Source: Figure from P. Lindsay & D. Norman (1972). *Human Information Processing.* Copyright © 1972 by Harcourt Brace Jovanovich, Inc., reprinted by permission of the publisher.

outer coat of the eyeball. The **ciliary muscles** change the shape of the lens so that the eye can focus on objects at varying distances. In the normal mature eye, no muscular effort is necessary to see clearly objects 20 feet or more away. When the eye looks at an object closer than 20 feet, the ciliary muscles increase the convex curvature of the lens so that the closer object is still focused on the retina. This change in the shape of the lens is called **accommodation**.

Extrinsic muscles control the movement of the eyeball in the socket. The change made by these muscles is known as **convergence**.

CAUSES OF VISUAL IMPAIRMENTS

A wide variety of conditions can cause serious visual impairments in children from birth to age 5. Figure 10.2 lists some of the most serious. It does not list common disorders—for example, **hyperopia** (farsightedness) or **myopia** (nearsightedness)—that are almost always correctable with glasses.

Figure 10.2

Causes of Legal Blindness from Birth to Age 5

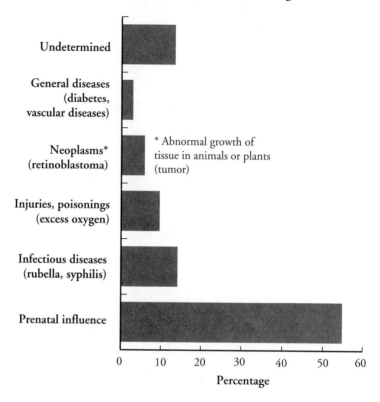

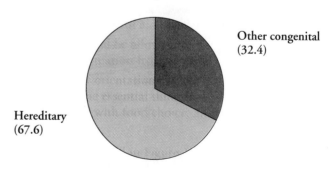

Breakdown of prenatal influences

Source: Adapted from M. Ward (1986). The visual system. In G. Scholl (Ed.), *Foundations of Education for Blind and Visually Handicapped Children and Youth.* New York: American Foundation for the Blind. Reprinted by permission of the American Foundation for the Blind, 11 Penn Plaza, Suite 300, New York, NY 10001. Copyright © 1986.

Heredity is by far the largest causal factor, responsible for more than 37 percent of profound visual disabilities in young children. Infectious diseases contracted by the mother during pregnancy account for about 15 percent of cases. Rubella (German measles) is an infectious disease that can cause serious birth defects, mental retardation, hearing loss, and other disabilities in addition to blindness. Improved control measures and education have reduced the percentage of children blinded by infectious disease and accidents.

Most of the approximately 10 percent of cases that stem from injuries and poisonings are due to a condition called **retinopathy of prematurity** (formerly called *retrolental fibroplasia*). This disorder was originally believed to be caused by the overadministering of oxygen to premature infants in an attempt to save the life of children threatened by other conditions. We now are not so sure. This condition turns out to be more complicated than originally believed (Silverman & Flynn, 1985; Hatton, 1991).

Another cause of visual impairment is **retinoblastoma**, a tumor of the eye that causes blindness. The condition is often found in the first years of life and is progressive, so radiation or chemotherapy is required to treat it. There is sometimes the need to remove the eye completely. Many children with retinoblastoma have sight for a year or more before the loss of vision. One odd characteristic of children with this condition is that they appear to show either very high or moderately low IQ scores. The reason for this unusual pattern is not known.

Characteristics of Children with Visual Impairments

One of the most serious obstacles to understanding children with visual impairment is the limited amount of scholarly work being done on the topic. Warren (1994) has done an admirable job of pulling together what is available, but on many significant topics information is scanty and dated. Warren is particularly concerned that parents do not misunderstand the general findings: Children with visual impairments tend to develop at a slower pace than children without disabilities; there is a wide variation in the development of children with visual impairments; and with a rich physical environment and with encouragement to take reasonable risks, parents can increase the adaptive skills of their children.

INTELLECTUAL DEVELOPMENT

In the 1940s and 1950s, educators generally believed that the intelligence of children with visual impairments was not seriously affected by their condition, except for their ability to use certain visual concepts (colors and three-dimensional space, for example). The thinking then was that intelligence unfolds on a genetically determined schedule and is affected by only the most severe environmental trauma. Samuel Hayes (1941) had modified the Stanford-Binet for children with visual impairments. His examination of more than two thousand youngsters revealed overall average intelligence quotient (IQ) scores.

Today, we hold a different view of intelligence. We recognize that what we measure as intelligence in school-age children has been notably affected by their cumulative experiences in the early years of development. Lack of vision, then, is both a primary impairment and a condition that can hamper cognitive development because it limits the integrating experiences and the understanding of those experiences that the visual sense brings naturally to sighted children (Kephart, Kephart, & Schwartz, 1974; Tillman & Osborne, 1969). These limitations are especially notable if the children do not receive early intervention in the preschool years.

One of the newest attempts to measure the intelligence of children with visual impairment—the Intelligence Test for Visually Impaired Children (ITVIC)—is based on Warren's (1994) primary factors. The designers of this test identified four measurable areas: orientation, reasoning, spatial perception, and verbal ability; verbal ability and reasoning are closely tied to school achievement (Dekker, Drenth, & Zool, 1991). The ITVIC is one of the few tests specifically designed for such children (as opposed to being adapted from tests designed for sighted children, such as the Hayes-Binet).

Visual impairment can hamper cognitive development.

A new test of intelligence (the ITVIC) has much promise for children with visual impairment.

LANGUAGE DEVELOPMENT

Sighted children acquire language by listening, reading, and watching movements and facial expressions. They express themselves first through babbling and later by imitating their parents and siblings. Children with visual impairments acquire language in much the same way, but their language concepts are not helped by reading or visual input. A sighted child develops the concept of a ball by seeing different balls; a child with blindness develops the same concept through tactile manipulation of different balls. Both are able to understand the word *ball,* and both are able to identify a ball.

A series of investigations into the language development of children with visual impairments yielded the following conclusions. Visual impairment does not interfere with everyday language usage or communication abilities. The language of children with visual impairments seems like that of their sighted peers (Civelli, 1983; Matsuda, 1984). However, the children with visual impairments had less understanding of words as vehicles, or as standing for, concrete experiences, and they were slower than sighted children to form hypotheses about word meaning. Children with severe visual impairment appeared to be restricted to word meanings from their own personal experience, whereas vision allowed children to broaden and generalize the meanings of words (Dunlea, 1989; Anderson, Dunlea, & Kekalis, 1984).

Warren (1994), in a review of the literature on the language of those with visual impairments, arrived at these conclusions:

Visual impairment limits children's conceptual understanding and generalizations in language and vocabulary.

> It is clear from the literature that the vocabulary of children with visual impairments is heavily grounded in their own perceptual experience and is not simply a parroting of sighted vocabulary. . . . This underscores the importance of the parents' role in ensuring not only that the child's perceptual experience is adequately rich, but also that it is embedded in a context of shared communication. (p. 326)

SENSORY COMPENSATION AND PERCEPTION

Vision is a continuous source of information. We depend on vision to orient our-selves, to identify people and objects, and to regulate our motor and social behav-ior. People without sight have to rely on other senses for information and for all the other tasks that vision performs. How this is accomplished has been the focus of much speculation and research.

The doctrine of **sensory compensation** holds that if one sense such as vision is deficient, other senses are automatically strengthened, in part because of their greater use. Although this may be true in certain cases, research does not show that the hearing or touch sensitivity of children with profound visual handicaps is superior to that of sighted children. For example, Gottesman (1971) tested chil-dren of ages 2 to 8 who were blind and who were sighted on their ability to identi-fy by touch such things as a key, a comb, a pair of scissors, and geometric forms (triangle, cross). He found no difference between the groups.

PERSONAL AND SOCIAL ADJUSTMENT

No personal or social problems *inevitably* follow from being visually impaired. However, the restricted mobility and consequent limited experiences of children who are visually impaired appear to cause, in some children, a state of passivity and dependency.

Tuttle (1984), in analyzing the self-esteem of children and adults who are blind, attributed their lack of self-confidence to their limited interaction with sighted people and to the attitude of sighted people toward blindness. He maintained that the impact of blindness on self-esteem should be temporary and can be alleviated by more sensitive interactions that visually impaired children receive from other people. Children who are congenitally blind do not recognize that they are differ-ent until people begin to treat them differently or to point out that they cannot do things because they cannot see. Those who lose their sight after having seen tend to go through several stages: mourning, withdrawal, denial, reassessment, and reaffirmation. Finally, with training and interaction with sighted people come self-acceptance and self-esteem.

Think about the special problems of Renaldo as he tries to learn how baseball is played. The child with vision who is learning watches the other players. She sees the pitcher throw the ball to the batter and sees the batter hit the ball and then run the bases. Gradually the patterns and rules become clear to her. All of this is lost on Renaldo, who has only his hearing and touch to help him understand.

Many youngsters with visual impairment give up trying to learn a game when there are so few cues for them to learn by. The easiest thing for them to do is to re-treat into a social silence and not even try. The tendency to retreat has to be com-bated if the child is to develop the social skills he or she needs to make a good adult adjustment.

The role of the teacher in the development of personal and social adjustment is critically important. Martin and Hoben (1977) offered the thoughts of some stu-dents with visual impairments about how they had been treated in school:

Self-esteem and self-acceptance in children with visual impairments are nurtured by positive interaction with sighted people. (© Ellen Senisi/The Image Works)

■ Teachers should learn what "legally blind" really means. Lots of legally blind kids can do all sorts of things.

■ If a teacher treats me different, the other kids think I'm a teacher's pet.

■ I don't want to see an "A" on my report card when I know I earned a "C."

■ It's more fun, more challenge when you have to compete. You don't feel like you're an outsider.

■ I appreciate the opportunity to get a better position in the classroom, but when the teacher asks me about it in front of the class it makes me feel like an idiot. I would tell teachers: if you want to tell me something that will help, don't make me feel like an idiot doing it. (p. 19)

Loosely translated, those students were saying, "Don't treat me like I'm helpless. Don't do me any special favors. Let me do it on my own." Many people who have not had experience with persons with disabilities react to them by lowering their expectations. But those students didn't want this kind of favor.

Many sighted people who have not worked with children who are visually impaired tend to have low expectations of those children's abilities.

After surveying the literature on the self-concepts of children who are blind, Warren (1994) stated that the studies found no overall differences. He noted, however, that "to the extent that people expect of the child that he will not differ from a sighted child, the tendency for the blind child's self-concept to be different from that of the sighted child will be decreased" (p. 232). There would seem to be nothing about visual impairment that increases the likelihood of behavior problems in this group. The sense of self for such youngsters seems similar to that of youngsters from the average community (Warren, 1994, p. 280).

Developmental Profiles

People with normal sight wonder from time to time what it would be like to be blind. It's obvious that adapting to sensory loss has implications that are profoundly personal and social as well as educational. A comprehensive special education program must involve all areas of development and adjustment. We introduce developmental profiles here of two visually impaired youngsters to highlight some of the problems children with visual handicaps have in adapting to their disability. Figure 10.3 shows the patterns of development of Renaldo and Susan. Renaldo has a severe visual disability; Susan, a profound visual disability. Both are being educated in public schools where special provisions, personnel, and equipment are available.

Renaldo is a tall, slim 11-year-old who has a serious visual impairment for which maximum correction has been obtained with the aid of thick glasses. He can read print material and, in the early grades, was able to make a reasonable academic adjustment. As the profile in Figure 10.3 shows, Renaldo scored slightly above average in intelligence as measured by an adaptation of the Stanford-Binet and is currently doing average work as measured by achievement tests administered with no time limits. Yet this profile, though favorable, tends to mask the academic problems Renaldo is likely to encounter. He will be required to use higher thought processes as he progresses through the educational system, and he is already beginning to experience the shift from concrete arithmetic to the more difficult (for him) abstractions of algebra and spatial concepts of geometry.

Renaldo spends most of his time in school with a regular sixth-grade class but leaves the program for about an hour a day to work with a specially trained resource teacher. Only three or four other youngsters are in the resource room with Renaldo, so the teacher can give him a good deal of tutoring in the academic areas in which he needs help.

Of more concern is how Renaldo feels about himself. His visual handicap is serious enough so that he is sometimes unsure whether he belongs to the sighted community or to the blind community. He feels deeply about his awkwardness and inability to perform in athletics—a very important dimension in the life of an 11-year-old—but he does not discuss this with his schoolmates.

Renaldo also has some interpersonal problems. He reacts with a sharp tongue and a quick temper to any slights or negative comments, real or imagined, about his impairment. Consequently, many of the other youngsters ignore or avoid him except when class participation requires interaction. Above all, Renaldo is beginning to wonder about his future: What is he going to do with his life when he grows up? How can he be independent? How will he establish friendships with girls? This is a topic of great importance to his older brother, Brian, who is in high

Figure 10.3
Profiles of Two Children with Different Degrees of Visual Impairment

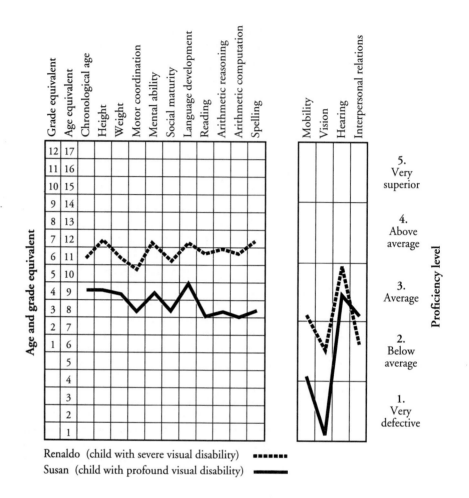

Renaldo (child with severe visual disability)   ▪▪▪▪▪▪▪▪

Susan (child with profound visual disability)   ▬▬▬▬▬

school and whose life seems to revolve around girls. Brian's behavior is a source of amusement to Renaldo now, but in a few years he will have to face social relationship problems more seriously.

Susan's profile is also shown in Figure 10.3. She is an average-looking 9-year-old who has been blind since birth. Like many children who are blind, she has limited light perception that helps her move around, but she cannot read print. She has mastered the Grade 2 braille system, which uses contractions, letter combinations, and shortened forms of words to save time and space in reading. In some respects, Susan is making a better adjustment than Renaldo, despite her more severe handicap. She has a warm, understanding mother who has given her strong emotional support and a professional father who provides a comfortable income for the family. Her mother has tried to be a companion for Susan and has read to her extensively from the time Susan was 3 or 4 years of age. She has helped Susan through some difficult times, particularly when Susan was having trouble mastering braille. Susan's father is more distant; he doesn't seem to know how to approach her.

In addition to her visual handicap, Susan shows some signs of mild neurological damage, which tends to make her physically awkward, but this condition is not serious enough to classify her as multiply disabled. As the developmental profile shows, Susan's performance on tests of mental ability and her development in speech and language are average, testimony perhaps to the intensive work with her mother in early years. But in arithmetic and spelling, her performance is somewhat below average.

Susan lives in an urban area with a large population where a number of children are visually impaired. The school system buses these children from around the district to a school that provides a special program for them. Susan is well accepted by her classmates and has one or two close sighted friends. She has not yet had to face problems in relationship with boys or to deal with the often cruel behavior of young adolescents.

Susan has been affected in an important way by the educational trend of placing exceptional children in the least restrictive environment. She does not have to attend a large state school for persons with blindness far from her home and family, as did many children a generation or so ago. Sometime in the next three or four years, her mother and father will have to decide whether they want her to attend a residential school that provides advanced curriculum and educational facilities for youngsters with visual impairments. But for now, they are happy that she is at home and able to get special help within the local school system.

■■■ *Early Intervention*

A child's experiences during the period from birth to age 5 are critical to subsequent development. It is especially important that the systematic education of visually impaired children begin as early as possible. Sighted children absorb a tremendous amount of information and experience from their environment in the ordinary course of events. Parents and teachers must specially design parallel experiences for children who are visually impaired (see Chapter 3 for more information).

The characteristics we observe in a 10-year-old who is visually handicapped are often a blend of the primary problem (loss of vision) and a number of secondary problems that have developed because the child has missed certain sequential experiences. For example, many youngsters with a visual disability are passive. Passivity is not a natural or inevitable byproduct of low vision; it is present because the child does not have a well-established motivation to move.

For the sighted child, the environment is filled with visual stimulation: toys, bottles, people, color, and shapes. The child has a natural impulse to move toward these elements. The child with a severe visual disability isn't aware of these elements unless someone points them out. For a child who is blind, the bottle appears magically. The child is not motivated to go after it; in fact, the child does not even realize that he or she can do something—be active—to get the bottle.

An easily understood concept for the sighted child is **object permanence**. By the age of 6 or 7 months, sighted children realize that even when objects disappear

When adapting instruction to the educational needs of children who are visually impaired, teachers should emphasize concreteness, unifying experiences, and learning by doing. (© *Steve Goldberg/Monkmeyer Press Photo Service*)

from their visual field (mother left the room; the ball rolled under the couch), they still exist. This knowledge makes the world more orderly and predictable. And it makes sense to go after objects even if they are not in the line of sight. Object constancy is a more difficult concept for children with visual disabilities to understand. They need deliberate instruction and an organized environment before they can understand the concept and begin to act on it.

It is important to let children take control of a task once they demonstrate an ability to do so.

Although it's important to help visually impaired youngsters learn tasks, it's also important to let them take over when they are able. Ferrell (1986) described a technique called **fading**, or gradually cutting back help as a child becomes competent at a task. She showed how the process works with the task of eating:

1. Begin by placing your hand completely around the child's hand as the child grasps the spoon. Move the child through the scooping and eating motions.
2. As the child gains control, continue the scooping and eating motions with your hand on the child's wrist.
3. Gradually move your hand from the wrist to the arm, and then to the elbow.
4. Eventually, just touch the arm to remind the child what he or she is supposed to do.

By teaching young children with visual disabilities to do things for themselves, we give these children some of the important experiences that sighted children get naturally.

It is important for parents and teachers to give the child with visual disabilities the opportunity to indicate what he or she wants, and not to anticipate the child's needs. "By doing so, they eliminate the child's choice and control of the situation and they foster his dependence. Independence training begins in infancy, not at age 2, 6, or when college is imminent" (Ferrell, 1986, p. 130).

So much of what is important for young children to learn is learned naturally through the visual sense (Piaget & Inhelder, 1969). For youngsters with visual disabilities, that same learning must come through careful planning and instruction. Parents and teachers must therefore work together to see that these children have important experiences and the independence to learn from them.

Part H of the Individuals with Disabilities Education Act, which mandates services for infants and toddlers with disabilities (see Chapter 2), provides for earlier identification and earlier professional services for children with vision problems. Such early intervention programs should reduce the number of secondary problems shown by children who did not have the advantages of earlier services. The work cited in Chapter 3 on early intervention provides additional evidence on the usefulness of early attention.

Educators have also become increasingly sensitive to the importance of the early emotional life of children who are blind. Barraga (1983) provided a representative point of view: "With the visually impaired infant, body play must replace eye play to communicate maternal concerns and love—the facilitators of developing a self-concept. More than the usual amount of time should be spent cuddling, holding, touching, stroking and moving the baby" (p. 31).

Identification

Most children with severe and profound visual disabilities are identified by parents and physicians long before they enter school. The most common exceptions are children with multiple handicaps. It is possible for another handicapping condition—for example, cerebral palsy or mental retardation—to mask a visual impairment. The key to identification is a comprehensive examination. Table 10.2 lists the components of this kind of assessment. Many of these components do not require formal testing, just the observations of those around the child. For example, the family can be very helpful in determining whether a child has mastered functional living skills. And a classroom teacher is a good source of information about a child's social and emotional development.

Most states require preschool vision screening, which identifies children with moderate vision problems. Throughout this textbook we discuss the importance of early experiences in cognitive development. Obviously, early identification allows us to broaden those experiences for the child with a visual disability through maximum correction and preschool programs.

Mild, correctable visual impairments often go undiagnosed until a child enters elementary school. School systems use different methods to detect visual impairments in children. Some refer children with suspected problems directly to an ophthalmologist or an optometrist. Others routinely screen youngsters to determine

TABLE 10.2 | **Components in a Comprehensive Assessment**

Vision

Eye examination by an ophthalmologist or optometrist
Functional vision assessment
Assessment of visual efficiency
Low-vision aids evaluation

Intelligence and aptitude

Cognitive development
Intellectual functioning

Sensory and motor skills

Gross and fine motor development
Perceptual learning

Academic skills and concept development

Achievement in reading, writing, spelling, and arithmetic
Language development
Listening skills
Temporal, quantitative, positional, directional, and sequential concepts
Study skills

Social, emotional, and affective skills

Behavioral control
Social and affective learning
Adaptive living skills
Recreation and leisure skills

Functional living skills

Daily living skills
Orientation and mobility skills
Community travel and use
Career and prevocational skills

Source: Adapted from A. Hall, G. Scholl, & R. Swallow (1986). Psychoeducational assessment. In G. Scholl (Ed.), *Foundations of Education for Blind and Visually Handicapped Children and Youth* (p. 192). New York: American Foundation for the Blind. Reprinted by permission of American Foundation for the Blind, 11 Penn Plaza, Suite 300, New York, NY 10001. Copyright © 1986.

whether they have vision difficulties, and they refer those who do not pass that screening for more comprehensive assessment.

The standard school screening instrument is the Snellen chart, which has rows of letters in gradually smaller sizes that children read at a distance of 20 feet. A variation that is useful for screening young children and people who do not know letter names consists of capital *E*s pointing in different directions. The individual is asked to indicate the direction in which the arms of the *E* are pointing. Scores are based on how accurately the subject identifies the letters (or directions of the *E*s) using one eye at a time. A reading of 20/20 is normal.

The National Society for the Prevention of Blindness is the oldest voluntary health agency involved in preventing blindness. For preschoolers and school-age children, it has developed a number of screening tests that use the Snellen chart or modifications of it. For infants, evaluation is based on observation of how the eyes are used. For 3- to 5-year-olds, both observation and the Snellen *E* chart are used. The consensus is that early diagnosis and treatment can prevent visual impairments in some children.

More extensive tests use elaborate equipment (such as the Keystone Telebinocular and the Bausch & Lomb Orthorater) to measure vision at far and near points and to test muscle balance, fusion, usable vision, and other characteristics. The Titmus Vision Tester (manufactured by Titmus, P.O. Box 191, Petersburg, VA 23804) is the most widely used test of visual acuity and is used to screen vision in preschool children, school-age children, and adults. Most people who have taken a driver's license test have been screened for vision problems by the Titmus.

Once a vision problem is discovered, the extent of the problem can be identified by using the Program to Develop Efficiency in Visual Functioning (Barraga, 1983). This scale assesses the level of visual functioning by presenting a series of increasingly smaller words, sentences, and pictures. The purpose of the test is to determine the extent to which a child is able to use his or her vision even though that vision is impaired.

Just as the pediatrician is the first line for identifying children with disabilities in preschool years, so the teacher is the prime source of identification of mild disabilities in school-age youngsters. Efforts have been made to sensitize classroom teachers to identify exceptional children.

Formal efforts in the United States to educate children with visual handicaps began in Boston in 1829 with the establishment of the residential school now called the Perkins School for the Blind. Not until 1900 was the first public school class for children who were blind organized—in Chicago. Some thirteen years later, another class for children with severe visual impairments was established.

The enormous increase of children with visual disabilities in public school programs in recent years reflects an increase in the actual number of students receiving services—from 18,000 in 1975 to more than 32,000 in 1988. This increase appears due in part to the provisions of the Education for All Handicapped

Educational
Adaptations

Children Act, which mandates the education of all children with disabilities and sent school systems in search of children needing service. Meanwhile, the population of visually impaired children in residential schools is placed at 8.8 percent of children with visual impairment.

Adaptations in both materials and equipment are needed to fully utilize the visually handicapped person's senses of hearing, touch, smell, residual vision, and even taste. Lowenfeld (1973) proposed three general principles that are important for adapting instruction to the educational needs of children who are visually impaired:

1. *Concreteness.* Children with severe and profound visual disabilities learn primarily through hearing and touch. To understand the surrounding world, these children must work with concrete objects that they can feel and manipulate. Through tactile observation of real objects in natural settings (or models of dangerous objects), students with visual handicaps come to understand shape, size, weight, hardness, texture, pliability, and temperature.

2. *Unifying experiences.* Visual experience tends to unify knowledge. A child who goes into a grocery store sees not only shelves and objects but also the relationships of shelves and objects in space. Children with visual impairments cannot understand these relationships unless teachers allow them the experience of a grocery store, post office, or farm. The teacher must bring the "whole" into perspective, not only by giving students concrete experiences but also by explaining relationships.

   Left on their own, children with severe and profound visual disabilities live a relatively restricted life. To expand their horizons, to enable them to develop imagery, and to orient them to a wider environment, it is necessary to develop experiences by systematic stimulation. We can lead children through space to help them understand large areas. We can expose them to different sizes, shapes, textures, and relationships to help them generalize the common qualities of different objects and understand the differences. Their verbalization of similarities and differences stimulates mental development.

3. *Learning by doing.* To learn about the environment, these children have to be motivated to explore that environment. A blind infant does not reach out for an object unless that object attracts the child through other senses (touch, smell, hearing). We have to stimulate the child to reach and to make contact by introducing motivating toys or games (rattles, objects with interesting textures).

Children with visual disabilities have the ability to listen, relate, and remember, and these skills must be developed to the fullest. These children have to learn to use time efficiently because the process of acquiring information or performing a task can be cumbersome and time-consuming. For the teacher, this means organizing material, giving specific directions, providing firsthand experiences, and using sound principles of learning.

Children with visual impairments need teachers to give them concrete experiences and to explain the relationships among those experiences.

Figure 10.4

Percentage of Students with Visual Impairments in Educational Environments, 1992–1993

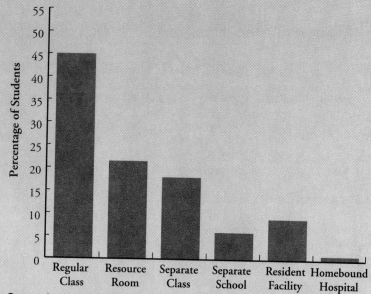

Source: Seventeenth Annual Report to Congress on the Implementation of the Individuals with Disability Education Act (1995). Washington, DC: U.S. Department of Education.

LEARNING ENVIRONMENT

The goal of moving students with visual impairments into the regular classroom or as close as possible (least restrictive environment) is proceeding, as Figure 10.4 indicates. Almost half of the students with visual impairments are found in the regular classroom, and another 21 percent are in a resource room program, which means they spend the majority of their time in the regular classroom. Only 9 percent of these children can now be found in a residential school—probably children who have a variety of disabilities requiring very specialized care.

As is true of children with other kinds of exceptionality, the various learning environments provided for children with visual impairments represent a continuum of care. The goal of full inclusion or integration is modified by the particular needs of the individual child and, sometimes, by the availability of services.

Inclusion

The philosophy of inclusion has always had a major impact on young children with visual impairments. The question of how thoroughly such children should be integrated into normal preschool settings has been raised. There are serious arguments within the profession about the merits of integration compared with the merits of specially trained personnel and special equipment that can be found in a residential or day school for the visually impaired. Lowenfeld (1982), one of the

For some children who are visually impaired, the least restrictive environment is a mainstreamed regular classroom; other children need some form of special resource room program. (© *Steve Goldberg/Monkmeyer Press Photo Service*)

Placement in a normal preschool requires careful planning and support personnel.

respected voices in the field, stated, "I believe uncompromisingly that integration of the blind into society is on all age levels in their and in society's best interest" (p. 69). But that view is not shared equally by others.

Erwin (1991) laid out a series of guidelines for the effective integration of young children with visual impairment. Not surprisingly, merely placing the child within a normal preschool setting, without careful planning and without support personnel, will not produce good results. An important aspect of the integrative approach that Erwin describes is a partnership and teamwork between the classroom teacher and the visual consultant teacher; otherwise, the visually impaired child may be socially isolated in integrated settings, particularly when the only focus in such a setting is academic (Kekelis & Sachs, 1988).

The curriculum framework for the preschool that focuses on cognitive development, language development, self-help, refining gross motor skills, and so on seems to fit the child with visual impairments as well as it fits other children. The preschool setting needs to be accepting of the philosophy of family involvement in the program as part of the total effort for all children in that setting. Finally, Erwin (1991) calls for research on the dynamics of blind children and their integration into various social groups beyond the immediate family, whether these groups include primarily blind children, primarily sighted children, or both.

Special Schools

Before the emphasis since the early 1980s on the least restrictive environment and the inclusive classroom, the education of children with visual impairments was often conducted in large residential state schools. With the rapidly growing trend for such students to be educated in the local schools, the question of what happens to the residential school and its often elaborate facilities arose.

Erin (1993) pointed out that the children attending residential schools may have additional disabilities and the schools have been redesigned to provide an effective environment for such children. Also, these schools provided outreach services, offering information, assessment, and technical assistance to students who are visually impaired and to their teachers in the public schools. Erin proposed a future in which such schools could play three distinct roles:

■ *Resource centers for students with visual impairments.* These facilities would function as state or regional sites to distribute materials and provide technical assistance and outreach services to neighborhood schools. They would also participate in professional preparation activities.

■ *Life skills centers for students with severe disabilities.* These centers would specialize in assisting students with severe and multiple disabilities, with an emphasis on those with visual impairments.

■ *Magnet schools for students with visual impairments.* These schools would provide direct instruction for the academic learner with a visual impairment. Short-term placements that would be arranged by contract with individual school districts and would address functional needs would be common.

In short, residential schools would address diverse needs as they play a role in the future education of children with visual impairments.

One argument for the continuation of special schools for children with visual impairment comes from parents. A survey of 985 parents of students in schools for the visually impaired reported widespread satisfaction with how the school was operating (AER, 1995). The parents stated clearly that they felt that a range of options should be available to educate children with visual impairment and that the needs of one child are very different from the needs of another child even though both have visual impairments. Over 70 percent of the parents responding to the survey reported that their local school system did not have specialized personnel or equipment.

Parents also mentioned the loss of the opportunity for social integration with children without disabilities. Some, however, downplayed the importance of such social integration. A few quotations will give the gist of their argument:

1. "At the school for the blind there is an opportunity to be 'typical' with peers, of not always being different—the chance to be average instead of being behind peers or 'remarkable.'"

2. "Being able to be with peers 'like yourself' and not having to feel 'you're the only one different' is important."

3. "My daughter is able to interact with peers like herself—not singled out as unusual or disabled. This is a more natural learning environment—she is not distracted or teased for her disability." (AER, 1995, p. 46)

The survey report strongly recommended that the continuum of services remain intact and be strengthened.

Orientation to possible careers is often part of the curriculum for children with visual impairments.

Another reason for placing a child with visual impairments in a special school is to receive a curriculum that cannot be provided in the regular classroom. The Texas School for the Blind and Visually Impaired, for example, is implementing a career education model that begins in the elementary school and continues through secondary school and beyond. At the elementary school level, the emphasis is on career awareness. Students may interview persons about their jobs and what they do to function in them (Lock, 1995). At the middle school level, the emphasis is on career investigation. Students take a course in Introduction to Work and assess their own abilities, aptitudes, and interests. At the secondary school level, students focus on career preparation and career specialization, and the academic subjects are tailored to those objectives.

Obviously, that curriculum would not be appropriate for nondisabled students in the public school, but it is beneficial for students with visual disabilities. For children with visual disabilities who attend public schools during the school year, the Texas School for the Blind and Visually Impaired also provides summer programs with an emphasis on career education.

Itinerant Teacher

The move toward mainstreaming has made the role of the itinerant teacher very important for children with visual disabilities. This teacher travels from school to school providing special materials, consultation with school personnel, and individualized instruction. Figure 10.5 shows a memo from an itinerant teacher to the regular classroom teachers of four children with visual disabilities. The memo highlights one of the important tasks of the itinerant teacher—to be sure that instructional materials for children with visual handicaps are in a form that they can effectively handle and to which they can respond.

The Need for Teamwork

An unsolved problem is how to provide within the framework of the ordinary school the specialized training that children with visual impairments need. It is clear from Figure 10.4 on p. 429 that the vast majority of children with visual disabilities are being educated in regular classrooms.

Bishop (1986) questioned groups of regular and special teachers, principals, parents, and students about the factors necessary for successful mainstreaming. The most important school factors were

■ An accepting and flexible regular classroom teacher

■ Peer acceptance and interaction

Figure 10.5
Memo from an Itinerant
Teacher to Regular Class
Teachers

September 30,1996

To teachers of the following visually impaired students:

George Harmon   Ann Sawyer   Susan Gifford   Kevin Smith

I now have a schedule at Belmont:

Monday:	Period 3 -	Kevin
	Period 7 -	Ann
Wednesday:	Period 7 -	Ann
Thursday:	Period 3 -	Kevin
	Period 4 -	George
	Period 5 -	Susan
Friday:	Period 7 -	Ann

I plan to be available for conferences regarding these students' participation in your class during lunch on Mondays or after school. Please contact me if your student experiences visual or academic difficulties in your class.

I have brought large-print copies of the New World Dictionary and Roget's Thesaurus to the library here. Please leave a note for me if your student will need to use an encyclopedia for research. I have a large-print copy that I could also put in the library.

Each of these students will benefit if you will provide materials, particularly worksheets, that have good contrast. For George, Susan, and Kevin, please make size-for-size copies of your ditto masters if the original print is no smaller than this. If your print is smaller than a pica, please enlarge the worksheets slightly.

Ann's worksheets need to be enlarged 154 percent. I have put 11' x 14" paper in the main tray of the office copier for this purpose. Additional paper is stored in the phone room next to the nurse's room. When you enlarge material on the 11" x 17" paper, please trim paper to a manageable size and staple them.

If you want me to enlarge or copy worksheets for you, put masters in my mailbox and include your name and the date you will use them in class. Check my Belmont schedule to make sure I'll be there in time to enlarge the work.

I've appreciated your cooperation in returning forms to me. I look forward to working with you this year.

Sincerely

Jean Olmstead

Jean Olmstead
Itinerant Teacher
Visually Impaired
320-4500

Source: J. Olmstead (1991). *Itinerant Teaching: Tricks of the Trade for Teachers of Blind and Visually Impaired Students.* New York: American Foundation for the Blind, 11 Penn Plaza, Suite 300, New York, NY 10001. Copyright © 1991 by American Foundation for the Blind.

■ Available support personnel
■ Adequate supplies and equipment (such as braille books)

We must say once again that the successful integration of the exceptional child does not happen by chance or accident. It requires a well-thought-out plan and capable people applying themselves to the task; otherwise, the possibility for social isolation of the child is great (Hoben & Lindstrom, 1980). An additional complicating factor is cultural differences between the child with visual difficulties and the school. A child who is blind and is from a Hispanic background has numerous challenges to overcome as well as, possibly, a language barrier and a set of family values differing from the values taught at school (Correa, 1987).

Whenever the child with visual impairments is placed, ideally one professional—often the classroom teacher or the teacher with special skills in instructing students with visual impairments—should take the role of **case manager** (or **service coordinator**). This individual brings together all the information that relates to the child (the comprehensive assessment, for example) and leads a team of professionals who, with the parents, develop an individualized education program (IEP) for the student. The creation of a working team made up of persons of different backgrounds and skills is of paramount importance if an IEP is to be written and executed.

The Need for Support Personnel

The greater the number of exceptional children placed in regular classrooms, the greater is the need for support personnel who have practical experience in the area of exceptionality to act as helpers and consultants. The following discussion is between Sarah, a classroom teacher, and Ellen, a specialist in visual impairment. Their conversation about Jackson, a child with a severe visual handicap, illustrates the variety of adaption problems that Jackson and his teachers must face to make mainstreaming work:

Sarah: Come on in and sit down. Since things have slowed down a little bit this week, I thought we could take time for a cup of coffee.
Ellen: Thanks. These first few weeks really have been hectic. But I know we're both glad to have finished Jackson's IEP at the conference with his parents last week. How have things been going in class? Is the arrangement we designed working out?
Sarah: It's great except for one thing. Jackson still can't see the chalkboard from where he's sitting and he doesn't really like having a friend copy the board work for him, so he keeps jumping up and down to read what's on the chalkboard.
Ellen: Well, at least I'm glad he doesn't feel self-conscious about not being able to see the board. However, there are a couple of things we can do to alleviate the problem. First, you can be sure to read aloud whatever you write on the chalkboard. That way, Jackson can write important things down from the oral input and go up to the board later to copy longer lists. Most teachers find that oral input helps the other kids, too. The other thing we can do is see if the janitor could put wheels on

Jackson's chair. He'd be able to get to the board without jumping up and down then. I'll check with Mr. Payne on my way out tonight.

Sarah: Those are both good ideas. Thanks, Ellen. But now let me tell you what's really got me concerned. It's the other kids. They were really excited about having Jackson in the class at first. Everybody wanted to take him around the school. I'll bet they showed him where the water fountain was at least fifty times! But lately the novelty seems to be wearing off. Today at recess Jackson just sat by the wall and listened to his portable radio while most of the others played softball.

Ellen: Lots of visually impaired youngsters do have a rough time being accepted. In fact, children with low vision, like Jackson, often find it harder to get along with sighted classmates than do children who are totally blind. I guess it's partly because the kids don't always know what Jackson can and can't see, what things he needs help with, and how they should act with him. But there are lots of other factors too, like how well Jackson does in his school work and how he handles group situations. It's hard to put your finger on a single cause.

Sarah: I know what you mean. The other day, Billy Turner—one of the real active tigers in my class—noticed that Jackson's handwriting was . . . well . . . kind of messy, and called the other kids over to look at it.

Ellen: Low vision students often write imperfectly because they see imperfectly. (*Looking at Jackson's paper*) Hmmm . . . it's certainly not beautiful handwriting, but this special boldline paper we ordered does seem to be helping. I'll plan to work with him on writing during the next few weeks. Another thing—Jackson is about ready to learn to type. Although he can't type class notes because of the noise, he can type assignments and that should help. (Orlansky, 1980, pp. 9–10)

Discussions like that are especially important for regular classroom teachers, most of whom have had limited experience in meeting the special needs of children who are visually impaired. Itinerant or resource room teachers can help classroom teachers understand the problems these children face.

For example, the classroom teacher of a boy with a severe visual disability was upset because he wanted to sit near the closed-circuit television monitor and because he tended to hold books close to his eyes. The teacher was afraid that he would damage his vision. The expert advice of a resource room teacher dispelled that misconception. Another classroom teacher believed that a very bright light should always be available for children with visual disabilities. In fact, dim light does not harm the eyes and may be more comfortable for students with cataracts, albinism, and certain other conditions.

Individualized Education Program

The IEP for children with visual disabilities should include a variety of goals—some focusing on the effective use of the learning environment, some on instructional content, and some on skills that the student will need to perform effectively in the mainstream. It will likely take a team of professionals to implement them. Some sample IEP goals for such children are as follows:

Goal: The student will receive adaptive materials and aids and instruction in their use.

Objective: The student will:

1. Use the following equipment at school or at home, when appropriate: large-print books, reading/writing stand, enlarged and darkened dittos, felt-tip pens, dome magnifier, and monocular and video magnifiers.

2. Locate information in a 12-volume thesaurus, a 24-volume dictionary, and a 30-volume encyclopedia (or a 7-volume math book).

3. Operate a video magnifier independently for reading and writing.

4. Demonstrate the ability to enlarge materials on a copier.

Goal: The student will take standardized tests under appropriate conditions.

Objective: The student will take standardized tests in large print (or braille or on tape) with extended time, and the teacher will mark the student's answer sheet.

(List tests, such as the Preliminary Scholastic Aptitude Test . . . and specify extended time as 1½ times for large print or 2 times for braille.)

Goal: The student will use adaptations to his or her environment.

Objective: The student will make appropriate changes in the environment to enhance his or her visual functioning (for example, use a magnifier or move to reduce the glare or to be able to see the chalkboard). (Olmstead, 1991, pp. 29–30)

SOCIAL ASPECTS OF INCLUSION

One of the most significant dimensions of the educational programs for children with visual difficulties should be the social needs of these children. Such needs are shortchanged in mainstream settings if the general education teacher knows little about the special needs of visually impaired children. We know that merely placing children with special needs in a classroom with other children does not guarantee good social interaction. And the same is certainly true for visually impaired children (Sacks, 1992). Some organized efforts to improve social skills are required, for visually impaired children are rejected by classmates more often than are other children (Jones & Chiba, 1985).

Training packages have been designed to help visually impaired children with posture, facial expressions, assertiveness, and speech (Kekelis, 1992). In one instance attempts were made to bolster the social skills of these children by means of teacher instruction and peer prompting. The training consisted of modeling, using prompts, discussing the need for social behaviors, and role-playing. The peer-mediated training turned out to produce more improvement than did the teacher instruction, and the social behavior that the children learned was maintained over time.

Sacks and Kekelis (1992) made some suggestions for regular education teachers and teachers of visually impaired students:

- Identify classmates whom the visually impaired student prefers.
- Encourage the visually impaired student to express positive feelings toward his or her classmates.
- Encourage the visually impaired student to choose a partner for play or academic tasks.
- Encourage the visually impaired student to help his or her sighted peers.
- Facilitate discussions about friendship with the visually impaired student to help him or her become more aware of the feelings of others.

Sacks and Kekelis (1992) pointed out that recess and lunchtime offer not merely breaks in the routine but opportunities for students to practice social skills and interactions.

The teacher may ask himself or herself a number of questions:

- Does the visually impaired student play with and talk to peers as much as his or her classmates?
- Do students talk with their visually impaired classmates in the classroom, play with them on the playground, and invite them to after-school and weekend activities?
- Does the visually impaired child show affection and display preferences for classmates?
- Do I observe interactions during recess and, when necessary, intervene so that the visually impaired child is not isolated on the playground? (Kekelis & Sells, 1988)

Negative answers to any of these questions call for constructive action by the special teacher working with the regular classroom teacher. One cannot count on a favorable social adaptation without some help and assistance from the teachers involved.

Although the field of educating children with visual disabilities was one of the first to mainstream, opinions differ about the usefulness of the integration approach as it is now being conducted. For example, educators disagree about whether the child with visual disabilities is harmed by being labeled as a student with special problems. Instead, the treatment program, for many professionals, includes the student's acceptance of his or her visual impairment as part of his or her identity (Harrell & Curry, 1987). Also, placing all services in a noncategorical program with children with other handicaps may result in children with visual disabilities not receiving the special services (such as braille and mobility) that they need to perform well in the educational setting. Hatlen and Curry (1988) asked, "Can 'generalists' in special education teach blind children to prepare lunch—let alone fulfill the children's basic instructional needs" (p. 7)?

The necessity for ongoing teamwork between professionals is clear. Teamwork is a prerequisite for a successful educational plan for the individual student with visual impairment. One problem that such students need to overcome is the tendency to lapse into passivity because they lack the skill to assert themselves in a socially acceptable way. The sample assertive statements listed in Table 10.3 can help students develop effective relationships with others. A clumsy statement can complicate social relationships considerably.

DEVELOPING ADAPTIVE SKILLS

Educators are increasingly recognizing that students who are blind require a modified curriculum, not just an adapted standard curriculum. Hatlen and Curry (1987) identified three areas of special instruction:

1. Concepts and skills that require more practice by those with visual handicaps (for example, teaching the concept *square* in a variety of settings, sizes, and functions)
2. Concepts and skills that are specific to the needs of those with visual handicaps (for example, reading by listening, a "gestalt" [overall understanding] for serial learning and self-advocacy)
3. Concepts that sighted children learn through incidental visual observation (for example, walking down the street, using public transportation)

Because they lack visual cues, children with visual impairments often have difficulty starting, maintaining, and not interrupting conversations.

The movement toward integrated education in the least restrictive environment has left many youngsters who are visually disabled with little explicit training in communication skills and the activities of daily living. Because they lack visual cues, youngsters with severe and profound visual disabilities often have trouble starting conversations, maintaining the interest of their conversation partners, and learning not to interrupt. Residential school programs taught not only communication skills but also personal hygiene, grooming, how to dress oneself, how to eat, and cooperative living.

All of those skills are important to the child's later adaptation. They should be taught in a carefully controlled and emotionally safe learning situation. Because many classroom teachers have neither the training nor the time to teach them, educators may have to fall back on some form of team teaching, or even separated programs, to tackle the job (Hatlen & Curry, 1987).

Communication Skills

Using Braille.   People with profound visual disabilities must develop a series of special communication skills. For children who are blind, using braille is a key skill for communicating with the sighted world.

Braille is a system of touch reading developed in 1829 by Louis Braille, a Frenchman who was blind. The system uses embossed characters in different combinations of six dots arranged in a cell two dots wide and three dots high (see Figure 10.6). The symbols are embossed on heavy paper from left to right, and users usually read with both hands, one leading, the other following. Advanced readers may use the second hand to orient themselves to the next line while reading the

TABLE 10.3 Teaching Assertive Behavior

The Situation	Assertive Statements
You want to ask for time or distance.	"I need to think about that one for a while."
You need to get a commitment from someone.	"When can you give me a firm answer?"
You want to make sure the receiver is getting your message.	"I want to make clear the point that _____."
You want to make sure you are getting the message.	"I'm confused; tell me again."
You want to share a positive feeling.	"I really like the way you _____."
You are feeling upset.	"I get embarrassed when _____."

line above, and they may read as much as one-third of the lower line with the second hand. Punctuation, music, and mathematical and scientific notations are based on the same system.

Standard English braille was accepted in 1932 as the system for general use, although many other communication systems have been tried. It has been developed on several levels of difficulty.

Even the most efficient braille reader has an average reading rate about two or three times slower than that of the average print reader. Thus, we can understand why students who are blind fall progressively farther and farther behind sighted students.

Braille Literacy. One of the concerns of teachers for children with visual impairments is that within the framework of the inclusive or mainstreamed class these children will not get sufficient instruction in the special communication skills they need. This feeling is so strong that it has spawned a movement to pass legislation requiring all children with visual impairments to be taught braille or at least be reviewed for the possibility of learning braille (Spungin, 1989).

In many communities, an unchanging number of itinerant teachers manage a growing caseload of children. These teachers have less and less time to teach braille or to translate print to braille for their students. Teachers in some communities have only three hours a week on average to provide direct services to children with visual impairments, and many teachers have even less time. Under such circumstances it is understandable why these children are not able to read rapidly or efficiently (Ferrell & Suvak, 1995). When highly specialized instruction is needed

Figure 10.6
Braille Alphabet and Numerals

The six dots of the braille cell are arranged and numbered thus: 1 ● ● 4
2 ● ● 5
3 ● ● 6

The capital sign, dot 6, placed before a letter makes it a capital. The number sign, dots 3, 4, 5, 6, placed before a character, makes it a figure and not a letter.

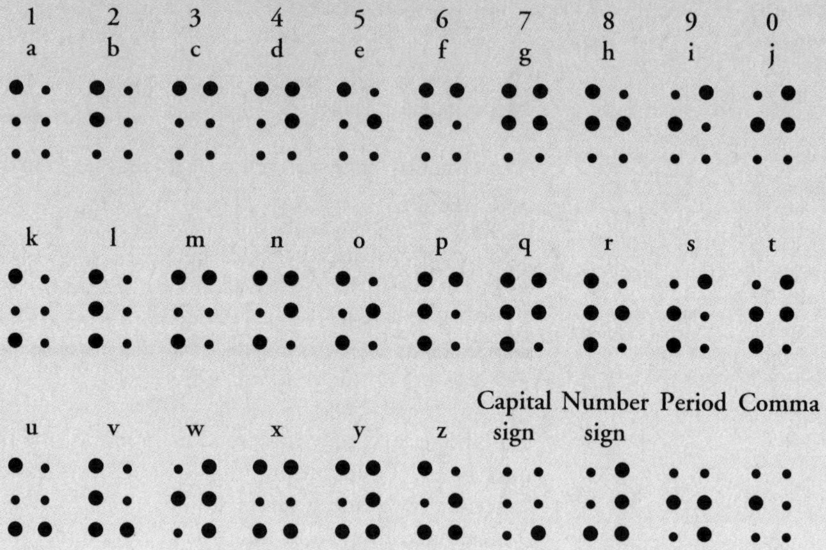

Source: Division for the Blind and Physically Handicapped, Library of Congress, Washington, DC 20542.

so that a youngster can learn other material—whether it is a child with auditory problems trying to learn total communication or a child with visual problems trying to learn braille—it becomes very important for the school to provide sufficient time and practice so that the children master these crucial skills at a functional level.

One of the most significant decisions to be made about a student with visual impairment is the primary reading method: print or braille? The decision is often made by a committee of people who bring together all the information known about the child. The decision is based on a number of factors. The child in question may have some residual distance vision but no near vision and thus could be instructed in braille. For some parents, however, accepting the notion that their child who has limited vision will be instructed in braille, which they consider to be a symbol of total blindness, is not easy. Extensive discussion with the family before instituting the program will be called for (Holbrook & Koenig, 1992).

Some students can be instructed in both print and braille. They learn readiness skills and word identification strategies in a style of parallel instruction, and the decision about which channel to emphasize is postponed until the teacher and the school gain experience with the child's learning style.

One of the most significant decisions for a student is whether to learn print or braille.

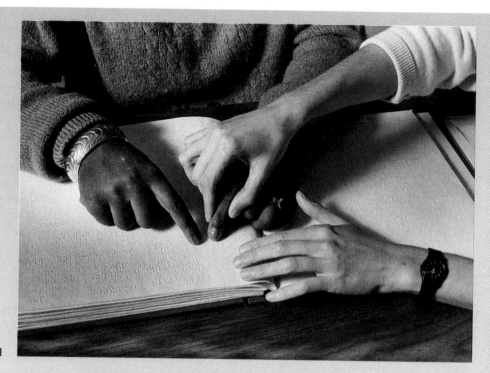

For children who are blind, learning to use braille is a key skill for communicating with the sighted world. (© *Jerry Speier/Design Conceptions*)

The learning experience approach to reading offers many advantages. It uses students' actual experiences as the basis for reading instruction and is a highly motivating approach for a student. But adaptations have to be made for children with visual handicaps. For example, the class visits a local fire station. Afterwards, the student with visual impairment dictates a story about the experience, and the teacher writes down exactly what the student says, using a braillewriter or a special slate and stylus. The student and teacher then read the story together. They can continue to discuss and elaborate on the story, and the teacher can develop reading strategy lessons using the story as a base—for example, thinking about the firefighters' various activities at the firehouse and when fighting a fire.

Braille writing is another part of the curriculum for children with profound visual handicaps. It is taught after the child learns braille reading. People can use various devices for writing the symbols. The easiest and fastest is the braille typewriter, or braillewriter. It has six keys corresponding to the six dots of the braille cell. A proficient user can type from 40 to 60 words a minute. Braille can also be written by hand, by means of a special slate and stylus.

Listening. Sykes (1984) defined *listening* as "the ability to hear, understand, interpret, and critically evaluate what one hears" (p. 99). Listening is the foundation of all language arts. It is an especially important skill for those with visual disabilities because they receive much of the information they process through listening (to talking books, tapes, verbal intercourse) and because of the importance of listening to the perception of obstacles.

Environment Skills

Mastering the Environment.　　Mastering the environment is especially important to children who are blind, for their physical and social independence. The ease with which they move about, find objects and places, and orient themselves to new physical and social situations is crucial in determining their role in peer relationships, the types of vocations and avocations open to them as adults, and their own estimation of themselves as people.

How do we help children who are blind master the environment? From a very early age we have to teach them not to be afraid of new experiences or injury. Sighted children skin their knees, bump their shins, fall from trees, and step in holes. Children who are blind must have the same chance if they are going to learn to control themselves and the environment. This means encouraging risk taking.

Children with visual impairment should be taught to feel the difference in the weight of their forks when they have successfully cornered a few peas and when they haven't. They also should learn a system of marking and organizing clothes for both efficiency and good grooming.

Models—of a room, the World Trade Center, or the neighborhood—can help children who are visually impaired understand the relationship of one place or size to another. Models are not a substitute for experience. But they are an extension of experience and a means of drawing perceptual relationships between areas too large to be included at one time in direct experience.

Table 10.4 lists a number of household and cooking skills that are within the easy reach of most children with visual disabilities. The child can even compile such a list. As the child begins to extend his or her repertoire, the list will grow longer and longer so that there is an impressive set of skills and knowledge that have been mastered.

Orientation and Mobility.　　The greatest limitations imposed by blindness are the problems of becoming oriented to one's environment and immobility. The situations that force dependence and can cause the greatest personality and social problems for individuals who have visual impairments usually involve mobility. Adults use tools for improving mobility such as long canes, guide dogs, and sighted guides. But children also must learn to move about their environment independently and safely, so orientation and mobility have become part of the curriculum in all programs for children with visual impairments.

Simply defined, **orientation and mobility (O&M)** involves an understanding of one's location in a given environment (orientation) coupled with the ability to physically move through that environment safely and independently (mobility) (Cioffi, 1995). It is not uncommon for young people to have one of these skills in greater amount than the other, so that attention has to be focused on one of them. The goal of any mobility program is to bring the individual to his or her highest

TABLE 10.4 Building Self-Esteem: What I Can Do!

Beginning Household Tasks	Beginning Cooking Skills
Sweeping the sidewalk	Washing little tomatoes and taking off the stems
Washing yard furniture	Making frozen lemonade or juice
Emptying wastebaskets	Opening potato chips and putting them in a bowl
Folding towels	
Setting the table	Making toast
Bringing in the mail	Buttering toast
Making the bed	Arranging presliced cheese on a plate
Taking silverware from the dishwasher and putting it away	Pouring breakfast food into a bowl
Washing the dishes	Taking ice cubes out of the tray and refilling the tray
Cleaning the sink and bathtub	Making instant pudding

Source: S. Mangold (1988). Nurturing high self-esteem in visually handicapped children. In S. Mangold (Ed.), *A Teacher's Guide to the Special Educational Needs of Blind and Visually Handicapped Children*. New York: American Foundation for the Blind. Reprinted by permission of the author.

The goal of an O&M program is to develop a child's mobility skills to the safest, most independent level possible.

desired level of safe, independent travel. Students with visual disabilities become independent when they can move about in the environment to meet their own needs. These skills are central to a strong curriculum stressing independence.

The role of the O&M specialist has many dimensions to it. He or she can contribute as a member of the educational team, provide developmentally appropriate goals for the educational plan, develop and implement educational activities for working with the child and family, analyze the child's travel environments for safety factors and possible modifications, and train other educational service providers in O&M principles (Anthony, Lampert, Fazzi, & Pogrund, 1992).

Because learning mobility with a degree of personal independence is one of the most desirable educational goals, special teachers provide O&M instruction to teach the child to use sensory information to establish and maintain his or her position in the environment and move safely, efficiently, and gracefully (Hill, 1992). The skill areas that are covered in such instruction include the following:

■ Ability to identify and make use of landmarks and clues

■ Knowledge and use of compass directions

A Braille trail such as this one helps a visually impaired person learn mobility and gain personal independence.

- Knowledge and use of indoor and city number systems
- Ability to align the body to objects and with sounds for the purpose of maintaining a straight line of travel
- Use of systematic search patterns to explore novel objects and environments
- Recovery skills
- Knowledge of where, when, and how to solicit aid (Hill, 1992, pp. 25–26)

Mobility training is a complex task requiring considerable skill, and not all teachers of visually impaired persons have had the special training that qualifies them to give O&M instruction.

A major focus in mobility training is learning how to avoid obstacles. Many people who are blind are able to avoid obstacles very well: They make turns in hallways. They stop before they run into a door. How do they do it? Do they sense a change of air pressure on their faces? Do they use residual light and dark vision? Do they use their sense of hearing? Over forty years ago, in a classic study, Cotzin and Dallenbach (1950) carried out a series of experiments to find the answer.

Cotzin and Dallenbach asked people with blindness to walk down a path and stop when they sensed an obstacle. Then the researchers began to systematically eliminate various possibilities. They put a velvet hood over the face to eliminate cues from air pressure; they used blindfolds to rule out residual vision; they plugged the ears to eliminate hearing—each in turn. Out of these experiments came a single definitive answer: The subjects' judgment suffered only when their ears were blocked. Clearly, they were using sound to detect barriers in their path, much as bats do. The knowledge that hearing is an essential element in obstacle perception has led educators to focus on enhancing (in natural and artificial ways) the use of hearing to increase mobility.

In the decades since Cotzin and Dallenbach's study, Juurmaa (1970, p. 386) and other scientists have worked to devise electronic aids to mobility. These have had some limited success, and the white cane is still widely used.

Personal mobility and independence have particular importance for adolescents who are ready to break away from family restraints and protection. The ability to control oneself and one's environment is essential to becoming independent and gaining the respect of peers. The schools are using physical education programs to sharpen the orientation and mobility skills of visually impaired youngsters.

In most cases, we increase the mobility of individuals who are visually impaired by teaching them ways to get around or to use available tools. But there is another way to ease the restrictions on those who are blind. Society has a responsibility to remove obstacles wherever possible. That responsibility became law in 1991 with the passage of the Americans with Disabilities Act, which directs businesses and public officials to remove barriers for persons with disabilities (see Chapter 2). Removing barriers includes attaching braille symbols to elevators, widening aisles for wheelchair access, and making public telephones accessible.

Map and Chart Reading. A favorite curriculum adaptation for children with visual impairments is models or tactile maps representing spatial relationships that students can master through their sense of touch. Berla (1981) discovered that students who are visually impaired, in particular younger pupils, can improve their ability to read maps if they are specifically taught systematic techniques for exploring maps. Teachers should not expect students to discover complex search techniques themselves. Just as sighted children need help in learning problem-solving techniques, children with visual impairments need instruction in specific search skills.

Special maps alone are not enough. Students must first understand what the maps represent. A map of one's neighborhood can be an important part of the orientation and mobility curriculum.

Skills in the Learning Environment

The itinerant or resource teacher in the public school must often instruct students and classroom teachers on some of the special skills that the child with visual disabilities should master. Some of these skills are important keys to the child's effectively mastering the learning environment (Torres & Corn, 1990):

■ *Fire drills.* The child with visual disabilities needs to be instructed to take hold of the nearest moving child or adult and quickly follow the others. No particular child should be assigned to the task of aiding the child because he or she might be absent or away when needed.

Taking Rachel Swimming

Several summers ago, I bought a pair of wings for my daughter Rachel, inflatable rings that fit around each upper arm. It took me until she was almost five years old to get them because I kept remembering my mother's advice of long ago, that tubes should be avoided because children depended on them and then never learned to swim properly. I bought them because at the time Rachel was getting hydrotherapy, and one day, when I looked in on her, I saw her splashing wildly, laughter echoing in the pool, water wings around her arms.

There isn't much that Rachel does well. She is legally blind, and although she gets around well enough to fool strangers into believing that her vision is perfect, we have seen her try to make conversation with a stone lawn ornament, and she has failed to recognize her father, ten feet away in the living room, unless he speaks out. Her motor skills aren't the best either; she is dyspraxic, which means she has motor-planning problems. She walks and runs clumsily, falling frequently; holds a pencil perfectly but often cannot seem to touch it to the paper, and when she does, the best she can make is a spidery line, or a circular scribble. She has many other problems, including a seizure disorder that had been well controlled, and at the time I first bought her water wings, we were slowly weaning her off one of the two medications she had been taking. Despite all this, she is a cheerful child, who has asked me for nothing, and whose desires, if she has them, have never been expressed.

We were at a pool party in June 1988 when I slipped the water wings on Rachel's arms for the first time. It seemed to me that she was transformed by the water, for my daughter, whose communication is limited in so many ways, was much like any five-year-old in the pool, making bubbles, asking me to watch her kick, to try to catch her. She was radiant, filled with energy.

My fingers were puckery, and her lips were blue when I tried to take her out. Rachel, my passive, uncomplaining child, yowled and fought so much that people at the poolside, who knew her, said, "Is *that* Rachel?"

We took the water wings with us to Maine, and that summer, whenever it was sunny, I went swimming with Rachel and her older sister, Charlotte. I can remember a splendid afternoon when we paddled out to a little island on our canoe. The tide was low, and we "hand swam" in shallow water, propelling ourselves forward in the muck—all of us, even Rachel. What an equalizer the water was, I had thought. For that hour, we were all the same. I suppose you can say I discovered what others have known for years, that, because of water's natural buoyancy, people with neurological, muscular, or joint problems can do in water what is difficult or impossible for them on land.

Later that summer, in a community pool where flotation devices such as water wings were not allowed, I watched Rachel hand swim in the smallest of three pools, then watched her slide beneath the water, never struggling. She never coughed when I picked her up, and she told me, when I asked, that she was fine. But she seemed woozy and out of it.

Several minutes later, she had a series of seizures that simply would not end. *Status epilepticus*, as it is known by physicians, is the kind of event that gives seizures a bad name, for it sometimes lasts for hours or even days, and can be life-threatening. The emergency squad entubed Rachel, to make sure she did not choke, and two physicians—a husband and wife on a rare afternoon off—administered intravenous Valium. She spent nearly a week in the hospital. ➡

I was assured that these alarming seizures were the result of her being undermedicated, that the episode was inevitable, and had absolutely nothing to do with the water. Further, that when her dosage was regulated, and she was fully recovered, she could swim again.

And so—cautiously we took her swimming again, and our daughter, awkward and hesitant on land, kicked and paddled, proud and vigorous.

It was midwinter when my husband decided to take the children for a swim at the Y in our town. They had been in the pool for 45 minutes when Rachel, who had been seizure-free for the six months since the *status epilepticus*, went limp in the water, her head thrown back. My husband took her from the pool, and within a minute she had roused and was begging to go in again. Nonetheless, we were concerned.

We had Rachel's drug levels checked, and found that she was within the normal range for both medications. We even arranged for her to have a 24-hour EEG, in which she wore electrodes and a small battery pack in a knapsack for a full day and night. The EEG showed no subclinical seizures.

"Take her swimming," said the neurologist, and so we did. This time I joined my family at the pool and saw the way Rachel swam with utter abandon and joy, the sudden limpness, the peculiar way she roused, with no postseizure grogginess, ready to go swimming again, furious that we said no.

"Was the water very cold?" the neurologist asked.

No. She had been in the smaller pool, which was heated like her hydrotherapy pool to nearly body temperature.

What about the temperature outside the pool—had it been hot?

No. The chill when stepping out of the pool was rather unpleasant.

Did she hyperventilate when she was swimming? Had she been sick? Did she swallow a great deal of water?

No to all of these.

What I felt then, along with the frustration of being unable to figure out what triggered these seizures, was a determination that Rachel continue to swim—a determination I feared was shared by neither neurologist nor husband, and that, when the summer was upon us again, I was forced to scrutinize. Why was I unable to let go of this desire in the face of her problems? Why was I so adamant that Rachel swim?

My first argument went like this: in the water she was radiant and energetic; what did any of us gain by depriving her of the only thing that she did well?

What complicated this was the fact that Rachel does not say, "Mommy, I want to swim," unless she hears others talking about it, and even then it is easy enough to reroute her, to trick her into thinking about something else. Therefore, if she was never again in the water, she might never ask to swim, and would never tell me that she missed it. Could I say, then, that I would not be depriving her of anything, that she did not really care? Or was this like saying that pleasure was only what one was able to recall and describe?

As we packed to leave for our cottage on Casco Bay, I wrestled with these questions, trying hard to separate my conception of pleasure from hers. I had to acknowledge that my insistence that Rachel swim was selfish, in part. I wanted her to swim because when she did, she was one of us, doing what we were able to do, equalized by the water. I only hoped that my attempt to have her live a normal life would not risk her well-being.

It seemed to me that this issue was far bigger than that of Rachel swimming. It had also to do with Rachel in her family's world, and beyond that, Rachel in the world of the unimpaired. As a disinterested person, I would like to imagine a society in which the able and disabled mix freely in child care centers and schools, and in the workplace, but as the mother of a child who *is* more vulnerable than most, I have the far more complicated task of figuring out how much to acknowledge her disabilities, and protect her because of them, and how much to push her into the world.

It is clear that I will continue to grapple with these issues for years to come, for Rachel is seven years old, and a child that age is still in a family's arms. The question of whether Rachel should swim is the first of many, and my adamance, with all its elements of stubbornness and denial, is my way of saying that I want to see how far my daughter will go before I use the world "never."

I only wish that the answers to these larger questions will be as simple as the one we settled on this summer. Rachel is swimming again, in the cold, clear water of Maine: in for 15 glorious minutes, and out despite her complaints. And so far she has thrived.

Source: Jane Bernstein, "Taking Rachel Swimming," *Ms.* (September–October 1991), pp. 40–41. Reprinted by permission of the Wallace Literary Agency, Inc.

---

commentary

What Is the Context? One of the contexts of this article is the environment itself and its challenges and risks for a child with disabilities. Overlaid on this is the protective context of family. Rachel's mother introduces her to the enjoyment and also the danger of swimming, then plays a strong role in mediating the environment and defending her child's independence.

Pivotal Issues. How do parents react to conflicting goals for their disabled child (promoting independence versus keeping the child safe)? What other recreational activities present these or similar issues of safety and independence (for all students, not necessarily those with disabilities)?

- *Field trips.* Giving prior notice to the place where these children will be visiting is important. The person in charge (such as the museum director) might be able to make adaptations that will aid the child with vision problems.

- *Auditorium.* The child should be allowed to sit close to the stage to get the maximum amount of information from the experience.

- *Lunchroom.* Some type of orientation is needed so that the child with visual disabilities learns where the essential things are. The cafeteria staff can be alerted to help the student with food choice, and peers can help with finding a seat.

Some daily living skills are noted in Figure 10.7. Thinking of a plate as the face of a clock facilitates finding food on a plate. Other useful adaptations of daily activities are the different ways of folding one-, five-, and ten-dollar bills and special arrangements of clothes in a closet. Such simple steps can make the daily life of the child with visual impairments easier. The things that sighted children learn as a matter of easy experience have to be planned. But, with such planning, the student with visual disabilities can perform effectively and truly become a member of the group.

How do visually handicapped people pay for things when they can't see their money?
Coins are very easy to recognize by feeling them. Dimes are very small and slim with ridges around the edges; pennies are small with smooth edges; nickels are bigger and thick; quarters have ridges and are even bigger but thinner than nickels.

Visually handicapped people use this trick in order to recognize dollar bills: In their wallet, dollar bills are left unfolded; five dollar bills are folded in half the short way; and ten dollar bills are folded in half the long way.

How do visually handicapped children find their toys and clothes?
Visually handicapped kids have to be very neat. They have to put their things in the same place every day in order to find them.

To pick out what to wear in the morning, visually handicapped kids may feel the texture of their clothes. They know jeans feel different than wool pants. Or they may remember in what order their clothes are hung in their closet.

In order to decide what top matches what bottom, aluminum clothing tags can be sewn in each piece of clothing. On the tags, there are braille markings indicating the color. Visually handicapped children must learn what colors go together.

How do visually handicapped children find the food on their plate?
To find the food on their plate, visually handicapped children imagine the plate is a clock. They are told **at what time** the food is placed.

On this plate, the hamburger is at 12 o'clock, the salad is at 3 o'clock and the french fries are at 8 o'clock.

Visually handicapped kids, just like you, think dessert should be all the time!

Figure 10.7
Life Skill Training for Children with Visual Disabilities

Source: R. Tannebaum (1988). *A Different Way of Seeing.* New York: American Foundation for the Blind. Reprinted with permission from the American Foundation for the Blind, 11 Penn Plaza, Suite 300, New York, NY 10001.

Figure 10.8 shows a page from a story designed to help sighted persons interact with a blind child without feeling strange or not knowing what to do. The theme is that, with only occasional help, the blind person can do many things that the sighted person can do. Helping the sighted person feel at ease is one step toward the integration of students with visual impairment into the general classroom.

Additional Skills Training

Some additional skills can help the child with visual disabilities respond more effectively to the educational program. The itinerant teacher can be of great help to the regular classroom teacher, who might not be familiar with how to teach such skills.

Skills should include keyboarding and daily living skills such as cooking, shopping, and orientation.

- *Keyboarding.* Students can learn keyboarding and word-processing skills for neater written assignments. Personal computers can be modified so there is both braille and large print output.
- *Daily living.* The child with visual impairment may need direct instruction to acquire skills that come more easily to sighted students, such as good grooming, cooking, and using a grocery store. The teacher should be able to assist the child in learning these skills.

In addition to the skills just noted, areas such as enhancing visual skills by the proper lighting and positioning of materials plus supplementary instruction in topics such as sex education, social skills, and the use of technology are often a part of the special education curriculum.

AIDS IN THE LEARNING ENVIRONMENT

A number of publications offer information to help teachers of visually impaired students. Corn and Martinez (1978), for example, described the use of special devices, ways in which children with visual disabilities can work with printed material, and suggestions for helping these students manage other activities. Among their suggestions were the following:

- *Lamps and rheostats.* With variable intensities and positioning, lamps can provide the additional or dimmed illumination that a child with a visual handicap may require.
- *Large-type books.* For comfort or for those children who cannot read regular print at close distance even with an optical aid, large type is helpful. Its quality or typeface is as important to legibility as its size. Spacing between letters and lines is also important.
- *Raised-line paper (writing paper, graph paper, and so on).* Raised-line paper allows a student to write script "on the line" or to maneuver a graph either by placing markers onto the graph paper or by punching holes to indicate specific points.

Figure 10.8
My Friend Jodi Is Blind

Jodi said, "You never walked with a blind person before, did you?" She held on to my elbow and asked me to walk one step ahead of her so she could follow. She said I should tell her when we got near steps, doors or holes in the ground.

Once I learned how, it was easy for us to get around together. Jodi said, "Now we are next to the cafeteria." I asked her how she knew that. She said, "Silly, my nose knows."

5

Source: Schwartz, N. (1987). *My Friend Jodi Is Blind*. New York: The Lighthouse, p. 5. Illustration by Peter Vey. Copyright © 1987 by The Lighthouse Inc., New York.

■ *Cassette tape recorders.* Children use the recorders to take notes, listen to recorded texts, or formulate compositions or writing assignments.

■ *More time.* Students who are blind will frequently need extra time to complete assignments and exams. Allowing time and a half is usually acceptable. The child may complete work in the resource room or school library. When you are certain that the child understands the work, it may be a good idea to shorten assignments: for example, you may request that a student do only the odd-numbered problems in the math homework. (pp. 9–15)

CONTENT

Most of the instructional material presented to children with visual disabilities is similar or identical to the material presented to sighted children, particularly when they spend the majority of their time in the regular classroom. However, some modifications can be made to address specific areas of adaptive difficulty.

Science

Malone, DeLucchi, and Thier (1981) attempted to bring special content in science to students with visual disabilities. Their program, Science Activities for the Visually Impaired (SAVI), was designed for children in the upper elementary grades. The project stresses hands-on activities that allow students with severe and profound visual disabilities to manipulate objects and conduct experiments. The activities can be challenging for both sighted children and children with visual disabilities working together, which makes them appropriate for use in a mainstreamed educational setting.

Figure 10.9 shows a sample activity, part of a unit on kitchen interactions, that allows students to measure the action of acids by using everyday objects plus a special plastic syringe with tactile notches. Special braille recording sheets enable students to quantify data. Through this kind of experience, students learn key scientific procedures such as observing, measuring, comparing, calculating, and drawing conclusions.

Other units in the SAVI program cover scientific reasoning, communications, magnetism and electricity, and structures of life. Each module has sets of activities, equipment, and detailed instructions for the teacher, including vocabulary terms and follow-up activities that students can do outside the classroom. Programs like SAVI provide concrete systematic experiences that allow students with visual impairments to make full use of their intellectual abilities by linking the physical environment to verbal interchange.

Mathematics

Another example of how specific content can be designed to help children with a profound visual disability master concepts was provided by Huff and Franks

Figure 10.9
A Scientific Experiment for
Students with Visual Impairments

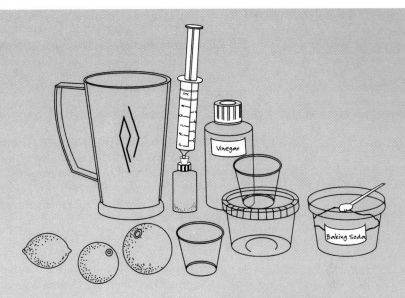

OVERVIEW

In *The Acid Test*, the students use baking soda to test for the presence of acid in common foods. They establish that when vinegar (an acid) is mixed with baking soda, a reaction occurs and a gas (carbon dioxide) is given off. When this reaction takes place in a bottle with a syringe stuck into the top, the carbon dioxide pushes the plunger out of the syringe barrel. The amount of acid in a measured amount of vinegar is the *standard* against which the amount of acid in other foods (orange juice, grapefruit juice, lemon juice) is compared.

Finally, the youngsters investigate the variables in the acid/soda reaction to help them "pop the top" (i.e. launch the plunger out of the syringe barrel.

BACKGROUND

How about a glass of acid with your peanut butter and jelly sandwich? Or how about tossing a little acid in the next batch of biscuits you bake? That sounds unappetizing to say the least, but acids are common in many of our favorite foods. The lemon juice is what we use to make our tangy glass of lemonade, the buttermilk we use in biscuit dough, and the vinegar bath used to preserve pickles are all examples of acid ingredients in the foods we eat.

A simple technique for testing the acid content of foods involves using baking soda as an indicator. When an acid reacts with baking soda two things happen. First, the acid is neutralized or converted into new substances that are not acidic; and second, a gas called carbon dioxide is liberated in the form of bubbles. The amount of gas produced by this reaction can be used to compare the strengths of

Source: L. Malone, L. DeLucchi, & H. Thier (1981). *Science Activities for the Visually Impaired: SAVI Leadership Trainer's Manual.* Berkeley: Center for Multisensory Learning, University of California. Reprinted with permission.

(1973) for teaching fractions. It is easy enough to understand fractions with a visual demonstration. But students who cannot see must acquire that understanding through the sense of touch. Huff and Franks demonstrated that blind children in kindergarten through third grade can master fractions by working with three-dimensional circles of wood and placing them in a form board nest that can include fractional parts to make up a full circle. Once they have placed a whole circle, the children can learn to assemble blocks representing a third of a circle and put them together in the nest to form the whole. This kind of tactile experience helps children who are blind not only master the idea of fractional parts but discriminate between the relative sizes of various fractional parts (halves versus quarters).

In the middle grades (fourth through eighth or ninth grade), students who are visually impaired work with supplementary materials to help themselves absorb the information that sighted children learn. They use talking books and recorded lessons, and they do remedial work when necessary.

A standard tool for learning mathematics is the abacus, used in many Asian countries to instruct all children. The Cranmer Abacus, a special version of the device, is a substantial help to persons who are visually impaired. The beads in the Cranmer Abacus do not move as rapidly as the beads in the usual abacus and thus can be read more easily by touch. Also, the rods are spaced farther apart for more convenient finger access to the beads. This is another example of the adaptation of devices to meet the special needs of these children.

THE USES OF TECHNOLOGY

Advances in electronics and computers are having an important impact on the education of those who are visually impaired by expanding their intellectual and physical worlds (Ashcroft, 1984).

Communication

Children may be reluctant to use machines that can assist persons who are visually impaired.

Today, many kinds of machines help persons with severe and profound visual handicaps communicate. Although some of these machines are both expensive and complex, often the biggest stumbling block to their use is the children's reluctance. Many youngsters are self-conscious about devices that make them look "strange" or "weird." To overcome this self-consciousness, it's important to introduce these tools in a positive way (by playing games, for example) when the children are young.

Technology has given us the capability to translate printed language into spoken language and braille. It also allows us to move easily from one form of communication to another, such as transferring from braille to written English and back again. Obviously, this technology has enormous potential for students who are visually handicapped and for their teachers:

Teachers can type a lesson or test and then, using the appropriate hardware or software, convert the material to large print, braille, regular print, or speech, depending

"The Reading Edge" uses synthetic speech to convert printed material into as many as seven languages in any of nine distinct voices. Evident in the background is the more costly and less convenient 1975 model. (*Courtesy Xerox Imaging Systems, Peabody, MA*)

upon the needs of the student. The student, on the other hand, could do homework or tests in braille and convert it to print for the teacher. (Todd, 1986, p. 292)

For Listening. **Synthetic speech** is the production of sound—of phonemes into words—by means of a computer. The process allows us to convert written words into speech so that those with severe and profound visual handicaps can listen to books, newspapers, and even typed letters and manuscripts.

The Kurzweil Reading Machine uses synthetic speech to convert printed material into spoken English. At this writing, it is extremely expensive (it is available only in libraries and colleges) and difficult to use (it requires extensive training), which limits its use to older youngsters and adults (Barraga, 1986). But it has the potential to open a new means of communication for those with visual disabilities.

The increasing popularity of talking books—books on tape—is a boon for those with visual handicaps. In addition to commercially made tapes, the Talking

Book program produces books on tape and makes them available at no charge to children and adults who are visually impaired.

The Speech Plus Talking Calculator is a hand-held calculator that announces (using a twenty-four-word vocabulary) each entry and the result of each operation. It is a relatively inexpensive device.

For Reading and Writing.   For those who have some vision, closed-circuit television can be a useful tool. By adjusting a lens, the user can magnify printed material that is within the range of the machine. The enlargement appears on a television screen on which size, brightness, and contrast can be adjusted. Closed-circuit television is also used for writing. As the student writes under the camera, an enlargement of the writing appears on the screen. Another print enlarger, the Viewscan, uses a small camera to track print on a page while the reader scans the screen.

The Optacon, developed at Stanford University, scans and converts print into 144 tactile pins. When activated by print, these pins produce a vibratory image of the letter on the user's finger. The machine is an optical-to-tactile converter, which makes available to those who are visually impaired books that are not in braille. Bliss and Moore (1974) found that to learn to read with the Optacon, a child must be highly intelligent, spend long periods in training, and be highly motivated. Barraga (1983) stated that the Optacon is a worthwhile technological invention because it allows print material to be read without modification or transcription. At present, however, the cost of the machine and the difficulty of learning how to use it limit its use.

At the Massachusetts Institute of Technology, a computer automation has been developed that translates ink print into Grade 2 braille. The procedure is being used extensively at the American Printing House for the Blind. An expansion of the computer braille translator, the MIT Braille Emboss, is used with a telewriter. When teachers of blind persons want braille output for new materials, they request it by telephone from a computer center, and it is returned in braille by means of a teletypewriter. Currently braille translations are made by microcomputers that are usually available in schools for the blind.

Although in the future even more exotic technology may provide help for students with visual impairments, a number of devices are available now. Portable computer devices allow students to take notes and do assignments without the need for a computer in each classroom. Both print and braille copies can be printed from these devices. With additions, they allow the student to listen to synthesized speech. Portable talking dictionaries are within financial reach and a welcome addition, for a braille dictionary can cost over $1,000. It would be good to get these devices in the hands of as many students as possible, because they will allow much more effective use of students' time than was previously possible.

Recreation

One area of investigation that has become more popular recently is the design of work and play areas to maximize the development of children with visual impair-

Figure 10.10

A Play Area for Children with Visual Impairments

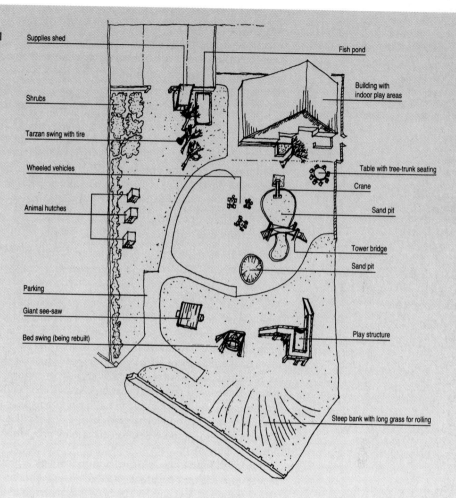

Supplies shed

Fish pond

Shrubs

Building with indoor play areas

Tarzan swing with tire

Wheeled vehicles

Table with tree-trunk seating

Crane

Animal hutches

Sand pit

Tower bridge

Sand pit

Parking

Giant see-saw

Bed swing (being rebuilt)

Play structure

Steep bank with long grass for rolling

Source: K. Blakely, M. Lang, & R. Hart (1991). *Getting in Touch with Play.* Illustration by Selim Iltus. New York: The Lighthouse Inc. Reprinted by permission.

ments. Figure 10.10 shows a play area for children with visual impairments. The purpose of such a plan is to provide a variety of physical experiences with swings, seesaws, climbing apparatus, sand pits, and so on, designed to encourage physical activity (Blakely, Lang, & Hart, 1991). Children with visual impairment are as energetic and interested in play as any child but often need special encouragement to overcome the inhibitions fostered by their visual problems. Such exploration done in a safe, carefully designed play area can encourage adventures and controlled risk taking.

TRANSITION FROM SCHOOL TO WORK

The transition from school to work is an extremely important aspect of the total educational program. Although there have been attempts to use sheltered workshops, where students produce goods in a protected setting that is publicly subsidized, the newer emphasis is on placement in real job settings whenever possible (Sacks & Bullis, 1988). The secondary school program then becomes a part-time academic and part-time workplace program to give the student a chance to experience employment while still in a supervised setting. The academic program focuses on functional reading and other skills that can enhance the student's chance of success in the workplace.

Figure 10.11 is a case study of John, a teenager with a visual disability who was exposed to several different jobs and learned a series of generic work skills (such as greeting and conversation skills). This type of experience should serve John in good stead in whatever occupation he finally decides to enter.

Figure 10.11
Case Study: John

John, age 17, has been visually handicapped since birth. Congenital cataracts, which were removed at age 2, left him with light perception in his left eye and usable residual vision in the right eye. John is able to read standard print with a hand-held magnifier or specially prescribed lenses, but his reading rate is slow and extremely labored. John has received the services of a teacher of visually handicapped students throughout his school years, first in an elementary resource room and later from itinerant teachers. John has been mainstreamed into regular education classes since the third grade, even though his skill levels range from fourth grade in math comprehension to eighth grade in spelling. His reading comprehension, organization, and note-taking skills are particularly weak and require constant support, yet his educational program has continued to emphasize academic pursuits.

Although John attends his neighborhood high school, he has few friends. He spends much of his leisure time alone and finds interaction with peers difficult and sometimes rather awkward. Encouraged by his VH teacher, John has begun to participate in the drama club. He is quite verbal and enjoys acting a variety of roles; however, he is easily intimidated when questioned about his visual impairment or difficulty with reading. At home, John is responsible for his personal needs, but does not consistently perform other job tasks around the house. He has repeatedly volunteered to help mow the lawn or prepare meals, but his parents are hesitant to allow him to perform such jobs because of his limited vision. Although John's parents recognize the importance of allowing him to become more independent, they are fearful of his safety and have not allowed him to travel by himself throughout the community or spend his own money as readily as his siblings or same-aged peers.

At a recent IEP meeting, John's VH teacher, along with other team members (orientation and mobility specialist, vocational coordinator, vocational rehabilitation counselor, school psychologist, John, and his parents) discussed future educational and vocational goals for him. As they spoke, it was apparent that John's parents perceived his academic performance much differently from other team members. His parents believed that John was functioning at or above grade level on most academic tasks and felt that he would be able to attend college. Conversely, team members did not recognize John's desire to develop more independent living and travel skills, as well as wanting to secure a job for himself. When questioned about job preference, John seemed interested in working at a radio station or developing his acting skills. At the suggestion of the vocational coordinator, John was asked to participate in a series of community vocational experiences, where he would be able to explore and to learn about a variety of jobs through hands-on experience. Reluctantly, John's parents allowed him to do so.

Instead of full participation in a regular education setting, John now spent half of his school day in a community classroom at a real job site. Assisted by a vocational special education teacher and his VH teacher, John gained exposure to landscape gardening, sorting and packaging, and basic office skills. Each experience lasted approximately three months. In addition, he developed a set of generic work behaviors and social skills (basic greetings and conversational skills through role plays and modeling) that transferred to other settings. In the community classroom environment, time was also spent developing functional math and reading skills that included money management, time management, and completion of job applications. John was expected to travel to work independently in the morning, and back to his local high school in the afternoon. As a result of this initial vocational experience, John's educational program has shifted from a purely academic focus to one that is more functionally based. He will continue to participate in the community classroom program during his final year of high school, while working with his special education teachers and vocational counselors to secure employment after high school.

Source: L. Kekelis & S. Sacks (1988). Guidelines for mainstreaming visually impaired children.

PROGRAM EVALUATION

Despite vigorous arguments about which setting is best for children with visual impairments, little data are available to support the various points of view. Does the child with visual disabilities profit from being integrated into a regular school program?

Some agree with Harrell and Curry (1987) that

There is no evidence that the provision of educational services to visually impaired students in regular classrooms and integrated settings is of greater benefit to the pupil than are more intensive segregated programs that offer carefully planned opportunities for successful interactions with nonhandicapped peers. (p. 372)

Falvey (1988), however, pointed out that if a great deal of money is spent on residential school programs, little is left for strengthening the delivery of services in local schools. Also, although residential schools allow children with visual disabilities to form friendships, these friendships are inevitably limited to others with visual disabilities. But the low incidence of children with visual disabilities means that many local schools will have few such children, so necessary, intensive special education in areas such as personal hygiene, grooming, eating, and cooperative living—to say nothing of mobility training—may be difficult to obtain in regular classrooms.

PREVOCATIONAL TRAINING

Technological advances have had an enormous impact on the ability of students with visual disabilities to communicate and move around. They have also opened a wide range of occupations (see Table 10.5). In many programs, young children are working with computers, gaining knowledge and skill that can help them move into computer-related jobs later.

TABLE 10.5	Jobs for Computer Users with Severe and Profound Visual Disabilities

Applications programmer
Assistant director of a rehabilitation center for the blind
Assistant engineer
Attorney
Claims representative
Computer programmer
Customer engineer
Customer service representative
Dispatcher
Editor of a technical magazine
Engineer
Liquor store owner
Marketing secretary
Materials expediter in a purchasing department
Medical transcriber
Occupational technician
Physicist
Programmer analyst
Programmer trainee
Radio station assignment editor
Receptionist
Research specialist
Secretary
Senior software manager
Software specialist
Software support specialist
Staff engineer
Staff supervisor
Systems analyst
Systems programmer (trouble shooter)
Tax analyst
Word processing operator (trainee)
Word processor

Source: Reprinted with permission from G. Goodrich (1984). Applications of microcomputers by visually impaired persons. *Journal of Visual Impairment and Blindness, 78* (November), pp. 408–414. Copyright © 1984 by the American Foundation for the Blind.

Note: This is not an exhaustive listing of all jobs in which computers are used, but it shows the diversity of jobs held by computer users who are visually impaired.

■■■ *Lifespan Issues*

In other chapters we have been concerned with what happens to exceptional children after they leave school and try to make their way in the world. After all, educational programs are supposed to prepare students for life in the community. We have the same concerns for children with visual impairments.

There is a limited supply of evidence available on this topic, but one longitudinal study (Freeman, Goetz, Richards, & Groenveld, 1991) provided a fifteen-year follow-up study of 69 legally blind persons who were 10 years old at the time of the original investigation. The follow-up data were collected through structured interviews conducted by the first two authors of the study.

The importance of multiple disabilities becomes clear in the results. Of the 40 participants in the study whose only disability was visual, 71 percent received a normal psychiatric diagnosis, and 44 percent were in open employment. However, of the 29 participants with other disabilities, only 24 percent received a normal psychiatric diagnosis, and only 17 percent were employed.

In education, 20 percent completed secondary school and went no further. Nineteen percent attended a university, and 6 percent graduated. Twenty percent did not complete secondary school, and another 17 percent were always in special classes. The authors felt that many of these subjects could have been employed, though they were not.

Among those with partial sight there was a strong tendency to try to "pass" as normal, to avoid the presumed stigma of blindness.

The authors felt that study of the resilience of some children needs to be pursued further—that is, students who appear to persevere against odds to reach a good adaptation. We know little about this topic and thus are unable to provide guidance about how to achieve the state of resilience. Certainly, there is sufficient evidence of good adult adjustment, given the right set of conditions and past experience.

■■■ *A Final Word*

We need to remember that comparisons of children with visual impairments and sighted children reveal only what *is,* rather than what could be with a more comprehensive intervention program. As Warren reminds us, "In virtually every area of development there are visually impaired children whose developmental progress is at least at the norm for, and at the high end of the distribution for, sighted children" (1994, p. 334). In this area as in others, individual differences should be used to guide educational strategies, not some general average that may not be applicable to the individual child.

Summary of Major Ideas

1. Children with visual impairments are classified in several ways. Educational classifications rest on the special adaptations that are necessary to help these children learn.

2. A moderate visual disability can be almost entirely corrected with visual aids. Aids are not as effective for a child with a severe visual disability, but the child can use residual vision to learn. A child with a profound visual disability cannot use vision as a learning tool.

3. The way we interpret the outside world is a function of our brain, experience, and eyes. A visual impairment can hamper the individual's understanding of the world, but such understanding can be enhanced through extending the experiential world of the child with vision impairment.

4. Hereditary factors are a primary cause of visual disabilities in young children. Other major causes are infectious diseases, injuries, and poisonings. Many of these children have multiple handicaps, not just visual disabilities.

5. Today most educators agree that the cumulative experiences of children as they develop affect intelligence. Youngsters with visual impairments lack the integrating experiences that come naturally to sighted children. The challenge for educators is to compensate for this through special instructional programs.

6. One of the byproducts of restricted mobility and limited experience can be a passive orientation to life. Teachers play a critical role in helping students with visual impairments be active and independent.

7. A growing number of children with visual impairments are being included in public school programs.

8. The educational program for students with visual disabilities should emphasize concrete learning, unifying experiences, and learning by doing, or directly teaching things that children with vision learn independently.

9. It is important for parents and teachers to help children with visual disabilities develop their skills. It is equally important to let these children do things for themselves and to experience as much as possible the things that sighted children experience.

10. The development of programs that will deliver services to children with developmental problems from birth on promises valuable early assistance to children with visual impairments and their families.

11. The many needs of students with visual impairments demand a continuum of special services, from preschool programs to special schools.

12. The trend toward mainstreaming or inclusion of children with disabilities has left many youngsters with visual disabilities without the special skills training they need to live independently.

13. Braille reading is slower than regular reading, and this fact affects the academic performance of students with profound visual impairments.

14. Orientation and mobility training are critically important parts of the curriculum for children with visual disabilities.

15. Technology is improving the means of communication and the mobility of those with visual disabilities. It has also broadened their occupational choices. Keyboarding and word processing are particularly useful skills for school and society.

Unresolved Issues

1. *Multiple disabilities.* The growing number of children who have two or more handicaps presents a serious issue for the schools. Some youngsters with visual impairments are either mentally retarded or deaf, or they have special learning or motor problems as well. We have to adapt educational programs to accommodate children with multiple disabilities, an adjustment that complicates an already serious challenge.

2. *Making technology accessible.* Technology is wonderful—when it is usable. The widespread distribution of technological developments for those with visual disabilities has been impeded by the cost and size of equipment. In the same way, we have to increase accessibility to the computers and word processors that are transforming the academic and work worlds of those with visual disabilities.

3. *Reform.* The new educational reform movement, which emphasizes the inclusion of students of all levels of ability and performance, places a special responsibility on general and special education teachers to operate as a team to provide services for children with visual disabilities.

Key Terms

accommodation p. 415
braille p. 438
case manager p. 434
ciliary muscles p. 415
convergence p. 415
cornea p. 414
extrinsic muscles p. 415
fading p. 424
hyperopia p. 415
iris p. 414
lens p. 414
moderate visual disability p. 413

myopia p. 415
object permanence p. 423
orientation and mobility (O&M) p. 442
profound visual disability p. 413
pupil p. 414
retina p. 414
retinoblastoma p. 417
retinopathy of prematurity p. 417
sensory compensation p. 419
severe visual disability p. 413
service coordinator p. 434
synthetic speech p. 455

Questions for Thought

1. Differentiate among moderate, severe, and profound visual disability.   p. 413

2. Describe these two causes of blindness: rubella and retinopathy of prematurity.   p. 417

3. Why is lack of vision both a primary disability and a condition that can hamper cognitive development?   pp. 417–418

4. How does a visual impairment impede the development of language?   p. 418

5. What effect do restricted mobility and consequent limited experiences have on the personal and social adjustment of children with visual disabilities?   pp. 419–421

6. When and how should preschoolers be screened for vision problems?   pp. 425–426

7. Briefly describe Lowenfeld's three general principles for adapting instruction to the educational needs of children who are visually impaired (concreteness, unifying experiences, and learning by doing).   p. 428

8. What are the key components of an effective program to integrate students with visual disabilities into general education classes?   pp. 429–430.

9. How are models used to help children who are visually impaired master their environment?   p. 442

10. List three devices that expand the communication capabilities of those with visual disabilities and three that affect their mobility.   pp. 438–445

References of Special Interest

Barraga, N., & Erin, J. (1992). *Visual handicaps and learning.* (3rd Edition). Austin, TX: Pro-Ed.

> A comprehensive, readable introduction to the problems of schoolchildren who have visual disabilities, this book provides good discussions of the impact of visual impairment on children, ways to conduct comprehensive assessments of individual children, and the nature of differential programming.

Dunlea, A. (1989). *Vision and the emergence of meaning.* New York: Cambridge University Press.

> This book analyzes in detail early language development in a group of children who are blind, partially sighted, and fully sighted. It indicates the convergence of conceptual development and early language.

Olmstead, J. (1991). *Itinerant teaching: Tricks of the trade for teachers of blind and visually impaired students.* New York: American Foundation for the Blind.

> This book is a detailed account of the role played by the itinerant teacher who serves in a supporting role to other teachers providing services to children with visual disabilities. It includes tips to improve integration for these children and shows how to organize services and consultation and how to help with the development of the individualized education program. It is a practical and informative publication.

Sacks, S., Kekelis, L., & Gaylord-Ross, R. (1992). *The development of social skills by blind and visually impaired students*. New York: American Foundation for the Blind.

> The eventual success or failure of an adult with visual impairments will rest in no small measure on the person's ability to form reasonable social relationships with other persons. This book provides an explanation of why it is so difficult for children with visual impairments to form effective social relationships and suggests useful intervention strategies. The authors demonstrate why the teaching of social skills is an integral part of the curriculum for visually impaired students.

Scholl, G. (Ed.). (1986). *Foundations of education for blind and visually handicapped children and youth*. New York: American Foundation for the Blind.

> This comprehensive volume incorporates much of the existing knowledge about educating children with visual disabilities. A large number of experts have contributed chapters in their own areas of expertise, and major sections are included on definitions, development and theory, the components of a quality educational program, and special curricula. The book stresses educational issues related to children with visual disabilities and raises curriculum issues of substantial importance to the special education community. It is an essential volume for those who want to educate themselves in this increasingly complex area.

Swallow, R., & Heubner, K. (Eds.). (1987). *How to thrive, not just survive*. New York: American Foundation for the Blind.

> This book is a guide to the development of independent living skills for children and youth who are blind and have visual impairments. It is a collection of suggestions from a large number of professionals who recognize that the curriculum for children who are visually impaired should go far beyond reading and arithmetic, to include daily living skills (eating, toileting, dressing, orientation, etiquette). The book is directed to both teachers and parents and is filled with practical suggestions for helping these children learn independent living skills.

Warren, D. (1994). *Blindness and children: An individual differences approach*. New York: Cambridge University Press.

> In this excellent review of what we know from research and scholarly review on the education of children with visual impairments, Warren reviews three major areas: the child's interaction with the physical world, the acquisition of cognitive skills, and adapting to the social world. A separate section surveys what longitudinal studies have told us. The reference section is a valuable source for those seeking to understand these students.

chapter 11

Children with Multiple and Severe Disabilities

focusing questions

Why is it necessary to determine the degree of functioning for each disability of a person with multiple and severe disabilities?

How is a dual diagnosis often made inappropriately?

Why are age-appropriate activities so important for students with severe disabilities?

Why is the curriculum for persons with multiple and severe disabilities so often a variation of the regular curriculum?

Throughout this text, we emphasize that children with disabilities do not always fit neatly into well-defined categories. There are individual differences among children with hearing, visual, cognitive, and emotional impairments. We also find children who have more than one impairment and children who are severely disabled. These youngsters are even more heterogeneous than other exceptional children.

This chapter focuses on children with disabilities that we also discuss in other chapters of this book. But the children who are the subject of this chapter have multiple disabilities (more than one), and the disabilities are so severe that the child needs some type of support for the rest of his or her life. Such support might include a driver for transportation, a companion to provide assistance in feeding or toileting, or a job coach working in the community.

Understand that not all of the individuals who have multiple disabilities are mentally retarded. Persons with multiple disabilities vary widely in cognitive abilities. Some have profound mental retardation and will need continuous caregiving to meet their needs. Some have disabilities so severe that they will never learn a language. A cognitively gifted child who is spastic may not be able to control his muscle movements. This individual may need assistance in controlling his body movements to be able to type to express his thoughts.

Andrew Rothstein, superintendent of the Henry Viscardi School for persons with physical disabilities and low-incidence disabilities, has suggested the classification shown in Table 11.1 when educating persons with multiple and severe disabilities.

If they are provided with early intervention and appropriate education and therapies, individuals in the first group—those with mild physical and mental disabilities—are able to attain full educational experiences, including college and independent living and working experiences. Individuals in the second group—those with severe physical disabilities but high cognitive abilities—need extensive therapies and probably prostheses in the form of wheelchairs, crutches, or leg

TABLE 11.1	**Examples of Multiple and Severe Disabilities**	
	Intellectual Capacity	
Physical Disability	**High**	**Low**
Low	1. Example: High cognitive functioning and mild cerebral palsy.	3. Example: Low cognitive functioning and mild cerebral palsy
High	2. Example: Severe cerebral palsy and high functional cognitive abilities	4. Example: Severe cognitive dysfunction and severe cerebral palsy

braces, and they may not be able to control their motor movements. To communicate, these children need augmented and alternative communication devices (computers, typewriters, and other devices). They are capable of completing their education and living independent lives with some support.

Individuals in the third group—those with mild physical disabilities and low cognitive abilities—require some physical therapies, but the degree of their retardation may limit their work experiences to activities supervised by a job coach. Those in the fourth group have such severe and multiple disabilities, including retardation, that they may never learn a symbol system (sign or vocal language), but they can learn to make requests and indicate refusal through gestures, facial expressions, body movements, and other nonverbal forms of communication (Brodalt, Gothelf, Crimmins, Mercer, & Finnochiaro, 1994; Dunst & Lowe, 1986). These persons require early and continuous intervention to enable them to live as fully as possible.

A Note About Terminology

In the field of multiple and severe disabilities, major advances have been made in recent years. Specialists in this field hold different opinions about the language to use to describe the individuals they serve. Clearly, throughout this book we favor terminology that reflects a humanistic, "people first" approach to writing about persons with disabilities—using, for example, the term *individual with cerebral palsy* rather than *cerebral palsy child*.

As the field of multiple and severe disabilities moves in the direction of nondiscriminatory language, professionals often disagree about what terms are appropriate. One example may serve to clarify this issue. The term *deaf-blind* is commonly used to refer to persons with both vision and hearing impairments, and it is used in federal legislation. However, 93.8 percent of individuals who are deaf-blind have either residual hearing or residual sight (Baldwin, 1993). Baldwin (1993) and others proposed the term *dual-sensory impairments* as a more accurate description of those with one or more disabilities of this nature. Some, however, want to do away with the *dual* designation and replace it with the all-purpose term *multiple-sensory impairments* (Meyer, Peck, & Brown, 1991). Although that form may be acceptable, it implies that the disabilities are in the senses (vision, hearing, touch, smell, and taste) and excludes disabilities such as malfunctioning of the brain, and the inability to learn, which are usually referred to as cognition. Cognition depends on sensory input, but it is not a sensory system.

Many of the references that we consulted for this chapter were published before changes in terminology were implemented. Thus, some of the quotations that we use here contain expressions no longer in widespread use among professionals in the field.

In any new movement, some individuals go to extremes, overusing language that has specific meanings and using words inaccurately. One example is the term *friendship* and the desirability of persons with multiple and severe disabilities being able to make friends by being included in regular classrooms. Friendship implies the establishment of intimacy, trust, secret-sharing, and loyalty. Some individuals with

Because children with severe disabilities have physical, cognitive, or emotional problems of an intense nature, they almost always require services beyond those traditionally offered by regular and special education programs. (© *Jerry Howard/Positive Images*)

multiple disabilities who do not possess a spoken or gestural language may be able to establish relationships with disabled and nondisabled people, but these are not friendships in the full sense. The individual with multiple disabilities may be able to produce a smile of recognition and allow another person to assist him or her. We call this interaction a *relationship*. Certainly, the distinction between friendship and relationship need not diminish the goals of allowing students with severe disabilities to be educated in regular classrooms and to interact with and relate to others in the school and the community.

One further issue: The words *train* and *teach* are synonyms. *Teach* is more widely preferred because it refers to any act of communication that imparts knowledge or skills. *Train* implies a concentration on particular skills intended to prepare a person for a desired role. Although the word *train* is more widely accepted in sports and the acquisition of physical skills, there is a movement in the field of multiple disabilities to use only the word *teach*, for some individuals in the field consider the word *train* demeaning. Accordingly, we avoid the use of the word *train* in this chapter.

Definition

Children with multiple and severe disabilities possess such a diverse combination of characteristics that it is difficult to give a succinct statement that includes them all.

Probably the most useful definition is the one adopted by the organization most concerned with this group of people and their families: The Association for Persons with Severe Handicaps (TASH). The definition accepted by TASH is as follows:

> Persons with severe handicaps include individuals of all ages who require extensive ongoing support in more than one life activity in order to participate in integrated community settings and to enjoy a quality of life that is available to citizens with fewer or no disabilities. Support may be required for life activities such as mobility, communication, self-care, and learning as necessary for independent living, employment, and self-sufficiency. (original Bureau for the Education of the Handicapped, April 1985; revised and adopted by TASH, December 1985, and revised November 1986; see Meyer, Peck, & Brown, 1991, p. 19)

Many children with severe disabilities have normal intelligence or are gifted.

In recent years The Association for Persons with Severe Handicaps changed its name to Association for Persons with Severe Disabilities. The name change indicates the rapid changes in terminology occurring in the field and the movement toward the use of nondiscriminatory language. The term *disability* refers to the state of the individual—that is, persons with vision, hearing, or other impairments. The term *handicapped* refers to environmental conditions that restrict a person with disabilities, such as lack of ramps or elevators for persons who use wheelchairs for mobility. This chapter is concerned with persons who have *multiple and severe disabilities*.

Fewell and Cone (1983) wrote that any definition of individuals with multiple and severe disabilities would "certainly include children often classified as deaf-blind, multiply disabled, autistic, schizophrenic, and mentally retarded, but in no way would it be limited to these groups" (p. 47). We should add that children who are severely retarded generally have other disabilities and are considered to be multiply disabled. However, not all children with multiple disabilities, or even with one severe disability, are mentally retarded. The motion picture *My Left Foot* (available on videocassette) tells the story of Christy Brown, a severely spastic man with cerebral palsy but without mental retardation, who learned to type with one toe and wrote several books (Brown, 1972). It took a long time for those in Brown's environment to realize that he had not multiple disabilities but one severe disability that almost completely disrupted his functioning. Fortunately, he received specialized assistance that allowed him to express his innate intelligence.

Note also that most multiple disabilities are disabilities that are considered sensory deficits, brain malfunctioning, or genetic disorders that interfere with the normal progression of development of cognitive, social, and physical skills.

■■■ *Prevalence of Multiple and Severe Disabilities*

It has been found that where one disability is present, the likelihood is high that an additional disability is also present (Shea, 1983). Teachers usually do not have many of these children in regular classes. They may encounter one or two children with physical disabilities or speech or language problems, or perhaps a child who is gifted and who has visual and hearing losses. Most of these children require so much specialized treatment that often they are educated either in special education classes in regular schools with a great deal of professional support from a multidisciplinary team (see Table 11.5 on p. 484) or in special schools.

Meyer (1991) suggested that students who have multiple disabilities account for only one-half of 1 percent of the total special education population. In 1983, the *Federal Register* reported that 67,539 individuals were receiving special education. Of that group, only 0.07 percent were considered to have multiple and severe disabilities (Evans, 1991).

Baldwin (1993) reported that there are 8,379 persons who are deaf-blind throughout the nation. He suspected that, because of underreporting, a more realistic total is between 7,657 and 12,274. Baldwin (1993) also reported that 2 out of every 1,000 individuals receiving special education have dual sensory impairments.

Causes of Multiple and Severe Disabilities

A discussion of causes of multiple and severe disabilities could go on at great length, for many conditions cause these problems, and many of these problems are rare. For example, as of the early 1990s, only five children had ever been diagnosed with Leigh disease, which causes widespread damage to the central nervous system, particularly to the brainstem (Behrman, Vaughn, & Nelson, 1987). These children appear normal at birth but then begin to exhibit weight loss, seizures, loss of vision, and severe retardation during the second year of life. After the onset of the disease, they may survive for a few weeks or for many years. Most low-incidence disorders—there are more than a thousand (Kopp, 1983)—are not highlighted in this text, but descriptions can be found in Behrman, Vaughn, and Nelson (1987). See Table 11.2 for a sampling of causes of multiple disabilities.

A number of things may cause multiple and severe disabilities: genes passed to the child by one or both parents; a negative influence during pregnancy, such as the mother's use of alcohol or harmful drugs; or events that occur during birth, such as breech birth (emerging feet first) or anoxia (lack of oxygen during birth). After birth, accidents or child abuse can cause multiple and severe disabilities (Cohen & Warren, 1987).

Characteristics of Children with Multiple and Severe Disabilities

In this section, we discuss some (not all) of the *major* categories in which the largest numbers of children with multiple and severe disabilities are found, including autism, deaf-blindness, behavior disturbance and hearing impairment, and mental retardation.

TABLE 11.2	Causes of Multiple Handicaps		
Time of Injury	**Affecting Agent**	**Agent Activity**	**Typical Results**
Conception	Genetic disorder; inherited; inborn errors of metabolism	Serious change in embryo and fetus; inability to carry out normal metabolic processes	Down syndrome; Tay Sachs; many other disorders that if untreated will lead to severe mental retardation
Prenatal	Mother has German measles or other viral infection; uses toxic substances (crack, heroin); or has RH blood incompatibility	Interferes with development of central nervous system	Visual, hearing, and motor impairments; mental retardation
Natal	Anoxia	Destroys brain cells	Cerebral palsy, mental retardation, and other defects
	Low birth weight (less than 5.5 lb); prematurity	Immature organism not ready for environmental stimulation	From normal to severe mental retardation and disabilities
	Very low birth weight (less than 3 lb)	Damage to brain organization	From normal to severe and profound disabilities
Postnatal	Encephalitis, meningitis, physical abuse	Damage to brain cells	Epilepsy, mental retardation, motor disabilities

AUTISM AND PERVASIVE DEVELOPMENTAL DISORDERS (NOS)

Autism and pervasive developmental disorders (not otherwise specified [NOS]) are two heterogeneous categories of developmental disabilities that are difficult to pinpoint because their origin is unknown. The disorders in both categories are neurological disorders that lead to deficits in the child's ability to communicate, understand language, play, develop social skills, and relate to others (NICHCY, 1994). The Individuals with Disabilities Education Act (IDEA) defines **autism** as a developmental disability significantly affecting verbal and non-verbal communication and social interaction usually evident before age 3, that adversely affects a child's educational performance. Other characteristics often associated with autism are engagement in repetitive activities and stereotyped movement, resistance to environmental change or change in daily routines, and unusual sensory experiences. (NICHCY, 1994, p. 1)

Three main groups can be identified: (1) infantile autism, (2) childhood onset of pervasive developmental disorder (after 30 months of age), and (3) atypical pervasive developmental disorder.

There are major disagreements in the field about the cause of autism. At one time, most professionals believed autism was caused by the mother's coolness and by emotional problems in the home. But few accept those theories today. Schopler and Bristol (1980) provided what is still an accurate summary of what we know about the causes of autism:

- For individual children the specific causes are usually unknown.
- There is probably no single underlying cause to account for autism; instead, there are probably multiple causes.
- Most likely the primary causes involve some form of brain abnormality or biochemical imbalance that impairs perception and understanding.

Based on their work with people with autism, Johnson and Koegel (1982) found that some individuals with the disorder

- Are unable to relate to others
- Have impaired or delayed speech and language and often repeat phrases again and again (echolalia)
- Show sensory disabilities and often are overresponsive or underresponsive to light, noise, touch, or pain
- Exhibit either inappropriate behavior (serious, prolonged temper tantrums) or flat affect
- Engage in repetitive self-stimulatory behaviors that can interfere notably with learning
- Fail to develop normal, appropriate play behaviors
- Exhibit obsessive ritualistic behaviors that make these individuals extremely resistant to change

Autism is one of the least understood of all disabilities.

The overall effect of these behaviors may be extremely upsetting to the family and individuals in the community.

Some individuals who are classified as autistic have high cognitive abilities that are undermined by their other behaviors and lack of language (Atwood, 1993). Several adults with autism have written books about their lives and how they perceive their problem (Williams, 1993). Williams writes that "none of us fit the stereotype" and suggests that persons who are classified as autistic have more personal, social, and written language skills than they have functional verbal skills (p. 196).

Autistic children are often withdrawn and unresponsive, but teachers and parents can reach them through a structured early educational program focusing on applied behavioral analysis and reinforcement in both school and home settings. (© Michael Weisbrot)

Many children with autism can attain normal cognitive functioning by age 7.

In an interesting book, a mother noted that her normally developing children "became" autistic between 18 and 22 months of age, displaying many of the behaviors associated with autism (Maurice, 1993). After many diagnoses and reviews by specialized personnel, she adopted Louvas's (1987) Applied Behavior Approach and with the assistance of trained personnel was able to return her children to normal development by ages 4 to 5. In his study, Louvas demonstrated that many children with autism could attain cognitive functioning by age 7. A follow-up study conducted when these children were 13 found that they had maintained the treatment gain (Eichen, Smith, & Louvas, 1994).

Note that the mother (family and support team) was successful with her two children, but Louvas was successful with slightly less than half of his sample. Some children with autism are capable of attaining "normal" functioning, but others are not. A puzzling question is how to treat those who do not respond to treatment. In essence, the most difficult question in the treatment of autism is yet to be answered. It is most likely that autism is a heterogeneous classification with subtypes not yet identified. The debate concerning facilitative communication is a good example of a technique that may work for some persons with autism but not for all persons with autism. (see whole volume TASH, Vol. 19, Fall 1994). Some children may be reached through this technique; some may not (see Chapter 8 for a discussion of facilitative communications).

Auditory integration training (AIT) is a form of treatment for children with autism and children with hypersensitive hearing. It requires the person to listen to the full range of sound frequencies for a minimum of ten hours (Rimland & Edelson,

1994). Behavioral improvements have been demonstrated, and the results are promising though not proven.

Teachers who work with children with autism find that the families of these children differ as much as the children do in their needs and abilities. Individual programs need to be developed to meet family needs as well as the needs of children with autism. Like many other disabilities, autism varies in form and severity.

DEAF-BLIND IMPAIRMENT

IDEA (PL 101-476) defines children who are deaf-blind functionally as

> having circulatory and visual impairments, the combination of which creates such severe communication and other developmental and learning needs that they cannot be appropriately educated in special education programs solely for children and youth with hearing impairments, visual impairments or severe disabilities, without supplementary assistance to address the educational needs due to these dual concurrent disabilities. (PL 101-476, 20 U.S.C. Chapter 33, Section 1422 [2]; see Everson, 1995, p. 6)

The Helen Keller National Center defines **deaf-blind** more specifically as someone

> (1) with central vision acuity of 20/200 or worse in the better eye with corrective lenses and/or a visual field of 20 degrees or less in the better eye . . . or with a progressive visual loss . . . ; (2) who has either a chronic hearing impairment so severe that most speech cannot be understood . . . ; (3) and for whom the combination of impairments . . . causes extreme difficulty in daily life activities . . . (Everson, 1995)

Common causes of deaf-blindness are listed in Table 11.3.

When one of the two major systems that bring information to the child is impaired, the special education program emphasizes the unimpaired sense. For the child who is hearing impaired, the visual channel is used to establish a communication system based on signing, finger spelling, picture communication systems, and lip reading. For the child who is visually handicapped, the program uses auditory aids to help compensate for the visual-channel problem.

In the education of children and adolescents who are deaf-blind, the focus has changed from multistate centers to allowing states to develop their own programs. The states are now responsible for both the education of youngsters with deaf-blind impairments and the transition of young adults (ages 22 and older) "from education to employment," including "vocational, independent living, and other postsecondary services" (U.S. Department of Education, 1985, pp. 2–3). These programs have brought comprehensive diagnostic processes and facilities and qualified personnel in contact with children and adolescents who are deaf and blind.

Concern for the infant who is deaf-blind begins with the family. A major disruption has occurred in the lives of these children. It should be met by the family, who will help establish realistic goals for the child and initiate special instructional techniques consistently (Murphy, 1983, p. 21). Visual evaluation and intervention are critical for infants who are deaf-blind for two main reasons: Efficient vision

TABLE 11.3	Common Syndromes Causing Deaf-Blindness
Syndromes	**Characteristics and Possible Medical and Health Care Concerns**
Congenital rubella syndrome (CRS)	• Visual defects (e.g., congenital cataracts; late-onset glaucoma; detached retina, possibly from self-injurious behaviors) • Congenital heart defects • Sensorineural severe to profound hearing loss • Diabetes • Hypertension • Mental retardation • (Rare) progressive rubella panencephalitis (PRP)—a slow, progressive, neurological deterioration with seizures, behavior outbursts, ataxia, and dementia
Usher syndrome	• *Type 1:* profound congenital hearing loss and retinitis pigmentosa (RP) • Abnormal vestibular functioning (poor balance) • Early childhood rod loss in retina (poor night vision) • Early teenage cone loss on sides of retina (peripheral field loss or "tunnel vision") • *Type II:* moderate to severe congenital hearing loss and retinitis pigmentosa • Early childhood to adolescent rod loss in retina (poor night vision) • Early teenage cone loss on sides of retina (peripheral field loss or "tunnel vision") • *Types III and IV:* less common than Types I or II; characterized by progressive hearing loss with symptoms of RP manifesting before adolescence; may be referred to as Hallgren syndrome • *Type IV:* characterized by moderate to severe hearing loss with symptoms of RP manifesting after adolescence (similar to Type II, but only occurring in males); may also be referred to as Laurence-Moon-Bardet-Biedl syndrome • Psychological concerns (e.g., depression) have been associated with Usher syndrome
Alstrom syndrome	• Atypical retinal degeneration resulting in a progressive and nearly total loss of central vision in early childhood • Congenital hearing loss beginning in early childhood and progressing through early adulthood • Diabetes • Obesity • Renal disease
Bardet-Biedl syndrome	• Retinitis pigmentosa • Hypogenitalism • Polysyndactyly • Mental retardation (usually mild) • Obesity • Congenital mild to severe hearing loss (sometimes progressive) • Urinary tract infections • Heart defects

TABLE 11.3	Common Syndromes Causing Deaf-Blindness (Cont.)
Syndromes	**Characteristics and Possible Medical and Health Care Concerns**
CHARGE association	• C = Colomba (incomplete fusion of the retina, iris, or optic nerve) • H = Congenital heart defects • A = Atresia choanae (blockage of the nasal passage) • R = Retarded growth and development • G = Genital and urinary tract abnormalities • E = Ear defects (e.g., abnormal ear development resulting in chronic ear infections, conductive hearing losses, sensorineural hearing losses, and/or central auditory processing problems) • Mental retardation • Cleft lip/palate

Source: N. Armstrong, T. Carr, J. Houghton, J. Belanich, and J. Mascia (1995). Supporting medical and health concerns of young adults who are deaf-blind. In J. Everson (Ed.), *Supporting Young Children Who Are Deaf-Blind in Their Communities: A Transition Planning Guide for Service Providers, Families, and Friends,* (p. 44, Table 3.1). Baltimore: Paul H. Brookes Publishing Co. P.O. Box 10624, Baltimore, M.D. 21285-0624. Reprinted with permission.

An infant who is deaf-blind needs to realize that he or she has needs.

use is important for learning, and visual functioning can be improved (Michael & Paul, 1990–1991, p. 201).

The first step with any individual, and particularly one who is multiply disabled, is to help the child maintain sufficiently focused attention to realize the following: (1) he or she exists; (2) others exist; (3) he or she has needs; (4) these needs can be met; (5) some of the needs will be met by himself or herself; and (6) some, if not most, of these needs will be met by others (Murphy & Byrne, 1983, p. 355). This is the genetic sequence of the development of the self. Many infants who possess deaf-blind impairments can go beyond point 6 and, as they develop, begin to meet many, if not most, of their own needs.

The key to all development is to begin joint attention—that is, transaction between the caregiver (usually the mother) and the infant (Donnellan, Mirender, Mesaros, & Fassbinder, 1984, p. 34). With the infant who is deaf-blind, this joint attention begins through touch. As communication develops through touch, it is augmented by any residual hearing or vision through the use of hearing aids and glasses or the more recently developed sonic directional devices that give the infant vibrational feedback about the location of objects (Bower, 1989).

Without intervention, infants who are deaf-blind focus on their own bodies and show little interest in object use. They do little exploration of the environment and resist new stimuli, becoming prone to self-stimulation (Taylor, 1988).

In addition, changes occur as the brain matures, and a child without the ability to see or hear is deprived of normal sensory stimulation that facilitates normal growth. Without early intervention to offset these lacks, the changes in the brain are degenerative and abnormal (Murphy & Byrne, 1983). Thus, immediate programming is needed for these children as soon as their condition is diagnosed.

The key to development is the transaction between the child and caregiver. (© *Mimi Forsyth/ Monkmeyer Press Photo Service*)

One early intervention approach that has been particularly successful with children who are deaf-blind is the Van Dijk method. The Van Dijk method is a movement-based approach that considers the sensorimotor experiences to be the foundation of all learning (Writer, 1987, p. 191). The aim is to enhance the quality of the child's interaction with people and objects. Van Dijk proposed that through body contact with others, children who are deaf-blind learn that they are separate persons and that other people are present in the environment. In addition, Van Dikj suggested that children with disabilities need to learn that their movements can affect others, a process he calls *resonance* (Van Dijk, 1986).

The Van Dijk method attempts to move the child through stages from signals by means of gestures to speech or signs (Writer, 1987). Caregiver-child interactions are important, for they constitute the beginning of the child's communication with the outer world. From this point, children with visual and hearing defects proceed through the normal stages of prelinguistic communication (see the section on normal development later in the chapter). Siegel-Causey and Guen (1985) adapted Van Dijk's system to teach prelinguistic behaviors to those with multiple and severe disabilities. Writer (1987) provided a full description of the Van Dijk method and positive outcomes in communication gains that children with multiple disabilities, particularly those who are deaf-blind, have made. Several authors in Everson (1995) recommend and suggest ways in which the person who is deaf-blind can be integrated into community settings and receive the job training necessary to become successfully employed (Everson, Burwell, & Killan, 1995).

Table 11.4 presents guidelines for vocational training. IDEA mandates transitional services, goals, and objectives for the individualized education program

TABLE 11.4	Jobsite Training Guidelines for Individuals Who Are Deaf-Blind

1. Always orient the worker to the setting, materials, and activities.
2. Ensure optimal positioning for efficient use of residual auditory and visual skills.
3. Always use task analyses to test and teach specific and related job skills.
4. Although it is always most desirable to have a worker respond to naturally occurring stimuli, for most individuals who are deaf-blind and have multiple impairments, it may be more efficient to provide a planned system of prompts and cues.
5. Selection of prompts and cues should consider types of visual and hearing losses, amount and extent of residual hearing and/or vision, age of onset of sensory losses, communication systems, and related disabilities (if any).
6. Prompts and cues include visual or tactual signed instruction, tactual cues, enhanced visual and/or auditory cues, model prompts, physical prompts, large print or braille cues, enlarged photographs, low vision aids, hearing aids, assistive listening devices, and other assistive technology.
7. Prompts and cues should be defined as permanent or temporary. All temporary cues and prompts should be faded along with the job coach or other employment personnel. Before presenting a temporary cue or prompt, know how you are going to fade it! Before presenting a permanent cue or prompt, ensure that it is site and age appropriate.
8. Choose an instructional format that includes a system of least-to-most intrusive prompts and/or time delay combined with whole task instruction, backward chaining, or forward chaining.
9. For individuals who have significant visual impairments or are blind but have some residual hearing, combine auditory prompts with tactual cues and prompts.
10. For individuals who have profound hearing losses or are deaf but have some residual vision, combine signed instruction with model prompts, enlarged visual cues, and physical prompts.
11. For individuals who are profoundly deaf and legally blind, combine tactual instruction and cues with physical (hand-over-hand) prompts.

Source: J. Everson, J. Burwell, and S. Killan (1995). Working and contributing to one's community. In J. Everson (Ed.), *Supporting Young Children Who Are Deaf-Blind in Their Communities: A Transition Planning Guide for Service Providers, Families, and Friends,* (p. 167, Table 7.2). Baltimore: Paul H. Brookes Publishing Co. P.O. Box 10624, Baltimore, M.D. 21285-0624. Reprinted with permission.

(IEP) of students who are deaf-blind. These IEPs should be outcome-oriented process objectives that promote movement from school to postschool activities (Everson, 1995).

BEHAVIOR DISTURBANCE AND HEARING IMPAIRMENT

A child with both a hearing loss and behavioral difficulties may have developed the behavioral problems because of the lack of environmental input resulting from the sensory disability.

Nothing inherent in a hearing deficit should create additional social or psychological problems (Schlesinger, 1983, p. 83). Most of the social and psychological problems found in persons with hearing deficits are secondary outgrowths of their lack of hearing in a speech-dominated world. Thus, Fredericks and Baldwin (1987) suggested that the term *dual diagnosis* be used with great care because an individual may have only one disability with secondary characteristics growing out of the lack of environmental input from the sensory disability.

Unfortunately, many children with hearing impairments have behavior problems. Many researchers believe that the secondary problem can be avoided if intervention is begun early and the strengths of the child are reinforced (Mencher & Gerber, 1983). Children who are deaf-blind and whose parents are deaf tend to have fewer problems than children who are deaf and whose parents have normal hearing (Moores, 1996).

Part of the problem for children with hearing losses is that so much of what they cannot hear they can feel vibrationally or see in shadow movements in the environment around them. This causes them to become confused and frustrated and to act out in consequence. Teaching caregivers to look at and explain by gesture, signing, or pointing to the event for the hearing-impaired child can keep some of the challenging behaviors from occurring. The aim of many intervention programs is to teach signing at an early age, so that the child who is deaf can communicate with others and therefore not be isolated.

In the past, many students with hearing losses were separated from their families and put into residential facilities. The intent was to promote their growth through intensive development of the visual and auditory skills. But separating a child from his or her family is likely to disrupt the development of the attachment system between child and caregiver, and this is one of the most common sources of emotional problems (Sroufe, 1979).

MENTAL RETARDATION WITH ANOTHER DISABILITY

In Chapter 5 we noted that a major problem for children who are mentally retarded is the slowness with which they learn or retain what they have learned. When this slowness is combined with other problems, the difficulty of teaching these children is compounded. Many special educators are very concerned with the excessive use of the term *dual diagnosis* to classify individuals, particularly those with mental retardation.

A child who has a hearing loss may be classified as mentally retarded because of a lack of appropriate teaching, not a lack of intelligence.

Some children do have more than one disability; an individual with a hearing loss may also possess mental retardation. However, a careful and appropriate assessment of a child with a hearing loss may reveal that the child's poor performance is due to the hearing loss and not to poor cognitive functioning. In other words, the second (or dual) disability is an outgrowth of the first disability. The child's low score on a standardized test may reflect that she is not able to accurately hear spoken language, or that she uses a sign language but the test was administered orally.

One of the Association for Persons with Severe Disabilities' major concerns is the faulty assumption that persons with mental retardation are mentally ill—an assumption based on these individuals' challenging behaviors. Individuals with mental retardation are prone to magical thinking and confusion of reality because of their cognitive deficits, but this is not mental illness (Menolasino, Levitas, & Greimer, 1986).

Persons with limited cognitive abilities also tend to be very rule oriented and rigid, applying a rule to all situations rather than being flexible. For example, a person with mental retardation who learns to open a door by pushing it may push all doors, even those that need to be pulled or to have a knob turned.

A teacher may believe that a person with mental retardation who is not following directions in the classroom is actively resisting the teacher's effort or is emotionally disturbed to the point of being unable to relate to reality. The teacher should investigate, however, whether the child is instead depressed because of his or her inability to understand instruction. The teacher can ask the parents if the child has poor sleep habits, has a poor appetite, and is generally sad and listless. If so, the child may need to be treated for depression and receive training in social skills to help solve what must be terrible emotional feelings beyond the cognitive understanding of a person with mental retardation (Evans, 1991).

In those examples, there is only one disorder, and the behaviors are an outgrowth of that disorder, not a separate disability. If there are separate disabilities, the treatment program must be very different, because it is necessary to treat both syndromes rather than to work on the complexities of one.

MENTAL RETARDATION AND CEREBRAL PALSY

People tend to assume that children with cerebral palsy are mentally retarded. A relationship does exist between the two conditions. Whatever genetic or environmental insult damages the motor control centers of the central nervous system sufficiently to cause **cerebral palsy** can cause enough damage to the cerebral cortex to create retardation. But the relationship is not universal.

Standardized intelligence testing often does not take into account a child's disability.

It is hard to justify a diagnosis of mental retardation in youngsters with cerebral palsy if we are using intelligence tests that are normed on children with adequate speech, language, and motor abilities. Many children with cerebral palsy have expressive problems in both speech and psychomotor areas. Their test results, then, are not necessarily valid. All we can conclude is that when these children are tested with instruments normed on other populations, about half of them show intelligence quotient (IQ) scores below 70 or 80. However, IQ tests have serious limitations in terms of evaluating children with multiple disabilities.

Often the poor speech and spastic movements of children with cerebral palsy give the layperson the impression that these individuals are mentally retarded. Actually, there is little relationship between the degree of physical impairment and intelligence in children with cerebral palsy. A child who is severely spastic may be intellectually gifted; another with mild physical involvement may be severely retarded. The assessment of mental retardation in children with cerebral palsy is extremely difficult and may take months. If after prolonged appropriate instruction a child does not make relatively average progress in most areas, a diagnosis of mental retardation may be valid. Recall, however, the motion picture *My Left Foot*, based on a book by Brown (1972), who, though severely spastic, learned to type with his toe and revealed a vast and poetic intelligence.

Although IQ tests—the most common instruments used to determine retardation—are inappropriate for those with disabilities in speech and motor areas, the

Parents and therapists need to teach children with severe disabilities to turn outward from their internal world to the outer world of the environment and other people for stimulation. (© Jerry Howard/Positive Images)

subtest scores on an IQ test can reveal more about a child's strengths than the total or derived score reveals. Thus, we find these subtest scores helpful when we must design an individualized teaching strategy to capitalize on those strengths (Boothroyd, 1983, p. 146). Keep in mind that most of the current remedial efforts in speech education focus on the children's strengths, not their weaknesses.

To assess adequately whether retardation exists, we need to be sure that whatever test of intelligence yields information on how to provide an intervention design that will lead to an outcome better than the outcome of an intervention design that we constructed solely on the basis of observation (Evans, 1991, p. 40).

Early Intervention

Parents and teachers need to teach these children how to transact with the world.

A critical need of children with multiple and severe disabilities is early intervention so that the parents can provide appropriate and consistent care. Parents and therapists need to help the child with severe disabilities recognize that he or she is a person in an environment. The adults need to teach the child to turn outward from his or her internal world to the external world of the environment and other people for stimulation. If they do not, these children tend to respond to internal rather than external stimuli and use their genetic capacity for curiosity to explore by manipulating their internal world through body movements. As Murphy (1983) wrote, once children fail to turn outward to the environment, it is almost impossible to get them to respond to the world around them. In addition, the child who responds to his or her internal world is likely to develop self-stimulating behaviors, some of which, such as head banging and eye poking, can be physically, psychologically, and socially damaging to the child and hard to eliminate.

An excellent example of this pattern is described in the work of Fraiberg (1977), who found that infants who are blind who were institutionalized appeared to be mentally retarded and developed problematic self-stimulating behaviors. On the other hand, children who are blind who were reared in regular homes and received ample physical stimulation did not develop these behaviors, and most were cognitively normal.

Considerable evaluation is required to determine the nature of the impairment and the kind of intervention needed to help the child function as effectively as possible. These evaluations have to be conducted periodically by a multidisciplinary team to determine if progress is being made and what changes, if any, are needed in the intervention process. Table 11.5 shows the types of professionals included on a multidisciplinary team and the services they provide (Rainforth, York, & MacDonald, 1992).

Coping skills need to be reinforced as they emerge.

Boothroyd (1983) suggested that the type of intervention chosen for the child after evaluation may be one of the following:

1. *Corrective:* Try to minimize the loss through medical procedures.

2. *Preventive:* Attempt to prevent the occurrence of secondary disabilities.

3. *Circumvention:* Enrich the environment to provide alternative stimulation for what the child cannot receive (for example, touch for sight).

4. *Compensatory:* Provide prostheses such as hearing aids and other types of technical assistance to help the child gain access to the environment.

5. *Remedial:* Fill in the gaps in development through frequent evaluations to determine what may have been missed in training and education.

Additionally, after evaluation, a decision is made about what type of classroom is most appropriate for the child. Some children with multiple and severe disabilities will be placed in regular settings. Many of these children may attend schools designed for persons with multiple and severe disabilities or other specialized classrooms in regular schools. Schools hire personnel especially prepared to work with and teach these individuals. Most of these specialized classrooms are located in regular schools. There are advocates who insist that all children, regardless of the severity of their disability, be included with their agemates in neighborhood schools (Helmstetter, Peck, & Giangreco, 1993). Many in the field disagree (Kaufmann & Hallahan, 1994). The major dispute between those advocating full inclusion and those who do not concerns children with low intellectual capacity and high physical disability (see number 4 in Table 11.1). These issues are discussed more fully in Chapter 2.

TABLE 11.5   Professional Members of a Multidisciplinary Team

Audiologist: To provide and coordinate services to children with auditory handicaps, including detecting the problem and managing any existing communication handicaps.

Early Childhood Special Educator: To ensure that environments for handicapped infants and preschoolers facilitate children's development of social, motor, communication, self-help, cognitive, and behavioral skills and enhance children's self-concept, sense of competence and control, and independence.

Physician: To assist families in promoting optimal health, growth, and development for their infants and young children by providing health services.

Nurse: To diagnose and treat actual and potential human responses for illness; for disabled infants and preschoolers, this means (1) promoting the highest health and developmental status possible and (2) helping families cope with changes in their lives resulting from the child's disabilities.

Nutritionist: To maximize the health and nutritional status of infants and preschoolers through developmentally appropriate nutrition services within family and community environments.

Occupational Therapist: To promote children's independence, mastery, and sense of self-worth in their physical, emotional, and psychosocial development. Purposeful activity is used to expand the child's functional abilities, such as self-help skills; adaptive behavior and play skills; and sensory, motor, and postural development. These services are designed to help families and other caregivers improve children's functioning in their environment.

Ophthalmologist: To determine the extent of the child's visual capacity.

Physical Therapist: To enhance the sensory motor development, neurobehavioral organization, and cardiopulmonary status of disabled or at-risk infants and preschool children within a family and community context.

Psychologist: To derive a comprehensive picture of child and family functioning and to identify, implement, or evaluate psychological interventions.

Social Worker: To improve the quality of life for infants and toddlers and their families who are served by PL 99-457 through the provision of social work services.

Speech-Language Pathologist: To promote children's communications skills in the context of social interactions with peers and family members, in school, and in the community.

Source: L. Rossetti (1990). *Infant-Toddler Assessment*. Boston: Little, Brown. Adapted from the Carolina Institute for Research on Infant Personal Preparation (1988). *Proceedings of a Working Conference*. Unpublished manuscript, revised.

Two or more appropriate members of a multidisciplinary team are needed for an accurate assessment.

A major question to be considered when planning intervention is how do multiple and severe disabilities influence each other and shape the individual's experience of the environment. For example, if a child is disabled both cognitively and physically, his or her academic accomplishments will be less than those of one who is mildly retarded and physically disabled. Multiple disabilities are not simple additions of disabilities. They interact with each other and confound the individual's condition (Mencher & Gerber, 1983).

As Mencher and Gerber (1983) suggested, helping to improve the functioning of an individual with a disability begins with identifying and developing the child's assets. Because 93.8 percent of the deaf-blind population have some residual vision or hearing (Baldwin, 1993), these residuals need to be identified and enhanced to improve the child's functioning. By encouraging the child's assets, the instructional staff hopes to avoid the development of negative challenging behaviors, such as self-stimulation or self-injury, tantrums, and aggression.

For a child with both deafness and blindness, the therapist needs not only to determine if there is residual hearing or vision but also to determine how the child responds to sensory stimulation (including touch and smell) and what kinds of therapy are needed. The next step is to recommend potential management procedures to the parents and teachers and inform them of the availability of needed resources, such as a hearing aid, special glasses, or a comprehensive intervention program. The parents also need to be made aware of the supports available in the community (Everson, Burwell, & Killan, 1995).

We must consider five axioms when providing service for the severely disabled:

■ *Axiom I:* Young children with severe disabilities have a right to services that improve the quality of life and maximize their developmental potential.

■ *Axiom II:* Early childhood services for children with severe disabilities are effective in improving the quality of life and maximizing developmental potential.

■ *Axiom III:* Intervention services that begin earlier in the child's life will be more effective than services that begin later.

■ *Axiom IV:* Early childhood services that involve families are more effective than those that do not. (Westlake & Kaiser, 1991, p. 432)

■ *Axiom V:* Including children with disabilities in regular classrooms increases their social skills and interpersonal relationships. (Helmstetter, Peck, & Giangreco, 1994)

The aim of special education is to support the person with disabilities so that he or she may become as independent as possible in the activities of daily life and work and develop the social skills expected by society. For most children with multiple disabilities, achieving these goals requires a long and specialized process, but much has been accomplished with these individuals in recent years.

Identification of Children with Multiple and Severe Disabilities

Most children with multiple and severe disabilities are identified at birth through simple screening techniques. The Apgar scoring system (Apgar & Beck, 1973), described in Chapter 3, is administered at one minute and five minutes after birth. It assesses the child's motor functioning, skin color, heart rate, respiration, and general appearance. The Brazelton Neonatal Behavioral Assessment Scale (Brazelton, 1973) may also be administered to assess the same areas.

Some vision defects such as cataracts are easy to spot. Most hearing defects are difficult to identify and may not be detected until the child is 2 or 3 months of age. Most physical defects can be diagnosed early by observing the infant's lack of normal reflex and body movement. Some physical disabilities may not be diagnosed until late in the first year of life, and autism may not be evident until the second year of life and, in some, not until adolescence (see above).

Infants who are premature or of low birth weight (usually both) may have experienced lack of oxygen during the birth process (anoxia), usually as a result of the umbilical cord's being wrapped around the neck), or are breech born (delivery feet first). Such children are monitored carefully, for these types of birth are often associated with disabilities.

Other defects such as some types of spina bifida (see Chapter 12 or Williamson, 1987) can easily be identified from obvious physical deformities. In some types of spina bifida, an opening is present on the spinal cord, and children who are affected may have enlarged heads from excess spinal fluid in the brain cavity (hydrocephalus). These children have surgery shortly after birth to drain the excess fluid from the brain because if the condition is allowed to continue, it will cause retardation. The process of draining is called *shunting*.

Children with Down syndrome can also be identified, from their flat facial profile and upwardly slanted eyes, as well as from their low Apgar scores (Batshaw & Perret, 1992). Children with Down syndrome may require immediate medical supervision for survival.

Individuals with spina bifida and Down syndrome can suffer from multiple disabilities and must be examined carefully at birth to determine their immediate needs. Children in both groups, however, vary across a wide range of cognitive functioning and will need intensive intervention to help them achieve their highest potential.

Educational Adaptations

A PHILOSOPHY OF TEACHING

Over the years, a philosophy of teaching students with multiple and severe disabilities has been evolving from research, experience, and common sense. Today the objective is to teach functional, age-appropriate skills in integrated school and nonschool settings and to base teaching on ongoing, systematic evaluation of the student's progress. The approach has become more age oriented; hence, it is more developmentally oriented. Recall that age appropriateness is defined by what the average individual without disabilities can do at a given age.

Keep in mind that many children with multiple and severe disabilities are cognitively normal; they are capable of mastering the regular curriculum when they receive the necessary supports (augmentative communication devices, motorized wheelchairs, low vision aids). Here, however, we focus on students who cannot follow the regular school curriculum and who have not mastered (usually at home) the self-help skills that lead to independence.

Functional Age-Appropriate Skills

Teaching functional skills that students will use in daily living is an important part of the curriculum.

The skills taught to students with severe disabilities must be both functional and age appropriate. Functional skills can be used immediately by the student, are necessary in everyday settings, and increase to some extent the student's independence. Folding a sheet of paper in half is not a functional skill; folding clothes is (Brown & Lehr, 1989).

Age-appropriate skills are appropriate to the student's chronological age, not mental age. A 16-year-old boy who is severely disabled is not taught how to solve a four-piece jigsaw puzzle of a dog, although it may correspond to his mental age. Instead, the focus is on activities the boy can carry out to some degree as his nondisabled agemates do—for example, eating, social or folk dancing, bowling, or operating the television set or personal stereo. If the skills are not age appropriate, they are not likely to be functional. Moreover, age appropriate skills give students with severe disabilities a measure of social acceptance.

Clearly, some youngsters with severe disabilities cannot do many tasks that their nondisabled agemates can do. Nevertheless, most of them can at least take part in certain activities. Partial participation enables students with disabilities to interact with their nondisabled agemates as much as possible (Brown, Nietupski, & Hamre-Nietupski, 1976); (Sailor, 1991).

Learning Environment

In the past, many children with multiple and severe disabilities were excluded from public schools because they did not fit into ongoing special education programs or because they were not toilet trained. Many of these youngsters were assigned to a residential institution for the more severe of their disabilities. For example, a child who was both mentally retarded and hearing impaired was placed in a residential institution serving people with mental retardation or mental illness; often the institution had neither the facilities nor the personnel to provide education for someone with a hearing loss.

Provisions for children with disabilities are different today because of parent involvement and the efforts of the Association for Persons with Severe Disabilities, the Council for Exceptional Children, the National Association for Retarded Citizens, the American Association on Mental Retardation, and other advocacy groups. The Civil Rights Act and the Education for All Handicapped Children Act of 1975 (Public Law 94-142) made it mandatory for public schools to educate all children.

According to Turnbull and Turnbull (1991), legislation and court decisions have guaranteed children with disabilities

- A free public education
- An objective evaluation of their strengths and weaknesses
- Appropriate and individualized education programs
- Education within the least restrictive environment

Students with multiple and severe disabilities can participate at least partially in most school and nonschool activities, increasing their confidence and their peers' perceptions of them as valuable, productive members of society. (© Gale Zucker)

■ The right to procedural due process so they can challenge the actions of state and local educational authorities

In addition, the parents, guardians, or surrogates of each child have the right to share with educators in making decisions that affect the child's education.

These laws and court decisions have also mandated the development of community programs for many children who previously were institutionalized. Brown, Nietupski, and Hamre-Nietupski (1976) advocated very early that "severely handicapped students should be placed in self-contained classes in public schools. . . . They have a right to be visible functioning citizens integrated into the everyday life of complex public communities" (p. 3). This thinking has been expanded to the idea of placing these students in a regular classroom for at least part of the day. In planning for children with multiple disabilities, Baumgart et al. suggest the following:

Students who are severely disabled should participate in regular classroom activities for at least part of the day.

■ Partial participation in chronological age-appropriate environments and activities is educationally more advantageous than exclusion from such environments and activities.

■ Students with multiple and severe disabilities, regardless of their degree of dependence or level of functioning, should be allowed to participate at least partially in a wide range of school and nonschool environments and activities.

■ The kinds and degrees of partial participation in school and nonschool environments and activities should be increased through direct and systematic instruction.

■ Partial participation in school and nonschool environments and activities should result in a student being perceived by others as a more valuable, contributing, striving, and productive member of society.

■ Systematic, coordinated, and longitudinal efforts must be initiated at a young age to prepare for at least partial participation in as many environments and activities with nondisabled chronological age-appropriate peers and other persons as possible. (Baumgart et al., 1982, p. 19)

Integrated Settings

Youngsters with severe and multiple disabilities should be taught in a variety of integrated environments, both in and out of school. An integrated setting is any setting where persons without disabilities and persons with disabilities are both present. These students have difficulty generalizing skills and applying skills they have learned in one setting to another. Mary Allen, a 16-year-old with severe disabilities, has just completed the bed-making program at school. But she cannot make her bed at home or at her grandmother's house because she is not able to generalize the skills across different environments, from school to home and to her grandmother's house.

There are many ways to help youngsters generalize skills. One is to teach the skill in the environment in which the person will use it. This kind of real-world training requires multiple integrated educational settings, both at school and in the community. This training is not classroom based; it is community based. If we want to teach shopping skills, we do not use a pretend store in the classroom. Instead, we go out into the community to grocery stores, department stores, and specialty shops.

Today, a growing body of literature supports the concept of integrating these students in public schools and community settings:

■ Positive changes have been reported in the attitudes of nondisabled individuals toward their peers with severe disabilities at various age levels (Grenot-Scheyer, 1994; Voeltz, 1980).

■ Integration has led to improvements in the social and communication skills of children with severe disabilities (Jenkins, Speltz, & Odom, 1985; Newton, Horner, Ard, LeBaron, & Sapperstein, 1994).

■ Integration has improved interaction between students with severe disabilities and their nondisabled agemates (Roberts, Burchinal, & Bailey, 1994).

To maximize the integration opportunities for students with severe disabilities, teachers should limit the ratio of disabled to nondisabled students in any setting and use students without disabilities as peer tutors. (© Spencer Grant/Monkmeyer Press Photo Service)

Interacting with students who have severe disabilities teaches tolerance to students who are not disabled.

■ Integration facilitates adjustment to community settings as adults (Hasazi, Gordon, & Roe, 1985; Helmstetter, Peck, & Giangreco, 1994).

One of the major findings about including persons with multiple and severe disabilities in regular classrooms is that the participation increases their social and interpersonal skills. They display increased responsiveness to others, an increase in reciprocal interactions, and increased display of affect toward others (Grenot-Scheyer, 1994). In addition, the inclusion of those with multiple and severe disabilities in regular classrooms has an impact on their peers who do not have disabilities. The latter show increased tolerance for others, increased tolerance for diversity, and growth in their own personal development (Helmstetter, Peck, & Giangreco, 1994).

Whatever the age of the students or the severity of their disabilities, integration provides them with a curriculum that is the most functional and age appropriate possible. Guiltinan (1986) suggested several ways for teachers and administrators to make integration work:

- Limit the ratio of disabled to nondisabled students in any setting.
- Highlight your student's strengths. If the student has well-developed gross motor skills but weak fine motor skills, integrate her or him into sports rather than art.
- Provide "extra help" at first to start the process.
- Encourage students with disabilities to dress like their peers. Send home dress tips to parents.
- Use students without disabilities to be peer tutors and friends to the student with disabilities.
- Be positive when talking to other teachers or students about the student with disabilities.
- Arrange the classroom schedule to maximize integration opportunities. (adapted from Guiltinan, 1986, pp. 4–5)

Data Collecting

Collecting data is an everyday activity for most people. We collect data about the weather to help us choose our clothes and plan for the weekend; we often compare prices before we make a purchase; the gauges and dials on our cars give us the data we need to keep them in good running condition. Without data, decisions are based on guesses and intuition. It is not surprising, then, that we need information to make intelligent programming decisions for children with disabilities. Wolery, Bailey, and Sugai (1988) suggested several reasons why data collection is necessary:

The ongoing collection of data about a student's responses is the core of an educational program.

- To pinpoint students' status
- To monitor progress and determine the program's effectiveness
- To provide feedback to students and parents
- To document efforts and demonstrate accountability

Teachers of students with multiple and severe disabilities collect data on all kinds of things: the number of steps a student making a sandwich completes correctly, the length of time it takes a student to complete a vocational assembly task (such as packaging drill bits), the percentage of community information signs a student reads correctly, and the amount of time a student spends on off-task behaviors. This kind of information enables teachers and other service providers to plan programs that meet a student's needs and to make decisions about the student's educational progress.

The teacher takes the individual through as many stages as possible by

1. Conditionally reinforcing simple responses related to causality, such as picking up a toy or touching someone to signal a need
2. Interactional coaching, turn taking, imitation of facial expressions, gestures, and sound
3. Individual teaching at the time of engaging in functional activities

The communication skills taught to persons with multiple and severe disabilities are functional in that they are relevant to the individual's survival and independent functioning in the community as appropriately (societally determined) as possible (Bradley, Ashbaugh, & Blaney, 1994; Goetz, Guess & Campbell, 1987).

Fuchs and Deno (1994) suggested that measurement of students' status and progress must

1. Be repeated on material of comparable difficulty (to curriculum taught) over time
2. Incorporate valid indicators of the critical outcomes of instruction
3. Rely on a data base that permits quantitative and qualitative descriptions of students' performance to assist teachers in adjusting and enhancing their instruction

TEACHING AND ASSESSING

Normal Development

Intervention begins with diagnosis, frequently at birth.

There are two approaches to teaching children with multiple and severe disabilities. One recognizes that development starts before birth, that it continues rapidly in the first year, and that the individual is more flexible and more easily influenced by environmental input during the early years. The other, newer approach uses knowledge of genetically determined development to decide what the child will need to know to function in a specific environment and what skills the child already possesses. The teacher then develops strategies to teach the child specific activities that will lead to mastery of a set of functional skills that support independence.

To understand these approaches, it is necessary to understand some of the basics of normal (ordinary) development.

One of the great achievements in human beings is the ability to communicate by using symbols—usually words or signs. A symbol is something that stands for something else—a person, event, attitude, feeling, concept. It usually refers directly to the thing signified—for example, "Mama" is mother, and usually a specific mother. A gesture is not a symbol unless it is part of a system, such as sign language, in which specific gestures always mean the same thing. Gestures that are not part of a sign language system usually have a variety of meanings. For example, the gesture of pointing can mean "See the dog," "Bring me a toy," or "I want to go outside."

It has been discovered that a symbol system grows out of genetically programmed prelinguistic behaviors such as cries, grunts, the social smile, eye contact, and interaction with another followed by babbling; finally, around 12 months of age, a child's oral sounds become words (Bates, 1979; Dromi, 1994). After 12 months of age, the average child proceeds rapidly from one word to the mastery of thousands by age 5, using them in a variety of ways to express logical communications and cognitive functioning.

Both speech and gestures can be part of a communication system. Persons who are most severely cognitively disabled, however, may never learn either speech or gestural system and have to rely on nonlinguistic systems to communicate their wants and needs (Sternberg, 1991).

At the beginning of the education process, an early intervention teacher does not know how far the individual with multiple disabilities will develop. The prelinguistic system usually begins at birth and definitely begins by 2 months of age for the individual with severe retardation. Therefore, education must begin early to identify the prelinguistic vocalizations and gestures so they can be developed into a communication system and ideally a symbol system consisting of signs or words.

Some type of communication system needs to be taught to children who otherwise would have difficulty communicating.

A major problem with children with multiple and severe disabilities is that they tend to lack the natural, genetically programmed inquisitiveness, curiosity, and desire to manipulate objects that come automatically to the average, nondisabled child. The facilitator (teacher or family member) must encourage children with multiple and severe disabilities to learn that they can use their genetically programmed prelinguistic skills and sounds to communicate—that is, they can use a gesture to show, to request, to accept, or to refuse. These simple sensorimotor patterns can help the individual move from internal worlds to the external world (Dunst & Lowe, 1986). Developing these genetically programmed gestures into a communication system enables the individual with severe and profound disabilities to relate to people in his or her environment.

The techniques of teaching persons with multiple and severe disabilities to use these genetically programmed sensorimotor patterns is called augmented or alternative communication (Baumgart, Johnson, & Helmstetter, 1990; Flippo, Inge, & Barais, 1995; Meyer, Peck, & Brown, 1991; Sternberg & McNerney, 1988). It is hoped that such teaching will move the child from the genetic reflex state of movements, signals, and gestures to pictures and signs and then to symbols, verbal speech, or sign language.

Generalization of Skills

The major problem for the teacher or facilitator of individuals with multiple and severe disabilities is to teach the individual that what he or she has learned can be applied in other settings. Traditionally, skills were taught in the classroom and were not transferred to or used in other settings by these individuals.

To understand the importance of this concept, consider a practical example. Most of us have forgotten how we learned to go to a store or to a fast-food restaurant to buy something. We learned it at some time, however, probably through guided instructions from our parents or by imitating them. Children with multiple and severe disabilities must be taught each step that is necessary to complete what to us might seem to be a simple task. They also must learn that they can apply these steps in other settings. It is not an easy process but one that requires persistence, repetition, and a variety of settings in which to use the skills.

The standard practice is to teach each step. Take, for example, buying a hamburger: You open the door, stand in line, ask for what you want, pay for it, wait until it is served, accept any change, move from the order line to the reception area, receive the food, take it to the accepted place for eating, and clean up afterward. Some students with autism and others with severe physical disabilities may be apraxic—that is, they cannot realize what to do when confronted with a situation such as opening a door and will stand in front of the door in confusion. Thus, teaching how to open different types of doors becomes the first step. After each step is mastered, the individual who has multiple and severe disabilities must be taught that the same (or very similar) procedures apply at the pizza parlor, the ice cream store, and so on. Preparation may begin in the classroom, but it must also be taught in the actual community for generalization and maintenance to take place (Brown & Lehr, 1993). Rewarding and reinforcing each successfully completed step are very important.

Assessment of Skills

Federal regulations about assessing or evaluating the skills of individuals with multiple and severe disabilities are quite clear: The evaluation must be appropriate to the needs of the individual, his or her family, and the recommended potential early intervention program. The regulations are also concerned with cultural and language issues. Any evaluation must be based on the reality of the family's culture and the individual's experience. Most normed tests assume uniform cultural experiences, and thus they are obviously biased against individuals whose life experiences vary from those of the dominant middle class.

Although commercial assessment devices are available, they sometimes fail to meet the individual needs of students with multiple and severe disabilities. Norm-referenced tests are not very helpful for classroom teachers. IQ scores and developmental-age quotients do not give us specific information about what students can and cannot do. **Criterion-referenced tests**—tests that compare students' levels of functioning to a standard of mastery—are more useful. Because children with multiple and severe disabilities are a very heterogeneous group, commercial assessment devices must be adjusted to each child's age and type of disabilities; to the teacher's qualifications; and to the characteristics and demands of the school, the community, and the student's home environment.

The constraints of many published assessment instruments have led many teachers to develop their own. Brown and his colleagues (1979) outlined a process called *ecological inventory* that teachers can use to develop and individualize functional curriculum for their students. The process consists of six phases:

1. Delineating the four curriculum domains: domestic skills, vocational skills, leisure and recreational skills, and community living skills
2. Identifying those environments in the community that require the use of these skills

3. Identifying the smaller environments (subenvironments) in which students with multiple and severe disabilities function or might function

4. Making an inventory of the age-appropriate and age-related activities that occur in the subenvironments (The activities related to the bathroom, for example, include toileting and cleaning the sink.)

5. Identifying the skills that must be taught to perform the tasks

6. Using special teaching procedures to instruct students with multiple and severe disabilities in the performance of the identified skill in a natural environment

Figure 11.1 shows part of an ecological inventory for an adolescent with a severe disability. The domain here is community living skills. One of the environments (a current environment) is the doctor's office. Subenvironments are all the settings in which the student must be able to function to get to the doctor's office and be examined. The focus here is on the examination room and the activity of removing one's clothes. The skills are the tasks that a person must carry out to remove his or her clothes.

Preparing an ecological inventory is time-consuming, but the information it provides is extremely valuable. The inventory can be used to assess a student's current level of functioning and to plan the educational agenda (skills that must be taught and the order in which to teach them). An ecological inventory, then, can be the basis of the individualized education program. Furthermore, because the curriculum is specific to a certain youngster, it is likely to be the most functional, most appropriate curriculum possible.

The assessment of a student's skill must take place in the setting where the student will use the skill.

CURRICULUM AND TEACHING APPROACHES

Preschool

Most young children with multiple and severe disabilities attend special pre-schools for half a day or a full day. Mastery of communication skills is usually the major aim of the curriculum. The ability it teaches to recognize the self as a person is also included (recall our discussion of Murphy and Byrne's [1983] six-step developmental sequence earlier in this chapter). The curriculum does not teach isolated skills; it teaches activities and routines that combine functional communication with physical and social needs. In addition, specialized personnel, such as physical, speech, and occupational therapists, will assist by providing appropriate therapies.

A major goal of the preschool is to move the children forward so that they will begin to act on the environment by manipulating objects, making requests to satisfy their needs, and exercising their natural curiosity—in other words, learning how to learn. The skills should relate to communication, mobility, social skills, and self-management. The best generalization and maintenance occurs when the skill

1. Has immediate utility to the individual

2. Produces something the student wants

3. Was acquired in the social context where it will be used

Figure 11.1

Partial Ecological Inventory for a Severely Handicapped Adolescent

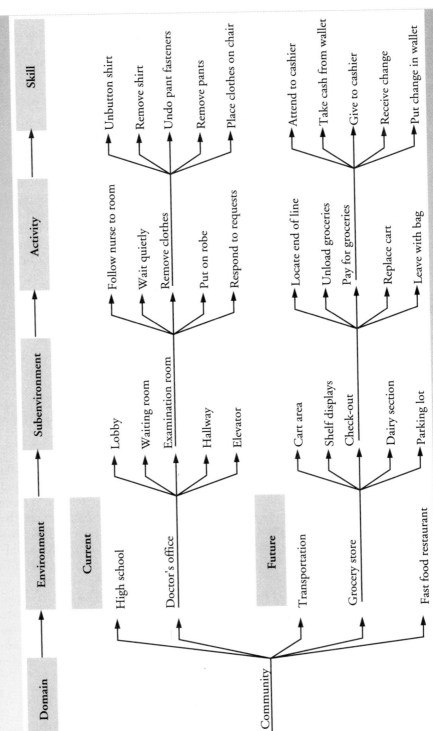

Source: M. E. Snell and N. C. Grigg (1993). *Systematic Instruction of Persons with Severe Handicaps*. Adapted by permission of Prentice-Hall, Inc., Upper Saddle River, NJ.

4. Is appropriate for the student's level of development
5. Is practical and useful
6. Is adaptable (Goetz, Guess, & Campbell, 1987)

Those characteristics are the guidelines for the development of any skill, from drinking from a cup or eating an apple to working in a fast-food restaurant.

In addition to overcoming the child's disabilities, the teacher or facilitator must overcome two other obstacles: (1) Caregivers usually are less flexible and less permissive than teachers in encouraging creative activity, and they are more intrusive in their interactions with children with multiple and severe disabilities. They tend to do things for the children, such as putting on their coats, instead of teaching them how to do things. This is a less-than-ideal learning strategy (Linden, Kankkunen, & Tjellstrom, 1983). (2) The child with multiple disabilities is usually less inquisitive, more withdrawn, less active, and less fun than a child without disabilities and engages in little play with objects. The teacher has to help families learn new strategies and also help the child overcome his or her lack of involvement with the environment. The teacher does so by teaching family members the meaning of their child's gestures and how to be more interactive with their child.

Primary and Secondary School

In elementary school, individuals with multiple and severe disabilities and those with severe retardation are likely to have similar curricula, which are continuations of efforts to teach functional skills that lead to clear communication and independence. If the child is moderately retarded, more complex skills can be taught—skills that are useful, practical, survival oriented, and socially appropriate.

An example of a curriculum for all ages is the Syracuse Community Referenced Curriculum Guide (Ford, Schnorr, Meyer, Davern, Black, & Dempsey, 1989). The curriculum stresses five areas of school concern: (1) self-management; (2) home living, including eating, food preparation, hygiene, and toileting; (3) vocational jobs at all levels, from cleaning blackboards to working at a fast-food chain or motel; (4) recreational leisure with family and friends, fitness, and travel; and (5) general community functioning, including shopping, eating out, and using community services.

A guide for planning inclusive education, *Choosing Options and Accommodation for Children (COACH)*, emphasizes collaborative teamwork with the family as the cornerstone of educational planning (Giangreco, Cloninger, & Iverson, 1994). The manual includes clear statements of goals, activities, and sample forms—including forms for interviews, assessments, IEPs, and community and school worksheets.

The key elements of the curriculum are to develop throughout elementary, middle, and high school individualized programs that lead to successful transition into the community and adult lifestyles. A teacher trained in alternative instructional strategies is necessary to accomplish these goals.

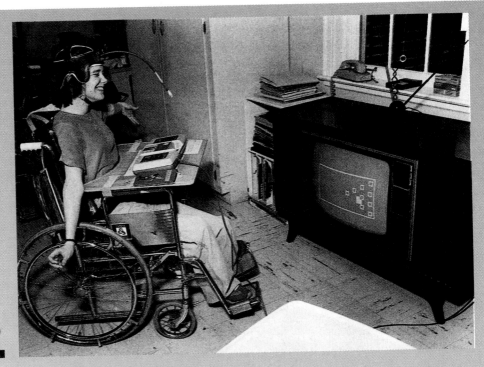

Communication boards and other augmentative systems have been developed to help the nonvocal student add to and supplement available speech. (© *Meri Houtchens-Kitchens/The Picture Cube*)

ADAPTATION FOR NONVOCAL STUDENTS

Many children with severe physical and cognitive disabilities have major communication impairments. They are often unable to use speech functionally. This inability to communicate is one of the most formidable obstacles that children with multiple and severe disabilities face. It prevents them from interacting successfully with their environments and impedes their ability to learn from interactive experiences—things that nondisabled children do readily.

Augmentative and alternative communication devices have been developed to help students who are nonvocal communicate. A simple device is the *communication board*, a piece of cardboard or other stable material on which pictures, words, or symbols can be written or attached. Computer screens also can serve as communication devices. These devices are designed not to replace speech but to add to and supplement available speech. With these devices the student can indicate needs, preferences, or responses by pointing to the item (direct selection). The student may also look in the direction of the item (scanning), and the teacher recognizes the student's response (Beukelman & Mirenda, 1994).

Technological advances have increased the sophistication of augmentative devices. There are wall charts that are battery operated, voice synthesizers in several different languages, and a wide range of devices for computer access. Beukeleman and Mirenda (1994) mention that a compact disc containing over sixteen thousand product descriptions can be obtained from Trace Research and Development Center, S-151 Waisman Center, 1500 Highland Avenue, Madison, WI 53705.

TRANSITION FROM HOME AND SCHOOL TO COMMUNITY AND WORK

The recent emphasis on transitional programming from high school to work and many plans for supportive employment (Bellamy, Rhodes, Mank, & Albin, 1988) have opened new vistas for persons with multiple and severe disabilities. Some of the newer perceptions about persons with multiple and severe disabilities favor empowering them to make decisions about their own preferences for work, living arrangements, and leisure activities (Brown & Lehr, 1993; Brown & Gothelf, in press; Gothelf, Crimmins, Mercer, & Finocchiro, 1994; Demchak, 1994). Authors looking favorably on such empowerment suggest moving toward supportive apartments, homeownership, and cooperative and shared living space (Brown & Gothelf, in press). They feel that the group home may not be the ideal housing model. Their articles indicate a shift from program-centered to person-centered decision making. An important aspect of this perspective is that the authors believe these new person-centered programs will improve the mental and physical health of persons with severe disabilities (Bradley, Ashbaugh, & Blaney, 1994; Newton, Horner, Ard, LeBaron, & Sapperton, 1994).

Transition programs from school to adult life aim for lifestyles for those with multiple and severe disabilities that develop their valued participation in the world of work with its routines, its monetary benefits, and its social relationships that build the self-confidence and self-efficacy of the individual (O'Neill, Gothelf, Cohen, Lehman, & Woolf, 1991). To be able to accomplish this participation, the individual needs to be taught to move from high school vocational skills development to the community setting in which the work is to take place. This requires a *transition coordinator*, who plans for and assists in the transition (Falvey, Coot, Bishop, & Grenot-Scheyer, 1989; Bellamy, Rhodes, Mank, & Albin, 1988; O'Neill, Gothelf, Cohen, Lehman, & Woolf, 1991).

Competitive paid employment at or above the minimum wage is still infrequent for persons with multiple and severe disabilities who may need ongoing support to perform in a work setting. Supportive employment is subsidized with government funds to encourage the employment of individuals with multiple and severe disabilities. It is conducted in a variety of settings (for example, fast-food restaurants, supermarkets, parks, and libraries) with additional support provided to include supervision and skills development for the individual.

The goal is to hold a paying job successfully (functional competence) and to live one's own life. Ideally, to support these goals, working side by side with those with multiple and severe disabilities, the nondisabled will perceive them as valued members of society (O'Neill, Gothelf, Cohen, Lehman, Woolf, & Ross, 1991). Public acceptance should lead to acceptance of these persons taking part in leisure activities, developing relationships with nondisabled persons, and pursuing interests of their own (O'Neill, Gothelf, Cohen, Lehman, Woolf, & Ross, 1991).

The goal of the transition coordinator is to find age-appropriate settings in the community, prepare the person in that setting, and teach the individual how to function in that setting in accordance with the expectations of nondisabled persons (Falvey, 1989; Kregel, 1994).

An individual transition plan (ITP) is now being developed for each individual in these programs. The ITP requires a great deal of information from the school, the individual, the parents, and the community. Questions to be answered include the following:

1. What will the student need to learn before leaving school?
2. Where will the person live as an adult?
3. What activities will replace school for recreation?
4. How will this individual support himself or herself?
5. What will he or she do in leisure time?
6. How will this person travel using community transportation?
7. How will he or she gain access to medical care?
8. What will be the relationship with his or her family? (adapted from O'Neill, Gothelf, Cohen, Lehman, Woolf, & Ross, 1991)

Persons with multiple and severe disabilities differ from one another. They have similar but different needs. No one set of treatments can cover everyone adequately. It is clear that the coordinator must have the skill to develop a plan for each person. The teacher or coordinator will need to collect information on the individual's past to find the most suitable community site, to conduct a task analysis of what will be required at that work site, and then to initiate a prescriptive program to meet these demands. To encourage persistence in work habits, the coordinator will try to match the individual to certain activities on the basis of the person's preferences.

COMPUTER TECHNOLOGY

A national commitment to support and encourage the development of computer technology for use by and with persons with disabilities is contained in IDEA as amended in 1994. The act encourages widespread use of computer technology with persons with disabilities for education, measurement, vocational training, and transition to the world of work (Greenwood, 1994).

A wide range of software is available to assist the teaching of persons with disabilities.

Computers are becoming standard equipment in classes for children with disabilities. Curriculum software—programs too numerous to mention—is being developed continuously. There are programs designed specifically for individuals with learning, hearing, vision, motor, and cognitive disabilities (see Council for Exceptional Children, Special Issue, *Exceptional Children*, Vol. 61, no. 2, October/November 1994).

Some children may need to use head pointers to type. Some can use a single finger to call up software (the curriculum) to read, and they can respond to it with single-finger pressure. Notebook computers, which are the size of a textbook and weigh from seven to eight pounds, are very useful for children with disabilities who possess a communication system (Cary & Sale, 1994).

Adulthood and Lifespan Issues

Attempts to normalize the lifestyles of children with multiple and severe disabilities would be largely a waste of time if we did not provide for the normalization of the lifestyles of adults in the community. Over the past twenty-five years, substantial efforts have been made to create community living and vocational arrangements to provide for adults who have been returned to the community from institutions and to prevent the institutionalization of youngsters who have been living in the community.

LIVING ARRANGEMENTS

The number of programs for community living has been growing since 1961, when President John F. Kennedy established the Presidential Committee on Mental Retardation (Rusch, Chadsey-Rusch, White, & Gifford, 1985). Today, these programs include living facilities, vocational and rehabilitation workshops, and recreational services. Coordinated team planning in the community is considered the appropriate manner to support people with disabilities so that they can live independently in their community (Bradley, Ashbaugh, & Blaney, 1994).

Major efforts are being made to enable persons with severe and profound disabilities to live and work as independently as they are able (Brown & Gothelf, in press; Burwell & Everson, 1995). The emerging trend emphasizes the involvement of the person with a disability and his or her family in decision making about work, leisure, and living arrangements (Bradley, Ashbaugh, & Blaney, 1994).

VOCATIONAL ARRANGEMENTS

Another step in the integration of adults with multiple and severe disabilities is providing appropriate vocational opportunities. Various options exist, among them day treatment programs, sheltered workshops, and supportive competitive employment. See Table 11.6 on p. 504 for others.

The Miracles of Brea

Our second child, Brea, was born three years ago with a muscle weakness. She had a club foot, a dislocated hip and some joint stiffness. She has a tracheostomy due to chronic respiratory problems and is fed via G-button because of swallowing difficulties. At night while Brea sleeps, we put her on a CPAP (continuous positive airway pressure) machine to put positive pressure into her lungs.

Brea says a few words and seems to understand almost everything. She can sit up when put in a sitting position, plays with her toys and loves books. She can scoot backwards on her bottom a little bit, but tires easily. That is the extent of her mobility. We are waiting for the insurance company to approve a wheelchair but for now we carry her everywhere. Brea is absolutely beautiful. She is happy and cheerful when healthy and entertained. She tends to get bored and irritable in the evening and it can be frustrating finally getting her to sleep. (She is very normal that way!)

BUSY DAYS

My husband, Gil, and I work full time—he is in land surveying and I am a first-grade teacher. For the last three years, Brea has had a nurse who arrives when I go to work and leaves when I get home. In addition to the normal household and family chores waiting for me when I get home, there are breathing treatments, lung suctioning, chest therapy and blended food therapy. There is always physical therapy to be done, not to mention cuddling and playing with Brea as well as our five-year-old, Ross, and our dog, Willie. Then, of course, there is bath time, dinner time and book time before bed. Often during the winter months, Brea has pneumonia and has to be rushed to the hospital or is at home connected to oxygen tanks with an IV in her arm. Needless to say, our stress level is high!

MAKING CHANGES & COPING

Gil and I have always been outdoors people—on the go, travelling a lot. It has been hard to lose that freedom. We like to do things as a family but sometimes Brea is just not well enough to participate. When she is well enough to join us, we choose our activities carefully because she cannot stay in one position for too long and she needs breathing treatments every four to six hours.

We try to choose things to do together that will not add to our stress. We avoid large, quiet groups and indoor restaurants. We boat, bicycle and go to the beach, zoo or the homes of close friends. We have taken vacations with Brea and all of her medical equipment. It is tiring but worth it just to have a change of scenery. Sometimes we leave Brea with her grandmother and go on day trips with Ross. We are very fortunate to have my mom so close.

It is very hard to successfully deal with the stress and heartbreak of having a child like Brea. You have to be "thick-skinned" (not my strong point) and you have to be able to "transcend" the pain (I tend to be earth-bound!). Taking Brea anywhere can be very painful for me, especially when I notice people's reactions to her or watch other little girls. But, not taking her places is equally painful because she is my child and she should be there with me. I am constantly having to push aside negative and painful feelings, focusing instead on the sweetness of Brea, who she is and all the love we share. I am not denying my feelings or pain, but I do not waste too much energy on them. ➜

Gil and I used to say maybe things will get easier. We finally realized that they probably won't. We just have to be happy with our lives now. I want to be happy and I want my family to be happy. This is a terrible blow but our lives will go on and I want them to go on happily.

Some days I have a bad attitude. I am embarrassed by my inability to handle things gracefully. On some of those days, I just go ahead and be a grump or feel sorry for myself and Brea all day. (I apologize to people later if necessary!) I cry, rant and rave—whatever I need to do. And then I feel better.

I take long runs four or five times a week. I go to church and have met a lot of supportive and inspiring people there. I read whenever I have time. I eat well, take vitamins and buy myself something nice whenever I can afford it! None of this takes away the pain but it helps me to deal with it.

Brea will have hip surgery this summer and will be in a body cast for eight weeks. In the fall she will be attending a preschool program for children with disabilities, which will be at my school for the first time ever. We are hoping that she will be healthy enough to attend on a regular basis.

DIFFERENT KINDS OF MIRACLES

Ever since Brea was born, I have been hoping to write a miracle story—the kind where the child beats all the odds, surprises all the doctors and lives a normal life. Although that miracle has not taken place, I can see other miracles at work here—the miracle of Brea who is happy and loving in spite of all her hardships. The miracle of my husband and I—basically immature and unprepared for this crisis—handling it (sometimes ineptly and other times well). And the miracle of my little boy, Ross—happy, healthy and telling his playmate on the way home from school, "Wait till you see my sister!"

Source: Chelle Howatt, "The Miracles of Brea," *Exceptional Parent* (April–May 1993), pp. 22–23. Reprinted with the expressed consent and approval of *Exceptional Parent*, a monthly magazine for parents and families of children with disabilities and special health care needs. Subscription cost is $28 per year for 12 issues; Call 1-800-247-8080. Offices are at 120 State Street, Hackensack, NJ 07601.

---

c o m m e n t a r y

What Is the Context? A mother explains the many difficulties and hidden rewards of having a child with multiple disabilities. Despite having to modify family activities to accommodate Brea's needs, the family remains active outdoors. The mother relies on emotional support from the family and community and has developed several ways to relieve the everyday stress of caring for Brea. The family's goal is to continue their lives with as much normalcy and happiness as possible.

Pivotal Issues. How has the family's attitude helped Brea develop? How has the family adapted its activities to accommodate Brea's disabilities? What kinds of support does the family need from the community and from social programs?

TABLE 11.6 Vocational Rehabilitation Services	
Service	**Description of Service**
Evaluation	To determine a person's interests, capabilities, aptitudes, and limitations, and the range of services needed to prepare the individual for employment
Counseling and guidance	To help the person aim for a job in keeping with his or her interests, capabilities, aptitudes, and limitations
Medical and hospital care	To attend, if needed, to mental or physical problems that are obstacles to job preparation
Job training	To provide training that fits the person's needs and that leads to a definite work goal; can include personal adjustment training, prevocational training, vocational training, on-the-job training, and training in a sheltered workshop
Maintenance payments	To cover increases in a person's basic living expenses because of participation in vocational rehabilitation
Transportation	To support and maximize the benefits of other services being received
Services to family members	To help the person achieve the maximum benefit from other services being provided
Interpreter services	To assist persons with hearing impairments
Reader services	To assist persons with visual impairments, including note-taking services and orientation and mobility services
Aids and devices	To provide the person with needed aids and devices, such as telecommunication devices, sensory aids, artificial limbs, braces, and wheelchairs
Tools and equipment	To provide the person with tools and equipment needed to perform the job
Recruitment and training services	To provide new work opportunities in public service employment
Job placement	To help the person find a job, taking into consideration the person's abilities and training; includes placement into supported employment
Job follow-up	To help the person make whatever adjustments are needed to succeed at the job into which he or she has been placed
Occupational licenses or permits	To provide the person with the occupational licenses or permits that the law requires a person have before entering an occupation
Other	To provide other services that an individual may need to become employable

Source: L. Kupper (Ed.) (1991). Options after high school for youth with disabilities. *NICHCY Transition Summary,* no. 7, p. 8. Available from the National Information Center for Children and Youth with Disabilities, P.O. Box 1492, Washington, DC 20013.

Day Treatment Programs

The day treatment program is the most restrictive setting for adults with multiple and severe disabilities. These programs are

> designed to provide therapeutic activities for disabled workers whose physical or mental impairment is so severe as to make their productive capacity inconsequential. Therapeutic activities include custodial activities (such as activities that focus on teaching basic living skills) and any purposeful activity so long as work or production is not the main purpose. (U.S. Department of Labor as cited in Bellamy, Rhodes, Bourbeau, & Mank, 1986, p. 260)

The purpose of these centers is to teach necessary life skills. Rather than providing vocational opportunities, the day treatment center provides continuing education.

Sheltered Workshops

The sheltered workshop provides vocational services to adults with disabilities (Bellamy, Rhodes, Bourbeau, & Mank, 1986). The U.S. Department of Labor defines a sheltered workshop as

> a charitable organization or institution conducted not-for-profit, but for the purpose of carrying out a recognized rehabilitation program for handicapped workers, and/or providing such individuals with remunerative employment or other occupational rehabilitating activity of an educational or therapeutic nature. (cited in Bellamy, Rhodes, Bourbeau, & Mank, 1986, p. 260)

Although the goal of sheltered workshops is to prepare individuals with multiple and severe disabilities to obtain and maintain competitive employment, placement out of the segregated work environment rarely occurs (Bellamy, Rhodes, Bourbeau, & Mank, 1986).

Supportive Competitive Employment

Day treatment centers and sheltered workshops violate many of the philosophical tenets of integration, supportive employment, and paid employment. The settings are segregated, and they do not fall within the boundaries of normalization, least restrictive environment, or partial participation. These shortcomings have increased the popularity of competitive employment training programs. These programs are attractive because both the individual and the public benefit (Bellamy, Rhodes, Bourbeau, & Mank, 1986).

Hill and Wehman (1983) presented an analysis of workshop versus competitive employment costs over a four-year period. They followed ninety adults labeled as having moderate or severe disabilities and measured many different variables, including the number of months each person worked, the number of staff hours needed at each workplace, the income earned, and the cost of operation. After four years, the competitive employment program had saved the public $100,000.

Data that encourage supportive competitive employment and discourage sheltered workshop employment are growing. But determining how to deliver the most effective and efficient vocational opportunities to people with multiple and severe disabilities remains an unsolved problem. Rush, Chadsey-Rush, and Johnson (1992, p. 146) described supportive employment approaches as follows:

1. *Individual placement model:*   The individual is hired by an employer, and a job coach assists the employee, gradually decreasing the amount of support until the employee is able to perform the task without assistance.
2. *Clustered placement model:*   A group of from six to eight individuals working for a company receives continuous guidance and supervision from a job coach employed by the company.
3. *Mobile work crew:*   A group works out of a van at several locations in the community under the supervision of a job coach who provides continuous guidance and direction.

One can see in those models the movement from independence to continuous supervision. The models allow many individuals with multiple and severe disabilities the opportunity to engage in meaningful work instead of spending their lives isolated within their homes. Currently, less than 30 percent of the population with multiple and severe disabilities are employed in some capacity, but it is hoped that this percentage can be greatly increased in the future.

Szymanski (1994) suggested that life span considerations for transition should include interventions that

1. Are designed to be maximally under the control of the individual rather than others
2. Are designed to facilitate independence or interdependence and autonomy
3. Use the least intrusive means that are effective
4. Use the most natural interventions for the particular work environment (pp. 406–407)

Families

Never underestimate the impact on a family of having a child with severe and multiple disabilities. Some families suffer grief and mourn because they do not have their ideal child. Others show amazing strength in coping with the emotional, physical, and economic demands placed on them.

Some families face the lifelong challenge of providing assistance to a wheelchair-bound child with sensory impairments. Consider the needs of a child who uses a wheelchair. One wheelchair will not serve for a lifetime. The child will require larger prostheses as he or she ages. Leg braces will need to be lengthened; wheelchairs will need to be larger; glasses and hearing aids will need to be replaced. From the outset, the family needs expert diagnosis and treatment plans, even though, as we have seen in the case of autism, much is not known and diagnosis can be erroneous.

The environmental issues for families that we discussed in Chapter 2 are relevant here. Having a child with severe and multiple disabilities causes added stress. It modifies the family's concept of itself and creates lifetime demands that can be anticipated from infancy. Consider a child with a speech deficit or a child with Down syndrome. For the former, there is a possibility of complete remediation; and the latter may attain nearly normal cognitive functioning, independent living, and supportive employment. Such accomplishments are very difficult to predict for children with multiple and severe disabilities.

Through intervention, questions will focus on how far the child can progress. Is the child likely to be able to master sign language, control a motorized wheelchair, or use a word processor or a communication board? Some children will be able, and some will not. Those who are can move on to independent living and supportive employment. The others may be their family's responsibility for life. Family resources will be siphoned into child care, equipment, and therapies. The needs of the child with multiple and severe disabilities will absorb large amounts of time that otherwise would be spent in husband-wife interactions or family-peer interactions. Brothers and sisters will be involved in caring for their disabled sibling and lose some of their playtime or peer-interaction time.

These families need expert counseling and a case coordinator who is fully aware of community resources and services. Counseling can assist family members in working through their grief and accepting their child's disabilities. Even so, the child may never have the status of other children in the family.

If the family is headed by a single parent, multiple supports will be needed. In many cases, the single caregiver may have to seek public assistance in order to survive economically and provide the therapies and education the child requires. A working parent (usually the mother) may have to give up her career (see Chapter 3). In a two-parent family, if it is an economic necessity for both parents to work, the loss of income will worsen their problems.

In *Down All My Life*, Brown (1972) says his father recognized him as his son only after he showed signs of cognitive awareness when he was of elementary school age. Such active and passive rejection of a child may be a serious issue that needs to be addressed. An additional problem is that so much is unknown about some of these disabilities, such as autism. The family may spend enormous amounts of time seeking an accurate diagnosis and placement for the child.

Finding a baby sitter who allows the family to have some respite or leisure time is a significant problem. Autistic children may be very rejecting of strangers. A child who is physically disabled and sensory impaired may need feeding and toileting assistance beyond what a baby sitter is willing to provide. Parents who need and seek respite care may require the services of a trained specialist for their child with behavior disorders and sensory impairments.

In essence, a family's needs and problems are intensified by a child with multiple and severe disabilities.

Summary of Major Ideas

1. Not all persons with multiple and severe disabilities are mentally retarded, and many can achieve an adult status of independent living and competitive work.

2. Some individuals with multiple and severe disabilities possess some degree of mental retardation. These individuals may need supportive employment and supervised living arrangements as adults.

3. The Association for Persons with Severe Handicaps definition of multiple and severe disabilities includes persons of all ages who need extensive, ongoing support in more than one life activity.

4. The current effort in the field of multiple and severe disabilities is to begin intervention as soon after birth as the disability has been diagnosed and to provide appropriate treatment, prostheses, family support, and education to assist the individual to develop to his or her full potential.

5. The current practice in the field of multiple and severe disabilities is to teach the person to perform functional activities in settings in which he or she will use these skills.

6. It is now recognized in the field that communication grows out of nonsymbolic cries, grunts, and gestures. The individual can be taught to use these sounds and gestures to make requests, indicate refusals, and communicate wants and needs. Some individuals will never reach the symbolic stage of communication by using sign language or words.

7. The major focus of all work with individuals with multiple and severe disabilities is to help them acquire, insofar as possible, the skills that their nondisabled peers of the same age possess.

8. Major curricula are available for most forms of multiple and severe disabilities. The field has advanced in important ways in recent years.

9. Educating individuals with multiple and severe disabilities and assisting them in the development of life adjustment skills is a lifelong process for both the individuals and their families.

10. The best hope for facilitating the normalization and development of persons with multiple and severe disabilities lies with family members and the professionals who work with these persons.

Unresolved Issues

1. *Community acceptance.* The special education profession has made significant advances in providing curriculum and teaching and intervention strategies, but not all workplaces or communities are prepared to accept

individuals with multiple and severe disabilities. Supportive employment is an attempt to open up workplaces to persons with multiple and severe disabilities. The goal of providing a variety of meaningful work and vocational opportunities that will benefit both individuals with multiple and severe disabilities and their employers has not been fully achieved.

2. *Cost of intervention and support.* The costs of intervention and life support are high. Persons with multiple and severe disabilities need specialized training from numerous professionals as well as specialized teaching tools and prostheses. They may require lifetime support. Funds for these services are not always readily available.

3. *Inclusion and its issues.* Not all special educators believe in inclusion, which aims to place all youngsters with disabilities in regular schools and enables them to spend some time in the regular classroom. Stainback and Stainback (1989), however, argued for a merger of regular education and special education. They and many other proponents of inclusion wish to see all children with disabilities in regular schools and classrooms. However, as Semmel, Abernathy, Butera, and Lesar (1991) wrote, "Both the regular and special education teachers are not generally dissatisfied with the *current* special education system" (p. 19). Other dissenters feel regular education teachers and administrators have not been involved with special educators in planning inclusion and attempting to implement it (Leiberman, 1985). Still other special educators question the political motivation that initiated the Inclusion movement (Kaufman, 1989). The debate will continue over whether the regular education classroom is the least restrictive environment for all students with disabilities. The arguments pro and con were nicely summarized by Thousands and Villa (1991), Jenkins and Pious (1991), and Halpern (1991–1992).

Key Terms

auditory integration training (AIT) p. 474
autism p. 472
cerebral palsy p. 481
criterion-referenced tests p. 494
deaf-blind p. 475

Questions for Thought

1. What are the four categories of multiple and severe disabilities? p. 471
2. What are the characteristics of children with autism? p. 472
3. Why should the term *dual diagnosis* be used with great care? p. 480
4. Why is early intervention particularly important for children with multiple and severe disabilities? p. 482
5. What are the five possible types of intervention, according to Boothroyd? p. 483

6. Why is it important to teach age-appropriate skills? p. 487
7. How can children be taught to generalize skills within an integrated environment? p. 489
8. How can the integration of students who are and are not disabled be made to work? p. 491
9. What are the guidelines for the development of skills relating to communication, mobility, social skills, and self-management? p. 497
10. What special means of communication have been developed to help nonvocal students? p. 498
11. What are the advantages and disadvantages of each of the following vocational arrangements for adults with multiple and severe handicaps: day treatment programs, sheltered workshops, and supportive competitive employment? p. 505

References of Special Interest

Bradley, V., Ashbaugh, J., & Blaney, B. (1994). *Creating individual supports for people with disabilities*. Baltimore: Paul H. Brookes Publishing Co.
   This guide helps individuals change community- and state-based agencies to organizations that become community supports for individuals with disabilities.

Brown, F., & Lehr, D. H. (1989). *Persons with profound disabilities*. Baltimore: Paul H. Brookes Publishing Co.
   Twenty leaders in the field discuss in twelve chapters issues of teaching, policy, integration, research, and suggestions for practice. This book presents current thinking on persons with multiple and severe disabilities.

Ford, A., Schnorr, R., Meyer, L., Davern, L., Black, J., & Dempsey, P. (1989). *The Syracuse community-referenced curriculum guide for students with moderate and severe disabilities*. Baltimore: Paul H. Brookes Publishing Co.
   This is a collection of curriculum suggestions from preschool and elementary, middle, and high school concerning transition into the community and community living suggestions.

Gerry, M. H., & McWhorter, C. M. (1991). "A comprehensive analysis of federal statutes and programs for persons with severe disabilities." In L. H. Meyer, C. Peck, & L. Brown (Eds.), *Critical issues in the lives of people with severe disabilities* (pp. 521–525). Baltimore: Paul H. Brookes Publishing Co.
   This chapter provides a current review of the varied federal statutes regarding persons with severe and multiple disabilities. It also describes some current operating programs.

Giangreco, M., Cloninger, C., & Iverson, V. (1994). *Choosing options and accommodations for children*. Baltimore: Paul H. Brookes Publishing Co.
   This is a manual of assessment and planning suggestions for the inclusion of students with disabilities into regular classrooms.

Meyer, L. H., Peck, C. A., & Brown, L. (1991). *Critical issues in the lives of people with severe disabilities*. Baltimore: Paul H. Brookes Publishing Co.

This book presents statements by The Association for Persons with Severe Disabilities containing TASH resolutions, the reasons behind their thinking, anecdotes, serious reviews of all research issues, and suggestions on how to organize the classroom and teach. It is highly recommended for anyone who works with individuals with multiple and severe disabilities or for anyone who wishes to know more about this topic and related issues.

chapter

12

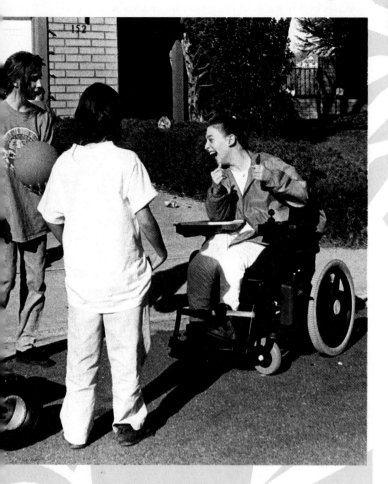

Children with Physical Disabilities and Health Impairments

focusing

Is every physical disability or health condition a disabling condition?

How does the age at which a child becomes physically disabled affect the child's adjustment to the condition?

What unique problems are faced by children with disabilities that are caused by accident or illness (disease)?

Why is it important for the classroom teacher to discuss a student's condition openly with the student's classmates?

Infants and young children without disabilities acquire cognitive, language, and social competence by interacting with their physical and social environments (Bower, 1989). They interact by using coordinated motor patterns that are genetically programmed to appear early in life and to assist them in learning what they need to know to adapt to their homes and environments (Bower, 1989).

This chapter is concerned with infants and children whose physical disabilities or health impairments interfere with their ability to interact with people and objects in their environment to the extent that they are not able to reach the normal milestones of development that their agemates reach easily. Some of the issues we discuss here you have encountered in other chapters, such as Chapter 11, on children with multiple and severe disabilities. However, only 20 percent of the children with chronic illnesses or physical disabilities have impairments that are classified as severe and profound (Lehr & Noonan, 1989). Due to the help of medical intervention and technology, many of these children are living normal, healthy lives and can function in regular environments. Until now, this has been a relatively small and diverse group. The situation may change, however, as technology helps to save the lives of very small premature infants (below 4 pounds) and the increase in severe child abuse cause the population of children with physical disabilities to grow.

A child's physical interaction with the environment is a major source of learning.

Definitions

The population of children with physical disabilities is very heterogeneous. It includes youngsters with many different conditions. Most of these conditions are unrelated, but for convenience, researchers often group them into two categories: physical disabilities and health impairments. A **physical disability** is a condition that interferes with a child's ability to use his or her body. Many, but not all, physical disabilities are *orthopedic impairments*—a term that generally refers to conditions of the muscular or skeletal system and sometimes to physically disabling conditions of the nervous system. A condition that requires ongoing medical attention is a **health impairment.**

According to the Individuals with Disabilities Education Act (IDEA), a person is disabled if he or she has a mental or physical impairment that substantially limits participation in one or more life activities. When a child's conditions—whether medical or physical—interfere with his or her ability to take part in routine school or home activities, the child has a physical disability. By this definition, a student with an artificial arm who takes part in all school activities, including physical education, is not physically disabled. But when a physical condition leaves a student unable to hold a pencil, walk from class to class, or use conventional toilets—when it interferes with the student's participation in routine school activities—the child is physically disabled. This does not mean that the child cannot learn. But it does place a special responsibility on teachers and therapists to adapt materials and equipment to meet the student's needs and help the student learn to use these adaptations and develop a strong self-concept.

Early intervention with a child who has physical disabilities and health impairments can minimize the severity of certain conditions and help the child participate in his or her environment, which in turn helps the child acquire the skills necessary for success in school. (© Michael D. Sullivan/Texas Stock)

Health impairments—for example, asthma, cystic fibrosis, heart defects, cancer, diabetes, and hemophilia—usually do not interfere with the child's ability to participate in regular classroom activities and do not require curricular adaptations. But these conditions can require medication or special medical treatment and can restrict physical activities and diet. Teachers should familiarize themselves with the student's medical history, first-aid procedures, and any restrictions recommended by the child's physician.

Prevalence of Physical Disabilities and Health Impairments

How many children have physical disabilities? The question is difficult to answer because of the way physical disabilities are defined and the way they are reported. Although we could determine the incidence of conditions that can result in physical disabilities, these figures would greatly overestimate the number of children whose participation in routine activities is actually limited by those conditions. The U.S. Department of Education (1992) estimated that about 0.5 percent of all school-age children have physical or health disabilities. This figure includes severely and profoundly disabled children as well as children with milder physical disabilities and health impairments described in this chapter.

For example, about 2 million persons in the United States have epilepsy (NICHCY, 1993). There are approximately 125,000 new cases each year, about 50 percent of which are children and adolescents (NICHCY, 1993). Medication can control seizures completely in most of the people with the disorder and reduce the number of seizures in most others. With regular medication, then, most children with epilepsy can participate in the same activities as their friends and classmates. Less than half of the total number of children with epilepsy are considered physically disabled.

This example applies to most other categories of physical and health disorders. Most of these children function well in regular classes, if the classrooms are accessible for wheelchairs or crutches or the support that persons with health impairments need is available (such as people who know how to clean and regulate oxygen tubes and other life-saving devices; discussed later in this chapter).

Local variations in the classification of disabilities further complicate the process of determining the prevalence of physical disabilities among schoolchildren. For example, one state may classify a large number of students as "other health impaired," and another state may classify similar students as "learning disabled." Or one state may classify students as "multihandicapped," and another may classify similar students according to the primary disabling conditions, such as "orthopedically impaired" (U.S. Department of Education, 1988).

Finally, at the national level there is no specific educational category for children with physical disabilities. Table 12.1 lists the number and percentage of children receiving special education and related services during the 1992–1993 school year who were classified as "orthopedically impaired" and "other health impaired." Taken together, the figures probably provide the best estimate of the number of school-age children with physical disabilities. Current figures reveal that only about 2.5 percent of all the children receiving special education and related services (or 0.27 percent of the entire school population) are physically disabled (U.S. Department of Education, 1994).

The low incidence of youngsters with physical disabilities limits the exposure of educators to their special needs. In the course of their careers, special education teachers might work with only a few students with physical disabilities, and these

TABLE 12.1	The Disability of Students Receiving Special Education in School Year 1992–93	
Disability	**Total**	**Percentage**
Orthopedic impairments	52,921	1.1
Other health impairments	66,054	1.4
Traumatic brain injury	3,903	0.1

Source: U.S. Department of Education (1994). *16th Annual Report to Congress on the Implementation of IDEA*. Section 618.

students' disabilities might be very different. Most of these children attend schools in which there is a staff of support personnel (occupational therapists, physical therapists, physicians, nurses, special educators). If a public school does not have the necessary support staff, it may contract for services in special schools.

Causes of Physical Disabilities and Health Impairments

Physically disabling conditions and health impairments can be either congenital or acquired. The cause of a condition and the age at which the condition develops influence the kinds of problems that children with physical disabilities and health impairments face as well as the implications for their teachers.

CONGENITAL DISABILITIES

The cause of a disabling condition and the age at which the child acquires it determine how the child will face it.

Children with congenital conditions are born with physical disabilities or develop them soon after birth. These children do not have the same developmental experiences that other children do. The extent of the differences depends on the type and severity of the condition. At one extreme, some youngsters never sit or walk. At the other extreme, some children with congenital conditions grow up and adapt with the help of prostheses or technical devices. Modern technology has provided devices and aids to help these children attain normal growth and development while they try to compensate for their disability (Schreiner, Donar, & Kettrick, 1987). What are these children feeling? Some feel badly because they have difficulty in playing with other children. But when they are placed in an accepting environment and provided with prosthetic devices that allow them to have access to that environment, most of these children have positive feelings of self-esteem and a positive self-concept (Orr, 1989).

ACQUIRED DISABILITIES

Not all physical disabilities are genetic. Some are acquired during the prenatal period and others upon or after birth.

Some children progress through normal developmental sequences and experiences and then develop or acquire—through injury or disease—a physically disabling condition. Some of these children are not able to use their preinjury experiences during rehabilitation. For example, a child with a traumatic brain injury may not be able to roll over, sit, or stand up, but remembers how to do it and tries to imitate the process. Most children with physical disabilities stemming from injuries are motivated to regain or replace their former abilities. When a child loses an ability, however, he or she usually goes through a period of mourning. The ability to adjust to a physical disability caused by injury depends on many factors, including the reactions of others, the importance of the lost abilities to the child's lifestyle, and the child's previously established style of coping (Heinemann & Shontz, 1984).

Children whose disabilities are caused by disease or terminal conditions (such as cancer and muscular dystrophy) face special problems. Often the process of a disease is poorly defined, and the extent of associated disabilities tends to change. Many diseases have acute or uncontrolled phases during which children are likely to miss school. Even when affected children return to school, pain and fatigue can interfere with learning. Although some diseases allow youngsters to live near-normal lives, others cause progressive deterioration and eventually death. The prospect of impending death is frightening for children as well as for their classmates and teachers. Some children become withdrawn, passive, or bitter. The children who understand their conditions, are encouraged to discuss them, and are held to the same general expectations and limits as their peers tend to cope best with progressive diseases (Hutter & Farrell, 1983).

Chronic diseases often require long-term medical treatments, which create difficulties. Cancer radiation and chemotherapy treatments cause nausea and hair loss. These side effects and their emotional impact can lead children to try to avoid treatment. Or youngsters with diabetes, wanting to be like other children, may eat the wrong foods or overexercise. These excesses can hasten the onset of irreversible problems associated with the disease.

Classification and Characteristics

Children with specific physical and health conditions are classified as physically (or orthopedically) disabled or as health impaired. This section provides an overview of the characteristics of children with common physical disabilities and health impairments.

CHILDREN WITH PHYSICAL DISABILITIES

Children with physical disabilities have many different types of conditions. Although there are important differences among these conditions, there are also similarities. Most affect one system of the body in particular: the **neurological system** (the brain, spinal cord, and nerves) or the **musculoskeletal system** (the muscles, bones, and joints).

The severity or degree of the child's physical involvement is a major component in classification. The severity of physical involvement can be described in functional terms according to the impact the disability has on mobility and motor skills:

■ A child with a *mild* physical disability is able to walk without aids and may make normal developmental progress.

■ A child with a *moderate* physical disability can walk with braces and crutches or a walker and may have difficulty with fine motor skills and speech production.

■ A child with a *severe* physical disability is wheelchair dependent and may need special help to achieve regular developmental milestones (see Chapter 11).

Clearly, the severity of the disability is a critical variable to consider when determining the amount of help and the kinds of adaptation a student needs. All children with physical disabilities have some limitations in their motor skills. For some, these limitations are severe: They cannot walk or sit independently or use their hands. Their dependence on others for getting around, for eating, and even for toileting can both frustrate and embarrass them. And conditions that affect appearance can increase these youngsters' social discomfort.

Neurological Conditions

The neurological system (often referred to as the *central nervous system*) is made up of the brain, the spinal cord, and a network of nerves that reach all parts of the body. The spinal cord and nerves carry messages between the brain and the rest of the body. Among its other functions, the brain controls muscle movement, and receptors in the muscles and joints send sensory feedback about speed, direction of movement, and body position to the brain.

With a neurological condition like cerebral palsy, the brain either sends the wrong instructions or interprets feedback incorrectly. In both cases, the result is poorly coordinated movement. With a spinal cord injury or deformity, pathways between the brain and the muscles are interrupted, so messages are transmitted but never received. The result is muscle paralysis and loss of sensation beyond the point where the spinal cord (or other nerve) is damaged. Children with these neurological conditions have motor skill deficits that can range from mild incoordination to paralysis from the neck down. The most severely involved children are totally dependent on other people or sophisticated equipment to carry out academic and self-care tasks.

Teachers can help students who have neurological conditions by adapting the learning environment to their needs. But because neurological conditions often affect the brain, teachers must first determine which behaviors the child can and cannot control and whether problems reflect a physical or social-emotional disability. They also have a responsibility to any exceptional child to create a supportive atmosphere that fosters the child's acceptance by providing classmates with information about the student's condition.

Cerebral Palsy.   **Cerebral palsy** is not a single disease but a number of disabilities caused by damage to the motor control centers of the brain (see Figure 12.1 on p. 522) (Batshaw & Perret, 1992). *Cerebral* refers to the brain and *palsy* to disorders of movement (NICHD, 1989). The damage that results in cerebral palsy can occur before birth, during the birth process, or after birth from an accident or injury (a blow to the head, lack of oxygen). The condition affects muscle tone (the degree of tension in the muscles), interferes with voluntary movement and full control of the muscles, and delays gross and fine motor development.

In **spastic (pyramidal) cerebral palsy,** muscle tone is abnormally high (hypertonia) and increases during activity. Muscles and joints are tight or stiff, and movements are limited to affected areas of the body (see Figure 12.1). Some children are *hemiplegic:* Just one side (left or right) of the body (either left arm and left leg or right arm and right leg) is affected. Others are *diplegic:* Their whole body is involved, but their legs are more severely involved than their arms. Still others are *quadriplegic:* Involvement is equally distributed throughout the body.

All children with cerebral palsy have problems with posture and movement.

With *extrapyramidal cerebral palsy* or *spastic quadriplegia,* all four limbs are spastic. The whole torso is involved and other disorders, such as visual and hearing impairment, almost always exist. The child has difficulty controlling movements (Batshaw & Perret, 1992).

In *choreoathetoid cerebral palsy,* muscle tone is constantly changing, usually from near normal to high. Movements are uncoordinated, uncontrolled, and jerky. The major problem is in initiating movement.

Children can have one or a combination of these types of cerebral palsy. The form and degree of physical involvement varies from child to child. In addition, the affected areas of the body also vary. A child with *mixed type cerebral palsy* has severe problems with balance and coordination, which affect ambulation.

Additional problems that can be associated with cerebral palsy include learning disabilities, mental retardation, seizures, speech impairments, eating problems, sensory impairments, and joint and bone deformities such as spinal curvatures and contractures (permanently fixed, tight muscles and joints). Scissor or toe walking is common among children with cerebral palsy who are able to walk.

Approximately 40 percent of children with cerebral palsy have normal intelligence; the remainder have from mild to severe retardation (Batshaw & Perret, 1992). Those classified as hemiplegic, the most common form of cerebral palsy, are most likely to have normal intelligence (Batshaw & Perret, 1992). The probability of normal intelligence decreases and the probability of secondary problems increases with the severity of the condition. But most children with cerebral palsy are not severely involved and do not have all or even some of the associated problems. This is an extremely heterogeneous group of children. Each child has unique abilities and needs. Technological advances in recent years have greatly improved the long-term well-being of these children (NICHD, 1989). They are more like their classmates who do not have a disability than they are different.

Epilepsy.   **Epilepsy** is a disorder that occurs when the brain cells are not working properly (March of Dimes, 1989). It is often called a seizure disorder. Epilepsy can occur in one hemisphere of the brain (*partial seizure*) or in both (*generalized seizure*). Some children may experience both types, and this condition is called *mixed seizure disorder.* Generalized seizures include the following types:

Mild or severe seizures can occur in epilepsy.

1. *Toxic-clonic seizures.* This is the most common type of seizure and involves major firing of neurons in both hemispheres of the brain. The child generally loses consciousness and falls to the floor. The clonic phase of the seizure is characterized by jerking of the body, sweating, and incontinence (Batshaw & Perret, 1992; NICHCY, 1993).

2. *Absence seizures.* During this seizure, the child has a blank expression, perhaps blinking before becoming unconscious, is unaware of the surroundings, and cannot be awakened. There may also be jerking of the arms. Afterward, the child is not aware of having had the seizure, which lasted less than ten seconds (Batshaw & Perret, 1992).

The Prison of Paralysis, the Freedom of Words

Christopher Nolan's body is his worst enemy. If he'd like to lift his right arm up from his wheelchair, his left arm is likely to shoot out in an uncontrollable jerk. He wants to smile for a photographer? His face collapses into a sleepy-looking stupor. Even the sacred act of taking Communion can turn into a farce: A vicious muscle spasm can force his jaw rigidly shut.

But inside Nolan's mute and almost useless body, plagued with cerebral palsy since his birth in Ireland 22 years ago, is an acute mind that has found its exuberant liberation in writing. Nolan's autobiography, *Under the Eye of the Clock,* won Britain's most prestigious literary award early this year and has zoomed to the top of the London bestseller lists. . . .

"Part of Nolan's value as a writer is that he comes from another planet—the planet of the paralyzed and speechless," says Oxford University literature Prof. John Carey.

The autobiography chronicles his struggle—ultimately successful—to attend high school with able-bodied boys and girls. While heaping praise upon his family, teachers and friends, Nolan writes unflinchingly of society's pity, intolerance and hypocrisy. Of those who vetoed his admission to a school: "Someone normal, someone beautiful . . . someone Christian worst of all, boasted ascetic, one of the head-strokers—poor child, God love him, ah God is good, never shuts one door but he opens another." And of the American journalist who hinted he was a fraud: "Giant-sized feet he seemed to put into the heart of the ear-sharp boy."

It is such imaginative use of language that has riveted the attention of critics. "Not merely another tale of brave strife against odds," says novelist Margaret Drabble in a recent review. "Nolan is a writer, a real writer who uses words with an idiosyncratic new-minted freshness."

Nolan was unable to make a meaningful mark on paper until age 11, when the drug Lioresal helped abate his muscle spasms. He approached words much as another child might approach an overturned truck of candy, says one critic. Just four years later, he published a book of poetry, *Dam-Burst of Dreams,* which won him comparisons with such literary giants as his compatriot James Joyce and 17th-century poet John Donne.

Nolan taps out letters on a typewriter with the help of a "unicorn" stick strapped to his forehead. His chin is supported by his mother, Bernadette, 53, who stands behind her wheelchair-bound son for hours at a stretch in a study in their middle-class Dublin home.

Nolan's family still must care for him as if he were a baby, washing and feeding him, sitting him on the toilet, carrying him up and down stairs. "His mother is heroic," says professor and poet Brendan Kennelly, who got to know the family during the year Nolan spent as a student at Dublin's Trinity College. "She has a capacity for devoted drudgery, drudgery transformed by love."

His mother is in demand as a speaker to groups aiding the disabled, a role she found very difficult at first. When Christy was 8, the family left its farm so that he could go to a special school for the disabled in Dublin. "We worked hard to give Christy a good education, but we thought it something we were giving him as a gift. Now he has turned around and made us famous." Bernadette does not underplay the strength required to care for a handicapped child. "A man's macho image is likely to be dented by fathering a less-than-perfect child. But a mother has to find acceptance for the child within herself."

Even these days, Nolan saves the typewriter for his creative work and for special tasks such as corresponding with his editor in London. He communicates with his family and friends through eye movements and a subtle sign language. "There wasn't anything he couldn't tell us before he was able to type," says Bernadette. "We've spent 22 years developing this language."

A visitor can catch on to what seems like an especially difficult game of charades. Nolan glances at a picture of a church on his livingroom wall, then at your throat, until the image of a white clerical collar pops into mind—a priest. He jiggles his feet, then glances at the electric heater. Think of an op-posite—a triumphal guess of "You got cold feet," is met with a joyous grin from Nolan.

Nolan's next project is a novel, but even some of his supporters are skeptical that Nolan's personal experience is wide enough to sustain fiction. His mother doesn't entertain any doubts. Nodding to a visiting journalist, she asks: "What do you think he is doing with all the people he meets?"

Regardless of what the future brings, Nolan's work already may have changed attitudes toward the disabled. Says his teacher Brendan Kennelly: "Christy experiences life so intensely, no one who reads his book could pity him."

Source: Pamela Sherrid, "The Prison of Paralysis, the Freedom of Words." Copyright *U.S. News & World Report,* March 14, 1988, p. 60. Reprinted by permission.

---

commentary

What Is the Context? Christopher Nolan's family provided him with the chance to attend school, developed ways for him to communicate and participate in the family life, and gave him the assistance he required without fostering feelings of self-pity or helplessness in him. His writing encourages the same response from society itself—to end intolerance, pity, and hypocrisy in its treatment of people with disabilities.

Pivotal Issues. How can or should society ensure that drugs such as Lioresal and technology such as the unicorn stick are available to all people who need them? Based on this article and your own experience, what other types of support do you think people with physical and health disabilities need, and how are they provided?

---

3. *Atypical absence seizures.* The onset of this type of seizure is more gradual than that of the absence type, but it lasts longer and creates greater confusion. It is more serious because a child who has atypical absence seizures is likely to have other types of seizures as well (Batshaw & Perret, 1992).

4. *Myclonic and atonic seizures.* These seizures start with abrupt jerking of the muscles, and in infancy they are called *infantile spasms.* Atonic seizures are the opposite of myclonic ones. They are characterized by a sudden loss of muscle tone, falling, and loss of consciousness (Batshaw & Perret, 1992).

Figure 12.1
Regions of the Brain Affected by
Various Forms of Cerebral Palsy
(The darker the shading, the more
severe is the involvement.)

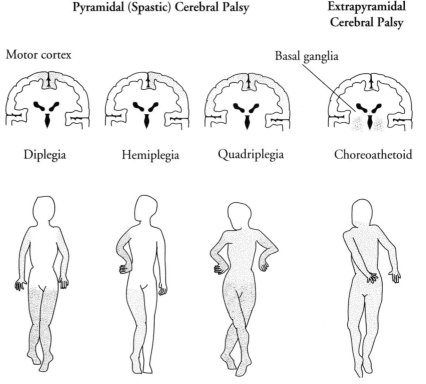

Source: M. I. Batshaw and Y. M. Perret (1992). *Children with Disabilities: A Medical Primer* (3rd ed., p. 444). Baltimore: Paul H. Brookes Publishing Co. Copyright © 1992. Used by permission of the author.

Partial seizures are limited to one hemisphere of the brain. When the individual loses consciousness, they are called *complex partial seizures*. When consciousness is not lost, they are called *simple partial seizures* (Batshaw & Perret, 1992).

Fortunately, once epilepsy is diagnosed, medication can completely control it in from 70 to 90 percent of cases. Surgery is often recommended for those who do not respond to medication (Freeman & Vining, 1990). Epilepsy does not interfere with performance in school. Most individuals with epilepsy have normal intelligence (Batshaw & Perret, 1986; Nealis, 1983). There are 2 million children and adolescents with epilepsy in the United States (NICHCY, 1989).

Tourette Syndrome.　Tourette syndrome should not be confused with epilepsy, although it is generally classified as a seizure disorder (Batshaw & Perret, 1992). This syndrome consists of multiple motor, facial, and vocal tics, which vary in intensity. Sometimes the child can control them. They appear to intensify when the child is tired, excited, or anxious (Batshaw & Perret, 1992).

Neural Tube Defects.　The most common types of neural tube defects (defects of the spinal cord and brain) are spina bifida and myelomeningocele.

Spina bifida is the separation of a portion of the backbone (spinal cord). *Myelomeningocele* is the protrusion from the spinal cord of a sac of fluids containing portions of the spinal cord itself. In cases in which both spina bifida and myelomeningocele occur, a portion of the backbone can be seen at birth. Damage to the spinal cord leads to paralysis and loss of sensation in portions of the body. In the most extreme case, *anencephaly*, the break occurs at the portion of the spinal cord that will develop into the brainstem. This is usually fatal.

The cause of spina bifida is considered unknown; however, if women who have given birth to a child with spina bifida or myelomeningocele are given folic acid (a type of vitamin B) before a subsequent pregnancy, they tend not to have another child with neural tube defects (Batshaw & Perret, 1992). The March of Dimes (1994) encourages women of childbearing age to take 0.4 milligrams of folic acid as a preventive measure, because spina bifida occurs in the first 26 to 28 days of pregnancy, usually before a woman is aware of her condition (Batshaw & Perret, 1992).

Folic acid taken by the mother before pregnancy tends to reduce the occurrence of spina bifida in the child.

The location and extent of injury to the spinal cord determine the degree of physical involvement and loss of function. Injuries to the upper segments of the spinal cord can leave the individual quadriplegic, with no function in the trunk, arms, or legs. Injuries to lower levels of the spinal cord result in varying degrees of paralysis in the legs (paraplegia).

Secondary or medical problems associated with myelomeningocele and spinal cord injury, as with cerebral palsy, include loss of bladder and bowel control (requiring catheterization or surgical intervention) and joint and bone deformities (spinal curvatures and contractures). In addition, children with myelomeningocele typically are hydrocephalic (hydrocephalus is the buildup of cerebrospinal fluid in the skull). A shunt is surgically inserted to drain excess fluid from the brain (see Figure 12.2).

Most children with myelomeningocele have normal intelligence, but these children may have learning disabilities, perceptual problems, and impaired fine motor skills. The degree of physical involvement determines the extent to which mobility and performance of daily activities are affected (March of Dimes, 1987; Williamson, 1987).

Spinal cord injuries are caused by car, motorcycle, in-line skating, and diving accidents and by disease. Adolescents older than age 15 and young adults are at the greatest risk for spinal cord injuries because of their active lifestyles and tendency to take risks (Gilgoff, 1983).

Musculoskeletal Conditions

The musculoskeletal system includes the muscles and their supporting framework, the skeleton. Conditions that affect the musculoskeletal system can result in progressive muscle weakness (muscular dystrophy); inflammation of the joints (arthritis), or loss of various parts of the body (amputation). Severe burns can lead to amputation, damage to muscles, or scars that impede movement. Severe scoliosis (curvature of the spine) can limit movement of the trunk, cause back pain, and eventually may compress the lungs, heart, and other internal organs.

Most children with musculoskeletal conditions have normal intellectual abilities (Batshaw & Perret, 1986). They do not necessarily encounter academic difficulties,

Figure 12.2
Ventriculoperitoneal Shunt

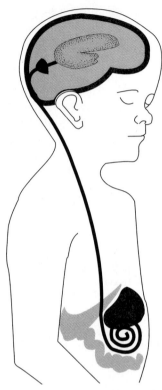

Source: G. Williamson (1987). *Children with Spina Bifida: Early Intervention and Preschool Programming* (p. 83, Figure 4.1). Baltimore: Paul H. Brookes Publishing Co., P.O. Box 10624, Baltimore, M.D. 21285-0624. Copyright © 1987. Used by permission of Paul H. Brookes Publishing Co. and the author.

Most children with musculoskeletal conditions have normal intelligence.

but their physical limitations and social and emotional adjustment can create educational problems.

Teachers can help students with musculoskeletal conditions by making adjustments for pain or poor endurance and encouraging as much physical activity as possible. They can arrange for a splint to hold a pencil or spoon or for a different faucet handle for a bathroom sink. They can be sensitive to the child's need for help with toileting and make arrangements for someone to respond quickly and competently. And they can encourage classmates to volunteer to help the child with difficult activities.

Muscular Dystrophy.   Muscular dystrophy is an inherited condition, occurring primarily in males, in which the muscles weaken and deteriorate. The weakness usually appears around 3 to 4 years of age and progressively worsens. By age 11, most victims can no longer walk. Death usually comes between the ages of 25 and 35 from respiratory failure or cardiac arrest (Lyle & Obringer, 1983).

Arthritis.   **Arthritis** is an inflammation of the joints. Symptoms include swollen and stiff joints, fever, and pain in the joints during acute flare-ups. Prolonged

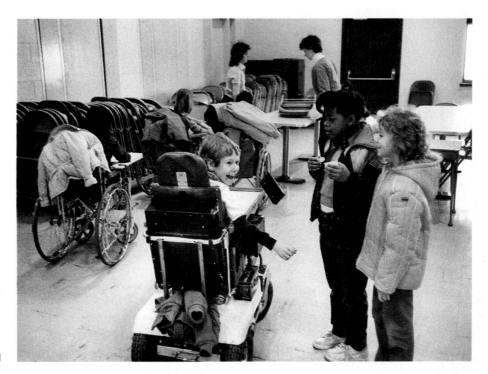

Musculoskeletal conditions affect the muscles and the skeleton. They often severely limit a child's motor skills and can increase the child's social discomfort but usually do not impair intellectual and academic abilities. (© Alan Carey/The Image Works)

inflammation can lead to joint deformities that eventually can affect mobility. Students may require frequent medication or miss school if surgery is needed.

Amputation. A small number of children are missing limbs because of congenital abnormalities, injury, or disease (malignant bone tumors in the limbs). These children can use customized prosthetic devices (artificial hands, arms, or legs) to replace limb functions and increase independence in daily activities. Teachers should be sensitive to the social and emotional needs of students with amputations, particularly when those amputations are acquired later in life. The child who acquires an amputation will have psychological stress adjusting to the loss.

Marfan Syndrome. Marfan syndrome is a genetic disorder that produces poorly developed muscles and a curved spine. Individuals with Marfan syndrome may have long, thin limbs, prominent shoulder blades, spinal curvature (scoliosis), and flat feet, or long fingers and thumbs. This syndrome affects about twenty thousand persons a year. The heart and blood vessels are usually affected. The greatest danger is damage to the aorta, which can lead to heart failure. Children with Marfan syndrome need to avoid heavy exercise and lifting heavy objects (March of Dimes, 1987).

Achondroplasia. Achondroplasia is a genetic disorder that affects 1 in 10,000 births. Children with this disorder usually develop a normal torso but have a straight upper back and a curved lower back (swayback). These children are at risk of sudden death during sleep from compression of the spinal cord interfering with their breathing. The disability may be lessened through the use of back braces or by surgery (March of Dimes, 1987).

Polio.   Polio was a common disease before the development of vaccines that offset the responsible virus. The virus could invade the brain and cause mild-to-severe paralysis of the body. There were also milder cases of partial paralysis. The virus is still present, and every child needs to be immunized for protection against this disease.

Post Polio Muscle Atrophy.   Post polio muscle atrophy appears in some individuals who had polio early in life. Muscles that were previously damaged weaken, and in some persons muscles that were not previously affected weaken as well (March of Dimes, 1986, 1987).

Club Foot.   Club foot is a major orthopedic problem affecting about nine thousand infants each year. The term is used to describe various ankle or foot deformities: twisting inward (*equinovarus*), the most severe form; sharply angled at the heel (*calcanel valgus*), the most common type; or the front part of the foot turning inward (*metatarsus varus*). These conditions can be treated with physical therapy, and a cast on the foot can solve the problem in most instances. In severe cases, surgery is necessary. With early treatment, most children can wear regular shoes and take part in all school activities (March of Dimes, 1986).

Cleft Lip and Cleft Palate.   Cleft lip and cleft palate are openings in the lip or roof of the mouth, respectively, that fail to close before birth. The cause is unknown. Most cleft problems can be repaired through surgery (March of Dimes, 1988; see also Chapter 8).

CHILDREN WITH HEALTH IMPAIRMENTS

Youngsters with health impairments require ongoing medical attention. Like physical disabilities, health impairments stem from a wide variety of conditions (see Table 12.2).

Cardiopulmonary Conditions

The **cardiopulmonary system** includes the heart, blood, and lungs. When a health problem affects the cardiopulmonary system, a child may have problems in breathing (for example, asthma, cystic fibrosis), or the heart may not pump blood properly (heart defects). Some children with these conditions cannot run, climb stairs, or even walk from one part of the school to another. Although it is possible to limit strenuous exercise for these children, simply sitting in school all day takes more energy than some of them can produce. Their inability to take part in normal activities with their agemates can create social problems for these youngsters. Adding to these problems is the high susceptibility of these children to illness. Frequent absences put them at an academic disadvantage in spite of their normal intelligence.

TABLE 12.2	Conditions That Can Result in Health Impairments				
	Primary System Affected		Cause of Condition		
	Cardiopulmonary	Other	Congenital Factors	Disease	Other
Asthma	x				x
Cancer		x		x	
Cystic fibrosis	x		x		
Diabetes		x		x	
Heart defects	x		x	x	

Health conditions often result in absences, forcing teachers to adjust their instructional plans.

Teachers can help a student with a cardiopulmonary condition by adapting instruction and the learning environment to the child's needs. For example, they can schedule the most important learning activities during the child's period of greatest energy, allow the child to rest at certain intervals, give the child extra time to complete assignments, arrange for locker space close to the classroom, or provide alternatives (and academic waivers) for physical education classes that exceed the child's capabilities.

Asthma.   **Asthma** is a condition affecting an individual's breathing. It usually has three features: Lungs are swollen, breathing is difficult, and the airways react negatively to a variety of environmental conditions (such as dust, smoke, cold air, and exercise). Asthma may also cause acute constriction of the bronchial tubes (Batshaw & Perret, 1992).

In children, the condition varies from mild to severe. Asthma usually does not pose a major problem for the teachers of children with this condition. Nevertheless, all teachers need to know how to deal with the frequent absences of children with severe asthma and what symptoms indicate that a child is having a severe attack. Teachers who have a child with asthma in their classes need a doctor's suggested plan of medication, a list of symptoms that indicate daily or emergency medical attention, and some indication of the degree to which the child can safely exercise and participate in classroom activities.

Asthma in a child can pose a serious problem for the parents. They need accurate diagnosis and treatment plans from appropriate medical personnel. Medication may be necessary throughout an individual's life, and those who are seriously affected are likely to require emergency treatment from time to time. A child with asthma may be a serious drain on the family's financial resources.

Cystic Fibrosis.   Cystic fibrosis is the most frequently occurring lethal genetic disease in the United States (*Science,* 1990). Children affected with this disorder have severe respiratory and digestive problems. Recently geneticists have identified the gene accounting for 70 percent of the cases (*Science,* 1990). Currently, an experiment is being conducted to determine if the problem can be avoided by supplying normal genes to a child afflicted with this disease. New techniques for screening prospective parents for the lethal gene are being developed (*Science,* 1990). It is hoped that in the future gene treatment can control both cystic fibrosis and muscular dystrophy.

Acquired Immune Deficiency Syndrome

Acquired immune deficiency syndrome (AIDS) is a breakdown of the body's immune system caused by the **human immunodeficiency virus (HIV).** Seventy percent of AIDS cases in children are the result of the virus being transmitted from an infected mother to the unborn child (Gee & Moran, 1988). A child may also become infected through a transfusion of contaminated blood.

Among adults, the disease is transmitted through sexual contact, by using contaminated needles to administer drugs intravenously, or through transfusions of infected blood. Adolescents exposed to any of these are as much at risk of contracting the disease as adults.

The outlook for children with AIDS is grim: severe developmental delays, brain damage, and early death (Gee & Moran, 1988). AIDS is a serious concern in our society, and communities are still formulating policies on how to work with infants and children who have the infection (including how those children are to be educated).

Regardless, because the incidence of the disease was expected to rise to four thousand children in 1992 (Crocker, 1989), professionals must respond to each child individually to best care for his or her health needs and to maximize his or her competencies. Infants need careful diagnosis, and individual family service plans (IFSPs) must be developed to ensure adequate medical and educational services (Crocker, 1989).

Cooley's Anemia and Sickle Cell Anemia

Cooley's anemia is a blood cell disease of genetic origin; it is most frequently found in persons living in the Mediterranean area or among those of Mediterranean stock. The child appears healthy at birth but soon becomes listless, has a poor appetite, and contracts frequent infections. Cooley's anemia is treated with frequent blood transfusions. At this time, there is no known cure.

Sickle cell anemia is an inherited blood disease most commonly found among African Americans and Hispanics of Caribbean ancestry. The oxygen-carrying red blood cells are usually round. In children with sickle cell anemia they are crescent or sickle shaped. The sickle cells are not as flexible as the round cells and can be trapped in body organs. When the red blood cells are trapped, oxygen is not carried through the body, and the resulting shortage of oxygen can leave the child highly vulnerable to infection. Currently, massive doses of penicillin are administered to children with sickle cell anemia to prevent the development of infections. The penicillin dosage continues throughout early childhood until the individual's immune system can fight the infections (summarized from March of Dimes, 1986, 1989).

Substance Abuse

It is estimated that in 1990, 4.8 million women of childbearing age used illicit drugs (Shriver & Piersal, 1994). This figure does not include the women who used legal drugs such as alcohol and tobacco—the 30.5 million women who consumed alcohol and the 17.4 million who used nicotine (Shriver & Piersal, 1994).

The media overemphasize the effects of maternal drug use in children born to these women, but some serious disabilities can occur. For example, although research has *not* demonstrated negative effects from prenatal exposure to heroin or marijuana, negative effects have been found in children whose mothers used cocaine or alcohol during pregnancy. The effect of alcohol on the fetus is the most thoroughly researched aspect of prenatal exposure to drugs.

Some disorders from fetal alcohol syndrome are not diagnosed until childhood or adolescence.

Alcohol.   The most adverse effects have been observed in the children of mothers who consumed alcohol heavily (more than 8 ounces per day) while they were pregnant. This consumption results in **fetal alcohol syndrome.** Children with this condition have disorders in three categories: growth deficiencies, facial malformations, and central nervous system effects in the form of mental retardation and challenging behaviors. These disorders are generally diagnosed in childhood and adolescence. Facial and physical abnormalities may require medical treatment (Batshaw & Perret, 1992; Shriver & Piersal, 1994). Generally, children exposed to alcohol (less than 8 ounces per day) have lower birth weight, decreased height, and smaller heads. There appears to be a relationship between an expectant mother's binge drinking (five or more drinks per day) and her child's lower cognitive functioning.

Cocaine.   An expectant mother's use of cocaine has been associated with her child's lower birth weight, shorter body length, and smaller head circumference. Some studies have also found cognitive deficits, challenging behaviors, and lower achievement; however, the results are not the same for all cocaine-exposed children. Cohen and Erwin (1994) found that only one-fourth of their sample of children exposed to cocaine prenatally exhibited problem-causing behavioral characteristics in the classroom. Moreover, half of the sample hardly resembled the cultural stereotype of the drug-exposed child at all (p. 248).

In summary, Shriver and Piersal's (1994) statement merits attention:

> Knowledge that a child has been exposed to drugs prenatally will not automatically qualify the child for early special education, *nor should it.* For example, information that children exposed in utero to crack cocaine will automatically have some type of learning disability, or that children exposed to alcohol will automatically be developmentally delayed is unsubstantiated by current research. (p. 176, emphasis added; see also Hansen & Ulrey, 1992)

Chronic diseases involving long-term medical treatments usually mean that a student will miss school, sometimes for prolonged periods, and that the individual may experience pain and fatigue, which can interfere with learning. (© *Audrey Gottlieb/Monkmeyer Press Photo Service*)

Other Health-Related Conditions

Other health-related conditions include chronic and sometimes life-threatening diseases such as cancer (leukemia, malignant tumors), diabetes, and hemophilia. Children with these conditions may require extensive medical treatment or periodic hospitalization. When working with a student who has a serious health disorder, teachers should obtain current information about the child's condition so that needed changes can be made in expectations and school activities. Also, teachers should be sensitive to the social and emotional status of the child, keep activities as normal as possible, and provide support. Children with diabetes or hemophilia may require regular medication or other medical treatment. Teachers working with these children should be knowledgeable about medical procedures needed at school, limitations on activities, and emergency procedures that may be necessary if problems arise.

TECHNOLOGY-DEPENDENT HEALTH CONDITIONS

Children who depend on technological devices to survive are increasingly included in regular and special education classes (Levine, 1996). Most of these children have chronic health or physical disabilities and will require technological assistance for long periods of their lives, although some outgrow the conditions in early childhood and do not require continued mechanical aids for survival.

Technology-dependent children are encouraged to live normal lives, for most of them can acquire academic, social, and language skills at an age-appropriate time. In 1984 the Supreme Court ruled that technology-dependent children have a right to live at home (instead of in a hospital or nursing facility) and to attend school and have nursing procedures provided for them. The reduction of cost in moving the child from the hospital to the home is enormous. Hospital costs can run to $270,830 a year, compared with $21,192 a year in the home (Schuman, 1990).

A Home-Care Success Story

By the end of his first day of life, Alex Hughes had been placed on a respirator and transferred from a community hospital to a neonatal intensive care unit (NICU). He had severe hyaline membrane disease, bronchopulmonary dysplasia, and multiple complications. Within days, Alex was baptized and given last rites.

With intensive care, though, his condition gradually improved. At 9 months he was transferred to Children's Memorial Hospital in Chicago, where he underwent a tracheostomy. At 15 months, the treatment team found a ventilator setting on which Alex was stable, and a joint decision was made to send him home. The alternative was two or three more years of high-tech hospital care. His mother, Ann Hughes, had practically been living at the hospital and at a nearby Ronald McDonald House; meanwhile, she was eight-months pregnant with her second child. Alex's father, Steve, was making regular visits from home, forty miles away.

"We had been thoroughly trained in using the ventilator, but all of a sudden the equipment looked very scary," Ann recalls. They maintained the ventilator, ordered supplies, changed the tracheostomy tube three times a week, and measured oxygen saturation with a pulse oximeter.

They worked closely with nurses and therapists and consulted by telephone with doctors at Children's Memorial and with their own pediatricians, who took responsibility for Alex's general care and reviewed the need for physical, speech, and occupational therapy. "Our pediatrician listened to us and believed what we had to say," Steve says. "They trusted our judgment and our ability to assess Alex's condition."

Alex was gradually weaned from the ventilator and from the need for in-house nursing care. He is off the ventilator entirely, and the tracheostomy has been closed. At 4 1/2 years of age, he is doing well physically but is still not talking and tends to be withdrawn. He is attending a school for physically and developmentally handicapped youngsters.

"Everything we went through has been worth every second just to have him home," his mother says. "His improvement has been extraordinary." Sister Katie,

2 1/2, is developmentally close to Alex and is his best friend. "She's a good influence," says Ann. "She's better than a therapist" (Goldberg, 1991, pp. 26–32).

In the following sections we discuss some of the devices that educators may encounter.

Tube Feeding

Some infants are born with or develop problems that prevent them from being able to eat. These children may have poorly developed sucking and swallowing reflexes; the sucking reflex is necessary to pull food into the mouth to be swallowed (Batshaw & Perret, 1992; Krajicek, 1991). They may also have abnormal muscle tone in the lips or tongue, which makes eating difficult or causes vomiting, or they may have a malformed breathing tube and esophagus, which allow food to enter the lungs.

Tube feeding allows children with severe eating problems to live regular lives.

When a child cannot receive enough nutrients through mouth feeding, a tube is inserted into the stomach, and food is fed directly into it. This is called *gastrostomy feeding* (Batshaw & Perret, 1992; Haynie, Porter, & Palfrey, 1989). As an alternative, the tube may be passed through the nose (nasogastric tube). The nasogastric technique cannot be used for longer than a few months, because the esophagus becomes irritated. Gastrostomy is usually the preferred treatment (Batshaw & Perret, 1992). See Figure 12.3 for examples of gastrostomy and nasogastric tube feedings. There are several types of tubes; a physician or specialist determines the best type for the child. Children who require tube feeding can live regular lives and engage in normal play and learning activities.

Parents and teachers need to learn how to manage the feeding and handle the equipment associated with it. In addition, careful monitoring is necessary to ensure that the child is receiving adequate nutrition. Two guides are very helpful in preparing parents and others to work with these children: *Handbook for the Care of Infants and Toddlers with Disabilities* (Krajicek, 1991) and *Children Assisted in Educational Settings: Guidelines for Care* (Haynie, Porter, & Palfrey, 1989). In addition, Smith and Krajicek (1991) prepared a video that demonstrates and describes the techniques, equipment, and care needed for gastrostomy feeding.

Intravenous Feeding

In some children, intravenous feeding is administered through a large, deep vein in the neck or chest (Haynie, Porter, & Palfrey, 1989). Children usually require this procedure if they need long-term care, such as chemotherapy or antibiotic therapy, or if the bowels are incapable of absorbing adequate nutrients (Haynie, Porter, & Palfrey, 1989).

Catheterization and Colostomy

Catherization and colostomy are used to remove wastes from the bladder and bowels when the nerves that normally stimulate their removal fail to function properly or a physical disability has damaged the signal area in the bladder or bowels. A child can be taught to insert a tube to remove the urine (catherization).

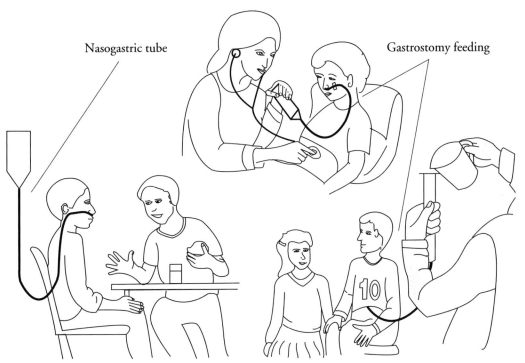

Nasogastric tube   Gastrostomy feeding

Figure 12.3
Gastrostomy and Nasogastric Feeding

Colostomy is a surgical procedure in which a doctor inserts a tube that allows waste from the bowels to be collected in a bag attached to the child's abdomen. The child can be taught to empty the pouch that contains the waste. Of course, when the child is an infant, the parents or caretakers have to learn to perform these procedures. These children usually possess normal intelligence and can take part in school activities.

The two manuals mentioned in the section on tube feeding contain pictures and instructions on how to carry out these procedures.

Oxygen-Dependent Children

Premature infants frequently suffer from severe respiratory distress. The therapy of providing oxygen to premature and low-birth-weight infants may cause a thickening and drying of the lung tissue (bronchopulmonary dysplasia), further complicating the problem and prolonging oxygen therapy (Krajicek, 1991). Children with cystic fibrosis (a dysfunction of mucous production), severe asthma, and some diseases of the heart also require oxygen therapy.

The most common method of treatment is providing oxygen through a nasal cannula. Other means of delivering oxygen are a nasal mask if the nasal passage is blocked or a tracheostomy (a tube inserted into the windpipe through a surgical opening).

Oxygen-dependent children require personnel trained in the proper use of their equipment.

Car seats and wheelchairs equipped with respirators and other oxygen-supplying equipment are available. They allow the infant and young child to be transported more easily from home to school or for out-of-home experiences. Parents and personnel who care for or teach these children need specialized training. The references previously mentioned provide guidelines on how to use the equipment effectively and safely (Haynie, Porter, & Palfrey, 1989; Krajicek, 1991). Smith and Krajicek (1989) have prepared a video on caring for children who are oxygen dependent and the proper use of the equipment involved. The video also illustrates how to transport these children to playgrounds, position them for normal play in their homes, and enable them to lead regular lives at home and in school.

CHILD ABUSE

Child abuse is a major cause of some children's disabilities.

Children who suffer from child abuse may acquire disabilities that are not caused by any genetic or birth disorder. Child abuse has become the leading cause of injury and death for children in the United States, outpacing the leader of the past, childhood accidents. Because they exhibit all the symptoms and disabilities of children with genetic or birth disorders, many of these children are misclassified by health-care workers. For example, Cohen and Warren (1987) found that about one-third of the children in a center for cerebral palsy were victims of child abuse and may or may not have had cerebral palsy before the abuse.

Money (1977) documented one of the more dramatic negative effects of child abuse, which he calls *abuse dwarfism*. The victims are children who were locked in closets, basements, or attics and were severely damaged physically, suffering abrasions and broken bones. As a result, they stopped growing and appear to be dwarfs. They also stopped developing in other ways and possess low intelligence quotient (IQ) scores and lack of verbal ability.

Children who are rescued from these environments are usually placed in a hospital for medical treatment and care. After two weeks, they begin to grow and develop. The amount of growth depends on the age of the child at the time of rescue. For example, if a girl is rescued at age 10, she may have a growth spurt of 12 inches over the next two years, reach menarche, and gain from 30 to 40 IQ points, although she will still be shorter than the average female. If she is rescued earlier, she will have a better chance of reaching the average height for her sex.

There is an epidemic of child abuse in the United States. There has been an increase of a million cases of reported child abuse since 1980, bringing the total to 2 million cases reported in 1987 (Zirpoli, 1990). Zirpoli writes that some professionals believe that the actual number of cases is at least twice the number reported (p. 6). Many abused children are placed in special education classes because their symptoms and needs are the same as those of children with genetic disabilities.

TRAUMATIC BRAIN INJURY AND ACCIDENTS

Accidents that involve the head are usually referred to as *traumatic brain injuries (TBI)*. The results of these injuries may resemble spina bifida, cerebral palsy, or other physical disabilities. TBI can result in cognitive, social, and language defects

Traumatic brain injuries can result in cognitive, social, and language defects that treatment sometimes reverses. (© *Spencer Grant/The Picture Cube*)

as well (National Head Injury Foundation, 1988). The current professional orientation is to attempt to distinguish these children from those with genetic dysfunctions. Although the two groups appear similar, treatment may reverse some of the disorders caused by TBI, but genetic disabilities such as paralysis are not able to be reversed. For example, Kevin Murphy, who was completely paralyzed in an automobile accident, had a full recovery and today is a leader in the field of special education, specializing in the severely and profoundly disabled.

Other accidents may lead to broken bones, the loss of limbs, or incurable paralysis. Car seats for infants have greatly reduced the number of fatal and damaging injuries to infants and preschoolers. Seat belts and air bags have further reduced the number of deaths and serious injuries resulting from car accidents.

■■ Developmental Profiles

Paolo and Margaritte are two children with physical disabilities. Their developmental profiles in Figure 12.4 show that they are like their classmates in many ways but very different in others.

Paolo was born with cerebral palsy, a condition that affects his nervous system and makes it hard for him to coordinate his muscles. Although he has average intelligence, he has never learned to sit by himself or walk. He cannot control the movements of his face and arms. And when he tries to speak, he makes grunts and groans instead of words.

Figure 12.4
Profiles of Two Children with
Physical Disabilities

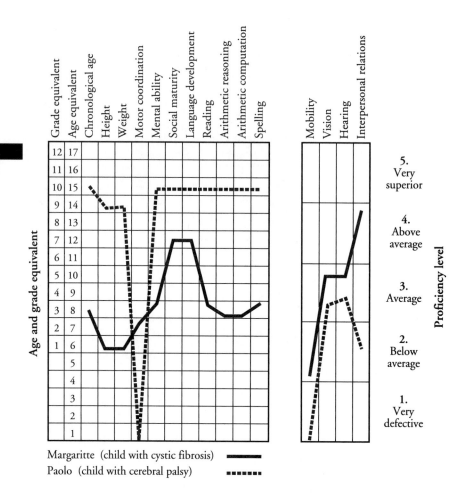

Margaritte (child with cystic fibrosis) ——————
Paolo (child with cerebral palsy) ■■■■■■■

For many years, Paolo's doctors and school personnel thought he was mentally retarded. When Paolo was 8, he learned to use an electronic communicating system. He has not stopped "talking" since. He now uses a Touch Talker that is programmed with the alphabet and about a hundred words and phrases. By touching squares on the keyboard, Paolo can construct sentences and "speak," using the device's voice synthesizer. Paolo's communication system is mounted on his wheelchair, so he is never at a loss for words.

Now 15, Paolo attends a regular tenth-grade class at a public high school. His schedule includes weekly occupational and physical therapy classes, which are focusing on the skills required for using the school bathrooms. These skills include maneuvering the electric wheelchair in and out of the bathroom, transferring to the toilet, and adjusting clothing. In other respects, Paolo is fairly independent. He has several pieces of specially designed equipment, and his therapists are continually looking for new devices to improve his communication and self-care abilities.

After Paolo was introduced to electric communication systems, he developed a strong interest in computers, a subject he hopes to study in college. His parents and sister are excited about his wanting to go to college and, as usual, will do what they can to help him achieve this goal. They have always been his greatest supporters and have helped him develop an optimistic outlook on life.

Paolo sometimes regrets that he has cerebral palsy. Although he has a couple of close friends, he believes that his appearance, his bulky equipment, and his inability to speak have limited his social relationships. His friends agree that he has a wonderful personality but that it does take a while to get to know him. Paolo looks forward to having girlfriends, getting married, and eventually having a family. He knows he will run into problems but feels confident about overcoming them.

Margaritte is 8 years old. She has cystic fibrosis, a disease that affects many organs in the body, especially the lungs. The disease has left her pale, thin, and short for her age. Her breathing problems have caused her chest to become barrel shaped, which is typical for children with cystic fibrosis. Margaritte has had frequent bouts with pneumonia since she was 3 months old. She is a regular patient at the local hospital, where she has become a favorite with the nurses.

Margaritte is in the third grade. She is a good student, but frequent absences have made it hard for her to keep up. Even when her health is better, she has trouble breathing and wheezes and coughs all day long at school. She is usually tired by lunchtime, so she has a regular appointment with the school nurse. The nurse "claps" Margaritte's chest to loosen the secretions in her lungs, letting her breathe more easily for a while. During lunch and recess, she rests, reads, or works on assignments she has missed. She would like to play with her friends, but their activity exhausts her. She chooses to save her energy for the afternoon.

Margaritte knows that cystic fibrosis is a progressive disease and that she may not live to adulthood. Her teacher has explained the condition to Margaritte's classmates and has always tried to answer their questions honestly. Whenever Margaritte is sick, the class sends letters to her. This gives the students another chance to ask the teacher questions or express their concerns, and it reminds Margaritte that they are her friends and are looking forward to her return.

EARLY INTERVENTION

Early intervention with children who have physical disabilities and health impairments is critical. The expression *early intervention* takes on two meanings in the context of children with physical disabilities and health impairments: (1) It means identifying a disorder at birth and in infancy. (2) It means identifying an acquired health disorder as soon as it is apparent, which may be in infancy, in early childhood, or later in life.

In some children, physical disabilities can be corrected with early medical treatment. In other children, early intervention can minimize the severity of certain physical disabilities and health conditions or present the development of additional disabling or medical conditions. For example, children with cerebral palsy who receive physical and occupational therapy may have fewer joint contractures or deformities that could decrease function in later years. In addition, correct physical management procedures, adaptations, and devices, if implemented by teachers, families, and others, can help the child participate in daily activities at home, at

Early intervention means starting therapy or treatment immediately following diagnosis.

school, and in the community and acquire needed motor and self-care skills to increase independence in preparation for public school placement. The early development of adequate skills also gives children a foundation for increasing interactions in their environments and helps them acquire the cognitive, language, and social skills that are necessary for success in school.

Identification of Children with Physical Disabilities and Health Impairments

The identification of children with physical disabilities and health impairments is primarily the responsibility of physicians: pediatricians; neurologists who specialize in conditions and diseases of the brain, spinal cord, and nervous system; and orthopedists and orthopedic surgeons, who are concerned with muscle function and conditions of the joints and bones. Other specialists involved in identification include physical and occupational therapists.

The identification process involves a medical evaluation, which includes a medical and developmental history (illnesses, medical history of family members, problems during pregnancy and labor, developmental progress), a physical examination, and laboratory tests or other special procedures needed for accurate diagnosis. The duration and complexity of the identification process depends on the specific disability (Whitehouse, 1987).

Educational Adaptations

CONTENT AND INSTRUCTIONAL ADAPTATIONS

The academic curriculum and academic skills do not necessarily present problems to children with physical disabilities. Children who miss school frequently or for long periods because of illness or surgery, however, may require special attention to catch up. Some children with health problems are unable to last a full day in school, so the teacher must teach the essentials over a shorter period of time or arrange for some home instruction. And instructional adaptations may be necessary for children with physical disabilities to participate fully and benefit from classroom instruction. Teachers may have to adapt existing instructional materials, modify skill sequences or performance requirements, or use adaptive and assistive devices. And they should work cooperatively with physical and occupational therapists when working with students who have physical disabilities. Therapeutic techniques must be integrated into daily programs.

Not all children need the same number or types of adaptations. The necessary adaptations depend on the child's physical capabilities and individual needs. In the following sections, we look at the role of related services in educating children with physical disabilities. Our discussion focuses on four areas of concern:

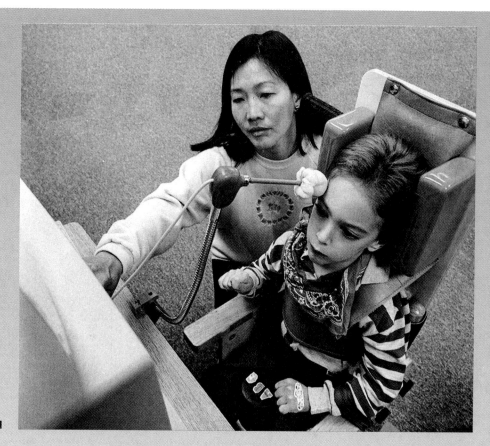

Students with physical disabilities may need to master augmented and alternative forms of communication to complete their schoolwork. (© Bob Daemmrich/Stock Boston)

communication, interaction with instructional materials, physical education, and emergency and medical procedures.

The Role of Related Services

For some students with physical disabilities, related services play a major role in the educational program. Occupational and physical therapists have recently started working in educational settings, and school nurses have begun expanding their traditional roles. These professionals support the efforts of teachers in three primary ways:

■ Providing direct services to students

■ Developing individualized educational programs (IEPs) and specific programs in cooperation with the classroom teacher

■ Preparing the classroom teacher to carry out or follow through on specific interventions

For example, Bridgit, a child with myelomeningocele, goes to physical therapy three times a week to work on increasing her walking speed and endurance. The occupational therapist is teaching her to manage her clothing more independently. The therapists have reported Bridgit's achievements to her teacher and have helped the teacher incorporate their method into Bridgit's routine trips to the bathroom. As a result, Bridgit practices her walking and dressing skills daily. Although she continues to need help going to the bathroom, trained aides are available to assist her.

Some teachers may be trained to provide direct services generally associated with another discipline. For example, a teacher might teach a child to perform clean intermittent catheterization (inserting a tube into the bladder to empty the urine) or teach a child to use a wheelchair. The nurse or therapist assesses the child's needs, determines the proper method of intervention, and then, with the educational team, decides who should carry out the intervention. The decision is based on the following factors:

- Who can perform the function legally?
- Who has the expertise now?
- Who else could learn the necessary skills?
- Who is consistently available to teach the task?
- When and where does it makes sense to teach the task?
- How quickly will the child learn to perform the task himself or herself?

If the classroom teacher is selected to carry out tasks outside his or her expertise, a nurse or therapist provides the teacher with training and ongoing consultation to ensure that the student's needs are being met. Usually, a support team is needed to provide the range of necessary services.

Members of the multidisciplinary team must assist the teacher in the day-to-day work with children who have health impairments and physical disabilities.

Just as it may not be appropriate for a teacher to carry out certain related services, it may not be appropriate to carry out all therapy or medical programs in a school setting. According to the Education for All Handicapped Children Act (PL 94-142), related services are "required to assist a child with disabilities to benefit from special education" (Section 121a.13). The courts have ruled that a health service such as clean intermittent catheterization must be provided in school when without it the student would be unable to receive an education in the least restrictive environment. Similarly, a child with cerebral palsy might need occupational therapy to achieve educational goals. In contrast, a child recovering from a broken leg would not be eligible to receive physical therapy in school because the child could remain in the least restrictive environment and make satisfactory educational progress without those services. Medical services that are not educationally relevant, then, remain the legal and financial responsibility of parents and health-care providers.

Communication

Students with physical disabilities who cannot acquire understandable speech or legible writing skills must be provided with augmented and alternative communication systems (Baumgart, Johnson, & Helmstetter, 1990). Some children with cerebral palsy, for example, have severe involvement of the oral muscles used in speech and limited fine motor abilities that hamper their writing skills. Muscular dystrophy or arthritis can leave children so weak that they tire easily when writing. These students need augmented and alternative forms of communication. Teachers and parents should work closely with speech therapists in selecting, designing, and implementing augmented and alternative communication devices for children with physical disabilities.

Speech: Boards and Electronic Devices.   The most common augmented and alternative methods for speech are communication boards and electronic devices with synthesized speech output. Most children use the board or electronic device by pointing with a finger or fist to a word or symbol. Children who are not able to point accurately use a hand-held pointer, a head-mounted wand, or a mouthstick. Youngsters with limited use of their hands may use their eyes instead, visually focusing on the intended word or letter.

A single switch may be necessary for students who have limited or no use of their hands. The type of switch depends on the child's movement abilities. Numerous commercial switches are available, and many can be made at home (Burkhart, 1986; Wright & Nomura, 1985). A switch is used with devices that light each possible selection on the board by rows, then columns. When the correct row is lit and the child presses the switch a second time, the correct sentence, phrase, word, or letter is "spoken." Although this method is slower than accessing the device by pointing or use of a keyboard directly, it does accommodate students with severe physical involvement. Many electronic communication devices can be connected to a computer for word processing or computer-assisted instruction.

Supplemental boards or overlays for electronic devices may be needed for academic content areas. For example, a mathematics board contains numbers, mathematics symbols, and words related to current classroom instruction. Other subject boards reflect the content and vocabulary of the specific academic subject (science, social studies, history). These boards should be revised or replaced as classroom content changes throughout the school year.

The provision of augmented and alternative communication devices for students with unintelligible speech is critical (Beukelman & Mirenda, 1992; Flippo, Inge, & Barcus, 1995). Many of these students may be denied placement in a less restrictive environment (resource room or regular classroom) because of their lack of spoken language. Professionals should work cooperatively with speech therapists, parents, and others to select an appropriate device, teach the student how to use it, and help others communicate with the student. (More specific information on the selection, design, and use of communication boards and other electronic devices is found in Chapters 8 and 11.)

Writing: Aids and Systems.   A variety of aids and augmented and alternative systems are available for written communication. Students with physical disabilities that cause muscle weakness, involuntary movements, and poor coordination of

Students with physical disabilities should participate as fully as possible in physical education, recreational, and play activities. (© Bob Daemmrich/Stock Boston)

Technological advances greatly facilitate learning for children with physical disabilities.

the fingers and hands may require a writing aid or an alternative system to complete written assignments in school and at home in a neat and timely manner.

Some students may benefit from the use of hand splints or special pencil holders to help them grasp a crayon, pencil, or pen. Other students may require a slant board, which supports the forearms. Students with severe physical involvement of their nondominant hand, who cannot use it to keep their paper secure while writing, may need to have their paper secured to a clipboard or to their desk with masking tape. Other adaptations include using heavy-weight paper, using paper with widely spaced lines, and allowing extra space for marking answers (Bigge, 1982).

Computers are another alternative means for written communication. Word-processing software can be used to complete written assignments and makes the computer more efficient than a typewriter. Keyguards are also available for most types of computer keyboard. For students who cannot use a standard keyboard because they lack fine motor skills, other methods may be needed. For the student with limited fine motor skills, expanded keyboards with large keys are easier to

A critical area of skill development for children with physical disabilities is motor skills and mobility, which are necessary to maintain upright postures, perform functional movements, and move around in the environment. (© Jerry Speier/Design Conceptions)

use. A student with muscular dystrophy, however, might use a miniature keyboard because he or she lacks the range of motion in the arms required to use a standard keyboard, yet has good finger movement within a limited range. Alternate keyboards are placed directly on the student's lap, desk, or lap tray for easy access. Students with a severe physical involvement may require a single switch to access the computer. The student scans the monitor screen, then selects the needed letter or symbol by pressing the switch as that letter or symbol is highlighted.

Instructional Materials and Classroom Equipment

Many students with physical disabilities have difficulty using common instructional materials and classroom equipment. They can't hold a book or turn pages. They can't use the classroom tape recorder, film projector, or slide projector.

Book stands can help these students hold a book. Elastic or rubber bands and larger paper clips can be used to secure pages on either side of the open book. An easy page-turning device is a rubber thimble attached to the end of a pencil. Also available are electric page turners that hold the child's book and turn the pages automatically when the child activates a switch.

Tape recorders can be adapted so children can use them independently. For example, cardboard can be placed over all buttons except the play and stop buttons to prevent accidental activation. These buttons can also be extended by attaching pieces of wood or plastic to them, enabling students who are weak to use the machine independently (Bigge, 1982). In addition, tape recorders can be turned on and off by means of a single switch (Burkhart, 1986; Levin & Scherfenberg, 1987).

Carousel slide projectors can be adapted to allow operation with a single switch so that the student can activate the projector (Goossens & Crain, 1985).

Physical Education

Before physical education or planned-play programs begin, the teacher should obtain from the child's physician information related to physical limitations, precautions, and restrictions on physical activities. School personnel should be aware of medical and emergency procedures related to the child's condition. Special adaptations may be needed in physical education programs or for playground activities to accommodate children with physical disabilities or health conditions. Classroom teachers should work closely with physical education teachers to help them design programs for children with physical disabilities or to include these children in games and playground activities.

Special equipment is available to help students. For example, a lowered basketball hoop can be used for wheelchair basketball, and a bowling ball ramp allows students in wheelchairs to bowl with their classmates. In many cases, all that's needed is a change in rules or procedures. For instance, a child in a wheelchair can play softball or baseball by batting and then having another child run the bases. The child with the disability can coach the runner to either run or stay on base. Students with physical disabilities should participate as fully as possible in physical education, recreational, and play activities. These students can play a major role in helping teachers and school personnel come up with ways to adapt activities for them.

Emergency and Medical Procedures

Teachers, therapists, and other school personnel who work with children who have physical disabilities or health conditions should know about the nature of the child's condition, restrictions on activities, medications, and emergency procedures. School districts should have a policy for handling medical procedures and emergencies. This policy should indicate what to do in case of seizures, severe falls or blows to the head, severe bleeding, fainting, choking, and other emergencies. Teachers should have this policy in writing and should know whom to notify first in case of emergency, how to notify them, how to have the rest of the class supervised during the emergency, and how to intervene during the emergency (Dykes & Venn, 1983). In addition, written records should be maintained, recording the administration of medications and instances of seizures, accidents, or injuries.

Some children with health disabilities require the presence of medical personnel (nurses or pediatricians) on site during the school day.

SKILL DEVELOPMENT

The unique needs of children with physical disabilities demand expansion of the traditional school curriculum into three areas: motor skills and mobility, self-care skills, and social and emotional adjustment.

Motor Skills and Mobility

Motor skills and mobility constitute a critical area of skill development for children with physical disabilities. These skills are necessary to maintain upright postures (sit, stand), perform functional movements (reach, grasp), and move around in the environment. The programming priorities for motor skill development should include developing functional movements and postures that are needed to perform classroom and school activities (Smith and Krajicek's 1989 video illustrates appropriate positioning techniques):

1. Development of head control and trunk control to maintain an upright sitting posture to perform needed activities throughout the school day (attending and listening, writing, using a computer or communication device, eating)

2. Development of arm movements and fine motor skills for performance of needed activities throughout the school day (holding a pencil and paper to write, holding a book and turning pages, using keyboards or switches to access a computer or communication device)

3. Development of standing and balance for assisted ambulation (using braces and crutches)

4. Development of skills needed to maneuver a wheelchair in the classroom and throughout the school environment (using arms to propel, learning to use an electric wheelchair with a joystick or other control, turning corners and entering doorways, negotiating ramps and curbs, crossing streets)

Physical and occupational therapists assume the primary responsibility for setting goals in motor development and mobility. They must work closely with teachers, other professionals, and parents, however, for the child to meet these goals. Teachers should become familiar with the basic working components of mobility equipment (wheelchairs, braces, crutches, walkers) and report needed repairs or adjustments to the child's therapist. Therapists should provide teachers and others with information related to the child's physical condition, limitations, and abilities.

Classroom teachers and others may be required to learn special techniques to help children perform motor tasks during the school day. These techniques can include physical management procedures and the use of adaptive positioning equipment. Positioning, handling, lifting, and transfer techniques are physical management procedures that teachers and others use to do the following: (1) help the student maintain good body alignment in a variety of positions (postures) and perform functional movements and skills in the context of daily activities, (2) prevent the development of secondary contractures and deformities, and (3) increase the benefits of therapy by implementing intervention programs throughout the day (Rainforth & York, 1987).

A child with spastic cerebral palsy who constantly leans sideways in the wheelchair will have tremendous difficulty reaching the keyboard on the computer and striking the correct keys. With help from a physical therapist or occupational therapist, the teacher can learn to position the student in the wheelchair, use a slant board to move the keyboard closer to the child, and relax the child's arms and bring them forward to rest on the keyboard.

Adaptive positioning equipment may be needed in the classroom to promote good body alignment in sitting, standing, and other positions. This equipment works as an adjunct to therapy and helps the child carry out necessary activities in the classroom. Teachers work cooperatively with therapists in using positioning equipment and selecting a position that matches the practical and movement demands of classroom activities (Rainforth & York, 1987).

Lifting and transfer techniques are used to help the child move from one position to another—for example, from the wheelchair to the toilet or into positioning equipment. To prevent injury to the teachers or the child, a therapist must train the teachers before they attempt to move the child. Many children can learn to help in this process or to move themselves independently if they have the ability to stand and adequate arm strength.

Self-Care Skills

Being able to take care of themselves is another critical area for children with physical disabilities. Self-care skills include eating, toileting, dressing, bathing, and grooming. Some children need assistive devices or physical help to perform many of these tasks. A child whose grasp is weak may need to use utensils with a built-up or larger handle. Other devices to increase independence in eating include special plates and cups and nonskid mats that stabilize the child's plate. Students with severe physical involvement may require physical assistance in eating or may have to be fed.

Skills to be developed in toileting include performing transfers from the wheelchair to the toilet or assisting others in accomplishing transfers. Children who lack sitting stability and trunk control need an adapted toilet seat that provides a more stable sitting surface or back supports with straps to help them maintain an upright position. Hand-held utensils and other aids can make toileting more convenient for the student.

Students who have health conditions that require medication on a routine basis (injections for diabetes) or a periodic basis (inhalants for asthma) should be taught as early as possible to administer the medication themselves. Teachers or school nurses must monitor the process closely, however, because they ultimately are responsible for seeing that the correct procedures are followed and that appropriate legal permission from parents, guardian, or physicians is secured before any medication is administered.

Social and Emotional Adjustment

Children with physical disabilities sometimes feel powerless. Christie knows that she has leukemia and that she will probably live only a few more months. She is frequently absent from school. She misses her friends when she is away from school, but when she returns, she no longer feels a part of the group. Besides being sick, she is lonely and is keeping to herself more and more. Josh faces an entirely different problem. He is recovering from a traumatic brain injury that has left him confined to a wheelchair. He is no longer able to do many things for himself, and he has discovered that temper tantrums are an effective way to get people to respond to his needs immediately. It seems that the more people try to help Josh, the more aggressive he becomes.

As we described in Chapter 3 on early intervention, Foley (Anastasiow, 1986) presented a theory about the stages that parents (or a child suddenly disabled by abuse or an accident) go through when dealing with a disability. Although withdrawal and aggression are normal stages in the process, children like Christie and Josh need support and help in accepting and adjusting to their handicapping conditions. Christie's and Josh's behavior patterns are similar to those of children who face continuing academic or environmental problems: Christie and Josh have lost control over certain aspects of their lives.

Harvey and Greenway (1984) found that children with physical disabilities have "a lower sense of self-worth, greater anxiety, and a less integrated view of self" than do children without handicaps (p. 280). Orr (1989), however, found children with physical disabilities in several settings who had positive self-concepts. Research shows that people are more likely to accept their physical disability when the environment is supportive (Heinemann & Shontz, 1984), when they achieve some sense of control over the handicapping condition (Rosenbaum & Palmon, 1984), and when they begin to demonstrate new competence (Patrick, 1984). In addition to using the methods described in Chapter 11, teachers can enhance the social and emotional adjustment of children with physical disabilities in several ways.

Assisting children with physical disabilities to achieve and maintain a positive self-concept is a major goal of education.

Increasing the Understanding of the Disabling Condition.

The teacher of a student with a physical disability should learn as much as possible about the condition—its cause, treatments, prognosis, and educational implications. Then, in cooperation with the child's parents, the teacher should help the child and other students understand relevant aspects of the condition. One of the major functions of organizations like the Epilepsy Foundation of America, the American Cancer Society, the March of Dimes Birth Defects Foundation, and United Cerebral Palsy is to provide information to the public. Many of these organizations offer teaching kits or help in developing educational workshops to increase children's and adults' understanding of a particular condition. Commercial materials are also available to help children learn about a variety of disabilities.

When teaching children about disabling conditions, teachers should help them understand that a physical disability is an individual difference, not something to fear, ridicule, or be ashamed of. One way to do this is to answer questions about a condition honestly. Another is to acknowledge and respect the way children (and adults) feel about disabling conditions without condoning maladaptive behaviors (teasing, name calling). A third way is to discuss the incidents that can occur at school—an epileptic seizure, an insulin reaction—and ask students to decide how they could help or how they should behave during such an incident.

Emphasizing the Quality of Life.　　Teachers can help students adjust to physical disabilities by helping them see their disabilities as just one aspect of their lives and of themselves. One elementary school approached this situation by offering a group counseling session, an hour each week, for children with physical disabilities (Williams & Baeker, 1983). One goal of the group was to develop a support system; another was to recognize individual limitations and strengths. Within the regular classroom a teacher might have students list what they like or admire about each of their classmates. This kind of exercise often gets surprising results, and it is a good starting point for illustrating that children have different assets. Although children with physical disabilities must be allowed to talk about their limitations, they should also be encouraged to inventory their abilities, including the ability to help others. A physical disability cannot be ignored, but these children can learn to focus on the more positive aspects of their lives.

For a child like Christie, who faces a terminal illness, the process can be very difficult. Her teachers must first overcome their own feelings about death, especially the death of a child. According to Kubler-Ross (1969), who has worked extensively with children and adults with terminal illnesses, focusing on life and living helps people accept the process of death and dying. Hospice, an organization founded on this philosophy, provides care and counseling to people with terminal illnesses and their families. Hospice groups are located in most cities throughout the United States and offer training to teachers and other school personnel to help them deal with children who are terminally ill.

Finally, teachers can improve the quality of life for a child like Christie by helping classmates show their interest and concern. When Christie is absent, her teacher has the other students send her letters, keeping her informed of the latest activities and reminding her that she is missed. When Christie returns to school, the teacher carefully avoids overprotecting and favoring the child and keeps her involved in as many activities as her condition allows.

Increasing the Sense of Control.　　Although Josh and Christie cannot control their physical disabilities, they can control many other aspects of their lives. It is very revealing to have children with physical disabilities list the aspects of their lives that they believe they cannot control. Josh knew he could no longer move independently, and he thought he was powerless. School personnel worked with Josh and his family to show the child that his temper tantrums were in fact one way to control people and events. They also helped Josh understand how he could achieve the same results in a more constructive way. Josh learned that his family and classmates were happy to help him when necessary and were interested in socializing with him when he took a more positive approach. He found that people understood his frustration and could help him find ways to express that frustration without damaging his relationships with others. Although he still has a severe physical disability, Josh now believes that he can control many aspects of his life.

Dealing with terminal illness and death is a major issue for the child, the caregivers, and all members of the multidisciplinary team.

LEARNING ENVIRONMENT

Inclusion

The many different needs of students with physical disabilities are met in a variety of learning environments. At one time, educators believed that the social, educational, and medical needs of these students could best be met by placing them in classes for the orthopedically impaired or in schools for the physically disabled. As public understanding and acceptance of people with physical disabilities increased, so did support for the concept of inclusion. Placement in integrated environments better prepares students to become well-adjusted contributing members of society.

In keeping with these goals, the Individuals with Disabilities Education Act (IDEA) encourages schools to educate students in the least restrictive environment and to offer the services necessary for students to succeed in that environment. Although changes in reporting methods make it difficult to compare past and current figures, the U.S. Department of Education (1984) reported that most students with physical disabilities are being educated in public school environments and that the number of students with physical disabilities in public schools is increasing. Delaware educates 90 percent of these children in regular classes, and Vermont educates 97 percent in regular classes. Most states use the regular classroom, resource room, and separate class (U.S. Department of Education, 1994).

Individualization requires that the learning environments that we discussed in Chapter 2 be available to students with physical disabilities. This means we find these students in regular classrooms, resource rooms, special classes, special schools, perhaps at home or in hospitals—according to their needs.

Students with physical disabilities who have no other learning impairments can achieve their greatest potential in the regular classroom. Here these children have the same learning opportunities and expectations as their handicapped peers. If children with physical disabilities are going to learn to live in integrated environments as adults, they must attend regular schools and classes to the greatest extent possible (Brown & Gothelp, 1996). Adjustments, like providing additional space to maneuver a wheelchair, extra time to change classes, or access to an elevator or a computer terminal, are often the key to enabling a child to participate in a challenging curriculum and in meaningful social interaction.

Some students may need tutoring by a resource room teacher to catch up with the class after a long absence. Others may go to adapted physical education or physical therapy while classmates go to physical education. These services are most effective as integral support to regular education rather than as separate entities. Some students, however, require such extensive adaptation that their needs can be met only in a separate class.

For students without learning impairments, placement in a special class should be temporary, and instruction should be geared toward reducing barriers that prevent participation in regular classes. For example, school personnel determined that Paolo had normal intelligence but could not communicate his needs or complete

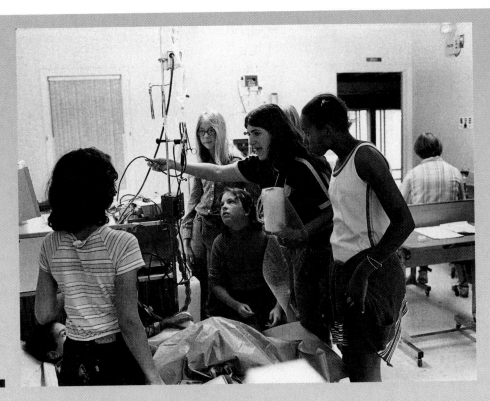

Students with physical disabilities but no specific learning impairment require adjustments—space to maneuver a wheelchair, time to change classes, or access to an elevator or computer terminal—before they can successfully participate in the regular school setting. (© Alan Carey/The Image Works)

academic tasks because of severe cerebral palsy. It took approximately two years of intensive training to teach Paolo to use an electronic communication system and to bring him up to grade level in essential reading, spelling, and math skills. During that time, he was assigned to a special class; it was understood, however, that the assignment was temporary. The goal of Paolo's educational program was to integrate him in the regular classroom. His special education teacher arranged for him to visit regular classes during a variety of activities and to have lunch with children his age. When Paolo was finally placed in the regular classroom, he knew his classmates and was prepared to enter the regular curriculum. Also his classroom teacher understood his needs, and the special education teacher and related services continued to be resources.

Children who are recovering from an acute illness, a serious accident, or surgery may have to continue their school program at home or in the hospital. In some cases, children's hospitals run their own schools. In others, an itinerant teacher maintains contact between homebound or hospitalized students and their regular teachers. Schools have also begun to use closed-circuit television and computers connected via telephone lines to maintain contact with homebound students.

Accessibility

Section 504 of the Rehabilitation Act of 1973 laid the groundwork for moving students with physical disabilities to less restrictive environments by requiring that public buildings be accessible to all people. School buildings built after the passage of this legislation should be accessible. Older buildings, however, may require renovations. Minimal renovations might include adding ramps at entrances. Extensive renovations might include installing an elevator in a two-story building and renovating the restrooms in addition to adding ramps. The American National Standards Institute (1980) has developed accessibility standards for new facilities; these guidelines also can be used to determine if facilities are accessible for students with impaired mobility:

- Walkways should be at least 36 inches wide and have a continuous surface that is not interrupted by steps or abrupt changes of more than one-half inch.

- Ramps should be at least 36 inches wide. Indoor and outdoor ramps should have a slope of not more than 1 foot for every 12 feet and 1 foot for every 20 feet, respectively.

- Entrances and doorways should be 32 inches wide to allow for easy passage of a wheelchair. The threshold should be beveled and have a maximum edge height of three-fourths inch.

- An accessible restroom should be available for both males and females on all floors. Stalls should be 60 inches wide and 60 inches deep and have stall doors that swing out to easily accommodate a wheelchair and allow for transfers to and from the toilet. Grab bars should be mounted on each side of the stall. Toilet seats should be from 17 to 19 inches from the floor. Sinks should be no more than 34 inches from the floor. The clearance underneath a sink should be at least 29 inches, so a wheelchair can fit. Mirrors, shelves, and towel dispensers should be no more than 40 inches from the floor.

Family and Lifespan Issues

TRANSITION

For all individuals with disabilities, the transition from school to work and independent living presents a range of challenges, such as obtaining a driver to take them to and from work, remodeling an apartment so that all appliances can be reached from a wheelchair, or having a live-in aide with special knowledge of how to deal with various kinds of equipment.

The National Center for Children and Youth with Disabilities (1991) has prepared a Transition Summary for parents, teachers, and individuals to assist individuals with disabilities in moving into work and independent living. The center indicates that research has demonstrated an enormous qualitative difference in the lives of people with disabilities because of recent legislation leading to changes to assist these individuals throughout the transition process. Postsecondary programs, on-the-job education, internships and apprenticeships, adult education, trade school, and technical schools as well as college and career education are all available with some support (NICHY, 1991, pp. 15–19).

LENGTH OF LIFE

Children with health impairments like diabetes, cystic fibrosis, AIDS, and cancer face shortened lives. These conditions follow different courses, however, which can present children with tremendous uncertainties. For youngsters with diabetes, even strict compliance with prescribed medication and diet does not guarantee good health or a normal lifespan, and violations often do not have immediate serious effects. Children with cystic fibrosis face a prognosis that is more certain but also more pessimistic: Few survive into adulthood; however, some recent treatments are increasing the lifespan of some individuals (*Science*, 1990). Children with advanced cancers face death daily.

Nevertheless, most children want to live as normally as possible. When a child with a terminal illness attempts to participate fully in life's activities, we may consider the child valiant. For a child with a condition like diabetes, which has a less certain course, efforts to live normally—eating the same foods as friends and family, strenuous exercise—may violate prescribed care. We may think this child is unaccepting, ambivalent, or noncompliant, but he or she may be experiencing a daily conflict between health needs and happiness. When we recognize the conflict, we can offer more effective support and accommodation (Bradley, Ashbaugh, & Blaney, 1994).

As a child with a terminal illness or progressive condition approaches the point where death becomes a certainty, he or she may face tremendous fear and grief—as may family members, classmates, and school personnel. Teachers must confront their own feelings about death and dying before they can offer support to children and their families.

DISCRIMINATION

People with physical handicaps face intentional and unintentional discrimination from other people and from the "system." Fear, ignorance, lack of experience, and inflexibility are the most common causes of discrimination. It is difficult to reconcile the fact that individuals limited by physical handicaps must also deal with limitations unnecessarily imposed on them by others.

Section 504 of the Rehabilitation Act of 1973 prohibits employers from discriminating against people with handicaps who are otherwise qualified for employment. The act further requires that all agencies receiving federal funds must make their programs and buildings accessible to those with handicaps.

The Americans with Disabilities Act (1990) went into effect in 1991. It mandated the removal of many of the obstacles that individuals with disabilities face and an end to the intentional or unintentional discrimination they face. The legislation requires employers to make reasonable efforts to hire people with disabilities. Although it has substantially reduced some types of barriers, violations and other types of discrimination persist. Public information and advocacy are still necessary to increase acceptance and access for people with physical disabilities.

■■■■■■■

Summary of Major Ideas

1. A physical disability is a condition that interferes with a child's ability to use his or her body; a health impairment is a condition that requires ongoing medical attention.

2. A physical disability or health impairment is not a handicap unless it limits the individual's participation in routine activities.

3. The cause of the disability or disorder has a large impact on the problems that children with physical handicaps face. Those with congenital conditions tend to make necessary adaptations to those conditions. Children whose disabilities are caused by injury generally go through a period of mourning before they finally accept and adjust to their conditions. Children whose conditions are caused by disease have the same adjustment problems as other physically disabled youngsters but also face uncertainty and the academic pressure that stems from frequent absence.

4. It is difficult to determine the prevalence of children with physical disability because of the way physical handicaps are defined and reported. Estimates place the proportion of children receiving special education services because of physical disability at 2.5 percent of all students enrolled in special education programs, or at 0.27 percent of the general school population.

5. Children with neurological conditions suffer from motor disabilities ranging from mild incoordination to total paralysis, and intellectual deficiencies sometimes complicate their development. Children with musculoskeletal conditions have motor skill deficits that in severe cases prevent walking or even sitting up. Children with cardiopulmonary conditions have breathing or heart problems that limit their participation in physical activities. Children with chronic life-threatening health conditions may require extensive medical treatment or hospitalization in acute stages.

6. Children with physical disabilities, like other exceptional children, should be taught in the least restrictive environment. For most of these children this means the regular classroom with extra attention in the resource room if needed. Special classes are a means of bringing children with normal intelligence up to grade level and equivalent capabilities and integrating them as quickly as possible into regular classrooms. Homebound or hospital

services are essential to the educational program of some children, if only temporarily.

7. Teachers can help students with physical disabilities by adapting the learning environment to individual needs. For example, by widening the aisles in the classroom to accommodate a wheelchair, the teacher can reduce the impact of the handicap on the student.

8. The implementation of the educational program for children with physical disabilities often involves physical therapists, school nurses, and occupational therapists. These specialists and others (speech therapists, parents) should work in close cooperation with the classroom teacher to reinforce skill learning.

9. Content and instructional adaptations for children with physical disabilities and health impairments may be needed in the areas of communication, use of instructional materials and classroom equipment, physical education, and emergency and medical procedures. The degree of adaptation varies from child to child.

10. Curricular changes for children with physical disabilities who have normal intelligence focus on motor skills and mobility, self-care skills, and social and emotional adjustment.

11. Teachers can facilitate the social and emotional adjustment of their students in several ways: by increasing the understanding of the condition, by emphasizing the quality of life, and by increasing feelings of self-control.

Unresolved Issues

1. *Participation in the mainstream (inclusion).* Professionals and laypeople continue to disagree about the extent to which children with physical disabilities can or should be mainstreamed. Much of the controversy stems from misconceptions and different experiences. In fact, there is no single "right" method. Decisions must be made case by case, based on individual needs, not on a diagnosis or disability. We cannot assume that certain children do not fit or cannot benefit from inclusion until they prove otherwise.

2. *Educational teamwork.* Students with physical disabilities often require an educational team consisting of members from diverse backgrounds. Professionals from traditional medical disciplines may have trouble adjusting to work in educational settings. Different terminology, methods, and philosophies further challenge the planning and implementation of coordinated educational programs. Unfortunately some training programs do not prepare teachers and other personnel to be effective team members. Individual school programs should work toward developing models of team service delivery that address the educational needs of individual students.

3. *Technology.* More than any group of exceptional children, students with physical handicaps use adaptive equipment and assistive devices. These

devices include specially designed spoons, customized electric wheelchairs, and electronic communication systems. For many people, adaptive equipment means the difference between dependence and independence. With technological advances have come new and better adaptations, but at a cost. School systems, insurance companies, and public assistance programs disagree about who should bear the cost of expensive equipment.

Key Terms

acquired immune deficiency syndrome (AIDS) p. 528
arthritis p. 524
asthma p. 527
cardiopulmonary system p. 526
cerebral palsy p. 518
epilepsy p. 519
fetal alcohol syndrome p. 529

health impairment p. 574
human immunodeficiency virus (HIV) p. 528
musculoskeletal system p. 517
neurological system p. 517
physical disability p. 513
spastic (pyramidal) cerebral palsy p. 518

Questions for Thought

1. What is the difference between a physical impairment and a disability? Provide examples of physical impairments that may not be disabilities. p. 513

2. Why are accurate prevalence figures for children with physical disabilities difficult to obtain? p. 514

3. What are several practical things that teachers can do to help children with physical disabilities caused by disease? p. 518

4. What problems do children face whose conditions are caused by disease or terminal illness? p. 518

5. To what extent is a child's intelligence affected by spina bifida? p. 523

6. What reasons would you give to a parent for recommending a prosthetic device for a child whose leg was amputated? p. 525

7. What role do related services play in the educational program for students with physical disabilities? p. 539

8. How do communication boards work? p. 541

9. What four types of motor skill development are necessary to master the functional movements and postures needed to perform classroom and school activities? p. 545

10. Name two of the stages that children with physical disabilities and other health impairments pass through, and explain the passage through them. p. 547

11. Under what conditions are people most likely to accept their physical disabilities? p. 547

12. What can individuals or organizations do to make the child, the family, and the public more understanding of physical disabilities? p. 547

13. The intellectual functioning of many people with physical disabilities is normal or above normal. Why, then, are these people not finding good jobs? p. 552

References of Special Interest

Batshaw, M., & Perret, Y. (1992). *Children with handicaps: A medical primer* (3rd ed.). Baltimore: Paul H. Brookes Publishing Co.

The third edition of this exemplary text explains how genetic abnormalities, problems during pregnancy and early infancy, and nutritional deficiencies can cause handicaps. It also describes how these problems affect the nervous and musculoskeletal systems and, in turn, child development. A small number of physically handicapping conditions also are discussed.

Bigge, J. (1991). *Teaching individuals with physical and multiple disabilities* (3rd ed.). Columbus, OH: Charles E. Merrill.

Bigge presents a detailed examination of problems that students with physical handicaps encounter and important components of education for these students. Chapters focus on assessment, methods of instruction, and components of the curriculum. Throughout the book are many examples of adaptations that minimize the impact of physical handicaps and help students benefit from the educational program.

Bleck, E., & Nagel, D. (Eds.). (1982). *Physically handicapped children: A medical atlas for teachers*. New York: Grune & Stratton.

Written primarily by physicians in lay terms, this book has chapters on approximately thirty different disabling conditions and on normal development, basic anatomy, non-oral communication, driving, counseling, and emergencies. It also includes extensive lists of print and organizational resources.

Krajicek, M. (1991). *Handbook for the care of infants and toddlers with disabilities and chronic conditions*. Lawrence, KS: Learner Management Designs.

This manual is designed to assist day-care and home-care workers in integrating children with physical disabilities and health problems into regular classes.

March of Dimes (1992–1993). Public health information sheets: *Clubfoot; Cleft lip and cleft palate; Polio; Post polio muscle atrophy; Spina bifida; Marfan syndrome; Thalassemia.* (Available from March of Dimes, Community Service Department, 1275 Mamaroneck Avenue, White Plains, NY 10605.)

Orelove, F. & Sobsey, D. (1991). *Educating children with multiple disabilities: A transdisciplinary approach* (2nd ed.). Baltimore: Paul H. Brookes Publishing Co.

This book includes chapters on team programming, motor development and cerebral palsy, handling and positioning, medical concerns, developing instructional adaptations, specific skill areas (self-care, communication), and working with families.

Rowley-Kelley, F. L., & Reigel, D. H. (1993). *Teaching students with spina bifida.* Baltimore: Paul H. Brookes Publishing Co. Also, Rosenthal, R., Dukes, B., Cosgrove, S.,

Rowley-Kelley, F. L., & Simpson, G. (1993). *Teaching students with spina bifida* (video). Baltimore: Paul H. Brookes Publishing Co.

> This book and video can be ordered as a set. The two together provide a comprehensive set of techniques, strategies, and information about positioning for those who work with students with spina bifida.

Schleichkorn, J. (1983). *Coping with cerebral palsy: Answers to questions parents often ask*. Austin, TX: PRO-ED.

> This book offers easy-to-understand information on cerebral palsy and its medical, educational, and psychological impact on children. One chapter deals with special issues, including financial assistance, respite care, access to special equipment, sex education, and marriage.

Umbreit, J. (Ed.). (1988). *Physical disabilities and health impairments: An introduction*. Columbus, OH: Charles E. Merrill.

> Information on the cause, treatment, prognosis, and educational implications of numerous handicapping conditions is included in chapters written in lay terms by physicians who specialize in treating the particular condition.

Williamson, G. (1989). *Children with spina bifida*. Baltimore: Paul H. Brookes Publishing Co.

> This is a complete and thorough discussion of all forms of spina bifida. A particular strength of this book is its examples of treatment and curriculum.

Perspectives on Educating Exceptional Children in the Future

In this text we examine the special educational knowledge, materials, and methods that are available to help educate students with special needs, and we document important advances that have taken place in special education over the past few years. But this is a period of considerable change in education. What pivotal issues and decisions have yet to be made? Where can we expect the field of special education to go from here? How might the regular or special education teacher expect to participate in making or implementing those decisions?

We expect to see the field of education evolve as much over the next few decades as it evolved in the past hundred years. The changes will affect everything and everyone connected with education: the roles that teachers play, the organization of local schools, the conduct of personnel preparation programs, assessment, and the curricula that schools follow. How will special education fare in the midst of such major changes?

Issues Affecting All School Systems

Reforms in education are a result of changes in educational theory and practice, but they are also a response to changes in society's expectations and needs. Changes in society that are currently influencing the educational system include the following:

1. *Children in poverty.* The number of children living in poverty has greatly increased over the last couple of decades. Many children often go to school without adequate food, clothing, and shelter and without proper preparation for learning in school. Educators need to understand how these deprivations affect children's abilities to learn and to grow physically, emotionally, and socially. School systems need to work with the community to address the needs of these children. The conditions of poverty certainly contribute to or increase the problems of exceptional children.

2. *Dual-career households.* Both parents in a family are likely to work outside the home these days. Thus many parents face employment-related distractions and pressures that keep them from working closely with schools to meet the educational and social needs of their children. Educators need to develop or revise programs to encourage and facilitate parents' participation, which is especially important for the parents of children who are exceptional.

3. *Diversity of students.* The number and size of diverse groups in American society have increased greatly, fostering a cultural diversity that raises questions about the Anglo-European emphasis of the traditional American curriculum. Educators need to work with communities to ascertain how members of those communities think that diversity, including physical as well as social and cultural differences, should be addressed.

4. *Drugs and crime.* Violence, drug abuse, and crime create major problems related to health, welfare, and discipline in the schools. Educators need to work with parents, law enforcement professionals, and other members of the community to identify the causes of these difficulties and to devise solutions to the problems they cause.

5. *High technology.* The evolution from an industrial-based economy to an economy based on information and service has changed the types of jobs that students can hope to fill. Fewer unskilled or semiskilled industrial jobs are available today than were available just a few decades ago. The pressure has increased greatly for students to learn sophisticated technical knowledge and skills. Educators need to work with high-tech companies and service industries to identify what basic knowledge and skills students will need when they enter the work force. Certain technologies have already benefited children who have exceptional needs, and improvements to those technologies may help these students become even more independent.

6. *Television and other popular media.* The role that popular media, notably television, play in community and family life has been increasing considerably. TV watching seems to undercut the discipline that students need to do homework and generally has caused a decrease in the amount of time students commit to formal education. Educators need to identify television's benefits as well as its detriments and to develop programs that counter its ill effects and build on its benefits.

Our educational system does not have the luxury of attacking these issues one at a time. Instead, it has to respond to them concurrently, even though doing so is a formidable challenge.

Issues for Exceptional Children

The issues listed above will affect students of *all* abilities. What issues are of particular concern to exceptional children? Each of the following issues deserves attention and healthy discussion so that any solutions that are reached are deliberate, productive, and genuinely beneficial to the children, their families, and society.

1. *Where will the child with special needs be educated?* Depending on the children's abilities and on the programs available in their school systems, we have seen from Chapter 2 and from discussions in the categorical chapters that the majority of exceptional children increasingly are being included in regular classrooms. Fewer children attend resource rooms, although a fairly consistent

number have been attending separate classrooms and a smaller but consistent number have been attending separate facilities. Will these trends continue?

2. *Who will educate the child with special needs?* The trend toward inclusion indicates that regular classroom teachers can expect to have increasing numbers of exceptional children in their classrooms. Does this mean that regular teachers will increasingly be called on to be the primary instructor? Does this mean a diminished role for the special education instructor or simply a changed role? What does this imply about the availability of instructors for the small but consistent number of children who need to be in a separate classroom or who need to attend a separate facility? Will the role or the makeup of the multidisciplinary team change?

3. *What goals should we hold for children with special needs?* Currently, the ideal set forth for exceptional children is for them to achieve the maximum abilities that they, as individuals, are capable of achieving. For some, this means living and supporting themselves independently; for others, learning basic skills and contributing to society by some means; for still others, merely learning basic survival and self-care skills. Are these goals likely to change? Will expectations increase or decrease for these children?

4. *How should we assess progress and success?* The methods of assessment depend on the goals that children are progressing toward and achieving. Current programs have the multidisciplinary team work with children and their parents to create an Individualized Education Program (IEP) and an Individualized Family Service Plan (IFSP). Will these processes prove to be valid for assessing the progress of exceptional children? How might the planning and evaluation process change?

Decision-Making Criteria

Each of those questions has a number of options or potential actions. How that choice will be made, and by whom, is a matter of serious concern to the parents and educators who care for exceptional children. In public decision making, many criteria often are brought to bear on an issue. Here are some of the most common ones:

1. *Cost.* The amount of money that a particular solution costs almost always affects the final decision. Helping children with special needs almost always costs more than general education, and we, both as the public and as educators, need to determine how much more a particular option will cost and whether we think it is worth the difference.

2. *Instructional effectiveness.* Our willingness to bear the additional costs for children with special needs depends, in part, on the confidence we have that something useful will happen as a result of our special efforts. If we can point to some success from research, case studies, or personal experience, we strengthen the probability that a particular option will be chosen.

3. *Personnel preparation needs.* How much and what kind of special personnel will be needed to staff our special program? We know it is not realistic to assign a therapist to every disturbed child. But how will our programs be individualized as well as supported in classroom settings for children with behavioral disturbance? Who will prepare these specialists for their work? Options that include the wholesale hiring of a new breed of professional such as early childhood interventionists will have to answer questions about where such professionals will come from, where they will be prepared for their tasks, and who is available to prepare them.

4. *Public opinion.* No matter what solutions are reached within the education professions, such answers must be received with some level of public acceptance. Today, for example, the concept of educating exceptional students in the least restrictive environment—the linchpin of PL 94-142, passed in 1975 —is supported by the public. Putting children with behavior problems in juvenile homes just so they won't negatively influence other students is no longer an option. This shift in public opinion continues to influence judicial decisions and legislation passed for exceptional children.

5. *Value: human worth and potential.* Our beliefs and values clearly influence our decision making and need to be considered along with information that is available. The universal recognition that every person is valuable and should be cherished has clearly and positively affected children with special needs and the desire to provide an opportunity for them to learn and develop.

6. *Value: self-interest and advocacy.* A value that sometimes is extrinsically motivated and can be less generous than the belief in human worth is self-interest. Self-interest shapes many policy decisions. The interests of organized groups and of individuals may conflict with one another. Professional turf and economic interests play a role in most public decisions, whether or not they are openly acknowledged.

Each of those criteria can play a role in special education policy decisions.

The issues facing us all—educators, administrators, parents, community leaders, legislators, political leaders—are complex and urgent. You can participate in the process of being an advocate or direct decision maker by using resources available to you to gather information. Such resources include direct sources (experience, consultation) as well as information in print and technology sources.

The future of children with exceptionalities appears to be bright, though somewhat undefined, within the framework of American public education. The battle for acceptance of these students as a legitimate and appropriate part of a public education framework appears to be won. The problem now is how best to tailor the rapidly changing educational services and programs to the needs of exceptional students. The central issues pivot on public and private economic support for quality education and innovation with all due speed! We hope that this text serves as a foundation and resource for all those involved in educating exceptional students.

glossary

Academic achievement learning disabilities Problems with academic subjects that are due to underlying disorders in information processing.

Academic aptitude The ability to perform tasks in school, usually measured by an intelligence test.

Accommodation Changes in the shape of the lens of the eye in order to focus on objects closer than 20 feet.

Acoupedic method See *auditory method.*

Acoustic method See *auditory method.*

Acquired immune deficiency syndrome (AIDS) A breakdown of the body's immune system, allowing the body to become vulnerable to a host of fatal infections that it normally is able to ward off.

Adaptive behavior The effectiveness or degree with which individuals meet the standards of personal independence and social responsibility expected for their age and cultural group.

Alpha-fetoprotein test A blood test given to pregnant women to detect fetal disabilities.

American Sign Language (ASL) A manual language used by many people with hearing impairments that meets the universal linguistic standards of spoken English.

Amniocentesis A procedure for analyzing the amniotic fluid (a watery liquid in which the embryo is suspended) to discover genetic defects in the unborn child.

Anxiety-withdrawal A pattern of deviant behavior in which children are shy, timid, reclusive, sensitive, submissive, overdependent, and easily depressed.

Apgar test A screening test administered to an infant at one minute and five minutes after birth.

Aphasia The loss of the ability to speak as a result of brain injury or trauma.

Applied behavioral analysis (ABA) A learning approach that is based on individual analyses of a student's functioning and relies on the learning of behaviors to remediate learning problems.

Aptitude-achievement discrepancy A discrepancy between a student's ability (measured on intelligence tests) and academic achievement; a factor in the diagnosis of learning disabilities.

Arthritis Inflammation of the joints that causes them to swell and stiffen.

Articulation The movement of the mouth and tongue that shapes sound into speech.

Articulation error Mispronunciation such as *ring* for *king.*

Assessment A process for identifying a child's strengths and weaknesses; it involves five steps: screening, diagnosis, classification, placement, and monitoring or discharge.

Assistive technology Tools that enhance the functioning of persons with disabilities.

Asthma A condition affecting a person's breathing.

At-risk infant An infant who has a greater chance of displaying developmental delays or cognitive or motor deficits due to a variety of factors.

Attention deficit disorder (ADD) A conduct disorder that leaves children unable to pay attention or work at a task; impulsiveness is another characteristic of the disorder. Often found in combination with hyperactivity (attention deficit hyperactivity disorder [ADHD]).

Attention-deficit hyperactivity disorder (ADHD) A disorder that causes children to have difficulty settling down to do a particular task, especially desk work.

Audiogram A graphic record of hearing acuity at selected intensities throughout the normal range of audibility, recorded from a pure-tone audiometer, which creates sounds of preset frequency or intensity.

Audiometer An instrument for testing hearing acuity.

Audition Thought transformed into words and received by a listener through hearing.

Auditory global method See *auditory method.*

Auditory integration training A form of treatment that requires 10 hours of listening to the full range of sound frequencies.

Auditory method A method of teaching deaf students that involves auditory training and makes extensive use of sound amplification to develop listening and speech skills. Also called *acoupedic method, acoustic method, auditory global method, aural method,* and *unisensory method.*

Augmented communication Methods of communicating that are based on symbols or gestures rather than speech.

Aural method See *auditory method.*

Authentic assessment Measuring a child's ability by means of an in-class assignment.

Autism A neurological disorder that leads to deficits in functioning, particularly in communication and social skills.

Behavior disorder A serious emotional disturbance.

Behavior modification Techniques designed to change behaviors and to increase the use of socially constructive behaviors.

Blindness See *profound visual disability.*

Bone-conductor test A measure of a person's ability to hear sounds by recording the sounds received in the brain.

Braille A system using embossed characters in different combinations of six dots arranged in a cell that allows people with profound visual impairments to read by touch as well as to write by using special aids.

Brainstorming A technique in which a group of people discuss a particular problem, trying to come up with as many solutions as possible; often used with gifted children.

Cardiopulmonary system The heart, blood, and lungs.

Case manager An individual who gathers all the information that relates to a child with a disability and heads up the team that prepares the child's individualized education program. Also called a *service coordinator.*

Central hearing loss Hearing loss that results from damage to sound-processing areas in the brain.

Central processing Classification of a stimulus through the use of memory, reasoning, and evaluation; the second step in the information-processing model.

Cerebral palsy A condition caused by damage to the motor control centers of the brain before birth, during the birth process, or after birth.

Choreoathetoid cerebral palsy A type of cerebral palsy in which changes in muscle tone cause uncoordinated, jerky movement.

Chorionic villus biopsy A test used to detect disabilities in a fetus during the first trimester.

Ciliary muscles Muscles that control changes in the shape of the lens so that the eye can focus on objects at varying distances.

Circle of friends A social contact technique that brings together disabled and nondisabled children to discuss their likes and dislikes under the leadership of a facilitator.

Class action suit Legal action that applies not only to the individual who brings the particular case to court but to all members of the class to which that individual belongs.

Classification The organization of information.

Cleft palate Failure of the bone and tissue of the palate (roof of the mouth) to fuse during early prenatal development; often associated with cleft lip.

Cognition The process of knowing and thinking.

Cognitive behavior modification A variation of behavior modification that focuses on the conscious feelings and attitudes of the individual.

Cognitive intervention strategy A strategy that focuses on the cognitive processes of learning to help remediate learning disabilities.

Cognitive strategies See *executive function.*

Combined method See *total communication method.*

Communication The exchange of thoughts, information, feelings, or ideas.

Communication board Chart containing symbols, letters, or words that nonspeaking students can point to in order to communicate their thoughts and needs.

Communication disorder An impairment in articulation, fluency, voice, or language.

Conduct disorder A pattern of deviant behavior in which children defy authority; are hostile toward authority figures; are cruel, malicious, and assaultive; and have few guilt feelings. This group includes children who are hyperactive, restless, and hyperkinetic.

Conductive hearing loss A condition that reduces the intensity of the sound vibrations reaching the auditory nerve and inner ear.

Congenital Present in an individual at birth.

Content acceleration Curriculum modification that moves students through the traditional curriculum at a fast pace.

Content enrichment Curriculum modification that expands the material for study, giving students the opportunity for a greater appreciation of a topic.

Content novelty Curriculum modification that introduces material that would not normally appear in the general curriculum, to help students who are gifted master important ideas.

Content sophistication Curriculum modification that challenges students who are gifted to use higher levels of thinking to understand ideas that average students of the same age find difficult or impossible to understand.

Contingent social reinforcement A behavior modification technique using a token system to teach appropriate social behavior.

Convergence Change in the extrinsic muscles of the eye.

Cooperative learning A set of instructional strategies that emphasize the use of groups for teaching students techniques of problem solving and working constructively with others.

Cornea The transparent anterior portion of the tough outer coat of the eyeball.

Creativity Mental process by which an individual creates new ideas and products or recombines existing ideas and products in a fashion that is novel to him or her.

Criterion-referenced tests A test designed to measure a child's development in terms of absolute levels of mastery, as opposed to the child's status relative to other children.

Cued commands A method of teaching children how to interact with their environment and the people around them.

Culture The attitudes, values, customs, and language that form an identifiable pattern or heritage.

Cumulative disorders Elements that gradually lower the functional intelligence of children and increase their adaptive problems.

Curriculum compacting   Content modification that allows students who are gifted to move ahead. It consists of three steps: finding out what the students know, arranging to teach the remaining concepts or skills, and providing a different set of experiences to enrich or advance the students.

Deaf   Having such severe hearing disorders (usually congenital) that understanding speech through the ear alone, with or without the use of a hearing aid, is impossible.

Deaf-blind   A person who possesses both a severe hearing loss and a severe loss of vision.

Decibels (dB)   A measurement of the relative intensity of sound.

Deinstitutionalization   Releasing as many exceptional children and adults as possible from the confinement of residential institutions into their local communities.

Developmental learning disabilities   Problems in processing information—attention problems, memory problems, disorders in thinking and using language. Also called *neuropsychological learning disabilities*.

Developmental scales   Instruments used to compare an infant's physical, emotional, and intellectual skills to other same-age children's development.

Developmental screening   A brief assessment of a child's developmental progress to determine if the child is at risk or is delayed.

Developmental therapy   An intervention strategy for children with behavior disorders that emphasizes the sequential learning of social behaviors and communication and academic skills.

Diagnostic achievement tests   Tests that help determine the process a student is using to solve a problem or decode a reading passage.

Diagnostic prescriptive model   A teaching approach that uses cognitive strategy instruction to address learning problems.

Dialect   A regional variation in pronunciation or language use.

Differential diagnosis   Pinpointing atypical behavior, explaining it, and distinguishing it from similar problems of other children with disabilities.

Differential reinforcement   A behavior modification technique that provides rewards if the student can increase the time between displays of unacceptable behavior.

Diplegic   Involvement of the entire body, especially the legs, in a physical condition.

Divergent thinking   The ability to produce many different answers to a question.

Down syndrome   A chromosomal abnormality that leads to mild or moderate mental retardation and, at times, a variety of hearing, skeletal, and heart problems.

Due process   A set of legal procedures designed to ensure that an individual's constitutional rights are protected.

Dyscalculia   The inability to perform mathematical functions.

Dyslexia   A severe reading disability involving difficulties in understanding the relationship between sounds and letters.

Dyslexic   Affected by dyslexia.

Dysphonia   A disorder in voice quality.

Early childhood intervention   Systematic efforts designed to prevent deficits or to improve an existing disability in children between birth and age 5.

Ecological inventory   A process that teachers can use to develop and individualize functional curriculum for their students.

Ecological model   A view of exceptionality that examines the individual in complex interaction with environmental forces and believes that exceptionalities should be remediated by modifying elements in the environment to allow more constructive interactions between the individual and the environment.

Educational assessment   The systematic gathering of educationally relevant information to make legal and instructional decisions about the provision of special services.

Environmental modification   A strategy creating an environment in which the child can succeed.

Epilepsy   A group of diseases of the nervous system marked primarily by seizures.

Exceptional child   A child who differs from the norm in mental characteristics, sensory abilities, communication abilities, social behavior, or physical characteristics to the extent that special education services are required for the child to develop to maximum capacity.

Executive function   The hypothesized decision-making element that controls reception, central processing, and expression.

Expression   The choice of a single response from a group of possible responses; the third step in information processing.

Extrinsic motivation   Motivating students to complete a task by promising a reward.

Extrinsic muscles   Muscles that control the movement of the eyeball in the socket.

Facilitative communication   Method of communicating in which an instructor holds the arms and wrists of a student to help him or her overcome tremors and communicate.

Fading   Gradually cutting back on help as a child becomes competent at a task.

Family-focused approach   Helping parents become more autonomous and less dependent on professionals.

Family harmony The perception that each partner in a marriage is taking his or her part in an acceptable manner.

Family life cycle The stages—couple, childbearing and preschool, school age, adolescence, launching, postparental, aging—through which the family moves.

Feedback The result of a response to a stimulus.

Fetal alcohol syndrome Defects in a child as a result of the mother's heavy use of alcohol during her pregnancy.

Finger spelling Spelling in the air or in the palm of another person using a manual alphabet.

Flexible pacing Allowing students to move through the school subjects or program at their own pace.

Fluency The flow of speech.

Fragile X syndrome A restriction at the end of the X chromosome that may result in mental retardation or learning disabilities.

Frequency The number of vibrations (or cycles) per second of a given sound wave.

Functional assessment A step by step assessment of the student's behavior to better understand the intent of the behavior.

Generalization Applying prior knowledge to new elements.

Genetic counseling A source of information for parents about the likelihood of their having a child with genetically based disabilities.

Gifted A term used to describe persons with intellectual gifts.

Grouping Bringing together students of similar abilities or levels of achievement for instruction.

Hard of hearing A person with a hearing loss and some residual hearing.

Head Start An educational preschool program for children living in poverty.

Health impairment A condition that requires ongoing medical attention.

Hearing impairment Any hearing loss, from mild to severe.

Helping teacher A direct-service special teacher who works in the classroom with the regular teacher to provide support, encouragement, and therapeutic tutoring.

Hemiplegic Involvement of one side of the body in a physical condition.

Human immunodeficiency virus (HIV) A virus that breaks down the body's immune system, causing AIDS.

Hyperactivity Excessive movement or motor restlessness, generally accompanied by impulsiveness and inattention.

Hyperbilirubinemia Incompatibility in the Rh factor of the mother's and fetus's blood that can lead to hearing loss.

Hyperopia Farsightedness.

Immaturity A pattern of deviant behavior in which children are inattentive, sluggish, uninterested in school, lazy, preoccupied, and reticent.

Incidence The number of new cases occurring in a population during a specific interval of time.

Inclusion The process of bringing children with exceptionalities into the regular classroom.

Individualized education program (IEP) A program written for every student receiving special education; it describes the child's current performance and goals for the school year, the particular special education services to be delivered, and the procedures by which outcomes are to be evaluated.

Individualized family services plan (IFSP) An intervention program for young children and their families that identifies their needs and sets forth a program to meet those needs.

Inert knowledge Knowledge stored in memory but not linked to other knowledge.

Instructional technology The computer and tools that support the use of the computer.

Integrated classroom A classroom administered jointly by regular and special education teachers. Usually one-third of the class is made up of youngsters with mild handicaps.

Intensity The relative loudness of a sound.

Interactive approach An approach to treating language disorders that uses the natural inclination of the child to talk about what he or she is doing to improve his or her language use.

Inter-individual difference A substantial difference among people along key dimensions of development.

Intra-individual difference A major variation in the abilities or development of a single child.

Intrinsic motivation Motivation that is internal to the student; self-motivation.

Invulnerability The concept used to explain how some at-risk children are able to develop without disabilities.

Iris The colored muscular partition in the eye that expands and contracts to regulate the amount of light admitted through the pupil.

Itinerant teacher A teacher who serves several schools, visiting exceptional children and their classroom teachers at regular intervals or whenever necessary.

Karyotyping A process by which a picture of chromosomal patterns is prepared to identify chromosomal abnormality.

Knowledge structure A bank of interrelated information in long-term memory that helps us recognize and recall patterns to use in solving problems.

Language An organized system of symbols that is used to express and receive meaning.

Language disorder   The impairment or deviant development of comprehension or use (or both) of a spoken, written, or other symbol system.

Learned helplessness   The belief that nothing one does can prevent negative things from happening.

Learning disability   A disorder that manifests itself in a discrepancy between ability and academic achievement. Learning disabilities do not stem from mental retardation, sensory impairments, emotional problems, or lack of opportunity to learn.

Least restrictive environment   The educational setting in which a child with special needs can learn that is as close as possible to the regular classroom.

Lens   The elastic biconvex body that focuses light on the retina of the eye.

Life space interview   A careful interview with a student directly after a crisis situation or event, in which the student discusses the event with the teacher and generates alternative solutions to the problem.

Low vision   See *severe visual disability.*

Mainstreaming   The process of bringing exceptional children into daily contact with nonexceptional children in an educational setting; the placement of exceptional children in the regular education program whenever possible.

Manual method   A method of communicating with persons with severe hearing impairments by using gestural signs.

Medical model   A view of exceptionality that implies a physical condition or disease within the patient.

Memory disorder   The inability to remember what has been seen, heard, or experienced.

Meningitis   An infection of the membranes covering the brain and spinal cord that can cause hearing loss.

Mental retardation   A combination of subnormal intelligence and deficits in adaptive behavior, manifested during the developmental period.

Metacognition   The ability to think about one's own thinking and monitor its effectiveness.

Mixed hearing loss   A condition involving problems in the outer ear as well as in the middle or inner ear.

Mnemonic   A rhyme or made-up system that helps students remember facts or concepts.

Modeling   Imitating the behavior of others.

Moderate visual disability   A visual impairment that can be almost entirely corrected with the help of visual aids.

Morphology   The structure of words and the way affixes change meaning or add information.

Multidisciplinary team   A group of professionals who work with children with disabilities to help them achieve their full potential.

Multisensory approach   A method for remediating reading disabilities that uses the child's hearing, vision, and motor skills.

Muscular dystrophy   A musculoskeletal disease that leads to the progressive deterioration of skeletal muscles.

Musculoskeletal system   The muscles, bones, and joints of the body.

Myelomeningocele   The protrusion from the spinal cord of a sac of fluids containing portions of the spinal cord itself.

Myopia   Nearsightedness.

Negative reinforcement   The process of reinforcing behavior by the withdrawal of an aversive stimulus.

Neurological system   The brain, spinal cord, and nerves.

Neuropsychological learning disabilities   See *developmental learning disabilities.*

Nondiscriminatory evaluation   A full individual examination appropriate to a student's cultural and linguistic background.

Normalization   The creation of a learning and social environment as normal as possible for the exceptional person.

Norm-referenced achievement   See *standard achievement tests.*

Object permanence   The understanding that objects that are not in the visual field still exist.

Operant conditioning   A technique of behavior modification that works by controlling the stimulus that follows a response.

Oral-aural method   An approach to teaching deaf students that uses residual hearing through amplified sound, speech reading, and speech to develop communication skills.

Orientation & mobility (O&M) training   Teaching a person with visual loss or a blind person how to move through space.

Otitis media   An infection of the middle ear that can cause hearing impairment.

Parental participation   The inclusion of parents in the development of their child's individualized education program, and their right to access to their child's educational records.

Parent empowerment   The expectation that parents will play a major role in decisions about their child's care.

Perceptual-motor disabilities   Difficulty in understanding or responding to the meaning of pictures or numbers.

Performance assessment   A measure of the application of knowledge.

Phenylketonuria (PKU)   A single-gene defect that that can produce severe retardation because of the body's inability to break down phenylalanine, which when accumulated at high levels in the brain results in severe damage. Can be controlled by a diet restricting phenylalanine.

Phonation The production of sound by the vibration of the vocal cords.

Phoneme A sound; the smallest unit of speech.

Phonological error Mispronunciation of speech sounds.

Phonology The sound system of a language; the way sounds are combined into meaningful sequences.

Physical disability A condition that interferes with the individual's ability to use his or her body.

Positive reinforcement The application of a positive stimulus immediately following a response.

Postlinguistic deafness The loss of hearing after spontaneous speech and language have developed.

Pragmatics The understanding of how language is used in communication in particular settings.

Preacademic instruction Instruction in the developmental skills that prepare children for reading, writing, and arithmetic.

Prelinguistic deafness The loss of hearing before speech and language have developed; referred to as *deafness*.

Prenatal care Monitoring of a pregnancy by the mother and her physician.

Prereferral services Services to help children at risk for disabling conditions to adapt to the regular classroom before they are singled out for special services.

Prevalence The number of people in a given category in a population group during a specified period of time.

Problem finding The ability to review an area of study and to perceive those elements worthy of further analysis and study.

Problem solving The ability to reach an appropriate answer by organizing and processing available information in a systematic way.

Profound visual disability A vision impairment that prohibits the use of vision as an educational tool; in legal terms, *blindness*.

Punishment The application of actions to reduce undesirable behavior.

Pupil The central opening of the eye through which light enters.

Pure-tone test Sounds produced mechanically to various levels of decibels to determine a person's range of hearing.

Reasoning The ability to generate new information through the internal processing of available information.

Reception The visual or auditory perception of a stimulus; the second step in information processing.

Reciprocal teaching A technique in which small groups of students and teachers take turns leading a discussion.

Regular education initiative (REI) The plan to integrate and educate all children with disabilities in regular schools.

Residential school A public or private institution for children with handicapping conditions.

Resonation The process that gives the voice its special characteristics.

Resource room An instructional setting to which an exceptional child comes for specific periods of time, usually on a regularly scheduled basis.

Respiration Breathing; the process that generates the energy that produces sound.

Respite care The services of a trained individual to relieve the primary caregiver of a child with disabilities on a short-term basis.

Retina The light-sensitive innermost layer of tissue at the back of the eyeball.

Retinoblastoma A tumor of the eye that causes blindness.

Retinopathy of prematurity A disease of the retina in which a mass of scar tissue forms in back of the lens of the eye. Both eyes are usually affected, and it occurs chiefly in infants born prematurely who receive excessive oxygen.

Rh incompatibility The condition that can develop when a mother who is Rh-negative carries an Rh-positive child; the mother's antibodies can cause deafness and other serious consequences for the fetus unless the condition is identified and treated.

Rochester method A method of teaching deaf students that combines the oral method and finger spelling.

Rubella German measles, which in the first three months of pregnancy can cause visual impairment, hearing impairment, mental retardation, and birth defects in the fetus.

Scaffolding A strategy in which a teacher models the expected behavior and guides the learning of the student.

Self-contained special class A separate class in which a special education teacher assumes primary responsibility for the education program of students with disabilities.

Self-evaluation A technique for behavior change that asks the student to compare his or her behavior to some criteria and make a judgment about the quality of the behavior being exhibited.

Self-instruction A technique for behavior change in which students talk to themselves, encouraging themselves with verbal prompts to persist in solving an academic or social problem.

Self-monitoring A technique for behavior change that requires students to determine whether a target behavior has occurred and then record its occurrence.

Self-reinforcement A technique for behavior change in which students reward themselves with a token or tally after meeting some performance standard.

Semantics The component of language that governs meanings of words and word combinations.

Sensorineural hearing loss   A defect of the inner ear or the auditory nerve in transmitting impulses to the brain.

Sensory compensation   The theory that if one sense avenue is deficient, other senses are automatically strengthened.

Service coordinator   See *case manager.*

Severe visual disability   A vision impairment that is only partially corrected by visual aids but allows the child to use vision as a channel for learning; in legal terms, *low vision.*

Sheltered workshop   A not-for-profit facility providing vocational services to adults with disabilities.

Simultaneous method   See *total communication method.*

Snellen chart   A chart consisting of rows of letters in graduated sizes that is used to determine visual acuity. A variation used with younger children and people who do not know the letter names consists of capital *E*s pointing in different directions.

Socialized aggression   A pattern of deviant behavior displayed by children who are hostile and aggressive and have few guilt feelings but who are socialized within their group, usually a gang.

Social language learning   An approach to treating language disorders that uses speech and language in a functional way to satisfy needs.

Social learning approach   A system designed to develop critical thinking and independent action by students with mild retardation.

Sonography   The use of sound waves to take a picture of a fetus in its mother's uterus.

Spastic (pyramidal) cerebral palsy   A form of cerebral palsy marked by tight muscles and stiff movements.

Special class   A class held for children who need more special instruction than the resource room can give them.

Special courses   Curriculum designed to meet students' diverse achievements and aptitudes.

Special education   The educational help devised for children who differ significantly from the norm.

Special Olympics   A program that allows children with disabilities to participate in competitions in a variety of physical events and games.

Special school   A day school, organized within a school system, for a group of children with specific exceptionalities.

Speech   The systematic oral production of words of a given language.

Speech disorder   A disorder of articulation (how words are pronounced), voice (how words are vocalized), or fluency (the flow of speech).

Speech-language pathologist   A trained professional who provides supervision and administration, diagnosis, consultation, and direct services for individuals who have communication disorders.

Speech reading   Lip reading; the visual interpretation of spoken communication.

Spina bifida   The separation of a portion of the spinal cord.

Standard achievement tests   Tests that measure the student's level of achievement compared with the achievement of students of similar age or grade. Also called *norm-referenced tests.*

Student acceleration   Passing students through the educational system as quickly as possible.

Stuttering   A disorder of fluency.

Syntax   The way in which words are organized in sentences.

Synthetic speech   The production of sound—of phonemes into words—by means of a computer.

Target behaviors   In behavior modification, the characteristics that we want to change or enhance.

Task analysis   A method that breaks down complex tasks into simpler component parts, teaches each of the components separately, then teaches them together; a procedure under which a child receives positive reinforcement for each step or part of the total task as it is completed.

Task training   A remediation strategy that emphasizes the sequencing and simplification of the task to be learned, using task analysis and teaching one skill at a time.

Teacher-consultant   A specially trained consultant who provides differentiated instruction for gifted students in the regular classroom.

Teratogen   A substance ingested by the mother that can damage the growth and development of the fetus.

Time-out   The physical removal of a child from a reinforcing situation for a period of time, usually immediately following an unwanted response.

TORCHS   An acronym given to a cluster of infections that can result in hearing loss and other disabilities: *t*oxoplasmosis, *r*ubella, *c*ytomegalo-virus, *h*erpes simplex virus, and syphilis.

Total communication method   A method of teaching deaf students that combines finger spelling, signs, speech reading, speech, and auditory amplification. Also called *combined method* and *simultaneous method.*

Transition services   Programs that help exceptional students move from school to the world of work and community.

Ultimate functioning   The degree to which severely handicapped people are able to take a productive part in a variety of community situations appropriate to their chronological age.

Unisensory method   See *auditory method.*

Verbal language   A spoken language, a language which is based on speech sounds.

Vicarious learning Learning that occurs to someone who observes how others' behaviors are reinforced while the learner himself is not an active participant of the event.

Visual acuity The ability to see details clearly or identify forms at a specified distance.

Visual-auditory-kinesthetic (VAK) method A phonic system for the remediation of reading disabilities.

Voice The production of sound in the larynx and the selective transmission and modification of that sound through resonance and loudness.

Voice disorder A variation from accepted norms in voice quality, pitch, or loudness.

Zero reject principle The principle that all children with disabilities must be provided a free and appropriate public education and that local school systems cannot decide not to provide needed services.

references

Abuelo, D. (1991). Genetic disorders. In J. Matson & J. Mulick (Eds.), *Handbook of mental retardation* (2nd ed.). New York: Pergamon Press.

Adlay, L. U., Aiken, M. J., & Wegener, D. (1988). *Pediatric home care: Results of a national evaluation of programs for ventilator-dependent children.* Chicago: Pluribus Press.

Adler, M. (1984). *The Paidaia program: An educational syllabus.* New York: Macmillan.

Affleck, G., Tennen, H., & Rowe, J. (1991). *Infants in crisis: How parents cope with newborn intensive care and its aftermath.* New York: Springer-Verlag.

Affleck, J. Q., Edgar, E., Levine, P., & Kortering, L. (1990). Postschool status of students classified as mildly mentally retarded, learning disabled, or non-handicapped: Does it get better with time? *Education and Training in Mental Retardation, 25,* 315–324.

Affleck, J., Madge, S., Adams, A., & Lowenbrau, L. (1988). Integrated classroom versus resource model. *Exceptional Children, 54,* 339–348.

Ahmann, E., & Lipsi, K. (1991). Early intervention for technology-dependent infants and young children. *Infants and Young Children, 3*(4), 67–77.

Allan, S. (1991). Ability grouping research reviews: What do they say about grouping and the gifted? *Educational Leadership, 48*(6), 60–65.

Allen T. (1986). A study of the achievement pattern of hearing impaired students: 1974–1983. In A. Schildroth & M. Karchmer (Eds.), *Deaf children in America* (pp. 161–206). San Diego: College-Hill Press.

Altshuler, K., & Baroff, G. (1983). Educational background and vocational adjustment. In J. Rainer, K. Altshuler, & F. Kallman (Eds.), *Family and mental health problems in a deaf population.* New York: New York State Psychiatric Institute.

America 2000. (1990). Washington, DC: U.S. Department of Education.

American National Standards Institute. (1980). *American national standards: specifications for making buildings and facilities accessible to and usable by physically handicapped people.* New York: Author.

Anastasiow, N. J. (1979). *Oral language: Expression of thought.* International Reading Association, 800 Barksdale Road, Newark, DE 19711.

Anastasiow, N. J. (1982). *The adolescent parent.* Baltimore: Paul H. Brookes.

Anastasiow, N. J. (1986). *Development and disability.* Baltimore: Paul H. Brookes.

Anastasiow, N. J. (1990). *A report to the State of Florida Center for Policy Options.* Tallahassee: Florida State University at Tallahassee.

Anastasiow, N. J. (1992). Overview and summary of the effects of early intervention. In N. J. Anastasiow & S. Harel (Eds.), *The at-risk infant.* Baltimore: Paul H. Brookes.

Anastasiow, N. J., & Nucci, C. (1994). Social, historical and theoretical foundations of early childhood special education and early intervention. In P. Safford (Ed.), *Early childhood special education: Vol. 5. Yearbook in early childhood education* (pp. 7–25). New York: Teachers College Press.

Anastasiow, N. J., Frankenberg, W., & Fandall, A. (1982). *Identifying the developmentally delayed child.* Baltimore: University Park Press.

Anastasiow, N. J., Hanes, M., & Hanes, M. (1982). *Language patterns in poverty children.* Austin, TX: PRO-ED.

Anderson, M., & Goldberg, P. (1991). *Cultural competence in screening and assessment.* National Early Childhood Technical Assistance System. Pacer Center, 4826 Chicago Avenue South, Minneapolis, MN 55417-1095.

Anthony, T., Fazzi, P., Lampert, J., & Pogrund, R. (1992). Movement focus: Orientation and mobility for young blind and visually impaired children. In R. Pogrund, D. Fazzi, & J. Lampert (Eds.), *Early focus: Working with young blind and visually impaired children and their families.* New York: American Foundation for the Blind.

Apgar, V., & Beck, J.. (1973). *Is my baby all right?* New York: Trident Press.

Arcia, E., Gallagher, J., & Serling, J. (1992). *But what about the other 93 percent?* Chapel Hill, NC: Carolina Policy Studies Program.

Armstrong, N., Carr, T., Houghton, J., Belanich, J., & Mascia, J. (1995). Supporting medical and health concerns of young adults who are deaf-blind. In J. Everson (Ed.), *Supporting young adults who are deaf-blind in their communities* (pp. 43–66). Baltimore: Paul H. Brookes.

Ashcroft, S. (1984). Research on multimedia access to microcomputers for visually impaired youth. *Education of the Visually Handicapped, 15* (4), 108–118.

Atkinson, J., (1993). The Cambridge assessment and screening of vision in high risk infants and young children.

In N. Anastasiow & S. Harel (Eds.), *The at-risk infant* (pp. 33–46). Baltimore: Paul H. Brookes.

Atwood, A. (1993, July). Movement disorders and autism acquired in review of communication abound. *American Journal of Mental Retardation, 99*(4), 450–451.

Badian, N. A. (1983). Dyscalculia and nonverbal disorders of learning. In H. R. Mykelbust (Ed.), *Progress in learning disabilities* (Vol. 5, pp. 235–264). New York: Grune & Stratton.

Badian, N. (1988). The prediction of good and poor reading before kindergarten entry: A nine-year follow-up. *Journal of Learning Disabilities, 21,* 98–103, 123.

Bailey, Jr., D. & Nelson, D. (in press). The nature and consequences of fragile X syndrome. *Mental Retardation and Developmental Disabilities Research Review.*

Bailey, Jr., D., Simeonsson, R., Winton, P., Huntington, G., Comfort, M., Isbell, P., O'Donnell, K., & Helm, J. (1986). Family-focused intervention: A functional model for planning, implementing, and evaluating individualized family services in early intervention. *Journal of the Division of Early Childhood, 10*(2).

Bailey, D. E., Simeonsson, R. J., Winton, P. J., Huntington, G. S., Comfort, M., Isbell, P., O'Donnell, K. J., & Helm, J. M. (1986). Family-focused intervention: A functional model for planning, implementing, and evaluating family services in early intervention. *Journal of the Division of Early Childhood, 11*(1), 156–170.

Baker, L., & Brown, A. L. (1984). Metacognitive skills in reading. In P. D. Pearson (Ed.), *Handbook of reading research* (pp. 353–394). New York: Longman.

Baldwin, A. (1987). Undiscovered diamonds. *Journal for the Education of the Gifted, 10*(4), 271–286.

Baldwin, V. (1991). Understanding the deaf-blind population census. *Traces.* Traces Project, Teaching Research Division, Western Oregon State College, Monmouth, OR 97361.

Baldwin, V. (1993, October). *Population/demographics.* Paper presented at the National Project Directors Meeting on Educational Services for Children and Youth with Deaf-Blindness, Washington, DC.

Baller, W., Charles, O., & Miller, E. (1966). Mid-life attainment of the mentally retarded: A longitudinal study. *Genetic Psychology Monographs, 75,* 235–239.

Bandura, A. (1989). Human agency in social cognitive theory. *American Psychologist, 44,* 1175–1184.

Barker, K., Baldes, Jenkinson, P., Wilson, K., & Freilinger, J. (1982). Iowa's severity rating scales for communication disabilities. *Language, Speech, and Hearing Services in the Schools, 13*(3), 156–162.

Barr, D. (1990). A solution in search of a problem: The role of technology in educational reform. *Journal for the Education of the Gifted, 14,* 79–95.

Barraga, N. (1986). Sensory perceptual development. In G. T. Scholl (Ed.), *Foundations of education for blind and visually handicapped children and youth.* New York: American Foundation for the Blind.

Batshaw, M. L., & Perret, Y. M. (Eds.). (1988). *Children with handicaps: A medical primer* (2nd ed.). Baltimore: Paul H. Brookes.

Batshaw, M. L., & Perret, Y. M. (Eds.). (1992). *Children with disabilities: A medical primer* (3rd Ed.). Baltimore: Paul H. Brookes.

Baumeister, A. (1987). Mental retardation: Some conceptions and dilemmas. *American Psychologist, 42,* 796–800.

Baumeister, A. (in press). Boom or bust. In W. McClean (Ed.)., *Handbook of mental deficiency: Psychological theory and research.* Hillsdale, NJ: Erlbaum.

Baumeister, A., Kuipstas, F., & Klindworth, L. (1992). The new morbidity. In T. Thompson & S. Hupp (Eds.), *Saving children at risk* (pp. 3–22). Newbury Park, CA: Sage Publications.

Baumgart, D., & Helmstetter, E. (1990). *Augmentative and alternative communication systems for persons with moderate and severe disabilities.* Baltimore: Paul H. Brookes.

Baumgart, D., Brown, L., Pumpian, I., Nisbet, J., Ford, A., Sweet, M., Messina, R., & Schroeder, L. (1982). Principle of partial participation and individualized programs for severely handicapped students. *Journal of the Association for Persons with Severe Handicaps, 7*(2), 17–26.

Bayley, N. (1993). *Bayley scales of infant development* (2nd ed.). San Antonio: Psychological Corporation.

Beckwith, L. (1988). Intervention with disadvantaged parents of sick preterm infants. *Psychiatry, 5*(1), 242–249.

Behrman, R., Vaughn, V., & Nelson, W. (1987). *Nelson textbook of pediatrics.* Philadelphia: Saunders.

Bellamy, G., Rhodes, L., Mank, D., & Albin, J. (1988). *Supportive employment.* Baltimore: Paul H. Brookes.

Bellinger, D., Leviton, A., Waternaux, C., Needleman, H., & Rabinowitz, M. (1987). Longitudinal analysis of prenatal and postnatal lead exposure and early cognition. *New England Journal of Medicine, 316,* 1037–1043.

Bellugi, U. (1988). Language development. *The Mind* (Vol. 7). New York: WNET, Educational Broadcasting.

Berger, N. (1978). Why can't John read? Perhaps he's not a good listener. *Journal of Learning Disabilities, 11,* 633–635.

Berla, E. (1981). Tactile scanning and memory for a spatial display by blind students. *Journal of Special Education, 15,* 341–350.

Bernard, G. (1993). *Hearing equals behavior.* Canaan, CT: Kents.

Bernthal, J., & Bankson, N. (1988). *Articulation and phonological disorders* (2nd ed.). Englewood Cliffs, NJ: Prentice-Hall.

Beukelman, D., & Mirenda, P. (1992). *Augmentative and alternative communication*. Baltimore: Paul H. Brookes.

Beyer, H. (1991). Litigation involving people with mental retardation. In J. Matson & J. Mulick (Eds.), *Handbook of mental retardation* (2nd ed.). New York: Pergamon Press.

Bigelow, A. (1992). Blind children's ability to predict what another sees. *Journal of Visual Impairment and Blindness, 86,* 181–184.

Bigge, J. (1982). Instructional adaptations. In J. Bigge (Ed.), *Teaching individuals with physical and multiple disabilities* (2nd ed., pp. 233–256). Columbus, OH: Charles E. Merrill.

Biklin, D. (1990). Communication unbound: Autism and praxis. *Harvard Educational Review, 60*(3).

Biklin, D., Ferguson, D., & Ford, A. (1989). *Schooling and disability* (Part II). Eighty-eighth Yearbook of the National Society for the Study of Education. Chicago: University of Chicago Press.

Biklin, D., Morton, M., Saha, S., Duncan, J., Gold, D., Hardadottir, M., Karna, I., O'Connor, S., & Rio, S. (1991). I AMN NOT A UTISIUC OH THSE TYP (I'm not autistic on the typewriter). *Disability, Handicap and Society, 6*(3), 161–180.

Biklin, D., & Duchan, J. (1994, Fall). "I am intelligent": The social construction of mental retardation. *The Journal of the Association for Persons with Severe Handicaps, 19*(3), 173–184.

Birley, D., & Nelson, D. (in press). The nature and consequences of fragile X syndrome. *Mental Retardation and Developmental Disabilities Research Review.*

Bishop, V. (1986, November). Identifying the components of success in mainstreaming. *Journal of Visual Impairment and Blindness,* pp. 939–946.

Blair, C., Ramey, C., & Hardin, M. J. (1995). Early intervention of low birthweight, premature infants: Participation and intellectual development. *American Journal of Mental Retardation, 99*(5), 542–544.

Blakely, K., Lang, M., & Hart, R. (1991). *Getting in touch with play*. New York: National Center for Vision and Child Development.

Blakeslee, S. (1991, September 15). Study ties dyslexia to brain flow affecting vision and other senses. *New York Times,* pp. 1, 10.

Blance, G., Stedal, K., & Smith, V. (1994, Winter). Stuttering: The role of the classroom teacher. *Teaching Exceptional Children, 26*(2), 10–12.

Bloom, B. (1985). *Developing talent in young people*. New York: Ballantine Books.

Bloom, L. (1991). *Language development from two to three.* New York: Cambridge University Press.

Bloom, L., & Capatides, R. (1987). Expression of affect and the emergence of language. *Child Development, 58,* 1513–1522.

Board of Education v. *Rowley,* 458 U.S. 176 (1982).

Bobarth, K., & Bobarth, B. (1984). The neurodevelopment treatment. In D. Scrutten (Ed.), *Management of motor disorders of children with cerebral palsy* (pp. 6–18). Philadelphia: Lippincott.

Boberg, E. (1986). Postscript: Relapse and outcome. In G. Shames & H. Rubin (Eds.), *Stuttering then and now.* Columbus, OH: Charles E. Merrill.

Bock, K. (1990, November). Structure in language. *American Psychologist, 45,* 1221–1236.

Boone, D., & McFarlane, S. (1988). *The voice and voice therapy.* Englewood Cliffs, NJ: Prentice-Hall.

Boothroyd, A. (1988). *Hearing impairments in children.* Washington, DC: Alexander Graham Bell Association for the Deaf.

Borkowski, J., & Day, J. (1987). *Cognition in special children: Comparative approaches to retardation, learning disabilities and giftedness.* Norwood, NJ: Ablex.

Bos, C. (1995). DLD president's message. *The DLD Times.* Reston, VA: Division for Learning Disabilities, Council for Exceptional Children.

Botuck, S., & Winsberg, B. (1991). Effects of respite on mothers of school-age and adult children with severe disabilities. *Mental Retardation, 29*(1), 43–47.

Bower, T. G. R. (1989). *The rational infant.* New York: W. H. Freeman.

Bradley, L., & Meredith, R. (1991). Interpersonal development: A study with children classified as educable mentally retarded. *Education and Training in Mental Retardation, 26,* 130–141.

Bradley, V., Ashbaugh, J., & Blaney, B. (1994). *Creating individual supports for people with developmental disabilities.* Baltimore: Paul H. Brookes.

Brady, M. (1984, October 1–2). *A critical review of the state of the art of high tech communication aids—1984.* Paper presented at the Conference on Technology for Disabled Persons, Chicago.

Brady, S., Shankweiler, O., & Mann, J. (1987). Speech perception and memory coding in relation to reading ability. *Journal of Experimental Child Psychology, 35,* 345–367.

Brambring, M., & Tröster, H. (1992). On the stability of stereotyped behaviors in blind infants and preschoolers. *Journal of Visual Impairment and Blindness, 86,* 105–110.

Brambring, M., and Tröster, H. (1994). The assessment of cognitive development in blind infants and preschoolers. *Journal of Visual Impairment and Blindness, 87,* 9–18.

Bransford, J., Sherwood, R., Vye, N., & Rieser, J. (1986). Teaching thinking and problem solving. *American Psychologist, 41*(10), 1078–1089.

Breske, S. (1994). Coping vulnerability in children with disabilities. *Teaching Exceptional Children, 27*(1).

Bricker, D. (1993, Spring). A rose by any name. Or is it? *Journal of Early Intervention, 17*(2), 89–96.

Bricker, D., & Carlson, L. (1981). Issues in early language intervention. In R. Schiefelbusch & D. Bricker (Eds.), *Early language acquisition* (pp. 477–510). Baltimore: University Park Press.

Bricker, D., & Cripes, J. (1992). *An activity based approach to early intervention.* Baltimore: Paul H. Brookes.

Brigham, F., Bakkan, J., Scruggs, J., & Mastropieni, M. (1992). Cooperative behavior management: Strategies for promoting a positive classroom environment. *Education and Training in Mental Retardation, 27,* 3–12.

Brinker, R. (1985). Interactions between severely retarded students and other students in integrated and segregated public school settings. *American Journal of Mental Deficiency, 89,* 58–59.

Bristol, M. (1987). Mothers of children with autism or communication disorders: Successful adaptation and the double ABCX model. *Journal of Autism and Developmental Disorders, 17,* 469–486.

Bristol, M., & Gallagher, J. (1986). Research on fathers of young handicapped children: Evolution, review, and some future directions. In J. Gallagher & P. Vietze (Eds.), *Families of handicapped persons* (pp. 81–100). Baltimore: Paul H. Brookes.

Bristol, M. G., Gallagher, J., & Schopler, E. (1988). Mothers and fathers of young developmentally disabled and nondisabled boys: Adaptation and spousal support. *Developmental Psychology, 24*(3), 441–451.

Bronfenbrenner, U. (1979). Content of child rearing: Problems and prospects. *American Psychologist, 34,* 844–850.

Brown, C. (1982). *My left foot.* London: Pan.

Brown F., & Lehr, D. (1989). *Persons with profound disabilities.* Baltimore: Paul H. Brookes.

Brown, F., and Lehr, D. H. (1993). Making activities meaningful for students with severe multiple disabilities. *Teaching Exceptional Children, 25*(4), 12–16.

Brown, F., & Gothelf, C. (in press). Self determination for all individuals. In D. Lehr and F. Brown (Eds.), *People with disabilities who challenge the system.* Baltimore: Paul H. Brookes.

Brown, J., & Burton, R. (1978). Diagnostic models for procedural bugs in basic mathematical skills. *Cognitive Science, 2,* 155–192.

Brown, L., Schwarz, P., Udvari-Solner, A., Kampschooer, E., Jolenson, F., Jorgensen, J., & Greenewald, L. (1991). How much time should students with severe intellectual disabilities spend in regular education classrooms and elsewhere? *Journal for the Association of the Severely Handicapped, 16*(1), 39–47.

Bruininks, R., Thurlow, M., & Gilman, C. (1987). Adaptive behavior and mental retardation. *Journal of Special Education, 21*(1), 69–88.

Bryce, R. L., Stanley, F. J., & Enkin, M. W. (1988). The role of social support system in the prevention of preterm birth. *Birth, 15*(1).

Bryen, D., & Joyce, D. (1985). Language intervention with severely handicapped: A decade of research. *Journal of Special Education, 19*(1), 7–39.

Burkhart, L. (1986). *More homemade battery devices for severely handicapped children with suggested activities.* College Park, MD: Author.

Butler-Por, N. (1987). *Underachievers in school: Issues and intervention.* New York: Wiley.

Cain, E. J., & Taber, F. (1987). *Educating disabled people for the 21st century.* Boston: Little, Brown.

Callahan, C., & McIntyre, J. (1994). *Identifying outstanding talent in American Indian and Alaskan native students.* Washington, DC: U.S. Department of Education.

Camarata, S. (1995). A rationale for naturalistic speech intelligibility intervention. In M. Fay, J. Windsor, & S. Warren (Eds.), *Language intervention: Preschool through elementary years,* pp. 63–84. Baltimore: Paul H. Brookes.

Camp, B., & Bash, M. (1981). *Think aloud: Increasing social and cognitive skills: A problem solving program for children.* Champaign, IL: Research Press.

Campbell, P. (1987). Programming for students with dysfunction in posture and severe handicaps. In M. Snell (Ed.), *Systematic instruction of persons with severe handicaps* (3rd ed.), pp. 188–211. Columbus, OH: Charles E. Merrill.

Cantwell, D. (1982). Childhood depression: A review of current research. In B. Lahey & A. Kazdin (Eds.), *Advances in clinical child psychology* (Vol. 5). New York: Plenum Press.

Carpignano, J., Sirvis, B., & Bigge, J. (1982). Psychosocial aspects of physical disability. In J. Bigge (Ed.), *Teaching individuals with physical and multiple disabilities* (2nd ed., pp. 110–137). Columbus, OH: Charles E. Merrill.

Cary, D., & Sale, P. (1994, Fall). Notebook computers increase communication. *Teaching Exceptional Children, 27*(1), 62–69.

Casper, A., & Fifer, W. (1984). Studying hearing in the womb. *Science, 45,* 302–303.

Castro, G. (1987). Plasticity and the handicapped child: A review of efficacy research. In J. Gallagher & C. Ramey (Eds.), *The malleability of children* (pp. 103–114). Baltimore: Paul H. Brookes.

Chalfant, J. (1985). Identifying learning disabled students: A summary of the national task force report. *Learning Disabilities Focus, 1,* 9–20.

Chalfant, J. (1987). Providing services to all students with learning problems: Implications for policy and programs. In S. Vaughn & C. Bos (Eds.), *Research in learning disabilities: Issues and future directions.* Boston: Little, Brown.

Chalfant, J. (1989). Learning disabilities: Public issues and promising approaches. *American Psychologist, 44*(2), 392–398.

Chalfant, J., Pysh, M., & Moultine, R. (1979). Teacher assistance teams: A model for within building problem solving. *Learning Disabilities Quarterly, 2,* 85–96.

Chase, W. G., & Chi, H. T. (1981). Cognitive skills: Implications for spatial skills and large scale environments. In J. Harvey (Ed.), *Cognition, social behavior, and environment.* Hillsdale, NJ: Erlbaum.

Chess, S., & Thomas, A. (1984). *Origins and evolution of behavioral disorders.* New York: Brunner/Mazel.

Chi, M. (1978). Knowledge structures and memory development. In R. Siegler (Ed.), *Children's thinking: What develops?* (2nd ed., pp. 73–96). Hillsdale, NJ: Erlbaum.

Children's Defense Fund. (1991). *The state of America's children: 1991.* Washington, DC: Author.

Chomsky, N. (1989). *Knowledge of language: Its nature, origin and use.* New York: Praeger.

Cioffi, J. (1995). Orientation and mobility issues and support strategies for young adults who are deaf-blind. In J. Everson (Ed.), *Supporting young adults who are deaf-blind in their communities.* Baltimore: Paul H. Brookes.

Cipani, E. (1991). Educational classification and placement. In J. Matson & J. Mulick (Eds.), *Handbook of mental retardation* (2nd ed.). New York: Pergamon Press.

Cipani, E., & Morrow, R. (1991). Educational assessment. In J. Matson & J. Mulick (Eds.), *Handbook of mental retardation* (2nd ed.). New York: Pergamon Press.

Civelli, E. (1983). Verbalism in young children. *Journal of Visual Impairment and Blindness, 77*(3), 61–63.

Clark, B. (1992). *Growing up gifted* (4th ed.). Columbus, OH: Charles E. Merrill.

Clark, D. B. (1988). *Dyslexia: Theory and practice of remedial instruction.* Parkton, MD: York Press.

Cohen, D. J., Donnellan, A. M., & Paul, R. (Eds.). (1987). *Handbook on autism and pervasive developmental disorders.* Silver Spring, MD: V. H. Winston & Sons.

Cohen, D. J., Paul, R., & Volkmar, F. (1987). Issues in classification of pervasive developmental disorders. In D. J. Cohen, A. M. Donnellan, & R. Paul (Eds.), *Handbook on autism and pervasive developmental disorders* (p. xvi). Silver Spring, MD: V. H. Winston & Sons.

Cohen, R., Harrell, L., Macon, C., Moedjono, S., Orrante, L., Pogrund, R., & Sacks-Salcedo, P. (1992). Family focus: Working with families of young blind and visually impaired children. In R. Pogrund, D. Fazzi, & J. Lampert (Eds.), *Early focus: Working with young blind and visually impaired children and their families.* New York: American Foundation for the Blind.

Cohen, S., & Warren, K. (1987). Preliminary survey of family abuse of children served by United Cerebral Palsy centers. *Developmental Medicine and Child Neurology, 29,* 12–18.

Coleman, M. R., & Gallagher, J. J. (1992). *State policies for identification of nontraditional gifted students.* Chapel Hill, NC: University of North Carolina, Gifted Education Policy Studies Program.

Coleman, M., & Gallagher, J. (1995, January). Middle schools and their impact on talent development. *Middle Schools Journal,* pp. 47–56.

Collins, B., Gast, D., Ault, M., & Wolery, M. (1991). Small group instruction: Guidelines for teachers of students with moderate to severe handicaps. *Education and Training in Mental Retardation, 26,* 18–32.

Conlon, C. (1992). New threats to development: Alcohol, cocaine and AIDS. In M. L. Batshaw, & Y. M. Perret (Eds.), *Children with disabilities: A medical primer* (3rd ed.). Baltimore: Paul H. Brookes.

Cooper, S. E., & Robinson, D. A. (1987). The effects of a structured academic support group on GPA and self-concept of ability. *Techniques, 3,* 260–264.

Coplan, J. (1985). Evaluation of the child with delayed speech or language. *Pediatric Annals, 14*(3), 203–208.

Correa, V. (1987, June). Working with Hispanic parents of visually impaired children: Cultural implications. *Journal of Visual Impairment and Blindness,* pp. 260–264.

Cotzin, M., & Dallenbach, K. (1950). "Facial Vision": The role of pitch and loudness in the perception of obstacles by the blind. *American Journal of Psychology, 63,* 485–515.

Council for Exceptional Children (1994, October–November). *Exceptional Children, 61*(2, Special Issue).

Cox, J., Daniel, N., & Boston, B. (1985). *Educating able learners.* Austin: University of Texas Press.

Cox, N. (1988). Molecular genetics: The key to the puzzle of stuttering. *ASHA, 30*(4), 36–39.

Cramer, J., & Oshima, T. (1992). Do gifted females attribute their math performance differently than other students? *Journal for the Education of the Gifted, 16*(1), 18–35.

Crnic, K., Friedrich, W., & Greenberg, M. (1983). Adaptation of families with mentally retarded children: A model of stress, coping and family ecology. *American Journal of Mental Deficiency, 88,* 125–138.

Crocker, A. C. (Ed.). (1989). Developmental disabilities and HIV infection. *Mental Retardation, 27*(4, Special Issue).

Cromer, R. (1978). The basis of childhood dysphasia: A linguistic approach. In D. Wyke (Ed.), *Developmental dysphasia*. New York: Wiley.

Cromer, R. K. (1987). Differentiating language and cognition. In R. Schiefelbusch & R. Lloyd (Eds.), *Language intervention strategies* (pp. 51–137). Austin, TX: PRO-ED.

Crossley, R. (1989). *Communication for training facilitated communications*. Melbourne, Australia: DEAL Communication Center.

Culp, D. (1984). The preschool fluency development program: Assessment and treatment. In M. Peins (Ed.), *Contemporary approaches in stuttering therapy*. Boston: Little, Brown.

Cummins, J. (1986). Psychological assessment of minority students: Out of content, out of focus, out of control? In A. Willig & H. Greenberg (Eds.), *Bilingualism and learning disabilities: Policy and practice for teachers and administrators*. New York: American Library.

Curry, S. A., & Hatlen, P. H. (1988). Meeting the unique educational needs of visually impaired pupils through appropriate placement. *Journal of Visual Impairment and Blindness, 82*(10), 417–424.

Curtis, S., & Talla, P. (1991). On the nature of impairment in language in children. In J. Miller (Ed.), *New directions in research on child language disorders* (pp. 189–210). Boston: College-Hill Press.

Davis, D. (1988). Nutrition in the prevention and reversal of mental retardation. In F. Menolascino & J. Stark (Eds.), *Preventive and curative intervention in mental retardation* (pp. 177–222). Baltimore: Paul H. Brookes.

Davis, J., Shepard, N., Stelmachonicz, P., & Gorga, M. (1981). Characteristics of hearing impaired children in public schools. Psychoeducational data. *Journal of Speech and Hearing Disorders, 46*, 130–137.

Daly, D. (1988). A practitioner's view of stuttering. *ASHA, 30*(4), 34–35.

Decher, S. N., & Defried, J. C. (1980). Cognitive abilities in families with reading disabled children. *Journal of Learning Disabilities, 13*, 517–522.

Dekker, R., Drenth, P., Zaal, J., & Koole, F. (1990). An intelligence test series for blind and low vision children. *Journal of Visual Impairment and Blindness, 84*, 71–76.

Dekker, R., & Koole, F. (1992). Visually impaired children's visual characteristics and intelligence. *Development Medicine and Child Neurology, 34*, 123–133.

Delisle, J. (1984). *Gifted kids speak out*. Minneapolis, MN: Free Spirit Publishing.

Delwein, P., Fewell, R., & Pruess, J. (1985). The efficacy of intervention at outreach sites of the program for children with Down syndrome and other developmental delays. *Topics in Early Childhood Special Education, 5*(2), 78–87.

DeMagistris, R., & Imber, S. (1980). The effects of life space interviewing on academic and social performance of behaviorally disordered children. *Behavior Disorders, 6*, 12–25.

Demchak, M. (1994, Fall). Helping individuals with severe disabilities find leisure activities. *Teaching Exceptional Children, 27*(1), 48–53.

Denckla, M. (1994). Measurement of executive function. In G. Lyon (Ed.), *Frames of reference for the assessment of learning disabilities* (pp. 117–142). Baltimore: Paul H. Brookes.

Denckla, M. B., & Chapman, J. (1985). Motor proficiency in dyslexic children without attention disorders. *Archives of Neurology, 42*, 228–231.

Deno, L. (1985). Curriculum-based measurement. *Exceptional Children, 52*(2), 219–232.

Deshler, D., & Schumaker, J. (1983). Social skills of learning disabled adolescents: A review of characteristics and intervention. *Topics in Learning and Learning Disabilities, 3*, 15–32.

Deshler, D., & Schumaker, J. (1986). Learning strategies: An instructional alternative for low achieving adolescents. *Behavioral Disorders, 7*, 207–212.

Deshler, D., Schumaker, J., & Lenz, B. (1984). Academic and cognitive intervention for LD adolescents, Part 1. *Journal of Learning Disabilities, 17*(2), 108–117.

Dichtelmiller, M., Meisels, S., Plunkett, J., Bozynski, M., Clafin, C., & Mangelsdorf, S. (1992). The relationship of parental knowledge to development of extremely low birth infants. *Journal of Early Intervention, 16*(3), 210–220.

Dickens, M., & Cornell, D. (1993). Parent influences on the mathematics of self concept of high ability adolescent girls. *Journal for Education of the Gifted, 17*(1), 53–73.

Dixon, R., & Carnue, D. (1994). Ideologies, practices and the implications for special education. *Journal of Special Education, 28*(3), 356–367.

Donnellan, A. M., Mirenda, P. L., Mesaros, R. A., & Fassbinder, L. (1984). Analyzing the communicative function of aberrant behaviors. *Journal of the Association for Persons with Severe Handicaps, 9*, 201–212.

Dore, J. (1986). The development of conversational competence. In R. L. Schiefelbusch (Ed.), *Language competence, assessment and intervention* (pp. 85–96). Boston: Little, Brown.

Dromi, E. (1993). The development of prelinguistic communication. In N. J. Anastasiow & S. Harel (Eds.), *The at-risk infant* (pp. 19–26). Baltimore: Paul H. Brookes.

Dryson, L. (1991). Families of young children with handicaps: Parental stress and family functioning. *American Association on Mental Retardation, 95*(6), 623–629.

Dunst, C. J., & Lowe, L. W. (1986). From reflex to symbol: Describing, explaining, and fostering communication competence. *Augmentative and Alternative Communication, 2,* 11–18.

Dunst, C. J., Lowe, L. W., & Bartholomew, P. (1990). Contingent social responsiveness, family ecology, and infant communication competence. *National Student Speech Language Hearing Association Journal, 17,* 39–49.

Dunst, C., Trivette, C., & Deal, A. (1988). *Enabling and empowering families.* Cambridge, MA: Brookline Books.

Dunst, G., & Dunst, C. (1988). Communicative competence: From research to practice. *Topics in Early Childhood Special Education, 6*(31), 1–22.

Dweck, C. (1975). The role of expectations and attributions in the alleviation of learned helplessness. *Journal of Personality and Social Psychology, 31,* 674–685.

Dykens, E., & Leckman, J. (1990). Developmental issues in fragile X syndrome. In R. Hodapp, J. Burock, & E. Zigler (Eds.), *Issues in the developmental approach to mental retardation* (pp. 226–245). New York: Cambridge University Press.

Edgar, E. (1987). Secondary programs in special education: Are many of them justified? *Exceptional Children, 53*(6), 555–561.

Edgerton, R. (1988). Perspectives on the prevention of mild mental retardation. In F. Menolascino & J. Stark (Eds.), *Preventive and curative intervention in mental retardation* (pp. 325–342). Baltimore: Paul H. Brookes.

Elinquest, D., Morgan, D., & Bolds, P. (1992). Substance use among adolescents with disabilities. *International Journal of the Addictions, 27,* 1475–1483.

Ellis, E. S., & Sabornie, E. J. (1986). Effective instruction with microcomputers: Promise, practices and preliminary findings. *Focus on Exceptional Children, 19*(4), 1–16.

English, R. (1995). *Educational audiology across the lifespan.* Baltimore: Paul H. Brookes.

Epilepsy. (1993). National Information Center for Children and Youth with Disabilities, P.O. Box 1492, Washington, DC 20013-1492.

Epstein, C. (1988). New approach to the study of Down syndrome. In F. Menolascino & J. Stark (Eds.), *Preventive and curative intervention in mental retardation* (pp. 35–60). Baltimore: Paul H. Brookes.

Epstein, M., Kinder, D., & Bursuck, B. (1989). The academic status of adolescents with behavioral disorders. *Behavior Disorders, 14*(3), 157–165.

Erikson, E. (1950). *Childhood and society.* New York: Norton.

Erikson, J. (1989). *The Connecticut infant and toddler assessment system (IDA).* New Haven: Yale University Institute for Child Study.

Erwin, E. (1993). Social participation of young children with visual impairments in specialized and integrated environments. *Journal of Visual Impairment and Blindness, 87,* 138–142.

Evans, I. M. (1991). Testing and diagnosis: A review and evaluation. In L. H. Meyer, C. Peck, & L. Brown (Eds.), *Critical issues in the lives of people with severe disabilities* (pp. 25–44). Baltimore: Paul H. Brookes.

Everson, J. (Ed.). (1995). *Supporting young adults who are deaf-blind in their communities.* Baltimore: Paul H. Brookes.

Everson, J., Burwell, J., & Killan, S. (1995). Working and contributing to one's community. In J. Everson (Ed.), *Supporting young adults who are deaf-blind in their communities* (pp. 131–158). Baltimore: Paul H. Brookes.

Executive Committee of the Council for Children with Behavioral Disorders. (1989). Position statement on the regular education initiative. *Behavioral Disorders, 14*(3), 201–207.

Falvey, M. (1989). *Community-based curriculum* (2nd ed.). Baltimore: Paul H. Brookes.

Falvey, M. A., Coot, J., Bishop, K. D., & Grenot-Scheyer, M. (1989). Educational and curricular adaptations. In S. Stainback, W. Stainback, & M. Forest (Eds.), *Educating all students in the mainstream of regular education.* Baltimore: Paul H. Brookes.

Farber, B. (1959). Effects of a severely mentally retarded child on family integration. *Monographs of the Society for Research in Child Development.* Serial 71.

Farber, B. (1976). Family adaptations to severely mentally retarded children. In M. Begab & S. Richardson (Eds.), *Mentally retarded in society.* Baltimore: University Park Press.

Farber, B. (1986). Historical context of research on families with mentally retarded members. In J. Gallagher & P. Vietze (Eds.), *Families of handicapped persons* (pp. 3–24). Baltimore: Paul H. Brookes.

Fazzi, D., Kirk, S., Pearce, R., Pogrund, R., & Wolfe, S. (1992). Social focus: Developing socioemotional, play and self-help skills in young blind and visually impaired children. In R. Pogrund, D. Fazzi & J. Lampert (Eds.), *Early focus: Working with young blind and visually impaired children and their families.* New York: American Foundation for the Blind.

Feldman, D. (1984). A follow-up of subjects scoring above 180 IQ in Terman's Genetic Studies of Genius. *Exceptional Children, 50,* 518–523.

Fernald, G. (1943). *Remedial techniques in basic school subjects.* New York: McGraw-Hill.

Ferrell, K. (1986). Infancy and early childhood. In G. Scholl (Ed.), *Foundations of education for blind and visually handicapped children and youth.* New York: American Foundation for the Blind.

Feuerstein, R., Rand, Y., Hoffman, M., & Miller, R. (1980). *Instrumental enrichment*. Baltimore: University Park Press.

Fewell, D., & Cone, J. (1983). Identification and placement of severely handicapped children. In M. Snell (Ed.), *Systematic instruction of the moderately and severely handicapped* (2nd ed.). Columbus, OH: Charles E. Merrill.

Fewell, R., & Rich, J. (1983). *Learning through play*. Austin, TX: DLM Teaching Resources.

Fey, M., Catts, H., & Larrivee, L. (1995). Preparing preschoolers for the academic and social challenges of school. In M. Fey, J. Windsor, & S. Warren (Eds.), *Language intervention: Preschool through elementary years* (pp. 3–58). Baltimore: Paul H. Brookes.

Fey, M., Windsor, J., & Warren, S. (Eds.). (1995). *Language intervention: Preschool through elementary years*. Baltimore: Paul H. Brookes.

Field, T. (1983). High risk infants "have less fun" during early interaction. *Topics in early childhood special education, 3,* 77–87.

Field, T. (1984). Affective and interactive disturbances in infants. In J. D. Osofsky (Ed.), *Handbook of infant development* (pp. 972–1005). New York: Wiley.

Field, T. (1989). Interaction coaching for high risk infants and their parents. *Prevention in Human Services, 1,* 8–54.

Finello, K., Hedlund-Hanson, N., & Kekelis, L. (1992). Cognitive focus: Developing cognition, concepts and language in young blind and visually impaired children. In R. Pogrund, D. Fazzi, & J. Lampert (Eds.), *Early focus: Working with young blind and visually impaired children and their families*. New York: American Foundation for the Blind.

Fischer, F. W., Liberman, I. Y., & Shankweiler, D. (1978). Reading reversals and developmental dyslexia. *Cortex, 14,* 496–510.

Flathouse, V. E. (1979). Multiply handicapped deaf children and Public Law 94–142. *Exceptional Children 45,* 560–565.

Flavall, J., Miller, P., & Miller, S. (1993). *Cognitive development* (3rd ed.). Englewood Cliffs, NJ: Prentice-Hall.

Fleishner, J. (1994). Diagnosing and assessment of mathematics learning disabilities. In G. Lyon (Ed.), *Frames of reference for the assessment of children with learning disabilities* (pp. 444–458). Baltimore: Paul H. Brookes.

Fletcher, J., & Forman, B. (1994). Issues in definitions and measurement of learning disabilities. In G. Lyon (Ed.), *Frames of reference for the assessment of children with learning disabilities* (pp. 185–202). Baltimore: Paul H. Brookes.

Fong-ruey, L., Meisels, S., & Brookes-Gunn, J. (in press). The effect of experience of early intervention on low birth premature children. *Early Childhood Research Quarterly.*

Ford, A., Schnorr, R., Meyer, L., Daver, L., Black, J., & Dempsey, P. (1989). *Syracuse community referenced curriculum guide*. Baltimore: Paul H. Brookes.

Ford, D., Harris, J., & Schuerger, J. (1993). Racial identity development among gifted black students: Counseling issues and concerns. *Journal of Counseling and Development, 71,* 409–417.

Forest, M., & Lusthaus, E. (1989). Promoting educational equality for all students: Circles and maps. In S. Stainback, W. Stainback, & M. Forest (Eds.), *Educating all students in the mainstream of regular education*. Baltimore: Paul H. Brookes.

Forness, S. (1992). Broadening the cultural-organizational perspective in exclusion of youth with social maladjustment. *Remedial and Special Education, 13*(1), 55–59.

Forness, S., & Kavale, K. (1984). Education of the mentally retarded: A note on policy. *Education and Training of the Mentally Retarded, 19*(4), 239–245.

Forness, S., & Kavale, K. (1988). Psychopharmacologic treatment: A note on classroom effects. *Journal of Learning Disabilities, 32,* 48–55.

Fox, L., Hanline, M., Vail, C., & Falant, K. (1994). Developmentally appropriate practices: Applications for young children with disabilities. *Journal of Early Intervention, 18*(3), 243–257.

Fraiberg, S. (1977). *Insights from the blind: Comparative studies of blind and sighted infants*. New York: Basic Books.

Frasier, M. (1987). The identification of gifted black students: Developing new perspectives. *Journal for the Education of the Gifted, 10*(3), 155–190.

Frasier, M. (1991). Disadvantaged and culturally diverse gifted students. *Journal for the Education of the Gifted, 14*(4), 234–245.

Fredericks, B., & Baldwin. (1987). Individuals with sensory impairments: Who are they? How are they educated? In L. Goetz, D. Guess, & K. Stremmel Campbell (Eds.), *Innovative program design for individuals with dual sensory impairments* (pp. 3–14). Baltimore: Paul H. Brookes.

Freeman, J. M., & Vining, E. (1990). Is surgery the answer for childhood epilepsy? *Contemporary Pediatrics, 5*(109), 88–95.

Freud, A. (1965). *Normality and pathology in childhood*. New York: International University Press.

Fuchs, D., Fuchs, L., Fernstrom, P., & Horn, M. (1991). Toward a responsible re-integration of behaviorally disordered students. *Behavioral Disorders, 16*(2), 133–147.

Fuchs, D., & Fuchs, L. (1994). Inclusive schools movement and the radicalization of special education reform. *Exceptional Children, 60*(4), 294–309.

Fuchs, L., & Deno, E. (1992). Effects of curriculum within curriculum-based measurement. *Exceptional Children, 58,* 232–243.

Fuchs, L., and Deno, S. (1994, September). Must instructionally useful performance assessment be based in the curriculum? *Exceptional Children, 6*(1), 15–24.

Fuchs, L., Fuchs, D., Hamlett, C., Phillips, N., & Bent, J. (1994). Classroom curriculum-based assessment. *Exceptional Children, 60*(6), 518–537.

Furuno, S., O'Reilly, K. A., Hosaka, C. M., Inatsuka, T. T., Allman, T., & Zeisloft, B. (1989). *Hawaii Early Learning Profile (HELP).* Palo Alto, CA: Vort Corp.

Gadow, K. (1986). *Children on medications: 1 & 2.* San Diego: College-Hill Press.

Gage, N., & Berliner, D. (1988). *Educational psychology* (4th ed.). Boston: Houghton Mifflin.

Gagne, R. (1985). *The conditions of learning and theory of instruction* (4th ed.). Fort Worth, TX: Holt, Rinehart and Winston.

Gallagher, J. (1989). The family as a focus for intervention. In S. Meisels & J. Shonkoff (Eds.), *Handbook of early intervention,* Boston: Houghton Mifflin.

Gallagher, J. (1991a). Educational reform, values and gifted students. *Gifted Child Quarterly, 35*(1), 12–19.

Gallagher, J. (1991b). Issues in gifted education. In N. Colangelo & G. Davis (Eds.), *Handbook of gifted education.* Boston: Allyn & Bacon.

Gallagher, J. (1991c). Longitudinal interventions: Virtues and limitations. *American Behavior Scientist, 34*(4), 431–439.

Gallagher, J. (1993). An intersection of public policy and social science: Gifted students and education in mathematics and science. In L. Penner, G. Batsche, H. Knoff & D. Nelson (Eds.), *The challenge in mathematics and science education: Psychology's responses.* Washington, DC: American Psychological Association.

Gallagher, J., & Bristol, M. (1988). Families of young handicapped children. In M. Wang, M. Reynolds, & H. Walberg (Eds.), *Handbook of special education: Research and practice: Vol. 3. Low incidence conditions.* Oxford, England: Pergamon Press.

Gallagher, J., & Coleman, M. (1994). Cooperative learning and gifted students: Five case studies. *Cooperative Learning, 14*(4), 21–26.

Gallagher, J., & Gallagher, S. (1994). *Teaching the gifted child* (4th ed.). Boston: Allyn & Bacon.

Gallagher, S. (1992). *Assessment in the science classroom.* Williamsburg, VA: Center for Gifted Education, College of William & Mary.

Gannon, J. (1981). *Deaf heritage: A narrative history of deaf America.* Silver Spring, MD: National Association of the Deaf.

Garber, H. (1988). *The Milwaukee project: Preventing mental retardation in children at risk.* Washington, DC: American Association on Mental Retardation.

Gardner, H. (1985). *Frames of mind: The theory of multiple intelligence.* New York: Basic Books.

Gardner, J. (1978). *Morale.* New York: Norton.

Gardner, J., & Bates, P. (1991). Attitudes and attributions on use of microcomputers in school by students who are mentally handicapped. *Education and Training in Mental Retardation, 26,* 98–107.

Garnett, K. (1989, Winter). Math learning disabilities. *The Forum,* pp. 11–14.

Gartner, A., & Lipsky, D. (1987). Beyond special education: Toward a quality system for all students. *Harvard Educational Review, 57,* 367–395.

Gartner, A., Lipsky, D. K., & Turnbull, A. P. (1991). *Supporting families with a child with a disability.* Baltimore: Paul H. Brookes.

Garwood, G., & Sheehan, R. (1989). *Designing a comprehensive early childhood system.* Austin, TX: PRO-ED.

Gates, C. (1985). Survey of multiply handicapped visually impaired children in the Rocky Mountain/Great Plains region. *Journal of Visual Impairment and Blindness, 79,* 385–391.

Gaylord-Ross, R. J., & Brower, D. (1991). Functional assessment: Dynamic properties. In L. H. Meyer, C. Peck, & L. Brown (Eds.), *Critical issues in the lives of people with severe disabilities* (pp. 45–66). Baltimore: Paul H. Brookes.

Gee, G., & Moran, T. (Eds.). (1988). *AIDS: Concepts in nursing practice.* Baltimore: Williams & Williams.

Genaux, M., Morgan, D., & Friedman, S. (1995). Substance use and its prevention: A survey of classroom practices. *Behavior Disorders, 20*(4), 279–289.

George, P. (1988). Tracking and ability grouping: Which way for the middle school? *Middle School Journal, 20,* 21–28.

George, P. (1992). *How to untrack your school.* Alexandria, VA: Association for Supervision and Curriculum Development.

Gerber, M. (1994). Post modernism in special education. *Journal of Special Education, 28*(3), 368–378.

Gilgoff, I. (1983). Spinal cord injury. In J. Umbreit (Ed.), *Physical disabilities and health impairments: An introduction* (pp. 132–146). Columbus, OH: Charles E. Merrill.

Gleason, B. (Ed.). (1993). *The development of language* (3rd ed.). New York: Macmillan.

Goetz, L., Guess, D., & Campbell, K. (1987). *Innovative programs for individuals with dual sensory impairments.* New York: Grune & Stratton.

Goldberg, A. (1991). Children on ventilators: Breathing easier at home. *Contemporary Pediatrics, 7,* 59–79.

Good, T. (1987). Teacher expectations. In D. Berliner & B. Rosenshine (Eds.), *Talks to teachers.* New York: Random House.

Goodlad, J. (1984). *A place called school.* New York: Mc-Graw-Hill.

Goossens, C., & Crain, S. (1985). Augmentative communication: Intervention resource. Birmingham, AL: Sparks Center for Developmental and Learning Disabilities, University of Alabama.

Gottfried, A. (Ed.). (1984). *Home environment and cognitive development.* New York: Academic Press.

Gothelf, C., Crimmins, D., Mercer, C., & Finocchiaro, P. (1994, Fall). Teaching choice-making skills to students who are deaf-blind. *Teaching Exceptional Children, 26*(1), 13–15.

Gottlieb, J., Alter, M., & Gottlieb, B. W. (1991). Mainstreaming mentally retarded children. In J. Matson & J. Mulick (Eds.), *Handbook of mental retardation* (2nd ed., pp. 63–73). New York: Pergamon Press.

Gray, D. B., & Kavanaugh, J. H. (1985). *Biobehavioral measures of learning disabilities.* Parkton, MD: York Press.

Green, A., & Shore, H. (1994, Fall). Science, reason and facilitative communication. *The Journal of the Association for Persons with Severe Handicaps, 19*(3), 151–172.

Greenwood, C. (1994). Advances in technology-based assessment within special education. *Exceptional Children, 61*(2), 102–104.

Gregory, H. (1986). Environmental manipulation and family counseling. In G. Shames & H. Rubin (Eds.), *Stuttering then and now.* Columbus, OH: Charles E. Merrill.

Grenot-Scheyer, M. (1994, Winter). The nature of interactions between students with severe disabilities and their friends and acquaintances without disabilities. *The Journal of the Association for Persons with Severe Handicaps, 19*(3).

Greschwind, N. (1985). The biology of dyslexia. In D. B. Gray & J. F. Kavanaugh (Eds.), *Biobehavioral measures of dyslexia* (pp. 1–120). Parkton, MD: York Press.

Groenveld, M., & Jan, J. (1992). Intelligence profiles of low vision and blind children. *Journal of Visual Impairment and Blindness, 86,* 68–71.

Grosenick, J., George, N., George, M., & Lewis, T. (1991). Public school services for behaviorally disordered students: Program practices in the 1980s. *Behavioral Disorders, 16*(2), 87–96.

Guetzloe, E. (1988). Suicide and depression: Special education's responsibility. *Teaching Exceptional Children, 20*(4), 24–28.

Guilford, J. (1967). *The nature of human intelligence.* New York: Fund for the Advancement of Education.

Guralnick, M. (Ed.). (1996). *The effectiveness of early intervention.* Baltimore: Paul H. Brookes.

Guralnick, M., & Bricker, D. (1987). The effectiveness of early intervention for children with cognitive and general developmental delays. In M. Guralnick & F. C. Bennett (Eds.), *The effectiveness of early intervention for at-risk and handicapped children* (pp. 115–168). New York: Academic Press.

Gustaitis, R., & Young, E. W. D. (1986). *A time to be born, a time to die.* Reading, MA: Addison-Wesley.

Hagerman, R., Schreiner, R., Kemper, M., Wittenberger, M., Zahn, B., & Habicht, K. (1989). Longitudinal IQ changes in fragile X males. *American Journal of Medical Genetics, 33,* 513–518.

Hale, C., & Borkowski, J. (1991). Attention, memory, and cognition. In J. Matson & J. Mulick (Eds.), *Handbook of mental retardation* (2nd ed.). New York: Pergamon Press.

Hall, L. (1994, Winter). A descriptive assessment of social relationships in integrated classrooms. *The Journal of the Association for Persons with Severe Handicaps, 19*(4), 302–313.

Hallahan, D., Kauffman, J., Lloyd, J., & McKinney, J. (1988). Introduction to the series: Questions about the regular education initiative. *Journal of Learning Disabilities, 21*(1), 3–5.

Hallenbeck, B., & Kauffman, J. (1995). How does observational learning affect the behavior of students with emotional or behavioral disorders: A review of research. *The Journal of Special Education, 29*(1), 45–71.

Halpern, A. (1991–1992, December–January). Transition: Old wine in new bottles. *Exceptional Children, 58*(3), 202–212.

Hammill, D., Brown, V., Larsen, S., & Weiderholt, L. (1987). *Test of adolescent language—2.* Austin, TX: PRO-ED.

Hansen, R., & Ulrey, G. (1992). Knowns and unknowns in the outcomes of drug-dependent women. In N. J. Anastasiow and S. Harel (Eds.), *The at-risk infant* (pp. 115–126). Baltimore: Paul H. Brookes.

Harbin, G. (1993). Family issues of children with disabilities. In N. J. Anastasiow and S. Harel (Eds.), *The at-risk infant* (pp. 101–114). Baltimore: Paul H. Brookes.

Harms, T., & Clifford, R. (1984). *Early childhood environmental rating scale.* New York: Teachers College Press.

Harrel, R., & Curry, S. (1987). Services to blind and visually impaired children and adults: Who is responsible? *Journal of Visual Impairment and Blindness,* pp. 368–376.

Hart, V., & Ferrell, K. (1992). Cooperative efforts with families in educating children with visual handicaps. *Division for the Visually Handicapped Quarterly, 37*(2), 18–19.

Harvey, D., & Greenway, A. (1984). The self-concept of physically handicapped children and their non-handicapped siblings: An empirical investigation. *Journal of Child Psychology and Psychiatry, 25,* 273–284.

Harvis, K., & Graham, S. (1994). Constructivism: Principles, paradigms and integration. *The Journal of Special Education, 28*(3), 233–247.

Hasazi, S., Gordon, L., & Roe, C. (1985). Factors associated with the employment status of handicapped youth exiting high school from 1979 to 1983. *Exceptional Children, 51,* 455–465.

Hatfield, E. (1979). Methods and standards for screening preschool children. *Sight Saving Review, 49*(2).

Hatlen, P., & Curry, S. (1987). In support of specialized programs for blind and visually impaired children: The impact of vision loss on learning. *Journal of Visual Impairment and Blindness, 81,* 7–13.

Hawley, R. (1987). School children and drugs: The fancy that has not passed. *Phi Delta Kappa, 68,* K1–K8.

Hayes, S. (1941). *Contributions to a psychology of blindness.* New York: American Foundation for the Blind.

Haynie, M., Porter, S., & Palfrey, J. (1989). *Children assisted by medical technology in educational settings: Guidelines for care.* Boston: Project School Care, Children's Hospital.

Hazel, J. F., & Schumaker, J. B. (1988). Social skills and learning disabilities. In J. F. Kavanaugh & T. J. Truss (Eds.), *Learning disabilities: Proceedings of the national conference* (pp. 293–362). Parkton, MD: York Press.

Heath, S. (1983). *Ways with words.* New York: Cambridge University Press.

Hechtman, L., & Weiss, G. (1985). Long-term outcome of hyperactive children. In S. Chess & A. Thomas (Eds.), *Annual progress in child psychiatry and child development—1984.* New York: Brunner/Mazel.

Heinemann, A., & Shontz, F. (1984). Adjustment following disability: Representative case studies. *Rehabilitation Counseling Bulletin, 28*(1), 3–14.

Heinicke, C. (1993). Factors affecting the efficacy of early family intervention. In N. J. Anastasiow and S. Harel (Eds.), *The at-risk infant* (pp. 91–100). Baltimore: Paul H. Brookes.

Heinicke, C. M., Beckwith, L., & Thompson, A. (1988). Early intervention in the family system: A framework and review. *Infant Mental Health Journal, 9*(2), 111–141.

Heinicke, C. (1992). Factors affecting the efficacy of early childhood family intervention. In N. J. Anastasiow & S. Harel (Eds.), *The at-risk infant.* Baltimore: Paul H. Brookes.

Heller, K., Holtzman, W., & Messick, S. (Eds.). (1982). *Placing children in special education: A strategy for equity.* Washington, DC: National Academy Press.

Helmstetter, E., Peck, C., & Giangreco, M. (1994, Winter). Outcomes of interaction with peers of moderate and severe disabilities: A statewide survey of high school students. *The Journal of the Association for Persons with Severe Handicaps, 19*(4), 260–276.

Henderson, L., & Meisels, S. (1994). Parental involvement in the developmental screening of their young children. *Journal of Early Intervention, 18(*2), 141–154.

Higgins, K., & Boone, R. (1991). Hypermedia computer-assisted instruction: Adapting a basal reading series. In J. Wilson & K. McBride, *Proceedings of the multimedia technology seminars.* Reston, VA: Council for Exceptional Children.

Hill, E. (1992). Instruction in orientation and mobility skills for students with visual handicaps. *Division for the Visually Handicapped Quarterly, 37*(2), 25–26.

Hill, N., & Wehman, P. (1983). Cost-benefit analysis of placing moderately and severely handicapped individuals into competitive employment. *Journal of the Association for Persons with Severe Handicaps, 8,* 30–38.

Hill, R. (1958). Generic features of families under stress. *Social Casework, 49,* 139–150.

Hobbs, N. (1970). Project Re-Ed: New ways of helping emotionally disturbed children. In Joint Commission on Mental Health of Children, *Crisis in child mental health: Challenge for the 1970's.* New York: Harper & Row.

Hobbs, N. (1979). *Helping disturbed children: Psychological and ecological strategies: II. Project Re-Ed, twenty years later.* Nashville: Vanderbilt University, Center for the Study of Families and Children.

Hoben, M., & Lindstrom, V. (1980, October). Evidence of isolation in the mainstream. *Journal of Visual Impairment and Blindness,* pp. 289–292.

Hodapp, R., Burack, J., & Zigler, E. (1990). *Issues in the developmental approach to mental retardation.* New York: Cambridge University Press.

Hollingsworth, L. S. (1942). *Children above 180 I.Q. Stanford-Binet: Origin and development.* New York: World Book Company.

Hoover, J., & Collier, C. (1991). Meeting the needs of culturally and linguistically diverse exceptional learners—prereferral to mainstreaming. *TESE, 14*(1), 30–34.

Horner, R. H., Dunlap, G., & Koegel, R. L. (Eds.). (1988). *Change in applied settings.* Baltimore: Paul H. Brookes.

Huber, A. (1991). Nutrition and mental retardation. In J. Matson & J. Mulick (Eds.), *Handbook of mental retardation* (2nd ed.). New York: Pergamon Press.

Hughes, C., Ruhl, K., & Misra, A. (1989). Self-management with behaviorally disordered students in school settings: A promise unfulfilled. *Behavioral Disorders, 14*(4), 250–262.

Humphrey, G., Dodwell, P., Muir, D., & Humphrey, D. (1988). Can blind infants and children use sonar sensory aids? *Canadian Journal of Psychology, 42,* 94–119.

Hutchinson, T. A. (1995, Winter). IDEA and the Provence profile-efficient early assessment. *ECO Letter, 4*(1), 11–13.

Huttenlocher, P. (1988). Developmental neurobiology: Current and future challenges. In F. Menolascino & J. Stark (Eds.), *Preventative and curative intervention in mental retardation* (pp. 101–111). Baltimore: Paul H. Brookes.

Hutter, J., & Farrell, F. (1983). Cancer in children. In J. Umbreit (Ed.), *Physical disabilities and health impairments: An introduction.* Columbus, OH: Charles E. Merrill.

Individuals with Disabilities Education Act of 1990, 20, U.S.C., Chap. 3 (1990).

Infant Health and Development Project. (1990). Enhancing the outcome of low-birth-weight premature infants. *Journal of the American Medical Association, 263*(22), 3035–3042.

Interagency Committee. (1990). *Learning disabilities: A report to Congress.* Washington, DC: U.S. Government Printing Office.

Iran-Nejad, A., Ortony, A., & Rittenhouse, R. (1981). The comprehension of figurative uses of English by deaf children. *Journal of Speech and Hearing, 24,* 551–556.

Jacobs, J. H. (1990). Child mental health: Service system and policy issues. *Social Policy Report: Society for Research in Child Development, 4*(2), 1–19.

Jamieson, J. (1994). Teaching as transaction: Vygotskian perspective on deafness and mother-child interaction. *Exceptional Children, 60*(5), 434–449.

Jenkins, J., & Pious, C. (1991, May). Full inclusion and the REI: A reply to Thousands and Villa. *Exceptional Children, 57*(6), 561–562.

Jenkins, J., Speltz, M., & Oldhom, S. (1985). Integrating normal and handicapped preschoolers: Effects on child development and social interaction. *Exceptional Children, 52*(1), 7–17.

Johnson, D. (1988). Review of research in specific writing and mathematical disorders. In J. F. Kavanaugh & T. J. Truss (Eds.), *Learning disabilities: Proceedings of the national conference* (pp. 79–180). Parkton, MD: York Press.

Johnson, D., & Johnson, R. (1989). *Cooperation and competition: Theory and research.* Edna, MN: Interaction Book Company.

Johnson, H. C. (1989). Behavior disorders. In F. J. Turner (Ed.), *Child psychopathology: A social work perspective* (pp. 73–140). New York: Free Press.

Johnson, J. (1988). The challenge of substance abuse. *Teaching Exceptional Children, 20*(4), 29–31.

Johnson, L., & Pugach, M. (1990). Classroom teacher's view of intervention strategies for learning and behavior problems: Which are reasonable and how frequently are they used? *Journal of Special Education, 24*(1), 69–84.

Johnson, L., Gallagher, R., LaMontagne, M., Jordan, J., Gallagher, J., Hutinger, P., & Karnes, M. (1994). *Meeting early intervention changes.* Baltimore: Paul H. Brookes.

Johnson, R., & Johnson, D. (1981). Building friendships between handicapped and nonhandicapped students: Effects of cooperative individualistic instruction. *American Educational Research Journal, 18,* 415–423.

Johnson-Martin, N., Attermeier, S., & Hacker, B. (1990). *Carolina curriculum for preschoolers with special needs.* Baltimore: Paul H. Brookes.

Johnson-Martin, N., Jens, K., & Attermeir, S. (1991). *Carolina curriculum for handicapped infants and infants at risk* (2nd ed.). Baltimore: Paul H. Brookes.

Jose P. v. Ambach, 699 F.2d 865 (2nd Cir. 1982).

Juurmaa, J. (1970). On the accuracy of obstacle detection by the blind. *New Outlook for the Blind, 64,* 104–117.

Kagan, S. (1990). The structural approach to cooperative learning. *Educational Leadership, 47,* 12–15.

Kaiser, A. (1994, Fall). The controversy surrounding facilitative communication. *The Journal of the Association for Persons with Severe Handicaps, 19*(3), 187–190.

Kaiser, A., & Gray, D. (1993). *Enhancing children's research foundation for intervention: Vol. 2. Communication and language series.* Baltimore: Paul H. Brookes.

Kauffman, J. (1986). Growing out of adolescence: Reflections on change in special education for the behaviorally disordered. *Behavioral Disorders, 12,* 290–296.

Kauffman, J., & Hallahan, D. P. (Eds.). *Handbook of special education.* Englewood Cliffs, NJ: Prentice-Hall.

Kauffman, J. (1994). One size does not fit all. *Beyond Behavior, 5*(3), 13–14.

Kaufmann, F. (1981). The 1964–68 presidential scholars: A follow-up study. *Exceptional Children, 48,* 164–169.

Kaufman, J. (1989). The regular education initiative as Reagan-Bush education policy: A trickle-down theory of education of the hard to teach. *Journal of Special Education, 23,* 256–278.

Kaufmann, J., & Hallahan, D. (1995). *The illusion of full inclusion.* Austin, TX: PRO-ED.

Kavale, K., Forness, S., & Bender, M. (Eds.). (1987). *Handbook of learning disabilities: Vol. 1. Dimensions and diagnoses; Vol. 2. Methods and intervention; Vol. 3. Programs and practices.* Boston: College-Hill/Little, Brown.

Kavale, K., & Nye, C. (1984). The effectiveness of drug treatment for severe behavior disorders: A meta-analysis. *Behavioral Disorders, 9*(2), 117–130.

Kekelis, L., & Sacks, S. (1992). The effects of visual impairment on children's social interactions in regular education programs. In S. Sacks, L. Kekelis, & R. Gaylord-Ross (Eds.), *The development of social skills by blind and visually impaired students* (pp. 59–82). New York: American Foundation for the Blind.

Kekelis, L. (1988a). Mainstreaming visually impaired children into regular education programs: The effects of visual impairment on children's interactions with peers. In S. Sacks, L. Kekelis, & R. Gaylord-Ross (Eds.), *The development of social skills by blind and visually impaired students* (pp. 103–132). New York: American Foundation for the Blind.

Kekelis, L. (1988b). Peer interactions in childhood: The impact of visual impairment. In S. Sacks, L. Kekelis, & R. Gaylord-Ross (Eds.), *The development of social skills by blind and visually impaired students* (pp. 103–132). New York: American Foundation for the Blind.

Kelly, L. (1995, February). Processing bottom-up and top-down information by skilled and average deaf readers and implications for whole language learning. *Exceptional Children, 61*(4), 315–334.

Kent, D. (1992, January). Ursula Bellugi receives neuroscience prize. *Observer.* American Psychological Association, Washington, DC.

Kephart, J., Kephart, C., & Schwartz, G. (1974). A journey into the world of the blind child. *Exceptional Children, 40,* 421–429.

Kerachsky, S., & Thornton, C. (1987). Findings from the STETS Transitional Employment Demonstration. *Exceptional Children, 53*(6), 515–521.

Kerr, M. M., & Nelson, C. M. (1989). *Strategies for managing behavior problems in the classroom* (2nd ed.). Columbus, OH: Charles E. Merrill.

Kerzner, Lipsky, D., & Gartner, A. (1989). School administration and financial arrangements. In S. Stainback, W. Stainback, & M. Forest (Eds.), *Educating all students in the mainstream of regular education.* Baltimore: Paul H. Brookes.

Khoury, A. F. (1988, September). Is it normal? A low Apgar score (Focus on 0–3 year olds). *Raising Kids.*

Kirchner, C. (1983). Statistical Brief No. 23. Special education for visually handicapped children: A critique of numbers and costs. *Journal of Visual Impairment and Blindness, 77*(1), 219–223.

Kirk, S. (1950). A project for pre-school mentally handicapped children. *American Journal of Mental Deficiency, 55,* 305–310.

Kirk, S. A., & Kirk, W. D. (1971). *Psycholinguistic learning disabilities* (Rev. ed.). Urbana, IL: University of Illinois Press.

Kirk, S., Kirk, W., & Minskoff, E. (1985). *The Phonic Remedial Reading Program.* San Rafael, CA: Academic Therapy Publications.

Kirk, S. A., McCarthy, J. J., & Kirk, W. D. (1971). *Illinois test of psycholinguistic abilities* (Rev. Ed.). Urbana: University of Illinois Press.

Kirst, M. W. (1990, April). *Improving children's services: Overcoming barriers, creating new opportunities.* Paper presented at the annual meeting of the American Educational Research Association, Boston.

Kitano, M. (1991). A multicultural education perspective on serving the culturally diverse gifted. *Journal for the Education of the Gifted.*

Kline, F. M., Deshler, D. D., & Schumaker, J. B. (1991). *Implementing learning strategies instruction in class settings, a research perspective: Barriers to strategy instruction.* Mimeo, University of Kansas Institute for Research in Learning Disabilities.

Knapczyk, D. (1988). Reducing aggressive behaviors in special and regular class settings by training alternative social responses. *Behavioral Disorders, 14*(1), 27–39.

Knitzer, J. (1989). Children's mental health: The advocacy challenge "and miles to go before we sleep." In R. M. Friedman, A. J. Duchnowski, & E. L. Henderson (Eds.), *Advocacy on behalf of children with serious emotional problems* (pp. 15–27). Springfield, IL: Charles C. Thomas.

Koch, R., Friedman, E., Azen, C., Wenz, E., Parton, P., Leduc, X., Fishler, K. (1988). Inborn errors of metabolism and the prevention of mental retardation. In F. Menolascino & J. Stark (Eds.), *Preventive and curative intervention in mental retardation* (pp. 61–92). Baltimore: Paul H. Brookes.

Kolb, B. (1989). Brain development, plasticity and behavior. *American Psychologist, 44*(9).

Kolvin, I., Miller, F. J. W., Scott, D. M., Gazonts, S. K. M., & Fleeting, M. (1990). *Continuities of depravation? The Newcastle 1000 family study.* Adershot, England: Arcburn Gover.

Koorland, M. A. (1986). Applied behavior analysis and the correction of learning disabilities. In J. K. Torgesen & B. Y. L. Wong (Eds.), *Psychological and educational perspectives on learning disabilities* (pp. 297–326). San Diego: Academic Press.

Kopp, C. (1983). Risk factors in development. In M. M. Haith & J. J. Campos (Eds.), *Handbook of child psychology* (Vol. 2, pp. 1081–1188). New York: Wiley.

Korinek, L., & Polloway, E. (1993). Social skills: Review and implications for instruction for students with mild mental retardation. In R. Gable & S. Warren (Eds.), *Advances in Mental Retardation and Developmental Disabilities, 5,* 71–92.

Krajicek, M. (1991). *Handbook for the care of infants and toddlers with disabilities and chronic conditions.* Lawrence, KS: Learner Managed Designs.

Krajicek, M., & Smith, A. (1990). *Positioning for toddlers and young children with motor problems.* Lawrence, KS: Learner Management Designs.

Krauss, M. (1990). New precedent in family policy: Individualized family service plan. *Exceptional Children, 56*(5), 388–395.

Kregel, J. (1994, Fall). *Natural support and the job coach: An unnecessary dichotomy*. Richmond: Virginia Commonwealth University, Rehabilitation and Research Training Center.

Krupski, A. (1986). Attentional problems in youngsters with learning disabilities. In J. K. Torgesen & B. Y. L. Wong (Eds.), *Psychological and educational perspectives on learning disabilities* (pp. 161–192). San Diego: Academic Press.

Krutetskii, V. (1976). *The psychology of mathematical abilities in school children* (J. Teller, Trans.). Chicago: University of Chicago Press.

Lamb, M. (1986). *The role of the father in child development* (3rd ed.). New York: Wiley.

Lambert, N., & Windmiller, M. (1981). *AAMD Adaptive Behavior Scale* (School ed.). Monterey, CA: McGraw-Hill.

Lane, H. (1995). The education of deaf children: Drowning in the mainstream and the sidestream. In J. Kaufman & D. Hallahan (Eds.), *The illusion of full inclusion* (pp. 275–288). Austin, TX: PRO-ED.

Larry P. v. Riles 343 F. Supp. 1306 (N.D. Cal. 1972), aff'd, 502 F.2d 963 (9th Cir. 1974).

LaSasso, C. (1986). A comparison of visual matching test-taking strategies of comparably aged normal hearing and hearing impaired subjects with comparable reading levels. *Volta Review, 88*, 231–235.

Lehr, D., & Noonan, M. (1989). Issues in the education of students with complex health care needs. In D. Ellis (Ed.), *Sensory impairments in mentally handicapped persons* (pp. 139–160). San Diego: College-Hill Press.

Leland, H. (1991). Adaptive behavior scales. In J. Matson & J. Mulick (Eds.), *Handbook of mental retardation* (2nd ed.). New York: Pergamon Press.

Leonard, L. (1986). Early language development and language disorders. In G. H. Shames & E. H. Wiig (Eds.), *Human communication disorders* (2nd ed., pp. 291–330). Columbus, OH: Charles E. Merrill.

Leonard, L. B. (1992). Intervention approaches for young children with communication disorders. In N. J. Anastasiow & S. Harel (Eds.), *The at-risk infant*. Baltimore: Paul H. Brookes.

Leone, P. (Ed.). (1990). *Understanding troubled and troubling youth*. Newbury Park, CA: Sage Publications.

Leone, P., Greenburg, J., Trickett, E., & Spero, E. (1989). A study of the use of cigarettes, alcohol and marijuana by students identified as "seriously emotionally disturbed." *Counterpoint, 9*(3), 6–7.

Leone, P., Luttig, P., Zlotlow, S., & Trickett, E. (1990). Understanding the social ecology of classrooms for adolescents with behavioral disorders: A preliminary study of differences in perceived environments. *Behavioral Disorders, 16*(1), 55–65.

Lerner, R. M. (1986). *The nature of human plasticity*. New York: Cambridge University Press.

Leskey, M., & Weldon, N. (1991). Identifying children with learning disabilities. *Journal of Learning Disabilities, 2*, 435–438.

Levin, J., & Scherfenberg, L. (1987). *Selection and use of simple technology in home, school work, and community settings*. Minneapolis: Abelnet.

Levine, J. (1996, Spring). Including children dependent on ventilators in schools. *Teaching Exceptional Children, 28*(3), 25–29.

Lewis, T., Chard, D., & Scott, T. (1994). Full inclusion and the education of children and youth with emotional and behavioral disorders. *Behavior Disorders, 19*(4), 277–293.

Liberman, I., & Shankweber, D. (1985). Phonology and the problem of learning to read and write. *Remedial Special Education, 6*, 8–17.

Liberman, I. Y., & Liberman, A. M. (1990). Whole language versus code emphasis. *Annals of dyslexia, 40*, 51–75.

Liberman, L. (1985). Special education and regular education: A merger made in heaven? *Exceptional Children, 51*, 513–516.

Linden, G., Kankkunen, A., & Tjellstrom, A. (1983). Multihandicaps and ear formation in hearing impaired children. In G. Mencher & S. Gerber (Eds.), *The multiply handicapped hearing impaired child* (pp. 67–82). New York: Grune & Stratton.

Linder, T. (1990). *Transdisciplinary play-based assessment*. Baltimore: Paul H. Brookes.

Lipsey, M., & Wilson, D. (1993). The efficacy of psychological, educational and behavioral treatment. *American Psychologist, 48*(12), 1181–1209.

Lloyd, J., Repp, A., & Singh, N. (Eds.). (1991). *The regular education initiative: Perspectives on concepts, issues and models*. Sycamore, IL: Sycamore.

Lomax, R. (1982). Causal model of reading acquisition. *Journal of Reading Behavior, 14*, 341–345.

Lowenfeld, B. (1982). In search of better ways. *Education of the Visually Handicapped, 14*(3), 69–77.

Lowenfeld, B. (1989, September). Professional self-esteem or the evolution of a profession. *Journal of Visual Impairment and Blindness*, pp. 336–339.

Lowenfeld, B. (Ed.). (1973). *The visually handicapped child in school*. New York: Day.

Lubker, B. (1986). Educational rehabilitation of persons with communication disorders in the United States. In K.-P. Becker & R. Greenberg (Eds.), *Educational rehabilitation for the handicapped in the German Democratic Republic and the United States of America*. Berlin: Verb Verlag Volk und Gesundheit.

Luetke-Stahlman, B. (1994). Procedures for socially integrating preschoolers who are hearing, deaf and hard-of-hearing. *Topics in Early Childhood Special Education, 14*(4), 472–487.

Lyle, R., & Obringer, S. (1983). Muscular dystrophy. In J. Umbreit (Ed.), *Physical disabilities and health impairments: An introduction* (pp. 100–109). Columbus, OH: Charles E. Merrill.

Lynch, E. W., Jackson, J. A., Mendoza, J., & English, K. (1991). The merging of best practices and state policy in IFSP process in California. In *Topics in early childhood: Special education and IFSP's. How are they working?* (pp. 32–53). Austin, TX: PRO-ED.

Lyon, G. (1985). Educational validation of learning disability subtypes. In B. Rourke (Ed.), *The neuropsychology of learning disabilities* (pp. 228–253). New York: Guilford Press.

Lyon, G. (Ed.). (1994). *Frames of reference for the assessment of learning disabilities.* Baltimore: Paul H. Brookes.

Maag, J., & Howell, K. (1992). Special education and the exclusion of youth with social maladjustments: A cultural-organizational perspective. *Remedial and Special Education, 13*(1), 47–54.

MacDonald, J., & Gillette, Y. (1986). Communicating with persons with severe handicaps: Role of parents and professionals. *Journal of the Association for Persons with Severe Handicaps, 11*(4), 255–265.

Mack, C., & Koenig, A. (1992). Access to technology for students with visual handicaps. *Division for the Visually Handicapped Quarterly, 37*(2), 24–25.

Malone, L., DeLucchi, L., & Thier, H. (1981). *Science activities for the visually impaired: SAVI leadership trainer's manual.* Berkeley: Center for Multisensory Learning, University of California.

Mann, V. A., & Liberman, A. M. (1984). Phonological awareness and verbal short-term memory. *Journal of Learning Disabilities, 17,* 592–599.

March of Dimes Defects Foundation. (1990). *Genetics Counseling.* (Available from March of Dimes Defects Foundation, 1275 Mamaroneck Avenue, White Plains, NY 10605.

Markoulis, D. (1988). Moral and cognitive reasoning features in congenitally blind children: Comparisons with the sighted. *British Journal of Developmental Psychology, 6,* 59–69.

Mastropieri, M., Balken, J., & Scruggs, T. (1991). Mathematics instruction for individuals with mental retardation: A perspective and research synthesis. *Education and Training in Mental Retardation, 26,* 115–129.

Mastropieri, M., Jenne, T., & Scruggs, T. (1988). A level system for managing problem behaviors in a high school resource program. *Behavioral Disorders, 13*(3), 202–208.

Mastropieri, M. A., Scruggs, T. E., & Shioh, S. (1991). Mathematics instruction for learning disabled students: A review of research. *Learning Disabilities Research and Practice, 6,* 89–98.

Matson, J., & Fee, V. (1991). Social skills difficulties among persons with mental retardation. In J. Matson & J. Mullick (Eds.), *Handbook of mental retardation* (2nd ed.). New York: Pergamon Press.

Matsuda, M. (1984). A comparative analysis of blind and sighted children's communication skills. *Journal of Visual Impairment and Blindness, 78*(1), 1–4.

Maurice, C. (1993). *Let me hear your voice.* New York: Fawcett Columbine.

McAnally, P., Rose, S., & Quigley, C. (1987). *Language learning practices with deaf children.* Boston: Little, Brown.

McCall, R. (1987). Developmental function, individual differences and the plasticity of intelligence. In J. Gallagher & C. Ramey (Eds.), *The malleability of children* (pp. 25–36). Baltimore: Paul H. Brookes.

McCarthy, M. (1994). Inclusion and the law: Recent judicial decisions. *Phi Delta Kappa Research Bulletin,* No. 13.

McCathren, R., Yoder, P., & Warren, S. (1995). The role of directives in early language intervention, *Journal of Early Intervention, 19*(2), 91–101.

McCubbin, H., & Patterson, J. (1983). The family stress process: The double ABCX model of adjustment and adaptation. *Marriage and Family Review, 6,* 7–37.

McCune-Nicolich, L. (1986). Play-language relationships: Implications for a theory of symbolic development. In A. Gottfried & C. Brown (Eds.), *Play interactions.* Lexington, MA: Lexington Books.

McIntosh, R., Vaughn, S., Schum, J., Hagger, D., & Lee, O. (1994). Observations of students with learning disabilities in general education classrooms. *Exceptional Children, 60*(2), 247–261.

McKinney, J., Hocutt, A. (1988). The need for policy analysis in evaluating the regular education initiative. *Journal of Learning Disabilities, 21*(1), 12–18.

McLaren, J., & Bryson, S. (1987). Review of recent epidemiological studies of mental retardation: Prevalence, associated disorders and etiology. *American Journal of Mental Retardation, 92*(3), 243–254.

McLaughlin, M., & Warren, S. (1992). *Issues and options in restructuring special education programs.* College Park: University of Maryland, Center for Policy Options in Special Education.

McLean, M., & Odom, S. (1988, June). Least restrictive environment and social integration. *The Division for Early Childhood Newsletter,* pp. 1–8.

McLoughlin, C. S., Garner, J. B., & Callahan, M. (1987). *Getting employed, staying employed: Job development and training for persons with severe handicaps.* Baltimore: Paul H. Brookes.

McLoughlin, J., & Lewis, R. (1991). *Assessing special students: Strategies and procedures* (3rd ed.). Columbus, OH: Charles E. Merrill.

McNulty, B., Soper, E., & Smith, D. (1984). *Effectiveness of early childhood special education of handicapped children.* Denver: Colorado State Department of Education.

McReynolds, L. (1986). Functional articulation disorders. In G. Shames & E. Wiig (Eds.), *Human communication disorders: An introduction* (2nd ed.). Columbus, OH: Charles E. Merrill.

Meisels, S. (1987, January). Uses and abuses of developmental screening and school readiness testing. *Young Children,* pp. 4–9.

Meisels, S., Jablon, J., Marsden, D., Dichtelmiller, M., & Dorfman, A. (1994). *The work sampling system* (2nd ed.). Ann Arbor, MI: Rebus Planning Associates.

Meisels, S., & Shonkoff, J. (Eds.). (1990). *Handbook of early intervention.* New York: Cambridge University Press.

Meisels, S., & Wiske, M. (1989). *The early screening inventory (ESI).* New York: Teachers College Press.

Meisels, S., Wiske, M., Henderson, L., Marsden D., & Browning, K. (1992). *The early screening inventory* (Rev. edition). Ann Arbor: University of Michigan.

Mencher, G., & Gerber, S. (1983). *The multiply handicapped hearing-impaired child.* New York: Grune & Stratton.

Menolascino, F. J., Levitas, A., & Greiner, C. (1986). The nature and type of mental illness in the mentally retarded. *Psychopharmacology Bulletin, 22,* 1060–1071.

Mercer, C. (1992). *Students with learning disabilities* (4th ed.). Columbus, OH: Charles E. Merrill.

Metz, I. (1991). Albuquerque, New Mexico. In M. Anderson & P. Goldberg (Eds.), *Cultural competence in screening and assessment* (pp. 8–10). National Early Childhood Technical Assistance System. Pacer Center, 4826 Chicago Avenue South, Minneapolis, MN 55417-1095.

Meyer, L. H. (1991, August). Personal communications.

Meyer, L. H., Peck, C. A., & Brown, L. *Critical issues in the lives of people with severe disabilities.* Baltimore: Paul H. Brookes.

Michael, M., & Paul, P. (1990–1991, December–January). Early intervention with deaf-blindness. *Exceptional Children, 57*(3), 200–210.

Millar, S. (1981). Crossmodal and intersensory perception and the blind. In R. Walk & H. Pick, Jr. (Eds.), *Intersensory perception and sensory integration.* New York: Plenum Press.

Miller, J., Colbert, A., & Osberg, J. S. (1990). Ventilator dependency: Decision making, daily functioning and quality of life for patients with Duchenne muscular dystrophy.

Developmental Medicine and Child Neurology, 32, 1078–1086.

Mills v. D.C. Board of Education, 348 F. Supp. 866 (D.D.C. 1972).

Montour, K. (1977). William James Sidis, the broken twig. *American Psychologist, 32,* 265–279.

Moore, G. (1986). Voice disorders. In G. Shames & E. Wiig (Eds.), *Human communication disorders: An introduction* (2nd ed.). Columbus, OH: Charles E. Merrill.

Moores, D. (1996). *Educating the deaf* (4th ed.). Boston: Houghton Mifflin.

Moores, D., Kluwin, T., & Mertens, D. (1985). *High school program for the deaf in metropolitan areas* (Research Monograph No. 3). Washington, DC: Gallaudet Research Institute.

Moroney, R., & Dokecki, P. (1984). The family and the professions: Implications for public policy. *Journal of Family Issues, 5,* 224–238.

Morse, W. (1976). The helping teacher/crisis teacher concept. *Focus on Exceptional Children, 8,* 1–11.

Mulick, J., Hammer, D., & Dura, J. (1991). Assessment and management of antisocial and hyperactive behavior. In J. Matson & J. Mulick (Eds.), *Handbook of mental retardation* (2nd ed.). New York: Pergamon Press.

Murphy, J. (1991). *Restructuring schools: Capturing and assessing the phenomena.* New York: Teachers College Press.

Murphy, K. (1983). The educator-therapist with deaf, multiply disabled children: Some essential criteria. In G. Mencher & S. Gerber (Eds.), *The multiply handicapped hearing-impaired child* (pp. 13–16). New York: Grune & Stratton.

Murphy, K., & Byrne, D. (1983). Selection of optimal modalities as avenues of learning in deaf, blind, multiply disabled children. In G. Mencher & S. Gerber (Eds.), *The multiply handicapped hearing-impaired child* (pp. 335–396). New York: Grune & Stratton.

Naglai, A. (1991). Manhattan, New York. In M. Anderson & P. Goldberg (Eds.), *Cultural competence in screening and assessment* (pp. 14–15). Pacer Center, 4826 Chicago Avenue South, Minneapolis, MN 55417-1095.

National Center for Children and Youth with Disabilities. (March 1994). *Learning Disabilities.* (Fact Sheet N. 7). Washington, DC: N. Amos.

National Council on Educational Standards and Testing. (1992). *Raising standards for American education: A report to Congress, the Secretary of Education, the National Education Goals Panel and the American people.* Washington, DC: Author.

National Joint Committee for Learning Disabilities. (1991). *A statement of the National Joint Committee for Learning Disabilities,* pp. 15–16.

Nealis, J. (1983). Epilepsy. In J. Umbreit (Ed.), *Physical disabilities in health impairments: An introduction* (pp. 74–85). Columbus, OH: Charles E. Merrill.

Neel, R., Meadows, N., Levine, P., & Edgar, E. (1988). What happens after special education: A statewide follow-up study of secondary students who have behavioral disorders. *Behavioral Disorders, 13*(3), 209–216.

Neidecker, E. (1987). *School programs in speech and language: Organization and management* (2nd ed.). Englewood Cliffs, NJ: Prentice-Hall.

Nelson, C., & Pearson, C. (1991). *Integrating services for children and youth with emotional and behavior disorders.* Reston, VA: Council for Exceptional Children.

Nelson, C. M., Rutherford, R. B., Center, D. B., & Walker, H. M. (1991). Do public schools have an obligation to serve troubled children and youth? *Exceptional Children, 57,* 406–415.

Newland, T. (1979). The blind learning aptitude test. *Journal of Visual Impairment and Blindness, 73,* 134–139.

Newman, P., Low, G., Creaghead, N., & Secord, W. (1985). Introduction. In P. Newman, N. Creaghead, & W. Secord (Eds.), *Assessment and remediation of articulatory and phonological disorders.* Columbus, OH: Charles E. Merrill.

Newman, R., & Simpson, R. (1983). Modifying the least restrictive environment to facilitate the integration of severely emotionally disturbed children and youth. *Behavioral Disorders, 8*(2), 102–112.

Newton, J., Horner, R., Ard, W., LeBaron, N., & Sapperton, G. (1994a). A conceptual model for improving the social life of individuals with mental retardation. *Mental Retardation, 32*(5), 383–391.

Newton, J., Horner, R., Ard, W., LeBaron, N., & Sapperton, G. (1994b). Social aspects and social relationship of individuals with disability. *Mental Retardation, 32*(5), 393–402.

Noble, J., & Conlery, R. (1987). Accumulating evidence on the benefits and costs of supportive and transitional employment for persons with severe handicaps. *Journal of the Association for Persons with Severe Handicaps, 12,* 167–174.

Nolan, C. (1987). *Under the eye of the clock.* London: Pan.

Norvich, R. (1993). Activity based intervention and developmentally appropriate practice: Points of convergence. *Topics in Early Childhood Special Education, 3*(4), 403–417.

Odom, S., & Karnes, M.(Eds.). (1988). *Early intervention for infants and children with handicaps.* Baltimore: Paul H. Brookes.

Odom, S., McConnell, S., & McEvoy, M. (1992). *Social competence of young children with disabilities.* Baltimore: Paul H. Brookes.

O'Donnel, L., & Livingston, R. (1991). Active exploration of the environment by young children with low vision: A review of the literature. *Journal of Visual Impairment and Blindness, 85,* 287–291.

Ogura, T. (1991). A longitudinal study of the relationship between early language development and play development. *Journal of Child Language, 18,* 273–294.

O'Hara, D., & Levy, J. (1987). Family intervention. In K. Kavale, S. Forness, & M. Bender (Eds.), *Handbook of learning disabilities* (pp. 215–235). Boston: College-Hill/ Little, Brown.

Oliver, J., Cole, N., Hollingsworth, H. (1991). Learning disabilities as function of familial learning problems and developmental problems. *Exceptional Children, 57*(5), 427–440.

Oller, D. K. (1985). Infant vocalizations. In S. Harel & N. J. Anastasiow (Eds.), *The at-risk infant* (pp. 323–332). Baltimore: Paul H. Brookes.

Olszewski, P., Kulieke, M., & Buescher, T. (1987). The influence of the family environment on the development of talent: A literature review. *Journal for the Education of the Gifted, 11*(1), 6–28.

O'Neil, J., Gothelf, C., Cohen, S., Lehman, L., & Woolf, S. (1991). *A curricular approach to support the transition to adulthood of adolescents with visual or dual sensory impairments and cognitive disabilities.* Albany: New York State Education Department, Office of Special Education and Rehabilitation Services.

Orelove, F., & Sobsey, D. (1987). *Educating children with multiple disabilities: A transdisciplinary approach.* Baltimore: Paul H. Brookes.

Orelove, F., & Sobsey, D. (1991). *Educating children with multiple disabilities.* Baltimore: Paul H. Brookes.

Orr, D. (1989). *Measurement of self-concept among disabled children.* Unpublished doctoral dissertation, Harvard University, Cambridge, MA.

Orton, S. T. (1937). *Reading, writing, and speech problems in children.* New York: Norton.

Osborn, A. (1957). *Creative imagination* (3rd ed.). New York: Scribner's.

Osofsky, J. (Ed.). (1987). *Handbook of infant development.* New York: Wiley.

Palfrey, J., Walker, D., Haynie, M., Singer, J., Porter, S., Bushey, B., & Cooperman, P. (1991, May). Technology's children: Report of a statewide census of children dependent on medical support. *Pediatrics, 87*(5), 611–618.

Papert, S. (1993). *The children's machine.* New York: Basic Books.

Pappas, D. (1985). *Diagnosis and treatment of hearing impairment in children.* San Diego: College-Hill.

Parette, H. (1991). The importance of technology in the education and training of persons with mental retardation. *Education and Training in Mental Retardation, 26,* 165–178.

Parke, B. N. (1989). *Gifted students in regular classrooms.* Boston: Allyn & Bacon.

Parmelee, S., & Sigman, M. (1983). Perinatal brain development. In J. J. Campos & M. M. Haith (Eds.), *Handbook of child psychology: Vol. 2. Infancy and developmental psychobiology* (pp. 95–155). New York: Wiley.

Parnes, S., Noller, R., & Biondi, A. (1977). *Guide to creative action.* New York: Scribner's.

Patrick, G. (1984). Comparison of novice and veteran wheelchair athlete's self-concept and acceptance of disability. *Rehabilitation Counseling Bulletin, 27,* 186–188.

Patton, J. R. (1986). *Transition: Curricular implications.* Honolulu: Project Ho-ko-ko, University of Hawaii.

Paul, J., & Epanchin, B. (Eds.). (1991). *Emotional disturbance in children* (4th ed.). Columbus, OH: Charles E. Merrill.

Paul, P., & Quigley, S. (1990). *Education and deafness.* White Plains, NY: Longman.

Pavenstedt, E. (1967). *The drifters: Children from disorganized families.* Boston: Little, Brown.

Pear, R. (1992, January 19). The hard thing about cutting infant mortality is educating mothers. *New York Times,* p. E5.

Pearl, R., Donahue, M., & Bryant, T. (1981). Learning disabled and normal children's responses to non-explicit requests for clarification. *Perceptual and Motor Skills, 53,* 919–925.

Pearpoint, J. (1989). Reflections on a quality education for all students. In S. Stainback, W. Stainback, & M. Forest (Eds.), *Educating all students in the mainstream of regular education.* Baltimore: Paul H. Brookes.

Peins, M. (Ed.). (1984). *Contemporary approaches in stuttering therapy.* Boston: Little, Brown.

Pennington, B. (1991). *Diagnosing learning disorders.* New York: Guilford Press.

Pennsylvania Association for Retarded Children (PARG) v. Commonwealth of Pennsylvania, 334 F. Supp. 1257; 343 F. Supp. 279 (E.D. Pa. 1971, 1972).

Perkins, D., & Simmons, R. (1988). The cognitive roots of scientific and mathematical ability. In J. Dreyden, G. Stanley, S. Gallagher, & R. Sawyer (Eds.), *The proceedings of the talent identification programs/National Science Foundation Conference on Academic Talent.* Durham, NC: Duke University Talent Identification Program.

Peters, J., Tampleman, T., & Brostrom, G. (1987). The school and community partnership: Planning transition for students with severe handicaps. *Exceptional Children, 53,* 531–536.

Peterson, N. (1987). Parenting the young handicapped and at-risk child. In N. Peterson (Ed.), *Early intervention for handicapped and at-risk children: An introduction to early childhood special education* (pp. 409–446). Denver, CO: Love.

Petitto, L., & Marentette, P. (1991, March). Babbling in the manual mode: Evidence for the ontogeny of language. *Science, 251,* 1493–1495.

Phillips, S. (1983). *The invisible culture: Communication in classroom and community on the Warm Springs Indian Reservation.* White Plains, NY: Longman.

Phillips, V., & McCullough, L. (1990). Consultation-based programming: Instituting the collaborative ethic in schools. *Exceptional Children, 56,* 291–304.

Piaget, J. (1926, 1955). *Language and thought in the child.* New York: Harcourt Brace Jovanovich.

Piaget, J., & Inhelder, B. (1969). *The psychology of the child.* New York: Basic Books.

Pindzola, M., & White, B. (1986). Protocol for differentiating the incipient stutterer. *Language, Speech, and Hearing Services in the School, 17*(1), 2–11.

Pinker, S. (1991). Rules of language. *Science, 253,* 530–535.

Pizant, B. M., & Rydell, R. J. (1984). Analysis of function of delayed echolia in autistics. *Journal of Speech and Hearing Research, 27,* 183–192.

Plomin, R. (1989). Environment and genes: Determinants of behavior. *American Psychologist, 44*(2), 105–111.

Plomin, R., & McClearn, G. (Eds.). (1993). *Nature, nurture and psychology.* Washington, DC: American Psychological Association.

Pogrund, R., Fazzi, D., & Lampert, J. (Eds.). (1992). *Early focus: Working with young blind and visually impaired children and their families.* New York: American Foundation for the Blind.

Pogrund, R., & Rosen, S. (1989). The preschool blind child can be a cane user. *Journal of Visual Impairment and Blind-ness, 83,* 431–439.

Polloway, E., Patton, J., Smith, J., & Roderique, T. (1991). Issues in program design for elementary students with mild retardation: Emphasis on curriculum development. *Education and Training in Mental Retardation, 26,* 142–150.

Polloway, E. A., & Smith, J. D. (1988). Current status of the mild mental retardation construct: Identification, placement, and programs. In M. C. Wang, M. C. Reynolds, & H. J. Walberg (Eds.), *The handbook of special education: Research and practice* (2, pp. 7–22). Oxford, England: Pergamon Press.

Powell, T., & Ogle, P. (1985). *Brothers and sisters: A special part of exceptional families.* Baltimore: Paul H. Brookes.

Premack, D. (1959). Toward empirical behavior laws: I. Positive reinforcement. *Psychological Review, 66,* 291–333.

Pressley, M., & Associate. (1990). *Cognitive strategy instructor*. Cambridge, MA: Brookline Press.

Pueschel, S. (1991). Ethical considerations related to prenatal diagnosis of fetuses with Down syndrome. *Mental Retardation, 29*(4), 185–190.

Pueschel, S., Scala, P., Weidenman, L., & Bernier, J. (Eds.). (1995). *The special child* (2nd ed.). Baltimore: Paul H. Brookes.

Pueschel, S., & Thuline, H. (1991). Chromosome disorders. In J. Matson & J. Mulick (Eds.), *Handbook of mental retardation* (2nd ed.). New York: Pergamon Press.

Pugash, M., & Johnson, L. (1995). Unlocking expertise among classroom teachers through structured dialogue: Extending research on peer collaboration. *Exceptional Children, 62*(2), 101–110.

Putman, A. H. (1988). Review of research on dysarthria. In H. Wintz (Ed.), *Human communication and its disorders* (pp. 181–193). Norwood, NJ: Ablex.

Quay, H., & Werry, J. (Eds.). (1986). *Psychopathological disorders of childhood* (3rd ed.). New York: Wiley.

Rainforth, B., & York, J. (1987). Handling and positioning. In F. Orelove & D. Sobsey (Eds.), *Educating children with multiple handicaps: A transdisciplinary approach* (pp. 67–104). Baltimore: Paul H. Brookes.

Rainforth, B., York, J., & MacDonald, C. (1992). *Collaborative teams for students with severe disabilities*. Baltimore: Paul H. Brookes.

Ramos-Ford, & Gardner, H. (1991). Giftedness from a multiple intelligences perspective. In N. Colangelo & G. David (Eds.), *Handbook of gifted education*. Boston: Allyn & Bacon.

Ramsey, E., & Walker, H. (1988). Family management correlates of antisocial behavior among middle school boys. *Behavioral Disorders, 13*(3), 187–201.

Rand, D., & Gibbs, L. (1989). A model program for gifted girls in science. *Journal for the Education of the Gifted, 12*(2), 142–155.

Raver, S. (1991). *Strategies for teaching at-risk and handicapped infants and toddlers: A transdisciplinary approach*. Columbus, OH: Charles E. Merrill.

Read, L. (1989). An examination of the social skills of blind kindergarten children. *Education of the Visually Handicapped, 20*, 142–155.

Redl, F. (1959). *Mental hygiene and teaching*. New York: Harcourt Brace Jovanovich.

Reid, D., Wilson, P., & Faw, G. (1991). Teaching self-help skills. In J. Matson & J. Mulick (Eds.), *Handbook of mental retardation* (2nd ed.). New York: Pergamon Press.

Reis, S., & Callahan, C. (1989). Gifted females: They've come a long way, or have they? *Journal for the Education of the Gifted, 12*(2), 99–117.

Renzulli, J., & Reis, S. (1991). The reform movement and the quiet crisis in gifted education. *Gifted Child Quarterly, 35*(1), 26–35.

Renzulli, J., Smith, L., & Reis, S. (1982). Curriculum compacting: An essential strategy for working with gifted students. *Elementary School Journal, 82*, 185–194.

Rettig, M. (1994). The play of young children with visual impairments: Characteristics and interventions. *Journal of Visual Impairment and Blindness, 88*, 410–420.

Reynolds, M., Wang, M., & Walberg, H. (1987). The necessary restructuring of special and regular education. *Exceptional Children, 53*, 391–398.

Richmond, J. (1990, June). Low birth weight infants: Can we enhance development? *Journal of American Medical Association, 13*, 3069.

Rimland, B., & Edelson, S. (1994a). Auditory integration training and autism. San Diego: Autism Research Institute. Also *Autism Research Review, 8*(2).

Rimland, B., & Edelson, S. (1994b). The effect of auditory integration training on autism. *American Journal of Speech and Language Pathology, 3*(2), 16–24.

Rittenhouse, R. (1985). *TTY language in deaf adolescents: A research report*. Normal: Illinois State University.

Robbins, F., Dunlap, G., & Plienis, A. (1991). Family characteristics, family training and the progress of young children with autism. *Journal of Early Intervention, 15*(2), 173–184.

Roberts, J., Burchinal, M., & Bailey, D. (1994). Communication among preschoolers with and without disabilities in same-age and mixed-age classes. *American Journal of Mental Retardation, 99*(3), 231–249.

Robertson, C., & Whytte, L. (1983). Prospective identification of infants with hearing loss and multiple handicaps. In G. Mencher & S. Gerber (Eds.), *The multiply handicapped hearing-impaired child* (pp. 27–54). New York: Grune & Stratton.

Robins, L. (1966). *Deviant children grow up*. Baltimore: Williams & Wilkins.

Romero, V. (1994). In C. Callahan & J. McIntire (Eds.), *Identifying outstanding talent in American Indian and Alaska's native students* (p. i). Washington, DC: U.S. Department of Education.

Rosen, S. (1992). Academics are not enough: Incorporating life skills into the curriculum for children and youth with visual handicaps. *Division for the Visually Handicapped Quarterly, 37*(2), 27–28.

Rosenbaum, M., & Palmon, N. (1984). Helplessness and resourcefulness in coping with epilepsy. *Journal of Consulting and Clinical Psychology, 52*, 244–253.

Rosenthal, E. (1991 September 29). As more tiny infants live, choices, and burdens grow. *New York Times*, Sec. 1, pp. 1, 16.

Ross, P. (Ed.). (1993). *National excellence*. Washington, DC: U.S. Department of Education.

Rossetti, L. (1986). *High-risk infants*. Boston: College Hill/Little, Brown.

Rossitti, L. (1990). *Infant-toddler assessment*. Austin, TX: PRO-ED.

Rourke, B. P. (Ed.). (1991). *Neuropsychological validation of learning disability subtypes*. New York: Guilford Press.

Rourke, B. P. (1994). Neuropsychological assessment of children with learning disabilities. In G. Lyon (Ed.), *Frames of reference for the assessment of learning disabilities* (pp. 475–514). Baltimore: Paul H. Brookes.

Rourke, P. (Ed.). (1995). *Syndrome of non-verbal learning disabilities*. New York: Guilford.

Rowitz, L. (1991). Social and environmental factors and developmental handicaps in children. In J. Matson, & J. Mulick (Eds.), *Handbook of mental retardation* (2nd ed.). New York: Pergamon Press.

Rusch, F., Chadsey-Rusch, J., & Lagomarcino, T. (1987). Preparing students for employment. In M. Snell (Ed.), *Systematic instruction of persons with severe handicaps* (3rd ed., pp. 471–490). Columbus, OH: Charles E. Merrill.

Rutter, M. (1988). Epidemiological approaches to developmental psychology. *Archives of General Psychology, 45,* 486–495.

Ryan, B. (1986). Operant procedures applied to stuttering therapy for children. In G. Shames & H. Wiig (Eds.), *Human communication disorders: An introduction* (2nd ed.). Columbus, OH: Charles E. Merrill.

Ryan, E. R., Weed, K. A., & Short, E. J. (1986). Cognitive behavior modification: Promoting active self-regulatory learning style. In J. K. Torgesen & B. Y. L. Wong (Eds.), *Psychological and educational perspectives on learning disabilities* (pp. 367–397). San Diego: Academic Press.

Sacks, S. (1992). The social development of visually impaired children: A theoretical perspective. In S. Sacks, L. Kekelis, & R. Gaylord-Ross (Eds.), *The development of social skills by blind and visually impaired students* (pp. 3–12). New York: American Foundation for the Blind.

Sacks, S., & Gaylord-Ross, R. (1992). Peer-mediated and teacher-directed social skills training for blind and visually impaired students. In S. Sacks, L. Kekelis, & R. Gaylord-Ross (Eds.), *The development of social skills by blind and visually impaired students* (pp. 103–132). New York: American Foundation for the Blind.

Safford, P., Sargent, M., & Cook, C. (Eds.). (1994). Instructional models in early childhood special education: Origins, issues and trends. In P. Safford (Ed.), *Early childhood special education* (pp. 96–117). New York: Teachers College Press.

Sailor, W. (1991). Teaching. In L. H. Meyer, C. Peck, & L. Brown (Eds.), *Critical issues in the lives of persons with severe disabilities*. Baltimore: Paul H. Brookes.

Sailor, W., Gee, K., Goetz, L., & Graham, N. (1988). Progress in educating students with the most severe disabilities: Is there any? *Journal of the Association for Persons with Severe Handicaps, 13,* 87–99.

Sailor, W., & Guess, D. (1983). *Severely handicapped students*. Boston: Houghton Mifflin.

Sale, P., & Carey, D. (1995). The sociometric status of students with disabilities in a full inclusion school. *Exceptional Children, 62*(1), 6–19.

Salvia, J., & Ysseldyke, J. (1991). *Assessment in special and remedial education*. Boston: Houghton Mifflin.

Sameroff, A. Neo-environmental perspectives on developmental theory. In R. Hodapp, J. Burack, & E. Zigler (Eds.), *Issues in the developmental approach to mental retardation* (pp. 93–130). New York: Cambridge University Press.

Sameroff, A. (1990). Neo-environmental perspectives on developmental theory. In R. Hodapp, J. Burack, & E. Zigler (Eds.), *Issues in the developmental approach to mental retardation*. New York: Cambridge University Press.

Samuelson, J. (1981). Individual differences in the interaction of vision and proprioception. In R. Walk & H. Pick (Eds.), *Intersensory perception and integration*. New York: Plenum Press.

Sattler, J. (1988). *Assessment of children* (3rd ed.). San Diego: Sattler.

Sawyer, R. (1988). In defense of academic rigor. *Journal of the Education of the Gifted, 11,* 5–19.

Scarr, S. (1982). Development is internally guided, not determined. *Contemporary Psychology, 27,* 852–853.

Schery, T., & O'Connor, L. (1995). Computers as a context for language intervention. In M. Rey, J. Windson, & S. Warren (Eds.), *Language intervention*. Baltimore: Paul H. Brookes.

Schill, W. (1988). *Five transition policy studies including pertinent literate synthesis: Transition research on problems of handicapped youth*. Seattle: University of Washington School of Education.

Schleichkorn, J. (1983). *Coping with cerebral palsy: Answers to questions parents often ask*. Austin, TX: PRO-ED.

Schlesinger, H. (1983). Early intervention: The prevention of multiple handicaps. In G. Mencher & S. Gerber (Eds.), *The multiply handicapped hearing-impaired child* (pp. 83–116). New York: Grune & Stratton.

Schloss, P. (1983). Classroom-based intervention for students exhibiting depressive reactions. *Behavioral Disorders, 8,* 231–236.

Schneekloth, L. (1989). Play environments for visually impaired children. *Journal of Visual Impairment and Blindness, 83,* 196–201.

Scholl, G. T. (Ed.). (1986). *Foundations of education for visually handicapped children and youth: Theory and practice.* New York: American Foundation for the Blind.

Schopler, E., & Mesibov, G. (Eds.). (1983). *Autism in adolescents and adults.* New York: Plenum.

Schopler, E., & Mesibov, G. (Eds.). (1984). *Effects of autism on the family.* New York: Plenum.

Schopler, E., & Mesibov, G. (Eds.). (1985). *Communication problems in autism.* New York: Plenum.

Schopler, E., & Mesibov, G. (Eds.). (1986). *Social behavior in autism.* New York: Plenum.

Schopler, E., & Mesibov, G. (Eds.). (1990). *High-functioning individuals with autism.* New York: Plenum.

Schrag, J. (1994). *Organizational, instructional and curriculum strategies to support the complementation of unified, coordinated and inclusive schools.* Reston, VA: Council for Exceptional Children.

Schreiner, M., Donar, M., & Kettrick, R. (1987). Pediatric mechanical ventilation. *Pediatric Clinics of North America, 34*(1), 47–60.

Schultz, R., William, W., Iverson, G., & Duncan, D. (1984). Social integration of severely handicapped students. In N. Certo, N. Haring, & R. York (Eds.), *Public school integration of severely handicapped students: National issues and progressive alternatives.* Baltimore: Paul H. Brookes.

Schum, J., & Vaughn, S. (1995). Getting ready for inclusion: Is the stage set? *Learning Disabilities Research and Practice, 10*(3), 169–179.

Schumaker, J., & Deshler, D. (1988). Implementing the regular education initiative in secondary schools: A different ball game. *Journal of Learning Disabilities, 21,* 26–42.

Schumaker, J. B., Deshler, D. D., & McKnight, R. C. (1991). Teaching routines for content areas at the secondary level. In G. Stover, M. R. Shinn, & H. M. Walker (Eds.), *Intervention for achievement and behavior problems* (pp. 473–494). Washington, DC: National Association of School Psychologists.

Schumaker, J., Hazel, J., & Sheldon, J. (1982). Social skill performance of learning disabled, non-learning disabled, and delinquent adolescents. *Learning Disability Quarterly, 5,* 388–397.

Schuman, A. (1990). Homeward bound: The explosion of pediatric home care. *Contemporary Pediatrics, 7,* 26–54.

Schuman, J., Vaughn, S., Haager, D., McDowell, J., Rothstein, L., & Saumell, L. (1995). General education teacher planning: What can students with learning disabilities expect? *Exceptional Children, 61*(4), 335–352.

Schwartz, N. (1987). *My friend Jodi is blind.* New York: The Lighthouse.

Science. (1990, January). To test or not to test. *Science, 247*(5), 17–18.

Scola, P. (1991). Infections. In J. Matson & J. Mulick (Eds.), *Handbook of mental retardation* (2nd ed.). New York: Pergamon Press.

Scott, K., & Carran, D. (1987). The epidemiology and prevention of mental retardation. *American Psychologist, 42*(8), 801–804.

Seitz de Martinez, B. (Ed.). (1995). *Understanding fetal alcohol syndrome.* Bloomington, IN: Hot Topic Series, Phi Delta Kappa.

Seligman, M., Peterson, C. (1986). A learned helplessness perspective on childhood depression. In M. Rutter, C. Izard, & P. Read (Eds.), *Depression in young people: Developmental and clinical perspectives.* New York: Guilford.

Semmel, N., Abernathy, T., Butera, G., & Lesar, S. (1991, September). Teacher perceptions of the regular education initiative. *Exceptional Children, 58*(1), 9–24.

Senf, G. M. (1986). Learning disability research in sociological and scientific perspective. In J. K. Torgesen & B. Y. L. Wong (Eds.), *Psychological and educational perspectives on learning disabilities* (pp. 27–54). San Diego: Academic Press.

Serna, L., & Patton, J. (1989). Science. In G. Robinson, J. Patton, E. Polloway, & L. Sargent (Eds.), *Best practices in mild mental retardation* (pp. 197–199). Reston, VA: Council for Exceptional Children.

Shames, G., & Rubin, H. (1986). *Stuttering then and now.* Columbus, OH: Charles E. Merrill.

Shames, G., & Wiig, H. (Eds.). (1985). *Human communication disorders: An introduction* (2nd ed.). Columbus, OH: Charles E. Merrill.

Shatz, M., & Ebeling, K. (1991). Patterns of language related behaviors: Evidence for self-help in acquiring grammar. *Journal of Child Language, 18,* 295–313.

Shea, R. (1983). Habilitation facilities at the Glenrose School Hospital. In G. Mencher & S. Gerber (Eds.), *The multiply handicapped hearing-impaired child* (pp. 45–50). New York: Grune & Stratton.

Shine, R. (1984). Assessment of fluency training with the young stutterer. In M. Peins (Ed.), *Contemporary approaches in stuttering therapy.* Boston: Little, Brown.

Shinn-Strieker, T. (1984). Trained communication assistants in the public schools. *Language, speech, and hearing services in schools, 15,* 169–174.

Shneidman, E. (1985). *Definition of suicide.* New York: Wiley.

Shonkoff, J. P., & Hauser-Cram, P. (1988). Early intervention for disabled infants and their families. *Pediatrics, 80,* 650–658.

Short, E. J., & Ryan, E. B. (1984). Metacognitive differences between skilled and less skilled readers: Remediating deficits through story grammar and attribution training. *Journal of Educational Psychology, 76*(7), 225–235.

Shriberg, L., & Kwiatowski, J. (1988). A follow-up study of children with phonological disorders of unknown origin. *Journal of Speech and Hearing Disorders, 53*(2), 144–145.

Shriver, M., & Pierseal, W. (1994, Summer). The long-term effects of intrauterine drug exposure: Review of recent research and implications for early childhood special education. *Topics in Early Childhood Special Education, 14*(2), 161–183.

Siegel-Causey, E., & Guess, D. (1990). *Enhancing nonsymbolic communication interaction among learners with severe disabilities.* Baltimore: Paul H. Brookes.

Siegler, R. (Ed.). (1986). *Children's thinking: What develops?* Englewood Cliffs, NJ: Prentice-Hall.

Silver, L. B. (1987). The magic cure: A review of the current controversial approaches for treating learning disabilities. *Journal of Learning Disabilities, 20*(8), 498–512.

Silver, L. B. (1990). Attention-deficit hyperactivity disorder: Is it a learning disability? *Journal of Learning Disabilities, 23,* 394–397.

Silverman, L. (Ed.). (1993). *Counseling the gifted and talented.* Denver, CO: Love.

Simeonsson, R., & Rosenthal, S. (1991). Qualitative-developmental processes. In J. Matson & J. Mulick (Eds.), *Handbook of mental retardation* (2nd ed.). New York: Pergamon Press.

Simon, H. (1979). Information processing models of cognition. *Annual Review of Psychology, 30,* 363–396.

Simpson, R., & Myles, B. (1990). The general education collaboration model: A model for successful mainstreaming. *Focus on Exceptional Children, 23*(4), 1–10.

Sizer, T. (1985). *Horace's compromise: The dilemma of the American high school.* Boston: Houghton Mifflin.

Skellenger, A., & Hill, E. (1994). Effects of a shared teacher-child play intervention on the play skills of three young children who are blind. *Journal of Visual Impairment and Blindness, 88,* 433–445.

Skinner, B. (1953). *Science and human behavior.* New York: Free Press.

Skrtic, T. (1991). *Behind special education.* Denver, CO: Love.

Slavin, R. (1988). Synthesis of research on grouping in elementary and secondary schools. *Education Leadership, 46,* 67–77.

Slavin, R. (1990). Achievement effects of ability grouping in secondary schools: A best evidence synthesis. *Review of Educational Research, 60,* 471–499.

Smelter, R., Rasch, B., & Yudewitz, G. (1994). Thinking of inclusion for all special needs students? Better think again. *Phi Delta Kappa Research Bulletin, 76*(1), 35–38.

Smith, S. D., & Pennington, B. (1987). Genetic influences: Paradigm. In K. Kavale, S. Forness, & M. Bender (Eds.), *Handbook of learning disabilities: Vol. 1. Dimensions and diagnoses* (pp. 49–75). Boston: College-Hill/Little, Brown.

Snowling, M. J., & Perrin, D. (1988). Cognitive processes in written language dysfunction. In R. L. Schiefelbusch & L. Lloyd (Eds.), *Language perspectives* (pp. 147–185). Austin, TX: PRO-ED.

Snowman, J. (1991, Fall). Memory and problem solving: The overlooked partnership. *Educational Forum,* pp. 9–11.

Solnit, G., Taylor, M., & Bednarczyk, A. (1992). *Access for all: Integrating deaf, hard of hearing and hearing students.* Washington, DC: Gallaudet University Press.

Spungin, S. (Ed.). (1981). *Guidelines for public school programs serving visually handicapped children* (2nd ed.). New York: American Foundation for the Blind.

Stainback, S., & Stainback, W. (1980). *Educating children with severe maladaptive behaviors.* New York: Grune & Stratton.

Stainback, S., & Stainback, W. (1988). *Understanding and conducting qualitative research.* Reston, VA: Council for Exceptional Children.

Stainback, S., & Stainback, W. (1989). No more teachers of students with severe handicaps. *TASH Newsletter, 19*(9).

Stainback, S., & Stainback, W. (1992). *Curriculum considerations on inclusive classrooms: Facilitating learning for all students.* Baltimore: Paul H. Brookes.

Stainback, S., Stainback, W., & Slavin, R. (1989). Classroom organization for diversity among students. In S. Stainback, W. Stainback, & M. Forest (Eds.), *Educating all students in the mainstream of regular education.* Baltimore: Paul H. Brookes.

Stanovich, K. (1986). Cognitive processes and the reading problems of learning disabled children. In J. K. Torgesen & B. Y. L. Wong (Eds.), *Psychological and educational perspectives on learning disabilities* (pp. 85–131). San Diego: Academic Press.

Stayton, V., & Karnes, M. (1994). Model program for infants and toddlers with disabilities and their families. In L. Johnson, R. Gallagher, M. LaMontagne, J. Jordan, J. Gallagher, P. Hutinger, & M. Karnes (Eds.), *Meeting early intervention challenges* (2nd ed.). Baltimore: Paul H. Brookes.

Stein, S. (1974). *About handicaps.* New York: Walker.

Sternberg, L., & McNerney, C. D. (1988). Prelanguage communication instruction. In L. Sternberg (Ed.), *Educating students with severe and profound handicaps* (pp. 311–363). Austin, TX: PRO-ED.

Stevenson, H., Cheri, C., & Lee, S. (1994). Motivation and achievement of gifted children in east Asia and the United States. *Journal for the Education of the Gifted, 16*(3), 223–250.

Stevenson, H. W., Lee, S., & Stigler, J. W. (1986). Mathematics achievement of Chinese, Japanese, and American children. *Science, 231,* 693–699.

Steward, L. (1982). Developing curriculum for severely disturbed learning-impaired students. In D. Tweedle & E. Stroyer (Eds.), *The multihandicapped hearing-impaired: Identification and instruction* (pp. 124–143). Washington, DC: Gallaudet University Press.

Stone, C., & Conca, L. (1993). The origin of strategy deficits in children with learning disabilities. In L. J. Meltzer (Ed.). *Strategy assessment and instruction for students with learning disabilities* (pp. 23–60). Austin, TX: PRO-ED.

Stroul, B. A., & Friedman, R. M. (1986). *A system of care for severely emotionally disturbed children and youth.* Washington, DC: CASSP Technical Assistance Center, Georgetown University Child Development Center.

Stroup, K., Wylie, P., & Bull, M. (1987). Car seats with mechanically assisted ventilation. *Pediatrics, 80*(2).

Subotnik, R., Kassen, L., Summers, E., & Wasser, A. (1993). *Genius revisited: High IQ children grow up.* Norwood, NJ: Ablex.

Sugai, G., Maheady, L., & Skouge, J. (1989). Best assessment practices for students with behavioral disorders: Accommodation to cultural diversity and individual differences. *Behavioral Disorders, 14*(4), 263–277.

Swanson, L. (1987). Verbal decoding effects on visual short-term memory of learning disabled and normal readers. *Journal of Educational Psychology, 70,* 539–544.

Szymanski, P. (1994). Transition: Life-span considerations for empowerment. *Exceptional Children, 60*(5), 402–410.

Tallal, P., Curtis, S., & Kaplan, R. (1988). The San Diego longitudinal study. In N. S. Garber & G. Mincher (Eds.), *International perspectives on communication disorders.* Washington, DC: Gallaudet University Press.

Tallal, P., Galaburda, A., Llinas, R., & Von Euler, C. (1993). *Temporal information processing in the nervous system.* New York: New York Academy of Science.

Tallal, P., Miller, S., & Fitch, R. (1993). Neurological bases of speech: A case for the preeminence of temporal processing. *Annals of New York Academy of Science, 682,* 27–47.

Taylor, R. (1988). Assessment policies and procedures. In L. Sternberg (Ed.), *Educating students with severe or profound handicaps* (pp. 103–118). Austin, TX: PRO-ED.

Taylor, R. (1989). *Assessment of exceptional children* (2nd ed.). Englewood Cliffs, NJ: Prentice-Hall.

Taylor, S. (1983). Adjustments to threatening events: A theory of cognitive adaptation. *American Psychologist, 38,* 642–630.

Taylor, S. J., & Racino, J. A. (1983). Community living: Lessons today. In L. H. Meyer, C. Peck, & L. Brown (Eds.), *Critical issues in the lives of people with severe disabilities* (pp. 235–238). Baltimore: Paul H. Brookes.

Terman, L., & Oden, M. (1947). *The gifted child grows up: Twenty-five-year follow-up of a superior group* (Vol. 4). Stanford, CA: Stanford University Press.

Thomas, A., & Chess, S. (1977). *Temperament and development.* New York: Brunner/Mazel.

Thousands, J., & Villa, P. (1991). A futuristic view of REI: A response to Jenkins, Pious, and Jewell. *Exceptional Children, 57*(6), 556–560.

Tindal, G., & Marston, D. (1986). Approaches to assessment. In J. K. Torgesen & B. Y. L. Wong (Eds.), *Psychological and educational perspectives on learning disabilities* (pp. 54–84). San Diego: Academic Press.

Todd, J. (1986). Resources, media, and technology. In G. Scholl (Ed.), *Foundations of education for blind and visually handicapped children and youth.* New York: American Foundation for the Blind.

Tomlinson, C., & Callahan, C. (1992). Contributions of gifted education to general education in a time of change. *Gifted Child Quarterly, 36,* 183–189.

Torgesen, J. (1988). Problems in the study of learning disabilities. In M. Hetherington & J. Hagen (Eds.), *Review of research in child development* (Vol. 5, pp. 162–184). Chicago: University of Chicago Press.

Torgesen, J. (1994). Issues in the assessment of executive function. In G. Lyon (Ed.), *Frames of reference for the assessment of learning disabilities* (pp. 475–514). Baltimore: Paul H. Brookes.

Torgesen, J., & Licht, B. (1983). The learning disabled child as an inactive learner. In J. McKinney & L. Feagens (Eds.), *Topics in learning disabilities* (Vol. 1, pp. 100–130). Norwood, NJ: Ablex.

Torgesen, J. K., & Wong, B. Y. L. (1986). *Psychological and educational perspectives on learning disabilities.* San Diego: Academic Press.

Torrance, E. (1981). Cross cultural studies of creative development in seven selected societies. In J. Gowan, J. Khateno, & E. Torrance (Eds.), *Creativity: Its education implications* (2nd ed.). Dubuque, IA: Kendall/Hunt.

Torres, I., & Corn, A. (1990). *When you have a visually handicapped child in your classroom: Suggestions for teachers.* New York: American Foundation for the Blind.

Trace, C. (1994). Ongoing studies of AIT. *Advance: For Speech-Language Pathologists and Audiologists, 4*(6), 5–19.

Treffinger, D. (1980). *Encouraging creative learning for the gifted and talented*. Los Angeles: National/State Leadership Training Institute.

Trieber, F. A., & Lahey, B. R. (1983). Toward a behavioral model of academic remediation with learning disabled children. *Journal of Learning Disabilities, 16*, 11–116.

Tröster, H., & Brambring, M. (1994). The play behavior and play materials of blind and sighted infants and preschoolers. *Journal of Visual Impairment and Blindness, 88*, 421–432.

Trybus, R., & Karchmer, M. (1977). School achievement scores of hearing impaired children: National data on achievement status and growth patterns. *American Annals of the Deaf, 122*, 35–53.

Tulving, E. (1985). How many memory systems are there? *American Psychologist, 40*, 385–398.

Turnbull, A., Summers, J., & Brotherson, M. (1984). *Working with families with disabled members: A family system approach*. Lawrence: Kansas University Affiliated Facility.

Turnbull, A., Summers, J., & Brotherson, M. (1986). Family life cycle: Theoretical and empirical implications and future directions for families with mentally retarded members. In J. Gallagher & P. Vietze (Eds.), *Families with handicapped children* (pp. 45–66). Baltimore: Paul H. Brookes.

Turnbull, A., & Turnbull, H. R. (1991). Family assessment and family empowerment. In L. Meyer, C. Peck, & L. Brown (Eds.), *Critical issues in the lives of people with severe disabilities* (pp. 485–488). Baltimore: Paul H. Brookes.

Turnbull, A. T., & Turnbull, H. R. (1989). *Parents speak out* (3rd ed.). Columbus, OH: Charles E. Merrill.

Turnbull, R., Turnbull, A., Bronickin, G., Summers, J., & Roeder-Gordon, C. (1989). *Disability and the family: A guide to decisions for adulthood*. Baltimore: Paul H. Brookes.

Tuttle, D. (1984). *Self-esteem and adjusting to blindness*. Springfield, IL: Charles C. Thomas.

U.S. Department of Education. (1984). *Sixth annual report to Congress on the implementation of Public Law 94-142: The Education of All Handicapped Children Act*. Washington, DC: U.S. Government Printing Office.

U.S. Department of Education. (1985, September 3). *New services for deaf-blind children program (SEP memorandum)*. Washington, DC: U.S. Government Printing Office.

U.S. Department of Education. (1988). *Tenth annual report to Congress on the implementation of the Education of the Handicapped Act*. Washington, DC: Author.

Umbreit, J. (Ed.). (1983). *Physical disabilities and health impairments: An introduction*. Columbus, OH: Charles E. Merrill.

Upsur, C. (1990). Early intervention as preventive intervention. In S. Meisels & J. Shonkoff (Eds.), *Handbook of early childhood intervention* (pp. 633–650). New York: Cambridge University Press.

Vadasy, P., Fewell, R., Meyer, D., Schell, G., & Greenberg, M. (1984). Involved parents: Characteristics and resources of fathers and mothers of young handicapped children. *Journal of the Division for Early Childhood, 8*, 13–25.

Vaillant, G., & Milofsky, M. (1980). Natural history of male psychological health: IX. Empirical evidence for Erikson's model of the life-cycle. *American Journal of Psychiatry, 137*(11), 1348–1359.

Valletutti, P. J. (1987). Social problems. In K. Kavale, S. Forness, & M. Bender (Eds.), *Handbook of learning disabilities: Vol. 1. Dimensions and diagnoses* (pp. 211–226). Boston: College-Hill/Little, Brown.

Vanderheiden, G. (1982). Computers can play a dual role for disabled individuals. *BYTE, 7*, 136–162.

Van Dijk, J. (1986). An educational curriculum for deaf-blind multiply handicapped persons. In D. Ellis (Ed.), *Sensory impairments in mentally retarded people* (pp. 375–382). San Diego: College-Hill Press.

Vaugh, S., McIntosh, R., & Spencer-Rowe, J. (1991). Peer rejection is a stubborn thing: Increasing peer acceptance of rejected students with learning disabilities. *Learning Disabilities and Practice, 6*, 83–98.

Veale, T. (1994). Auditory integration training: The use of a new listening treatment within our profession. *American Journal of Speech and Hearing, 3*(2), 12–15.

Vellutino, F. (1987, March). Dyslexia. *Scientific American, 256*, 3.

Voeltz, L. (1980). Children's attitudes toward handicapped peers. *American Journal of Mental Deficiency, 84*, 455–464.

Voeltz, L. (1982). Effects of structured interaction with severely handicapped peers on children's attitudes. *American Journal of Mental Deficiency, 86*, 380–390.

Vonnegut, K. (1970). Harrison Bergeron. In *Welcome to the monkey house* (pp. 7–14). New York: Delacorte.

Wagner, M., Newman, L., D'Amico, R., Jay, E., Buter-Nalin, P., Marker, C., & Cox, R. (1991). *Youth with disabilities: How are they doing?* Menlo Park, CA: SRI International.

Walker, H. M., & Bullis, M. (1991). Behavior disorders and the social context of regular class integration: A conceptual dilemma. In J. W. Lloyd, N. N. Singh, & A. C. Repp (Eds.), *The regular education initiative: Alternative perspectives on concepts, issues, and models* (pp. 75–94). Sycamore, IL: Sycamore Press.

Walker, H., & Fabre, T. (1987). Assessment of behavior disorders in the school setting: Issues, problems, and strategies revisited. In N. Harring (Ed.), *Assessing and managing be-*

havior disorders (pp. 198–234). Seattle: University of Washington Press.

Walker, H. M., Severson, H., Stiller, B., Williams, G., Haring, N., Shinn, M., & Todis, B. (1988). Systematic screening of pupils in the elementary age range at risk for behavior disorders: Development and trial testing. Remedial and Special Education, 9(3), 8–14.

Wang, M. C. (1989). Accommodating student diversity through adaptive instruction. In S. Stainback, W. Stainback, & M. Forest (Eds.), Educating all students in the mainstream of regular education. Baltimore: Paul H. Brookes.

Wang, M., & Walberg, H. (1988). Four fallacies of segregationism. Exceptional Children, 55, 128–137.

Ward, M. E. (1986). The visual system. In G. T. Scholl (Ed.), Foundations of education for visually handicapped children and youth: Theory and practice. New York: American Foundation for the Blind.

Warren, D. (1994). Blindness and children: An individual differences approach. New York: Cambridge University Press.

Warren, S. F., & Kaiser A. P. (1988). Research in early childhood language intervention. In S. L. Odom & M. B. Karnes (Eds.), Research in early childhood special education (pp. 89–108). Baltimore: Paul H. Brookes.

Washington, V., & Gallagher, J. J. (1986). Family roles, preschool handicapped children and social policy. In J. J. Gallagher & P. M. Vietze (Eds.), Families of handicapped persons: Research, programs, and policy issues. Baltimore: Paul H. Brookes.

Webber, J. (1992). A cultural-organizational perspective on special education and the exclusion of youth with social maladjustment. Remedial and Special Education, 13(1), 60–62.

Weinstein, L. (1974). Evaluation of a program for re-educating disturbed children: A follow-up comparison with untreated children. Washington, DC: U.S. Department of Health, Education and Welfare. (Available through ERIC Document Reproduction Service, ED-141–966.)

Werner, E. E. (1988). Individual differences needs: A thirty-year study of resilient high-risk infants. Zero to Three, 8, 1–5.

Werner, E. E., & Smith, R. S. (1992). Overcoming the odds. Ithaca, NY: Cornell University Press.

Westlake, C. P., & Kaiser, A. (1991). Early childhood services for children with severe disabilities: Research, values, policies and practice. In L. Meyer, C. Peck, & L. Brown (Eds.), Critical issues in the lives of people with severe disabilities (pp. 429–458). Baltimore: Paul H. Brookes.

Wheeler, D., Jacobsen, J., Paglieri, R., & Schwartz, A. (1993). An experimental assessment of facilitative communication. Mental Retardation, 31, 49–60.

Whitehouse, D. (1987). Medical services. In M. Esterson & L. Bluth (Eds.), Related services for handicapped children (pp. 41–52). San Diego: College-Hill Press.

Whitehurst, G. J. (1980). Language development. In B. Wolman (Ed.), Handbook of developmental psychology (pp. 367–386). Englewood Cliffs, NJ: Prentice-Hall.

Whitmore, J. R. (1980). The etiology of underachievement in highly gifted young children. Journal for the Education of the Gifted, 3(1), 38–51.

Wier, C. (1980). Habilitation and rehabilitation of the hearing impaired. In T. Hixon & J. Saxon (Eds.), Introduction to communication disorders. Englewood Cliffs, NJ: Prentice-Hall.

Wilhelm, J. (1989). Fear and anxiety in low vision and totally blind children. Education of the Visually Handicapped, 20, 163–172.

Will, M. (1984a). Let us pause and reflect—but not too long. Exceptional Children, 51(1), 11–16.

Will, M. (1984b). OSERS programming for the transition of youth with disabilities: Bridges from school to working life. Programs for the handicapped. Washington, DC: U.S. Department of Education.

Will, M. C. (1986). Educating children with learning problems: A shared responsibility. Exceptional Children, 52, 411–415.

Williams, D. (1994). In the real world. The Journal of the Association for Persons with Severe Handicaps, 19(3), 196–199.

Williams, K., & Baeker, M. (1983). Use of small groups with chronically ill children. Journal of School Health, 53, 205–208.

Williams, M. (1968). Superior intelligence of children blinded from retinoblastoma. Archives of Diseases of Childhood, 43, 204–210.

Williamson, G. (1987). Children with spina bifida. Baltimore: Paul H. Brookes.

Wilson, R. (1984). A review of self-control treatments for aggressive behavior. Behavioral Disorders, 9, 131–141.

Wilson, W. University of Washington Child Development and Mental Retardation Center. Newsletter, 1994. Seattle, Washington.

Wing, D. M., & Heimgarter, L. J. (1973). Articulation carry over procedure immediately by parents. Language, Speech and Hearing Services in Schools, 4, 182–195.

Wingate, M. (1986). Physiological and genetic factors. In G. Shames & H. Rubin (Eds.), Stuttering then and now. Columbus, OH: Charles E. Merrill.

Winton, P., & Turnbull, A. (1981). Parent involvement as viewed by parents of preschool handicapped children. Topics in Early Childhood Special Education, 1(3), 11–20.

Wolery, M. (1992). Preschoolers with learning disabilities. *Topics in Early Childhood Special Education, 12*(2).

Wolery, M., Bailey, D., & Sugai, G. (1988). *Effective teaching: Principles and procedures of applied behavior analysis with exceptional children*. Boston: Allyn & Bacon.

Wolf, A., & Harkins, J. (1986). Multihandicapped students. In A. Schildroth & M. Karchmer (Eds.), *Deaf children in America*. San Diego: College-Hill Press.

Wolf, M. (1981). Talent search and development in the visual and performing arts. In I. Sato (Ed.), *Balancing the scale of the disadvantaged gifted* (pp. 103–116). Los Angeles: National/State Leadership Training Institute on the Gifted and Talented.

Wolfensberger, W. (1972). *The principles of normalization in human services*. Toronto: National Institute on Mental Retardation.

Wong, B. (1986). Problems at issue of identification of learning disabled. In J. K. Torgesen & B. Y. L. Wong (Eds.), *Psychological and educational perspectives on learning disabilities* (pp. 3–22). San Diego: Academic Press.

Wood, D. (1989). Homeless children: Their evaluation and treatment. *Journal of Pediatric Care, 3*(4), 194–199.

Wood, F. (1982). Defining disturbing, disordered, and disturbed behavior. In F. Wood & K. Laken (Eds.), *Disturbing, disoriented, or disturbed?* Reston, VA: Council for Exceptional Children.

Wood, F., & Smith, C. (1985). Assessment of emotionally disturbed/behaviorally disordered students. *Diagnostique, 10*, 40–51.

Wood, M., Combs, C., Gunn, A., & Weller, D. (1986). *Developmental therapy in the classroom*. Austin, TX: PRO-ED.

Wright, C., & Nomura, M. (1985). *From toys to computers: Access for the physically disabled child*. San Jose, CA: Authors.

Writer, J. (1987). A movement-based approach to the education of students who are sensory impaired/multihandicapped. In L. Goetz, D. Guess, & K. Stremel-Campbell (Eds.), *Innovative program design for individuals with dual sensory impairments* (pp. 191–224). Baltimore: Paul H. Brookes.

Wrobel, G., & Wood, F. (1992). Students and parents discuss time-out: A preliminary analysis of group interview data. *Severe Behavior Disorders Monograph, 15*, 88–97.

Wyatt v. Stickney, 344 F. Supp. 373, 387, 396 (M.D. Ala. 1972).

Yell, M. L. (1989). *Honig v. Doe:* The suspension and expulsion of handicapped students. *Exceptional Children, 56*, 60–69.

Yell, M. L. (1995). Least restrictive environment, inclusion and students with disabilities: A legal analysis. *The Journal of Special Education, 28*(4), 389–404.

Yin, R., & White, J. (1984). *Microcomputer implementation in schools*. Washington, DC: Cosmos.

Yule, W., Rutter, M., Berger, M., & Thompson, J. (1974). Over and underachievement in reading. *British Journal of Educational Psychology, 44*, 1–12.

Zeitlin, S., & Williamson, G. (1994). *Coping in young children*. Baltimore: Paul H. Brookes.

Zetlin, A., & Turner, J. (1985). Transition from adolescence to adulthood: Perspectives of mentally retarded individuals and their families. *American Journal of Mental Deficiency, 89*, 570–579.

Zigler, E., & Hoddap, R. (1986). *Understanding mental retardation*. New York: Cambridge University Press.

Zigmond, N., & Baker, J. (1990). Mainstream experiences for learning disabled students. *Exceptional Children, 57*, 176–185.

Zigmond, N., Jenkins, J., Fuchs, L., Deno, S., Fuchs, D., Baker, J., Jenkins, L., & Contino, J. (1995). *Phi Delta Kappan*, 531–540.

Zill, N., & Nord, C. (1993). *Running in place*. Washington, DC: Child Trends Inc.

Zill, N., & Schoenborn, C. (1990). Development, learning, and emotional problems: Health of a nation's children, United States, 1988. *Advance Data, 190*, 1–17.

Zirpoli, T. (1990). Physical abuse: Are children with disabilities at greater risk? *Intervention in School and Clinic, 26*(1), 6–12.

Zwerleir, R. A., Smith, M., & Diffley, J. (1990). *Vocational rehabilitation for learning disabled adults*. National Center on Employment of the Handicapped, Human Resource Center, Albertson, NY 11507.

author/source

subject

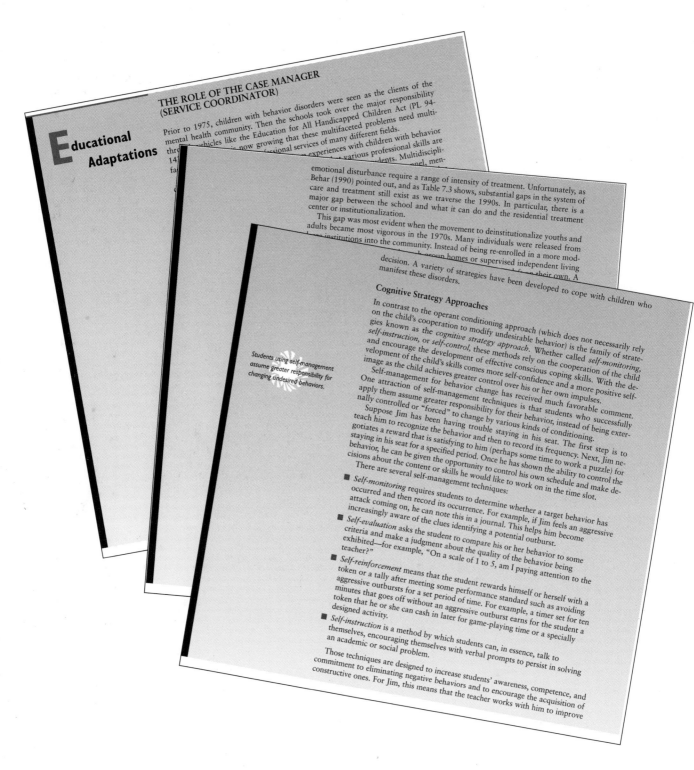

**THE ROLE OF THE CASE MANAGER
(SERVICE COORDINATOR)**

Prior to 1975, children with behavior disorders were seen as the clients of the
mental health community. Then the schools took over the major responsibility
through vehicles like the Education for All Handicapped Children Act (PL 94-
14...). It is now growing that these multifaceted problems need multi-
fa... ...essional services of many different fields.
...t experiences with children with behavior
... various professional skills are
...dents. Multidiscipli-
...anel, men-

emotional disturbance require a range of intensity of treatment. Unfortunately, as
Behar (1990) pointed out, and as Table 7.3 shows, substantial gaps in the system of
care and treatment still exist as we traverse the 1990s. In particular, there is a
major gap between the school and what it can do and the residential treatment
center or institutionalization.

This gap was most evident when the movement to deinstitutionalize youths and
adults became most vigorous in the 1970s. Many individuals were released from
... institutions into the community. Instead of being re-enrolled in a more mod-
... group homes or supervised independent living
decision. A variety of strategies have been developed to cope with children who
manifest these disorders.

Students using self-management
assume greater responsibility for
changing undesired behaviors.

Cognitive Strategy Approaches

In contrast to the operant conditioning approach (which does not necessarily rely
on the child's cooperation to modify undesirable behavior) is the family of strategies known as the *cognitive strategy approach*. Whether called *self-monitoring,
self-instruction,* or *self-control,* these methods rely on the cooperation of the child
and encourage the development of effective conscious coping skills. With the development of the child's skills comes more self-confidence and a more positive self-
image as the child achieves greater control over his or her own impulses.

Self-management for behavior change has received much favorable comment.
One attraction of self-management techniques is that students who successfully
apply them assume greater responsibility for their behavior, instead of being externally controlled or "forced" to change by various kinds of conditioning.

Suppose Jim has been having trouble staying in his seat. The first step is to
teach him to recognize the behavior and then to record its frequency. Next, Jim negotiates a reward that is satisfying to him (perhaps some time to work a puzzle) for
staying in his seat for a specified period. Once he has shown the ability to control the
behavior, he can be given the opportunity to control his own schedule and make decisions about the content or skills he would like to work on in the time slot.

There are several self-management techniques:

■ *Self-monitoring* requires students to determine whether a target behavior has
occurred and then record its occurrence. For example, if Jim feels an aggressive
attack coming on, he can note this in a journal. This helps him become
increasingly aware of the clues identifying a potential outburst.

■ *Self-evaluation* asks the student to compare his or her behavior to some
criteria and make a judgment about the quality of the behavior being
exhibited—for example, "On a scale of 1 to 5, am I paying attention to the
teacher?"

■ *Self-reinforcement* means that the student rewards himself or herself with a
token or a tally after meeting some performance standard such as avoiding
aggressive outbursts for a set period of time. For example, a timer set for ten
minutes that goes off without an aggressive outburst earns for the student a
token that he or she can cash in later for game-playing time or a specially
designed activity.

■ *Self-instruction* is a method by which students can, in essence, talk to
themselves, encouraging themselves with verbal prompts to persist in solving
an academic or social problem.

Those techniques are designed to increase students' awareness, competence, and
commitment to eliminating negative behaviors and to encourage the acquisition of
constructive ones. For Jim, this means that the teacher works with him to improve

EDUCATIONAL ADAPTATIONS, easy-to-find tabbed
sections in every categorical chapter, offer extended teaching